Women Writing Antiquity

Women Writing Antiquity

Gender and Learning in Early Modern France

HELENA TAYLOR

Great Clarendon Street, Oxford, OX2 6DP,
United Kingdom

Oxford University Press is a department of the University of Oxford.
It furthers the University's objective of excellence in research, scholarship,
and education by publishing worldwide. Oxford is a registered trade mark of
Oxford University Press in the UK and in certain other countries

© Helena Taylor 2024

The moral rights of the author have been asserted

All rights reserved. No part of this publication may be reproduced, stored in
a retrieval system, or transmitted, in any form or by any means, without the
prior permission in writing of Oxford University Press, or as expressly permitted
by law, by licence or under terms agreed with the appropriate reprographics
rights organization. Enquiries concerning reproduction outside the scope of the
above should be sent to the Rights Department, Oxford University Press, at the
address above

You must not circulate this work in any other form
and you must impose this same condition on any acquirer

Published in the United States of America by Oxford University Press
198 Madison Avenue, New York, NY 10016, United States of America

British Library Cataloguing in Publication Data

Data available

Library of Congress Control Number: 2023949211

ISBN 9780192870445

DOI: 10.1093/oso/9780192870445.001.0001

Printed and bound by
CPI Group (UK) Ltd, Croydon, CR0 4YY

Links to third party websites are provided by Oxford in good faith and
for information only. Oxford disclaims any responsibility for the materials
contained in any third party website referenced in this work.

Contents

List of Illustrations	vi
Acknowledgements	vii
A Note on the Text	ix

1. Introduction	1
2. Authorship, Authority, and Agonism: Antiquity and Writing the Self	25
3. The Paradoxes of Modesty: Historical Fiction and the Female Line	67
4. 'Classics' as Commodity: Antiquity and the Literary Market	103
5. Salon Verse and the Philosopher-Poet	135
6. Ancients and Moderns: *Conteuses* as Literary Critics	176
7. The Career Classicist: Gender and Translation	203
8. Conclusion	243

Bibliography	252
Index	282

List of Illustrations

Figure 1. Frontispiece, Anne Dacier, *L'Iliade d'Homère*, 3 vols (Paris: Rigaud, 1711), i, np. Image reproduced with the permission of The Provost and Fellows of Worcester College, Oxford.   227

Figure 2. Frontispiece, Antoine Houdar de La Motte, *L'Iliade, poëme avec un discours sur Homère* (Paris: Dupuis, 1714). Image reproduced with the permission of The Provost and Fellows of Worcester College, Oxford.   228

Acknowledgements

Sincere thanks are due first and foremost to the Leverhulme Trust for awarding me an Early Career Fellowship which made it possible to write this book. I also note with gratitude both the Trust's response to the disruption caused by the COVID-19 pandemic and its fair and exemplary parental leave policy which meant that, although this was a fixed-term role, my leave was recouped so I did not have to choose between taking leave and continuing with research work when I had a baby during this fellowship. Thanks also to the University of Exeter's Department of Languages, Cultures, and Visual Studies for supporting my career before, during, and after my fellowship.

Part of Chapter 7 originally appeared as 'Polemical Translation, Translating Polemic: Anne Dacier's Rhetoric in the Homer Quarrel', *Modern Language Review*, 116.1 (2021), 21–41; and part of Chapter 6 originally appeared as '"Gracieuse et Percinet" de Madame d'Aulnoy: un conte programmatique', *Op. cit. revue des littératures et des arts*, *"Agrégation 2022"*, 23, 2021: I thank both journal editors for permission to include this work here in its revised form.

I'm grateful to everyone who read parts—or in some cases, all—of this book: Fiona Cox, Emma Herdman, Katherine Ibbett, Lisa Nicholson, Hugh Roberts, David Sergeant, Kate Tunstall, and the anonymous OUP readers. I appreciate the time, attention, and energy that went into the constructive comments and advice, and hope to pay forward (and back!) this generosity.

For offering advice at key moments, I thank Emma Claussen, Anne Debrosse, Esther van Dyke, Lise Forment, Peta Fowler, Emma Gilby, Emily Hauser, Tom Hinton, Michael Moriarty, John O'Brien, Jenny Oliver, Marine Roussillon, Gemma Tidman, Alain Viala, and Rosie Wyles. Thanks also to Valerie Worth-Stylianou for her interest and engagement and for coming to my aid with the much-needed edition of Marie de Gournay's complete works that was then out of print. Any errors or inaccuracies are my own.

There are so many other people who have supported me and this project and I note them here with gratitude. For community, conversation, and guidance, I thank Katie Brown, Ruth Bush, Emily Butterworth, Freyja Cox Jensen, Paul Earlie, Felicity Henderson, Rebecca Langlands, Ina Linge, Muireann Maguire, Henry Power, Beatrijs Vanacker, and Adam Watt. Thanks also to the wider community of scholars in early modern French studies, and members of my department at Exeter. I was fortunate to present material from this book at a range of events where I received invaluable feedback and would like to thank the participants and organisers of the following: the Oxford Early Modern French seminar in 2016; the MLA in Chicago in 2019; 'Portraits and Poses' in Leuven in 2019; 'Women and *Querelles* in Early Modern France' in Exeter in 2019; 'Research in Rhetoric' in Bristol in 2019; SE17 in Charlotte, North Carolina, in 2019; 'Between Self and State: Exile in the Early Modern World' at Cambridge in 2021; 'Antiquity in Early Modern France' at Princeton in 2022; the Society for French Studies Conference 2022 in Belfast; the Society for Early Modern French Studies Conference 2022 in St Andrews; the Cambridge Early Modern French Seminar in 2022; and 'Feminism and (Early Modern) History' at KCL in 2023. Thank you also to the OUP editors and production team.

I couldn't have written this book without the childcare provided by nursery, preschool, and teaching staff and wish to record my gratitude here. I would also like to thank my family—my parents and their partners, my siblings, and my in-laws. Finally, for everything, thank you to David, Leo, and Zac: my loves.

HT, Exeter, July 2023

A Note on the Text

I have used the same spelling conventions as the editions used, although when quoting early modern texts, the uses of i, j, u, and v have been modernised, ampersands replaced, and modern accents added in cases where confusion might arise (à, là, où, etc.). Long titles have been curtailed, particularly in the footnotes. With regards to the Quarrel of the Ancients and Moderns, I use Ancients and Moderns with capital letters to refer to the seventeenth-century quarrellers and the taste and ideology associated with their positions; ancient and modern in lower case refer to the respective periods and their cultures. Unless otherwise stated, all translations from French and Latin are my own.

1

Introduction

In 1626 Marie de Gournay—translator, essayist, and Montaigne's first editor—complained of the category error she represented as a female intellectual. She did not qualify as either 'docte' or 'ignorante'; her version of knowledge did not fit normative definitions:

> Puis qu'il est veritable, ou que je ne sçay rien, tant par oubli qu'autrement, ou que ce que je sçay se qualifie, se cognoist et se practique si peu pour Science en nostre temps que tous les jours mon ignorance en sert de risée aux esprits guaillards d'entre les sçavans, comme ma Science en sert aux autres [...] Que ne me permet donc le babil du monde, de me reposer sans contredit, au siege des Doctes ou des Ignorans, des hommes ou des bestes?[1]

> For it is a fact that either I know nothing, as much on account of a faulty memory as otherwise, or what I do know is so little judged, recognized and practised as being learning in our time that every day my ignorance serves as an object of ridicule for the high-spirited among the learned, just as my knowledge does for the others. [...] So why will the babbling of the world not permit me to rest, without opposing me, in the seat of the learned or of the ignorant, of human beings or of beasts?[2]

This category error will form the subject of this book. By the end of Gournay's century, debates about women's learning had become a key issue. While fear of women's learning and scepticism about their capacities were nothing new, the problems posed by the female intellectual along with the freedoms this figure represented had come to be expressed in a type, described variously as the 'savante femme', the 'femme savante', and the 'savante'. This study shows how 'savante', as a pre- or postnominal adjective and a substantive noun, emerged as a site of contested meaning, a term we might designate as a 'cultural keyword', that is, as an 'active agent in social and intellectual change, rather than a passive reflector

---

[1] Marie de Gournay, 'Apologie pour celle qui escrit', in *Œuvres Complètes*, ed. by Jean-Claude Arnould, Évelyne Berriot, Claude Blum, Anna Lia Franchetti, Marie-Claire Thomine, and Valerie Worth-Stylianou, 2 vols (Paris: Champion, 2002), II, pp. 1375–1429 (pp. 1394–95).
[2] Marie de Gournay, *Apology for the Woman Writing and Other Works*, trans. by Richard Hillman and Colette Quesnel, The Other Voice in Early Modern Europe (Chicago: Chicago University Press, 2002), p. 126 (with minor modifications).

Women Writing Antiquity. Helena Taylor, Oxford University Press. © Helena Taylor (2024).
DOI: 10.1093/oso/9780192870445.003.0001

2   WOMEN WRITING ANTIQUITY

of that change'.[3] In the Renaissance, 'savant', which was defined primarily in the masculine, meant 'learned'; by the end of the seventeenth century, it had both a feminine definition and a pejorative one. 'Savante' could be a term of praise or an insult, a definition women denied or claimed—it is thus more complex than its parallel, 'précieuse', a derogatory term which women never used to describe themselves. It could designate a pedantic scholar spouting Latin and Greek or it could refer to a more French-orientated, sociable, and 'modern' articulation of learning; it could refer to women engaged in literary pursuits, as well as much broader categories of intellectuals and leaders: queens, saints, philosophers, and patrons.[4] As an unstable referent, 'savante' mirrored wider questions about women's purpose and authority, and, as Gournay intimates, about what constituted learning itself. After all, any categorisation of learning entails a definition of its adherents, its community: to define one is to define the other.[5]

This study seeks to examine the shifting identities of the female intellectual as they were articulated by women, exploring the relationship between the representation of this figure, an individual's authorial ethos, and wider dynamics of cultural change in this period. As the female intellectual became a figure of debate, France was also undergoing a shift away from the dominance of classical cultural models, the transition towards a standardised modern language, the development of a national literature and literary canon, and the emergence of the literary field. This book examines the intersection of these phenomena by analysing one domain of learning—'literature'—and looking at women's most 'savant' of literary activities: their receptions of antiquity. Even as women espoused intellectual identities that played down knowledge of ancient Greek and Roman culture (e.g. they denied being 'savante' or turned 'savante' into a term that designated learning that was French rather than Latin or Greek), they often did so in texts which engaged directly with the literature of ancient Greece and Rome. Greco-Roman culture still possessed significant cultural capital for women entering the literary field even at a time when this capital was being questioned in the Quarrel of the Ancients and Moderns, that is, the longstanding debate which compared classical Greek and Roman culture with French culture, and encompassed questions of authority and imitation; of readership, taste and intellectual value; of authorship and legitimacy.[6] I explore how the early modern attempt to define the female intellectual tracks various dichotomies: the seventeenth-century version of the struggle between a

---

[3] Emily Butterworth and Rowan Tomlinson, 'Scandal', in *Renaissance Keywords*, ed. by Ita Mac Carthy (Leeds: Legenda, 2013), pp. 80–100 (p. 82).

[4] For examples of this range, see Jean de La Forge, *Le Cercle des femmes savantes* (Paris: Loyson, 1663); Jacquette Guillaume, *Les Dames Illustres où par bonnes et fortes raisons il se prouve que le sexe féminin surpasse en toutes sortes de genres le sexe masculin* (Paris: Jolly, 1665); Marguerite Buffet, *Nouvelles Observations sur la langue Françoise [...] avec Les Eloges des Illustres Sçavantes, tant anciennes que modernes* (Paris: Cusson, 1668).

[5] I take my cue from Rebecca Wilkin's argument that 'to define an epistemological program was also to define an intellectual community'. Rebecca Wilkin, *Women, Imagination and the Search for Truth in Early Modern France* (Aldershot: Ashgate, 2008), p. 1.

[6] For two interpretations, see Joan DeJean, *Ancients against Moderns: Culture Wars and the Making of a Fin de Siècle* (Chicago: University of Chicago Press, 1997); and Larry F. Norman, *The Shock of the Ancient: Literature and History in Early Modern France* (Chicago: University of Chicago Press, 2011).

feminism of difference and a feminism of equality; the oppositions contained in the Quarrel of the Ancients and Moderns between classical and French culture in defining and valorising 'savoir'; and methodological problems of confronting self-identification and historiographical categorisation (what are the implications of accepting that women who denied they were 'savante' were not 'savante', as is suggested in the imposed division of 'savante' and *salonnière*?).

The corpus spans the long seventeenth century, from the debates about poetics in its early decades to the *Querelle d'Homère* of the early eighteenth century, from Marie de Gournay to Anne Dacier, by way of Madeleine de Scudéry, Antoinette Deshoulières, Madame de Villedieu, Anne de La Roche-Guilhen, Catherine Bernard, Charlotte-Rose Caumont de La Force, Henriette-Julie de Murat, Marie-Catherine d'Aulnoy, and Marie-Jeanne L'Héritier de Villandon. By bringing together a wide range of authors and genres, from those who paraded traditional learning, in the form of philological knowledge of Latin (and Greek), to those who advocated French culture and more adaptive approaches to antiquity, I examine the construction of intellectual value—both at the time and since, by the authors themselves and in their reception. The intentions of this book are twofold, speaking to its dual audience of early modernists and Classicists. The first relates to content: to shine light for the first time on the classical reception by women not usually regarded as Classicists, and to explore in fine detail the uses of Western ancient culture in the writing of the women in my corpus whose work has received only selective, isolated attention in this regard. The second is more historical: to tell a story of the relationship between the figure of the 'learned woman' and the period's struggle over the definition of literature. By bringing these diverse authors together, this study re-evaluates the ideologies underpinning the categories of 'woman writer', often used to define those who wrote in feminised genres or with a female cause in mind, and 'Classicist', that is, traditionally, those literate in Latin (and possibly Greek).[7] This book thus reveals the significance of Greco-Roman culture to authorial self-fashioning and shines new light on the gendering of learning in this period and its historiography.

Savants, Savantes, and Salonnières

At the book's core is an exploration of the relationship between gender and knowledge, by which I mean specifically learning.[8] As scholars such as Linda Timmermans have shown, the question of women's education, or what she and others

For a transnational study of the Quarrel and the influence of ancient Greece and Rome on eighteenth-century culture and politics, see Floris Verhaart, *Classical Learning in Britain, France and the Dutch Republic, 1690–1750: Beyond the Ancients and Moderns* (Oxford: Oxford University Press, 2020).

[7] I use 'classics' and 'classical' in English as recognisable terms to refer to what at the time was called 'ancien' or 'antiquité' and which in this corpus refers to Greek and Roman culture and history, as well as to the 'ancient Near East' as described by Xenophon and Herodotus in particular. I use 'Classics' to refer to the modern discipline.

[8] Following Peter Burke, *A Social History of Knowledge: from Gutenberg to Diderot* (Cambridge: Polity Press, 2000).

4   WOMEN WRITING ANTIQUITY

call 'la querelle de la femme savante', brought together key issues of contention and concern in the second half of the seventeenth century.[9] Articulated in treatises, satires, novels, poetry, and theatre, the debate ranged from practical arguments about what form women's education should take (or be confined to), to more abstract discussions of whether the mind is sexed.[10] The problem of women's education was not a new one: these debates renewed and built on long-standing questions of women's equality that were articulated in France from the time of Christine de Pizan and the original 'querelle des femmes'.[11] However, the seventeenth-century version of this debate was prompted by women's increasing professional cultural activity, especially within the domain of literature, and their increasing cultural authority in salons: this has been explored in excellent detail by scholars such as Linda Timmermans, Myriam Dufour-Maître, Joan DeJean, Anne E. Duggan, and Domna Stanton.[12] This activity was related to a wider shifting—and mingling—of literary publics and practitioners, due to the sociocultural changes occurring in seventeenth-century France, notably the rise of what Alain Viala calls the 'nouveaux doctes' and the decreasing authority of *savant* culture (an encyclopaedic Humanist tradition of scholarship that was philological and founded on the study of antiquity) and increasing authority of *mondain* culture (amateur, French-orientated, invested in distinguishing 'literature' from other domains of learning).[13]

With these new or newly dominant literary publics and practitioners came new terms and terminology that were infused with particular weight and complexity: notable is the word 'savante' and its different uses and inflections.[14] I argue that 'savante' came to be associated primarily with the figure of the pedantic female intellectual in a way that became culturally recognised and influential in

---

[9] Linda Timmermans, *L'Accès des femmes à la culture (1598–1715)*, 2nd edn (Paris: Champion, 2005), pp. 239–80 and pp. 319–92.

[10] See Derval Conroy, ed., *Towards an Equality of the Sexes in Early Modern France* (London: Routledge, 2021) and Marie-Frédérique Pellegrin, *Pensées du corps et différences des sexes à l'époque moderne* (Lyon: ENS-Editions, 2020). Studies on women and curiosity also intersect with this field: see Neil Kenny, *The Uses of Curiosity in Early Modern France and Germany* (Oxford: Oxford University Press, 2004), pp. 367–380, pp. 384–424; and Line Cottegnies, John Thompson and Sandrine Parageau, eds, *Women and Curiosity in Early Modern England and France* (Leiden: Brill, 2016).

[11] For a recent study which challenges patriarchal approaches to literary and fictional women in the texts of the Grand Siècle, see Jennifer Tamas, *Au non des femmes: libérer nos classiques du regard masculin* (Paris: Seuil, 2023).

[12] Myriam Dufour-Maître, *Les Précieuses: naissance des femmes de lettres en France au XVIIe siècle*, 2nd edn (Paris: Champion, 2008); Joan DeJean, *Fictions of Sappho: 1546–1937* (Chicago: University of Chicago Press, 1989) and *Tender Geographies: Women and the Origins of the Novel in France* (New York: Columbia University Press, 1991); Anne E. Duggan, *Salonnières, Furies, and Fairies: The Politics of Gender and Cultural Change in Absolutist France* (Newark: University of Delaware Press, 2005); Domna Stanton, *The Dynamics of Gender in Early Modern France: Women Writ, Women Writing* (New York: Routledge, 2014). For a transnational approach to women's intellectual communities, see Carol Pal, *Republic of Women: Rethinking the Republic of Letters in the Seventeenth Century* (Cambridge: Cambridge University Press, 2012).

[13] Alain Viala, *Naissance de l'écrivain: sociologie de la littérature à l'âge classique* (Paris: Minuit, 1985), pp. 7–40.

[14] On the phenomenon of crises and *querelles* creating new terms or infusing old terms with new meanings, see Joan DeJean, *Ancients against Moderns*, and Gemma Tidman, *The Emergence of Literature in Eighteenth-Century France: The Battle of the School Books* (Liverpool: Liverpool University Press, 2023).

Georges and Madeleine de Scudéry's *Artamène ou le Grand Cyrus* (1649–53), and its interpolated 'Histoire de Sapho', in which Madeleine de Scudéry distinguishes between a positive prenominal adjective, 'sçavante fille', who is modest and hides her learning (although this term is rarely used), and a much more commonly used negatively connoted postnominal adjective, 'fille sçavante', and substantive noun, 'une femme qui fait la sçavante' (a woman who plays the learned lady), associating this figure and what Scudéry calls 'ce terrible nom' with overt demonstrations of knowledge, pedantry, and failed aspiration (as was then echoed famously by Molière in his 1672 *Les Femmes savantes*).[15] Gournay, writing in the early decades of the seventeenth century articulated, as noted, the challenge of categorising the female intellectual, but she did not solely use the term 'savante', alternating it with 'femmes studieuses', and 'femmes lettrées', nor did she invest it with dual positive and negative meanings, rendering it a term of praise or (positive) aspiration only. We can see Scudéry's hugely influential derogatory usage of 'savante', and her related vaunting of the modest female intellectual, as not only a turning point or threshold, to use Terence Cave's terms, in the history of this word and its referents, but also a watershed moment in ideologies surrounding female learning.[16] While it has much in common with the Humanist model of cultivated elegance, Christian ideals of the good woman as obedient and acquiescent, and contemporary ideas of women's 'civilising' influence and *politesse*, Scudéry's exemplary intellectual—and its foil, the 'savante'—stand out for their detail and their considerable influence on the next two generations.[17] From the middle of the century, this particular polyptoton, that is, the series of words derived from the root 'savoir', was, as Karen Newman argues, characterised by different grammatical derivations that had diverse and loaded 'cultural meanings' so specific to this moment in French culture that the term as it was used in the Scudérys' novel proved untranslatable into English.[18] That is not to say that there were no positive uses of the term 'savante'—three key texts from 1660s, which celebrated literary and illustrious women, used positively the postnominal and substantive 'savante'—but it is to stress both its contested definition and the influence of Scudéry's charged usage.[19]

The term 'sçavant' in the Latin-French dictionaries of the sixteenth century is defined positively as 'doctus', 'literatus', 'eruditus', with a sub-definition connoting

[15] Madeleine and Georges de Scudéry, 'Histoire de Sapho', *Artamène ou le Grand Cyrus* (Paris: Courbé, 1656), x, pp. 329–608 (p. 333, p. 380, p. 401). 'Galant' also differs in meaning in this period as an adjective according to whether its use is prenominal or postnominal, with the former a term of praise and the latter an insult. See Alain Viala, 'D'une politique des formes: la galanterie', *Dix-septième siècle*, 182 (1994), 143–51 (p. 143).

[16] Terence Cave, *Pré-histoires: textes troublés au seuil de la modernité* (Geneva: Droz, 1999).

[17] On these traditions, see Anne R. Larsen, 'A Women's Republic of Letters: Anna Maria van Schurman, Marie de Gournay, and Female Self-Representation in Relation to the Public Sphere', *Early Modern Women*, 3 (2008), 105–26 (p. 106); and Danielle Haase-Dubosc, 'Intellectuelles, femmes d'esprit et femmes savantes au XVIIe siècle', *Clio. Histoire, femmes et sociétés*, 13 (2001), <https://doi.org/10.4000/clio.133>. Curiosity could also be both positively and negatively associated with women, but as Kenny shows the association was primarily negative, even though Scudéry's own discussion of curiosity in her 1661 *Célinte* refrains from judgement. See Kenny, *Uses of Curiosity*, pp. 367–75, 384–424.

[18] Karen Newman, 'The French Disease', *Comparative Literature*, 64.1 (2012), 33–48 (p. 42).

[19] La Forge's *Le Cercle des femmes savantes* (1663), Jacquette Guillaume's *Les Dames illustres* (1665), and Marguerite Buffet's *Nouvelles Observations* (1668).

6 WOMEN WRITING ANTIQUITY

expertise ('estre sçavant en' or 'gnarus').[20] Frédéric Godefroy offers 'savant', the pre- and postnominal adjective, as an attribute of one 'qui a de la science';[21] for Edmond Huguet, 'sçavant' means 'habile'.[22] Godefroy and Huguet also both note derived pejorative terms: 'savantas' as 'savant ennuyeux, pédant';[23] and 'sçavanteau' is a 'dérivé péjoratif de sçavant'.[24] By the end of the seventeenth century, we witness a shift in the dictionary definitions. 'Savant' in the masculine has a first-level adjectival meaning akin to these earlier definitions: 'Docte; qui a beaucoup lû et étudié; qui a beaucoup de science et d'érudition' and 'habile' (learned, one who has much read and studied; who has much knowledge and erudition);[25] 'Qui a de la science, et de l'érudition, qui a de belles et de solides connoissances dans de certaines matieres' (who has knowledge, erudition, good and solid understanding of certain subjects);[26] 'Qui sçait beaucoup en matiere d'erudition, de litterature' and 'Qui est bien instruit, bien informé de quelque chose, de quelque affaire' (who knows much in terms of erudition and cultural knowledge; who is well instructed, well informed of something or some matter).[27] However, the adjective in the masculine can also mean 'pédant' in certain contexts: 'Les sçavants de profession sont souvent fort sots, et très ridicules, parce qu'ils affectent trop de faire connoître qu'ils sont sçavans' (Those who are learned by profession are often very stupid and ridiculous because they strive too much to make it known that they are learned).[28] Most significantly, the term now occurs in the feminine as both an adjective and a substantive, *and* when the feminine use is distinguished it is with pejorative connotations: 'Les femmes qui affectent le titre de sçavantes ne sont pas sur un bon pied dans le monde' (women who feign the title of learned are not well regarded) and 'elle fait la scavante' (she plays the learned lady),[29] which is clarified by a cross-reference to 'pédante': 'Pedante, se dit, d'une femme qui fait la sçavante et la capable'.[30]

---

[20] Robert Estienne, *Dictionnaire françois-latin* (Paris: Estienne, 1539), p. 448; Jean Nicot, *Dictionnaire françois-latin* (Paris: Du Puys, 1573), p. 560.

[21] Frédéric Godefroy, *Dictionnaire de l'ancienne langue française et de tous ses dialectes du 9e au 15e siècle*, 10 vols (Paris: Vieweg and Bouillon, 1881–1902), x: *Complément. Inaccoutumé-Zoophyte* (Paris: Bouillon, 1902), p. 634. Edition used: <https://www.classiques-garnier.com/numerique-bases/godefroy>.

[22] Edmond Huguet, *Dictionnaire de la langue française du seizième siècle*, 7 vols (Paris: Champion and Didier, 1925–67), xi (Paris: Didier, 1965), p. 720. Edition used: <https://www.classiques-garnier.com/numerique-bases/huguet>.

[23] Godefroy, p. 634.

[24] Huguet, p. 712. 'Savantas' is also included as a separate entry in the seventeenth-century dictionaries.

[25] Antoine Furetière, *Dictionnaire universel* (Amsterdam: Leers, 1690), np.

[26] Pierre Richelet, *Dictionnaire de la langue française* (Geneva: Wider, 1680), np.

[27] *Dictionnaire de l'Académie française*, 2 vols (Paris: Coignard, 1694), ii, p. 447.

[28] Furetière, *Dictionnaire universel*, np.

[29] Ibid.; *Dictionnaire de l'Académie française*, ii, p. 447.

[30] *Dictionnaire de l'Académie française*, ii, p. 207. This cross-reference occurs also in Furetière under 'pédant': 'Il y a aussi des femmes *pedantes*, qui font les sçavantes à la manière du College.' Furetière, *Dictionnaire universel*, np.

The *femme savante*, given cultural weight in the Scudérys' novel, emerged therefore as a recognised figure in the second half of the century, as is also attested by the numerous satires and fictional representations of it.[31] This figure has received critical attention: Domna Stanton, focusing in particular on the education treatises by François Poullain de la Barre and François Fénelon, argues that this figure replaced 'la précieuse' to become 'a privileged object of struggle in gender ideology' and stresses that its varying signification from positively connoting *belle-lettrists* and philosophers to its use as a term of pedantry and ridicule attests to this struggle. Stanton locates its various definitions and the related debates about women's learning in a wider picture of the creation of—and departure from—gender norms in this period.[32] Timmermans identifies the complexity of this category and its opposing meanings of pretension and learning; its dichotomous uses of ridicule and aspiration; and its shifting referents in terms of the sort of knowledge it designates.[33] Looking in particular at the satirical uses of this figure, she suggests that as a 'type' it enjoyed immense success.[34] The collected volume by Colette Nativel focuses on the wide range of domains of learning—scientific, religious, legal, philosophical, literary—and includes different case studies to highlight exceptional women's engagements with cultures of learning.[35] Looking at the long eighteenth century, and commencing in 1690, Adeline Gargam tracks historical and fictional 'femmes savantes, lettrées et cultivées', placing them in the context of debates about women's education and sexual difference.[36]

This present study builds on this excellent scholarship that has treated the figure of the 'savante' but takes a different approach: rather than directing its conclusions towards an understanding of shifting gender norms, it explores how the struggle to define the female intellectual—a struggle that is represented in part by the word history of the term 'savante' but also, as I show, by broader attempts to define this figure—shaped and reflected wider debates over the nature, value, and practices of literature.[37] In so doing, it resonates with other significant studies that

[31] For a collected study of these representations, see the chapters under the section 'Savants and Savantes' in *Le Savoir au XVII siècle*, ed. by John D. Lyons and Cara Welch (Tübingen: Narr, 2002), pp. 183–235.

[32] Stanton, *The Dynamics of Gender*, pp. 96–97. On Buffet, see also Faith E. Beasley, 'Marguerite Buffet et la sagesse mondaine', in *Le Savoir au XVII siècle*, ed. by Lyons and Welch, pp. 227–35.

[33] Timmermans, *L'Accès des femmes*, pp. 338–52. Nathalie Grande also shows that 'femme savante' could refer to both literary and scientific learning: 'Qui furent les femmes savantes? Réflexions sur l'accès des femmes à la science au temps de Louis XIV', in *Femmes de sciences de l'Antiquité au XIX* siècle. Réalités et représentations, ed. by Adeline Gargam (Dijon: Editions universitaires de Dijon, 2014), pp. 57-67.

[34] Timmermans, *L'Accès des femmes*, pp. 338–52; see also pp. 319–37.

[35] Colette Nativel, ed., *Femmes savantes, savoirs des femmes: du crepuscule de la Renaissance à l'aube des Lumières* (Geneva: Droz, 1999). For a similar case studies-based approach to the eighteenth century, see Roland Bonnel and Catherine Rubinger, eds, *Femmes savantes et femmes d'esprit: Women Intellectuals of the French Eighteenth Century* (New York: Peter Lang, 1994).

[36] *Les femmes savantes, lettrées et cultivées dans la littérature française des Lumières ou La conquête d'une légitimité: 1690-1804*, 2 vols (Paris: Champion, 2013).

[37] The various different meanings of 'savante' depending on its grammatical function are not directly addressed in the Nativel collection or by Timmermans or Stanton—and indeed, Gargam deliberately

8 WOMEN WRITING ANTIQUITY

have looked at the relationship between women (as subjects and as an idea) and cultural and political change in France.[38] 'Savant/e' has particular resonance in this period because of the tension it contains between erudite, traditional forms of learning, which include literacy in Latin and a classical education, and more 'modern', French forms of learning. For instance, where for Gournay a 'femme savante' was necessarily learned in Latin and this was positive; for Scudéry, the 'femme savante' was a pedant for her demonstration of classical knowledge; for Poullain de la Barre, who associated the 'dame sçavante' and the 'sçavante' positively with the new science of self-knowledge, influenced by the inclusive philosophy of Descartes's *Discours de la méthode*,[39] this figure abhorred Latin and her knowledge had nothing to do with antiquity.[40] Both the term 'savante' and the figure of the female intellectual more widely—a figure I show to preoccupy all of the women in my corpus—are therefore deeply entwined with the reception of antiquity and the ideologies underpinning this reception.[41]

The word history of the term 'savante' can be compared to that of 'autrice', a feminine noun that also proved contentious in this period: in both cases the contested definitions are an example of 'le mot' absorbing the debates prompted by 'la chose'. The resistance to certain feminine nouns (a resistance that was only officially overcome in 2019 when the *Académie française* gave approval to the use of feminine terms for most *métiers* and *fonctions*)[42] is to be placed in the linguistic context

avoids endogenous uses of this term, preferring exogenous categories. Inevitably there was sometimes some slippage between 'femme savante', 'femme auteur', 'femme cultivée', 'femme illustre', and 'précieuse', etc. See also Timmermans, *L'Accès des femmes*, pp. 338–48.

[38] For instance, Duggan reads works by Scudéry and d'Aulnoy in relation to political, social and cultural changes in *Salonnières, Furies, and Fairies*; Rebecca Wilkin has examined the centrality of ideas of 'women and gender difference' to the 'epistemological experimentation that culminated in the "new science"' of this period' in *Women, Imagination and the Search for Truth* (p. 1); Dufour-Maître examines the relationship between 'précieuses' and the literary field in *Précieuses*; and DeJean has argued that many of the questions at the heart of the Quarrel of the Ancients and Moderns were propelled by women's cultural presence and practice in *Ancients against Moderns*.

[39] For a nuanced intervention in the question of Descartes and the representation of women, see Wilkin, pp. 183–222, and Marie-Frédérique Pellegrin, 'Equality, Neutrality, Differentialism: Descartes, Malebranche, and Poulain de la Barre', in *Towards an Equality of the Sexes*, ed. by Conroy, pp. 22–38. On Cartesianism, see Marie-Frédérique Pellegrin, 'Cartesianism and Feminism', in *The Oxford Handbook of Descartes and Cartesianism*, ed. by Steven Nadler, Tad M. Schmaltz, and Delphine Antoine-Mahut (Oxford: Oxford University Press, 2019), pp. 565–79.

[40] Poullain de la Barre, *De l'égalité des sexes; De l'éducation des dames; De l'excellence des hommes*, ed. by Marie-Frédérique Pellegrin (Paris: Vrin, 2011), p. 79, p. 82, p. 76. See Marie-Frédérique Pellegrin, 'La science parfaite: savants et savantes chez Poulain de la Barre', in *Penser au féminin au XVIIe siècle*, ed. by Vicent Guillin and Marie-Frédérique Pellegrin (= *Revue Philosophique de La France et de l'Étranger*, 138.3 (2013)), pp. 377–92 (p. 391). See also Stanton, *The Dynamics of Gender*, pp. 98–103.

[41] My emphasis on this preoccupation runs counter to what Julie Crawford suggests in relation to England—'yet the women who produced literary texts in the early modern period did not do so primarily in order to "find a voice" in print, nor to make cultural space for such a phenomenon as "the woman writer"'—although I agree that they also had many other motivations for writing as she delineates. Julie Crawford, *Mediatrix: Women, Politics, and Literary Production in Early Modern England* (Oxford: Oxford University Press, 2014), p. 3.

[42] <https://www.academie-francaise.fr/sites/academie-francaise.fr/files/rapport_feminisation_noms_de_metier_et_de_fonction.pdf>.

INTRODUCTION 9

of the seventeenth century—a period credited not only with being a transitional moment because of the standardisation and codification of the French language,[43] but also with ushering in the masculinisation of French, evident from the shift towards the preferred use of the universal masculine pronoun and agreement. As Éliane Viennot and others remind us, grammar is never a neutral or objective phenomenon, and there were exclusionary strategies at play in its development.[44] Related to this masculinisation was movement against the feminisation of terms used to designate certain activities: this debate crystallised in particular around the term 'autrice'. This is a term Marie de Gournay used liberally in her œuvre, both as a scholar of Latin (it has its roots in the Latin feminine noun 'auctrix', meaning female creator or originator, used in the feminine from the first century CE) and as a (proto)-feminist intellectual, trying to find a name, and thus a place, for herself. In contrast, Guez de Balzac, engaging directly with Gournay, was critical of the use of this term.[45] He was actually in favour of '-rice' female-gendered suffixes (and so calls Gournay a 'traductrice') and against the '-esse' suffix (Gournay, for him, is a poète not a poétesse; a philosophe not a philosophesse)—although one might be minded to consider these preferences as already imposing a gendered hierarchy with translation an activity deemed suitable for women, but poetry and philosophy less so. Despite this preference for the '-rice' suffix, he argued against the use of 'autrice', criticising its use in Latin by Tertullian and praising Virgil's use of the masculine 'auctor' to describe Juno in the *Aeneid*.[46] Feminist linguistics scholars, such as Viennot and Aurore Evain, persuasively suggest that the bias against this referent indicates a wider one against its referee: 'une lecture en creux prouve qu'il s'agit moins de censurer un féminin que de condamner la femme qui écrit' (a detailed reading shows that it is less a question of censuring the feminine than of condemning women who write).[47] They credit Balzac's stance as influential:[48] the term 'autrice' in the feminine is not included in the dictionaries of later in the century, its usage no longer current.[49]

---

[43] See Antoine Adam, *Histoire de la littérature française au XVIIe siècle* (Paris: Albin Michel, 1997) and Anthony Lodge, *French: from Dialect to Standard* (London: Routledge, 1993).

[44] See Éliane Viennot, *Non, le masculin ne l'emporte pas sur le féminin! Petite Histoire des résistances de la langue française* (Paris: Éditions iXe, 2014).

[45] Guez de Balzac, 'Lettre à Monsieur Girard', 7 May 1636, *Œuvres de Monsieur de Balzac*, 2 vols (Paris: Billaine, 1665), I, p. 257. On his *Lettres*, see Mathilde Bombart, *Guez de Balzac et la querelle des Lettres: écriture, polémique et critique dans la France du premier XVIIe siècle* (Paris: Champion, 2007).

[46] Balzac, 'Lettre à Monsieur Girard', p. 257.

[47] Aurore Evain, 'Histoire d'autrice, de l'époque latine à nos jours', *SÊMÉION, Travaux de sémiologie*, 6 (2008), 53–62 (p. 58). See also Éliane Viennot, 'La Querelle de la langue', in *La France, les femmes et le pouvoir, 2. Les résistances de la société (17e–18e siècles)* (Paris: Perrin, 2008), pp. 78–84; and 'La guerre des mots' section on the website of the Société internationale pour l'étude des femmes de l'ancien régime: www.siefar.org.

[48] For instance, Gilles Ménage quotes his letter in the *Observations sur la langue française*, 2 vols (Paris: Barbin, 1676), II, pp. 367–70.

[49] For example, Furetière says 'On dit aussi d'une femme qu'elle s'est erigée en auteur quand elle a fait quelque livre ou pièce de théâtre' (One also says of a woman that she assumes the role of author

'Savante' has a different fate: for a start, the term *is* included in the *Dictionnaires*. There are two reasons for this: one socio-linguistic and one linguistic. 'Savante', as this study will explore and as I have intimated above, became a commonly used word at the very moment it was also a term of ridicule, so that the character and activity it describes are not valorised by the act of naming them, unlike the process entailed by the term 'autrice'. Having a name, therefore, is not enough in itself to ensure an accepted place in literary culture; and, as Scudéry's gesture shows, a feminised term is not necessarily an equalising one: it can also work within an excluding grammatical logic if its gendering conveys inequality. Secondly, 'savante' is both a substantive and an adjective—and feminine adjectival endings posed no problem for conversative grammarians in this period—and the substantive derives from the adjective: in other words, it does not as unambiguously designate a *métier* or *fonction* in the same way as, for example, 'autrice' does. It is precisely because 'savante', by virtue of its social usage and its grammatical function, avoids the banishment from use suffered by other feminised nouns that it proves a rich and fascinating object of study.

This study also differs from previous scholarship by focusing on instances of self-presentation or self-naming (or instances where self-identification and fictional representations blur, as in Scudéry's 'Sapho'), and relates this construction of authorial ethos to an author's practice, and specifically to her classical reception. This allows us to prioritise the gestures and reflections of individuals instead of concentrating on how these women were received, or ridiculed, as is more commonly the case in relation to studies of the 'femme savante'. While my focus on self-representation may appear to risk rehearsing what Chris Kraus describes as the world divided into 'poet-man, presenter of ideas, and actress-woman, presenter of themselves',[50] I do not read the ethos and postures of the authors studied biographically or in isolation: my intention is rather to trace the relationship between constructions of a female intellectual self and wider notions of literature and authorship. This emphasis on authorial ethos also allows for more scope for difference between the women studied and resists the tug of collectivity that can sometimes shape scholarship on 'women's writing', including the work of feminist historians in the 1990s.[51] Instead, I follow more recent work that is wary of the

---

when she has written a book or a play). Furetière, *Dictionnaire universel*, np. The 1694 *Dictionnaire de l'académie française* includes no feminisation under its entry for 'autheur' (I, 73). The second edition of 1718 states: 'En parlant d'une femme qui aura composé un livre, ou fait quelque ouvrage d'esprit, on dit, qu'elle est l'autheur d'un tel livre, d'un tel ouvrage' (Describing a woman who has composed a book or other work, one says that she is the author of that book or that work). *Nouveau dictionnaire de l'académie française*, 2 vols (Paris: Coignard, 1718), I, p. 119.

[50] Chris Kraus, *I Love Dick* (London: Serpent's Tail, 2016), pp. 161–62. As quoted in Hannah Dawson, *The Penguin Book of Feminist Writing* (London: Penguin, 2023), p. 44. For a recent study of early modern women's self-presentation see Beatrijs Vanacker and Lieke van Deinsen, eds, *Portraits and Poses: Female Intellectual Authority, Agency and Authorship in Early Modern Europe* (Leuven: Leuven University Press, 2022).

[51] For example, DeJean, *Tender Geographies*. In contrast, Stanton raises questions of individual distinction: 'the case of Scudéry raises vexing questions about the relation (and tensions) between gender

category of the 'woman writer', either because this appears, if left unpacked, to have essentialising connotations, and/or because it assumes a common orientation towards feminised genres or women's causes.[52] Taking its cue from scholarship, such as that by Hilary Brown, that seeks to go beyond a 'female tradition', this study brings women together as much to challenge ideas of unity as to explore them.[53] Like Brown, I build on long-standing work that has foregrounded gender as a category of analysis, which sees gender as one category alongside others, such as class, education, and faith;[54] and allows us to avoid essentialising notions of 'man' and 'woman'.[55]

The figure of the seventeenth-century 'savante' is haunted by the spectre of a late nineteenth-century neologism: 'salonnière'. *Le Grand Robert* defines this as 'une femme qui fréquente les salons' (a woman who attends salons) and dates its first use to Maupassant in the 1880s. *Le Petit Robert* suggests: 'Propre aux salons, à l'esprit mondain des salons' (pertaining to salons, to their mondain esprit), and the *Oxford English Dictionary*: 'A woman who holds a salon; a society hostess'.[56] As these definitions suggest, 'salonnière' is associated with 'mondain' activities and the social, facilitating role played by the women it designates. Gargam, who uses this term throughout her study, acknowledges that it is not used by any of the texts in her corpus but argues that it is 'une commodité de langage postérieure, qui nous permet de rassembler les femmes cultivées sous un concept qui est défini en littérature comme typiquement féminin ou presque' (a convenient retrospective term which allows us to group together all cultivated women under an umbrella term which is defined in literature as more or less typically feminine), showing how 'salonnière' usefully describes a 'femme de bel esprit', a 'précieuse', or a 'savante', and essentially connotes any woman connected to salon culture.[57] That approach is justifiable; however, there is potentially a danger of imprecision.

---

normativity and individual practice, and correlatively, the importance of deciphering the signs of conformity to gender codes and those of a subject's resistance, which delineates the nature and extent of agency'. Stanton, *The Dynamics of Gender*, p. 23.

[52] For work questioning this category, see, for instance, Laura Lunger Knoppers, 'Introduction: Critical Framework and Issues', in *The Cambridge Companion to Early Modern Women's Writing*, ed. by Laura Lunger Knoppers (Cambridge: Cambridge University Press, 2009), pp. 1–18 (p. 8).

[53] See Hilary Brown, *Women and Early Modern Cultures of Translation: Beyond the Female Tradition* (Oxford: Oxford University Press, 2022), in particular the Introduction, pp. 1–18. See also Danielle Clarke, *The Politics of Early Modern Women's Writing* (Harlow: Pearson, 2001).

[54] Joan W. Scott, 'Gender: A Useful Category of Historical Analysis', *The American Historical Review*, 91.5 (1986), 1053–75. For an overview of the field in relation to early modern Britain, see Lara Dodds and Michelle M. Dowd, 'Happy Accidents: Critical Belatedness, Feminist Formalism, and Early Modern Women's Writing', *Criticism*, 62.2 (2020), 169–93.

[55] See also Laura Knoppers: such a focus enables us to 'ground our work in historical particulars' with gender as 'the socially constructed roles, behaviours and activities that a given society considers appropriate for men and women, based on perceptions of biological [assigned] sex'. Knoppers, 'Introduction', pp. 8–9. See also Merry Wiesner-Hanks, *Women and Gender in Early Modern Europe*, 4th edn (Cambridge: Cambridge University Press, 2019), pp. 1–16.

[56] *Le Grand Robert* online: <https://www.lerobert.com/dictionnaires/francais/langue/dictionnaire-le-grand-robert-de-la-langue-francaise-edition>; *Le Petit Robert* online, <https://petitrobert-lerobert-com; Oxford English Dictionary Online: https://www.oed.com/>.

[57] Gargam, II, p. 587.

Firstly, the problems with the term 'salonnière' as a nineteenth-century coinage overlap with the problems caused by the fact that the 'salon', as the designation of a gathering—with assumptions about the nature of those gatherings—is also a nineteenth-century term (the first definition of 'salon' as figurative, meaning 'la bonne compagnie' and 'les gens du beau monde', occurs in the 1835 *Dictionnaire de l'Académie française*).[58] Whether pre-Revolutionary gatherings or salons were in fact as they were represented in certain seventeenth-century sources, and those of the nineteenth century such as by Victor Cousin and Pierre-Louis Roederer,[59] has been the subject of scholarly debate, with some scholars suggesting that the compelling notion of the salon as an egalitarian Republic of Letters that privileged intellectual exchange, dominant in particular in Anglophone criticism,[60] replicates the ideological inventions of the likes of Roederer and Cousin.[61] Instead, others argue, 'salons', or rather *ruelles*, to use the contemporary term, were not necessarily privileged spaces of conversation over other social locations;[62] they were primarily elite social and leisure, rather than intellectual, spaces, marked by social hierarchy and opportunism where *professionnels des lettres* and urban elites did not mix equally but in a dynamic of power and exchange.[63] Such professionals often mimicked the overtly amateur *mondain* sociable practices of the urban elites to hide their professional status, but their roles and powers were different.[64]

Although salons are not the object of this study, I engage with this debate in two ways, without necessarily taking a partisan approach: firstly, as I will develop further in the body of this book, I am interested in how social spaces of literary exchange are represented in certain texts in my corpus (in the treatises of Gournay, the novels of Scudéry, the poems of Deshoulières, the correspondence

---

[58] *Dictionnaire de l'Académie française*, 2 vols (Paris: Firmin-Didot Frères, 1835), II, pp. 697–98.

[59] Pierre-Louis Roederer, *Fragments de divers mémoires pour servir à l'histoire de la société polie en France* (Paris: Didot Frères, 1834) and Victor Cousin, *La Société française au XVIIe siècle d'après Le Grand Cyrus de Mlle de Scudéry* (Paris: Didier, 1858), and *La Jeunesse de Mme de Longueville: études sur les femmes illustres et la société du XVIIe siècle* (Paris: Dider, 1853). See Antoine Lilti, 'Les salons d'autrefois: XVIIe ou XVIIIe siècle?', *Les Cahiers du Centre de Recherches Historiques*, 28–29 (2002), <http://journals.openedition.org/ccrh/1032>.

[60] See, for instance, Dena Goodman, *The Republic of Letters: A Cultural History of the Enlightenment* (Ithaca: Cornell University Press, 1994); and Daniel Gordon, *Citizens without Sovereignty: Equality and Sociability in French Thought, 1670–1789* (Princeton: Princeton University Press, 1994).

[61] See Lilti, 'Les salons d'autrefois: XVIIe ou XVIIIe siècle?'.

[62] Nicolas Schapira, 'Écrivains et élites urbaines au XVIIe siècle: peut-on se passer du modèle du salon?', in *La ville et l'esprit de société*, ed. by Katia Béguin and Olivier Dautresme (Tours: Presses Universitaires François-Rabelais, 2004), pp. 17–32.

[63] See Ibid. and Antoine Lilti, *Le Monde des salons: sociabilité et mondanité à Paris au XVIIIe siècle* (Paris: Fayard, 2005). On this debate, see Elena Russo, review [of Antoine Lilti], *The World of the Salons: Sociability and Worldliness in Eighteenth-Century Paris* (Oxford: Oxford University Press, 2015), *Reviews in History*, <https://reviews.history.ac.uk/review/2041>. On debates about the material culture of the salon, see Alain Niderst, Delphine Denis and Myriam Dufour-Maître, eds, Madeleine de Scudéry, Paul Pellisson et leurs amis, *Chroniques du Samedi. Suivis de pièces diverses* (Paris: Champion, 2002) and Geoffrey Turnovsky, 'Chroniques des *Chroniques du Samedi*: l'invention d'un manuscrit', *Les Dossiers du Grihl* [Online], 11-2 | 2017, https://doi.org/10.4000/dossiersgrihl.6795.

[64] Schapira, 'Écrivains et élites urbaines au XVIIe siècle'.

and *mémoires* of Murat)—and how sociability affects literature, as evident in the poetic games of Deshoulières—particularly to consider how the female intellectual is constructed as a social identity and its purchase on the dynamics of the literary field. I draw both on scholarship that sees the 'salon' as a vibrant intellectual community—and am particularly persuaded by Faith E. Beasley's recent elaboration of the central place of the salon, and of conversation, in intellectual culture in her study of the role played by Marguerite de la Sablière's salon in the image of India in the French imaginary—and on scholarship which stresses the posturing and power dynamics at play.[65] Secondly, I treat with caution the term 'salonnière', wary of the conflation of seventeenth-century salons with 'préciosité', and thus frivolity, in much eighteenth- and nineteenth-century historiography.[66] As Beasley and Elena Russo have also shown, the role of the *salonnière* shifted from the seventeenth to the eighteenth centuries, from a figure actively involved in writing to more of a mediator or facilitator, so that a seventeenth-century *salonnière* is not the same as an eighteenth-century one.[67] When the term is used to designate women writers who attended or hosted salons, with the intention to focus less on the hosting and more on the writing, it often refers implicitly to a particular ideological grouping—the modern, *mondain*, writers of 'leisure literature' (often female-coded and also vaunting aristocratic amateurism over professionalism)—and forms an implicit contrast with 'savant' culture. That usage is justifiable if it is that leisure culture which is of interest; however, there is a danger of not only missing an author's masking of professional strategies under a posture of elite urbanity (or *mondainité*), but also of upholding a (gendered) hierarchy of intellectual value attributed across genres and forms of learning: would we call Marie de Gournay, a salon host, or Anne Dacier, an attendee, *salonnières*? Indeed, would we call Balzac or Racine, also attendees, *salonniers*?

Underpinning my approach is a concern to push beyond some of the normative paradigms of formalist classical reception studies: namely the prioritising of fidelity, shaped by an implicit focus on an author's literacy in ancient languages. Criticism has often focussed on classical reception in the work of Latinate women and on forms that are obviously reception, such as translation: in so doing it brings to light crucial and important work by women, and shows how some women used these elite forms of knowledge to question the very power dynamics and exclusion they represent. However, this approach also necessarily structures early modern women's engagements with Greco-Roman culture around literacy

---

[65] Faith E. Beasley, *Versailles meets the Taj Mahal: François Bernier, Marguerite de la Sablière and Enlightening Conversations in Seventeenth-Century France* (Toronto: University of Toronto Press, 2018). For a study of intellectual circles earlier in the century, see Robert A. Schneider, *Dignified Retreat: Writers and Intellectuals in the Age of Richelieu* (Oxford: Oxford University Press, 2019).

[66] See Lilti, 'Les salons d'autrefois: XVIIᵉ ou XVIIIᵉ siècle?'.

[67] Faith E. Beasley, *Salons, History and the Creation of Seventeenth-Century France* (Aldershot: Ashgate, 2006), pp. 174–248 (p. 181); Elena Russo, *La Cour et la ville: de la littérature classique aux lumières* (Paris: Presses Universitaires de France, 2002), pp. 107–08.

in Latin.[68] For instance, significant work by Jane Stevenson and Laurie Churchill has focussed on women Latinists; and the important and chronologically wide-ranging *Women Classical Scholars*, which examines women's classical reception from the Renaissance to the twentieth century, defines a female classicist as a 'philologist', foregrounding linguistic knowledge.[69] This would (and does) include Anne Dacier, but exclude Madeleine de Scudéry. Alongside this, there is a growing corpus of research on post-1800 European and American women's classical reception, in which a much broader range of cultural products by authors both literate in Latin and not are accepted as legitimate forms of reception.[70] In contrast, scholarship on early modern France has tended to overlook classical presences in the more 'popular' genres of novels, certain forms of theatre, and poetry by non-Latinate women, genres which fall into what Viala describes as the 'cultural category' of *galant* writing: Modern, French, and female-orientated.[71] In this respect, early modern genres have been a site of implicit or explicit judgement according to their degree of learning: with traditional forms of reception (translation, imitation, commentary), in the hands of 'savantes', valued more highly than new genres that took the ancient world as their subjects (historical novels or romances, imagined lives, incidental verse, epistolary novels) and were products of a female-orientated salon culture, by so-called *salonnières*.

With this book, I address this gap in scholarship and hope to equalise the literary value of these different forms of culture, not only as cultural products but, crucially and originally, as valid forms of classical reception, showing how non-scholarly genres, such as the novel, constitute legitimate forms of learning, alongside women's translations and imitations of ancient texts. This methodology breaks from the current approaches to early modern women and Greco-Roman

---

[68] For scholarship on the gendering of knowledge, see Lorraine Code, *What Can She Know? Feminist Theory and the Construction of Knowledge* (Ithaca: Cornell University Press, 1991), Londa Schiebinger, *The Mind Has No Sex? Women in the Origins of Modern Science* (Cambridge, MA: Harvard University Press, 1989), and Michèle Le Dœuff, *Le Sexe du savoir* (Paris: Aubier, 1998). On the historiography of women and the history of philosophy, see, for instance, Sarah Hutton, '"Blue-eyed Philosophers Born on Wednesdays": An Essay on Women and History of Philosophy', in *The History of Women's Ideas*, ed. by Karen Green and Ruth Hagengruber (= *The Monist*, 98.1 (2015)), pp. 7–20.

[69] Jane Stevenson, *Women Latin Poets* (Oxford: Oxford University Press, 2005); Laurie J. Churchill, Phyllis R. Brown and Jane E. Jeffrey, eds, *Women Writing Latin: from Roman Antiquity to Early Modern Europe*, 3 vols, III: *Early Modern Women Writing Latin* (London: Routledge, 2002). Rosie Wyles and Edith Hall, eds, *Women Classics Scholars: Unsealing the Fountain from the Renaissance to Jacqueline de Romilly* (Oxford: Oxford University Press, 2016), p. 13.

[70] Isobel Hurst, *Victorian Women Writers and the Classics: The Feminine of Homer* (Oxford: Oxford University Press, 2006); Tracey L. Walters, *African American Literature and the Classicist Tradition: Black Women Writers from Wheatley to Morrison* (Basingstoke: Palgrave Macmillan, 2007); Fiona Cox, *Sibylline Sisters: Virgil's Presence in Contemporary Women's Writing* (Oxford: Oxford University Press, 2011) and *Ovid's Presence in Contemporary Women's Writing: Strange Monsters* (Oxford: Oxford University Press, 2017); Yopie Prins, *Ladies' Greek: Victorian Translations of Tragedy* (Princeton: Princeton University Press, 2017); Fiona Cox and Elena Theodorakopoulos, eds, *Homer's Daughters: Women's Responses to Homer in the Twentieth Century and Beyond* (Oxford: Oxford University Press, 2019).

[71] Alain Viala, *La France galante: essai historique sur une catégorie culturelle, de ses origines jusqu'à la Révolution* (Paris: Presses Universitaires de France, 2008).

culture by foregrounding the ideologies at stake in reception and by taking a different angle on the very question of literacy: one that explores not only historical literacy—that is, women's education and access to ancient learning—but also literacy as a symbolic value.[72] I will examine women who paraded their literacy in ancient languages (particularly Marie de Gournay and Anne Dacier) and those who claimed not to possess such literacy, even when writing about the ancient world, preferring an overtly 'modest' approach to knowledge (Madeleine de Scudéry; Madame de Villedieu). Thus, rather than dividing women according to their (apparent) linguistic ability—an ability which is notoriously difficult to judge accurately—I will instead analyse how this literacy and the knowledge it represented were used as tools for fashioning authorial identities.

Ancients, Moderns, and Literary Value

A key premise of my study is that any notion of this projected intellectual self is entangled with, and informed by, an idea of the public, and more specifically, by patronage and/or the literary market, driven by the 'economic imperative' that shaped the careers of the women studied here.[73] This study builds on what Geoffrey Turnovsky describes as the symbolic order of the literary market, and his emphasis on the literary market as a site for establishing legitimacy (and not just making money). I show how Greco-Roman culture becomes, for the writers studied here, key to how they present themselves and therefore to how they shape their relationship with the public.[74] Particularly important is the tension between the professionalisation of the writer, and the related necessity to earn a living by one's pen, and what Viala calls 'le tropisme nobiliaire', that is, the aristocratic vaunting of amateurism over money-making (such detachment was especially expected of women).[75] Most of the authors in my corpus shared the need to navigate this tension because of financial difficulties, resulting in complex career strategies and, significantly, complex representations of their own intellectual activities: for instance, Scudéry, aspiring to aristocracy, and dependent on favours and patronage, played down the professionalism of her literary activity, and the labour of her learning (and thus her Latinity), even though she did also (and did need to)

---

[72] Margaret W. Ferguson also approaches literacy in Latin in this light by looking at its social value, considering the relationship between claims to (and denials of) literacy and social performance, particularly in relation to gender. Margaret W. Ferguson, *Dido's Daughters: Literacy, Gender, and Empire in Early Modern England and France* (Chicago: Chicago University Press, 2003).

[73] On the broader trends of this 'material turn' towards women's finances, see Carme Font Paz and Nina Geerdink, eds, *Economic Imperatives for Women's Writing in Early Modern Europe* (Leiden: Brill, 2018).

[74] Geoffrey Turnovsky, *The Literary Market: Authorship and Modernity in the Old Regime* (Philadelphia: University of Pennsylvania Press, 2010).

[75] Viala, *Naissance*, pp. 261–64. On this risk, see Elizabeth C. Goldsmith and Dena Goodman, eds, *Going Public: Women and Publishing in Early Modern France* (Ithaca: Cornell University Press, 1995).

16 WOMEN WRITING ANTIQUITY

profit from it financially; Gournay, on the other hand, needed to prove her worth, through her knowledge of classical culture, in order to court her patrons; whereas Villedieu, with her publisher, Claude Barbin, developed her own lucrative and influential conception of ancient historical fiction that was geared to public and commercial success.

Underlying some of these different positions was the Quarrel of the Ancients and Moderns and its debates about ideologies of learning, classical reception, especially vulgarisation and adaptation, and literary value. I show how the women in this corpus were all engaging with the Quarrel, usually in forms or genres that we are not necessarily accustomed to understanding as interventions—occasional verse, novels, fairy tales, rather than treatises—with their practice, that is, how they interpreted antiquity, as well as their representations of this practice, key to their polemical gestures. Classical languages and culture, particularly Latin, were (still) the epitome of what constituted learning within the literary field in seventeenth-century France, and whereas men had the cultural privilege to deny the importance of Latinity and Greco-Roman culture (the Modern position), the path to legitimacy for women was more complicated. For those women who espoused Modern views in particular, this path was freighted by a negotiation of belonging through both their demonstration of classical learning and their denial of it. In many respects, the gestures analysed here constitute versions of a 'stratégie de multiple alliance' as authors targeted and accommodated both erudite and 'worldly' readers to secure and legitimise their place in the literary field.[76]

This Quarrel has long roots into the Renaissance, and emerges throughout the seventeenth century in the guise of other instances of confrontation and debate.[77] The *Querelle des anciens et des modernes* proper—a name that was conferred by historians, but in the period 'querelle', 'dispute', 'guerre', and 'duel' were used to define the confrontations it entailed—also refers to two particular moments. The first is from 1687 with the public confrontation between Charles Perrault (the Modern) and Nicolas Boileau (the Ancient) in the *Académie française* when the latter stormed out at Perrault's reading of his poem, 'Le Siècle de Louis le Grand', which argues that French culture surpasses that of antiquity, and which prompted a flurry of texts back and forth. It also refers to the years 1711–16 and the specific *querelle* between Anne Dacier, Antoine Houdar de La Motte, and others over how to translate Homer and whether to 'foreignise' or to assimilate the culture of his epics. Contained within this Quarrel, often seen as both a 'mega-quarrel',

---

[76] This term derives from Viala, *Naissance*, pp. 167–68; it has been used recently by Marine Roussillon to describe the uses of the medieval past in works by Georges and Madeleine de Scudéry in the 1640s and 1650s, whereby what she calls 'l'imaginaire médiéval' also had a dual purchase on learned and worldly cultures of reading. Marine Roussillon, *Don Quichotte à Versailles: l'imaginaire médiéval au grand siècle* (Ceyzérieu: Champ Vallon, 2022), pp. 32–33.

[77] On the longer history, see Marc Fumaroli, 'Les Abeilles et les araignées', in *La Querelle des anciens et des modernes*, ed. by Anne-Marie Lecoq (Paris: Gallimard, 2001), pp. 7–218.

in that it engulfed others, and a 'meta-quarrel', in that it was also about how to argue—about agonistic rhetoric and polemic—as much as it was about its subject matter,[78] are a number of other related Quarrels that I study in this volume, which include the *querelle d'Homère*, and of course the broad *querelle des femmes*, as well as a range of other smaller interconnected ones (about language reform in the early part of the century; tragic historical theatre; inscriptions; pastoral verse; troubadours; and the animal soul).

I develop scholarship of the Quarrel of the Ancients and Moderns, and the interconnected quarrels I analyse, particularly in relation to gender. This study joins the recent work exploring the limitations of the 'feminism' of the Moderns, who appropriated female taste as an example of spontaneous, natural expression in contrast to book learning;[79] and work analysing the association and connections between the Quarrel of the Ancients and Moderns and the *querelle des femmes*—starting from Joan DeJean's argument that the Quarrel was propelled by the vulgarisation of knowledge represented by women, and evident most obviously in the battle over female taste and cultural authority waged between the Modern, Charles Perrault in his *Apologie des femmes*, and the Ancient, Nicolas Boileau in his *Satire X, Contre les femmes*.[80] I build on this to show that many of the characteristics or positions we understand to be 'Modern' are usually derived from only a selection of Modern texts. Looking at how women engaged in the Quarrel destabilises this paradigm, questioning the constitution of a quarrel's corpus, given that women were not expected to quarrel and their gestures in quarrels were sometimes met with a delegitimising silence.[81]

More broadly, this study also benefits from and builds on the extensive recent work in early modern French studies that has attended specifically to the many intellectual and literary *querelles* that marked this period.[82] It particularly draws on work which emphasises the relationship between literary *querelles* and the wider

---

[78] Alexis Tadié, 'The Language of Quarrels', in *Theories of Quarrels*, ed. by Alexis Tadié (=*Paragraph*, 40.1 (2017)), pp. 81–96.

[79] See, for example, Myriam Dufour-Maître, 'Trouble dans la galanterie? Préciosité et questions de genre', *Littératures classiques*, 90.2 (2016), 107–18.

[80] Joan DeJean, *Ancients against Moderns*. On the limitations of *galanterie* as egalitarian, see Lewis C. Seifert, *Manning the Margins: Masculinity and Writing in Seventeenth-Century France* (Ann Arbor: University of Michigan Press, 2009), pp. 89–91; see also Helena Taylor, 'Ancients, Moderns, Gender: Marie-Jeanne L'Héritier's "Le Parnasse reconnoissant, ou, le triomphe de Madame Des-Houlières"', *French Studies*, 71.1 (2017), 15–30 and Anne E. Duggan, 'The *Querelle des femmes* and Nicolas Boileau's *Satire X*: Going beyond Perrault', *Early Modern French Studies*, 41.2 (2019), 144–57.

[81] See Myriam Dufour-Maître, 'Femmes, querelles galantes du dix-septième siècle et histoire littéraire', in *Women and* Querelles *in Early Modern France*, ed. by Helena Taylor and Kate E. Tunstall (= *Romanic Review*, 112.3 (2021)), pp. 372–88.

[82] In particular, I take my cue from the work produced as part of the Agence Nationale de la Recherche-funded project on early modern French *querelles*, 'AGON': <http://www.agon.paris-sorbonne.fr/fr>. See also Gérard Ferreyrolles, ed., *La Polémique au xviie siècle* (= *Littératures classiques*, 59 (2006)); Christophe Prochasson and Anne Rasmussen, eds, *Comment on se dispute: les formes de la controverse* (= *Mil neuf cent. Revue d'histoire intellectuelle*, 25.1 (2007)). See also 'Modernités en Querelle', <https://modernites.hypotheses.org>.

literary field—that is, the way in which such *querelles* both expressed and shaped the dynamics of the role of the author and the values attributed to literature, as well as its very constitution.[83] I use the English term 'literature' in this study to refer primarily to what in the period was described as 'belles-lettres', that is, an emergent and unstable category that comprised texts which were aesthetically pleasing, which reflected certain ideas about taste, value, practitioners, and right judgement and which came increasingly to be associated with a national canon—questions that were debated in the *Querelle des anciens et des modernes*. As Gemma Tidman shows, the primary meaning of 'littérature', by contrast, for most of the seventeenth century was 'erudition' or 'cultural knowledge'.[84] However, since my corpus includes texts which clearly engage in literary culture but might not be defined as 'belles lettres'—for instance, Gournay's writings, Dacier's translations—and my interest lies in the hybridity of knowledge cultures, I use the term 'literature' in English as it offers more flexibility than the French *belles-lettres*.[85]

Critics have long argued that the seventeenth century witnessed the emergence of the relatively autonomous and distinct 'literary field', with its own institutions and forms of production, circulation, and consumption. Michael Moriarty has shown that with this literary field 'a specifically literary criticism took shape';[86] and Larry Norman has persuasively linked the development of such criticism to the Quarrel of the Ancients and Moderns and its focus not only on national French literary history but also on questions of the properties of literature, such as alterity, affect, and imagination.[87] Joan DeJean has suggested that the sociable practices of the salon can be seen as forms of literary criticism.[88] I engage with this scholarship and approach many of the works studied here as forms of literary criticism as they seek to define French literary history and literary value in relation to, or in contrast with, Greco-Roman culture. Where other studies have engaged with 'literary' representations of the 'femme savante', I am concerned with how conceptions of the 'savante' informed notions of the value and ideologies of literature.

---

[83] See, for instance, Alexis Tadié and Anne-Lise Rey, 'Introduction', in *Disputes et territoires épistémiques*, ed. by Tadié and Rey (= *Revue de Synthèse*, 137 (2016)), pp. 223–26. See also Alain Viala, *L'Adhésion littéraire* (Montreuil: Le Temps des Cerises, 2022).

[84] Tidman, *The Emergence of Literature*, p. 10. Tidman shows that the term 'littérature' came to replace *belles-lettres* in the 1760s to refer to writing that was pleasing, erudite, part of a national canon, and, significantly, constituted a discipline.

[85] In this usage I follow many critics, for instance, Norman, *The Shock of the Ancient*.

[86] Michael Moriarty, 'French Criticism in the Seventeenth Century', in *The Cambridge History of Literary Criticism*, III: *The Renaissance*, ed. by Glyn P. Norton (Cambridge: Cambridge University Press, 2008), pp. 555–65 (p. 555).

[87] Larry F. Norman, 'La Querelle des anciens et des modernes, ou la métamorphose de la critique', in *Naissance de la critique littéraire*, ed. by Patrick Dandrey (= *Littératures classiques*, 86 (2015)), pp. 95–114. For a French–English comparison of the way the Quarrel developed a language of criticism, see Alexis Tadié, 'Ancients, Moderns and the Language of Criticism', in *Ancients and Moderns in Europe: Comparative Perspectives*, ed. by Paddy Bullard and Alexis Tadié (Oxford: Voltaire Foundation, 2016), pp. 37–54.

[88] Joan DeJean, 'Rooms of their Own: Literary Salons in Seventeenth-Century France', in *The Cambridge History of Literary Criticism*, pp. 378–83.

Corpus, Methods, and Chapters

My decision to bring women authors together in this study and my approaches to them and their work are not essentialising: I do not presuppose that they are necessarily all interested in advancing a cause for women's learning or collectivity or that they write from a shared position.[89] Rather, I take gender to be a useful category of analysis because in this case the restrictions to women's access to a classical education shaped both/either the conditions of their use of antiquity and/or the reception of that usage. This study traces the varieties of learning possessed by elite French women at this time (autodidactism; family education, and tutoring; salons and learning through friendship): the variety here should therefore resist any notion that a systemic exclusion from formal education resulted in the same education; it also resists a sense that such exclusion always resulted in any sort of inferior learning.[90] And yet, where gender does prove a unifying factor for the authors studied here is in the relationship between their work and the expectations of their reading public and the—divergent but nevertheless similarly self-conscious—self-presentation that comes from navigating such expectations.

In bringing the different authors of my corpus together, I pay attention to and acknowledge the divisions in forms of knowledge as they were constructed by women at the time in part so that they could navigate these expectations, but I also show that we need to be careful not to replicate such divisions in our methodological approach to these authors' works, if that replication results in categorising learning in a way that perpetuates a limited conception of it and excludes a whole range of female intellectuals from cultures of classical reception. This book thus offers a similar approach to the feminist scholarship that has called for the inclusion of 'nontraditional intellectual-history sources' in the study of intellectual history;[91] and endorses Beasley's argument that 'salon sociability was as strongly implicated in knowledge creation as the various academies'.[92]

There are two further principles governing the selection of the corpus for this study. The first is the primary focus on the reception of Greco-Roman literature, as a broad category (that is, poetry, including philosophical poetry, novels, and also oratory and history): it does not directly treat the reception of texts we would

---

[89] Scholars have long stressed that women often upheld class or gender restrictions: see Knoppers, 'Introduction', p. 14. See also Jaime Goodrich and Paula McQuade, eds, *Beyond Canonicity: the Future(s) of Early Modern Women Writers* (= *Criticism*, 63 (2021)).

[90] On the variety of women's learning despite exclusion from formal spaces in England, see Caroline Bowden, 'Women in Educational Spaces', in *The Cambridge Companion to Early Modern Women's Writing*, ed. by Knoppers, pp. 85–96. See also John J. Conley, 'Tutor, Salon, Convent: The Formation of Women Philosophers in Early Modern France', *British Journal for the History of Philosophy*, 27.4 (2019), 786–805.

[91] Katherine J. Hamerton, 'A Feminist Voice in the Enlightenment Salon: Madame de Lambert on Taste, Sensibility and the Feminine Mind', *Modern Intellectual History*, 7.2 (2010), 209–38 (p. 213).

[92] Beasley, *Versailles meets the Taj Mahal*, p. 19.

20   WOMEN WRITING ANTIQUITY

designate as philosophy (Aristotle, Plato, etc.). The second is the focus on vernacular writing: some women wrote in Latin, even some of the women in this corpus, but those works will not be discussed in detail here.[93] Those decisions have as weaknesses a potential for perpetuating gendered divisions of knowledge, whereby literary and vernacular genres often have less intellectual value because of their association with women's work than philology and philosophy. And it would be interesting, for example, to explore further Marie de Gournay's receptions of ancient philosophy, building on the work of Marguerite Deslauriers, or to bring in a figure not included in this corpus, Gabrielle Suchon, and explore her uses of ancient philosophy.[94] However, by focusing on the literary and the vernacular, this study hopes to achieve the opposite of perpetuating those gendered divisions: to reinstate some of this work to reception studies and to show how the struggle for (self-)definition of the woman intellectual was crucial to the major cultural debates in this period over the nature and value of literature.

Each chapter takes an author or several authors as its focus, but is structured around a larger theme. The second chapter, 'Authority, Authorship, and Agonism: Antiquity and Writing the Self', analyses the place of classical reception in the construction of an author's ethos through the works of Marie de Gournay. Marie de Gournay (1565–1645) was a self-declared autodidact of Latin, prolific essayist, translator of Latin, theorist of women's equality and capacity for an education equal to men's, and perhaps mostly famously known as Michel de Montaigne's 'fille d'alliance', and first posthumous editor of his essays, for which she also provided translations of the Latin quotations. In this chapter I argue that antiquity was essential to the construction of her authorial ethos: she used her knowledge of Greco-Roman culture to present herself as an authoritative and engaged 'femme savante' or 'femme studieuse', a category she also shows to be an aporia, and, grounded in an urgent need to solicit favour, she made her own case exemplary for female education, as is particularly evident in her autobiographical writing. Central to that ethos, I then show, was her stance as a polemicist: her translations of Cicero's *Second Philippic*, Sallust's oration by Marius to the Roman people, and Tacitus's speech of Galba, and their prefaces, demonstrate how she ventriloquised the (male) polemical and persuasive voice in order to gain her own authority as an intellectual and as a polemicist, using these texts about succession, corruption, and merit as a way into exploring ideas of good governance and meritocratic (literary) practice. I then explore how her translation of extracts from Virgil's *Aeneid* allowed her to intervene in debates about poetics, language reform, and

---

[93] For a study of Latin literacy and Latin writing by women in this period, see Stevenson, *Women Latin Poets*, pp. 324–35; and Churchill, Brown and Jeffrey, eds, *Women Writing Latin: from Roman Antiquity to Early Modern Europe*, III: *Early Modern Women Writing Latin*.

[94] Marguerite Deslauriers, 'Marie de Gournay and Aristotle on the Unity of the Sexes', in *Feminist History of Philosophy: The Recovery and Evaluation of Women's Philosophical Thought*, ed. by Eileen O'Neill and Marcy P. Lascano (New York: Springer, 2019), pp. 281–99.

male-female equality. The chapter closes by examining her reception, probing the reasons (sociological; taste; gendered) why, although highly regarded in many circles, Gournay was subject to significant and sustained ridicule both in her lifetime and afterwards. Gournay proves an apt starting point for this study as she represents an important transitional moment, looking back to the Ronsardian poetics of the Renaissance at a time when they were already becoming outmoded.

The third chapter, 'The Paradoxes of Modesty: Historical Fiction and the Female Line', considers the alternative and hugely influential model for a female intellectual as espoused by Madeleine de Scudéry (1607–1701) and links this to her development of the modern genre of historical fiction. Madeleine de Scudéry heralded a break from the poetics and gender politics of Gournay with an influential modest version of female 'savoir', defined in opposition to what she saw as a pedantic 'savante'. This chapter explores the paradox that Scudéry's modesty hinged on a denial of classical knowledge for reasons of social mores, but that she frequently turned to Greco-Roman literature and history as models while establishing her career. Focusing on her early works—the Sappho letter from the *Les Femmes illustres* (1642); the 'Histoire de Sapho' in *Le Grand Cyrus* (1649–53); and *Clélie* (1654–60), her Roman history—I examine how she influenced literary taste with modern and feminised versions of ancient history. The chapter first treats the tensions between learning and modesty in her own ethos of amateurism and in the portrayal of her exemplary female intellectual 'Sapho', and her counterpart, the 'savante', and examines the literary genealogies represented by 'Sapho' (and her double, Anacreon), which anchor Scudéry's poetics of the novel to both a female-orientated line of lyric as well as the more traditional masculine epic. Showing how Scudéry creatively engaged with ancient sources and the exemplarity tradition, it then considers her revisionist representation of the role of masculinity in the founding of the Roman Republic through her rewriting, in *Clélie*, of the characters of Lucrèce, Clélie, and particularly Brutus. This reading complicates the prevailing view that sees Scudéry as a precursor of a feminism of 'difference' and establishes her as a key figure in traditions of ancient historical fiction that continue today.

Chapter 4, '"Classics" as Commodity: Antiquity and the Literary Market', analyses the place of ancient historical fiction in the commercial success of an author's career. Using Turnovsky's conceptions of the 'literary market' as a symbolic order as much as an economic one, and drawing on book history methodologies, it considers how writers made their name (as well as their living) by 'cashing in' on the appeal of historical fiction set in antiquity. The chapter focuses in particular on Madame de Villedieu (1640–1683), another professional writer, whose complex and at times antagonistic relationship with her publisher, Claude Barbin, as well as her prolific output of bestselling fictions set in antiquity, make her an important test case. Focusing on paratextual material, including the multiple *privilèges d'auteur* she solicited in her name, her self-conscious authorial naming, and the *querelle* involving her play, *Manlius*, this chapter explores her explicit manoeuvres

22 WOMEN WRITING ANTIQUITY

vis-à-vis the market and her dedicatees and patrons, to suggest that together she and Barbin defined a lucrative Modern aesthetic that in part hinged on Villedieu's self-presentation as *galante* rather than *savante*. Challenging Turnovsky's assertions that the 'success' valued in this period was not commercial, but predicated on a distance from commerce, I argue that she positioned her authorial identity and her *galant* ancient historical fiction in such a way as to celebrate commercial success and to exploit the opposition between *savant* and *galant* culture, thus remodelling literary value, questioning the dichotomy between commercial and intellectual prestige. The chapter closes by stressing Villedieu's influence in redefining women's relationship to profit by examining the cases of Catherine Bernard, who had great success rewriting antiquity for the stage, and the novelist, Anne de La Roche-Guilhen, the first to openly state that money-making was her object. It thus stresses the enduring commercial appeal of ancient history to an author positioning herself in the literary market.

In Chapter 5, 'Salon Verse and the Philosopher-Poet', I analyse the place of ancient philosophical poetry in 'salon verse' by looking in particular at Antoinette Deshoulières (1638?–1694). The poetry of Antoinette Deshoulières, a figure who has received comparably little critical attention among the authors of my corpus, and one of the few female poets of this time to publish a full collection of poetry, is replete with classical intertext. I focus on her nonsense version of Lucretius, her Virgilian pastoral, and her reworkings of Anacreon, Horace and Ovid, to analyse her philosophical scepticism and her interest in ancient atomism and Epicurus, which has its origins in her education by the Gassendist, Jean Dehénault. I explore the playful hermeneutics of her 'Imitation de Lucrèce en galimatias fait exprès', as her irony and burlesque style allow her to use this philosopher-poet to reflect on poetry's capacity to make meaning. She revisits this question in her eclogues which I show engage with quarrel surrounding the eclogue in the 1680s: a version of Ancients and Moderns, it was a quarrel about whether certain forms of poetry (namely the 'simple' pastoral) can or should be philosophical. This scepticism extends to her scrutiny of man's reason in her pastoral verse, particularly her idylls, where she takes an innovative approach to the classical and Renaissance genre of pastoral to engage in the debates about the animal-machine and to question the supremacy of man's reason, favouring an anti-Cartesian view. I then demonstrate how she uses ancient models (Anacreon and Horace) to reflect on salon verse and the status of the (female) poet. Showing that she takes an elusive position in the Quarrel of the Ancients and Moderns, I argue that she 'thinks with' a range of ancient texts to explore 'authority' as both authorial and epistemological.

The sixth chapter, 'Ancients and Moderns: *Conteuses* as Literary Critics', turns to four writers of fairy tales (and other genres) to analyse how they used Greco-Roman culture to explore questions of literary value and, approaching their work as metadiscursive, understands it as literary criticism. It analyses the work of the *conteuses*, Marie-Catherine d'Aulnoy (1650/51–1705), Charlotte de La Force

(1650–1724), Henriette-Julie de Murat (1668–1716), and Marie-Jeanne L'Héritier (1664–1734). Based on the premise that the *conteuses* were self-consciously Modern, it explores the differences in their conceptions of modernity from those of Charles Perrault, so-called father of the fairy tale, to emphasise the more complex genealogies that include classical and medieval, folklore and fable, traced by the *conteuses* in their quest to find legitimacy for their genre and their authorship, to trouble hierarchisations of genre, and to define 'French literature'. I first examine d'Aulnoy's *Gracieuse et Percinet* (1697) and La Force's *Plus belle que fée* (1698) as rewritings of the story of *Cupid and Psyche*. I suggest that although they incorporate into their version the Modern elements of the fairy tale as delineated by Perrault—morality and the triumph of virtue—they both nevertheless deliberately chose as source text a story that Perrault had derided, in a complex assertion of independence that also complicates the ancient/modern divide he was advocating. I then consider how Marie-Jeanne L'Héritier self-consciously incorporated both Modern gestures and classical intertext into her fairy tales (1696), her 'Parnassus' fictions, and her periodical, *L'Érudition enjouée*, in ways that distinguish her from Perrault, and analyse her coining of the term 'savante moderne'. In the last section I look at how Henriette-Julie de Murat develops some of the tensions between ancient and modern when she classes Perrault as 'ancient' in the preface addressed to the 'Fées Modernes' from her *Histoires sublimes et allégoriques* (1699). I show how she continues to play with tropes of modernity in her 1708 *Journal pour Mademoiselle de Menou* which contains a 'dialogue des morts' between 'Madame de Villedieu' and the ancient Roman 'Junie' from Villedieu's *Les Exilés de la cour d'Auguste* (1672–76). The chapter reflects on how these works question the masculinist boundaries of our understanding of what it meant to be a Modern and explores the relationship between these writers' articulations of 'savoir mondaine', the figure of the 'savante moderne', and definitions of literature.

The final chapter, 'The Career Classicist: Gender and Translation', analyses the only figure from this period to be vaunted—both then and now—as a Classicist and a 'savante': Anne Dacier (1647–1720). To date there has been little sustained analysis of Dacier's use of antiquity and its relationship to her self-fashioning across her œuvre, or contextualisation of her practice within a wider focus on gender, learning, and women's classical reception in this period. In this chapter I examine how Dacier unsettles gendered norms—as a female Ancient, as a scholar of Latin and Greek, and as an accepted quarrel participant. I argue that, progressively, across her translations and her prefaces, she moved from a more *galant* (even Modern) approach in her first translation of Sappho and Anacreon of 1681 through to an increasingly strident Ancient voice in her translations of Plautus (1683), Aristophanes (1684), and Terence (1688), culminating in her involvement in the *Querelle d'Homère* with her Homer translations and essays (1711–16). I argue for the importance of understanding this *Querelle* not as a mere accident or vocation but rather as a strategic move to strengthen her literary reputation:

her identity as a 'savante' was linked to her identity as a quarreller. For all the respect she commanded, Dacier also had to navigate expectations of her gender, making an apparently successful distinction between social and authorial identities. The chapter then considers her reception, emphasising that in her lifetime she was subject to fewer overtly gendered criticisms than after her death, but that at all times her position as a woman engaging in polemic proved problematic. Her exceptionalism has meant that more recently she has been classed among Classicists and thinkers, but not 'women writers', a category generally reserved for those who wrote in feminised genres or advocated for female causes, which I suggest reveals an inherited bias that eclipses the complexity of her position—and reveals the limitations of how those categories are sometimes used.

The Conclusion reflects on the study's contributions. It then broadens the enquiry beyond the seventeenth century and beyond France to trace the legacy of the '(femme) savante'. It tracks the influence of this figure in England, in particular on the 'Bluestocking' movement of the eighteenth century and its French counterpart, the 'Bas-Bleu', and moves forward to the late nineteenth- and early twentieth-century 'Girton Girl'. The study closes by thinking more broadly about how some of the seventeenth-century questions analysed here continue to influence contemporary concerns about the gendering of learning, of language, and of professions.

2

Authorship, Authority, and Agonism

Antiquity and Writing the Self

Marie de Gournay (1565–1645) explores everywhere in her multi-genre writing the challenges faced by the female intellectual, challenges also attested to by her chequered reception. As a figure unafraid of using '[s]a propre expérience' as a test case for the general, Gournay exposed herself to considerable criticism and slander in her lifetime, as has been documented.[1] She was an autodidact in Latin, who argued for women's right to, and capacity for, an education equal to men's in the *Égalité des hommes et des femmes* (1622). She was a significant voice in the question of the 'sexed mind', arguing against this proposition on numerous occasions, as articulated in this image: 'il n'est rien plus semblable au chat sur une fenestre, que la chatte' (nothing so resembles a (male) cat on a windowsill as a female one).[2] She was associated with the intellectual circle surrounding Marguerite de Valois and a prized attendee of the salon of Madame des Loges; in her later years she held important salons at her home in the rue de l'Arbre sec and then in the rue Saint-Honoré, attended by prominent intellectuals, including Michel de Marolles and La Mothe Le Vayer. She was also a staunch defender of classical and Renaissance poetics against the language reform and standardisation of French proposed by François de Malherbe and others and consolidated by the *Académie française*. Knowledge of ancient Greek and Roman culture is held up throughout her work—notably her essays, translations, and poetry—as the pinnacle of learning. Her authorial ethos and authority are thus almost always dependent on her demonstration of her knowledge of ancient literature and philosophy. This knowledge was a fraught site of both legitimacy and inadequacy as Gournay grappled with her lack of Greek, her ad hoc schooling in ancient philosophy, and her self-taught Latin, aware that, as a woman, her footing in intellectual culture was already compromised. Throughout her work, she explores and represents the inadequacy of the female intellectual faced with a masculine conception of learning.

---

[1] Marie de Gournay, 'Grief des Dames', in Marie de Gournay, *Œuvres complètes*, ed. by Jean-Claude Arnould and others, 2 vols (Paris: Champion, 2002), I, pp. 1074–80 (p. 1075). All subsequent references to this edition will be given in the text. On the slander, see in particular Emily Butterworth, 'Marie de Gournay and the Abuse of Mockery', in *Poisoned Words: Slander and Satire in Early Modern France* (Leeds: Legenda, 2006), pp. 60–75.

[2] Marie de Gournay, 'Égalité des hommes et des femmes', in *Œuvres complètes*, I, pp. 965–88 (p. 978).

Women Writing Antiquity. Helena Taylor, Oxford University Press. © Helena Taylor (2024).
DOI: 10.1093/oso/9780192870445.003.0002

The ancients and their authority are therefore everywhere in her œuvre, published as her complete works in 1626 as *L'Ombre de la Damoiselle de Gournay* (as she entered her sixties and perhaps wanted to take stock of her career); and then again, in augmented form, in 1634 as *Les Advis ou les presens de la Damoiselle de Gournay*, and finally again under the same title in 1641 as a definitive version.[3] This work is clearly envisaged as a complete œuvre, as she makes clear in the prefatory 'Discours à Sophrosine'—the figure for soundness of mind and good judgement, attributes so lauded by her 'adopted father', Montaigne—added from 1634.[4] Antiquity features in Gournay's work in two key ways: as a source of authority—political, moral, poetic—and, related to this, as the subject of her extensive translation work (she translated extracts from Cicero, Sallust, Tacitus, Ovid, and Virgil). Where the construction of her ethos has been approached in relation to her autobiographical writings and to her identity as a translator, little work has explicitly considered the relationship between antiquity, learning, and authorial ethos in Gournay's writing.[5] In this chapter, I analyse her figuration of the female intellectual in her autobiographical writings; then I turn to her translations, first of prose (Tacitus, Sallust, Cicero) and then of Virgil's *Aeneid*, before considering the place of classical reception and Latin in her poetry.[6] I argue that Gournay's representations of ancient culture and her self-conscious awareness of the prestige associated with knowledge of this culture offer a crucial insight into her ethos, her agonistic rhetoric, and her polemical and provocative theories of poetics.

Publication and authorial self are closely entwined in Gournay's work: not only does she make herself the subject or test case for many of her reflections on gender and learning, but she also makes it clear that her work is her textual monument.[7] She added this postscript to her definitive 1641 edition:

---

[3] *L'Ombre de la Damoiselle de Gournay* (Paris: Libert, 1626); this was reprinted in 1627; *Les Advis ou les presens de la Damoiselle de Gournay* (Paris: Tousssaint du Bray, 1634); *Les Advis ou les presens de la Damoiselle de Gournay, troisiesme édition* (Paris: Toussaint du Bray, 1641). On the stages of this composition, see in particular Anna Lia Franchetti, *L'Ombre discourante de Marie de Gournay* (Paris: Classiques Garnier, 2006), pp. 15–38.

[4] 'Discours sur ce livre à Sophrosine', in *Œuvres complètes*, I, pp. 553–67. She describes it as her 'œuvre' (p. 557) and claims the change in title was to satisfy her publisher and critics (p. 565).

[5] On the construction of her ethos as a translator, see Jean-Philippe Beaulieu, '"Moy Traductrice": le façonnement de la figure auctoriale dans le paratexte des traductions de Marie de Gournay', in *Women's Translations in Early Modern England and France*, ed. by Marie-Alice Belle (= *Renaissance and Reformation*, 35.4 (2012)), pp. 119–34. And more widely, on her autobiographical writing, see Domna Stanton, 'Auto-gynography: The Case of Marie de Gournay's *Apologie pour celle qui escrit*', in *Autobiography in French Literature* (Columbia, SC: University of South Carolina, 1985), pp. 18–31.

[6] On her uses of ancient philosophy, see Marguerite Deslauriers, 'Marie de Gournay and Aristotle on the Unity of the Sexes', in *Feminist History of Philosophy: The Recovery and Evaluation of Women's Philosophical Thought*, ed. by Eileen O'Neill and Marcy P. Lascano (New York: Springer, 2019), pp. 281–99.

[7] See Jean-Philippe Beaulieu, 'Marie de Gournay ou l'occultation d'une figure auctoriale', *Renaissance and Reformation*, 24.2 (2000), 23–34.

Si ce Livre me survit, je deffends à toute personne, telle qu'elle soit, d'y adjouster, diminuer, ny changer jamais aucune chose, soit aux mots ou en la substance, soubs peine à ceux qui l'entreprendroient d'estre tenus aux yeux des gens d'honneur, pour violateurs d'un sepulchre innocent. (II, p. 1864)

If this book survives me, I forbid anyone, whoever they may be, from adding to it, removing anything from it, or changing anything, either the words or the meaning, for those who do so risk being regarded by honourable people as violators of an innocent tomb.

Turning her work into a monument to herself has clear figurative implications—of self-aggrandisement, of authority and projection, of posterity and lineage, which themselves take on a new force given that they are in the hands of a woman—and her particular wording also articulates a somewhat fraught envisaged relationship with future readers, which I will explore. But the connection between self and text was also more pragmatic and immediate in Gournay's writing: her learning needed to be monetised as she found herself in a difficult financial position at the outset of her career. Much has been made of her status as 'fille d'alliance' of Montaigne, whom she befriended upon reading his *Essais*, and for whom she acted as posthumous editor for the 1595 edition, referencing and translating the majority of his Latin quotations for seventh edition she oversaw in 1617. Her edition would prove definitive until the end of the eighteenth century when an alternative manuscript (known as the Bordeaux copy) was discovered and became the primary source—although her 1595 edition still retains its authority (it was used for the 2007 Pléiade edition of the *Essais*).[8] Some attention has also been paid to what has been described as a mother-daughter relationship with the younger Dutch 'savante', Anna Maria van Schurman, with whom Gournay corresponded, advising on her learning.[9] However, it is her biological family and the state they left

---

[8] *Les Essais de Michel Seigneur de Montaigne, Édition nouvelle* (Paris: L'Angelier, 1595), which includes the 'Preface sur les Essais de Michel de Montaigne, par sa fille d'alliance', np. On this and her substantial editorial work, see *Marie de Gournay et l'édition de 1595 des Essais de Montaigne*, ed. by Jean-Claude Arnould (Paris: Champion, 1996). The Pléiade edition is Michel de Montaigne, *Les Essais*, ed. by Michel Magnien, Catherine Magnien-Simonin, and Alain Legros (Paris: Gallimard, 2007).

[9] On her relationship with Schurman, see Carol Pal, 'Marie de Gournay, Marie du Moulin, and Anna Maria van Schurman: Constructing intellectual kinship', in *Republic of Women: Rethinking the Republic of Letters in the Seventeenth Century* (Cambridge: Cambridge University Press, 2012), pp. 78–109; see also Anne R. Larsen, *Anna Maria van Schurman, 'The Star of Utrecht': The Educational Vision and Reception of a Savante* (London: Routledge, 2006), pp. 121–22; and on Schurman's appreciation of Gournay's learning and advocacy for female education, see Anne R. Larsen, 'A Women's Republic of Letters: Anna Maria van Schurman, Marie de Gournay, and Female Self-Representation in Relation to the Public Sphere', *Early Modern Women*, 3 (2008), 105–26. On their different strategies (Schurman's as more socially conforming and thus less confrontational, resulting in less damage to her reputation), see ibid., and Linda Timmermans, *L'Accès des femmes à la culture (1598–1715)*, 2nd edn (Paris: Champion, 2005), p. 307.

her in which will underly this chapter and its interest in how she used antiquity to create and maintain her reputation.[10]

Although Gournay was from a minor aristocratic background—her father, Guillaume le Jars, had a successful career in the service of Charles IX and Henri III, notably as the former's Treasurer; his wife, Jeanne de Hacqueville came from a successful family of jurists—she had to supplement her income with her writing by the time she was in her late twenties, given the complex and indebted state of the family finances after her mother died in 1591. Gournay's father's untimely death some thirteen years earlier, in 1578, had left his widow and their seven children in difficulty. Various factors (rising living costs, property damage, increasing taxes, political turmoil) meant that Jeanne le Jars had to borrow money; with debts increasing, she decided around 1580 to leave the expensive life in Paris and move to the Gournay estate, in Gournay-sur-Aronde in Picardy—the feudal rights to which her husband had purchased in 1568—with her (now) four daughters and her younger son (the elder son, Charles, was in Italy where he also required financial support). When Jeanne le Jars died in 1591, the family finances were in an even worse state: the debts were now considerable and, as the eldest, Marie had to find situations for her siblings and meet her liabilities. She did so by reducing her own portion of the estate (and so accepting a life of relative financial restraint) and through family connections which provided for her younger brother, Augustin, and sister, Marthe (the other sister, Madeleine, had married and the third, Léonore, we assume, had entered a convent).[11] Gournay resolved to live in Paris, independently: an unusual decision for a woman of her class. Her financial difficulties persisted as she lived at five different addresses in the ten years from 1601 to 1611.[12] She herself explains much of this financial situation in punctilious detail in the second part of her 'Apologie pour celle qui escrit' (1626). She provides such an explanation because, as she also describes, she needed to garner support and patronage, reassuring her 'investor' that she was careful with her money and yet still in need of support. Her reputation, and defending it, as she tirelessly did against her critics, especially those who suggested she squandered her money (her practice of alchemy was considered profligate), was for Gournay as practical as it was symbolic, as moral as it was connected to her intellectual abilities: self and authorship, the individual and the general, correspond throughout her work. Her connection with an author as celebrated as Montaigne provided her with a certain legitimacy—her editions of his work were important early steps in her career, and indeed continued throughout. She exploited and paraded this connection in the title of her early and only work of fiction, *Le Proumenoir de*

---

[10] There are two biographies: Michèle Fogel, *Marie de Gournay: itinéraires d'une femme savante* (Paris: Fayard, 2004) and Marjorie Henry Ilsley, *A Daughter of the Renaissance: Marie le Jars de Gournay, her Life and Works* (The Hague: Mouton, 1963).

[11] See Ilsley, *A Daughter of the Renaissance*, pp. 16–17 and pp. 38–39.

[12] See Fogel, *Marie de Gournay*, pp. 149–61.

Monsieur de Montaigne (1594), published with Montaigne's Parisian publisher, a picaresque tale that has nothing to do with her adopted father, save its dedication to him and apparent provenance from a story she told him while they were walking together.[13] And yet, as Emily Butterworth notes, Gournay was unusual as an early modern woman writer in that she was not married, had no family in publishing, and was not of the high nobility. She also did not aspire to the Humanist model of the educated woman, in which education was 'elegant cultivation' not studious competence; nor did she espouse the model of 'controlled and sophisticated *politesse*' emerging in the salons of the aristocrats, Madame de Rambouillet and Madame des Loges.[14] Gournay, then, as we will see, was a pioneer.

Ethos and Learning

Possessing the learning that knowledge of classical texts represents was fundamental to Marie de Gournay's construction of her authorial ethos: erudition for Gournay was measured by classical knowledge. Her self-representation in her autobiographical works is marked by a fragile tension between expressions of her own inadequacy with her lack of Greek, her position as an autodidact in Latin, and evident extensive knowledge of the Latin language and of Greek and Roman literature and philosophy; between her acute awareness of her exclusion from elite cultures of knowledge, and her mastery of elements of that knowledge. In the *Égalité des hommes et des femmes*, she puts forward a theoretical argument for why women should be educated, based on a premise that they possess equal capacities to men. In her autobiographical writing, which has been approached particularly from the perspective of feminism,[15] and in relation to slander,[16] she offers an insight into the relationship between ethos, authority, and classical learning: in gestures that mingle the individual and the collective, she offers herself as a test case for what she reveals to be the aporia or category error of the female intellectual.

Gournay provides her readers with three autobiographies, although she also includes autobiographical references in the prefaces that accompany her translations, and in her feminist treatises, the 'Grief des dames' (1626), and even the *Égalité des hommes et des femmes*. Her three 'autobiographies' are 'Copie de la Vie de la Damoiselle de Gournay, envoyée à Hinhenctum Anglois' (1641); 'La Pincture des mœurs' (composed 1616, published 1626), a verse account of her

---

[13] Marie de Gournay, *Le Proumenoir de Monsieur de Montaigne, par sa fille d'alliance* (Paris: L'Angelier, 1594).

[14] Butterworth, 'Marie de Gournay and the Abuse of Mockery', p. 61.

[15] See, in particular, Marie de Gournay, *Apology for the Woman Writing and Other Works*, trans. by Richard Hillman and Collette Quesnel, The Other Voice in Early Modern Europe (Chicago: Chicago University Press, 2002); Stanton, 'Auto-gynography'. See Franchetti, *L'Ombre discourante*, pp. 39–70, for a discussion of how Gournay works her image throughout her œuvre.

[16] See Butterworth, 'Marie de Gournay and the Abuse of Mockery', pp. 60–75.

character, rather than a narrative of her life, dedicated to Jean d'Espagnet, conseiller d'état, and fellow alchemist; and the 'Apologie pour celle qui escrit' (1626), in which she justifies her learning, particularly her interest in alchemy, and defends her household management against critics.[17] The 'Copie de la Vie de la Damoiselle de Gournay, envoyée à Hinhenctum Anglois' was allegedly initially written as the result of a prank: according to Tallemant des Réaux's *Historiettes*, in 1616 three friends of Malherbe (the Comte de Moret, the Chevalier de Bueil, and Yvrande) forged a letter from King James of England asking for an account of her life; she wrote this only to be humiliated.[18] However, in a defiant gesture of reclaiming the narrative and redefining it on her own terms, she published it anyway: that she thus has the 'last word' is literalised by the position of this 'Vie' as the conclusion to her complete works.

It is primarily the question of legitimacy, respect, and the problem posed by the female intellectual in the eyes of society that consumes most of Gournay's prose autobiographical writing, which I will examine here. In her 'Copie de la Vie de la Damoiselle de Gournay', of which half is devoted to a description of how her encounter with Montaigne and his family changed the course of her life, she alludes to the challenges she faced in accessing education:

> à des heures pour la pluspart desrobées, elle aprit les Lettres seule, et mesme le Latin sans Grammaire, et sans ayde, confrontant les Livres de cette Langue Traduicts en François, contre leurs originaux. Et fit son estude ainsi, tant par l'aversion que sa mere aportoit en telles choses, que parce que cette authorité maternelle l'emmena soudain après le trespas du pere en Picardie à Gournay, lieu reculé des commoditez d'apprendre les Sciences par enseignement ny par conference. (II, p. 1862)

> in mostly stolen hours, she studied letters on her own, and even Latin without a grammar, and without help, comparing books in this language translated into French with their originals. And she did so as much because her mother expressed distaste for this sort of thing, as because this maternal authority had taken her suddenly to Gournay in Picardy after her father's death, a place far from the amenities needed for learning, whether teaching or discussion.

Her use of the third person here highlights that she was writing in what was normally a biographical rather than autobiographical genre (the 'vie') and it also underscores how far writing her life thus contributes to her self-fashioning as a

---

[17] The common English translation of which, *Apology for the Woman Writer*, misses the nuance in the French 'celle', which captures the tension between the indvidual and the general in her work, giving: *Apology for the/this Woman who Writes*.

[18] See an account of this in Gédéon Tallemant des Réaux, 'Mlle de Gournay', *Historiettes*, ed. by Michel Jeanneret and Antoine Adam (Paris: Gallimard, 2013), pp. 257–60.

public intellectual since this genre was necessarily reserved for the illustrious of history. Gournay depicts her learning as a form of defiance against expectations (maternal, in this case), and explains that her method of learning Latin by comparing original with translation was the only one available to her without other resources. The autodidactism in Latin described here, which is also mentioned defensively in the prefaces to her translations, as I explore below, recurs in her autobiographical writing as a focal point for her discussions of the difficulties faced by women in accessing knowledge, the problem posed by the female intellectual for wider society, and her extra-institutional knowledge. This is most clearly the case in her 'Apologie pour celle qui escrit':

> Est-il au demeurant, un tel but particulier à caquets, en nostre climat, que la condition des amateurs de Science, s'ils ne sont d'Eglise ou de robe longue? Il n'est rien pour luy de sot ny de ridicule, après la pauvreté, comme d'estre clair-voyant et sçavant: combien plus d'estre clair-voyante et sçavante, ou d'avoir simplement, ainsi que moy, desiré de se rendre telle? Parmy nostre Vulgaire, on fagotte à fantasie l'image des femmes Lettrées: c'est-à-dire, on compose d'elles une fricassée d'extravagences et de chimeres: et dit-on en general, sans s'amuser aux exceptions ou distinctions, qu'elles sont jettées sur ce moule. Quelle que soit après celle de ce mestier, qui se presente, et pour contraire que sa forme soit à cella-là, ce Vulgaire ne la comprend en façon quelconque: et ne la voit-on plus, qu'avec des presumptions injurieuses, et soubs la figure de cét épouventail. (II, pp. 1391–92)

> All things considered, isn't the condition of lovers of learning, if they are not of the Church or of the law, a particular target of cacklers in our climate? There is nothing as foolish or ridiculous for them, after poverty, as being clear-sighted and learned; how much more so to be a clear-sighted and learned woman, or simply, like me, to have desired to make oneself so? Among our vulgar class, they fantastically prank up the image of an educated woman—that is, they make of her a stew of extravagancies and chimeras, and they say in general, without bothering with exceptions and distinctions, that such women are shaped on this mould. Whatever may present itself beyond this stereotype to disprove her conformity to it, those vulgar people in no way understand her, and she is no longer seen except in the light of wrongful presumptions and as the image of such a scarecrow.[19]

Poverty, learning, and being a woman make one vulnerable to ridicule. Her terminology is worthy of note: 'clair-voyant' here serves as an opposition to those whose social standing has provided them with a formal education through the church or schooling; she interchanges 'sçavante' with 'femmes lettrées' (and later 'femme studieuse'); she also identifies a difference between what she implies are

---

[19] Gournay, *Apology*, trans. by Hillman and Quesnel, pp. 124–25.

32 WOMEN WRITING ANTIQUITY

true 'sçavantes' and those, like her, who are aspirational. 'Sçavante' in her usage of the term is not negatively inflected in the way we will see it become in the writing of Madeleine de Scudéry, analysed in the next chapter, whose aspirational 'savante' figure, Damophile, is the pedantic fool later echoed in Molière's *Les Femmes savantes* (1672). However, Gournay does attend to the negative stereotypes pertaining to the word and its referent: she later adds that to the 'mespriseurs du sexe' 'les Sçavantes sont des escervelées' ('the disdainers of this sex', 'learned women are scatterbrained') (II, p. 1392).[20] There is no place for women who are 'sçavante' other than the 'moule' of the mocked 'image': the female intellectual is only ever ridiculed; there is no positive category or comfortable space for her.[21]

The unresolved question of her own identity as a 'sçavante' is at the heart of Gournay's self-presentation in the 'Apologie' which Anna Lia Franchetti describes as the 'lieu de l'émergence du sujet' (the place in which the subject emerges).[22] It is unresolved because Gournay considers herself to be outside this category as she aspires to 'savoir', although she is at pains to demonstrate that she deserves this status (her work is full of erudite references), and she casts herself as a gatekeeper of taste and knowledge, scathing as she is towards the 'Vulgaire' 'en nostre climat'. It is also unresolved because she is aspiring to an identity, as she expresses it, that has no place in the socio-literary regime of her time. Rather than a portrait led by the negative views of others, as Franchetti suggests it is, Gournay's description identifies the aporia, and thus identifies the problem:[23]

> Or quant aux Lettres et Sciences, soit en homme ou en femme, je n'ay pas entrepris de m'amuser à faire une Apologie en ce lieu, pour establir leur valeur ny leur estime. Mais, mon Dieu! Que ne me laisse t'on jouir du passeport de l'ignorance? Puis qu'il est veritable, ou que je ne sçay rien, tant par oubli qu'autrement, ou que ce que je sçay se qualifie, se cognoist et se practique si peu pour Science en nostre temps que tous les jours mon ignorance en sert de risée aux esprits guaillards d'entre les sçavans, comme ma Science en sert aux autres? Pourquoi ne riroient ceux-la, s'ils trouvent une sçavante pretendue, sans Grammaire, pour s'etre instruicte soy-mesme au Latin par routine, aydée de la confrontation des Versions aux Originaux, et qui partant n'oseroit parler ceste Langue de crainte de se defferrer: sçavante qui ne peut cautionner nettement la mesure d'un Vers Latin, sçavante sans Grec, sans Hebreu, sans faculté d'illustration sur les Autheurs, sans Manuscrits, sans Logique, Physique, ny Metaphysique, Mathematique ny sa suite. Disons après, sans vieilles medailles en cabinet, puis qu'on loge assez souvent en

---

[20] Ibid., p. 125.

[21] See also Butterworth, 'Marie de Gournay and the Abuse of Mockery', pp. 62–63. On the question of the ontological existence of the 'femme savante' and especially the '"je" féminin, savant et philosophe' in relation to Scudéry's *Conversations*, see Laura J. Burch, 'Madeleine de Scudéry: peut-on parler de la femme philosophe?', *Revue philosophique de la France et de l'étranger*, 138.3 (2013), pp. 361–7 (p. 363).

[22] Franchetti, *L'Ombre discourante*, p. 44.

[23] Ibid., pp. 47–48.

leur possession l'une des principales suffisances de nostre Siecle. Que ne me permet donc le babil du monde, de me reposer sans contredit, au siege des Doctes ou des Ignorans, des hommes ou des bestes? (ɪɪ, pp. 1394–95)

Now as for letters and learning, whether in men or women, I have not undertaken to busy myself with making an Apology here to establish their value or standing. But for heaven's sake, why won't they let me profit from the passport of ignorance? For it is a fact that either I know nothing, as much on account of a faulty memory as otherwise, or what I do know is so little judged, recognized and practised as being learning in our time that every day my ignorance serves as an object of ridicule for the high-spirited among the learned, just as my knowledge does for the others. Why would they not laugh, such people, if they come across a woman pretending to learning without formal schooling, because she instructed herself in Latin by rote, aided by setting the translations side by side with the originals, and who therefore would not dare to speak that language for fear of making a false step—a learned woman who cannot unequivocally guarantee the meter of a Latin verse; a learned woman without Greek, without Hebrew, without aptitude for providing scholarly commentary on authors, without manuscripts, without Logic, without Physics or Metaphysics, Mathematics or the rest? Let us add, without old medals in a cabinet, since possessing them is regularly set up as one of the chief accomplishments in our age. So why will the babbling of the world not permit me to rest, without opposing me, in the seat of the learned or of the ignorant, of human beings or of beasts?[24]

She articulates forcefully here how her knowledge, outside the mainstream and outside disciplines of knowledge as organised at her time, makes her a hybrid case, too learned for some, and too ignorant for others. By identifying that what she knows 'is not judged, recognized and practised as knowledge', Gournay anticipates much feminist scholarship in the history of knowledge which has argued that the only way to access women's voices is to widen what we understand science and scientific practice, for instance, to mean.[25] However, her primary referent is still the exclusive masculinist world of letters: her very protest that she is not considered learned enough is couched in highly learned (classical) terms. She continues:

Moy vrayement encore, à qui viendroit à poinct en toutes ces Sciences, comme violons à nopces, si l'on m'en interrogeoit, la plaisante deffaite d'Aristipus sur une seule, la Logique: 'Pourquoy delierois-je ceste difficulté, si toute liée elle m'empesche?' (ɪɪ, p. 1395)

[24] Gournay, *Apology*, trans. by Hillman and Quesnel, pp. 125–26 (with minor modifications).
[25] See, for instance, Sarah Hutton, 'Science and Natural Philosophy', in *The Routledge History of Women in Early Modern Europe*, ed. by Amanda L. Capern (London: Routledge, 2021), pp. 386–403.

34 WOMEN WRITING ANTIQUITY

And this, moreover, when I am someone to whom in all these fields, if I were questioned, there would duly come, like violins at a wedding, the amusing defeat that Aristippus met with Logic alone: 'why would I untie that difficulty if it baffles me when it is tied up?'[26]

In a gesture that beautifully exemplifies the tensions Gournay is exploring, she claims that she finds 'toutes ces sciences' baffling: why try to unpick something she cannot grasp when it is already complex enough (she is quoting Diogenes Laertius who has Aristippus say: 'why, you simpleton, do you want it untied seeing that it causes enough trouble as it is?'; Montaigne also uses this quotation from Aristippus[27]). And yet, to represent this exclusion, she uses a learned reference to Aristippus which is also—intentionally, given the complexity of what she is exploring—obfuscatory, showing the impossibility of resolving the problem she has identified.

Gournay's personal defence in this 'Apologie', and her justification of her well-intentioned desire to learn, also have a pragmatic function: when this was first published in 1626, she was, as ever, attempting to solicit patronage and favour. It was also written in the context of sustained attack and satire: after she wrote her *Adieu de l'âme du roi* (1610), in which she defended the Jesuists after François Ravaillac's assassination of Henri IV, she was subject to all manner of backlash: several pamphlets targeted her.[28] She apparently attempted to have one of these banned with little success.[29] The backlash to her defence of the Jesuits opened the floodgates for attacks, pranks, and ridicule that she would endure throughout her life (for example, she was fictionalised in two satires targeting the *Académie française*: these satires also acknowledge her close connections to the networks and social circles from which the *Académie* was founded).[30] Her writing, along

---

[26] Gournay, *Apology*, trans. by Hillman and Quesnel, pp. 126–27 (with some modifications).

[27] Diogenes Laertius, *Lives of Eminent Philosophers, Volume I: Books 1–5*, trans. by R. D. Hicks, Loeb Classical Library 184 (Cambridge, MA: Harvard University Press, 1925), 2.8.70. Montaigne describes this quotation as 'une plaisante contrefinesse' which might enable children to deal with a 'subtilité sophistique'. Montaigne, 'De l'institution des enfants', *Essais*, ed. by Alexandre Micha, 3 vols (Paris: Flammarion, 1969), I, p. 218.

[28] *Remerciment des Beurrières* (Niort, 1610); and *L'Anti-Gournai, ou l'Anti-Gontier, servant de response à l'adieu de l'ame, fait par le pere Gontier sous le nom de la Damoiselle de Gournai* ([n.p.]: [n. pub.], [n.d.]). See Michèle Fogel, 'La Damoiselle de Gournay, qui a tousjours bien servi au public', in *Les Femmes et l'écriture de l'histoire, 1400–1800*, ed. by Sylvie Steinberg and Jean-Claude Arnould (Mont Saint-Aignan: Publications des Universités de Rouen et du Havre, 2008), pp. 205–17; Derval Conroy, 'A Defence and Illustration of Marie de Gournay: Bayle's Reception of "Cette Savante Demoiselle"', *French Studies Bulletin*, 40.152 (2019), 51–54; and Claude-Gilbert Dubois, 'Autour de l'*Adieu de l'ame du roy Henry de France* (1610) de Marie de Gournay', *Journal of Medieval and Renaissance Studies*, 25.3 (1995), 477–87. See also Constant Venesoen, *Marie de Gournay: Textes relatifs à la calomnie* (Tübingen: Narr, 1998), although there is some confusion of pamphlets here.

[29] See Ilsley, *A Daughter of the Renaissance*, p. 118.

[30] Antoine Gaillard, *La furieuse monomachie de Gaillard et de Braquemart (1634)*, in *Œuvres du Sieur Gaillard* (Paris: Dugast, 1634), pp. 1–26; and Charles de Saint-Évremond, *La Comédie des Académistes* ([n.p.]: [n. pub.], [n.d.]). On the Gournay and the *Académie française*, see Ilsley, *A Daughter of the Renaissance*, pp. 217–31 and 232–42, and Giovanna Devincenzo, '"On ne parle plus ainsi":

with her social connections, seems to have paid off as she benefited from Richelieu's financial support: in August 1635 she and her servant were able to move into larger quarters from the rue de l'Arbre sec to the rue Saint-Honoré, as she writes to Richelieu 'la liberalité de notre Roi suffisait à me tenir à mon aise' (the King's generosity has allowed me to live more comfortably).[31] The 'Apologie' has a slightly different function once it is included in the 1641 edition, published when she was in her late seventies: at this point the 'Apologie' becomes more the textual monument discussed above, its currency now posterity rather than immediate reward.

Money, professionalism, and her erudition are thus connected: it is by her pen that she hoped to make money and to gain favour. She explains that she has relied on the money she earnt by her 'inventions' and 'labeurs, non de [s]on patrimoine' ('wits and labours, not from my inheritance') (II, p. 1397) and justifies some small expense incurred in attracting visitors to her house so that she might curry favour and acquire financial support.[32] However, the connection of erudition and money has also been damaging: it is in part because of, as she puts it, 'mes lettres' (II, p. 1392) and 'mon Latin' (II, p. 1426), that she has been so ridiculed; as she states, this ridicule has gone some way to jeopardising her chances at patronage or a pension, which is why it is imperative that she defend herself.[33]

There is one point against which she is at particular pains to defend herself: that she has excessively and irresponsibly squandered her meagre means on her pursuit of alchemy. In the 'Apologie', she writes: 'A ce descry general des femmes studieuses, on adjouste en mon fait un poinct particulier, c'est de pratiquer l'Alchimie, qu'ils croyent en soy folie parfaicte' ('to that general condemnation of intellectual women a particular point is added in my case—that is, my practice of alchemy, which they deem absolute folly in itself') (II, p. 1395).[34] She adds that it was as much the 'mauvais estat de [s]a fortune' ('poor state of [her] fortune') (II, p. 1396), as her learning or scientific endeavour, that tarnished her

---

Marie de Gournay et le destin de la langue française', *Cahiers de recherches médiévales et humanistes*, 43 (2022), 497–510 and Devincenzo, 'Les "après-diners" de la Rue Saint-Honoré ou Marie de Gournay, amoureuse de la langue française', *Bulletin de la société internationale des amis de Montaigne*, 68 (2018), 105–116. For evidence that the idea for the *Académie française* originated in her salon, see Michel de Marolles, *Mémoires de Michel de Marolles*, 2 vols (Paris: Sommaville, 1656–57), II, 289.

[31] See the Letter dated June 16 1634? in Ilsley, *A Daughter of the Renaissance*, p. 218. Mary Hays also discusses this royal favour in detail in her biography of Marie de Gournay, 'Mary of Jars, Lady of Gournay', in *Female Biography; or Memoirs of Illustrious and Celebrated Women of All Ages and Countries*, 6 vols (London: Phillips, 1803), II, 445–51 (p. 446).

[32] Gournay, *Apology*, trans. by Hillman and Quesnel, p. 128.

[33] 'Mais la malignité de ceux qui m'accusent de la ruine de mes affaires, ou d'autres extravangences à leur poste, m'arrache encore la vie en consequence' ('But the malice of those who accuse me of ruining my finances, or of other kinds of extravagances, as they see fit, further entails taking my livelihood from me'). 'Apologie', *Œuvres complètes*, II, 1400–01; Gournay, *Apology*, trans. by Hillman and Quesnel, p. 130.

[34] Gournay, *Apology*, trans. by Hillman and Quesnel, p. 127. She defends this again in her verse portrait, the 'Pincture des mœurs', where she objects to public opinion and ridicule (II, p. 1786).

36   WOMEN WRITING ANTIQUITY

reputation.[35] She explains in detail that she was not profligate in her pursuit of this science and justifies this with painstaking precision: 'la calomnie me force à conter ce monceau de sornettes' ('calumny compels me [...] to recount this heap of trivialities') (II, p. 1399).[36] In the second part of the 'Apologie' in particular, she accounts for the way her family came to be in such debt and details with precision the state of her finances. This minutely detailed account of her own finances mingled with a defence of her learning is significant because it allows her to represent herself as a reliable investment: she is both learned, and so the worthy object of literary patronage, and adept at managing her household finances, two skills which, as she points out, are not usually held in tandem: 'joinct que les personnes qui sçavent lire en Latin ont besoin d'une telle justification parmy nostre monde: qui croid que ceux qui sont bons aux Livres ne sont bons qu'à cela ('Besides which, persons who know how to read Latin have need of such a justification in our society, which believes that those who are suited to books are suited only to that') (II, p. 1426).[37] She claims to have found the balance between living modestly, having good household management skills and nevertheless, despite her own financial stability, being worthy of investment, an investment she needs. Her exposition here of the necessity of a social network for esteem, as well as the fragilities of such networks and the challenges faced by those who do not already fit an established 'mould' chimes with her other writing on slander, including her 'De la médisance' of 1626.[38]

The 'Apologie' is thus driven by a certain pragmatism; however, it also has more self-aggrandising characteristics (here too perhaps with posterity in mind) in the way it is modelled on the *Apologia* genre, and particularly the apologia by Plato for Socrates. Gournay makes this intended comparison explicit as she represents Socrates, like herself, as a figure assailed by calumny and slander in her 'Apologie'.[39] (Elsewhere she also mentions a translation she produced of Diogenes Leartius's 'Vie de Socrate', which, although lost and the attribution not certain, would attest to her interest in this figure.)[40]

Socrates is one of many classical figures referred to as a parallel for her own experiences in her 'Apologie': Aeneas's personal pride is offered as justification for her making positive remarks about herself;[41] Polyxena is an example of self-sacrifice

---

[35] Gournay, *Apology*, trans. by Hillman and Quesnel, p. 128.

[36] Ibid., p. 130.

[37] Ibid., pp. 150–51 (with some modifications).

[38] 'De la médisance', *Œuvres complètes*, I, pp. 702–36; see also Butterworth, 'Marie de Gournay and the Abuse of Mockery', p. 69.

[39] She mentions Socrates explicitly as an example of a figure well able to disdain criticism of his faults and vices, 'Apologie', *Œuvres complètes*, II, p. 1377.

[40] 'Je traduisis un jour la Vie de Socrate en Laertius', 'De l'impertinente amitié', in *Œuvres complètes*, I, p. 1040. She then once more mentions her lack of ancient Greek, but laments the Latin translation of Diogenes Laertius and asserts the value of her own (p. 1041).

[41] 'Apologie', *Œuvres complètes*, II, p. 1416.

and honourable failure to parallel Gournay's endeavours to salvage her reputation.[42] These parallels feature in other texts: in her 1626 'Grief des dames', she compares intelligent women (and clearly herself) with Carneades of Cyrene, the second-century Skeptic philosopher highly praised by Cicero,[43] although, as she shows, women do not enjoy his success in being taken seriously:

> Eussent les Dames les raisons et les meditations de Carneades, il n'y a si chetif qui ne les rembarre avec approbation de la pluspart des assistans, quand avec un souris seulement, ou quelque petit branslement de teste, son éloquence muette aura dit: 'C'est une femme qui parle'. (I, p. 1075)

> If women possessed the arguments and the profound thoughts of Carneades, there is no man, however mediocre, who does not put them in their place with the approval of most of the company, when, with merely a smile or some slight shaking of his head, his mute eloquence pronounces, 'It's a woman speaking'.[44]

Furthermore, ancient female philosophers and the esteem in which they have been held provide the exemplar which proves Gournay's argument in her *Égalité des hommes et des femmes* and implicitly form a comparison with herself. She references Hypatia; Aspasia; Arete; Themistoclea, Pythagoras' sister; 'la Sage Theano', his wife; and Damo, his daughter; Cornelia, mother of the Gracchi brothers, and Laelia, daughter of the Roman orator, both praised by Cicero (I, p. 970).[45] She also lists a number of female poets as proof of women's intellectual contributions: she mentions Sappho, Corinna, and Erinna. Sappho, Corinna, Hypatia, and Arete are also all evoked in her prefatory dedication to Sophrosine as examples of women whose work has not been favoured by the 'ravages' of time and men, in comparison with the long posterity she hopes for her own work (I, p. 558).[46] In the *Égalité*,

---

[42] Ibid., p. 1424.

[43] Cicero, *On Ends*, trans. by H. Rackham, Loeb Classical Library 40 (Cambridge, MA: Harvard University Press, 1914), 5.2.4.

[44] Gournay, *Apology*, trans. by Hillman and Quesnel, p. 101–02. See further Helena Taylor, 'Introduction: "C'est une femme qui parle"', in *Women and* Querelles *in Early Modern France*, ed. by Helena Taylor and Kate E. Tunstall (= *Romanic Review*, 112.3 (2021)), pp. 363–71.

[45] See also Ruth Hagengruber, 'Cutting through the Veil of Ignorance: Rewriting the History of Philosophy', in *The History of Women's Ideas*, ed. by Karen Green and Ruth Hagengruber (= *The Monist*, 98.1 (2015)), pp. 34–42. Gournay also references Mademoiselle de Schurman, with whom she had corresponded on the question of women's education, and makes the association between Schurman and the ancient figures clear: 'l'emulatrice de ces illutres Dames en l'eloquence, et de leurs poetes lyriques encores, mesmement sur leur propre langue Latine, et qui possede avec celle-la, toutes les autres antiques et nouvelles et tous les Arts liberaux et nobles' ('the rival of those illustrious ladies in eloquence, and of their lyric poets too, even in their own Latin language, and who, besides that language, possesses all the others, ancient and modern, and all the liberal and noble arts'). 'Égalité', in *Œuvres complètes*, I, p. 969; Gournay, *Apology*, trans. by Hillman and Quesnel, p. 78.

[46] Her main sources for these catalogues of illustrious ancient women are Louis Le Berman's *Le Bouclier des dames*, Diogenes Laertius' *Vies et doctrines des philosophes illustres* and Plutarch's *Moralia*,

38   WOMEN WRITING ANTIQUITY

ancient women also provide proof of women's equal capacity to rule (Gournay explains that Salic law is outdated, having been devised at the time of Pharamond when the leader needed to excel in physical strength, as she cites the Lacedaemonians, 'ce brave et genereux peuple', who 'consultoit de toutes affaires privées et publiques avec ses femmes' ('Lacedaemonians, that brave and generous people, consulted with their wives on all business, public and private') (I, p. 976)).[47] She uses Dido to show that women have been accepted as rulers (I, p. 977); and gives the examples of how the ancient Gauls and Cartheginians used 'les Dames Gauloises' as 'arbitres de leurs differens' ('they established the women of Gaul to serve as arbiters of their quarrels') (I, p. 977).[48] She likewise lists famous female warriors, including Penthesilea and Camilla, exemplary in their resilience and patriotism.

With these examples from the *Égalité*, we have strayed away from Gournay's autobiographical works, even if she implicitly casts herself in these catalogues of illustrious women. Women are models for learning and authority, but she also indicates her own learning in discussing these exempla at all, casting herself as both a member of an illustrious catalogue and as the learned author of such a catalogue, as both the author and the subject—a gesture echoed strongly in her *Vie* analysed above. Gournay creates an authorial ethos that is closely, though fraughtly, bound up with knowledge of antiquity; this ethos is necessarily assertive as well as fragile because, as she shows, it has no stable or accepted referent in her socio-literary culture. Her personal and familial situation adds to that fragility, given that she did not have the wealth to live well independently of financial support or the status to ignore personal attacks. Through her own extensive self-justification, the parallels she makes between herself and ancient intellectuals, her defensiveness about her learning, Gournay exposes the aporia represented by the female intellectual at this time. She strives to be an example for something that exists only as a category error. Her exemplarity, and thus her being recognised as a female intellectual, is essential because for Gournay her intellectual identity is socially constituted: as Butterworth suggests, 'for Gournay, to go unrecognized, is in some way not to exist at all, or to exist only outside a social structure that has the power to affirm existence.'[49] Gournay's self-portrait thus provides us not only with a compelling account of the female intellectual in the first half of the seventeenth century, but also with a bold and intensely personal experiment in writing the identity of that intellectual.

---

but she also recalls earlier *Nef des dames* traditions, and particularly Christine de Pizan's *Cité des Dames*.

[47] Gournay, *Apology*, trans. by Hillman and Quesnel, p. 84.
[48] Ibid., p. 86.
[49] Butterworth, 'Marie de Gournay and the Abuse of Mockery', p. 72.

Polemical Prose Translations

As we have seen, Gournay's abilities to read and translate Latin were key to her representation of her learning: she published translations of Sallust, Tacitus, Cicero, Ovid, and Virgil.[50] Translation was a significant part of her scholarly enterprise and occupied her throughout her career: her first published translation was *Aeneid* 2 in 1594;[51] and in the 1634 edition of her works and the definitive version of 1641, all her translations are gathered together, taking up the majority of the second volume. She also translated the majority of the Latin quotations in Montaigne's *Essais* for the edition of 1617, having undertaken the arduous task of identifying the sources in the 1611 edition. In the preface to the 1617 edition, she claims that the 'imprimeur' encouraged her to produce these translations so that those 'ignorans de ce langage' (I, p. 347) can understand the quotations.[52] This is, however, the only time Gournay explicitly makes mention of translation as a vulgarising enterprise (which compares strikingly to the claims made by Anne Dacier, who posits female readers as the main target audience of her illustrative translations). And although Gournay states in the Montaigne preface that her translations are to help the reader, she also then goes onto question their utility for aiding understanding: translations might tell you what the quotation says but they do not necessarily explain its meaning or context.[53]

Translation for Gournay was instead philological, an activity centred on enriching and exploring the French language.[54] Although she, by her own avowal, learnt Latin by comparing translations and originals, she does not explicitly suggest that her own translations are intended for the purpose of access and education, and indeed, often assumes a learned reader. In this respect, Gournay continues

---

[50] I discuss all here apart from her translation of Ovid's *Heroides* 13, Laodamia to Protesilaus, 'Epistre de Laodamia à Protesilaus', in *Œuvres complètes*, II, pp. 1455–64. For discussion of this translation, see Helena Taylor, 'Belle and fidèle? Women Translating Ovid in Early Modern France', in *Ovid in French: Reception by Women from the Renaissance to the Present*, ed. by Fiona Cox and Helena Taylor (Oxford: Oxford University Press, 2023), pp. 67–87.

[51] It was included with the *Proumenoir de Monsieur de Montaigne*.

[52] She omits about twenty translations from the 1617 edition and several more from the later 1635 one, out of prudence. See Valerie Worth-Stylianou, 'Marie de Gournay et la traduction: défense et illustration d'un style', in *Marie de Gournay et l'édition de 1595 des Essais de Montaigne*, ed. by Jean-Claude Arnould (Paris: Champion, 1996), pp. 193–206 (p. 203), and Valerie Worth-Stylianou, 'Marie de Gournay, traductrice', in *Œuvres complètes*, I, pp. 56–79 (pp. 64–79).

[53] 'Ce désir est assez creu: veu qu'un Lecteur qui cognoist ces passages-là n'est pas plus prest de demesler ce Livre à poinct, que celuy qui ne les cognoist pas' (this desire [to enlighten readers] is rather crude, given that a reader who knows these quotations is no more likely to make sense of the book than one who does not know them) (I, p. 347). See also Valerie Worth-Stylianou, '"Bugge-Beares" or "Bouquets"?: Translations of the Latin Quotations in Florio's and Gournay's Versions of the *Essais*', in *Montaigne in Transit: Essays in Honour of Ian Maclean*, ed. by Neil Kenny, Richard Scholar, and Wes Williams (Cambridge: Legenda, 2016), pp. 155–70.

[54] Worth argues that, for Gournay, 'la traduction était une activité vouée par excellence à l'enrichissement de la langue' (translation was an activity devoted to language enrichment), Worth, 'Marie de Gournay et la traduction', p. 199.

40 WOMEN WRITING ANTIQUITY

the nation-building project of translation as articulated by Joachim Du Bellay, whereby translation, particularly of Latin and Greek into French, can shape the vernacular language and literature, even though the translation is always inferior to the original text.[55] This approach which shies from accommodating her reader also chimes with her oftentimes oppositional construction of that reader, from whom she does not necessarily expect a favourable response,[56] and who is envisaged as exclusive, elite, and explicitly contrasted with the 'vulgaire': she fears her reader's ability to destroy her reputation, thus seeks their approval, and erects this reader as elite, and hard to please, thus capturing in this relationship her vulnerable status and need for recognition.[57]

That focus on linguistic enrichment was part of a wider polemic: her translations and their prefaces are important sites for Gournay to make heard her views against contemporary language reform.[58] The early seventeenth century ushered in codification and standardisation of French.[59] François de Malherbe (1555–1628), who had joined Louis XIII's court as poet in 1610, was a key architect, among others, including Guez de Balzac, Jean Chapelain, Nicolas Conrart, and Antoine Godeau, of a new language use and poetics, which sought a standard language based primarily on usage, and thus were seen to tend towards purifying French of loan words, repetitions, obscenities, certain stylistic features considered excessive, such as diminutives, imperfect rhymes, and the imaginative hinterlands of metaphor and allegory.[60] Gournay (and others, such as Mathurin Régnier and Claude Garnier) resisted these changes: recent work has justifiably framed Gournay's writing on language within the history of linguistics.[61] She makes these arguments in a number of essays, 'Deffence de la poésie et du langage des poetes';[62]

---

[55] For the wider context of translation and women, see Jean-Philippe Beaulieu, ed., *D'une écriture à l'autre. Les Femmes et la traduction sous l'Ancien Régime* (Ottawa: Ottawa University Press, 2004).

[56] In the preface 'Au Lecteur', she declares 'ainsi donc, Lecteur, mon Livre n'espere pas de rencontrer souvent une oreille favorable (my book, therefore, reader, does not expect to encounter often a favourable ear). Gournay, 'Au Lecteur', *Œuvres complètes*, I, pp. 568–70 (p. 570).

[57] On this dynamic, see also Butterworth: 'the care of reputation renders the self vulnerable to others; dependent, to a certain extent, on others for the affirmation of the self'. Butterworth, 'Marie de Gournay and the Abuse of Mockery', p. 71.

[58] See also Franchetti, *L'Ombre discourante*, pp. 90–93.

[59] See Anthony Lodge, *French: From Dialect to Standard* (London: Routledge, 1993).

[60] Malherbe himself did not write a formal grammar: his 'theory' of language and poetics comes from his critical comments on the poet Philippe Desportes. On these networks, see Emma Gilby, 'The Paris Context', in *Descartes's Fictions: Reading Philosophy with Poetics* (Oxford: Oxford University Press, 2019), pp. 47–64. On Gournay and Malherbe, see Robert A. Schneider, *Dignified Retreat: Writers and Intellectuals in the Age of Richelieu* (Oxford: Oxford University Press, 2019), pp. 46–54.

[61] For example, Giovanna Devincenzo, *Des mots et des femmes à l'origine de la langue française. XVIe–XVIIe siècles* (Paris: Hermann, 2018), which gives Gournay a central place; and Wendy Ayres-Bennett, 'Women as Authors, Audience, and Authorities in the French Tradition', *Women in the History of Linguistics*, ed. by Wendy Ayres-Bennett and Helena Sanson (Oxford: Oxford University Press, 2020), pp. 91–120. On Gournay and the language debate, see Mathilde Bombart, *Guez de Balzac et la querelle des Lettres: écriture, polémique et critique dans la France du premier XVIIe siècle* (Paris: Champion, 2007), pp. 146–55, and pp. 195–97.

[62] This essay originated as the *Traité sur la Poésie* published in her 1619 *Versions de quelques pieces de Virgile, Tacite et Salluste avec L'Institution de Monsieur, frère unique du roi, à sa majesté* (Paris: Fleury, 1619).

'Sur la version des poètes antiques ou les métaphores';[63] 'Des Rymes'; 'Des Diminutifs François'; and 'Du langage français',[64] as well as in significant translation prefaces, namely her 1626 'De la façon d'escrire de Messieurs L'Eminentissime Cardinal Du Perron et Bertaut Illustrissime Evesque de Sées' (II, pp. 1524–79), which introduces her translations of Virgil, as I explore in more detail in the next section, and her 1626 'Advis sur la traduction de la Seconde Philippique de Ciceron' (II, pp. 1464–70), which I consider here.

Gournay makes her polemic clear: she is scathing towards those whom she terms variously 'ces nouveaux docteurs' ('Façon', II, p. 1528), 'cette troupe nouvelle' ('Façon', II, p. 1575), and 'nouveaux rethoriciens' ('Poètes antiques', I, p. 941); and although she refrains in 'Poètes antiques' from naming Malherbe, albeit targeting him specifically, 'l'un d'eux ...' (I, p. 959), he is named as the main object of her attack at the end of 'De la façon' (II, p. 1577). Translation for Gournay is thus intrinsically intermingled with ideology and with polemic and dissent: in taking this view, I draw on work that has approached early modern translation as a political activity, and as a site for tracing the agency of the translator.[65] And although she figures herself as learning Latin through translation as a private activity, Gournay's translations are a public endeavour, far from the image of the modest woman translator working for her private interest.[66] As Jean-Philippe Beaulieu has argued, her ethos as a translator is based on 'la rhétorique eristique'.[67] We even could say that for Gournay, most discourse is aligned with some form of dissent: it is constructed as an agonistic enterprise; for example, in her 'Grief des dames', 'conferance' (public discussion) is figured as a 'duel', 'querelle', 'dispute', 'combat', and 'coup'.[68]

In this section, building on recent work on Gournay as polemicist, and as translator, I examine the construction of the combative or agonistic voice in her prose translations from Latin, all of which have received very little attention: the political

---

[63] First published in *L'Ombre*, 1626.

[64] First published in *L'Ombre*, 1626. On her linguistics, see Devincenzo, *Des mots et des femmes*; see also Wendy Ayres-Bennett, *Sociolinguistic Variation in Seventeenth-Century France: Methodology and Case Studies* (Cambridge: Cambridge University Press, 2004), pp. 111–80; Marie-Claire Bichard-Thomine, 'Des métaphores chez Marie de Gournay: réflexion linguistique et practique littéraire', in *Marie de Gournay et l'édition de 1595*, ed. by Arnould, pp. 175–92; Marie-Claire Bichard-Thomine, 'Les Traités linguistiques', in *Œuvres complètes*, I, pp. 44–55; Franchetti, *L'Ombre discourante*, pp. 71–114, and John Conley, 'Against Uniformity: Gournay's Philosophy of Language and Literature', in *Women Philosophers in Early Modern France*, ed. by Derval Conroy (= *Early Modern French Studies*, 43.1 (2021)), pp. 21–38.

[65] For instance, Danielle Clarke, 'The Politics of Translation and Gender in the Countess of Pembroke's *Antonie*', *Translation and Literature*, 6.2 (1997), 149–66.

[66] For discussion of this private figure, see Brenda M. Hosington, 'Women Translators and the Early Printed Book', in *A Companion to the Early Printed Book in Britain 1476–1558*, ed. by Vincent Gillespie and Susan Powell (Cambridge: Brewer, 2014), pp. 248–71. See also Marie-Alice Belle, 'Locating Early Modern Women's Translations: Critical and Historiographical Issues', in *Women's Translations in Early Modern England and France*, ed. by Belle, pp. 5–23 (p. 11).

[67] Beaulieu, '"Moy traductrice"', p. 121.

[68] 'Grief des dames', in *Œuvres complètes*, I, pp. 1075–77.

42 WOMEN WRITING ANTIQUITY

speeches by Galba (Tacitus) and Marius (Sallust), published together in 1619, and Cicero's Second Philippic against Mark Anthony, published in her *L'Ombre de la Damoiselle de Gournay* in 1626.[69] Aside from some exploration of their prefaces, such as by Beaulieu, there has been little work on the prose translations themselves and their relation to the ethos Gournay constructs.[70] Jean-Claude Arnould has approached Gournay as a polemicist and affirmed how her identity is shaped by this; however, he takes a more 'macro' approach to the place of polemic within the disposition and accumulation of her work as a whole, and does not focus on how her polemical voice is constructed within particular texts, especially those which are not written in the 'traité' genre.[71]

Her selection of these three speeches, their contextualisation in her œuvre, and their prefatory material, as well as textual details of their translation, offer key examples of Gournay's self-conscious philosophy of merit and of its relation to her ethos. Political speeches, military speeches, and speeches in law courts were de facto realms of discourse from which women were excluded, but they also constituted official, accepted, and institutional forms of dissent and polemic. Uniting these particular speeches is their eristic tone, but all three speeches also advocate meritocracy, good governance, and citizenship and warn against the dangers of the abuse of power. With these prose translations, Gournay is ventriloquising discourse usually gendered as male: these translations also provoke reflection on gender, polemic, authority and merit, lineage, and succession.

The two speeches from Tacitus and Sallust are among her earliest published translations and were included in her 1619 *Versions de quelques pieces de Virgile, Tacite et Salluste avec l'Institution de Monsigneur, frère unique du Roy*: a text which combined these translations with her advice on the education of royal princes. The speeches hold an important place in Gournay's translation canon. They are introduced by the 'Lettre à Monseigneur de Gelas sur la version des deux Oraisons Latines' (II, pp. 1430–39), which constitutes one of Gournay's earliest prefatory statements regarding translation and, as such, is a key document for the assertion of her authorial position. This preface allows Gournay to elaborate her authority and identity as a translator and a Latinist, complementing the portrait of (herself as) a female intellectual in her autobiographical works we studied above. My arguments here draw on the considerable work that has placed the apparently liminal space of the translation preface at the forefront of 'authorial, social and cultural negotiation', revising Gérard Genette's neat distinctions 'between text and paratext, authorial and allographic interventions' (not to mention his more general

---

[69] Jean-Claude Arnould, 'Marie de Gournay polémique', *Littératures Classiques*, 59.1 (2006), 237–50; Beaulieu, '"Moy traductrice"'; and Franchetti, *L'Ombre discourante*, pp. 93–114.

[70] They are treated in brief by Worth-Stylianou in 'Marie de Gournay, traductrice', in *Œuvres complètes*, I, pp. 56–79.

[71] Arnould, 'Marie de Gournay polémique'.

dismissal of translations as paratextual additions to the originals).[72] I build on work that has shown how prefaces attempt both to guide interpretations of readers and are themselves sites of contested meaning, posing new ideas and theories, and demonstrating a complex engagement with the context of other translators, patrons, and the market.[73]

The art of translation elaborated in her 'Lettre à Monseigneur de Gelas' is anchored in merit and good judgement; translation requires linguistic skill and intellectual comprehension: 'car ce sont deux facultez tres-distinctes, estre capable d'entendre et de parler la langue Latine, et capable de la conception de Tacite, ou de ses égaux' (for these are two very distinct capacities: to be able to understand and to speak Latin, and to be able to grasp Tacitus and others like him) (II, p. 1431). Gournay emphasises the need to match the original in style and tone: to express one's own language 'aussi vigoureusement, richement, figurément, succinctement et delicieusement qu'ils parlent la leur' (as vigorously, richly, figuratively, succinctly and deliciously as they speak their own) (II, p. 1432). While there may be nothing particularly new in this assertion, building as it does on Du Bellay's translation theories, Gournay stresses the particular challenge faced by women whose merits and capabilities as translators are not recognised:[74]

Il y a pis pour moy: c'est que quelques-uns croyent qu'une femme ne peut entendre le Latin, et que je traduis sur les Traducteurs: mesmement pource qu'ils sçavent que je l'apris de moy-mesme, et par simple routine, confrontant des Traductions aux Originaux. (II, p. 1436)

And it is worse for me: there are some who believe that a woman cannot understand Latin and that I have only produced translations by copying other translators because they know that I taught myself and my simple habit of comparing translations with originals.

Gournay makes it clear here that the challenge she faces is not so much the obstacles to learning Latin posed by her sex as the—related—prejudice of her readers. While scholarship has shown that women did engage in translation and were not excluded from this practice, with translation valued as a skilled activity, it has tended to focus on vernacular translation: as Gournay intimates, a new set of prejudices needed confronting with regard to Latin and the skills and education

---

[72] Marie-Alice Belle and Brenda M. Hosington, eds, *Thresholds of Translation: Paratexts, Print, and Cultural Exchange in Early Modern Britain (1473–1660)* (Palgrave Macmillan, 2018), p. 3 and p. 9.

[73] See also Julie Candler Hayes, *Translation, Subjectivity, and Culture in France and England, 1600–1800* (Stanford: Stanford University Press 2008), p. 7.

[74] Joachim Du Bellay, *La Deffence et illustration de la langue française* (Paris: L'Angelier, 1549). On their interconnection, see Worth-Stylianou, 'Marie de Gournay et la traduction'.

required to know this language.[75] She treats this prejudice directly in the rest of the preface which she also uses as an occasion to defend her translation of the quotations in Montaigne's *Essais* (published only two years before the first publication of this preface):

> Tant ils ignorent generalement l'art de traduire, si ces menues fantaisies meritent response, et tant ils mécognoissent encores particulierement la delicatesse des allegations dont il est question [...] Ce que je vous conte en passant chemin, parce, Monseigneur, que vous avez daigné regarder ces Versions-là de bon œil; et parce aussi que je ne puis assez souvent rire, si rire se doibt, de la litterature du Siecle, et de l'équité dont les femmes sont traictées par telles personnes. (II, p. 1436)

> They know so little about the art of translation, if their petty fantasies even merit a response, and they struggle in particular to understand the subtlety of the citations in question. I tell you this in passing, Monseigneur, since you have taken the time to look favourably at those translations and because I cannot laugh often enough (if laughter is the appropriate response) at the erudition of this century and the equity with which women are treated by such people.

Gournay thus anticipates readers' criticism, and defends herself against criticism already received, through her eristic rhetoric and explicitly personal defence. She lays claim to her own authority and correct judgement as sufficient to determine her (and other women's) fitness to translate.

With this in mind, it might seem that these translations are merely linguistic exercises allowing her to rival her male intellectual counterparts and elaborate on her philosophy of language. However, given her emphasis on merit and her use of polemic, her decision to translate the Galba and Marius speeches in particular seems deliberately driven by a desire to explore and expose questions of merit and equality, as well as to enable a self-conscious reflection on how to voice dissent: after all, as 'quarrel studies' have shown us, early modern *querelles* were often as much about how to quarrel as about the subject of dispute at hand.[76] Both Galba and Marius characterise themselves as right, as risk-takers and as outsiders, pushing against norms and traditions, an ethos that chimes with Gournay's own repeated self-characterisation as both correct and outside formal and respected institutions of learning.

---

[75] See Belle, 'Locating Early Modern Women's Translations'; Danielle Clarke, 'Translation', in *The Cambridge Companion to Early Modern Women's Writing*, ed. by Laura Lunger Knoppers (Cambridge: Cambridge University Press, 2010), pp. 167–80; Hilary Brown, *Women and Early Modern Cultures of Translation: Beyond the Female Tradition* (Oxford: Oxford University Press, 2022). See also Hannah Fournier, 'Women Translators in France', in *The Encyclopedia of Women in the Renaissance: Italy, France and England*, ed. by Diana M. Robin, Anne Larsen, and Carole Levin (Santa Barbara: University of California Press, 2007), pp. 373–74.

[76] For an overview of quarrel studies, see the Introduction.

The Emperor Galba, who had assumed the throne following Nero's suicide and whose short-lived reign of seven months in AD 68–69 is described in Book 1 of Tacitus's *Histories*, adopted Piso as his heir on 10th January 69, only to be killed five days later by Otho, who had hoped to succeed him, and whom Galba had been advised to appoint, and who then became Emperor. In the speech Gournay translates from its retelling in Tacitus (1.15–16)—and she includes this Latin text in her edition—Galba names Piso as his successor. Galba uses this speech to advocate for selection based on merit over hereditary succession. Galba advises on the course of good governance, using Nero as an example of the abuses of power: he warns against flatterers and the dangers of being corrupted by success, and he inclines towards favouring what he sees as the freedoms that non-hereditary succession of power represent. In her *Institution du prince*, the first version of which was published with her 1619 Tacitus, Sallust, and Virgil translations (the *Versions*), Gournay similarly emphasises the desirability of merit in a ruler for eliciting obedience and asserts that a monarch needs to be 'instruit et sage' to deserve such obedience.[77] She is aware that this virtue is harder for a monarch to achieve than a private citizen and that it requires committed attention, particularly because of the obsequiousness of the court. It is significant that these two prose translations are included with her reflection on sovereignty.[78] Given the political turmoil Gournay had witnessed growing up in the throes of the Wars of the Religion, made complicated by the often ineffective rules of Charles IX and Henri III, and given the assassination of the two most recent monarchs, Henri III and Henri IV, the topic of princely education was of key political and cultural importance: the selection of speeches was surely intended to complement her reflections on education and to form an education in themselves. Good governance for Gournay derives from learning; for instance, she promotes mythology as aiding the quest for virtue and Alexander the Great emerges in her *Institution du Prince* as exemplary, not only because of his merit, virtue, and accountability but also because, like all the best leaders, he respected arts as well as arms—'l'honneur des armes et des Grands estoit inseparable des Lettres' (I, p. 832)—and celebrated writers.[79]

That Gournay is particularly interested in Galba's speech as an elaboration of the qualities of merit and of practices of good governance is evident from her

---

[77] 'Institution du Prince', *Œuvres complètes*, I, pp. 818–40 (p. 839).

[78] On Gournay's politics and theories of sovereignity, see Derval Conroy, 'Engendering Equality: Gynæcocracy in Gournay, Poullain de la Barre and Suchon', in *Ruling Women: Government, Virtue and the Female Prince in Seventeenth-Century France*, 2 vols (Basingstoke: Palgrave Macmillan, 2016), I, pp. 83–91; and Isabelle Flandrois, *L'Institution du Prince au début du XVIIe siècle* (Paris: Presses Universitaires de France, 1992) pp. 47–49, 62–65, and 134–40.

[79] On her *Institution du prince* and notions of governance, see Jacqueline Broad and Karen Green, 'From the Reformation to Marie le Jars de Gournay', in *A History of Women's Political Thought in Europe 1400–1700* (Cambridge: Cambridge University Press, 2009), pp. 110–39 (pp. 125–39); and Marie-Claire Bichard-Thomine, 'Les traités sur l'éducation du prince', in Gournay, *Œuvres complètes*, I, pp. 98–108.

46 WOMEN WRITING ANTIQUITY

translation choices. While her translation is mostly close to the original, she deviates from the Latin on occasion to expand Galba's stance against corruption and stress the importance of consensus and approval: for instance, she explicates the term 'ambitione' and expands on Galba's reference to his judgement: 'sed neque ipse imperium ambitione accepi, et iudicii mei documentum sit non meae tantum necessitudines, quas tibi postposui, sed et tuae'[80] becomes 'mais je n'ay pas moy-mesme acquis l'Empire par brigue ny par faveur, ou par droict de sang ny d'amitié: et je veux que mes amis et mes proches et les tiens encore, ausquels je te prefere, servent d'argument à verifier l'intention et le prix de mon choix' (But I have not acquired the Empire by intrigue or favour, by blood right or friendship: and I want my friends, those close to me and your friends and those close to you, all of whom I overlook to prefer you, to provide the argument that proves the intention and the price of my choice) (II, p. 1442). She develops the notion of merit and accountability, for instance, inserting the word 'citoyen': 'et finita Iuliorum Claudiorumque domo optimum quemque adoptio inveniet' becomes 'la tige des Cesars et des Claudes perie, l'adoption choisira desormais le meilleur entre les Citoyens' (The Cesearean and Claudian line has died out, and adoption from now on will choose the best among the citizens) (I, p. 1443).[81]

Similar concerns with merit, expressed this time against the entitled advancement and nepotism of nobles, are also present in the speech Gournay translates from Sallust's *Jugurthan Wars*: the address to the Roman people by Marius—self-described as an 'homme nouveau' (I, p. 1450), Roman general, and seven-time consul, who faced hostility for not being from an old noble family.[82] Following his election in 107 BC to the consulship of Numidia, a country with which Rome had recently been at war, Marius was preparing for war to erupt again: he used this speech to encourage men to enrol and to criticise the nobility. As in the speech by Galba, but this time in the context of the Republic, issues of good governance, leadership, the pitfalls of hereditary succession, and the abuse of power form key themes in Marius's speech. He argues for self-sufficiency and meritocracy; he criticises noble elites who can make mistakes but rely on 'leur antique noblesse, les actions memorables de leurs ayeuls' and contrasts this with himself: 'au lieu que toute mon esperance est en moy-mesme, laquelle il faut que j'appuye necessairement d'innocence et de valeur me trouvant foible du reste' (Their old nobility, the memorable actions of their ancestors [...] instead, I place all my hope in myself,

---

[80] 'But I did not myself gain this power by self-seeking and I would have the character of my decision shown by the fact that I have passed over for you not only my own relatives, but yours also.' Tacitus, *Histories: Books 1–3*, trans. by Clifford H. Moore, Loeb Classical Library 111 (Cambridge, MA: Harvard University Press, 1925), 1.15.

[81] 'And since the houses of the Julii and the Claudii are ended, adoption will select only the best', ibid., 1.16.

[82] Sallust, *The War with Catiline: The War with Jugurtha*, ed. by John T. Ramsey and trans. by J. C. Rolfe, Loeb Classical Library 116 (Cambridge, MA: Harvard University Press, 2013), 85.

and necessarily support this with my innocence and valour, having little else to rely on) (II, pp. 1448–49).[83]

The tone of persuasion and defiance present in these two speeches, along with their parallel concerns with merit and with guarding against corruption, are matched, even surpassed, in the oration Gournay chose to translate for her 1626 *L'Ombre*: Cicero's second Philippic against Mark Anthony, one of the most the condemnatory, aggressive, and attacking speeches from this orator and indeed of all Latin prose. Cicero is a defender of good governance, due procedure, and meritocracy, and he castigates Marc Anthony for his corruption (fraud, false acquisition of goods, and appropriation of inheritance), poor leadership, bringing the Republic into disrepute, and personal debauchery and vice. As with the Sallust and Tacitus translations, we can map a correlation between the ancient voice of the defender of justice that she is translating and the stance Gournay is taking with this translation. In the preface that introduces this translation, the 'Advis sur la traduction de la Seconde Philippique de Ciceron', Gournay casts herself as the defender of 'la majestueuse antiquité' against changing tastes and the rule of politeness which have resulted in inaccurate and misleading translations: 'Quelle prophanation du sacré mystere des Muses! [...] Voilà donc en fin, comme on travestit à la gaillarde mode qui trotte, cette venerable et majestueuse Antiquité' (What irreverence towards the sacred mystery of the Muses [...] This, therefore, how one travesties, according to a jolly, fashionable way, the venerable and majestic antiquity) (II, p. 1466). She is scathing about translators' habits of translating according to contemporary mores; she complains:

> lesquels [translateurs de ce temps] outre la licence que je nottois n'agueres, de remaçonner à leur fantasie, le stile et les textes, pour les enricher de ce qui leur semble d'art et de bon sens, s'efforcent de baptiser de nos termes et de depeindre soubs l'image de nos moeurs et de nos façons de faire et des mediocritez des estats modernes, tant de choses si loin de nostre usage, loin de nostre cognoissance encores le plus souvent, et ces immenses indeterminées Grandeurs Romaines ? (II, p. 1468)

> in addition to the licence I have just noted, to rebuild, according to their whims, style, and texts, thinking that they enrich them with art and good sense, do they not [translators of our time] strive to baptise in our own terminology and paint in the image of our own mores, and manners, and the mediocrities of modernity, so many things which are so far from our habits, and—even more often—far from our knowledge, including the immense unlimited Roman greatness?

[83] 'vetus nobilitas, maiorum fortia facta, cognatorum et adfinium opes [...] mihi spes omnes in memet sitae, quas necesse est virtute et innocentia tutari' ('their ancient nobility, the brave deeds of their ancestors, the powers of their relatives and in-laws [...] *my* hopes are all vested in myself and must be maintained by my own worth and integrity'). Ibid., 85.4.

48   WOMEN WRITING ANTIQUITY

This presentism is imputed to the translators' (false) notion that to accommodate female readers and 'damoiseaux' ('effeminate men' or courtiers, a reference
to the civility and politeness that was gendered as feminine), such changes are
necessary:

> tout ce change et toutes ces bricoles, dis-je, aux versions des ouvriers
> d'aujourd'huy, parce qu'à leur advis les Dames et les Demoiseaux qui les liront
> ne cognoissent point ces bestes-là par leur propre nom. (II, p. 1468)

> [we find] all these changes and all these ruses in the versions of today's writers
> because in their opinion the women and courtiers reading them do not know
> those beasts by their own names.

Gournay's comments also engage with the debates about obscenity so topical in the
late sixteenth and early seventeenth century: is obscenity semantic or lexical? Does
it lie in the 'mot' or the 'chose'; in the description or the thing described?[84] Significant here is her use of the term 'damoiseaux' to define a certain sort of effeminate
courtier, alongside the 'dames'. This places emphasis on gendered behaviour rather
than essential categories: she is not attacking women's speech as such, not deploying a deterministic conception of women's language use, as some critics suggest,
but rather attacking the association of femininity with civility and politeness.[85] Her
disparaging tone is not towards the women themselves but the translators' opinions of women ('à leur advis'). Such a position is also articulated in her 'Sur la
version des poètes antiques ou les métaphores'. She takes issues with equivocation
and the use of euphemism for the sake of *bienséance*, protesting the tyranny of
politeness: 'Que nous proffite aussi, d'estre riches en politesse, si nous polissons
une crotte de chévre?' (What benefit is there to being rich in politeness if we are
polishing goat droppings?) ('Poètes antiques', I, p. 954) and she explicitly blames
the (perceived) need to placate women for this. Here too her criticisms are not
against women, as such, rather a particular group (just as she criticises a particular
group of male courtiers), and also against the way women's language has been used
or influenced by the architects of reform: 'mais pourquoy m'amuse-je à remarquer ce que porte le langage des femmes, hors l'intention des nouveaux poetes,

---

[84] See also Montaigne, *Essais*, III, 5, 'Sur des vers de Virgile', on the ridiculousness of preserv-
ing women from the 'mot' (sex) given their familiarity with the 'chose' (and, if only men realised,
quite probably with several 'mots' as well). Montaigne, *Essais*, ed. by Micha, III, pp. 56–112. See
also *Obscénités Renaissantes*, ed. by Hugh Roberts, Guillaume Peureux, and Lise Wajeman (Geneva:
Droz, 2011).

[85] Cathleen Bauschatz, 'Marie de Gournay and the Crisis of Humanism', in *Humanism in Crisis:
The Decline of the French Renaissance*, ed. by Philippe Desan (Ann Arbor, MI: University of Michigan
Press, 1991), pp. 279–94; and see also Cathleen Bauschatz, 'Marie de Gournay's Gendered Images for
Language and Poetry', in *Montaigne et Marie de Gournay*, ed. by Marcel Tétel (Paris: Champion, 1997),
pp. 251–67. For further discussion of her 'antifeminism', see also Franchetti, *L'Ombre discourante*,
pp. 200–11.

veu que c'est quelque chose comme infinie' (but why should I amuse myself in discussing what women's language consists of, beyond the intention of the new poets, given that it is infinite) ('Deffence', I, p. 1171). For Gournay, women are the inadvertent instruments of a change that is introduced by those who also deny them access to the forms of culture that are being rejected (as the Moderns do later on: women's exclusion from institutions of learning is the basis for the Moderns vaunting of the 'spontaneity' and 'natural genius' of female-gendered taste).[86]

Given the focus of the 'Advis sur la traduction de la Seconde Philippique de Ciceron' on topical questions of language reform, her defence of her authority as a translator is less marked in this preface than in the 'Lettre à Monsieur Gelas' analysed above. However, she is at pains to explain which Latin text she used and to explain differences between her version and other translations;[87] and, as is customary in translation prefaces, she acknowledges that she received advice from her intellectual friend, Jean de Simond, and the theologian and writer, François Ogier, friend of the translator Michel de Marolles,[88] but asserts that she had not known about two recent French versions by François Joulet de Chastillon and Antoine de Laval until later, thus stressing that her version is her own working of Cicero's text and not influenced by those of others (II, pp. 1468–69).[89] She also justifies small modifications she made for the sake of making the historical context more comprehensible—unlike the previous orations, this time Gournay does include a brief explanatory note on the animosity between Marc Anthony and Cicero, on his first Philippic, and Cicero's assassination as a result of this enmity. Gournay uses her own authority and judgement as a translator to justify these small changes and her occasional contextual explanations: 'Si moy traductrice manquant de ces rayons de lumiere pour m'exprimer, ne les eusse cherchez à ma nécessité dans cette sobre paraphrase, j'eusse avec peu de peine, faict d'une tres-belle Oraison un tres-impertinent galimathias' (If I, as translator, lacking these rays of light to express myself, had not sought them, out of necessity, in this sober paraphrase, I would have, with little effort, turned a beautiful piece of oratory into a perfect piece of nonsense) (II, p. 1467).[90] It is a feature of Gournay's own rhetoric

---

[86] This chimes with her *Égalité des hommes et des femmes* where she says Aristotle criticises women only for their lack of education. Gournay, 'Égalité', in *Œuvres complètes*, I, p. 973.

[87] The version used is that of the Italian Humanist, Caelius Secondus Curio, *M Tulli Ciceronis Philippicae Orationes XIIII* (Bale: Froben, 1551).

[88] In a dedicatory letter prefacing Marolles's *Heroides*, Ogier describes her to Marolles as 'vostre bonne amie et la mienne' (Marolles, *Les Épistres Héroïdes d'Ovide* (Paris: Lamy, 1661), np); we know that Marolles frequented her salon and thought very highly of her. See Michel de Marolles, *Mémoires de Michel de Marolles*, 2 vols (Paris: Sommaville, 1656), I, p. 58.

[89] François Joulet de Chastillon, *Six oraisons de Ciceron* (Paris: Estienne, 1609); Antoine de Laval, *Desseins de professions nobles et publiques* (Paris: Langelier, 1605).

[90] Beaulieu shows how in this preface she both asserts her individualism and shows the support and respect of her networks, in '"Moy Traductrice"', p. 122. See also Jean-Philippe Beaulieu and Hannah Fournier, '"Les interests du sexe": dédicataires féminins et réseaux de sociabilité chez Marie de Gournay', *Renaissance and Reformation*, 28.1 (2004), 47–59.

50 WOMEN WRITING ANTIQUITY

to make self-aggrandising parallels (we encountered this with her Socrates): does she cast herself as defender of the just representation of antiquity and an un-purged French language, as Cicero was of the Republic, thereby proposing stakes of parallel proportions?

For all that she says she has 'paraphrased' to help with specific clarity of the argu-ment, the translation is, in keeping with her discourses on translation, close to the original, to the extent that it demands a learned reader, schooled in this moment of history of the Republic, the political roles and some understanding of Roman law and customs. The only changes she makes beyond rare moments of clarification serve to amplify Cicero's already powerful rhetoric, lending weight to my argu-ment that there is slippage between Gournay's preference for polemical rhetoric and her decision to translate this speech. For example, she translates 'O teste, per-due d'insolence, d'arrogance et de folle entreprise' (O what a man, lost to insolence, arrogance and a foolish undertaking) (II, p. 1490) for 'homo audacissime'.[91] The amplification of incendiary rhetoric is strengthened by the way she upholds in this translation her arguments about language use. Key to Gournay's position is her rejection of the 'purification' of language: as we might expect, then, Gournay does not shy away from the more sexual aspects of Cicero's speech, namely the charges against Marc Anthony of being a sodomite, of having prostituted himself in offering sexual services to older men, such as Curion: 'jamais garçon achepté pour servir de bardache ne fut si servilement soubmis à son maistre que tu l'étois à Curion' (never was a boy, purchased to serve as a sexual slave for a man, so servile and submissive towards his master as you were towards Curion) (II, p. 1490), for 'Nemo umquam puer emptus libidinis causa tam fuit in domini potestate quam tu in Curionis'; and she translates all the allusions to his perceived sexual deviancy faithfully.[92]

A link can therefore be made between her interest in meritocracy, evident from the selection of speeches, and her approach to translation and learning more widely. Gournay advocates for equal education between men and women and, as we have seen, makes a case for social acceptance on the grounds of her learning. On numerous occasions, she also questions the standing of those considered as intel-lectuals simply because they have 'medals in their cabinets' and other signifiers of rank. In these political speeches, meritocracy and succession come as a pair: we know Gournay was interested in the gender politics of succession in her writing against Salic Law and in favour of women in positions of governance; but I think we can also read ideas of succession and lineage as intellectual, as inscribed into her work. As Neil Kenny has shown in relation to the Dames des Roches, literary

[91] 'You insolent wretch', Cicero, *Philippics 1–6*, ed. and trans. by D. R. Shackleton Bailey, rev. by John T. Ramsey and Gesine Manuwald, Loeb Classical Library 189 (Cambridge, MA: Harvard University Press, 2010), 2.43.

[92] 'No slave boy bought to satisfy lust was ever so completely in his master's power as you were in Curio's.' Ibid., 2.45.

work, conferred in this case from mother to daughter to posterity, can be a form of transmission or lineage and can also be framed in such a way as to resist patrilinear lines of inheritance. Gournay makes it clear, as explored, that her work is what she leaves behind of herself and of her family name (as she says in the closing note, 'si ce Livre me survit', and associates it with her tomb). Like the Des Roches in Kenny's analysis, Gournay also creates a 'renown that is unusual in that it will not be attached to future patrilinear bodies'.[93] Her name 'Gournay' does come from her father but not his line: Guillaume Le Jars purchased the lordship and estate of Gournay becoming 'le Sieur de Gournay'; her publishing as 'La Demoiselle de Gournay' rather than using 'Le Jars de Gournay' signifies to an extent a break from her father's line, a reinvention of a name to suit the intellectual legacy she leaves behind. In relation to translation and so in particular to these three prose texts in which succession, merit, and inheritance are significant, lineage also looms large. As she makes clear, merit is the basis for Gournay's activity and authority as a translator; translation is a form of transmission: Gournay's translations thus represent succession based on merit, and she—and by extension other women—are worthy successors.[94]

Poetics: Gournay's *Aeneid*

Gournay's prose translations established the link between translation and dissent and allowed her to articulate her authority as a translator; they also gave her some opportunity to reflect on the French language and resist linguistic reform. That resistance is most strongly articulated in her verse translations of Virgil's *Aeneid* and their accompanying prefatory material. These are the translations for which she is best known, and they make up the majority of her translations from Latin: she translates into verse near-complete extracts from Books 1, 2, and 4, and the whole of Book 6.[95] These translations were published at different points in her career, accompanied by different prefaces and significant dedications, before all being integrated into the 1634 edition of her *Advis*. In this section, I look first at her prefaces and then at the translations to explore in detail her poetics. From the 1626 first edition of her complete works, her translations of

[93] Neil Kenny, *Born to Write: Literary Families and Social Hierarchy in Early Modern France* (Oxford: Oxford University Press, 2020), p. 117.
[94] My thanks to Emma Herdman for helping me think this section through.
[95] On her *Aeneid* translations specifically, see Worth-Stylianou, 'Marie de Gournay, traductrice', in *Œuvres complètes*, I, pp. 56–79; Worth-Stylianou, 'Marie de Gournay et la traduction'; Jonathan Patterson, 'Marie de Gournay, Poetry and Gender: In Search of "La vraye douceur"', *Seventeenth-Century French Studies*, 32:2 (2010), 206–20; Sheldon Brammall, 'The Politics of the Partial Translations of the *Aeneid* by Dudley Digges and Marie de Gournay', *Translation and Literature*, 22.2 (2013), 182–94; and Fiona Cox, 'An Amazon in the Renaissance: Marie de Gournay's Translation of *Aeneid 2*', in *Virgil and his Translators*, ed. by Susanna Braund and Martirosova Torlone (Oxford: Oxford University Press, 2018), pp. 97–106.

52 WOMEN WRITING ANTIQUITY

Aeneid 1, 2, and 4 are prefaced by her essay, 'De la façon d'escrire de Messieurs L'Eminentissime Cardinal Du Perron et Bertaut Illustrissime Evesque de Sées' 'qui sert d'advertissment au lecteur sur les poemes de ce Volume' (II, p. 733); this essay complements another, also first published in 1626, 'Sur la version des poètes antiques ou des métaphores', discussed above. In both works, she combines her praise for Virgil with a defence of Pléiade poetics: her allegiance is towards the poetics of 'Ronsard et sa bande' ('Poètes antiques', I, p. 957)—namely Pierre de Ronsard, Du Bellay, Philippe Desportes—and to post-Pléiade poets, Jacques Davy Du Perron and Jean Bertaut.

In both these essays Gournay also makes it clear that she valorises the ancients as authorities: she is enabled to repeat subject matter because 'les Anciens n'espargent pas les repetitions frequentes et multipliées, quand le sujet les exige' (the ancients do not refrain from frequent and multiple repetitions if the subject requires them) ('Façon', II, p. 1528); she defends the different elements of poetic speech by citing usage by ancient writers; and she argues that ancient works are at the source of all poetic inspiration and invention. She criticises her contemporaries for not holding these views:

> Au lieu de s'excuser de la foiblesse de leurs efforts, à comparaison de ces insignes poëtes, ils ont entrepris de les degrader eux-mesmes: au lieu de s'excuser de bassesse, ils veulent que les autres s'excusent de hautesse. Ce que je ne dis pas pour diffamer eux ou leurs œuvres tout du long, car certainement il se void par fois des poëmes de la main de ces poëtes nouveaux, qui peuvent faire honneur à leurs autheurs, pourveu qu'ils peussent pardoner aux grands poëtes Grecs, Latins et François, d'estre leurs superieurs ou pour mieux dire leurs maitres, et la principale source de leurs inventions et de leurs conceptions. ('Poètes antiques', I, p. 958)

> Instead of excusing themselves for the feebleness of their efforts, in comparison to these remarkable poets, they have undertaken to degrade them themselves; instead of apologising for their baseness, they want others to apologise for their greatness. I do not say this to defame them or their works in their entirety, because sometimes one encounters poems by these new poets that do afford their authors some merit, provided that they forgive these great Greek, Latin, and French poets for being their superiors, even, to put it better, their masters, and the principal source of their inventions and ideas.

For Gournay, the problem with the 'poètes nouveaux' is their attitude, what she perceives to be a sort of arrogant presentism that does not show proper respect towards the greats of the past. By making ancient poetics exemplary in her resistance to contemporary taste, Gournay anticipates some of the questions that will be revisited in the late-century Quarrel of the Ancients and Moderns (reminding us that the temporal parameters of that Quarrel extend beyond the flashpoint of Boileau and Perrault). But we also grasp how some of the poetic parameters have shifted by this later flashpoint as there is widespread acceptance of the language reform Gournay rails against: Boileau, an Ancient in the Quarrel, is also well-known for his praise of Malherbe (evident from the famous 'enfin Malherbe vint', from his *Art poètique*) and, like his adversary, Perrault, was also disparaging of the Pléiade poets. And yet, there are some parallels to be drawn: for instance, in an image that will be echoed strikingly by Dacier to defend Homeric morals, Gournay describes ancient epic as uplifting in its 'estrangeté': a characteristic 'qui semble un monstre à ceux qui n'y sont habituez' (strangeness, which seems monstrous to those who are not used to it) ('Façon', II, p. 1530).

This evocation of the 'strangeness' of antiquity 'for those who are not used to it' suggestively recalls the tensions in the expectations of her readers, as described above. Because, despite this statement, her translations are not necessarily aimed at readers who would not know or be able to read the original Latin. For her *Aeneid* translations, unlike the common sixteenth-century practice, she provides no parallel text of the Latin (after all, it is a text every schoolboy would have studied);[96] but she does draw attention to her translation choices by including, with her own translation, extracts from two of the most recent translations of Virgil into French: by Jacques Davy Du Perron and Jean Bertaut. She includes Du Perron's translation from Book 1 and from Book 4, before continuing in her own words, and she intersperses extracts from Bertaut's translation throughout her version of Book 2. Bertaut's version from 1603 and Du Perron's from 1610 were the most recent translations into French of Virgil, but there were a significant number of prominent ones from across the sixteenth century, notably by Octavien de Saint-Gelais.[97] Gournay's decision to refer to those of her contemporaries rather than earlier ones is important for connecting her to this group of intellectuals (and is an example of what Sheldon Brammall describes as 'communities of Virgil translation'[98]). As Beaulieu persuasively argues, and as I will explore, her association with established and contemporary translators was a way of suggesting her inclusion and belonging, a means of showing respect, but also a declaration of independence and distinction: 'l'hommage tourne à la rivalité' (homage slips into rivalry).[99] Indeed, the fact that her final translation, of Book 6, her latest from 1634, contains no other translator's voice (and few notes) is perhaps a mark of her confidence and maturity.

[96] Valerie Worth-Stylianou, 'Virgilian Space in Renaissance French Translations of the *Aeneid*', in *Virgilian Identities in the French Renaissance*, ed. by John P. Usher and Isabelle Fernbach (Cambridge: Boydell & Brewer, 2012), pp. 117–40.

[97] Jean de Bertaut, *Traduction un peu paraphrasée du deuxiesme livre de l'Aeneide de Virgile* ([n.p.]: [n. pub], 1603); Jacques Davy Du Perron, *Partie du premier livre de l'Ænéide de Virgile* (Paris: Estienne, 1610).

[98] Brammall, 'The Politics of the Partial Translations of the *Aeneid*', p. 182.

[99] Beaulieu, '"Moy traductrice"', p. 129; see also Worth-Stylianou, 'Marie de Gournay et la traduction', p. 200.

54 WOMEN WRITING ANTIQUITY

The question of her authority as a translator is made evident in the first translation of the *Aeneid* that she published: her translation of Book 2, prefaced by a 'Lettre au Roy' and first published in 1594, before being published again in revised form in 1619. As her first published translation of the *Aeneid*, her version of Book 2 stands out from her later ones for its extensive scholarly notes and justifications. As explained, for Book 2 she inserts short extracts from translations by Jean Bertaut (set pieces; speeches; ekphrasis) to follow her own version. Bertaut becomes someone who represents state-of-the-art of Virgil's translations, a figure of authority, institution, and legitimacy; in the prefatory 'Lettre au Roy', Gournay 'dares' compare her work to his: 'l'une de ces Versions, estant la meilleure qui se soit veue sur le second de l'Aeneide, l'autre de ma façon si je l'ose advouer' (one of these versions is the best translation ever produced of the second book of the Aeneid; the other is my own if I may say so) (II, p. 1604). This daring is performative and marked, intended to lift her own version beyond the status quo. She uses a well-known gendered image to make this clear:

> Quelle temerité, SIRE, une quenouille attaque une crosse, et la crosse illustre d'un Bertault ? duquel à parler sérieusement neantmoins, je ne m'approche, qu'affin de porter en reverence le Livre devant luy dans le sainct mystere des Muses; bien qu'il fust raisonnable que soubs un Monarque si brave et si magnanime que LOUIS treizieme, les Dames osassent entreprendre des gestes d'Amazone. (II, p. 1604)

> What boldness, Sir, a distaff attacks a crosier, and the crosier of the illustrious Bertaut, no less? To whom nevertheless speaking seriously I dare not come near, except to carry the book reverently before him in the sacred mystery of the Muses, even though it would be reasonable that under a monarch as brave and magnanimous as Louis XIII, women might dare to undertake the gestures of an Amazon.

Here her distaff meets Bertaut's crosier; but she also appropriates for herself a much more violent weapon, that of an Amazon, which counters the domestic reference to the 'quenouille'.[100] The modesty of the 'quenouille' is thus undermined by the 'geste d'Amazone'. We will hear echoes of this sort of rhetoric in Anne Dacier's translation prefaces. Gournay is not an explicit reference for Dacier who did not translate Virgil; however, there are parallels in their use of images of warriors to describe their own endeavour, particularly as it relates to the translation of epic.

---

[100] She critisises the limitations represented by the quenouille in her 'Égalité', in *Œuvres complètes*, I, p. 965. Anna Maria van Schurman characterises Gournay in military terms as a 'virago' in a poem in Latin praising her as defender of women. Anna Maria van Schurman, *Opuscula Hebreae, Graeca, Latina, Gallica. Prosaica et Metrica* (Leiden: Elzevir, 1648), p. 264. See Larsen, 'A Women's Republic of Letters', pp. 108–09.

Her bold term, 'd'Amazone', was in fact replaced after the first edition of this preface to make the epic reference clearer: from 1620 it became 'gestes heroïques' (heroic gestures) which has a double function of referring to epic poetry (verse gendered as male) and to the male heroism it celebrates. Gournay aspires to the attributes of epic, but also associates them with female power, offering a hybrid poetics. This is evident from her insistence on translating Mars (2.440) or even the nouns of war 'arma' (2.655) and 'belli' (6.842) consistently with the term 'Bellonne', the ancient Roman Goddess of war.[101] She also retains this identification with the 'Amazone' after the removal of this reference through the addition of a quotation from Book 1 of the *Aeneid* (1.493) at the end of her Book 2 translation: 'audetque viris concurrere Virgo': 'and the maid [the Amazon warrior Penthesilea] dared to fight with men' (II, p. 1677).

The notion of 'hardiesse' captured in this preface in the term 'témérité' recurs in a number of her other prefaces, such as in the short letter dedicated to Du Perron which precedes her translation of *Aeneid* Book 1, the next work of Virgil that she translated, first published in 1620. She defends herself against temerity, claiming she has acted out of love and a duty to her readers: 'cette hardiesse toutesfois, me seroit reprochée à tort: car il faut recognoistre qu'elle est fondée directement sur l'amour et sur le service du Public' (I have nevertheless wrongly been reproached of this boldness, for we must note that it is based directly on love and service to the people) (II, p. 1580). Such boldness is also picked up in the strikingly violent image with which she closes her longer preface, 'De la façon ...':

> J'entends bien que tu veux dire, Lecteur, que travaillant à ce premier et à ce quatriesme, après un si suffisant personnage, je conduis, au Premier, Aenée à Port-de-salut, pour faire naufrage moy-mesme, et qu'au Quatriesme j'ensevelis Didon, pour enterrer mon nom en son sepulchre. Quel remede? *In magnis voluisse sat est.* Encores est-ce quelque chose, de se tuer d'un beau couteau. (II, p. 1579)

> I understand that you want to say, reader, that by working on the first and fourth books, after such a capable figure, I lead, in the first one, Aeneas, to his port of safety, only to shipwreck myself, and that in the fourth, I bury Dido, only to bury my own name on her tomb. What remedy? *In great things, it is enough to have wanted.* And it is still something, to kill oneself with a beautiful knife.

Here she compares her act of translation to the dangers Aeneas faced in the ship-wreck (she saves him to leave herself exposed) and buries Dido to bury her own

---

[101] *Œuvres completes*, II, p. 1647; II, p. 1665; II, p. 1751. Fiona Cox stresses that Gournay 'employs very vivid imagery for the depiction of anger' in 'An Amazon in the Renaissance', p. 104. See also Jonathan Patterson who argues that she privileged 'forceful, oratorical vehemence' in 'Marie de Gournay, Poetry and Gender', p. 209.

56 WOMEN WRITING ANTIQUITY

name in Dido's sepulchre. She then adds, after her quotation from Propertius ('in great things it is enough to have wanted to') that it is 'quelque chose' to kill oneself with a beautiful knife, evoking Dido's own (male-gendered) death.[102] In all these comparisons—Penthesilea, Dido and the shipwreck that nearly ruins Aeneas, the bold Amazons—Gournay makes the grand parallel gestures we encountered in her self-projection as Cicero and Socrates, but here she interjects physical violence. This powerfully evokes the personal stakes entailed by Gournay in the act of publication, its relation to her intellectual identity, and the investment of herself (to the point of obliteration) in her works, an investment which Beaulieu argues was one of the reasons for her being shunned because it strays far from the modesty expected of (women) writers.[103] The self-reference, the linking of self to textual monument, the way her œuvre constitutes what Beaulieu describes as her 'textual alter-ego', is powerfully evoked in the note she adds to the end of the 1641 edition, quoted above, warning readers against tampering with her work.[104] This closes with 'Les insolences, voire les meurtres de reputation que je voy tous les jours faire en cas pareil dans cét impertinent siècle, me convient à lascher cette imprecation' (the insolence, even the destruction of reputation that I see every day to happen in this way in this impertinent time, compels me to unleash this warning) (II, p. 1864). The emotive language which conjures personal and physical violence, entwining her person, her reputation and her text, evokes the violent metaphors she uses to describe her act of translation.

What of the comparison she invites between her work and that of Bertaut for her *Aeneid* 2 translation? This comparison veers between homage and contest, as noted, but also serves to put into practice her arguments about language.[105] Linguistically, the translation remains close to Virgil's original text: there are many instances in this translation when she mimics or even amplifies Virgil's stylistic features, in keeping with her valorisation of ancient poetics. To take one example, she captures Virgil's repetition: Anchises' 'iam iam nulla mora est' (2.701) becomes 'marchon, marchon, mon fils, je consens à la fuitte' (let us advance my son, advance, I consent to flee) (II, p. 1669).[106] This valorisation is particularly evident in the passages which are similar to Bertaut's version: while his already exemplifies the language use she vaunts, her translations go even further. She tends to use more

---

[102] Dido kills herself with a knife like a male warrior, rather than hanging herself with bedsheets as tragic women more commonly did. See Nicole Loraux, *Façons tragiques de tuer une femme* (Paris: Hachette, 1985).

[103] Beaulieu, 'Marie de Gournay, ou l'occultation d'une figure auctoriale'.

[104] Ibid., p. 23.

[105] See, for instance, the way she explains her use of the word 'plaints', which Malherbe had criticised as 'mal' and old-fashioned (II, p. 1634). As Franchetti shows, she litters her work with such rejected terms, including, for instance the 'Grief' of her 'Grief des dames'. Franchetti, *L'Ombre discourante*, p. 90.

[106] 'Now, now, there is no delay'. Virgil, *Eclogues. Georgics. Aeneid: Books 1–6*, trans. by H. Rushton Fairclough, rev. by G. P. Goold, Loeb Classical Library 63 (Cambridge, MA: Harvard University Press, 1916), 2.701.

of the 'poetic' features she defends in her essays on poetics, evident in her use of names. For example, when Aeneas starts to tell Dido of his adventures, where the Latin is 'et iam nox umida caelo / praecipitat suadentque cadentia sidera somnos' (2.8–9),[107] which Bethaut replicates fairly closely: 'Desjà l'humide nuict du Ciel se precipite, / Et maint astre tombant au sommeil nous invite' (The dewy night hurries on / and many falling stars invite us to sleep) (II, p. 1610), Gournay introduces mythology: 'l'humide nuict du Ciel se precipte / Et l'Ourse desja basse au sommeil nous invite' (The dewy nightsky advances / And the Bear, already dropped low in the sky, invites us to sleep) (II, p. 1609); for 'Troei' in the Latin (Troye by Bertaut), Gournay uses 'Ilion' (II, p. 1609). These sorts of amplifications can be traced throughout all the books she translates; her need to associate her work with contemporary versions—and her assertion of her own distinction—occurs again in relation to Books 1 and 4, which she introduces with extracts from Du Perron's translation, then followed by her own.

Gournay's *Aeneid* also allows her to expand on her gender politics, notably in the representation of Dido and Aeneas. As Brammall argues, the fact that Gournay has produced a partial translation both of the whole of the *Aeneid*, which is 12 Books in total, and of the Books she chooses to translate (1, 2, 4; only Book 6 is complete), means that her selection is all the more significant: it allows her to more quickly highlight the themes that interest her.[108] Her representation of Dido in particular is notable as she chooses to translate all the Books in which Dido features (1, 4, and 6). She draws on the tradition established by Christine de Pizan which sees Dido as a dignified and noble queen (rather than, for example, the helpless abandoned woman or impious for her suicide), and integrates this portrayal explicitly into the *querelle des femmes*.[109] Gournay's portrayal complements her use of Dido as an example of female rule when criticising Salic Law in her *Egalité des hommes et des femmes*. As Valerie Worth-Stylaniou has shown, the *Aeneid* in the Renaissance was almost always taken up for political means, especially notions of nationhood and civil war, meaning that Gournay's inflection of gender politics into the poem was by no means an unusual gesture.[110]

---

[107] 'And now dewy night is speeding from the sky and the setting stars counsel sleep', Ibid., 2.8–9.

[108] Brammall, 'The Politics of the Partial Translations of the *Aeneid*', p. 183. See also Cox, 'An Amazon in the Renaissance'.

[109] On Dido's contradictory reception, see, for instance, Marilynn Desmond, *Reading Dido: Gender, Textuality, and the Medieval Aeneid* (Minneapolis: University of Minnesota Press, 1994). She is also portrayed sympathetically in the other translation of Virgil's *Aeneid* by a woman, Hélisenne de Crenne's *Eneydes* (1541), although this version is not mentioned by Gournay. Hélisenne de Crenne, *Les Quatre premiers livres des Eneydes du treselegant poete Virgile. Traduictz de Latin en prose Françoyse* (Paris: Janot, 1541). On this, see Pollie E. Bromilow, 'Power through Print: The Works of Hélisenne de Crenne', in *Women and Power at the French Court, 1483–1563*, ed. by. Susan Broomhall (Amsterdam: Amsterdam University Press, 2018), pp. 287–305; and Sharon Marshall, 'The *Aeneid* and the Illusory Authoress: Truth, Fiction and Feminism in Hélisenne de Crenne's *Eneyde*' (unpublished doctoral thesis, University of Exeter, 2011).

[110] See Worth-Stylianou, 'Virgilian Space in Renaissance French Translations', pp. 126–39; on political uses of Virgil in the English context, see Ian Calvert, *Virgil's English Translators: Civil Wars to Restoration* (Edinburgh: Edinburgh University Press, 2021).

58 WOMEN WRITING ANTIQUITY

Gournay's translation choices in Book 4, first published in 1620, demonstrate in particular her sensitivity to the emotive dynamics of this book and to the characterisation of Dido and Aeneas.[111] Here she draws out the pathos of the relationship between the two. Readers have been cued to anticipate a sympathetic interpretation of Dido from Gournay's comments in the 'Lettre à Bassompierre', added to introduce her translations of Book 4: Gournay praises Dido as being endowed with 'esprit, beauté, bien-séance, courage, affabilité' (wit, beauty, bienséance, courage and affability) and as someone whom Aeneas should have treated 'moins durement' (less harshly) (ii, p. 1680). Her translation is to confer 'la gloire' onto this queen: forgiving her for her suicide and instead emphasising her dignity and governance (ii, p. 1680). Gournay's subtle adaptations mean that Aeneas does treat Dido less severely; not only does Gournay emphasise Dido's pathos but she tempers Aeneas's inflexibility. When he wonders how to tell Dido of his impending departure—'quae prima exordia sumat?' (4.284)[112]—Gournay expands this: 'Ou quel discours subtil peut-il onques tramer, / Qui puisse dextrement le depart entamer?' (Or what subtle speech can he ever spin / Which can deftly initiate his departure?) (ii, p. 1686), following through, as is her tendency, the logic behind his question and fleshing out Aeneas's perspective. Likewise, when he finally does speak to Dido, once she has discovered his plan to leave, his tone is softer than in the Latin: where he addresses her as 'regina' (4.334), Gournay adds 'Reyne fleur de beauté' (The Queen, flower of beauty) (ii, p. 1689), and slightly nuances Aeneas's line towards the end of his speech: 'desine meque tuis incendere teque querelis' (4.360),[113] becomes 'cesse donc d'enflammer, Princesse Tyrienne / De plainctes et de pleurs ta douleur et la mienne' (Cease, therefore, Tyrian Princess, to inflame with compaints and tears your grief and my own) (ii, p. 1691). He now emphasises his own 'douleur' rather than the more ambiguous state of being 'inflamed'. She also expands the description of his silent suffering after Dido's speech: 'linquens multa metu cunctantem et multa parantem / dicere (4.390–91):[114] 'Seulet et desolé delaissant son Ænée: / Qui pressé du respect naissant de trop aimer / Maint propos veut ouvrir et ne l'ose entamer' (Leaving Aeneas alone and aggrieved; he who, with the growing respect for his deep love, many speeches attempted to start but did not dare broach) (ii, p. 1693).

Gournay heightens the pathos and drama in Dido's final monologue as she prepares to kill herself as she sees Aeneas leaving. When Dido asks herself 'infelix

---

[111] Worth-Stylianou suggests that her version is more emotive, 'Marie de Gournay, traductrice', in *Œuvres complètes*, i, p. 64; Brammall emphasises that her version is almost twice as long as original, with this expansion allowing for heightened tragedy. Brammall, 'The Politics of the Partial Translations of the *Aeneid*', p. 192.

[112] 'What opening words choose first?' Virgil, *Aeneid: Books 1–6*, trans. by Fairclough, rev. by Goold, 4.334.

[113] 'Cease to inflame yourself and me with your complaints.' Ibid., 4.360.

[114] 'Leaving him in fear and much hesitance and ready to say much.' Ibid., 4.390–91.

Dido, nunc te facta impia tangunt?'(4.596),[115] Gournay expands: 'Te precipite, Ô Reyne en si profonde erreur? / Pauvrette il faut mourir: la sentence éternelle / De ton fatal destin au dernier jour t'appelle' (Do you throw yourself, O Queen, into such a great mistake? / Poor thing, you must die: the eternal sentence / of your fatal destiny calls you on your final day) (II, p. 1706). The series of four questions in Virgil's lines 600–04 of Dido's final monologue in which she regrets how she welcomed Aenaes is amplified in Gournay's version with seven short questions (II, p. 1707), four of which are given in a particularly staccato and arresting manner, all opening with 'que'. The repetitive structure here, which is not in Virgil's original, both affords Dido an urgency and accentuates the frantic crescendo of passions at play. Dido's death in Virgil's account is narrated with a distance: 'Dixerat, atque illam media inter talia ferro / conlapsam aspiciunt comites, ensemque cruore / spumantem sparsasque manus' (4.663–5).[116] Gournay keeps some of this distance but gives Dido an active verb 'enfoncer': 'Elle enfonce à ces mots le fatal coutelas / On la void trébucher sur ce funebre amas' (With these words, she drives in in the fatal sword / She could be seen to falter on the funeral pyre) (II, p. 1711). The gendering of Dido's death is already significant in Virgil's version—by killing herself with a sword she effects a soldier's death; Gournay underscores this by making her agency evident through the active verb.

Gournay's characterisation of Aeneas in her translation of Book 6, also makes for a more dignified representation of Dido. She elaborates on the speech Aeneas makes to Dido when he encounters her in the underworld. For Aeneas's 'quem fugis? extremum fato, quod te adloquor, hoc est' (6.466), Gournay writes, 'Fuis-tu ce cher amant? la haute Destinée / Pour la dernière fois t'ameine ton Ænée' (Do you flee your dear love? Great Destiny brings you your Aeneas for the last time) (II, p. 1734).[117] The softer tone that we encountered in Book 4 is continued here as Gournay's Aeneas depicts himself as a 'cher amant', emphasising his emotion, and describes himself as being hers. Likewise, Gournay emphasises Aeneas's perspective and grief where Virgil prioritises his pity for Dido: 'nec minus Aeneas, casu percussus iniquo / prosequitur lacrimis longe et miseratur euntem' (6.475–76);[118] using an epithet again, Gournay writes 'Le Troyen cepandant qu'un si cruel malheur / Percé des ayguillons d'une amere douleur / Haste ses pas bien loin après la triste Reyne / Lamentant tout en pleurs et sa suyte et sa peine' (The Trojan, however, whom such great misfortune pierces with the needles of a bitter pain, hastens his steps far behind the sad Queen, lamenting in tears both her fate and her pain)

---

[115] 'Unhappy Dido, do only now your sinful deeds come home to you?' Ibid., 4.596.
[116] 'She ceased, and even as she spoke her handmaids see her fallen on the sword, the blade reeking with blood and her hands bespattered.' Ibid., 4.663–5.
[117] 'Whom do you flee? This is the last word Fate suffers me to say to you.' Ibid., 6.466.
[118] 'Yet none the less, stricken by her unjust doom, Aeneas attends her with tears afar and pities her as she goes.' Ibid., 6.475–76.

60   WOMEN WRITING ANTIQUITY

(II, p. 1735) and thus subtly shifts the emphasis onto their shared grief with 'cruel malheur' being applicable to both parties. With these characterisations, Gournay injects lyrical lament into the epic genre, thus troubling the gendered binaries associated with those poetic modes: as Jonathan Patterson has argued convincingly (in relation to *Aeneid* 2, and her conceptualisations of 'douceur' and 'vigueur'), Gournay advocates a 'gender-neutral poetic style'.[119]

Gournay's translations of the *Aeneid* need to be situated alongside her essays on poetics and language, her other classical translations, and her reflections on her learning and authority: doing this allows us to grasp the coherence of her œuvre in which she constructs herself as a female intellectual and vigorous, even violent, defender of classical and Renaissance poetics against language reform. In her translation of the *Aeneid*, we also glimpse a further aspect of her polysemic and polymathic intellectual endeavour: her resistance to norms of gendered behaviour which result in a creativity that is not usually recognised in Gournay scholarship. Gournay's approach to Dido and Aeneas is subtle and sensitive: he is afforded more interiority and is more able to express his grief; and she is given dignity in death. This creativity, and her use of antiquity as source of inspiration for gender politics, is also evident in Gournay's poetry, analysis of which will form the final section of this chapter.

Poetry and Latinity

The last part of Gournay's *Les Advis* which immediately follows her translation of Book 6 of the *Aeneid* is devoted to her poetry, entitled the *Bouquet de Pinde, composé de fleurs diverses* (II, pp. 1754–1860), gathering together work written and published from 1594 onwards, some included in a previous collection entitled 'Bouquet poétique'.[120] 'Pinde' here refers to Pindus, the Greek mountain range, associated with the Muses; it possibly also evokes 'Pindar' (Pindare in French), the ancient Greek lyric poet to whom Ronsard, one of Gournay's great models, compared himself. This collection is dedicated to Montaigne's daughter, Leonor, whom Gournay calls her 'sœur d'alliance'. These poems have received little criticism, apart from the analysis devoted to her verse self-portrait, 'La Pincture des

---

[119] Patterson, 'Marie de Gournay, Poetry and Gender', p. 210. Her portrayal of Dido and Aeneas also echoes some of the characterisations in her novel *Proumenoir de Monsieur de Montaigne* (1594). For analysis of this novel, see Domna C. Stanton, 'Woman as Object and Subject of Exchange: Marie de Gournay's "Le Proumenoir" (1594)', *L'Esprit Créateur*, 23.2 (1983), 9–25. See also Franchetti who focuses on this work throughout her study, *L'Ombre discourante*, but see especially pp. 15–31, and for its representation of the female condition see pp. 117–70. On the links between this novel and her *Aeneid* 2, see Martine Debaisieux, 'Marie de Gournay cont(r)e la tradition: du *Proumenoir de Monsieur de Montaigne* aux versions de l'*Énéide*', *Renaissance and Reformation*, 21.2 (1997), 45–58.

[120] 'Bouquet poetique, ou meslanges', in *Le Promenoir de Monsieur de Montaigne*.

mœurs'.[121] And yet, these poems form a significant epilogue to Gournay's carefully curated œuvre: in her definitive 1641 edition, this collection is followed only by a letter to M. Thévenin (who might be Jean Thévenin, the family lawyer) introducing the 'Copie de la Vie de la Damoiselle de Gournay'. There are well over a hundred poems included here, ranging from short, often humorous, verse epigrams addressed to or about different characters—for instance, 'Pour une fille qui sert une Dame sçavante' (For a girl serving a learned lady) (ii, p. 1813) and 'D'un aveugle né Joueur d'espinette' (Of a born-blind espinette player) (ii, p. 1811)— dedicatory poems, longer epitaphs, 'cantiques', and dialogues. For the purposes of this chapter, I will only look at a very small proportion of her poems and not at the most typical selection (the majority being the shorter epigrams): I treat those which demonstrate Gournay's skills as a Latinist and demonstrate her engagement with classical poetry. In this collection, there are four translations from neo-Latin poems, for three of which Gournay places the Latin text first, including 'Hermaphrodite', which I analyse below; there is one poem in Latin, which she translates herself,[122] as well as another praising her in Latin by the Dutch polymath, Hugo Grotius, who had translated some of her poetry;[123] two poems called 'Eclogues'; and a translation of Horace 3.9 (here she also includes a parallel Latin text). I will focus in this closing discussion on the four that demonstrate most her uses of classical poetry: the two Eclogues, 'Hermaphrodite', and her Horace translation.

Gournay's two 'Eclogues'—'Eclogue pour une grande dame, absente de Monsieur son mary' (ii, pp. 1755–62) and 'Autre Eclogue, pour la mesme Dame' (ii, pp. 1762–63)—were both originally published in the 1594 'Bouquet poétique'. Both stage the shepherdess, Cléophile: in the first she laments the absence of her lover, Cléophon; in the second, they are reconciled. The eclogue, genre of classical pastoral, harking back to Theocritus, then Virgil, was also a significant Renaissance poetic mode, as its influence was felt in poetry by Clément Marot and by Ronsard.[124] It is thought that Gournay's first 'Eclogue' was influenced by Marco Giralamo Vida's *Bucolica* and particularly his 'Eclogua prima, Daphnis'.[125] However, as we will see again in Chapter 5 in relation to Antoinette Deshoulières's eclogue poems, Gournay's inclusion of a female speaker is significant: as Ellen Osiensis argues, 'in the world of Virgilian pastoral, girls are not singers; they do

---

[121] For some analysis, see Ilsley, *A Daughter of the Renaissance*, pp. 182–99; and Giovanna Devincenzo, *Marie de Gournay: un cas littéraire* (Paris: Presses de l'Université de Paris-Sorbonne, 2002), pp. 65–86.

[122] 'De eo qui natavit ab insula, Rhea ad castra Regis Christianissimi', 'Bouquet de Pinde', in *Œuvres complètes*, ii, p. 1796.

[123] 'Bouquet de Pinde', in *Œuvres complètes*, ii, p. 1823.

[124] Marot translated Virgil's first Eclogue at the opening of his *L'Adolescence clémentine* of 1513: *Œuvres complètes*, ed. by François Rigolot, 2 vols (Paris: Flammarion, 2007–08), i (2007), pp. 38–43. Florian Preisig, *Clément Marot et les métamorphoses de l'auteur à l'aube de la Renaissance* (Geneva: Droz, 2004), pp. 109–26, p. 159. See also Chapter 5 on Antoinette Deshoulières.

[125] See Note A, 'Bouquet de Pinde', in *Œuvres complètes*, ii, p. 1755.

62 WOMEN WRITING ANTIQUITY

not perform; and while they are sometimes quoted, we never hear them speak.'[126] Female speakers were not traditional in the Renaissance tradition either: indeed, Vida's first Eclogue stages two male shepherds, Lycidas and Amyntas. In addition to this marked use of a female-gendered voice, Gournay's Eclogues powerfully demonstrate her commitment to the poetics she defends in the essays analysed above. In her recycling of the typical tropes of the shepherd's lament, we encounter diminutives ('seulette' (little alone one): II, p. 1756); and an emphasis on physicality and sensuality that is not typical in the classical tradition, but which does chime with her insistence on frankness and her resistance to *bienséant* language: 'j'ay ma chemise ouverte où le tetin la baise' (my blouse is open where the breast kisses it) (II, p. 1762).

Gournay's Eclogues offer a suggestive interpretation of a classical (and Renaissance) tradition. She makes her Latinity even more evident in the translation she offers of a neo-Latin poem, 'Hermaphroditus', for which she includes the Latin before her translation. It is thought she would have accessed this poem from a manuscript and the poem is thought to be by an Italian, Pulci de Costozza.[127] This playful poem (II, p. 1815), told from the perspective of the hermaphrodite, starts with the description of the oracle predicting their undetermined sex at birth (Phoebus suggesting a son; Mars a daughter; and Juno neither one or the other); then discusses how these three figures suggested the hermaphrodite should be killed (sword; drowning; hanging) before ending with the description of how the hermaphrodite did in fact die (by climbing a tree and falling on their own dagger). It seems to owe little to Ovid's tale of Hermaphroditus and Salmacis (*Met.* 4.247–388), in which the two characters fuse to become the original hermaphrodite as Hermaphroditus struggles against the rape by Salmacis.[128] It perhaps owes more to Narcissus, the parallel/antithetical tale of self-recognition, in the fatal prediction at birth, and the references to downing. Does it stretch interpretation too far, and deploy a reductive framework of conceiving of all her work through a gendered lens, to suggest she is interested in the hybrid gender politics of the hermaphrodite myth? Learning and gender (and their tensions) are present in this poem in a further way: Gournay's translation follows the Latin text, underscoring the tension in the expectations she has of her readers that we have traced thus far. Is this a learning device to aid a reader unfamiliar with Latin or an invitation to a learned reader to scrutinise Gournay's knowledge of Latin?

---

[126] Ellen Oliensis, 'Sons and Lovers: Sexuality and Gender in Virgil's Poetry', in *The Cambridge Companion to Virgil*, ed. by Charles Martindale (Cambridge: Cambridge University Press, 2006), pp. 294–331 (p. 297).

[127] See the 'Dissertation sur la fameuse epigramme latine de l'hermaphrodite', in *Menagiana*, 4 vols (Paris: Delaulne, 1715), IV, pp. 322–34, which mentions Gournay's poem (p. 330).

[128] See Emma Herdman, 'Folie and Salmacis: Labé's Rewriting of Ovid', *The Modern Language Review*, 108.3 (2013), 782–801. I'm grateful to Emma Herdman for her suggestions regarding Gournay's poem.

A similar interest in gender binaries, and equality, is present in Gournay's translation from Horace's Ode 3.9, the dialogue between Lydia and Horace, which is dedicated to a M. Pasquier, and to Nicolas de Neufville, secretary of state (II, pp. 1816–17).[129] This poem, first published in 1622, is also offered as a parallel text, but the Latin and French are included together, with her translation following each quatrain. The poem opens with the two speakers reflecting on their past love, then moves on to the fact that both have found new love, and closes with the prospect of their reconciliation. Most significant is the location of its original publication: it was placed at the end of the *Égalité des hommes et des femmes* when it was first published in 1622. Given how carefully she curated her œuvre, it can hardly be a coincidence that this poem, in which male and female voices jostle, or compete, first in conflict and then in reconciliation, follows her essay about male and female equality: the paralleling exemplifies her concern with reciprocity and fairness. Its position also complements and indeed proves the argument in the *Égalité*, that a woman can possess the learning and ability (and temerity) to translate the words of a great male poet. This combination of creativity, self-conscious demonstration of erudition and of her gender, and strategic and ideological use of adaptation is typical of Gournay's approach to classical texts, which underpins her *Advis*.

**

Gournay sets up the key threads of this study: as a writer self-conscious about her status as an intellectual woman, for whom money was important and whose reputation as a (female) thinker and a moral person was implicated in her precarious economy and self-representation, and who engaged in the enduring question of the status and authority of antiquity compared to French taste and aesthetics. However, she also represents a rupture or discontinuity: the leap from her to Scudéry, who will be studied in the next chapter, is a significant one in terms of ideology. Not only does Gournay aspire (like Dacier later in the century, who, as we see, because of her family and because of her nods to modesty, fares better) to be a 'savante' who demonstrates her learning—and so forms a contrast with the ideal modest female intellectual promoted by Scudéry—but, connected to this, the term 'savante' is not charged in her work with the same force as it is in the works of later writers, especially, but not only, those who deny this title.

As a figure who fell between two periods of taste (and landed on the wrong side, from the perspective of the 'Grand Siècle'), Gournay has been written out of the seventeenth-century canon, and indeed has even been marginalised in the recovery of female authors of the Grand Siècle, although she does feature prominently in accounts of Renaissance women writers.[130] This categorisation echoes

---

[129] It is entitled 'Dialogue d'Horace et de Lydie, traduict en faveur des muses du sieur Pasquier, autrefois premier commis de Mr de Villeroy'.

[130] For example, Cathleen Bauchatz, 'To Choose Ink and Pen: French Renaissance Women's Writing', in *A History of Women's Writing in France*, ed. by Sonya Stephens (Cambridge: Cambridge University

the way she was received by women in the seventeenth century: for instance, Marie-Jeanne L'Héritier, in her catalogue of illustrious French women thinkers, casts Gournay not with women of her century, but with Christine de Pizan.[131] These divisions, however, risk overdetermining periodisation (her 1641 *Advis* came out a year before Scudéry's *Les Femmes illustres* and we would include, for instance, Corneille's 1636 *Le Cid* in discussions of seventeenth-century aesthetic changes) and undervalue Gournay's direct engagement with the very emergence of new aesthetics and poetics. In this present study, she opens analysis of seventeenth-century women's uses of antiquity: pushing against the periodisation that has often partitioned her off from writers of the next two generations offers a new perspective on the ruptures she navigated.

As will be evident by now, Marie de Gournay was a respected figure in her own time: she hosted a successful salon, was an important guest at salons in Paris and the Netherlands, and was a correspondent of Anna Maria van Schurman.[132] However, as critics have long argued, her uncompromising stances, her polemic, her aggression, her self-exposure all made her vulnerable to attack, ridicule, and criticism, all the worse because she did not espouse the demure modesty expected of a female writer: in her demonstration of her knowledge and in her frankness, she was, as she says, 'loin de bienséance'.[133] That Madeleine de Scudéry's strategy of modesty was enabling (albeit compromised) is all the more evident when contrasted with Gournay: Scudéry (along with Deshoulières, Villedieu, Dacier) was made a member of the *Accademia dei Ricovrati* in Padua, founded in 1599, and won a prize from the *Académie française*. The practical jokes made at Gournay's expense, the slander she suffered, are often woven into descriptions of her life, such that the two are inseparable. Tallemant des Réaux, source of the anecdote about the origins of her *Vie*, is scathing, mixing agism, misogyny, and satire; his description opens: 'Mademoiselle de Gournay était une vieille fille de Picardie, et bien demoiselle' (Mademoiselle de Gournay was a spinster from Picardy, and certainly an old maid). He mocks the pension she received from Richelieu, noting that

---

Press), pp. 41–63. She features in Emily Butterworth, 'Women's Writing in the Sixteenth Century', in *The Cambridge History of French Literature*, ed. by William Burgwinkle, Nicholas Hammond, and Emma Wilson (Cambridge: Cambridge University Press, 2011), pp. 211–19, but does so only briefly in the chapter on seventeenth-century women's writing. Devincenzo does draw a line between Gournay, Buffet, and Scudéry as prominent linguists, in *Des mots et des femmes*, pp. 159–60.

[131] On this see Helena Taylor, 'Marie de Gournay et le Parnasse des femmes', in *Littéraire: pour Alain Viala*, ed. by M. M. Fragonard and others, 2 vols (Arras: Artois Presses Université, 2018), ii, pp. 227–37.

[132] In some (less typical) corners of her reception, this activity has eclipsed her writing: Mary Hays suggests that Gournay 'was more valuable for her good nature, her generosity and other admirable virtues than for her learning'. Hays, *Female Biography*, p. 449. On the role of this text in determining a philosophical canon, see Sarah Hutton, '"Context" and "Fortuna" in the History of Women Philosophers: A Diachronic Perspective', in *Methodological Reflections on Women's Contributions and Influence in the History of Philosophy*, ed. by Sigridur Thorgeirsdottir and Ruth Edith Hagengruber (Cham: Springer, 2020), pp. 29–42.

[133] On the ridicule she endured and her own writing about slander, see Butterworth, 'Marie de Gournay and the Abuse of Mockery'.

extra was needed for her faithful cat's kittens, and is unsparing in his portrait.[134] He lists others who mocked her, the Comte de Moret, Malherbe, Boisrobert, and suggests that 'Perrette', the old Sibylle who lives with her cat and translated Virgil in Saint-Amant's satirical *Le Poète crotté*, is based on Gournay.[135]

Even those who admired her, such as Michel de Marolles and Pierre Bayle, made allusion to this ridicule: in his *Mémoires*, Marolles, who praises her and was a close acquaintance, refers to 'ceux qui l'ont voulu railler' (those who sought to mock her).[136] Pierre Bayle describes her as 'célèbre par son savoir' (celebrated for her learning) in his article devoted to her, and refutes the very unfavourable portrait of her in the *Le Remerciment des Beurrières de Paris* in which she is described as a 'une femme qui a bien servi le public' (a woman who served the public well), with connotations of prostitution, reprised again in the *Perroniana* (a collection of anecdotes relating to Perron and his circle), as part of a jibe suggesting this would be unlikely given her physical appearance.[137] Bayle also describes her disagreements with Gilles Ménage and Malherbe over language reform and recounts another practical joke played on her by some friends of the poet, Honorat de Racan. She was expecting him, but a friend turned up impersonating him; when Gournay realised she had been tricked, she attacked him 's'armant d'une de ses pantoufles' (arming herself with slippers). Describing her as 'un peu bilieuse', Bayle echoes the particular misogyny that Gournay faced, as an old, unmarried, childless, fairly impoverished, opinionated, learned woman. The two 'jokes' played on her which emerge from these anecdotes (the story about her being asked to send a version of her life to the English king; and this one involving Racan) are similar: they both mock her aspirations to inclusion in learned culture. Although Gournay is not usually categorised with the 'précieuse'—the term being coined in 1654 and in relation to Scudéry and her salon—the attack on aspiration it entails chimes with the humiliations Gournay suffered.

For a long time, Gournay was studied solely in relation to Montaigne, and while this led to valuable scholarship on her, and identified her crucial contributions to his reception, it was always relational, until her feminism, feminist discourse, and autobiography became a subject of critical interest and dominated work on her. Recent work has looked more widely at her writing, and begun to restore her to the history of linguistics, has recognised the key role her salon and its attendees played in the linguistics debates of the early seventeenth century and indeed to the founding of the *Académie française* (even though she did not agree with many of its reforms), and has identified her importance to the history of political thought and

---

[134] Tallemant des Réaux, 'Mlle de Gournay', in *Historiettes*, p. 257.

[135] Ibid., p. 257.

[136] Marolles, *Mémoires*, I (1656), p. 58.

[137] Pierre Bayle, *Dictionnaire historique et critique*, 4 vols (Amsterdam: Brunel, 1740), II, pp. 585–87. See also Fogel, 'La Damoiselle de Gournay, qui a tousjours bien servi au public', pp. 214–17, and Conroy, 'A Defence and Illustration of Marie de Gournay'.

66 WOMEN WRITING ANTIQUITY

of philosophy in a broad sense.[138] The relative neglect of the full range of Gournay's work in criticism also speaks of Gournay's inaccessibility. She writes in a very dense and difficult French; she is closely and intricately engaged with debates of her period that do not always translate easily to readers; and her work can be opaque in its learned references. But it is also testament to the enduring power of the gossip and slander that beset her reputation. In her quest to define and exemplify the figure of the female intellectual, Gournay took considerable risk, exposing herself to attack. As we have seen, Gournay strove to be an example for a category that was not self-evident, that did not even really exist; a pioneer by necessity, she also brought into view the risks to personal reputation that were entailed by taking such a stance.

---

[138] To give some examples, Deslauriers, 'Marie de Gournay and Aristotle'; Devincenzo, 'Les "après-diners"'; Ayres-Bennett and Sanson, *Women in the History of Linguistics*; Pal, 'Marie de Gournay, Marie du Moulin, and Anna Maria van Schurman'; Broad and Green, 'From the Reformation to Marie le Jars de Gournay'.

3

The Paradoxes of Modesty

Historical Fiction and the Female Line

Ancient history and literature played a complex role in Madeleine de Scudéry's fiction and the construction of her authorial ethos. Her early works, which form the subjects of this chapter, *Les Femmes illustres* (1642), *Artamène ou le Grand Cyrus* (1649–53), *Clélie: histoire romaine* (1654–60), all use antiquity as a setting and constitute creative reworkings of Greek and Roman historical and literary sources.[1] Co-authored with her brother, Georges, *Les Femmes illustres* stages rhetorical speeches of ancient women from history and myth, and generically is influenced by Ovid's *Heroides*; *Artamène ou le Grand Cyrus*, also thought to be co-authored, draws on Xenophon and Herodotus and tells of Cyrus the Great's adventures in the ancient Near East; and *Clélie, histoire romaine*, considered to be her first single-authored work, is based primarily on the first two books of Livy, recounting the early history of Rome.[2] At the same time, across these very works, particularly in her (self) portraits of (or as) 'Sapho' in the *Femmes illustres* and in *Le Grand Cyrus*, Scudéry heralded a shift from the poetics and gender politics espoused by Marie de Gournay, studied in the previous chapter, to a hugely influential version of a modest 'savoir' in which women should not parade their learning, but rather cultivate the art of discreet conversation and sociability.[3] The ultimate example of

---

[1] [Madeleine and] Georges de Scudéry, *Les Femmes illustres ou les harangues héroïques de Mr de Scudéry* (Paris: Sommaville, 1642); [Madeleine and] Georges de Scudéry, 'Histoire de Sapho', *Artamène ou le grand Cyrus par Mr de Scudéry*, 10 vols (Paris: Courbé, 1649–53); [Madeleine de Scudéry], *Clélie, histoire romaine par Mr de Scudéry*, 10 vols (Paris: Courbé, 1654–1660).

[2] On attribution: *Ibrahim ou le grand Bassa* is generally attributed to Georges although Madeleine is considered to have made some contribution: see Georges de Scudéry, *Ibrahim ou le grand Bassa*, ed. by Rosa Pellegrini and Antonella Arrigoni (Paris: Presses de l'Université de Paris-Sorbonne, 2003); for *Les Femmes illustres*, see Joan DeJean's argument that the Sapho letter was by Madeleine though the collection was co-authored: Joan DeJean, *Fictions of Sappho: 1546–1937* (Chicago: University of Chicago Press, 1989), p. 103; and Donna Kuizenga, 'L'Arc de triomphe des dames: Héroïsme dans Les Femmes Illustres de Madeleine et Georges de Scudéry', in *Les Trois Scudéry*, ed. by Alain Niderst (Paris: Klincksieck, 1993), pp. 301–10 (p. 301). *Le Grand Cyrus* is considered to be co-authored: see Georges and Madeleine de Scudéry, *Artamène ou le grand Cyrus*, ed. by Claude Bourqui (Paris: Flammarion, 2005) with Madeleine writing the 'Histoire de Sapho'. See also Myriam Dufour-Maître, *Les Précieuses: naissance des femmes de lettres en France au XVIIe siècle*, 2nd edn (Paris: Champion, 2008), p. 398; and on the attribution of *Clélie* to Madeleine, see Madeleine de Scudéry, *Clélie; histoire romaine*, ed. by Delphine Denis (Paris: Gallimard, 2006), and see Dufour-Maître, *Les Précieuses*, p. 398.

[3] On Sapho as self-portrait of Scudéry, see Anne Debrosse, *La Souvenance et le désir: la reception des poétesses grecques* (Paris: Classiques Garnier, 2018), pp. 344–56. For examples of her use of this pseudonym, see Alain Niderst, Delphine Denis and Myriam Dufour-Maître, eds, Madeleine de

Women Writing Antiquity. Helena Taylor, Oxford University Press. © Helena Taylor (2024).
DOI: 10.1093/oso/9780192870445.003.0003

68 WOMEN WRITING ANTIQUITY

such learning, as she makes evident, is classical knowledge, particularly literacy in ancient Greek and Latin; she explicitly figures her ideal modest female intellectual in opposition to an aspirational 'savante' who quotes Latin and Greek.[4] In this chapter, I will explore what I suggest to be a paradox: that Scudéry's modesty hinged on a disavowal of classical knowledge in order to achieve desired social mores, but that she frequently turned to the classical past to establish her literary career. For all that Scudéry cultivated a way of knowing that required discretion regarding erudite knowledge of antiquity, she also emphatically drew on ancient historians, such as Plutarch, Herodotus, and Livy, and classical figures, such as Sappho and Cloelia, as vehicles to establish her career across her early works. Because of this contradiction, Scudéry's reception of antiquity represents a singular and illuminating negotiation of her own place in the literary field.

Of course, this contradiction could be neutralised and the paradox explained away, to some degree, by the discreet way Scudéry uses the ancient past: she does not cite her sources, she mixes history and fiction, she modernises, often making 'antiquity' so seventeenth century, so 'galant' in flavour that it is hardly recognisable. Her long novels are characterised as being 'à clè' and thus about contemporary figures and events. She does not, therefore, parade her knowledge: indeed, she claims not to be able to read Latin (we do not know whether she could or not, but her use of certain Latin sources suggests she had some access either from her own abilities or thanks to help from her brother or perhaps her friend, Paul Pellisson). We know she had received a good education under the guardianship of her uncle, an ecclesiastic in Rouen, who took in Madeleine and her brother when they were orphaned at a young age and allowed her to access his extensive library, and particularly his collection of books in Spanish and Italian. Her discretion is further reinforced by the fact that it was her brother's name which appeared on all of the works discussed here, even though socially her contribution was well known.[5] However, the main point (and the paradox it implies) stands: why use ancient history at all? Why launch her career with works set in the classical past?

I propose two connected ways of tackling these questions. The first is extratextual and relates to how Scudéry uses classical intertext to modulate questions of literary value. The second relates to the details of what Scudéry does with antiquity in her early works. Scudéry intended her work to impart classical knowledge. She famously wrote to Pierre-Daniel Huet in 1670 on the publication of his *Discours sur l'origine des romans*:

Scudéry, Paul Pellisson et leurs amis, *Chroniques du Samedi. Suivis de pièces diverses* (Paris: Champion, 2002), an edition based on the BnF Arsenal MS 15156, and see the Introduction to this edition, pp. 17–18.

[4] For a discussion of her later figuration of the female intellectual, particularly in 'De l'incertitude' of her *Conversations morales* (1686), see Laura J. Burch, 'Madeleine de Scudéry: peut-on parler de la femme philosophe?', *Revue philosophique de la France et de l'étranger*, 138.3 (2013), 361–75.

[5] See Dufour-Maître, *Les Précieuses*, p. 398. See Tallemant des Réaux, *Historiettes*, ed. by Antoine Adam, 2 vols (Paris: Gallimard, 1961), II, p. 685.

car comme l'histoire et la fable sont mêlées aux romans dont la scène est tirée de l'antiquité, les femmes qui ont de l'esprit doivent raisonnablement chercher à lire les originaux de ces sortes de choses dont elle trouvent des passages dans les romans: et j'ai une amie qui n'eût jamais connu Xenophon ni Hérodote, si elle n'eût jamais lu le Cyrus, et qui en le lisant s'est accoutumée à aimer l'histoire et même la fable.[6]

for since history and fable are mixed in novels set in antiquity, curious women may well reasonably seek to read the originals of the sorts of things they find described in novels: and I have a female friend who would never have known Xenophon or Herodotus if she hadn't read *Cyrus* and reading it made her become keen on history as well as fable.

Historical fiction was often an important source of knowledge of ancient culture, particularly for women.[7] Drawing on the recent collective study, 'La galanterie des anciens', in which, as Claudine Nédélec and Nathalie Grande argue, 'les nouveaux doctes s'efforcent de "valoriser" leur capital culturel, en le mettant au goût du jour, et en imaginant une *transaltio studii* entre l'Antiquité et la galanterie' (the new learned elites attempt to 'valorise' their cultural capital by aligning it with contemporary taste and effecting a *translatio studii* between antiquity and *galanterie*), I will examine how with these gestures Scudéry attempted to shift notions of literary value from the elite cultures of knowledge to Modern, feminised genres.[8] She did so not by denying antiquity but by placing it—in its renewed form—at the heart of her fiction and making this very innovation key to her authorial strategy for recognition and legitimacy. I argue that Scudéry's gestures have important implications for our understanding of what constitutes 'modernity' in this period, as she reveals the centrality of appropriation and adaptation to the Modern project, which is sometimes lost by the focus on the progress and superiority later advanced by Charles Perrault.

The second response to the question of why Scudéry turned to ancient history lies in what she does with these sources and stories. She inscribes the questions of power, knowledge, and gender that structure the literary field into her classical reception. Given that Scudéry so often worked literary and socio-literary theories into her writing, approaching her use of antiquity to illuminate her representation of contemporary dynamics of writing and publication is justified. The differences

---

[6] Edmé-Jacques-Benoît Rathery and Boutron, eds, *Mademoiselle de Scudéry: sa vie et sa correspondence* (Paris: Techener, 1873), p. 295.

[7] As Nathalie Grande argues, 'Il ne faut donc pas sous-estimer la part de culture antique véhiculée par les ouvrages de fiction galante'. Nathalie Grande, 'La métamorphose galante de l'histoire antique: modalités et enjeux d'une poétique', in *La Galanterie des anciens*, ed. by Nathalie Grande and Claudine Nédélec (= *Littératures classiques*, 77 (2012)), pp. 229–44 (p. 242).

[8] Nathalie Grande and Claudine Nédélec, 'Avant-propos', in *La Galanterie des anciens*, ed. by Grande and Nédélec, pp. 5–13 (p. 6).

70   WOMEN WRITING ANTIQUITY

between Scudéry and Gournay have been paralleled with the twentieth-century division between a feminism of 'difference' and that of 'equality'.[9] However, while this difference can be traced in her advancing of a distinct type of female intellectual, Scudéry's rewriting of ancient history also, I will argue, nuances her commitment to 'difference' over 'equality' in male–female relations, identifying ways of reading her early works which advocate a modulation of both femininity and masculinity, equalising the positive attributes of both. This in turn enriches our understanding of Scudéry's attempts to recalibrate literary value because her literary complicating of gender boundaries maps onto—and offers a theory for—her attempts to equalise the value of elite (masculine) and vulgar (feminine) forms of knowledge. I show that Sappho and the female-gendered Greek lyric tradition become as important a genealogy in Scudéry's theorisation of the novel as the more traditional (and masculine) epic. Attending to her innovative characterisations of Brutus, Lucrèce, and Clélie, I then show that rather than simply advocating female heroism, as has generally been argued, she deliberately intermixes masculine and feminine ideals to unpick the patriarchy inherent to the story of the founding of Rome, and thereby, as Lewis C. Seifert argues, she 'offers a radical vision of gender in which the boundaries between masculinity and femininity are blurred'.[10]

Underpinning Scudéry's navigations of genre, literary value, and classical texts also lies the context of the inverse relationship between cultural and economic capital: this inverse relationship is manifest particularly clearly in relation to the seventeenth-century historical novel and its reception. Widely read, published serially, and intended for a mixed-gendered reading public, the long historical novels of the mid-century, such as those by the Scudérys, and Gauthier de La Calprenède, often located in antiquity and drawing—loosely—on ancient history, were famously derided and lambasted by critics such as Nicolas Boileau. In his much-discussed *Dialogue des héros de roman* (1666; published 1688), set in the underworld, Boileau satirises Georges and Madeleine de Scudéry's *Le Grand Cyrus* and Madeleine de Scudéry's *Clélie*. He singles out the 'effeminacy' of the heroes, who so little resemble their military historical counterparts and instead are concerned with conversation, dancing, poetry, and falling in love.[11] Boileau also mocks the fictionalisation of these accounts: Pluton complains that many of the characters are simply made up, exclaiming, 'Je sçais aussi bien mon Herodote qu'un autre' (I know my Herodotus as well as anyone else).[12] Boileau thus attacks

[9] Karen Green, 'Women's Writing and the Early Modern Genres Wars', *Hypatia*, 28.3 (2013), 499–515 (p. 504).

[10] Lewis C. Seifert, *Manning the Margins: Masculinity and Writing in Seventeenth-Century France* (Ann Arbor: University of Michigan Press, 2009), p. 118. See also Debrosse, *La Souvenance et le désir*, p. 352: 'Scudéry a pour idéal une société où hommes et femmes se ressembleraient davantage, où les vertus valorisées ne dépendraient pas du sexe de la personne' (In Scudéry's ideal society, men and women resemble each other and the valued virtues do not depend on one's sex).

[11] Nicolas Boileau, 'Dialogue des héros de roman', in *Œuvres complètes*, ed. by Françoise Escal, introduction by Antoine Adam (Paris: Gallimard, 1966), pp. 447–89 (p. 445).

[12] Ibid., p. 454.

the two elements that were salient features of the genre: a shift in heroic values and the mixing of fiction and history. The underlying premise here, which is explored further in his *Art poétique* of 1674—that these novels are, for their success and vulgarisation, less prestigious—exemplifies for Alain Viala that the French seventeenth-century literary field was structured by the two, opposing, spheres of market and symbolic value which Pierre Bourdieu locates in the nineteenth century.[13] The more a book sold, the less distinctive a literary value it possessed. Boileau also implicitly links the vulgarising aspects of the historical novel—fictionalising of history, modernising of mores, feminising of taste—to its commercial success, conflating these traits with a loss of value. He thus places 'pure' classical knowledge and its elite reception at the heart of an exclusive intellectual prestige.[14]

The tension between the promises of the commercial sphere and the more restrictive social sphere is one that Scudéry also negotiated in her career, and for all that she came to writing as part of a salon collective, as Joan DeJean shows, there is a case to be made for attending to her individual career strategy, as Nathalie Grande makes clear.[15] She navigated the narrow route between dependence on economic success and the aspiration for aristocratic detachment from it. Scudéry, although a minor noble—her father had been governor at the port of Le Havre where she was born—was attached to her name and measured in her involvement with the book trade in order to retain her aristocratic prerogative, even if this was to her financial detriment, mostly accepting royal handouts while her publisher made a profit.[16] Such detachment is not only manifest extra-textually in her relationship with money-making, but is also present in her representation of the activities of writing and publishing texts in her novels. This detachment underpins her praise of modesty and discretion, her praise of women's spontaneous abilities over the (unattractive, and unattractive-making) exertions of the hard-graft of learning.[17] This modesty was also strategic, a way of deflecting accusations of 'préciosité'— that is, of striving for intellectual distinction—a term first used a year after the final volume of *Cyrus* was published.[18]

---

[13] Alain Viala, 'The Theory of the Literary Field and the Situation of the First Modernity', in *Theory and the Early Modern* (=*Paragraph*), 29.1 (2006), 80–93; and *Naissance de l'écrivain: sociologie de la littérature à l'âge classique* (Paris: Minuit, 1985).

[14] Joan DeJean reads the Quarrel of the Ancients and Moderns in this light in *Ancients against Moderns: Culture Wars and the Making of a Fin de Siècle* (Chicago: University of Chicago Press, 1997).

[15] Joan DeJean, *Tender Geographies: Women and the Origins of the Novel in Early Modern France* (New York: Columbia University Press, 1991), p. 77. On strategy, see Nathalie Grande, *Stratégies de romancières: de 'Clélie' à 'La Princesse de Clèves': 1654–1678* (Paris: Champion, 1999), pp. 268–72.

[16] Dufour-Maître, *Les Précieuses*, p. 400.

[17] See for example Nicolas Boileau, 'Satire X', in *Œuvres complètes*, ed. by Escal, pp. 62–80.

[18] On modesty as rhetorical, see Patricia Pender, *Early Modern Women's Writing and the Rhetoric of Modesty* (Basingstoke: Palgrave, 2012). 'Précieuses' was first used to characterise groups of women in 1654 in a letter from the Chevalier de Sévigné to Christine de France, the Duchess of Savoy: 'il y a une nature de filles et de femmes à Paris que l'on nomme "Précieuses" qui ont un jargon et des mines' (there are types of girls and women in Paris that one calls 'précieuses' with a particular jargon

72 WOMEN WRITING ANTIQUITY

This chapter focuses, therefore, on the interrelation of three perspectives: the place of antiquity in Scudéry's construction of her authorial ethos; the complex relationship between this and her adaptations of classical texts; and how her ethos and her adaptations have shaped her place in the classical reception canon. These perspectives have been underexplored by critics who tend to treat her use of ancient history, which itself has received scant attention among the extensive criticism on Scudéry, and her career strategies separately.[19] My intention here is not to suggest that only a classical reception reading can access the full range of Scudéry's work or that it offers any form of superior critique in itself. Nor do I want to 'save' Scudéry from Boileau's accusations by showing that 'in fact' she did know a lot about ancient culture: to take that line is to enter the framework of Boileau's debate (and in any case, she hardly needs saving). Likewise, I do not mean to suggest that because Scudéry had an obvious predilection for Greco-Roman culture she was an Ancient and not a Modern.[20] *Clélie*, for instance, can be read, as Myriam Dufour-Maître argues, as a 'belle infidèle', and a 'coup de force' against Latinity, with all the complexity that this entails.[21] Rather I stress that there is cause for looking—in considerable detail—beyond the smoke screen of (strategic) modesty by approaching Scudéry as a 'Classicist'. Doing so not only sheds new light on details in her text, but it also reframes some of our wider approaches to gender and learning, stressing the need to go further than noting the socially strategic nature of her modesty, as it has often been described, to consider the other currents that work in opposition to it. By offering this analysis, I intend to undo some of the negative impact of Boileau's accusation by positioning Scudéry as an important figure in the history of classical reception. I argue that her novels must be seen in the tradition of what Emily Wilson describes as ideological 'creative responses' to antiquity.[22]

---

and countenance). Letter XC, 3 April 1654, *Correspondance du chevalier de Sévigné et de Christine de France, duchesse de Savoi*, ed. by Jean Lemoine and Frédéric Saulnier (Paris: Laurens, 1911), p. 246.

[19] On her engagement with Roman history, see for example Anne E. Duggan, 'Clélie, Histoire Romaine, or Writing the Nation', in *Le Savoir au XVIIe siècle*, ed. by John Lyons and Cara Welch (Tübingen: Narr, 2003), pp. 71–79; Alain Niderst, 'L'histoire romaine dans les romans de Madeleine de Scudéry', in *Le Roman Historique*, ed. by Pierre Ronzeaud (Tübingen: Narr, 1983), pp. 11–22; Noémie Hepp, 'L'utilisation d'Hérodote et de Xénophon dans *Le Grand Cyrus* ou les tabous de Sapho', in *Les Trois Scudéry*, ed. by Niderst, pp. 359–66; Laurence Plazenet, 'What did Heliodorus's Name Stand for in the Works of Mlle de Scudéry?', in *Re-Wiring the Ancient Novel. Volume 1: Greek Novels*, ed. by Edmund Cueva and others (Groningen: Barkhuis, 2018), pp. 289–312. On career strategies, see Grande, *Stratégies de romancières*, pp. 268–72; and Dufour-Maître, *Les Précieuses*, pp. 395–404.

[20] For an argument that sees the Ancients and Moderns as having many shared preferences, see Larry F. Norman, *The Shock of the Ancient: Literature and History in Early Modern France* (Chicago: University of Chicago Press, 2011), pp. 11–34.

[21] Dufour-Maître, *Les Précieuses*, p. 318.

[22] Emily Wilson, 'Epilogue: Translating Homer as a Woman', in *Homer's Daughters: Women's Responses to Homer in the Twentieth Century and Beyond*, ed. by Fiona Cox and Elena Theodorakopoulos (Oxford: Oxford University Press, 2019), pp. 279–98 (p. 282).

THE PARADOXES OF MODESTY   73

Sapho's Strategies

Scudéry's early career followed a three-stage trajectory that can be mapped onto her first works and which is exemplified in the portrait of Sappho in each of these texts.[23] The *Femmes illustres* (1642), co-authored with Georges, in which the Sapho harangue is thought to be by Madeleine alone, signalled her arrival on the literary scene.[24] *Le Grand Cyrus*, also co-authored with her brother, of which it is thought that Madeleine penned the 'Histoire de Sapho' in the tenth volume, articulates some of the tensions of women's place in the public sphere in its criticisms of the 'savante'; and *Clélie*, solo-authored and an assertion of independence, features a brief vignette of Sapho's life. Joan DeJean has provided the most comprehensive account of Scudéry's representations of 'Sapho' as a key moment in the history of the Greek poet's reception.[25] In this section, I emphasise instead how Scudéry used the different depictions of Sapho as part of her authorial strategy across her early publications, showing that her Sapho reveals the tension at the heart of Scudéry's early work between modesty and learning. Her depictions work on two, sometimes opposing, levels. Intradiegetically, the values that Sapho espouses map onto Scudéry's ethics and aesthetics, especially as they pertain to the ideal modest female intellectual. Where Marie de Gournay aspired to be classed as a 'savante' and used this term interchangeably with 'femmes lettrées' and 'femmes studieuses', as we saw in the previous chapter, Scudéry established a more complicated relationship with the 'savante' identity through her characterisation of Sapho. Extradiegetically, however, Scudéry's depiction of Sapho reveals a close engagement with, and a bold revision of, classical sources, which has not been analysed in detail by critics, but which enriches our understanding of both Sap(p)ho and of Scudéry's complex representation of her own learning.[26]

The Renaissance Sappho that Scudéry inherited was in part a problematic figure, whose poetic achievements were sometimes lost in the scandal surrounding her life. Scudéry simplifies this by drawing on a tradition dating from Boccaccio's *On Famous Women* and Christine de Pizan's *City of Ladies* which present Sappho

---

[23] On the three stages of her early career, see Dufour-Maître, *Les Précieuses*, pp. 395–404. Joan DeJean has argued that the *Lettres amoureuses de divers auteurs de son temps* (Paris: Courbé, 1641), a series of fictional male-authored complaints to women, which inverts the Ovidian *Heroides*, and was published anonymously (but with 'Le Sieur de Scudéry' as author on the *privilège*) was her first publication (DeJean, *Fictions of Sappho*, pp. 98–99). See also Madeleine de Scudéry, *Selected Letters, Orations, and Rhetorical Dialogues*, trans. by Jane Donawerth and Jane Strongson, The Other Voice in Early Modern Europe (Chicago: Chicago University Press, 2004), pp. 44–55. Because of the uncertainty around attribution and its lack of direct classical engagement, I do not examine this text here.

[24] She also wrote letters to Anna Maria van Schurman and Guez de Balzac securing their support. See Dufour-Maître, *Les Précieuses*, pp. 395–96.

[25] DeJean, *Fictions of Sappho*, pp. 96–115.

[26] DeJean suggests that 'every detail of [her portrait of Sapho] is based on ancient commentaries of Sappho' (*Fictions of Sappho*, p. 103), but includes very little further discussion.

primarily as a learned lady, but Scudéry also nuances Sapho's learning to accommodate the social demands of the seventeenth-century salon. This is evident firstly in Sapho's 'harangue' in the *Femmes illustres* which asserts women's capacities to write.[27] Sapho addresses her female friend, Erinne (rather than Phaon, the lover for whom she kills herself in Ovid's version in *Heroides* 15). Scudéry almost entirely rewrites Ovid's Sappho, turning her from the abandoned lover to a renowned poet, writing to her female disciple, Erinne, and encouraging her (and other women) to take up poetry (Erinne also evokes the ancient Greek poet, Erinna). As Anne Debrosse argues, this epistle contains 'une portée polémique et sociale [...] très forte' (a strong social and polemical stance)[28] in relation to contemporary culture and, as DeJean notes, it also entails a radical revision of, or 'resolute opposition to', the Ovidian source text, and 'a positive valorization of the female heroic'.[29]

And yet, a certain modesty pervades even this 'polemical' text. If compared to the case for women's education and equality that Gournay was making and which we explored in the previous chapter, Scudéry takes a moderate approach. She delineates certain areas of study that are suitable for women: 'on pourroit mesme dire que si les choses estoient ordonnées comme il faut, l'estude des belles lettres devroit plustot estre permise aux femmes qu'aux hommes' (one could even say that were things as they should be, the study of *belles lettres* would be more permitted to women than to men).[30] That Erinne should deflect attention from her own beauty to 'belles lettres' epitomises for Myriam Dufour-Maître how the dominant feminine ethos in this period, characterised by modesty and discretion, was both enabling for women in terms of giving them an acceptable way in to literary culture and restrictive in that this access was governed by gendered constraints.[31]

The complex negotiation of modesty and learning is most prominent, however, in Scudéry's next representation of Sapho, in the 'Histoire de Sapho', narrated by Démocède, Sapho's friend, to Cyrus who has met her in the past and asks for news about her; Démocède relays this news, also addressing the Queen of Pontus. It is included in the second book of the tenth and final part of *Artamène ou le Grand Cyrus* (1653), written during the tumultuous time of the Fronde, or aristocratic rebellion, which saw Georges on the side of Condé in rebellion against the King. The novel's main sources for the stories about Cyrus the Great, the Persian King who founded the Achaemenid Persian Empire, were Xenophon's *Cyropaedia*, the

---

[27] See also Jane Stevenson, 'Women Writers and the Classics', in *The Oxford History of Classical Reception in English Literature*, ed. by Patrick Cheney and Phillip Hardie, 5 vols (Oxford: Oxford University Press, 2015), II, pp. 129–43 (p. 131).

[28] Anne Debrosse, 'Promenades désenchantées en "mer Dangereuse": Madeleine de Scudéry, Sapho et Erinne aux prises avec le monde', *Études Épistémè*, 27 (2015), <http://journals.openedition.org/episteme/464>.

[29] DeJean, *Fictions of Sappho*, p. 102.

[30] Scudéry, 'Sapho à Erinne', *Les Femmes illustres*, I, pp. 421–42 (p. 431).

[31] See Myriam Dufour-Maître, 'Les "antipathies": académies des dames savantes et ruelles des précieuses, un discours polémique dans l'espace des Belles-Lettres', *Bonnes lettres / Belles lettres*, ed. by Claudine Poulouin et Jean-Claude Arnould (Paris: Champion, 2006), pp. 271–92.

fictionalised biography of Cyrus's imperial ventures, and Herodotus's *Histories* of the Persian Empire and Greco-Persian wars. Although both written in ancient Greek, by Scudéry's time they had been translated into Latin and French, with the most recent French translations from the mid to late 1640s, by Nicolas Perrot d'Ablancourt and Pierre Du Ryer respectively.[32] Interest in the 'ancient Near East' was also expressed in a range of French texts from the 1640s and 50s, from theatre to compendia, tracing the lives of Queens and rulers, including Cyrus's adversary, Tomyris, as Derval Conroy has shown.[33] *Le Grand Cyrus* recounts some of the titular Cyrus's adventures, but, as we might expect, retells his story as one of love, following him as he pursues his love, Mandane, daughter of the King of Media. Its many characters, subplots and intercalated stories, of which the 'Histoire de Sapho' is one, have been read as a contemporary chronicle of the Fronde, a *roman à clé*, with Cyrus as Condé and Mandane as the Duchesse de Longueville.

Although the novel as a whole was co-authored, critics think that the 'Histoire de Sapho' was probably by Madeleine alone, as it bears evidence of her desire to make references to her own participation in writing, in order to assert herself and her authority over the text.[34] However, it was written at a time when Scudéry was frequenting the Hôtel de Rambouillet, an aristocratic circle to which, as a minor noble of relatively modest means, she had an uncertain claim: for Scudéry, protecting her name and cultivating an aristocratic ethos, in which modesty, discretion, and some distance from the vulgarity of publishing and money, became priorities.[35] The interpolated 'Histoire de Sapho' reveals both gestures: it can be read as an allusion to her negotiation of authorship and to her modesty. In this portrait of Sapho, Scudéry articulates most forcibly and influentially her ideals of women's learning and does so by constructing a negative counterpart to Sapho, Damophile, the 'savante' pedant. However, as I will show, Scudéry's depiction of Sap(p)ho also reveals her own learning through her evident use of Sappho's fragments: her portrait is thus emblematic of the tensions entailed by 'modest learning'.

---

[32] Xenophon hailed from Athens and Herodotus from Halicarnassus, a Greek city in the Persian empire. The first French translation of Xenophon was published in 1470; and of Herodotus in 1556. *La Retraite des Dix-Mille, de Xénophon, ou l'Expédition de Cyrus contre Artaxerxès*, trans. by Nicolas Perrot d'Ablancourt (Paris: Vve Camusat and Le Petit, 1648); and *Les Histoires de Herodote*, trans. by Pierre Du Ryer (Paris: Sommaville, 1645). See Noreen Humble, 'The Well-Thumbed Attic Muse: Cicero and the Reception of Xenophon's Persia in the Early Modern Period', in *Beyond Greece and Rome: Reading the Ancient Near East in Early Modern Europe*, ed. by Jane Grogan (Oxford: Oxford University Press, 2020), pp. 29–52; and Benjamin Earley, 'Herodotus in Renaissance France', in *Brill's Companion to the Reception of Herodotus in Antiquity and Beyond*, ed. by Jessica Priestley and Vasilika Zali (Leiden: Brill, 2016), pp. 120–42.

[33] Derval Conroy, 'Casting Models: Female Exempla of the Ancient Near East in Seventeenth-Century French Drama and Gallery Books (1642–62)', in *Beyond Greece and Rome*, ed. by Grogan, pp. 212–34.

[34] Dufour-Maître, *Les Précieuses*, p. 399.

[35] Ibid., p. 398.

76 WOMEN WRITING ANTIQUITY

The multiple inflections of the term 'savante' to be found in the *Dictionnaires* of
the 1690s, and which we explored in the Introduction, are articulated in Scudéry's
'Histoire de Sapho'. Sapho is introduced positively by the narrator, Démocède, as
a 'sçavante fille':[36] when the term is used as a prenominal adjective it has positive
connotations.[37] However, this is one of very few occasions when 'scavante' is used
in this way: Sapho is most frequently described as 'admirable' and in opposition
to 'sçavante'. In the description that follows, we encounter the first negative use of
the term 'savante', as a substantive when it is coupled with 'faire': 'Mais ce qu'il
y a d'admirable, c'est que cette personne qui sçait tant de choses differentes, les
sçait sans faire la sçavante: sans en avoir aucun orgueil; et sans mespriser celles
qui ne les sçavent pas' (But what is admirable is that this person who knows so
many different things knows them without acting the learned lady, without vanity, and without disdain towards those who do not have the same knowledge)
(p. 334).[38] 'Faire la sçavante' connotes an excessive demonstration of knowledge,
pedantry, and aspiration (and this is echoed in other pejorative phrases, 'passer
pour sçavante' and 'parler en sçavante').[39] Sapho uses the phrase 'faire la sçavante'
to distance herself from such women: 'Encore que je sois ennemie déclarée de toute
femmes qui font les sçavantes [...]' (Although I continue to be the declared enemy
of all women who play the learned lady ...) (p. 397).

For all that this phrasing ('passer pour' or 'faire') seems to single out 'savante'
as a target when describing one who is playing or acting something one is not,
when 'savante' is used as a predicative adjective with 'être' in Scudéry's 'Histoire'—
and so when it describes what someone is rather than what someone pretends
to be—it still, more often than not, has negative connotations.[40] There are occasional examples of a positive usage, for instance when Democède states that Sapho
'estoit sçavante' (p. 375), but this connotation is contingent and needs to be

---

[36] *Artamène ou le Grand Cyrus*, p. 333. The edition used in this chapter is from http://www.
artamene.org, which is based on *Artamène ou le Grand Cyrus* (Paris: Courbé, 1656). All references
to this edition will hereafter be included in the text.

[37] See the Introduction.

[38] See also the translation of Madeleine de Scudéry, *The Story of Sapho*, trans. by Karen Newman,
The Other Voice in Early Modern Europe (Chicago: Chicago University Press, 2003). This excellent
translation alternates between 'pedant' and 'play the learned lady' to translate the many uses of the term
'faire la savante': for consistency and an understanding of the specific uses of the term, translations are
my own and will use 'learned'. For Newman's discussion on the seventeenth-century 'untranslatability'
into English of the term 'savante' with its gendered connotations and specific cultural history, see Karen
Newman, 'The French Disease', *Comparative Literature*, 64.1 (2012), 33–48 (p. 42).

[39] Sapho declares: 'je ne veux point passer pour sçavante' (I do not want to seem learned) (p. 395);
Sapho says: 'je ne veux pourtant jamais qu'elles agissent ny qu'elles parlent en sçavantes (I do not want
women to act or speak as learned ladies) (p. 401).

[40] This use is echoed later: 'Les femmes qui affectent le titre de sçavantes ne sont pas sur un bon pied
dans le monde.' Antoine Furetière, *Dictionnaire universel* (La Haye and Rotterdam: Leers, 1701), np;
and, from the *Dictionnaire de l'Académie française*, 2 vols (Paris: Coignard, 1694), II, p. 447: 'Sçavant.
Est aussi quelquefois subst. les *scavants disent. Elle fait la scavante.*' See also the definition of 'pédante':
'Pedante, se dit, d'une femme qui fait la sçavante et la capable', Ibid., p. 207. For further discussion see
the Introduction.

contextualised: we know already that Sapho is the right kind of 'sçavante' in that in her terms she is not one. More usually in this 'Histoire', the predicative adjective has a negative force, conjuring the pedantic, demonstrative type of learning that echoes the implication of the phrase 'faire la sçavante': as in 'il estoit presques impossible qu'une femme pûst estre sçavante sans estre ridicule, ou du moins incommode ou peu agréable' (it was almost impossible for a woman to be learned without being ridiculous, or at least awkward or unpleasant) (p. 375). Crucially, Sapho does not want to be described as *being* 'savante' because she *is not* one. This is evident from her exchange with Themistogene:

> 'y a-t'il rien de plus beau, que d'entendre dire qu'une fille fait mieux des vers qu'Homere n'en a fait, et qu'elle est plus sçavante que tous les sept Sages de Grece?' 'Quoy qu'il en soit', dit Sapho, 'je n'aime nullement qu'on parle de moy en ces termes [...] car enfin comme je ne suis point sçavante, je ne veux pas qu'on me die que je le suis; et quand je le serois, je ne le voudrois pas non plus.' (pp. 381–82)

> 'is there anything more pleasant than to hear it said that a young woman writes verse better than Homer did and that she is more learned than all the seven sages of Greece?' 'In any event', said Sapho, 'I do not wish anyone to describe me in those terms [...] Since I am not a learned lady, I do not wish to be described as such; if I were, I would not want to be either.'

'Sçavante' as a postnominal adjective also has negative connotations: Phaon is surprised that 'une fille sçavante' might also be 'agréable' (p. 380). Using the postnominal adjective, Sapho states that she does not want to be treated as 'une fille sçavante' (p. 370); and that the 'femme sçavante' is a woman who does not know how to be modest about her learning:

> Je veux donc bien qu'on puisse dire d'une personne de mon sexe, qu'elle sçait cent choses dont elle ne se vante pas; qu'elle a l'esprit fort esclairé; qu'elle connoist finement les beaux Ouvrages; qu'elle parle bien; qu'elle escrit juste; et qu'elle sçait le monde; mais je ne veux pas qu'on puisse dire d'elle, c'est une Femme sçavante: car ces deux caracteres sont si differens, qu'ils ne se ressemblent point. Ce n'est pas que celle qu'on n'apellera point sçavante, ne puisse sçavoir autant et plus de choses que celle à qui on donnera ce terrible nom: mais c'est qu'elle se sçait mieux servir de son esprit, et qu'elle sçait cacher adroitement, ce que l'autre montre mal à propos. (p. 401)

> I want someone to be able to say of a person of my sex that she knows a hundred things but does not boast of them; that she has an enlightened mind and that she knows finely great works; that she speaks well, that she writes correctly and that she knows the world; but I do not want anyone to say of her that she is a learned

lady: these two characters are so different that they do not resemble each other. It is not that the woman whom we will not call 'learned' is not permitted to know as much or even more than the one whom we will describe with this terrible name: but she knows better how to use her intelligence and she is skilful at hiding what the other shows in a clumsy way.

Scudéry offers a counter-example to Sapho in Damophile, who is a clumsy imitator of Sapho, ostentatious in her knowledge, pedantic, striving for intellectual distinction. Sapho instead epitomises the modest form of learning so vaunted by Scudéry. This modesty is made evident particularly in relation to knowledge of antiquity:

En effet on peut sçavoir quelques Langues Estrangeres; on peut avoüer qu'on a leû Homere, Hesiode, et les excellents Ouvrages de l'illustre Aristhée, sans faire trop la sçavante: on peut mesme en dire son advis d'une maniere si modeste, et si peu affirmative, que sans choquer la bien-seance de son sexe, on ne laisse pas de faire voir qu'on a de l'esprit, de la connoissance, et du jugement. (p. 402)

Indeed, she can know foreign languages; she can admit to having read Homer, Hesiod, and other excellent works of the illustrious Aristaeus, without acting too much the learned lady; she can even offer an opinion in a modest, unassuming way that does not challenge the modesty expected of her sex, and still reveal her wit, knowledge, and good judgement.

Although Scudéry uses several adjectives as terms of praise for Sapho, and certainly delineates in this text her vision for the ideal female intellectual by offering an example in the character of Sapho, Scudéry provides no substantive noun to connote this figure: Scudéry's ideal intellectual has no signifier; she is 'celle qu'on n'apellera point sçavante'. Sapho is an exemplar, but language cannot adequately categorise her.

Scudéry's insistence on modesty has made her a complex figure in the history of feminist discourse, with some criticising her for her accommodations;[41] some arguing that Damophile is actually a projection of men's anxieties, and so directs the satire at them, rather than at other women;[42] and with others suggesting that modesty is itself a form of empowerment, especially as it might authorise Scudéry to challenge other aspects of elite women's lives.[43] Lisa Nicholson has persuasively analysed the mechanics of Scudéry's use of satire, in line with her formulations

---

[41] Madeleine Alcover is critical of Scudéry: 'The Indecency of Knowledge', *Rice University Studies*, 64 (1978), 25–39 (p. 34). See also Erica Harth, *Cartesian Women: Versions and Subversions of Rational Discourse in the Old Regime* (Ithaca: Cornell University Press, 1992), pp. 50–56.

[42] DeJean, *Fictions of Sappho*, p. 108.

[43] Siefert, *Manning*, p. 123; Domna Stanton, *The Dynamics of Gender in Early Modern France: Women Writ, Women Writing* (London: Routledge, 2014), p. 98.

of *raillerie*, showing that it is directed towards Damophile, to underscore the fact that 'salon women were writing satires aimed at would-be salon women'.[44] Noting, as I do, the ambivalence of Scudéry's modest version of the female intellectual—in that it created the double-edged gendered identity that Gournay so railed against—also invites us to frame Scudéry's approach as individualistic and contingent rather than as primarily collective, considering what she stands to gain from this position.

Less examined in relation to the 'Histoire de Sapho', however, is the performance of Sapho's accommodation in this portrait. Scudéry takes pains to demonstrate that Sapho acquiesces to social pressure, showing how her intellectual self is socially constituted, necessarily relative, reminding us of the very contingency of that self.[45] As is clear from her conversation with Themistogene quoted above, Sapho does not want to be described by others as 'savante', she does not want to be seen as such. Much of her grievance centres on her perception of being hounded by 'gens du monde' (p. 383) who want to talk to her about books. This also explains her desire for a new sort of social life with Phaon in the court of Phylire in the Land of the Sarmatians, framed as a 'repos' (retreat) (p. 504), from which visitors are banished for ten years. Being 'savante' is a problem because of how other people respond to this distinction. Scudéry's female intellectual, therefore, is also represented, as in Gournay's work, as a social identity determined relationally, by others' perceptions, in a constant state of negotiation:

> A ce que je voy, répliqua froidement Phaon, la belle Sapho ne pouvait acquerir l'estime de Themistogène et de moy: car je l'estime infiniment apres luy avoir entendu dire toutes les bagatelles qu'il luy reproche: mais je ne l'aurois guere estimée si elle avait dit toutes ces grandes choses qu'il s'imagine qu'elle devait dire: ainsi il s'enfuit de nécessité, qu'elle ne nous pouvait satisfaire tous deux. (pp. 390–91)

> 'As far as I see it', replied Phaon coldly, 'the beautiful Sapho cannot gain the esteem of both Themistogene and myself: for I esteem her greatly after having heard her say all the light-hearted things for which he reproaches her; but I would have hardly esteemed her at all if she had said all the great things that he thinks she should have. So it is: she cannot satisfy us both'.

The capitulating acceptance implied in 'ainsi il s'enfuit de nécessité', and in the way that Sapho does acquiesce to the modest version Phaon prefers, contrasts strongly with Gournay's frustrated identification of the impossibility of categorising the female intellectual. However, Scudéry does acknowledge the restrictions of

---

[44] Annalisa Nicholson, 'The Satire of the Salonnière: Women and Humour in Seventeenth-Century France', *Australian Journal of French Studies*, 59.4 (2022), 361–75 (p. 365).

[45] On this stategy of modesty more generally as deployed by several writers, see Dufour-Maître, *Les Précieuses*, pp. 390–95.

80   WOMEN WRITING ANTIQUITY

society's pressures, particularly in her exploration of Sapho's own desire to leave this learned company; she also shows how attempts to define the female intellectual challenges categories. Sapho's discomfort at being hounded by literary society also touches on the dangers of being read autobiographically—she laments that her doctor thinks he knows the cause of her illness from her poetry.[46] This discomfort reveals self-reflexive playfulness on Scudéry's part because her portrait of Sapho is based on such a reading, and because Sapho is also a self-portrait of Scudéry.

Scudéry's own modesty is tempered by the learning that underpins her Sapho story: for instance, the figure of Damophile has a classical counterpart and is a learned reference from Philostratus.[47] This learning is most evident from the knowledge Scudéry demonstrates of versions of Sappho's life and some of Sappho's fragments.[48] Much of this tradition was only available to Scudéry in Latin, because there were very few translations of Sappho into French by this point.[49] Two fictional poems by 'Sapho' feature in the 'Histoire de Sapho' of *Le Cyrus*, one which is only talked about and one which is represented in full, and both of which seem to draw on two of the best-known poems attributed to Sappho, now known as fragment 31, 'He seems to me equal to Gods', reprised by Catullus in his Ode 51, which recounts the speaker's physiological sensations of jealousy of the man who gets to sit next to her (female) love at a dinner party, often interpreted as 'friend'; and Poem 1, the 'Ode to Aphrodite' calling on her to help the narrator in the pursuit of her beloved, for which the pronoun is now accepted to be feminine, but in the Renaissance tradition the Greek text presupposed a male lover.[50] Henri Estienne included Latin translations of both fragments in his edition

[46] For an argument that Damophile represents some of the jealous reaction to the success of Scudéry's own salon, see Niderst, Denis and Dufour-Maître, eds, *Chroniques du Samedi*, p. 28.

[47] 'A clever woman named Damophyla was said to have had girl companions just like Sappho and to have composed love poems just as she did.' Philostratus, *Apollonius of Tyana, Volume I: Life of Apollonius of Tyana, Books 1–4*, ed. and trans. by Christopher P. Jones, Loeb Classical Library 16 (Cambridge, MA: Harvard University Press, 2005), 1.30. See also DeJean, *Fictions of Sappho*, p. 108. She also features in Lilio Gregorio Giraldi's *Historiae poetarum tam Graecorum quam Latinorum dialogi decem* (Basel, 1545) where she is described as a friend of Sappho (p. 377). On the fact that the learned references to historical Sappho have been overlooked, see Newman, *The Story of Sapho*, p. 8.

[48] DeJean, *Fictions of Sappho*, p. 103.

[49] Rémi Belleau was the first to translate Sappho's fr. 31 into French in 1556 an appendix to his *Odes d'Anacréon*. Rémi Belleau, *Les odes d'Anacréon ... traduites de grec en françois* (Paris: Wechel, 1556), pp. 61–62. Other poets also imitated Sappho 31, such as Jean Antoine de Baïf, Ronsard, Amyot: see Robert Aulotte, 'Sur quelques traductions d'une ode de Sappho au XVIe siècle', *Bulletin de l'Association Guillaume Budé: Lettres d'humanité*, 17 (1958), 107–22. Louise Labé also engages with fr. 1 in her first elegy, stressing the pain and suffering of Sappho's love: see DeJean, *Fictions of Sappho*, pp. 30–42, and Debrosse, *La Souvenance et le désir*, pp. 332–36. Later in the seventeenth century, as we will explore further in Chapter 7 on Anne Dacier, Sappho's fragments became more widely known thanks to Tanneguy Le Fèvre's *Abrégé des vies des poètes grecs* (Paris: Sercy, 1665); Claude-Denis Du Four de la Crespelière's *Odes amoureuses, charmantes et bachiques des poètes grecs Anacreon, Sappho et Théocrite* (Paris: Loyson, 1670), and Anne LeFèvre's (Dacier), *Les poésies d'Anacréon et de Sapho* (Paris: Thierry, 1681).

[50] For a detailed discussion, see Chapter 7 on Dacier.

of nine Greek lyric poets from 1560 in which he also included a Life of Sappho, which is an abbreviated version of that included in Lilio Gregorio Giraldi's *Lives of Greek and Latin Poets* (1545), influenced by Ovid's *Heroides* 15.[51] Giraldi, and also Estienne, were key sources for Scudéry.[52] The Giraldi *Vita* contains an allusion to Sappho's lesbianism in a comment about her promiscuity with both men and women, but he also singles out Phaon as her lover and cause of her suicide and closes with Ovid's poem. Estienne also includes other fragments attributed to Sappho, of which a couple are also mentioned by Giraldi in his *Vita*, namely what is now fragment 121, addressed to a younger man refusing marriage (which Scudéry would have known), and fragment 55, Sappho's poem to another woman of Lesbos, informing her that she will never be remembered as, it is implied, she, Sappho, will be.[53] This poem might have influenced the sort of rivalry Scudéry fictionalises in her portrayal of Damophile, offering a context for Sapho's desire to flee the company at Lesbos. Some of the sentiments of this fragment are echoed in Horace's *Ode* 2.13 where he figures Sappho in the underworld 'bewailing her ungrateful sex.'[54]

The two fictional poems in Scudéry's 'Histoire de Sapho' bear evidence of Scudéry's knowledge of this tradition, and her interpretations strengthen the case for her allusion to Sappho's ambiguous sexuality, showing that Sappho is a useful figure for Scudéry to explore alternatives to heterosexual marriage relations.[55] The fictional poem that is discussed represents jealousy in a female friendship so strong that it resembles love; Démocède narrates:[56]

---

[51] Fragment 1 survives through its quotation in Dionysus of Halicarnassus, first printed in 1508 by Aldus Manutius, *Rhetores Graeci* (Venice: Aldus, 1508), which was first printed in Paris in 1547 in Robert Estienne's Greek edition of Dionysus of Halicarnassus, *De compositione* (Paris: R. Estienne, 1547); and then again in Henri Estienne's 1554 Latin-Greek edition of Anacreon, *Anacreon. Odae* (Paris: H. Estienne, 1554). Fragment 31, which we know thanks to its inclusion in Longinus' *On the Sublime*, was first published in 1554 in Basel in Robortello's edition of Longinus and in Venice in Muret's commentary on Catullus. *Dionysii Longini rhetoris praestantissimi liber de grandi, siue sublimi orationis genere* (Basel: Robortello, 1554); *Catullus, et in eum commentarius M. Antonij Mureti* (Venice: Muret, 1554).

[52] *Pindari Olympia, Pythia, Nemea, Isthmia. Caeterorum octo lyricorum carmina, Alcaei, Sapphus, Stesichori, Ibyci, Anacreontis, Bacchylidis, Simonidis, Alcmanis, nonnulla etiam aliorum* (Paris: H. Estienne, 1560). See also Giraldi, *Historiae poetarum tam Graecorum quam Latinorum dialogi decem* (Basel, 1545), pp. 972–80. See Mary Morrison, 'Henri Estienne et Sappho', *Bibliothèque d'Humanisme et Renaissance*, 24.2 (1962), 388–91; and P. J. Finglass, 'Editions of Sappho since the Renaissance', in *The Cambridge Companion to Sappho*, ed. by P. J. Finglass and Adrian Kelly (Cambridge: Cambridge University Press, 2021), pp. 247–60.

[53] Fr. 121, p. 47, and fr. 55, p. 45, in *Carminum poetarum novem lyricae*.

[54] Both of these fragments are from the Stobeaus anthology, first edited by Trincavelli (Venice, 1536). Horace, *Odes and Epodes*, ed. and trans. by Niall Rudd (Cambridge, MA: Harvard University Press, 2004).

[55] DeJean also notes a queering of lineage in that Scudéry changes the name of Sapho's father from the 'historically verifiable, Scamandronymus' to 'Scamandrogine', and with this new suffix, serves to 'undermine the stability of the familial description' (*Fictions of Sappho*, p. 105).

[56] On Scudéry's portrayals of female friendship in this novel, see Marianne Legault, *Female Intimacies in Seventeenth-Century French Literature* (Abingdon: Routledge, 2012), pp. 121–38.

82 WOMEN WRITING ANTIQUITY

> Je le forçay de lire des vers que Sapho avoit faits sur une jalousie d'amitié, qui avoit esté entre Athys et Amithone. Mais Madame, cette jalousie avoit le veritable carractere de l'amour: et tout ce que cette tirannique passion peut inspirer de plus violent dans un coeur amoureux, y estoit exprimé si merveilleusement, qu'il estoit impossible de le faire mieux. (p. 456)

> I forced him to read some of Sappho's verses on the subject of the jealous friend-ship of Athys and Amithone. But Madame, this jealousy was really like love; and possessed all the violence that this tyrannical passion can inspire in a person in love, and it was expressed so beautifully that it would be impossible to say it better.

This poem seems to echo the jealousy that permeates fragment 31. Given that Athys and Amithone are both female, we might read the invocation of a jealous friendship that borders on love as a knowing reference by Scudéry to Sappho's lesbianism, or at least to this famous poem about female 'friendship'.

Scudéry also uses learned reference to Sappho's fragments to emphasise the poet's influence, which is important for the lineage between the historical Sap-pho and Scudéry as Sapho. The poem we read in full in the 'Histoire de Sapho' also seems to echo fragment 31, and perhaps also fragment 1, in its articulation of the intensity and pain of love; it is made contemporary by its inclusion in the novel as part of social reading, akin to salon activity. It stresses the physiological effects of love (as in fr. 31): 'Ma peine est grande, et mon plaisir extréme; Je ne dors point la nuit, je resve tout le jour; je ne sçay pas encor si j'aime, Mais cela ressemble à l'amour' (My pain is great and my pleasure extreme: I cannot sleep at night, I dream all day; I do not know if I love but this seems like love) (pp. 472).[57] It could also be argued that Scudéry is bringing in a further—playful—intertext in the way the first line and last lines evoke Catullus 85 'Odi et amo' ('I hate and I love. Why I do this, perhaps you ask. I know not, but I feel it happening and I am in torment').[58] If so, this could be construed as a knowing gesture to the way Catullus 51, his rewriting of Sapho's fragment 31, tended to partially eclipse, or at least be yoked to, versions of Sappho's fragment produced in the mid-sixteenth century. Reading this Catullan intertext into Scudéry's work also draws attention to the tradition of Sappho reception and implicitly places Scudéry and her novels within this.

In the 'Histoire de Sapho', just as in the *Femmes illustres*, Scudéry also self-consciously revises the traditional ending which sees the poet commit suicide by

---

[57] The last two lines are quoted by 'Acante' (Pellisson) in 'Acante à Sapho' in the *Chroniques du Samedi*, pp. 112–13 with a marginal note indicating this. There are a number of other occasions where the 'Histoire de Sapho' is quoted in the *Chroniques*, such as pp. 133–34.

[58] Catullus, *Catullus*, trans. by Francis Cornish, 2nd edn by G. P. Goold, Loeb Classical Library 6 (Cambridge, MA: Harvard University Press, 1988).

leaping off the Leucadian cliffs. This revision reinforces Scudéry's use of Sapho to question norms, particularly around marriage. Sapho's evident homosociality is clear from her unconventional approach to her relationship with Phaon—to his discontent, she insists that the love they share is not to be consummated sexually by the tyranny of marriage; Phaon is consistently placed as secondary to her female companions. Instead of marriage, the story ends with Sapho and Phaon leaving Lesbos for the land of the Sarmatians, descendants of the Amazons, which is female-led. Her preference is given a legal framework when she manages to plead her case to the judges at court in Phylire who initially think that her relationship with Phoan should be formalised by marriage. Sapho's need to leave Lesbos in order to flourish, as Debrosse reads it, is a rejection of the marriage plot, and an emphasis on female sociability.[59] After all, the 'repos' Sapho finds in Phylire is not a straightforward retreat, in that she continues a social life in the land of the Sarmatians, who are presented as social and interested in conversation.[60] Scudéry also makes a point of marking her revision of the story with performative rhetoric: the ship in which Sapho and Phaon are sailing to Phylire is knocked off course in a storm and reaches Epirus at Leukas.[61] A different passionate suicide is referred to, that of Deucalion, thus drawing attention to the absence of the suicide we might expect. Sapho's portrait in *Le Cyrus* is suggestive, therefore, of the tensions in Scudéry's relationship to the knowledge represented by ancient texts: it is infused with learned intertext, but also demonstrates her endeavour to modernise and vulgarise this knowledge; it also reveals how Scudéry embeds in her reception contemporary questions relating to marriage and women's literary and intellectual practice.

A final portrait of Sappho features in Scudéry's next novel, *Clélie*, in the 'Songe d'Hésiode', a catalogue set in the underworld, in which Calliope guides Hesiod through poets and writers, from Homer to the Comtesse de La Suze; much of this catalogue and the descriptions of the poets are based closely on the collected *Lives* by Giraldi. Given that this was Scudéry's first solo-authored novel, written at the height of her influence, while she presided alone over the *samedi* salon when her brother was in exile, there was less need to give coded references to her authorship as she had done when she was composing *Cyrus* with Georges. What was needed instead was an assertion of authority: her brief depiction of Sapho in the 'Songe d'Hésiode' is a persuasive means by which Scudéry articulates this authority.[62] Although the version is in line with Modern practices, in that there is no citation of sources, the account follows the Humanist Giraldi closely. Sapho features as one

---

[59] Debrosse, 'Promenades désenchantées'.

[60] See Dufour-Maître, *Les Précieuses*, p. 305.

[61] See Rebecca Bullard, *The Politics of Disclosure, 1674–1725: Secret History Narratives* (London: Pickering and Chatto, 2009), pp. 1–25.

[62] *Clélie, Histoire romaine*, ed. by Chantal Morlet-Chantalat, 5 vols (Paris: Champion, 2001–05), IV (2004), pp. 286–328. References to this edition will hereafter be given in the text.

of three female poets from antiquity (with Phemonoe and Corinne). The account of Sapho's 'life' here is brief:

> Hésiode vit une île, et sur le haut d'un rocher une femme brune de médiocre taille, et de médiocre beauté. Elle avait pourtant les yeux vifs, et pleins d'esprit, et la taille assez bien faite. 'Celle que tu vois', dit alors Calliope à Hésiode, 'est la fameuse Sapho de Mytilène, qui sera célèbre dans tous les siècles, par la beauté de ses vers, principalement par un certain caractère amoureux et passionné, qui sera presque inimitable. Elle inventera l'usage de l'archet sur la lyre, qui en perfectionnera le son, elle aimera un infidèle qui sera cause de sa mort, mais quoique presque tous ces ouvrages doivent périr, son nom vivra pourtant éternellement, elle sera nommée la dixième Muse, et d'âge en âge on lui fera de nouveaux honneurs.' (IV, pp. 293–94)

> Hesiod saw an island and on the top of a rock a dark-haired woman of mediocre stature. She had, however, keen eyes, full of life, and a fine waist. 'The one you see there', said Calliope to Hesiod, 'is the famous Sapho of Mytilene, who will be famous throughout the centuries because of the beauty of her poetry, which is characterised by an almost unparalleled expression of love and passion. She will invent the use of the bow on the lyre, which will perfect its sound, she will love one who is unfaithful and will cause her death, and even though most of her works will not survive, her name will live in eternity, she will be called the tenth muse and through the ages will be honoured anew.'

While this might be the most conservative of the versions of Sapho's life, it also shows Scudéry at her least restrained, in that here she pushes the limits of being able to show her knowledge of the tradition of Sappho's Life and thus it constitutes an assertion of authority.[63] The 'Songe d'Hésiode' itself stages precisely a transfer of authority: it is a story about genealogy that takes a Modern approach as a story of progress and transmission. A legitimising lineage is constructed from Sapho to La Suze. As Dufour-Maître argues, the lineage is reinforced through the prosopopoeia: Calliope, muse of eloquence and epic, singer of Kings, is Apollo (Louis XIV)'s spokesperson but she is also a spokesperson for Scudéry herself, firmly anchoring a historical line from Sappho to Scudéry, and also shoring up Scudéry's own position of authority.[64] As we will see in the next section, Sapho also appears as guide or figure of influence throughout *Clélie*, in which Scudéry

---

[63] Debrosse argues in contrast that this change in perspective marks regression in Scudéry's progressive agenda for women. She also suggests that the reference to the other two poets, Phemonoe and Corinne, is much less creative and inventive than her evocation of the more obscure Erinne and Damophile in the *Femmes illustres* and *Le Grand Cyrus* ('Promenades désenchantées').

[64] Dufour-Maître, *Les Précieuses*, p. 318.

continues to pursue her interest in sociable knowledge, conversation, and male-female relations that underpin her 'Histoire de Sapho', but instead of figuring the female intellectual, she offers models for women in political roles of power, using her rewriting of the story of the founding of Rome's Republic to examine patriarchal structures.

Writing Rome: *Clélie*

With *Clélie*, Scudéry brings her focus to the early history of Rome, and, specifically, the founding of the Republic (509 BC). It entails a fictionalised version of the story of the Roman heroine, Cloelia, who is known for being sent with other women by the consul, Publius Valerius Publicola, as a bond for peace to the camp of Porsenna, leader of the Clusians, Rome's neighbours and enemies. She then threatens that peace by leading her fellow hostages across the Tiber back to Rome, only to be returned, but her actions so impressed Porsenna that peace is guaranteed and the women freed. Scudéry's fictional version, which follows the (invented) love story of Clélie and Aronce, starts before the Republic is founded and opens in Capua, where this community of Romans, who have gathered to escape from Tarquin the Proud's tyranny in Rome, make preparations for the couple's marriage.[65] Before they can marry, they are separated by an earthquake; they are reunited and part again at points throughout the novel and marry at the end of its tenth volume. The novel is structured by a series of interpolated stories, some of which track the rise and fall of Tarquin and the early history of the Roman Republic. It is thus modulated by the fates of two women: Lucretia, whose rape triggers the expulsion of Tarquin by Brutus who then founds the Republic in 509 BC; and Cloelia, who establishes peace between Rome and its Clusian neighbours by her escape from hostage, thus consolidating the Republic's power (508 BC). The principal ancient sources are Livy's *History of Rome*, Books 1 and 2,[66] Plutarch's *Life of Publicola*,[67] Dionysus of Halicarnassus's *Antiquities*, and Giraldi's *Lives*, with the latter two texts only available to Scudéry in Latin.[68]

---

[65] 'Aronce' may also refer to Aruns, the son of Porsenna as described by Plutarch and Dionysus of Halicarnassus (though he is not named here): both authors afford him a political role (in Plutarch it is Aruns who urges Porsenna to ally with the Romans and Aruns defends Cloelia against Tarquin). Confusingly, the son of Tarquin in Livy is also called Aruns. See Nicole Aronson, 'Mademoiselle de Scudéry et l'histoire Romaine dans "Clélie"', *Romanische Forschungen*, 88 (1976), pp. 183–94 (p. 185). Gaines argues that the name also recalls the 'Arons' character from Pierre Du Ryer's *Scévole* (1644), James F. Gaines, 'Lucrèce, Junie and Clélie: Burdens of Female Exemplarity', *Journal of the Western Society for French History*, 17 (1990), 515–21 (p. 518).

[66] Livy, *History of Rome, Volume 1, Books 1–2*, trans. by O. B. Foster, Loeb Classical Library 114 (Cambridge MA: Harvard University Press, 1919).

[67] Plutarch, *Lives, Volume I: Theseus and Romulus. Lycurgus and Numa. Solon and Publicola*, trans. by Bernadotte Perrin, Loeb Classical Library 46 (Cambridge, MA: Harvard University Press, 1914).

[68] Dionysus of Halicarnassus, *Roman Antiquities*, trans. by Earnest Cary, Loeb Classical Library 319 (Cambridge, MA: Havard University Press, 1937). She shows extensive and detailed knowledge of

Scudéry's novel is best known for the 'Carte de Tendre', a cartographical depiction of courtship and male-female friendship, imagined visually in an illustration by François Chauveau. As one of the most important discussions of *galanterie*, the Carte has understandably been the most studied aspect of Scudéry's novel, with considerable attention also paid to the novel's related representations of contemporary French society and its character as a *roman à clé*.[69] As Chantal Morlet-Chantalat argues, it is in part a historical fiction and part a 'gazette' or chronicle of contemporary culture.[70] Because of its generic hybridity and the self-reflexive discussions included in the novel about history and fiction, *Clélie* has also received considerable attention for its place in the history of the novel genre.[71]

Less attention has been paid to Scudéry's rewriting of Roman sources, and where critics have considered the historical dimensions of the novel, they have mostly been interested in what its Republican framework reveals about Scudéry's own political views in relation to the Fronde, divided as to whether or not we can read into it any anti-monarchical positioning on Scudéry's behalf, with more convincing accounts stressing that Scudéry was supportive of the monarchy (but against tyranny).[72] Where attention has been focused on the more obvious Roman elements, such as the stories of Tarquin le Superbe, and particularly Lucrèce and Clélie, the emphasis has tended still to consider their affective dimensions: the relationship to *galanterie* and depictions of sentiment and mores. Scudéry's engagements with her sources—that is, the nature and the effect of her creative rewritings—are taken to be self-evident, with changes seen as proof of her approach to historical fiction and prioritising of contemporary mores, or simply bypassed.[73] Sharon Nell's recent translation of the Lucretia and Brutus episodes

---

Roman customs and includes details which only feature in Dionysus of Halicarnassus's *Antiquities*. See Aronson, 'Mademoiselle de Scudéry et l'histoire Romaine dans "Clélie"', p. 185.

[69] See, for instance, DeJean, *Tender Geographies*, pp. 65–93; and Anne E. Duggan, 'Love Orders Chaos: Madeleine de Scudéry's *Clélie, Histoire Romaine*', in *Salonnières, Furies, and Fairies: The Politics of Gender and Cultural Change in Absolutist France* (Newark: Delaware University Press, 2005), pp. 50–90 (pp. 62–77). On the origins of the Carte de Tendre, see the *Chroniques du Samedi*, pp. 34–38.

[70] See Chantal Morlet-Chantalat, *La Clélie de Mademoiselle de Scudéry: de l'épopée à la gazette: un discours féminin de la gloire* (Paris: Champion, 1994).

[71] See, for instance, Faith E. Beasley, 'Seventeenth-Century Women Writers and the Novel: A Challenge to Literary History', in *The History of the Novel in French*, ed. by Adam Watt (Cambridge: Cambridge University Press, 2021), pp. 95–112.

[72] As Dufour-Maître argues, the Republican framework 'géne visiblement la romancière' (*Les Précieuses*, p. 318). Marlies Mueller also argues that it is pro-monarchy (though suspicious of absolutism) and against revolution which she associates with political chaos in *Les Idées politiques dans le roman héroïque de 1630 à 1670* (Lexington, KT: French Forum, 1984), pp. 149–65: the dedication to the Duchesse de Longueville seems in line with this thesis. In contrast, Anne E. Duggan suggests that Scudéry's valorising of the Republic in this novel, along with her depiction of the relationship between the individual and the state, offers a nuanced and aristocratic-orientated model of republicanism. ('Clélie, Histoire Romaine', p. 79). See also Duggan, 'Love Orders Chaos: Madeleine de Scudéry's *Clélie, Histoire Romaine*', pp. 86–89.

[73] This is the effect of a number of essays, such as Robert Nunn, 'The Rape of Lucretia in Madeleine de Scudéry's *Clélie*', in *Violence et fiction jusqu'à la Révolution*, ed. by Martine Debaisieux and Gabrielle Verdier (Tübingen: Narr, 1998), pp. 245–49; James F. Gaines, 'Lucrèce, Junie and Clélie: Burdens of Female Exemplarity', *Journal of the Western Society for French History*, 17 (1990), 515–21; and Megan

from *Clélie* unites the thread of the story of the two lovers and gathers together Scudéry's ancient sources, which are given in an appendix; her excellent analysis focuses on how their story intersects with Scudéry's ideals of tender friendship and of 'gloire', but does not explore the consequences of the reception of those sources for Scudéry's ethos or the status of antiquity in this period.[74]

In this section, by examining Scudéry's use of sources, I want to mobilise more explicitly what she is doing with ancient history to analyse her representations of gender and to think about her career strategies. I suggest that Scudéry deliberately blurs masculine and feminine ideals to unpick the patriarchy inherent to the story of the founding of Rome; she does so in her characterisations of Brutus, Lucrèce, and Clélie. I argue that rather than showing an anti-monarchist bent, Scudéry's narrative engages with the gendered history of the founding of Rome: the founding is inaugurated by the rape of Lucretia, which creates military bonds of masculinity, and is cemented by the virile heroism of Cloelia. The episodes of *Clélie* which have been read as depicting the episodes from the Fronde, especially which relate women's roles in these military encounters, have a political charge, but that charge is best contextualised as being in dialogue with patriarchy rather than monarchy.

There were also literary, rather than political, reasons for choosing to retell the story of the founding of the Republic: Du Ryer's translation of Livy's history was published in 1653, a year before the publication of the first part of *Clélie*. This was a major text, the first new translation since 1606, and it became the authoritative version of the seventeenth century.[75] The story of early Rome and of the founding of the Republic was a topic treated with success and acclaim by Scudéry's contemporaries, notably Corneille with his *Horace* (1640) and *La mort de Pompée* (1642), and, as we will see, Lucretia proved a figure of particular interest in the 1630s and 40s. Given that *Clélie* is Scudéry's first solo-authored novel in which she was asserting her full authority and enjoying cultural influence, taking on a major canonical topic can be seen as a legitimising, authoritative gesture. It is therefore all the more important to attend to how her version differs from traditional accounts.

Such assertion of authority can be seen in the genealogy Scudéry constructs for the genre of the historical novel in the conversation included in *Clélie*, later entitled

---

Kruer, 'The End of Marriage: Sexual Violence after *Clélie*', *Papers on French Seventeenth Century Literature*, 83 (2015), pp. 313–25. Plazenet, 'What Did Heliodorus' Name Stand for?' proves to be an exception to this.

[74] *Madeleine de Scudéry, Lucrèce and Brutus: Glory in the Land of Tender*, ed. and trans. by Sharon Nell, The Other Voice in Early Modern Europe: The Toronto Series 84 (Toronto: Iter Press, 2021). On Scudéry's redefinition of 'gloire' in this text, see also Duggan, 'Love Orders Chaos: Madeleine de Scudéry's *Clélie, Histoire Romaine*', pp. 55–62.

[75] Pierre Du Ryer, *Les Décades de Tite-Live* (Paris: Sommaville, 1653), 2 vols. This was reprinted in 1669, 1694, 1700, and 1722. The previous translation was by Blaise de Vigenère from 1606 published with Abel L'Angelier, to which Malherbe added supplements for the 1616 version printed with L'Angelier's widow. Prior to this, the complete translation *Les Décades* by Antoine de la Faye (1540–1615) was published in 1582. On the Renaissance tradition of Livy translations in France, see Jean-Mark Philo, *An Ocean Untouched and Untried: The Tudor Translations of Livy* (Oxford: Oxford University Press, 2020), pp. 22–28.

'de la manière d'inventer une fable' (on inventing a fable) (IV, pp. 410–21), in which Scudéry has the ancient Greek lyric poet, Anacreon, play a fundamental role.[76] This conversation follows shortly after the 'Songe d'Hésiode' (IV, pp. 288–328), analysed above, in which Anacreon is constructed, with Ovid, Catullus, Horace, and Moschus, as *galant*: Scudéry's presentation of Anacreon in the 'Songe' is thus a Modern gesture.[77] Such a gesture is then reinforced by the innovative way Scudéry uses 'Anacréon' in the conversation on the fable, which constitutes a defence of the novel. In this conversation, she is deliberately engaging with the preface written by her brother (perhaps by her as well) to *Ibrahim ou le Grand Bassa* (1641),[78] in which the historical novel is theorised. Classical epic and the ancient novel, such as by Heliodorus, whose *Aethiopica* was first translated into French by Jacques Amyot in 1547, are seen as its antecedents, carried through a tradition continued by Honoré d'Urfé.[79] Using Anacréon as spokesperson, Scudéry echoes many of this preface's points in defence of the novel: Anacréon draws on theories of Tasso, as Georges de Scudéry had done, when he argues for the centrality of love (p. 411), and Aristotle, when he argues for the importance of following 'les règles de l'art' (p. 412); both Anacréon and Herminius (a character thought to figure Scudéry's friend, Paul Pellisson) defend the virtue that the novel teaches (p. 417–18); and Anacréon emphasises the key tenet of both Madeleine's and Georges's theory of the novel: that it is beneficial to mix history and fiction as long as it is within the bounds of vraisemblance.

However, by using Anacréon as spokesperson Scudéry differs from the *Ibrahim* preface as she introduces ancient Greek lyric, as well as epic, as the novel's antecedent.[80] In this very figuration of Anacréon, Scudéry puts theory into practice. She has, in accordance with *vraisemblance*, reinvented the Greek lyric poet, whose persona in the poetry attributed to Anacreon, which we know call pseudo-Anacreon or the Aanacreontea, is frequently a lubricious and sometimes

---

[76] It was reprised with some modifications as 'De la manière de bien inventer une fable', in *Conversations sur divers sujets*, 2 vols (Paris: Barbin, 1680), II, pp. 451–90. Although this episode has been examined by critics, very little attention is paid to Anacreon. See Morlet-Chantalat, *La Clélie de Mademoiselle de Scudéry*, p. 126, and Delphine Denis, 'De la manière d'inventer une fable', in *'De l'air galant' et autres conversations (1653–1684)* (Paris: Champion, 1998), pp. 161–80. On her approach to history, fable, and vraisemblance, see also Duggan, 'Love Orders Chaos: Madeleine de Scudéry's *Clélie, Histoire Romaine*', pp. 59–62.

[77] See Claudine Nédélec, 'Lyriques anciens et lyriques modernes à l'aune de la galanterie', *Littératures Classiques*, 77.1 (2012), 319–31.

[78] On attribution of this preface see Plazenet, 'What did Heliodorus' Name Stand for?', pp. 291–92. On Heliodorus and the ancient novel, see Laurence Plazenet, *L'Ébahissement et la délectation: réception comparée et poétiques du roman grec en France et en Angleterre aux XVIe et XVIIe siècles* (Paris: Champion, 1997).

[79] Georges de Scudéry, 'Preface', *Ibrahim ou le Grand Bassa*, 4 vols (Paris: Sommaville, 1641–4), I, p. 5.

[80] Scudéry's shift away from the formalities and erudition associated with epic towards sociable literary forms is also evident in her decision to place her theorisation of the novel not in a preface or essay but in a fictional conversation. See also Denis, 'De l'air galant', p. 165.

homoerotic old man, and whose work depicts bodily pleasure.[81] While she maintains his association with pleasure by making him the 'roi du festin' (king of the festival) at the fête galante (IV, pp. 263), she also creatively responds to Anacreon's poetry by reimagining the bodily pleasure that characterises his work as intellectual and social pleasure in the way he theorises the novel. Although she valorises epic models in this conversation, with Anacréon as spokesperson she offers an additional lyric genealogy, explicitly reorienting her historical fiction from the muscular 'arms and the man' to narratives of sentiment and social interaction.[82] References to Anacreon also implicitly evoke Sappho, given her position as his double or counterpart in early modern taxonomy (and book history: they are frequently included together in editions).[83] Scudéry thus aligns her novel with both the masculine genre of epic and a feminised lyric, establishing a hybridity which we will also now see as present in her characterisations of heroism.

Shifting Masculinities: Brutus, Sapho, and Lucrèce

The historical centrepiece of *Clélie* is the well-known story of Lucretia's rape by Sextus Tarquin, her subsequent suicide, and Brutus's revenge. In Scudéry's version, Lucrèce's rape, the actions leading up to it, and its consequences are told in the main narrative and in the retrospective interpolated and fictionalised story Scudéry adds of Lucrèce and Brutus's amorous relationship told by Herminius, the 'Histoire de Lucius Junius Brutus' (II, pp. 70–235). Rather than confirm the virility at the heart of the ancient historical tradition in which rape and revenge are necessary for the Republic's founding, and the forming of the male bonds which catalyse this, as critics suggest Livy's version does, I argue that Scudéry's rewriting complicates the patriarchal norms inherent in this story and engages creatively with the exemplar tradition of both Lucretia and Cloelia.[84] The traditional

---

[81] Her reinvention of Anacreon would prove influential to salon culture, and can be traced in the writing of Antoinette Deshoulières, as we will examine in Chapter 5. Sophie Tonolo describes the 1670s and early 1680s as having an 'atmosphère anacréontique'. 'Les métamorphoses d'Anacréon chez Mme Deshoulières: effets d'une tradition philologique et philosophique sur son lyrisme pastoral', *Revue Fontenelle*, 10 (2012), 181–97 (p.182). Marie-Jeanne L'Héritier recognises this when she has Ovid and Anacreon guide Scudéry to the temple for deification in her fictional apotheoisis. Marie-Jeanne L'Héritier, *L'Apothéose de Mademoiselle de Scudéry* (Paris: Moreau, 1702), p. 31.

[82] She valorises Homer in stronger terms than Georges de Scudéry does in his Preface to *Ibrahim*, p. 4.

[83] It was also reported by Athenaus that Anacreon was in love with Sappho (but since they did not live at the same time this cannot be true, as is made clear in the *Lives* by Tanneguy Le Fèvre and Dacier).

[84] On the rape and Rome's founding, Stephanie Jed has argued that 'the rape of Lucretia is transformed into an injury against the honour of her male survivors'. Stephanie Jed, *Chaste Thinking: The Rape of Lucretia and the Birth of Humanism* (Bloomington: Indiana University Press, 1989), p. 11. Melissa Matthes argues that the violence against women at the founding of Rome is seen as necessary for the male bonds that will spur the rejection of the tyrant. Melissa Matthes, *The Rape of Lucretia and*

90   WOMEN WRITING ANTIQUITY

accounts, from antiquity through to the vogue for Lucretia's story in the 1630s, evident from the tragedies by Pierre Du Ryer (1638) and Urbain Chevreau (1637), as well as the version of Lucrèce's 'harangue' to her husband, Collatin, in the *Femmes illustres*, are united by two key elements: the connection between the rape and the founding of the Republic, as it spurs vengeance against the Tarquins and their tyranny, with this vengeance being coded as masculine; and the role of Brutus as agent in this revenge.[85] In Livy's version, as well as the two plays by Scudéry's contemporaries, Du Ryer and Chevreau, Brutus takes the lead in avenging Lucretia, famously chastising Collatinus and Lucretius (her father) for their tears, spurring them instead to action and vengeance (Livy 1.59.4: 'tum Brutus castigator lacrimarum').[86]

Beyond the detail of the love of Brutus and Lucrèce, Scudéry develops the traditional story of Lucretia's rape in two crucial ways: firstly, in her complex gendering of Brutus, which has received little critical attention, and secondly in her portrayal of the rape and its relationship to the founding of Rome.[87] Her gendering of Brutus prompted particular contemporary scorn: Boileau suggests in his *Art poétique* that in *Clélie*, Scudéry has represented Brutus as 'dameret', that is, 'qui veut paroistre de bonne mine pour plaire aux Dames' (one who wants to present himself well so as to please women) (as Furetière has it), and 'd'une élégance efféminée' (Godefroy).[88] However, I show that with her version of Brutus, Scudéry makes a dramatic shift away from the patriarchal undertone of this founding narrative. By shifting the role played by codes of masculinity in his characterisation, and, as we will see, by shifting the narrative of the rape to offer Lucrèce a more empowering legacy, she

---

the *Founding of Republics: Readings in Livy, Machiavelli and Rousseau* (University Park: Penn State University Press, 2000), p. 42–44.

[85] These accounts include Livy, *Histories* 1.57–59; Dionysus of Halicarnassus, *Antiquities*, 4.67; Valerius Maximus, *Memorable Doings and Sayings, Volume II: Books 6–9*, ed. and trans. by D. R. Shackleton Bailey, Loeb Classical Library 493 (Cambridge, MA: Harvard University Press, 2000), 6.1.1; Urbain Chevreau, *La Belle Lucresse romaine, tragédie* (Paris: Quinet, 1637); Pierre Du Ryer, *Lucrèce, tragédie* (Paris: Sommaville, 1638), Jacques Du Bosc, *L'Honnête femme* (Paris: Billaine, 1632), pp. 162–63; Pierre Le Moyne, *Gallerie des femmes fortes* (Paris: Sommaville, 1647), pp. 162–75.

[86] This is also the case in the version by Dionysus of Halicarnassus: 'You will have countless opportunities, Lucretius, Collatinus, and all of you who are kinsmen of this woman, to bewail her fate; but now let us consider how to avenge her, for that is what the present moment calls for.' Dionysus of Halicarnassus, *Roman Antiquities*, trans. by Cary, 4.70.

[87] For instance, Gaines only focuses on Brutus as Lucrèce's lover ('Lucrèce, Junie and Clélie', p. 519); Marie-Gabrielle Lallemand has focused on how Cyrus is made *galant* in *Le Grand Cyrus*, but does not analyse Brutus in 'Galanterie des conquérants: l'Alexandre de la Calprenède et le Cyrus des Scudéry', in *La Galanterie des anciens*, ed. by Grande and Nédélec, pp. 99–112; Alain Niderst keeps his analysis of Brutus as 'galant' brief in 'Le Brutus de Madeleine de Scudéry', in *Bruto il maggiore nella letteratura francese e dintorni*, ed. by Franco Piva (Fasano: Schena, 2002), pp. 75–87; and Nell reads Brutus in relation to the Carte de Tende, usefully emphasising Brutus as a *galant*, who navigates tender friendship, but does not focus her analysis on his gendering and its effects on the myth of Rome's founding (Madeleine de Scudéry, *Lucrèce and Brutus*, ed. and trans. by Nell, pp. 109–20, pp. 241–45).

[88] Furetière, *Dictionnaire universel*; Frédéric Godefroy, *Dictionnaire de l'ancienne langue française et de tous ses dialectes du 9e au 15e siècle*, 10 vols (Paris: Vieweg and Bouillon, 1881–1902), IX: *Complément. Carrel–Inaccostable* (Paris: Bouillon, 1898), p. 272. Edition used: <https://www.classiques-garnier.com/numerique-bases/godefroy>.

changes the gendered balance at the heart of this foundational story. Her version also, as we encountered in her 'Histoire de Sapho' analysed above, subtly and indirectly demonstrates her own learning.

The first development to Lucrèce's story in Scudéry's version is the retrospective 'Histoire de Lucius Junius Brutus', in which she modifies Brutus's character and tells the story of his relationship with Lucrèce. The early parts of this story which open with Brutus as an adult in Tarquin's Rome follow Livy quite closely: for instance, the important trope of his character—that he pretended to be more stupid than he was in order to beguile the Tarquins—is retained. Initially, then, in accounting for Tarquin's crimes, the Brutus story follows on from the interpolated 'Histoire de Tarquin le Superbe' (I, pp. 307–80), similarly told by Herminius, which also follows Livy Book 1 closely to chart the founding and early history of Rome, from Romulus and Remus through to the rise of Tarquin. The Brutus story thus appears to rehearse the typical version which pits Brutus against Tarquin in a male-on-male battle and presents him as military founder of the Republic. Soon, however, in the 'Histoire de Brutus', Scudéry moves away from this template to cast Brutus in a different light, when the story moves back to Brutus's childhood and upbringing in Métapont (Metapontum).

At Métapont, Brutus receives a female-led education by Damo, 'la sage et savante fille de Pythagore' (the wise and learned daughter of Pythagoras) (II, p. 77)—we might note, too, the positive use of the prenominal adjective here.[89] Metapontum was known for its community modelled on the one which Pythagoras had founded at Crotone in Greece, according to Aristoxenus of Tarento. Pythagoras was considered by Diogenes Laertius to have had a daughter called Damo (and Scudéry may have come across Diogenes Laertius' *Lives of Philosophers* in her *samedi* salon, because one of its attendees, Gilles Ménage, who later penned a *History of Women Philosophers*, was particularly interested in this work).[90] However, the inclusion of Brutus here in this community is fictitious. With this fiction Scudéry depicts Brutus, avenger of Lucrèce, instigator of the Roman Republic, as having been educated by a woman who also, it is stressed, cultivates in him a love of Sappho:

Je vous dirai seulement que Brutus eut la savante Damo pour guide de sa première jeunesse et que les premiers disciples de Pythagore furent ses maîtres. Je lui ai

---

[89] On the representation of Pythagoras in this text, see Chantal Morlet-Chantalat, 'Pythagore et Sapho: reincarnation galante d'un philosophe mythique', in *Madeleine de Scudéry: une femme de lettres au XVIIe siècle*, ed. by Delphine Denis and Anne-Élisabeth Spica (Arras: Artois Presses Université, 2002), pp. 123–31.

[90] Although this had been translated into French in 1601, it is more likely that Scudéry knew of this text in Latin. See François Fougerolles, *Le Diogène français tiré du grec ou Diogène Laërtien touchant les vies traduites et paraphrasées sur le grec par M. François de Fougerolles* (Lyon: Huguetan, 1601) and Gilles Ménage, *Historia Mulierum Philopharum* (The History of Women Philosophers) (Lyon: Rigaud, 1690). See also *Clélie*, ed. by Morlet-Chantalat, II, p. 77.

92 WOMEN WRITING ANTIQUITY

ouï assurer que les ingénieuses louanges, ou les douces et adroites réprimandes de cette prudente fille, lui servirent plus que tous ses livres. (II, p. 81)

I will only tell you that Brutus had the learned Damo for his guide in his youth and that the first disciples of Pythagoras were his tutors. I have heard him swear that the inventive praises, as well as the sweet and deft reprimands of this prudent woman, were more instructive to him than any book.

The role of feminine taste in cultivating and rendering Brutus 'poli' (II, p. 81) is emphasised in the homage Brutus pays to Sappho. He then travels to Greece for a year to complete his education: 'l'amour qu'il eut pour les vers de Sapho fut si forte que cette passion lui apprit à en faire, qui valent mieux que ceux de cette célèbre Lesbienne. De plus, il était courageux, doux, civil, complaisant et agréable' (the love that he had for Sappho's verse was so strong that this passion taught him to write verse of his own that excelled those of this famous woman from Lesbos. Moreover, he was brave, gentle, civil, obliging, and aimable) (II, p. 81). It is Damo who then encourages him to return to Rome to try to combat Tarquin by pretending to be stupid, so Scudéry shifts one of his key 'strategic' military moves from being of his own initiative to being a result of the advice of his female teacher. The references to the Pythagorean tradition, through the evocation of Damo, evoke a society in which women were equal as scholars: Pythagoras apparently allowed his wife, Theano (also Damo's mother in Scudéry's version); sister, Thémistoclée; and daughters, Myia, Arignote, and Damo, to be part of his inner circle of scholars. Ménage emphasises the uniqueness of this philosophy for its inclusion of women: 'il y a eu tant de femmes pythagoriciennes que le grammarian athénien Philochore a écrit, d'après Suidas, un ouvrage entier sur elles intitulé *Recueil des femmes héroïques*' (there were so many Pythagorean women that the Athenian grammarian Philocorus wrote, according to Suidas, a whole book on them, called the 'Catalogue of heroic women').[91]

Once he is back in Rome, Brutus finds himself in the same circles as Lucrèce, and, because she sees through his guise of stupidity, they fall for each other. Poetry and, in particular, the Greek lyric tradition (and so Sappho again) are central to their burgeoning love. Brutus hopes to write poems to Lucrèce in ancient Greek and in the style of Sappho in order to express his love, but proves too much in despair to be able to do so. He hopes that she might understand them because of her Greek slave, Cléobuline, who 'leur avait récité cent belles choses de Sapho et de Phocilide' (has recited to them the beautiful words of Sappho and Phocylidus) (II, p. 128). Phocylides de Coes, a Greek lyric poet and philosopher from the sixth century BC, proves no incidental reference. Shortly after this episode, Lucrèce initiates a poetry game (II, pp. 132–33), in which she gives a series of jumbled words

[91] Gilles Ménage, *Histoire des femmes philosophes* (Paris: Arléa, 2006), p. 79.

which the group has to reorder to generate sense. Brutus is the one who finally cracks the code: the lines are from two verses of the aforementioned Phocylides.[92] Although Brutus's characterisation was a cause for ridicule for its distortion of classical knowledge, what we see here is a highly learned vision of Brutus that draws on a range of ancient texts and which claims for *galanterie* and the Moderns a place in a *savant* culture.

We also see in Brutus's characterisation an exploration of questions of gender and power. This can be seen from the contrast between Scudéry's portrait of Brutus and her depiction of a powerful woman, Tullia the Younger, the ambitious wife of Tarquin the Proud who plotted to kill her older sister (Tarquin the Proud's first wife, Tullia the Elder), her first husband (Arruns Tarquins, his brother), and, with Tarquin the Proud, also killed her father, Servius Tullius, the King, running her chariot over his dead body. This tale, told in Livy Book 1, is one of the elements of the ancient historian that Scudéry follows most closely in her 'Histoire de Tarquin le Superbe', although, as we might expect, she offers a long digression on the courtship of the two sisters and brothers and the murderous plotting of Tullia and Tarquin. She retains key elements of Livy's text that pertain to the characterisation of the younger Tullia: the notion that Tullia the Younger is the driving force behind Tarquin the Proud's actions and Tullia's defilement of her father's body, to which Scudéry adds the gory detail that she looked back 'avec joie' (I, p. 371). Scudéry also emphasises Tullia's lack of femininity. In conversation with her sister, she expresses dissatisfaction with the restrictions of her sex: 'j'aimerais mieux être le soldat que la princesse, tant je suis peu satisfaite de mon sexe' (I would prefer to be a soldier than a princess: that is how little I am satisfied with my sex) (I, p. 322), and she is defined as preferring male company: 'elle méprisait même extrêmement les femmes et ne pouvait souffrir la conversation que des hommes' (she was extremely disdainful towards women and could only endure the conversation of men) (I, p. 359). Scudéry offers a critique of aggressive masculinity by questioning the model which constructs power as male in her exaggerated and monstrous portrait of Tullia. This portrait works in opposition to Brutus who represents an ideal leader, civil rather than overtly military, lyric rather than epic. While the attributes are clearly gendered with Scudéry valorising feminised traits (and disproving of an immodest woman), her depiction allows for fluidity in terms of who possesses these characteristics.[93]

---

[92] Kruer has also discussed this riddle, suggesting that it implies that Lucrèce is more worldly and experienced that she might at first appear. Kruer, 'The End of Marriage', p. 322.

[93] On Tullia, see also Jacqueline Broad and Karen Green, 'The Fronde and Madeleine de Scudéry', in *Women's Political Thought in Europe 1400–1700* (Cambridge: Cambridge University Press, 2009), pp. 180–98 (p. 198). Broad and Green also suggest we might read Tullia as representing Christina of Sweden, the 'strong, ambitious and masculine woman that Madeleine de Scudéry opposed'. Broad and Green, 'Women of Late Seventeenth-Century France', ibid., pp. 247–64 (pp. 253–4).

94 WOMEN WRITING ANTIQUITY

Male violence is most evident in the next and most important episode of the story of Brutus and Lucrèce: her rape by Sextus Tarquin. As critics have noted, the description of the rape in Scudéry's novel occurs as an ellipsis. Collatin and Lucretius see Sextus leaving Lucrèce's apartments: he looks shifty, and they wonder what he has been up to. Lucrèce does not name what happened to her: 'mais tout ce que la modestie peut souffrir que je vous en dise, c'est que l'infâme Sextus est venu dans ma chambre et qu'il est le plus criminal, et le plus insolent de tous les hommes et que je suis la plus malheureuse personne de mon sexe, quoique je sois la plus innocente' (but the only thing modesty will allow me to say is that the vile Sextus came into my bedroom; and that he is the most criminal and insolent of all men and that I am the most unfortunate person of my sex, although I am the most innocent) (II, p. 484). The ellipsis is then repeated by the slave who explains what has happened, but we only have this as reported: 'une fidèle esclave de cette belle affligée racontait en deux mots à Lucretius le crime de Sextus' (a faithful slave of this beautiful afflicted woman explained in brief Sextus's crime to Lucretius) (II, p. 485). The ellipsis is performative as Lucrèce identifies that she cannot name the crime given its gravity: 'si le malheur qui m'est arrivé se pouvait dire, il ne serait pas aussi grand qu'il est' (if the misfortune that has befallen me could be named, it would not be as serious as it is) (II, p. 484). This ellipsis and the simplification of the story have, for the most part, been equated with Scudéry's 'sensitive' and 'polite' approach whereby the rape is effaced or censored.[94] However, as I will show, Scudéry in fact foregrounds the violence, through her distinct retelling of this ancient story.

Livy's well-known description explains that Sextus Tarquin coerced Lucretia by offering her an ultimatum: that she either stop resisting or he would kill her, strip her, and leave her lying naked on a bed with a naked male slave, thus destroying her reputation as a faithful wife. By stopping resisting, Lucretia surpasses the confines of her body in order to choose to control the narrative: she 'overlives', to use Emily Wilson's term, and endures the rape in order to keep her reputation intact.[95] Her suicide, once she has conveyed the truth, is not motivated by guilt but because, having told the truth, it allows her to preserve her reputation. In Livy, she asks: 'quid enim salvi est mulieri amissa pudicitia?' ('for what can be well with a woman when she has lost her honour?').[96] She kills herself to prove her innocence and set an example to other women. The moral problem of Lucretia's story hangs

---

[94] This is the argument made by Gaines, Kruer, and Nunn; Nunn argues that 'all she can do is divert our attention from it, first by supressing the details of rape as they are known to the traditional version of the story and second by incorporating it into one of the many love stories that make up much of the novel' ('The Rape of Lucretia', p. 249). Niderst states, 'le viol de Lucrèce, dont la romancière élude pudiquement le récit ...' (the rape of Lucretia, which the novelist modestly eludes) ('Le Brutus de Madeleine de Scudéry', p. 80).

[95] Emily Wilson, *Mocked with Death: Tragic Over-living from Sophocles to Milton* (Baltimore: Johns Hopkins University Press, 2005).

[96] Livy, *History of Rome, Volume I: Books 1–2*, trans. by B. O. Foster, Loeb Classical Library 114 (Cambridge, MA: Harvard University Press, 1919), 58.8.

on the question of intention (was it rape or adultery?) and her death then becomes proof of her innocence.[97] This logic of innocence in Livy's version is complex: she is innocent in mind, though not in body—'ceterum corpus est tantum violatum, animus insons; mors testis erit' ('Yet my body only has been violated; my heart is guiltless, as death shall be my witness')—and innocent of the crime but not eligible to avoid the punishment—'ego me etsi peccato absolvo, supplicio non libero' ('though I acquit myself of the sin, I do not absolve myself from punishment').[98] Lucretia is therefore a self-consciously exemplary figure, for whom exemplarity is a motivator for her actions: she wants to *set* an example and is not simply received as one.

In the subsequent tradition, these complexities are extended by the fact that her suicide needed excusing for a Christian audience. St Augustine was the prominent figure who would grant her no such excuse or pardon, but instead viewed her suicide as an admission of her guilt at her act of adultery, suggesting that she enjoyed the assault.[99] Boccaccio, by contrast, casts Lucretia as an 'outstanding model of Roman chastity and sacred glory of ancient virtue' whose death restores her reputation.[100] On the whole, the French tradition, with which Scudéry was also engaging, resolves the problem of her suicide in her favour: Le Moyne argues that she should not be held to Christian standards, but be judged instead as pagan;[101] Du Ryer shows her intentions to be innocent, as he echoes the mind/body split present in Livy's version: 'Mon esprit, cher espoux, ny peut estre qu'en guerre / Il déteste ce corps comme une infâme terre' (my soul, dear husband, can only be at war / it hates this body as a vile land).[102] There was one prominent French retelling of this story which followed St Augustine and which bears its trace in the Lucrèce harangue of the *Femmes illustres*: Du Bosc's *L'Honnête femme*. He condemns her suicide, and gives her as an example of 'fausse probité'.[103] He considers her to be a suspicions case, aligning her with debauched women, and suggests that she killed herself to hide her criminal adultery.

Although the version in the *Femmes illustres* echoes elements of Du Bosc's condemnation—Lucrèce is judged more severely for her suicide and for 'overliving' to tell the tale, and her crime chiefly lies in her decision to preserve her reputation (an earthly, vain pursuit) rather than, in the terms of this version,

---

[97] See Rebecca Langlands, *Sexual Morality in Ancient Rome* (Cambridge: Cambridge University Press, 2006), pp. 85–96. Complexity is also typical of exemplarity: as Susan Wiseman has argued, exemplarity always involves a complex dynamic of 'praise and dispraise'. Susan Wiseman, 'Exemplarity, Women and Political Rhetoric', in *Rhetoric, Women, and Politics in Early Modern England*, ed. by Jennifer Richards and Alison Thorne (London: Routledge, 2007), pp. 129–48 (p. 146).

[98] Livy, *History of Rome*, trans. by Foster, 58.7 and 58.10.

[99] See Ian Donaldson, *The Rapes of Lucretia: A Myth and its Transformations* (Oxford: Clarendon Press, 1982), pp. 21–39.

[100] Giovanni Boccaccio, *On Famous Women*, trans. by Guido Guarino (London: Allen and Unwin, 1964), pp. 102–03.

[101] Le Moyne, *Gallerie des femmes fortes*, p. 169.

[102] Du Ryer, *Lucrèce*, p. 85. On Du Ryer's play and his adaptations of the story, see James F. Gaines, *Pierre Du Ryer and His Tragedies: From Envy to Liberation* (Geneva: Droz, 1987), pp. 61–111.

[103] Du Bosc, *L'Honnête femme*, p. 162.

96 WOMEN WRITING ANTIQUITY

remain true to her actual honour and die innocent, though thought to be guilty—in *Clélie*, Scudéry removes the key element of the story that provides this ambiguity.[104] Sextus does not threaten to kill Lucrèce and ruin her reputation: there is no ultimatum. Lucrèce does not 'choose' to endure the rape and live to tell the tale. As Rebecca Langlands describes it, in Livy's account (and all the versions which include the ultimatum), the encounter is one of coercion, 'he has forced her (but metaphorically, not physically) into a position where she is constrained to give this consent.'[105] In *Clélie*, Scudéry depicts what is rape as rape, removing the detail that has allowed for questions into Lucrèce's actions and thus making the lack of consent that is implied in the original account more stark.[106] While Scudéry's version urges on the side of *politesse*, it is not necessarily a censoring gesture: in removing the key element of Sextus's threat from the story, she emphasises the non-consensual violence that lies at the heart of this story, and emphasises Lucrèce's status as a victim by removing the moral quandary that she 'overlived' to save her reputation.

Lucrèce's death in Scudéry's version does not confirm the bonds of masculinity as in the traditional accounts. Brutus is no longer the stony-faced castigator of tears; he is not, as Stephanie Jed reads him in Livy, afraid of libidinal energy but rather, socialised by women, in love with Lucrèce, he is both empathetic and presented empathetically. We witness Lucrèce's death through his eyes: 'elle tomba [...] aux pieds du malheureux Brutus qui eut le funeste avantage d'avoir le dernier de ses regards et d'entendre son dernier soupir' (she fell at the feet of the unfortunate Brutus who had the unhappy advantage of receiving her final glances and of hearing her last gasp) (II, p. 485).[107] He does not chide Lucretius and Collatin for their tears.[108]

---

[104] As the opening 'argument' of the harangue establishes: 'l'on n'a pû decider encore si elle fit bien de se tuer apres son mal-heur, et si elle n'eust pas mieux faict de souffrir que Tarquin l'eust tuée et de mourir innocente, bien qu'elle n'eust pas esté cruë telle' (it is yet to be decided whether she was right to kill herself after her misfortune or whether she would have done better to let Tarquin kill her and to die innocent, although presumed otherwise) (*Les Femmes Illustres*, p. 206). The ensuing harangue is then presented as a sort of defence which the readers are invited to judge: 'mais puis qu'elle va parler, ne la condamnez pas sans l'entendre' (since she is about to speak, do not condemn her without hearing her first) (ibid.). The rhetorical thrust of this harangue, with the oppositions of guilt and innocence, also exemplifies what Susan Wiseman picks out as a feature of telling the Lucretia story: 'at times, indeed, as with many uses of Lucretia, there seems to be a display of virtuosity involved in the author's ability to balance positive and negative versions of the example' ('Exemplarity, Women and Political Rhetoric', p. 147). On the contrast in the portrayal of Lucrèce in the *Femmes illustres* and *Clélie*, see Madeleine de Scudéry, *Lucrèce and Brutus*, ed. and trans. by Nell, pp. 47–53.

[105] Langlands, *Sexual Morality in Ancient Rome*, p. 91.

[106] For a discussion of women's consent and its interpretation in fiction by male authors of this period, see Jennifer Tamas, *Au non des femmes: libérer nos classiques du regard masculin* (Paris: Seuil, 2023).

[107] Nell persuasively suggests that this is influenced by Ovid's account of the moment of her death in his *Fasti* 2.685–852 (Madeleine de Scudéry, *Lucrèce and Brutus*, ed. and trans. by Nell, p. 243).

[108] Later, in Scudéry's discussion of Brutus as consul having to oversee the trial and execution of his sons for treachery, Scudéry interprets the sympathy present in Livy's version and exaggerates this: 'si bien que ramassant alors toutes les forces de son âme, il se tint ferme, et cachant le désordre de

With the moral problem of intention and glory removed, Scudéry also focuses attention on Lucrèce's demands for vengeance, which are presented in stronger terms than in Livy: 'mais promettez-moi généreusement que vous me vengerez, que vous exterminerez toute la famille des Tarquins' (but promise me magnanimously that you will have revenge on me, that you will exterminate the whole Tarquin family) (II, p. 484). Scudéry then emphasises this agency by showing Lucrèce as continuing to influence the action: she appears as a vision to Brutus when he is in battle with Sextus and encourages him (III, p. 531); and later appears to Clélie in a dream encouraging her to leave the Clusian camp, as I discuss below (V, pp. 322–23). The ambiguously coded gender that is often attributed to Lucrèce, who is described by Valerius Maximus as having a 'masculine soul' ('virilis animus') but a 'woman's body' ('muliebre corpus'), is removed from Scudéry's portrayal of Lucrèce: she has a courage and agency of her own that do not need to be valorised as male.[109] The ambiguity is instead transferred to Brutus.[110] By shifting away from the military male response, Scudéry reframes the effects of Lucrèce's rape to grant her a legacy which is not present in Livy's version where her death prompts no change for the women who succeed her. As we will see in the next and final section of this chapter, in Scudéry's version, it *does* change things for the women who come after her.

Clélie: Imitation and Example

In the final part of Scudéry's *Clélie*, we come to the moment for which our eponymous heroine is known. As Matthew Roller emphasises, in the classical accounts by Plutarch, Dionysus Halicarnassus, and Valerius Maximus, Cleolia is normally shown as an imitator of other male heroes, particularly Horatius Cocles, who defended Rome from the Clusians at the Sublicius bridge, and Mutius Scaevola who attempted to kill Porsenna, the Clusian leader. Valerius Maximus describes her as 'viris puella lumen virtutis praeferendo' ('a girl, holding the light of valour before men').[111] This tradition is continued in the more recent versions: Boccaccio

---

son esprit, il sembla regarder avec beaucoup de constance, le plus funeste objet du monde' (so that, gathering all the strength of his soul, he stood firm, and hiding the disorder of his spirit, he seemed to look with steadfastness upon the most dire sight in the world) (III, p. 233). Plutarch represents Brutus with little sympathy: 'it is said that the father neither turned his gaze away nor allowed any pity to soften the stern wrath that sat upon his countenance.' Plutarch, 'Life of Publicola', in Plutarch, *Lives I*, trans. by Bernadotte Perrin, Loeb Classical Library 46 (Cambridge, MA: Harvard University Press, 1914), 6.3.

[109] Valerius Maximus, *Memorable Doings and Sayings*, 6.1.1. See Langlands, *Sexual Morality in Ancient Rome*, p. 177.

[110] Lucretia's 'manliness' is also implied in Ovid's *Fasti* where she is described as a 'matrona animi virilis' ('matron of manly courage'). Ovid, *Fasti*, trans. by James G. Frazer, rev. by G. P. Goold, Loeb Classical Library 253 (Cambridge, MA: Harvard University Press, 1931), 2.847.

[111] Matthew Roller, 'Exemplarity in Roman Culture: the Cases of Horatius Cocles and Cloelia', *Classical Philology*, 99.1 (2004), 1–56 (p. 28). Valerius Maximus, *Memorable Doings and Sayings*, 3.2.2.

mentions her actions in sequence with those of Horace and Mutius, suggesting that she 'armed her breast with a manly courage' in his *On Famous Women*; and Le Moyne presents her action as inspired by that of Mutius in his *Gallerie des femmes fortes*.[112] It is also perpetuated in the *Femmes illustres*: Cloelia's inspirations are shown to be the Roman heroes, Mutius, Horace, and Brutus, to whom Cloelia refers several times.[113] In *Clélie*, however, Scudéry complicates the male gendering of Clélie's heroism present in these versions by removing any notion of her imitating male heroes and instead emphasises her exemplarity. And, if she is inspired by anyone, it is Lucrèce.

Parallels are established early between Clélie and Lucrèce, even before Lucrèce's appearance in Clélie's dream: we know that Sextus was also in love with Clélie and her desire to flee Porsenna's camp is initially sparked by Sextus making overtures which she perceives as threatening (v, p. 98). Livy does not give her motivation for wanting to leave the camp (it is presumably self-evident) and in later accounts it is suggested that it was unseemly for women to be in a military camp full of men.[114] Scudéry is innovative in casting Sextus as motivator. The connection with Lucrèce is then strengthened when Clélie recounts to her friend, Valérie, her vision of Lucrèce urging her flight:

> ses cheveux étaient négligés, elle était couverte d'un grand manteau blanc, et elle tenait un poignard sanglant à la main. En cet état, j'ai cru entendre sa voix qui avait quelque chose d'effrayant. 'Fuyez, Clélie, fuyez', m'a-t-elle dit, 'mais fuyez promptement, car je vous avertis que le tyran qui me fit avoir recours à ce poignard, en veut à votre gloire comme il en voulait à la mienne.' (v, pp. 322–23)

> her hair was in disarray, she was wrapped in a large white cloak, and she was holding a bloody dagger in her hand. In this state, I thought I heard her voice, which had a terrifying tone: 'Flee, Clélie, flee', she said to me, 'and quickly, for I am warning you that the tyrant who forced me to use this dagger is after your glory as he was after mine.'

When Clélie then persuades the other women to cross the Tiber with her, she uses Lucrèce as a motivating example: 'si nous mourrons, nous mourrons encore avec plus de gloire que Lucrèce, puisque ce sera pour éviter un malheur, après lequel elle ne voulut plus vivre' (if we die, it will be with more glory than Lucrèce; as it will be to avoid the misfortune after which she no longer wanted to live) (v, p. 325). Clélie also explicitly evokes Sextus as threat: 'il s'agit de s'empêcher d'être sous la puissance du bourreau de la vertueuse Lucrèce' (we need to remove ourselves from the power of virtuous Lucretia's executioner) (v, p. 325). James Gaines argues that

---

[112] Boccaccio, *On Famous Women*, p. 115; Le Moyne, *Gallerie des femmes fortes*, pp. 182–96 (p. 185).
[113] *Les Femmes illustres*, I, p. 364, p. 368.
[114] See Le Moyne, *Gallerie des femmes fortes*, p. 184; Boccaccio, *On Famous Women*, p. 115.

shifting the motivation for Clélie's escape onto her fear of Sextus is an example of the personal and psychological changes Scudéry effects to ancient history.[115] Be that as it may, the effect of this is also to strengthen Lucrèce's legacy and her influence on the women who came after her. Linking Clélie and Lucrèce further allows Scudéry to strengthen her attack on aggressive forms of masculinity: where, with Lucrèce, the founding of the Roman Republic was catalysed by Sextus's rape, in Clélie's case it is the *threat* of rape that also prompts the actions which sealed Rome's peace with its neighbours.[116]

In addition to having her imitate Lucrèce, Scudéry also places Clélie in a line of female 'viragos' by evoking the Amazons, thus also echoing the Sapho story of *Le Grand Cyrus*, where Scudéry has Sapho depart for the land of the Sarmatians (who were associated with the Amazons). Scudéry portrays Clélie's crossing of the Tiber in much more detail than her ancient sources. Before they cross, a soldier helps the women by providing planks and bundles of wood as rafts but Clélie prefers to trust in her courage and the river gods: 'mon courage m'y soutiendra et les dieux m'assisteront' (my courage will support me and the gods will aid me) (v, p. 327). Katherine Ibbett persuasively reads this as an echo of Odysseus's raft and as an example of Scudéry's re-gendering of resourcefulness.[117] Scudéry then incorporates the detail of Clélie crossing on horseback from Plutarch, Valerius Maximus, and Dionysius of Halicarnassus, though this is not included in Livy's account. Representing Clélie thus on horseback is unexpected in that it deviates from Scudéry's main source (Livy); it is surely therefore intended to evoke the Amazons.[118] Scudéry ironically nods to the male gendering of Clélie's heroism in some of the ancient sources, but draws attention to this very gendering. The soldiers on the near side who helped the women were 'bien surpris' to see them crossing given that they were women (v, p. 328) and those on the other side thought they were men in disguise (v, p. 328). Scudéry then strengthens the association with the horse-riding Amazons by granting Clélie all the horses mentioned across the various sources: Livy has Valerius Publicola erect an equestrian statue in Clélie's honour; Scudéry includes this as a consolatory gesture when Publicola sends Clélie and the other hostages back; she also echoes Plutarch when Porsenna gives Clélie a gift of a horse; and she adds a further horse as he also erects a statue of a horse in her honour in Clusium, 'pour témoigner qu'il lui trouvait le cœur d'un héros' (to show that he found she had the heart of a hero) (v, p. 462).[119] All these horses evoke the Amazons, so Scudéry encourages readers to make a

---

[115] Gaines, 'Lucrèce, Junie and Clélie', p. 520.

[116] Nell suggests that Clélie can claim some superiority over Lucrèce (can claim to be a better example) because in Scudéry's version Lucrèce tolerated Brutus's love for her even though they were not married. Madeleine de Scudéry, *Lucrèce and Brutus*, ed. and trans. by Nell, p. 120.

[117] Katherine Ibbett, *Liquid Empire* (forthcoming).

[118] See Grande, *Stratégies*, p. 33.

[119] Plutarch, 'Life of Publicola', in Plutarch, *Lives I*, trans. by Perrin, 14.4.

100   WOMEN WRITING ANTIQUITY

connection with Sapho in *Cyrus*, which links Sapho and Clélie and reinforces the subtle influence of Sa(p)pho we have encountered throughout *Clélie*. Clélie is also deliberately twinned with Brutus because both are shown in Scudéry's novel as being influenced by Lucrèce from beyond the grave. Scudéry's representation of Clélie serves as a counterpoint to the re-gendering of heroism we saw with Brutus: Brutus with his 'soft masculinity' and Clélie with her exemplary authority could be seen to constitute an example of Scudéry's blurring of gendered boundaries.

By granting Clélie two statues in her account, Scudéry also emphasises the memorialisation of Clélie, anchoring her position as an exemplar rather than as an imitator of men. But, as I have indicated, in Clélie's story we get a double legacy: both that of Clélie and of Lucrèce. Lucrèce is shown as empowering Clélie to her heroic act. Rather than simply leaving women confined to the 'domus', as Melissa Matthes has argued to be the case in Livy's version, the effect of Lucrèce's action is to initiate an act of heroism that questions the gendered restrictions placed on women.[120] In his analysis of the tradition of Lucretia stories, Ian Donaldson has divided the political interpretations from the ones which focus on rape and suicide (highlighting Brutus's role in the former);[121] such division has been criticised by Susan Wiseman who shows that it is Lucretia's 'potential to draw on both strands of representation that makes her a key example'.[122] Scudéry's interpretation lends weight to that criticism in so far as she identifies Lucrèce as a political agent, as critics have noted.[123] However, by tracing threads of interconnection between and within her early works of historical fiction, we see that Scudéry also challenges the broader patriarchal structures underpinning the story of Rome's founding. She does so in her rewriting of Brutus's character and her re-routing of the effect of the rape from bonds of masculinity to female agency; in her emphasis on female legacy and memorialisation; and, on a meta level, in her reorientation of the novel genre towards a lyric, rather than epic, tradition. Where her portrayal of the ideal female intellectual in *Le Grand Cyrus* was grounded in gender difference, her depiction of gender in *Clélie* seems less essentialising and more dynamic: both explorations are underpinned by an approach to ancient sources that is adaptive, that draws on both traditional learning and Modern practices of fictionalisation, thus effecting shifts in taste and literary practice.

**

Scudéry's mixed reception attests to the complexity of her relationship with antiquity and with the *savoir* that it represented. Scudéry was lauded in some circles: Tanneguy Le Fèvre describes her as 'la plus Sçavante fille' (with the prenominal adjective used positively again) in his *Life of Anacreon* in 1665 and Anne

---

[120] Matthes, *The Rape of Lucretia*, p. 43.
[121] Donaldson, *The Rapes of Lucretia*.
[122] Wiseman, 'Exemplarity, Women and Political Rhetoric', p. 135.
[123] Lucrèce and Clélie 'shape history itself'. Gaines, 'Lucrèce, Junie and Clélie', p. 521.

Dacier describes her as 'l'illustre Mademoiselle de Scuderi'.[124] Her learning, modesty, and decorum are also praised, for instance in the *Éloge* written on her death by the Abbé de Bosquillon in the *Journal des sçavans*, and Marie-Jeanne L'Héritier described her as 'la sçavante fille' in her *L'Apothéose de Mademoiselle de Scudéry*.[125] Her novels were translated into a number of languages and she was an influential figure in eighteenth-century England.[126] For some time now, academic work has emphasised Scudéry's reputation as a key cultural influence in this period; and she is included in studies from disciplines outside literature, such as moral and political philosophy.[127] However, there remains some hesitation over her contribution to classical reception studies: she still remains only a passing reference, if that, in broader studies of classical reception, with all attention paid to her Sapho.[128] Her erudite learning is often valorised for being relational, for instance through her correspondence with Anna Maria van Schurman.[129] Her novels or 'romances', as they are described in the English tradition, do not tend, as we have seen, to be highly regarded as classical reception.[130] Henry Power has shown the importance of epic tradition in popular male-authored novels and the consumerism of early eighteenth-century print culture, but we have yet to take the further leap into the more complex territory of the female-authored romances.[131]

It is more complex because of the gendering of intellectual value that still operates in relation to the early modern period and has its origins in the ridicule that Scudéry received on account of her representation of ancient history. The condemnation of Boileau's *Dialogue des héros de roman*, mentioned above, culminates in his much-commented-upon prescriptive remark that these are novels 'qu'on ne [...] lit presque plus' (that are hardly read anymore), credited with determining the long exclusion of such *galant* novels from the canon, which lasted through the better part of the twentieth century.[132] This ridicule was echoed in the eighteenth century and beyond France, for instance in Charlotte Lennox's *The*

---

[124] Tanneguy Le Fèvre, *Abrégé des vies des poètes grecs*, p. 54; Anne Dacier [Le Fèvre], 'Vie d'Anacréon', in *Les poésies d'Anacréon et de Sapho*, np.

[125] *Journal des sçavans*, July 1701, pp. 315–22. Marie-Jeanne l'Héritier, *L'Apothéose de Mademoiselle de Scudéry* (Paris: Moreau, 1702).

[126] Karen Green, 'Eighteenth-Century Debates: From Anne Dacier to Catharine Trotter Cockburn', in *Women's Political Thought in Europe 1700–1800* (Cambridge: Cambridge University Press, 2014), pp. 14–42.

[127] See, for instance, Broad and Green, 'The Fronde and Madeleine de Scudéry'.

[128] See, for instance, Jane Stevenson, 'Women Writers and Classics'; Scudéry does not feature in *Women Classical Scholars: Unsealing the Fountain from the Renaissance to Jacqueline de Romilly*, ed. by Edith Hall and Rosie Wyles (Oxford: Oxford University Press, 2016).

[129] She features only briefly in Pal's study, and only for her correspondence with Schurman. Carol Pal, *Republic of Women: Rethinking the Republic of Letters in the Seventeenth Century* (Cambridge: Cambridge University Press, 2012), p. 15.

[130] There is more work to be done tracing the ancient influences on her later works, particularly her essays and *Conversations*.

[131] Henry Power, *Epic into Novel: Henry Fielding, Scriblerian Satire and the Consumption of Classical Literature* (Oxford: Oxford University Press, 2015).

[132] Boileau, 'Dialogue des héros de roman', p. 446. See DeJean, *Tender Geographies*, pp. 165–67; and for a discussion of Boileau's role in canon formation, see Faith E. Beasley, 'Disseminating a National

Female Quixote (1752) in which the heroine Arabella's unconventional knowledge of classics, entirely derived from romances, especially those by Scudéry, who is mentioned explicitly, is subject to mockery.[133] As Faith E. Beasley has shown, Boileau's opinion of Scudéry became dominant into the nineteenth century when, despite some favourable comments by Sainte-Beuve, for example, much criticism dismissed her work as unreadable.[134] But, as I have also suggested in this chapter, such exclusion from the classical reception canon also has its origins in how critics respond to Scudéry's own posturing as modest. We have seen how it is particularly in relation to classical knowledge that the equivocation of this strategy is made evident: modesty and erudition compete as women's tickets for entry to the public sphere.

In this chapter I have shown that Scudéry's rewriting of ancient history, her creative response to antiquity, places her securely as a precursor to female-orientated fictional rewritings currently so in vogue and highly regarded (by Margaret Atwood, Madeline Miller, or Pat Barker, to name but a few in the Anglophone tradition). That is not to over-valorise the position of precursor, but the comparison is intended to reveal how much more readily scholars of the modern period accept a wide range of media and genres, by those both literate in ancient languages and those who are not, as valid reception.[135] Thinking of Scudéry as a precursor to this current mainstream interest in women's classical reception also usefully draws attention to the market dynamics of this phenomenon: there is no doubt that this subgenre is currently also a site of commercial success, just as it was for Scudéry. In the next chapter we will explore more fully this commodification of antiquity through analysis of Madame de Villedieu's (and her publisher, Claude Barbin's) hugely successful exploitation of the historical fiction literary market.

Past: Teaching *Le Grand Siècle*', in *Salons, History and the Creation of Seventeenth-Century France* (Aldershot: Ashgate, 2006), pp. 261–313.

[133] Charlotte Lennox, *The Female Quixote*, ed. by Margaret Dalziel (Oxford: Oxford University Press, 2008), pp. 61–62.

[134] See Faith E. Beasley, 'From Critics to Hostess: Creating Classical France', in *Salons, History and the Creation of Seventeenth-Century France*, pp. 175–260.

[135] For example, see Lorna Hardwick and Stephen Harrison, eds, *Classics in the Modern World: A Democratic Turn?* (Oxford: Oxford University Press, 2013).

4

'Classics' as Commodity

Antiquity and the Literary Market

This chapter examines the relationship between the literary market, reception of antiquity, and an author's career by focusing on Madame de Villedieu (Marie-Catherine Desjardins). Villedieu wrote in a range of genres (theatre, poetry, *nouvelles*, and novels) and explicitly drew on ancient history for seven of her published works. Like a number of the other women in the corpus of this book, Villedieu was a professional writer, that is, a person for whom writing was determinant of their income and foundational to their role in society.[1] She relied on two streams of income: favour and patronage, evident particularly in the dedications of her early works, and, increasingly through her career, commercial success. Given that she was of minor nobility with little wealth, both of these sources were essential. The extent of that professionalism has been emphasised recently in work by Edwige Keller-Rahbé who has highlighted that Villedieu stands out among her (female) peers and predecessors for the number of 'privilèges d'auteur' granted to her. 'Privilèges d'auteur', the royal permission to publish, which protected the work by allowing the author to choose the publisher(s), were afforded to the author, as opposed to the more typical 'privilège de libraire', where the permission was granted directly to the printer/publisher.[2] A significant number of other women, many of whom are studied here, also solicited author *privilèges* (including, from early in the century, Marie de Gournay, and, from the 1680s, Antoinette Deshoulières, Catherine Bernard, Marie-Jeanne L'Héritier, Marie-Catherine d'Aulnoy), but Villedieu is distinctive for pioneering this approach in the 1660s and 1670s, when it had become less common for a woman, and for the regularity with which she solicited such *privilèges*.[3]

Building on Geoffrey Turnovsky's conceptions of the 'literary market' as a symbolic order as much as an economic one, in this chapter, I shall consider how

---

[1] This follows the definition of 'écrivain de profession' offered by Alain Viala in 'Des stratégies dans les lettres', in *On ne peut pas tous réduire à des stratégies: pratiques d'écriture et trajectoires sociales*, ed. by Nicolas Schapira and Dinah Ribard (Paris: Presses Universitaires de France, 2013), pp. 183–200 (p. 186).

[2] Edwige Keller-Rahbé, 'Pratiques et usages du privilège d'auteur chez Mme de Villedieu et quelques autres femmes de lettres du XVIIe siècle', *Œuvres & Critiques*, 35.1 (2010), 69–94. I have found the resources of the Madame de Villedieu website, https://madamedevilledieu.huma-num.fr, run by the Groupe Renaissance et Âge Classique at Université Lyon II, invaluable in writing this chapter.

[3] Keller-Rahbé, 'Pratiques et usages du privilège d'auteur', p. 77.

Women Writing Antiquity. Helena Taylor, Oxford University Press. © Helena Taylor (2024).
DOI: 10.1093/oso/9780192870445.003.0004

104 WOMEN WRITING ANTIQUITY

Villedieu made her name and made her name a brand by 'cashing in' on the popular appeal of historical fiction set in antiquity.[4] I show that Villedieu did not follow the paradigmatic posture of amateur, aristocratic detachment towards the business of the book trade and instead argue that she positioned her authorial identity and her *galant* ancient historical fiction in such a way as to celebrate commercial success. She played with the opposition between *galant* and *savant* culture, in which antiquity acts as a flashpoint, by capitalising on a projected identity as a 'woman writer' and by her fictionalising approach to ancient history. I analyse prefatory material, including her *privilèges*, to examine how Villedieu (and her chief publisher, Claude Barbin) defined a lucrative aesthetic and exploited the market for her fiction, and in so doing legitimised it and its commercial success.

Villedieu's historical fiction, and particularly her novels set in antiquity, have received considerable analysis in relation to the ways in which she fictionalised ancient history. Studies have analysed the implications of this historical fiction for a Modern and *galant* aesthetic, for the history of the novel, for the 'demolition' of the epic qualities of the hero in favour of sentiment, for her centring of women's lives and stories, and for comments on contemporary politics.[5] And critics have analysed this work in relation to changing practices in historiography, evident in the writings of François-Eudes de Mézeray, the theories of César Vichard de Saint-Réal, and the emergence of the secret history genre.[6] The fiction–history question has thus dominated criticism of Villedieu's writing about antiquity: I propose to shift the focus onto the literary market, mindful also that this is not often appraised in studies on the receptions of antiquity. Much of what follows in this chapter is unique to Villedieu's particular situation and career path; however, I also suggest that Villedieu broke new ground: at the end of this chapter, I briefly examine two comparable authors, Catherine Bernard and Anne de La Roche-Guilhen, who are able to shed further light on the influence of Villedieu's commercial practice.

Madame de Villedieu's career has been well documented, but a brief summary is useful here.[7] Her father came from the lower nobility, but had little wealth;

---

[4] Geoffrey Turnovsky, *The Literary Market: Authorship and Modernity in the Old Regime* (Philadelphia: University of Pennsylvania Press, 2010).

[5] Edwige Keller-Rahbé, "Je crois déjà les entendre dire que je viole le respect dû à la sacrée Antiquité": Mme de Villedieu et la galanterie des anciens, ou le savoir-faire d'une mondaine', in *La Galanterie des anciens*, ed. by Nathalie Grande and Claudine Nédélec (= *Littératures Classiques*, 77.1 (2012)), pp. 161–75 (pp. 174–75); Domna Stanton, 'The Demystification of History and Fiction in "Les Annales Galantes"', in *L'Image du souverain dans le théâtre de 1600 à 1650. Actes de Wake Forest*, ed. by Milorad R. Margitić and Byron R. Wells (Tübingen: Narr, 1987), pp. 339–60; Gérard Letexier, 'Des nouvelles historiques exemplaires: *Les Annales galantes*', in *Madame de Villedieu romancière: nouvelles perspectives de recherche*, ed. by Edwige Keller-Rahbé (Lyon: Presses Universitaires de Lyon, 2004), pp. 201–18; Christian Zonza, 'La houlette et le sceptre: une écriture entre fiction et histoire', *Littératures classiques*, 61.3 (2006), 219–34.

[6] See, for instance, Nathalie Grande, 'La métamorphose galante de l'histoire antique: modalités et enjeux d'une poétique', in *La Galanterie des anciens*, ed. by Grande and Nédélec, pp. 229–44.

[7] For a fuller biography, see Perry Gethner, ed. and trans., 'Nitetis', in *Challenges to Traditional Authority: Plays by French Women Authors, 1650–1700*, The Other Voice in Early Modern Europe: The Toronto Series 36 (Toronto: Iter Academic Press, 2015), pp. 101–63 (pp. 101–04).

her mother was lady-in-waiting to the Duchess of Rohan-Montbazon: their marriage secured him a position in government and after their separation in 1655, when Villedieu's mother returned to Paris from Alençon with her two daughters, the Duchess's connections proved useful. In 1658, at the age of eighteen, Marie-Catherine Desjardins met Antoine Boësset, le Sieur de Villedieu, with whom she had an affair. Around this time, she wrote her first work, a sonnet, 'Jouissance', which circulated anonymously with some notoriety before it was published in 1660. She launched her career with the *Récit en prose et en vers de la farce des précieuses* in 1659, a two-volume but unfinished novel, *Alcidamie* (1661), and a collection of poetry (1662). This was followed by her three plays: her Roman *Manlius* (1662), which was subject to a quarrel about its historical veracity; *Nitetis* (1664), set in ancient Egypt during the reign of Cambyses, as told by Herodotus (and recently translated into French by Du Ryer);[8] and a contemporary piece, *Le Favory* (1665), which Molière produced, thought to be about Nicolas Fouquet. In the relatively short time span of 1668 to 1675, her output was prolific with some thirteen different texts, many of them long novels: she was writing an average of 1500 pages per year.[9] She separated from le Sieur de Villedieu in 1667 when he married an heiress and he died a year later. After his death she decided to publish as 'Madame de Villedieu', having previously used the name 'Desjardins': they had never married, but a formal promise of marriage had been signed in Provence and witnessed by a priest and notary in June 1664; his parents would never have provided the required consent, and in 1667 the promise was retraced to enable his marriage, but his family appear not to have objected to her use of his name.[10] As we will see, Villedieu's choice of authorial name had a role to play in her career strategy and in the way she made a name for herself.[11] In addition to her two ancient plays, five of her narrative fictions were set in antiquity and drew on ancient history, all of which were published by Claude Barbin: a *nouvelle*, *Carmente, histoire Grecque* (1668), 'ancient' primarily in setting and drawing largely on the atmosphere of the Honoré d'Urfé's pastoral, *L'Astrée*, although it has been argued that the characters of Théocrite and Timoléon are influenced by Plutarch; the fictional compendium, *Les Amours des grands hommes* (1671), tracing the loves of Solon, Socrates, Julius

---

[8] Pierre du Ryer, *Les Histoires de Hérodote* (Paris: Sommaville, 1645). It was re-edited at least four times before the century's close.

[9] Nathalie Grande, *Stratégies des romancières: de Clélie à La Princesse de Clèves (1654–1678)* (Paris: Champion, 1999), p. 268. On the professionalism of her novel output in particular, see Linda Timmermans, *L'Accès des femmes à la culture (1598–1715)*, 2nd edn (Paris: Champion, 2005), p. 215.

[10] See Micheline Cuénin, *Roman et société sous Louis XIV: Madame de Villedieu (Marie-Catherine Desjardins, 1640–1683)*, 2 vols (Paris: Champion, 1979), i, 127. Tallemant des Réaux reported that she had wanted Molière to use the name Madame de Villedieu for *Le Favory* in 1665, but he had turned her down since it had already been advertised as being by Marie-Catherine Desjardins. Gédéon Tallemant des Réaux, *Historiettes*, ed. by Antoine Adam, 2 vols (Paris: Gallimard, 1961), ii, p. 908.

[11] 'se faire un nom, c'est aussi lui faire de la publicité' (making one's name is also to create publicity for oneself). Nathalie Grande and Edwige Keller-Rahbé, 'Villedieu, ou les avatars d'un nom d'écrivain(e)', *Littératures Classiques*, 3.61 (2006), 5–32 (p. 13).

106 WOMEN WRITING ANTIQUITY

Caesar, and Cato; the long novel, *Les Exilés de la Cour d'Auguste* (1672–73), telling the story of Ovid, Livia, and Augustus among others; as well as the two she wrote after 1675 from her retirement and which were published posthumously, the novels, *Portrait des faiblesses humaines* (1685), detailing various Greco-Roman lives (including Livia, Agripinna, Pericles); and *Annales galantes de Grèce* (1687), which draws on Herodotus.[12] Some characters recur across these texts, as if she were writing a 'comédie humaine à l'antique'.[13] In 1676 she received a royal pension and stopped publishing: she married Claude-Nicolas de Chaste in 1677 (and became widowed—again—two years later), and retired to Clinchemore where she lived until her death in 1683.

Villedieu's publishing career reveals the tensions and complexities in the relationship between author and 'imprimeur-libraire'. Guillaume de Luyne had published her *Récit de la farce des précieuses* without permission in 1659; she then had Claude Barbin publish a corrected, sanctioned version a year later. This was Barbin's first successful publication, meaning that they effectively launched their careers together.[14] Barbin was unusual in that most of the works he published had a *privilège d'auteur*, not *de libraire*; and Villedieu, as noted, was unusual for the number she obtained when she did, particularly as a woman.[15] It was more typical for *privilèges* to be afforded to printers or booksellers, although *privilèges d'auteur* were not rare (Michèle Clément and Keller-Rahbé count over 200 for the sixteenth century and the number significantly increases in the seventeenth century).[16] A *privilège d'auteur* meant that the author probably solicited the *privilège* themselves (with more complex questions of access and social norms in place for women); having an author *privilège* affirms the author's ownership of the work, allowing them to negotiate better contracts with the publisher.[17] A *privilège d'auteur* also meant the author could transfer the *privilège* to the printer-publisher of their choosing which gave them a certain amount of control and in principle reduced the risk of pirate editions. Villedieu solicited author *privilèges* for five of her works from throughout her career: *Le Favory, Carmente, Les Amours des*

---

[12] On *Carmente*, see Keller-Rahbé, '"Je crois déjà les entendre dire"', p. 162; and see also Edwige Keller-Rahbé, 'L'île de Théras dans *Les Annales galantes de Grèce* (1687) de Madame de Villedieu. Une réécriture libertine d'Hérodote?', in *L'Île au XVIIᵉ siècle: jeux et enjeux*, ed. by Christian Zonza (Tübingen: Narr, 2010), pp. 205–23.

[13] Keller-Rahbé, '"Je crois déjà les entendre dire"', p. 162.

[14] Grande, *Stratégies des romancières*, pp. 265–66.

[15] Authors did not have 'legal rights' in France until 1777; however, scholars have long argued that ideas around author rights and professional authorship date back to 1505 when *privilèges* came into use. See Laurent Pfister, 'L'Auteur, propriétaire de son oeuvre? La formation du droit d'auteur du xvie siècle' (unpublished doctoral thesis, Université Robert Schuman, Strasbourg, 1999). See also Alain Viala, *Naissance de l'écrivain. Sociologie de la littérature à l'âge Classique* (Paris: Minuit, 1985).

[16] Michèle Clément and Edwige Keller-Rahbé, 'Introduction', *Privilèges d'auteurs et d'autrices en France (XVI–XVII siècles). Anthologie critique* (Paris: Garnier Classiques, 2017), pp. 7–63 (p. 8).

[17] See Nicolas Schapira, 'Quand le privilège de librairie publie l'auteur', in *De la publication: entre Renaissance et Lumières*, ed. by Christian Jouhaud and Alain Viala (Paris: Fayard, 2002), pp. 121–37 (p. 125); see also Viala, *Naissance*, p. 99.

grands hommes, *Les Galanteries Grenadines* (1672–73), and *Les Exilés*. Her transferring of these *privilèges* to Barbin, her publisher of choice, further attests to the mutually beneficial nature of their relationship.

However, despite this apparent agency, her relationship with Claude Barbin was also complex, as is attested by their various skirmishes: he apparently pressurised her into finishing *Les Exilés*—evident from the note introducing tome 5; he published some of the volumes of *Le Journal Amoureux* without her permission (she only recognised volumes 2, 5, and 6); and he published posthumously, against her wishes, apparently, the two novels she wrote from her 'retirement', *Portrait des faiblesses humaines* in 1685 (in the *avis* Barbin states that although published against her wishes, its success would have prompted forgiveness) and *Les Annales galantes de Grèce* in 1687—although questions remain as to how he acquired them and why she kept writing in retirement if she did not intend to publish.[18] The entangled nature of their relationship and the role commercial success played in it is also attested by the funeral *éloge* written in the *Mercure Galant* on Villedieu's death: Barbin gets a mention here, as it provides an opportunity to plug her forthcoming posthumous volume.[19] And, there is the well-known scandal of the *Lettres et billets galants* of 1668—letters that she claims were private, to her lover, Villedieu, but which he had apparently sold to Barbin who published them without her consent for commercial reasons. Whatever the truth in this story, these *lettres* and their notoriety served Villedieu's career—and that of Barbin.

Villedieu and Barbin: a mutually beneficial commercial relationship. Keller-Rahbé argues persuasively that Villedieu, dubbed Barbin's 'poule aux œufs d'or' by Louis Ménard in the nineteenth century, was not in fact Barbin's puppet or his bestseller-producing machine and, despite Barbin's unfavourable reputations (dubbed in turn 'chien de Barbin' by Madame de Sévigné and 'ce terrible homme de Barbin' by Esprit Fléchier), there was an element of collaboration and mutual success that underpinned their relationship.[20] This is evident from the place Villedieu held in his own catalogue. Between 1659 and 1698 Barbin published more than 626 works, of which over sixty were by the fourteen different women whose work he published, making him the leading publisher of women in the second half of the century.[21] Villedieu was the first female author he published

---

[18] See Edwige Keller-Rahbé, 'Madame de Villedieu, "la poule aux œufs d'or" de Claude Barbin?', in *Les Arrières-Boutiques de la Littérature: auteurs et imprimeurs-libraires au XVIe et XVIIe siècles*, ed. by Edwige Keller-Rahbé (Toulouse: Presses Universitaires de Toulouse-Le Mirail, 2010), pp. 87–111.

[19] 'Le sieur Barbin qui a imprimé tous ces ouvrages, en a encore beaucoup d'elle, et le premier qu'il mettra au jour, a pour titre, *Le Portrait des faiblesses humaines*. Ils ont tous eu un si grand succès, qu'on peut en attendre un pareil de ce dernier' (Mr Barbin, who printed all her works, has more from her and the first of these which he will publish is called *Le Portrait des faiblesses humaines*. All her works have enjoyed great success, and we can expect the same from this latest one). *Mercure Galant*, November 1683, pp. 164–65.

[20] Marie de Rabutin-Chantal, de Sévigné, *Lettres de Madame de Sévigné de sa famille et de ses amis* (Paris: Hachette, 1862), p. 535. Edwige Keller-Rahbé, 'Madame de Villedieu, "la poule aux œufs d'or"'.

[21] See Nathalie Grande, 'Claude Barbin, un libraire pour les dames', *Revue de la BNF*, 3 (2011), 22–27.

108 WOMEN WRITING ANTIQUITY

and he went onto publish work by many of the writers studied here, including later works by Scudéry, Deshoulières's play, *Génseric*, many of Anne Dacier's translations, and work by Madame d'Aulnoy and Madame de Murat. His literary output is associated strongly with *galanterie* and this was shaped by the success he had with Villedieu: in her corpus alone, the sheer number of titles containing 'galant' is notable. Most of his books were published in a cheaper, portable, duodecimo format, with a preference for large type and multiple volumes to appeal to less-accustomed readers.[22] Indeed, *galant* writing, even with its diminished intellectual prestige because of its associations with women, became his brand, as is clear from these two satirical comments. The first, by Esprit le Fléchier:

> Le terrible homme que Barbin,
> Il ne songe soir et matin
> Qu'à débiter livre sur livre,
> Recueil sur recueil amoureux,
> Et si Dieu ne nous en délivre,
> Un jour il nous vendra tous deux.
> Sottise en vers, sottise en prose,
> De demoiselle qui compose
> Et de galant qui veut être caché,
> Il vend tout [...][23]

> That terrible man Barbin
> All he dreams of day and night
> is selling book after book
> collection after collection of love stories
> and if God does not spare us
> one day he will sell us both.
> Idiocy in verse, idiocy in prose
> whether by a young lady
> or a *galant* man who wishes to hide
> He'll sell anything.

The second is the term 'Barbinade'. The *Dictionnaire de Trévoux* has the following entry:

> BARBINADE, s.f. J'appelle des *barbinades* ces nombreux colifichets de
> petits livres qui ne servent qu'à faire perdre inutilement
> du temps, et après la lecture desquels on se trouve l'esprit

---

[22] See Grande, 'Claude Barbin', p. 26; and Gervais Reed, *Claude Barbin: libraire de Paris sous le règne de Louis XIV* (Geneva: Droz, 1974), pp. 51–52.
[23] Quoted in Grande, 'Claude Barbin', p. 26.

> aussi peu rempli que si l'on n'avait rien lu, et qui
> n'ont pas laissé d'enrichir Barbin.[24]

BARBINADES describes the innumerable trinket books which only serve to waste time; after having read them, one feels so little fulfilled that one might as well not have read them at all, although they still manage to make Barbin endlessly rich.

These satires remind us of the inverse relationship between cultural and economic capital and the limited prestige afforded to historical fiction.

Villedieu's 'Barbinades' saw huge commercial success. She was capitalising on the momentum of her achievements and doing something right. That success is demonstrated by her ancient history novels which saw a number of re-editions—both official and unofficial. It is notable how the interest extended beyond Paris, with a version of the *Portrait des faiblesses humaines* (1685) coming out in Amsterdam with Henry Desbordes in 1686 and of the *Annales galantes de Grèce* (1687) in The Hague in 1688, Lyon in 1697, and Toulouse in 1702. Two of her ancient history novels stand out: *Les Amours des grands hommes*, which, as Rudolf Harneit shows, was her second most widely disseminated volume after the *Mémoires de Henriette Sylvie de Molière* (which saw twenty-six editions), with some fourteen different editions, of which eight were Dutch;[25] and *Les Exilés de la cour d'Auguste* (1672–78), saw thirteen different editions, of which four were Dutch; and was the most translated into English of all her novels.[26] *Les Exilés*, *Les Amours des grands hommes*, and the *Annales galantes de Grèce* also feature most frequently in the collections of her *Œuvres* published throughout the first half of the eighteenth century.

What I want to explore here is how Villedieu and Barbin exploited this *galant* branding across a range of forms to succeed in the literary market. Turnovsky has persuasively argued that the 'literary market' as a concept, that is, a site in which authors projected themselves, and not simply an economic market, played a key role in defining literary value and in turning individuals into autonomous authors. He stresses that the distinction between an old model predicated on patronage and the modern profit-making of book sales was not always evident as there was not a clear internalised distinction between commercial and non-commercial pay. He

---

[24] *Dictionnaire universel françois et latin [Dictionnaire de Trévoux]*, 4th edn, 6 vols (Paris: Vve Delaulne, 1743), I, p. 1029.

[25] Rudolf Harneit, 'Diffusion Européenne des Œuvres de Madame de Villedieu au siècle de Louis XIV', in *Madame de Villedieu romancière*, ed. by Keller-Rahbé, pp. 29–70 (p. 49); see also Nathalie Grande, 'Introduction générale', in Madame de Villedieu, *Les Amours des grands hommes*, ed. by Nathalie Grande (Paris: Garnier, 2015), pp. 7–49 (p. 42).

[26] Harneit, 'Diffusion Européenne des Œuvres de Madame de Villedieu', p. 50. On English translations, see Donna Kuizenga, 'Madame de Villedieu englished: les traductions en anglais des ouvrages de Villedieu au XVIIe siècle', in *Madame de Villedieu romancière*, ed. by Keller-Rahbé, pp.145–60 (p. 152).

110 WOMEN WRITING ANTIQUITY

argues for the agency a writer had in shaping the 'commerce des livres' and the institution of literature into a site for self-projection and aspiration.[27] These points stand for Villedieu. He also stresses the paradoxical 'quandary facing seventeenth-century *gens de lettres*': that they had to appear to be distant from the commerce of the book trade in order to acquire cultural legitimacy and to adhere to values of aristocratic social identity.[28]

Madeleine de Scudéry, explored in the previous chapter, fits this paradigm; Villedieu, I show, does not. I build on Turnovsky's work, but suggest that the distinction between commercial success and social prestige is less clear-cut in the case of Madame de Villedieu and her close and complex dealings with Barbin and the market. To be sure, she never states explicitly that she wants to make money, but, I want to argue, her literary identity, her claims to prestige, and even her articulation of what constitutes 'literature' are modelled on an involvement in the business of the book trade and a widespread appeal that was predicated on commercial success. Villedieu was not alone in pushing against the paradigm of aristocratic detachment: as Christophe Schuwey argues, Jean Donneau de Visé also had an entrepreneurial and commercial attitude towards his literary career; Schuwey recognises that Donneau de Visé was not unique in this approach which he shows can similarly be seen in the attitudes of Molière, Edmé Boursault, and, indeed, Villedieu.[29] The fact that Villedieu solicited her own *privilèges*, including her name at strategic points within these documents; her signing of the majority of her works; and, as I will explore, the way she frames her works all attest to her willingness to associate her literary identity and her fiction with the book trade in a way that would have been unthinkable for Scudéry.[30] Villedieu's approach also differs significantly from the approach of Madame de Lafayette whom Joan DeJean uses as a test case for exploring the relationship between the salon and the literary market in the 1660s and 1670s. DeJean argues that Lafayette's case shows how aristocratic women who did not sign their works played an important role in the development of the space of literary production, and that their anonymity was not purely driven by the norms of their class, but was deliberately intended to 'introduce a concept of authorship not based on a signature with a unique,

---

[27] Turnovsky, *The Literary Market*, p. 19.

[28] Ibid., p. 21.

[29] Christophe Schuwey, *Un entrepreneur des lettres au XVII siècle: Donneau de Visé, de Molière au 'Mercure Galant'* (Paris: Classiques Garnier, 2020). On Molière, see also Nicholas Hammond, 'Authorship and Authority in Molière's *Le Misanthrope*', in *Essays on French Comic Drama from the 1640s to the 1780s*, ed. by D. Connon and G. Evans (Bern: Peter Lang, 2000), pp. 55–70 and C. E. J. Caldicott, *La carrière de Molière: entre protecteurs et éditeurs* (Amsterdam: Rodopi, 1998).

[30] Published anonymously were 'Jouissance'; *Récit de la Farce des Précieuses*; *Lettres et billets galants*; *Les nouvelles affriquaines*; *Mémoires de la vie de Henriette-Sylvie de Molière*; and the *Annales galantes*. For explanations for this, see Keller-Rahbé and Grande, 'Villedieu ou les avatars d'un nom d'écrivain(e)', p. 16.

stable referent', in favour instead of 'collective strength'.[31] Villedieu takes a different, far more individualistic, and far less detached approach: in so doing, I show,
she remodels 'literary value' by linking it with commercial success, troubling the
Bourdieusian dichotomy between commercial value and cultural prestige.

Villedieu operates in a similar way across all of her works, but it is particularly her versions of ancient history that have a loaded purchase on ideas of
literary value because of the prestige of Greco-Roman culture and because of
the charged question of historical veracity versus *vraisemblance*. Keller-Rahbé
has suggested, in passing, that the 'galantisation' of ancient history we encounter
across Villedieu's ancient fictions, which come in a variety of genres (tragedy,
tragi-comedy, pastoral, historical novels), 'est un domain presque exclusivement
villedieusien' (is an almost exclusively Villedieusian domain) to the extent that 'le
nom Villedieu est devenu un label de qualité', 'une marque de fabrique' (Villedieu's
name became a label of quality, a trademark) for tales which mix ancient history
and fiction.[32] I take this as a starting point to delve into her commerce-orientated
approach. I first analyse the *querelle* (that did not quite) surround her play, *Manlius*, which, I argue, launched Villedieu's successful approach to ancient history,
and which she used to shape her career. By then analysing Villedieu's prefatory
material, including her *privilèges d'auteur*, I show how she positioned her ancient
historical fiction in such a way as to celebrate its success alongside its status as
explicitly *galant* rather than *savant*, celebrating the very hybridity and range of
galant fictional genres. My contention is that she and Barbin navigated this literary market together, cultivating an approach to antiquity that could be seen, in the
context of the Quarrel of the Ancients and Moderns and its wider questions, as ideological, not only because, as critics have noted, she reorientates ancient history
towards women's stories, but also because she valorises the commercial success of
her fictions.

The *Manlius* 'Querelle'

By April 1662, when her successful *Manlius* was the first play by a woman to be performed at the Hôtel de Bourgogne, Villedieu had an emerging position in Paris's
literary scene.[33] Her poem 'Jouissance' had circulated from 1658; her 1659 *Récit de
la farce des précieuses* was well-known; she had published *Alcidamie* (1661), and
her poetry collection. With *Manlius*, Villedieu turned to Roman history and—like

---

[31] Joan DeJean, *Tender Geographies: Women and the Origins of the Novel in Early Modern France*
(New York: Columbia University Press, 1991), pp. 94–126 (pp. 95–96). Her discussion of Villedieu is
not focused on her relationship with the literary market, but examines her status as notorious and the
fictional model of her representation of history (pp. 127–40).

[32] Edwige Keller-Rahbé, '"Je crois déjà les entendre dire"', p. 162.

[33] It was on for a whole month; on its success, see Valerie Worth-Stylaniou, '"C'est, pourtant, l'œuvre
d'une Fille": Mlle Desjardins à l'Hôtel de Bourgogne', *Littératures Classiques*, 51 (2004), 105–20 (p.106).

112 WOMEN WRITING ANTIQUITY

Scudéry—to Livy: indeed, like Scudéry, Villedieu probably depended on Du Ryer's 1653 translation of Livy's *History of Rome*.[34] Villedieu made a key intervention in the story of Manlius: she has his father, the famous consul, Manlius Torquatus, spare the life of his son, the titular Manlius, thus changing historical fact to suit her play. In Livy's version the young Manlius is found guilty of disobedience by his father who orders his execution for boldly waging a (successful) war against the Latians. The striking change to historical truth was part of the play's success when it was first performed in spring 1662. It was published that October, with her name, 'Mademoiselle Desjardins', on the title page, a *privilège de libraire* dated to September 28th, and a dedication to Mademoiselle de Montpensier. In this dedication Villedieu develops the theme of 'témérité' that recurs later in her other prefaces, and aligns that of Manlius with her own:[35]

> Il dit que par tout l'univers
> On sait que Manlius était un téméraire
> Qu'il eût toujours ce caractère,
> Et dans l'histoire, et dans mes vers,
> Et que, dût-il servir mille fois de victime
> A l'austère sévérité
> Il veut faire avouer à la postérité,
> Que souvent ce n'est pas un crime
> Qu'une heureuse témérité.

C'est, Mademoiselle, dans cette pensée qu'il a eu l'audace d'abuser de votre bonté en dérobant à votre Altesse Royale quelques heures de son loisir, et c'est par ce même mouvement qu'il ose aujourd'hui vous demander l'honneur de votre protection.[36]

> He says that throughout the whole universe
> Manlius is known for being bold
>> and that he was always thus
>> in both history and my verse,
> And that, if he must serve as a victim
>> a thousand times to austere severity,
>> He wants to make posterity admit

---

[34] Pierre Du Ryer, *Les Décades de Tite-Live*, 2 vols (Paris: Sommaville, 1653).

[35] See Nathalie Grande, 'Discours paratextuel et stratégie d'écriture chez Madame de Villedieu', in *Madame de Villedieu romancière*, ed. by Keller-Rahbé, pp. 163–74; and 'Madame de Villedieu, 1640?–1683', in *Théâtre de femmes de l'Ancien Régime, Tome II, XVIIè siècle*, ed. by Aurore Evain, Perry Gethner, and Henriette Goldwyn (Paris: Classiques Garnier, 2016), pp. 309–452 (pp. 317–18). See also Charlotte Simonin, 'Des seuils féminins? Le péritexte chez Mme de Villedieu', *Littératures Classiques*, 61 (2006), 151–72.

[36] Marie-Catherine Desjardins, *Manlius* (Paris: Barbin, 1662), np.

> That sometimes what is thought to be a crime
> is rather a favourable act of temerity.

It is, Mademoiselle, in this vein that he had the audacity to abuse your goodness in taking some hours away from Your Majesty's leisure, and it is by this same feeling that he dares today demand the honour of your protection.

If Manlius 'vient audacieusement se jetter aux pieds de la plus merveilleuse princesse' (comes boldly to throw himself at the feet of the most marvellous princess) (np), then he only does so thanks to Villedieu's mediation. His 'témérité', 'both in history and in [her] verse', phrasing which acknowledges the distinction between the two, is not a crime but 'heureuse', which Villedieu repeats at the end of this dedication: 'Après cela n'est-il pas vrai de dire, qu'il y a des témérités si heureuses qu'elles ne sont jamais criminelles?' (After all, is it not true to say that some acts of boldness are so favourable that they cannot be called criminal?). That favourable boldness can also be read as a reference to her own rewriting of history.

Having enjoyed considerable success, *Manlius* was caught up in the *querelle* about Corneille's play *Sophonisbe* (performed in January 1663 at the Hôtel de Bourgogne), and to a lesser degree, his earlier *Sertorius* (February 1662, Marais), that lasted from February to July 1663: *Manlius* was used by each side as foil to explore history–fiction relations on stage. This was a curious *querelle* in that Villedieu seems to have taken no part in it: the main actors were the Abbé d'Aubignac on the offensive, and Jean Donneau de Visé who defended Corneille. And yet, as I will show, this *querelle*, known now as the *querelle de Sophonisbe*, played a key role in launching Villedieu's particular approach to antiquity, anchoring the success of her fictionalisation of history. For all the work on this *querelle*, we are yet to piece together the references to *Manlius* within it: doing so reveals it as a key point of contention throughout the whole quarrel; it confirms the centrality of the history–fiction issue to *Manlius*'s success and notoriety; and sets a crucial context for the strategies Villedieu used to establish herself and to position her later work. Let us delve into this *querelle*.[37]

Although there had been animosity between d'Aubignac and Corneille for a number of years (since the latter omitted to quote d'Aubignac's work of dramatic theory, *La Pratique du théâtre*, in his *Discours sur le poème dramatique* of 1660), Tallemant des Réaux explains that this particular quarrel was sparked by something rude Corneille had said about Villedieu's *Manlius* which d'Aubignac, who had acted as a sort of mentor to Villedieu—at the least, reading a draft of the play,

---

[37] *Manlius* is treated in brief by Bernard J. Bourque, *All the Abbé's Women: Power and Misogyny in Seventeenth-Century France, through the Writings of Abbé d'Aubignac* (Tübingen: Narr, 2015), p. 182. For recent work on the *querelle de Sophonisbe*, which sees it as key in the development of literary criticism, see Cinthia Meli, 'La Critique dramatique à l'épreuve de la polémique: l'abbé d'Aubignac et la querelle de *Sophonisbe*', *Littératures classiques*, 89, (2016), 43–54.

114 WOMEN WRITING ANTIQUITY

at the most, crafting it—took personally.[38] Corneille's original criticism has not been recovered (if it ever occurred or was written down), so the first mention of Villedieu's play is d'Aubignac's defence of it in the February 1663 *Remarques sur la tragédie de Sophonisbe de Mr Corneille*, also the first text in this quarrel.[39] Here d'Aubignac praises Jean Mairet's 1634 version of *Sophonisbe* in which some changes were made to historical truth for the sake of *bienséance*: Mairet had killed off Syphax, Sophonisbe's husband, to stop her marriage to Massinisse from being bigamous and has Massinisse commit suicide after Sophonisbe does so herself to enhance the play's *vraisemblance*. The reference by d'Aubignac to Mairet was provocative: Corneille had written his version in explicit contrast to that of Mairet, his great rival from the *Querelle du Cid*, whose *Sophonisbe* was the most successful version of this story to date, still being performed in 1663.[40] *Manlius* is then introduced and defended by way of comparison:

> Ainsi pour n'avoir pas voulu faire comme Mairet, il n'y a pas si bien fait que Mairet; et si l'on a blâmé injustement Mademoiselle Desjardins d'avoir sauvé la vie à Manlius, qui par les raisons de la nature et de l'humanité ne devait point mourir, on ne louera pas Monsieur de Corneille d'avoir laissé Massinisse vivant et sans peine dans un état si déplorable, qu'il ne pouvait conserver aucun reste de gloire qu'en mourant: et voilà qu'il ne faut jamais s'attacher aux circonstances de l'histoire, quand elles ne s'accordent pas avec la beauté du théâtre; il n'est pas nécessaire que le poète s'opiniâtre à faire l'historien, et quand la vérité répugne à la générosité, à l'honnêteté, ou à la grâce de la scène, il faut qu'il l'abandonne, et qu'il prenne le vraisemblable pour faire un beau poème au lieu d'une méchante histoire.[41]

> Thus in not wanting to do the same as Mairet, he has not done as well in this matter as Mairet; and if Mademoiselle Desjardins was unjustly blamed for having saved Manlius' life, who by the laws of nature and humanity ought not to have died, one will not praise Corneille for having left Massinisse alive and without punishment in such a lamentable state that the only way he could recover some glory was by dying: this shows that one should never follow the details of history

---

[38] Tallemant des Réaux, *Historiettes*, ii, pp. 900–09.

[39] *Remarques sur la tragédie de Sophonisbe de Mr Corneille envoyées à Madame la Duchesse de R** par Monsieur L. D.* (Paris: Sercy, 1663). The permission is dated to 8th February but there is no 'achevé d'imprimer' so we do not know if d'Aubignac authorised the publication (he says not). It was reprinted with consent and some small changes in April/May along with an essay against *Sertorius*, as *Deux dissertations concernant le poème dramatique, en forme de Remarques sur deux tragédies de M. Corneille intitulées Sophonisbe et Sertorius* (Paris: Brueil, 1663).

[40] See Nina Ekstein, 'Sophonisbe's Seduction: Corneille Writing against Mairet', in *Studies in Early Modern France*, viii: *Strategic Rewriting*, ed. by D. L. Rubin (Charlottesville: Rookwood Press, 2002), pp. 104–18.

[41] 'Première Dissertation', in L'Abbé d'Aubignac, *Dissertations contre Corneille*, ed. by Nicholas Hammond and Michael Hawcroft (Exeter: University of Exeter Press, 1995), pp. 12–13.

when they do not match the beauty of theatre. It is not necessary for the poet to insist on being a historian and when truth clashes with generosity, honesty, and the grace of a scene, he should abandon this role and invent something believable to write a beautiful poem instead of a cruel history.

The play is introduced not, as Tallemant des Réaux might have us think, to be defended on its own right, but as a way of further attacking Corneille's version: it is thus offered as an authoritative piece of contemporary theatre. Villedieu, like Mairet and unlike Corneille, preserved *vraisemblance* and 'the beauty of theatre' over 'cruel history'. The following month, March 1663, Donneau de Visé defended Corneille's play in his anonymous *Défense de la Sophonisbe de M. de Corneille*— to complicate matters, he had actually criticised it in a publication the previous month—and responding to d'Aubignac's defence of *Manlius*, attributed the play's plot, and thus the decision to tamper with history, to him. Comparing *Manlius* to a different play, *Erixène*, also attributed to d'Aubignac and performed with little success in 1661, he writes:

> Si le Manlius de Mademoiselle Desjardins, dont il a fait tout le sujet, a eu plus de succès, la gloire n'en est due qu'à la beauté des vers de cette incomparable fille, et aux comédiens qui les ont si bien fait remarquer, qu'ils ont fait réussir la pièce, malgré tous les défauts du sujet. Je ne perdrai de temps à les faire remarquer.[42]

> If the Manlius of Mlle Desjardins, the plot of which he wrote, has been more successful, the glory is only due to the beauty of the verses of this incomparable young woman and to the actors who speak them so well, making the play a success despite all the problems with the story. I will not waste time listing them all.

Donneau de Visé then goes on precisely to enumerate these faults, reiterating the distinction between the poorly executed 'sujet' and the qualities of the verse.[43] (In June 1663, when Donneau de Visé penned his *Défense du Sertorius*, he likewise suggests that d'Aubignac designed the plot of *Manlius*.)[44] The anonymous *Lettre sur les remarques qu'on a faites sur la Sophonisbe de M. Corneille*,[45] probably also published in March 1663, which also takes Corneille's side, picks up directly

---

[42] *Jean Donneau de Visé et la querelle de Sophonisbe: écrits contre l'abbé d'Aubignac*, ed. by Bernard J. Bourque (Tübingen: Narr, 2014), pp. 42–43. See also F. Granet, *Recueil de dissertations sur plusieurs tragédies de Corneille et de Racine*, 2 vols (Paris: Gissey, 1739), I, pp. 145–95 (pp. 157–58). It was originally published as *Deffense de la Sophonisbe de Monsieur de Corneille* (Paris: Barbin, 1663).
[43] *Jean Donneau de Visé et la querelle de Sophonisbe*, ed. by Bourque, p. 44.
[44] *Deffence du Sertorius de Monsieur de Corneille* (Paris: Barbin, 1663), p. 41.
[45] *À Monsieur D.P.P.S. sur les remarques qu'on a faites sur la Sophonisbe de M. Corneille* (1663). This original is lost and the only version we have is in F. Granet, *Recueil de dissertations*, I, pp. 195–212.

116 WOMEN WRITING ANTIQUITY

on d'Aubignac's argument, refuting the premise that it is acceptable for a poet to change history:

> Il [d'Aubignac] dit que si l'on a blâmé injustement Mademoiselle des Jardins d'avoir sauvé la vie à Manlius, qu'on ne louera pas Monsieur Corneille d'avoir laissé Massinisse vivant dans un état si déplorable, et qu'il ne faut point que le poëte s'attache si fortement aux circonstances de l'histoire. Je ne suis pas pour cette maxime et je tiens que quand le Poëte met sur le Théatre une histoire connue, il en doit conserver la vérité.[46]

> He [d'Aubignac] said that if Mlle DesJardins was blamed unfairly for having saved Manlius' life, one will not praise Corneille for having left Massinisse in such a lamentable state and that a poet should not be so attached to the details of history. I do not follow this precept and I think that when a poet puts on stage a history whose details are known, he should conserve its truth.

The author then argues that part of the problem lies in the name of Desjardins's play which advertises the centrality of Manlius; and then twice refers to the 'savant' who interfered with this plot: 'J'ai oüi dire à plusieurs personnes que si elle n'avoit déféré trop aveuglément aux sentiments d'un savant qui s'est mêlé de conduire la pièce, elle eût fait mourir Manlius et qu'elle eût conservé à Torquatus la fermeté et le caractère que l'histoire lui donne' (I have heard said that if she had not been so blindly deferential to the feelings of a learned gentleman who interfered in producing her play, she would have had Manlius killed and would have preserved the resolve and character that history affords Torquatus).[47] The author then suggests, surely in a tongue-in-cheek fashion, that this 'savant' (by which he means d'Aubignac) went against the advice of Horace and d'Aubignac himself.[48]

When Corneille came to publish *Sophonisbe* in April 1663, he included in the Preface a remark which critics consider to be pointed at *Manlius* and at d'Aubignac for his involvement with it:

> J'aime mieux qu'on me reproche d'avoir fait mes femmes trop héroïnes, par une ignorante et basse affectation de les faire ressembler aux originaux qui en sont venus jusqu'à nous, que de m'entendre louer d'avoir efféminé mes héros, par une docte et sublime complaisance au goût de nos délicats, qui veulent de l'amour partout.[49]

---

[46] Granet, *Recueil de dissertations*, p. 206.
[47] Ibid., p. 207.
[48] Ibid., p. 208.
[49] Quoted in L'Abbé d'Aubignac, *Dissertations contre Corneille*, ed. by Hammond and Hawcroft, xxii; see also Georges Couton, *La Vieillesse de Corneille* (Paris: Maloine, 1949), p. 51.

I prefer to be blamed for having made my women too heroic, through an ignorant and simple affectation that makes them resemble the originals as they have come to us, than to hear myself being praised for having made my heroes effeminate, in a learned and sublime acquiescence to the taste of our most delicate audience members who want to see love everywhere.

So far, then, entangled with the questions of the fictionalisation of history, we also have allusion to Villedieu's commercial strategy in the way she chose to name her play; and to the feminisation of heroes associated with *galanterie*. The next text in this *querelle* was d'Aubignac's *Deux dissertations* of April/May 1663: in the *Seconde Dissertation*, d'Aubignac refers again to Desjardins's play, responding in particular to the comment in the anonymous *Lettres sur les remarques* which, along with the *Défense de la Sophonisbe*, he attributes to Corneille. He opens by suggesting that Desjardins has nothing to do with their quarrel and that as a woman she ought to be spared his jealousy, but adds that she could easily defend herself since this maxim of not changing history is hardly one that Corneille himself had followed. He once again draws a comparison between *Manlius* and *Sophonisbe*, using phrasing that suggests he had no part in the play's design, arguing that where Desjardins could have fixed any fault, Corneille could not do likewise:

> Et quand même, elle aurait failli en sauvant Manlius dont le nom et les aventures n'étaient pas si connus que de César et d'Alexandre, il lui serait facile de tout réparer avec quinze ou vingt vers qui contiendraient le récit de sa mort; au lieu que M. de Corneille pour rétablir les manquements de ses Pièces, aurait peine d'en conserver la moitié des vers.[50]

> And in any case, even if she had made an error in saving the life of Manlius, a figure much less well-known than Caesar or Alexander, it would be easy for her to repair her fault with a few verses that would recount his death; whereas M. de Corneille, to make up for the faults in his plays, would have struggled to keep half of their lines.

It was not until d'Aubignac's fourth dissertation, published with his third in July 1663 and after Donneau de Visé's *Défense du Sertorius*, which d'Aubignac also attributed to Corneille, that he addressed directly the question of his involvement in the plot, denying that he had any:

> Vous avez une étrange aversion contre Mademoiselle Desjardins; il vous fâche qu'une fille vous dame le pion, et vous lui voulez dérober son Manlius par l'effet d'une jalousie sans exemple. Je confesse bien qu'elle m'en a montré le dessein, et

---

[50] L'Abbé d'Aubignac, *Dissertations contre Corneille*, ed. by Hammond and Hawcroft, p. 63.

118   WOMEN WRITING ANTIQUITY

que je lui en ai dit mon avis en quelques endroits, dont elle a fait après ce qu'elle a jugé pour le mieux, et sa seconde Pièce la justifie assez contre votre calomnie. Je ne prétends pas ici faire son apologie, mais je suis obligé de vous dire qu'il est faux que j'aie fait son Manlius, et jamais un petit conseil n'a donné droit à personne de s'attribuer l'ouvrage d'autrui [...].[51]

You have a strange aversion towards Mlle Desjardins; it annoys you that a young woman can outdo you and you want to undermine her Manlius out of unparalleled jealousy. I confess that she showed me the storyline and I offered her my advice at certain points, and she judged herself afterwards what to do with it, and her second play sufficiently makes her case against your calumny. I do not claim to defend her here but I am obliged to tell you that it is not true that I wrote her Manlius and a small word of advice was never reason enough to attribute to anyone authorship of someone else's work.

Having declared in the *Seconde dissertation* that Villedieu should not be brought into the *querelle*, although he carries on doing so, and that she would easily be able to defend herself, here d'Aubignac suggests that he will not 'faire son apologie', except in the personal way he does in the opening of this paragraph when he suggests that Corneille is jealous of a 'young woman', and instead focuses on denying his authorship of the plot.

There is much that is curious about this '(non)querelle' of *Manlius*: firstly, was d'Aubignac involved in writing the plot of her play?[52] We do not know, but, as Keller-Rahbé argues, it would go against Villedieu's usual autonomy, and the way she framed the play on the title page and in the dedication. Equally, it is possible, given that this was her first piece of theatre, that it was a collaboration. There is no clear answer.[53] The interest nevertheless lies in d'Aubignac playing down his involvement, although he only does so after having defended Villedieu's play and having used it to attack Corneille. Secondly, where is Villedieu in this quarrel? Not quarrelling, but letting d'Aubignac do so on her behalf, because, as he implies, she ought to be spared this as a woman; perhaps she thought it better to keep out of the fray.[54] She nevertheless took advantage of this spotlight by having her next play *Nitetis*, another retelling of ancient history, performed at the Hôtel de Bourgogne in April 1663, right in the middle of this *querelle*. Perhaps d'Aubignac had hoped to boost Villedieu's reputation by involving her play in this quarrel (surely this is possible): we do not know for certain how successful this second play was

---

[51] Ibid., pp. 137–38.

[52] Chloé Hogg, 'On Not Cutting Off Manlius's Head: Villedieu's (Non) Querelle and the Politics of Literary Reconciliation' (unpublished paper, Modern Languages Association Conference, Chicago, January 2019).

[53] Keller-Rahbé, '"Je crois déjà les entendre dire"', p. 166.

[54] On women and quarrelling, see Helena Taylor and Kate E. Tunstall, eds, *Women and Querelles in Early Modern France* (= *Romanic Review*, 112.3 (2021)).

(there are mixed contemporary reports), but Perry Gethner argues that the delay between performance and publication for both *Nitetis* and *Manlius*—eight and six months respectively—suggests that both plays did fairly well.[55] Both Donneau de Visé's *Défences* were published by Barbin, suggesting that perhaps he too saw the commercial advantage of this *querelle*.

However, the question at stake here—whether a writer has the licence to change history—became, as I will show, central to Villedieu's definition of historical fiction and so played a key role in her longer-term success. As she knew from her poem 'Jouissance', controversy was commercially useful. And while we cannot know whether she was involved in discussions with d'Aubignac as he penned her defence, just as we cannot know for certain how involved he was in the plot of *Manlius*, it is clear that every time she was mentioned, she was getting useful publicity. The use of *Manlius* as a constant reference in this *querelle* also underscores the most significant point: that Villedieu *was* present in this quarrel, in so far as *Manlius* itself was an intervention in the question of theatrical adaptation of ancient history in the way it deliberately fictionalised and changed that history.[56] I propose, therefore, that if *Manlius* might be Villedieu's opening salvo in the questions about the adaptation of ancient history, then, as we will see in the following section, she was actively participating in this quarrel in all her subsequent ancient publications, using the stance this entailed to shape her claim to the literary market.

Prefaces and *Privilèges*

Villedieu was a prolific writer of peritexts and used peritext to make a name for herself and connect this name to her brand of historical fiction: twenty-one of her sanctioned twenty-two works contain some form of peritext.[57] This includes various types of traditional prefatory material (dedications, *avis*, prefaces); to this, as I will explore, we might add the *privilèges* and, in particular, the five *privilèges d'auteur* she was granted (for *Le Favory*, *Carmente*, *Les Amours des grands hommes*, *Les Galanteries Grenadines*, and *Les Exilés*). Recent work has persuasively argued for understanding *privilèges* as forming an integral part of a book, to be read alongside and intertextually with the other prefatory material.[58]

---

[55] Perry Gethner, ed. and trans., 'Nitetis', in *Challenges to Traditional Authority*, pp. 101–63 (p. 112).

[56] It has also been analysed for its revisions of Corneillian heroism towards a more faulted and *galant* model: see Cinthia Meli, 'L'Audace pour mot d'ordre: l'invention de l'intrigue et des caractères dans le *Manlius* de Marie-Catherine Desjardins', in *Madame de Villedieu et le théâtre*, ed. by Nathalie Grande and Edwige Keller-Rahbé (Tübingen: Narr, 2009), pp. 107–17; and Henriette Goldwyn, 'Manlius—l'héroïsme inversé', in *Actes de Wake Forest*, ed. by Margitic and Wells, pp. 421–37.

[57] For a detailed break-down and analysis, see Simonin, 'Des seuils féminins?'.

[58] Claire Lévy-Lelouche, 'Quand le privilège de librairie publie le roi', in *De la publication: entre Renaissance et Lumières*, ed. by Christian Jouhaud and Alain Viala (Paris: Fayard, 2002), pp. 139–59 (p. 150). For a wider discussion of book history in this period, see Henri-Jean Martin, *Livre, pouvoirs et société à Paris au XVIIe siècle, 1598–1701*, 3rd edn (Geneva: Droz, 1999).

120 WOMEN WRITING ANTIQUITY

Such scholarship has also drawn our attention to reading *privilèges* as rhetorical. While the *privilège* was a legal document, it could, as Nicolas Schapira has shown, 'publish an author' in the way it established legitimacy;[59] and was also a 'literary' document, as Keller-Rahbé argues, in so far as it can bear the scrutiny of rhetorical analysis.[60]

Although some of the language of the *privilèges* was formulaic, it was not entirely standardised: *privilèges* show considerable diversity and are thus worth scrutinising. Villedieu's *privilèges d'auteur*, of which three were for her ancient texts, are also key sites for her willingness to be associated with authorship. Turnovsky argues, using Schapira, that the *privilège d'auteur* did not derive from 'an attachment to intellectual property or profits' but rather that it was part of a more abstract and symbolic system 'for advertising the social, political and cultural legitimacy of writers before a public', in particular in soliciting and conveying the favour of the King.[61] Schapira and Claire Lévy-Lelouche figure the King as royal reader whose presence meant the *privilège* constituted a sign of royal approval.[62] Shapira and Turnovsky cite as a salient example of the importance of this approval the *privilèges* accorded to Georges de Scudéry in which the wording underscores his activities as a soldier faithful to the King, thereby presenting his literary work as an aristocratic form of leisure, a homage to the King and not a professional activity. This is persuasive; however, I suggest that in Villedieu's case, while the *privilèges* did show the King's sanction, they were also a pragmatic gesture designed to enable her to acquire better contracts and more money; and their wording underscores professionalism, not aristocracy or leisure. The anecdote offered by Schapira of Descartes writing to Mersenne to say that he did not want a *privilège d'auteur* because he did not want to be associated with making money, to be a 'faiseur et vendeur des livres', is illuminating in this regard.[63] That letter is shown to be tactical—he did not mind so much acquiring such a *privilège* as being seen to want to acquire it—exemplifying that for Descartes in the 1630s at least, the *privilège d'auteur* was associated with a professionalisation which he did not want to be seen to seek. As Keller-Rahbé has shown, Villedieu's *privilèges d'auteur* affirm the 'partenariat professionnel auctrice/libraire, reconnu et "autorisé" d'abord par le roi, puis par le syndic des libraires, et au terme de la chaîne, par les lecteurs' (the professional partnership between the author and the bookseller, recognised and 'authorised' by the King, then by the syndic of booksellers, and, at the end of the chain, by

---

[59] Schapira, 'Quand le privilège de librairie publie l'auteur', pp. 124–29.

[60] Clément and Keller-Rahbé, 'Introduction', p. 8.

[61] Turnovsky, *The Literary Market*, p. 44. On the King as the royal reader, see Claire Lévy-Lelouche, 'Quand le privilège de librairie publie le roi', p. 147.

[62] Schapira, 'Quand le privilège de librairie publie l'auteur', p. 123.

[63] Descartes to Mersenne, 27 April 1637, in *Œuvres complètes de Descartes*, ed. by Charles Adam and Paul Tannery, 12 vols (Paris: Vrin, 1982), I, p. 363–65. Quoted in Schapira, 'Quand le privilège de librairie publie l'auteur', p. 126.

the readers).[64] I argue that the *privilèges d'auteur* for Villedieu are both practical, giving her greater agency in the world of print, and symbolic of her willingness to be seen to engage in that commerce. In this section, I read in tandem the prefaces and *privilèges* of her plays and novels set in antiquity in order to trace how she connects her conception of authorship to her historical fiction.

In the prefaces to the works that follow *Manlius*, Villedieu frames her approaches to ancient history in such a way as to anticipate a critical audience, continuing the *querelle* that had surrounded *Manlius*, and continuing to ride the wave of its publicity. Her Modern and fictionalising approach to antiquity becomes associated with her name, which, at this point in her career, was Marie-Catherine Desjardins. In the preface introducing her 1664 *Nitetis*, she includes a verse *Billet* addressed to the Duc de Saint-Aignan in which she anticipates the reactions of the 'messieurs les sçavants' who, she suggests, will protest her use of the letter as opening:[65]

> Quelle faute contre l'usage!
> Juste ciel! quel dérèglement!
> Quoy! renverser ainsi la belle économie,
> Dont Voiture et Balzac ont tracé leurs écrits?
> Et que dira l'Académie?
> Que diront tous les beaux esprits? (np)

> What a violation of convention!
> Good Heaven! What a great disorder!
> What! Overturn the fine, harmonious pattern,
> That Voiture and Balzac laid out in their writings!
> What will the Academy say?
> What will all the refined wits have to say?[66]

She then claims to agree with one she describes as 'ce docte', suggesting that 'en bonne police, la République des Lettres devrait me condamner à l'amende' ('The Republic of Letters ought, according to proper policy, sentence me to pay a fine') (np).[67] Significant is the way in which she suggests she has avoided any judgement by having placed her name at the top of the *Billet*:

> Que pour mieux éviter cette punition
> J'ai d'abord mis mon nom en tête,
> Car on sait que sur la requête

---

[64] Keller-Rahbé, 'Pratiques et usages du privilège d'auteur', p. 83.
[65] Marie-Catherine Desjardins, *Nitetis* (Paris: Barbin, 1664), np.
[66] Gethner, ed. and trans., *Challenges to Traditional Authority*, p. 115.
[67] Ibid.

> Desjardins n'est pas trop sujet à caution.
> Bien que ma fortune soit basse,
> Et qu'on croit rarement un poète sur sa foy,
> Sitôt qu'en quelque lieu vous lirez que c'est moy,
> À ce nom, poursuivez, de grâce [...]

> That the better to avoid any prejudging,
> I at once put my name at the top,
> For it's well known that on petitions,
> Desjardins is not a name to be wary of.
> Although I have but little wealth
> And a poet's word is rarely credited
> As soon as anywhere you read that it is I,
> Seeing this name, I beg, keep on reading.[68]

Her name vouches against the 'punition', even though poets are never (to be) believed. It is tempting to read her comments about the violation of prefatory convention as also extending to her fictionalising approach to ancient history. In this reading, the recourse to her name takes on a certain irony: by 1664 her name had been associated with the (notorious) poem 'Jouissance' and the *Manlius* controversy: perhaps other instances where she affronted the 'messieurs les sçavants'. Her gesture also indicates an awareness of her name as a sign of both authority and a style, as having a certain currency, one that she associates with displeasing the 'savants'.[69]

The importance placed here on her name is consolidated by her decision to solicit for the first time in 1665 a *privilège d'auteur* for her next work, the contemporary play, *Le Favory*. The *privilège* is presented to 'Notre bien aimée LA DEMOISELLE DESJARDINS' (our beloved DEMOISELLE DESJARDINS) and, as Keller-Rahbé describes, it 'resembles an enthronement' in its lengthy description of royal favour, with her name and that of the King in capital letters.[70] Far more than the skeleton judicial-economic text, this *privilège* announces the author as a figure of favour and esteem.[71] In this *privilège* it is also specified that one copy of the book will be given to the royal library, and another to the library of the Chancellor,

---

[68] Ibid., p. 116.

[69] The language she uses in this preface, such as 'Nitetis prend la liberté de vous rendre une visite' (np) ('Nitetis is taking the liberty of paying you a visit') (Gethner, p. 114), whereby she figures Nitetis as personally coming to visit Saint-Aignan (a trope she also uses in the *Manlius* preface), recalls the tropes of *belles infidèles* translation prefaces and constitutes another way of anchoring her poetics to a style that openly takes liberties with classical sources.

[70] Keller-Rahbé, 'Pratiques et usages du privilège d'auteur', p. 85.

[71] It is an example of a *privilège* that falls into the category of what Schapira describes as the 'privilège avec louange', Schapira, 'Quand le privilège de librairie publie l'auteur', p. 131.

Pierre Séguier. This gives an additional shape to that royal favour: the royal library becomes a sort of copyright library, inclusion in this collection indicating prestige and approval.[72]

Villedieu also solicited a *privilège* for her next publication, her first complete novel, and first ancient historical fiction, *Carmente, histoire Grecque* (1668), dedicated to the Duchesse de Nemours, and prefaced with a dedication to the Reader. The first page of the story, which starts just after the *privilège*, explicitly links it to *Manlius*: 'par l'auteur de Manlius', with 'l'auteur' reinforcing the status imparted by the *privilège*.[73] This *privilège d'auteur* is less ostentatious (there is no capitalisation at all here and no lengthy description of royal favour); and yet, the more legal-economic chord also underscores the formal nature of this document, making more striking its female *exposante*: her name is figured twice—'Mademoiselle Desjardins' and 'Ladite Demoiselle Desjardins'—and her professional and legal actions underscored.[74]

The presence of two dedications, to the Duchess and to the Reader, confirms Turnovsky's assessment that there sometimes was not a clear-cut distinction between patronage and commerce. As Nathalie Grande has also shown, it was around this time that Villedieu shifted from relying on primarily patronage to appealing to commerce.[75] The language of the two dedications also recalls approaches taken in *Manlius* and *Nitetis*: she thanks the Duchess for her support, figuring the 'témérité' of her own 'zèle'.[76] In the address to the reader, whom she figures intimately in the second person singular, she affirms her approach to history:[77]

> Assez d'autres auteurs ont pris le soin de peindre des héros fabuleux, pour moi, je ne sais figurer que des hommes ordinaires, mais pour peu que tu aies d'indulgence pour eux, peut-être les trouveras-tu assez tendres et galants, pour ne leur souhaiter aucune des qualités, que mon sexe, et mon ignorance dans le métier de la guerre, me défendent de leur donner.[78]

> Enough other authors have taken pains to paint legendary heroes; I only know how to depict ordinary men, but as long as you have some indulgence towards them, maybe you will find them *galant* and tender enough and not wish for them any of those qualities, which my sex and my ignorance in matters of war prevent me from giving them.

---

[72] My thanks to John O'Brien for his guidance here.

[73] Marie-Catherine Desjardins, *Carmente, histoire Grecque par Mademoiselle Desjardins* (Paris: Barbin, 1668), p. 1. On the history of the term 'auteur' and its feminine 'autrice', see the Introduction.

[74] Desjardins, *Carmente*, np.

[75] Grande, *Stratégies*, pp. 266–67.

[76] Desjardins, *Carmente*, np.

[77] On the use of the second person, see Grande, 'Discours paratextuel et stratégie d'écriture', p. 173.

[78] Desjardins, *Carmente*, np.

124   WOMEN WRITING ANTIQUITY

This approach is once again presented as oppositional, framed in contrast to 'autres auteurs'. She also genders her stance, linking the 'tendre' and 'galant' nature of it to her ignorance of war.

In these examples from *Manlius*, *Nitetis*, *Le Favory*, and *Carmente*, we encounter the shaping of historical fiction that also informs and is informed by her authorial persona: this persona was to be recognised, and so was marshalled as a way of marketing her books in a certain way. I suggest that if we read her *privilèges* alongside and in combination with her prefatory material, they construct an authorial ethos that is entrepreneurial and commerce-orientated (with the King's sanction crucial, but towards her as author, not aristocrat at leisure); this orientation is explicitly linked to her *galant* version of ancient history. This aesthetic is present across other prefaces to her historical fictions set in different periods, but the stakes are particularly significant for ancient history where the modernising and even subversive effect of her *galantisation* is keenly felt.

She makes this clear in the *Épistre au Roy* introducing her next ancient historical novel, *Les Amours des grands hommes* (1671–72).[79] She once again figures the 'savants', this time who object to the changes she has made to history, as her enemies. She anticipates the attack, harking back to the *Manlius querelle*: 'Je ne doute pas que les savants ne se révoltent contre cette métamorphose, et je crois déjà les entendre dire que je viole le respect dû à la sacrée antiquité. Mais je ne sais s'ils trouveraient autant d'exemples pour soutenir leur censure, que j'en ai pour autoriser ma licence' (I imagine that the savants will revolt against this metamorphosis and I think I can already hear them saying that I have violated the respect due to sacred antiquity. But I do not know if they would find as many examples to justify their censure as I have to authorise my licence).[80] She links this approach clearly to her own authorial persona: 'Quoiqu'il en soit, mon sexe sera mon retranchement. Il est permis aux dames de chercher des endroits sensibles dans les cœurs les plus illustres, et celles qui ne peuvent y parvenir par leurs charmes, sont en droit de se tracer un autre chemin' (be that as it may, I will double down on my sex. Women are allowed to uncover the sensitivities of the most illustrious, and women who cannot acquire these through their charms are permitted to find another route).[81] She appropriates a learned vocabulary—'métamorphose' is surely intended to evoke Ovid—in her anticipation of the attacks she will receive; her comment also reveals her savvy exploitation of the association between fictionalised history and 'women's writing', such that her gender becomes part of the branding. But there is also a sense of irony here: 'retranchement' suggests that in

---

[79] On this preface, see Grande, 'Introduction générale' to *Les Amours des grands hommes* (pp. 11–14), and Edwige Keller-Rahbé, '"Je crois déjà les entendre dire"'.

[80] *Les Amours des Grands Hommes, par M. de Villedieu* (Paris: Barbin, 1671), np.

[81] Ibid., np.

making her 'sexe' her defence, she is turning to her profit and advantage the very degrading of 'women's writing' she and others endured.[82]

Her *Amours des grands hommes* was also afforded a *privilège d'auteur* and her name once again proves significant. By 1671 she was publishing under the name of 'Madame de Villedieu'—this change had taken place in her 1669 novel *Cléonice* and is evident on both its title page and the *privilège de libraire*.[83] Keller-Rahbé and Grande suggest several reasons for her shift in name: the most obvious is the emotive and personal one, which is that she may have taken on this name after the death of her lover in an act of homage and mourning. However, as they show, her adoption of 'Madame de Villedieu' as signature also coincides, largely, with a shift in her career, from the poetry and plays of her early days as 'Marie-Catherine Desjardins' to the novels of 'Madame de Villedieu'. The new name also carried more respectability: both the title and the name itself afforded Villedieu a social status she had thus far lacked, given that Antoine de Boësset had been the son of a well-known court musician and superintendent of music. And an elevated social status mitigated against the risks of publishing.[84]

And yet, Villedieu's name was still not a stable entity: indeed, she plays with its instability, in part, perhaps, gesturing to the playful salon practices of naming and pseudonymity, and to their reflection in the literary *romans à clé* which she herself also wrote. For instance, *Les Amours des grands hommes* is presented on the title page as being by 'M. de Villedieu' (which is also the case for her 1675 *Les Desordres de l'amour*); however, the dedication to the King is signed in the feminine with 'la tres fidele servante et sujette Desjardins de Villedieu' and the two separate *privilèges d'auteur* afforded for this text (for tomes 1 and tome 3) are for 'La Dame Desjardins'. The first of these is very similar to that of *Le Favory* in its ostentatious descriptions of the King's favour: she is described as 'Nostre chere & bien amée la Dame DESJARDINS, veuve du feu Sieur DE VILLEDIEU' (our beloved Lady Desjardins, widow of the late Sieur de Villedieu).[85]

Les Amours des grands hommes, attributed on the title to M. de Villedieu, with a dedication signed in the feminine as 'Desjardins de Villedieu' and a *privilège* for 'la Dame Desjardins, veuve du feu sieur de Villledieu', thus represents the peak of her playful naming. It can hardly be the case that this pseudonym of M. de Villedieu was intended in any way to mask the real author, give that her name is then offered, but it may be an ironic nod to the norms of attributing work by women to male relatives. Her playful variations here emphasise, ironically, the

---

[82] Her discussion here of modifying ancient history also expands on the theorisation of historical fiction explicated in her *Annales galantes*, published a year earlier in 1670.

[83] The novel she published after *Cléonice*, the *Annales galantes* (1670), has no author name on the title page or in the *privilège de libraire*.

[84] Keller-Rahbé and Grande, 'Villedieu ou les avatars d'un nom d'écrivain(e)', pp. 12–21. For a brief discussion of her name, see also DeJean, *Tender Geographies*, p. 130.

[85] *Les Amours des grands hommes, par M. de Villedieu*, np. See Keller-Rahbé, 'Pratiques et usages du privilège d'auteur', pp. 92–93.

126 WOMEN WRITING ANTIQUITY

patrilinear relationship of women to names, and perhaps also parallel the many names to which intellectual women were subject in this period (*précieuse*, 'femme savante', etc.).[86] Pragmatically, gathering together all the names associated with her was a way of making it clear that there was one author behind these identities, so that despite the plurality they in fact affirm her authorship. In so doing, Villedieu draws attention to the connection between (self)-naming and authorship, in a way that chimes with the notion of the 'author-function', that is, the practice of the attribution of works to a sole author, a figure who is to an extent an imaginary construction. Where Foucault does not pay much attention to naming itself, Villedieu's acts remind us of the centrality of naming to the creation of an author.[87] She nods ironically to the place of naming in the act of making one's name.

Her name continues to take on a significant role in the twin *privilèges d'auteur* for *Les Galanteries grenadines* and *Les Exilés*, afforded together (6 February 1672),[88] in which she is credited in this legal document as 'La Dame de Villedieu'.[89] This name is placed, as Keller-Rahbé notes, 'triumphantly', second only to the King (and thus not preceded by the usual list of other officials).[90] In soliciting an author *privilège*, Villedieu willingly parades her involvement in the commerce of the book trade; she also marks, with all these names, both the process of self-naming and her gender. The authorial ethos Villedieu constructs not only values the commercial success of *galant* ancient historical fictions but also exploits the expectations of 'women's writing', both in her self-conscious focus on sentiment within her works and, as we have seen, in the emphasis on the processes of coming to authorship that her naming reveals.

Villedieu makes the link between gender and her approach to history in her late, posthumously published *Annales galantes de Grèce* (1687). It has no preface but the opening paragraphs provide a theoretical statement of intention:

> Assez d'auteurs celebres ont pris le soin d'écrire les actions mémorables des anciens grecs et de les faire passer jusques à nous. Ils en portent la gloire si haut, qu'ils nous ont donné sujet de douter si ce qu'ils rapportent comme des vérités

---

[86] For a discussion of this in more general terms, see Keller-Rahbé and Grande, 'Villedieu ou les avatars d'un nom d'écrivain(e)', p. 6; and in relation to Villedieu's gesture, see also DeJean, *Tender Geographies*, p. 130.

[87] Michel Foucault, 'Qu'est-ce qu'un auteur?', *Bulletin de la société française de philosophie*, 63 (1969), 73–104. See Kate E. Tunstall and Wilda Anderson, eds, *Naming, Un-Naming, and Re-Naming in Early Modern and Enlightenment Europe* (= *Romance Studies*, 31.3–4 (2013)), especially the 'Introductory Note' by Kate E. Tunstall, pp. 137–38. See also Neil Kenny on the 'family function' for ways in which names and the 'author function' coincide in early modern France. Neil Kenny, *Born to Write: Literary Families and Social Hierarchy in Early Modern France* (Oxford: Oxford University Press, 2020), pp. 35–42.

[88] Keller-Rahbé, 'Pratiques et usages du privilège d'auteur', p. 87.

[89] This is in the 1679 Lyon edition of *Les Exilés* by Amaulry—the *privilège* concludes: 'et ledit Claude Barbin a fait part de son droit de privilège à Thomas Amaulry.'

[90] Keller-Rahbé, 'Pratiques et usages du privilège d'auteur', p. 85.

historiques, en sont en effet, ou si ce sont d'agréables fictions, mais aucun ne s'est encore avisé de parler des Grecques fameuses.[91]

A sufficient number of famous authors have taken care to write the memorable actions of ancient Greek men and to pass them down to us. They present their glory in such a way that we might doubt whether what they relay are historical facts or pleasant fictions, but no one has thought to talk about famous Greek women.

She emphasises: 'cependant il me semble que les nations étant composées des deux sexes, on ne peint la Grèce qu'à demi, quand on n'en peint que les grands hommes; ajoûtons quelques traits à cette peinture, et disons aujourd'hui quelque chose des dames' (however, it seems to me that since nations are composed of two sexes, we are only getting half the picture of Greece when it is only great men who are described: let us add some detail to this image and say something today of the women).[92] Villedieu thus consciously links questions of women's presence and visibility in literary culture with her own *galant* approach. She then anticipates accusations of temerity and of a lack of factual accuracy using a familiar formula:

Au pis aller, je ne commets que moi, et ne m'expose qu'au péril d'être blâmée d'un peu de témérité, ou de n'avoir pas mis les matières assez fidellement en œuvre; le hasard n'est pas mortel, embarquons-nous sur cette risque, et commençons nos Annales de Grèce par les malheurs de la Princesse Phronine.[93]

At worst, I risk only myself and expose only myself to the peril of being blamed for a little bit of temerity or for having not faithfully rendered matters in my work; the danger is not life-threatening, let us take this risk and start our Annals of Greece with the story of the Princess Phronine.

By this point in her career, there is surely very little 'péril', and yet the term here, linked with her 'témérité', traces a line back to her *Manlius* and reminds readers of her long career as a writer of a certain kind of historical fiction.

With this very notion of an aesthetic associated with her name comes a shift from the approaches we encountered in Scudéry's writing. While Villedieu also distances herself from *savant* culture, this gesture is not, as it was for Scudéry, part of an elaborate presentation of modesty which corresponded to Scudéry's detachment towards the book trade. Instead, Villedieu's opposition to *savant* culture is couched in terms that promote her commercial prowess, her popularity,

---

[91] Madame de Villedieu, *Annales galantes de Grèce* (Paris: Barbin, 1687), pp. 1–2.

[92] *Annales galantes de Grèce*, p. 3. For a discussion, see Sophie Houdard, 'Les fictions du non-mariage: Mme de Villedieu et le personnage de la femme naturelle et publique', *Littératures classiques*, 55.3 (2004), 225–42.

[93] *Annales galantes de Grèce*, pp. 4–5.

128 WOMEN WRITING ANTIQUITY

and her authorial identity. She makes a direct link between that success and the broad appeal of her historical fiction as *galant*, as changing ancient history to update it to suit and reflect contemporary society. While that approach of fictionalising ancient history and making a success of it owes a debt to Scudéry, Villedieu is distinct in the way she frames and values such an approach as commercially successful. In the next section, I explore Villedieu's legacy by considering the cases of two of her successors in this field, Catherine Bernard and Anne de La Roche-Guilhen.

Legacies: Catherine Bernard and Anne de La Roche-Guilhen

Villedieu consolidated the commercial value of ancient historical fiction and made a space for women in this market. This is evident from the fact that, after her writing, ancient historical fictions by women continued to be a route for literary success. That success can be traced in particular by looking (briefly) at two case studies: Catherine Bernard (1662–1712) and Anne de La Roche-Guilhen (1644–1707/10), both authors of novels and theatre, who both turned productively to ancient historical fiction.[94] Unsurprisingly Claude Barbin figures in their careers: he published all of La Roche-Guilhen's narrative fictions in Paris before she left France definitively for London in 1685 to live as a Huguenot exile; he also published Catherine Bernard's third novel *Le Comte d'Amboise* in 1687.

La Roche-Guilhen, along with Villedieu and Scudéry, is defined by Grande as a professional novelist: she too was from minor nobility and unmarried (Villedieu was unmarried at least at the time of her publications)—circumstances which underpinned their need to make profit from their work.[95] Unlike Villedieu and Scudéry (who were Catholic) and unlike Catherine Bernard and Anne Dacier, who converted to Catholicism just before the Revocation of the Edict of Nantes, in 1685 La Roche-Guilhen became a Huguenot refugee, selling her manuscripts to various publishers in Holland and living in exile in London; her works circulated clandestinely in France.[96] She primarily wrote narrative fiction, but also translated from Spanish and wrote one theatrical comedy, *Rare-en-tout*, in 1677.[97] Although attribution of her work has been inconsistent and often unreliable, in particular with

[94] René Démoris also sees Anne de La Roche-Guilhen, Marie-Catherine d'Aulnoy, and Catherine Durand as Villedieu's 'héritières'. René Démoris, 'Écriture féminine en *je* et subversion des savoirs chez Mme de Villedieu (*Les Mémoires d'Henriette-Sylvie de Molière*)', in *Femmes savantes, savoir des femmes: du crépuscule de la Renaissance à l'aube des Lumières*, ed. by Colette Nativel (Geneva: Droz, 1999), pp. 197–208 (p. 202).

[95] Grande, *Stratégies des romancières*, p. 299.

[96] See Alexandre Calame, *Anne de La Roche-Guilhen: romancière huguenote, 1644–1707* (Geneva: Droz, 1972).

[97] See 'Anne de La Roche-Guilhen (1644–1707)', in *Théâtre de femmes de l'Ancien Régime*, ed. by Evain, Gethner, and Goldwyn, pp. 253–513.

some of her works having been wrongly attributed to Villedieu, La Roche-Guilhen was also a significant voice in the 'galantisation' of ancient historical fiction, capitalising on the viability of its commercial success as established by Villedieu.[98] A third of her works were set in antiquity, of which the most well-known and studied is her 1697 *Histoire des favorites*.[99]

Her ancient fictions also explicitly trace a line back to Villedieu and to Scudéry: she places herself in their tradition. As I have explored elsewhere, the Livie story in her *Histoire des favorites*, which centres on Ovid, reworks and responds to Villedieu's portrayal of 'Ovide' in her *Exilés*. In the 1695 *Sapho ou l'heureuse inconstance*, for which the attribution to La Roche-Guilhen remains uncertain, Scudéry is evoked in the preface dedicated to the Reader, as communicator of the *savant* stories about Sappho to the 'beau sexe':[100]

Le nom de Sapho est si célébre et chez les sçavans et parmi le beau sexe même, après les vives peintures que l'illustre Madamoiselle de Scuderi en a faites dans son *Grand Cyrus*, que ce sera inspirer de la curiosité de reste aux lecteurs amoureux des galanteries Grecques, que de leur dire qu'ils trouveront ici une circonstance anecdote de cette dixieme muse, dont nos auteurs modernes se sont point encore avisez de faire aucune mention.[101]

Sappho's name is so famous among the learned and among women, thanks to the vivid portraits by the illustrious Mlle de Scudéry in her *Grand Cyrus*, that it will stir the curiosity of readers who admire Greek *galanteries* to tell them that they will encounter here an anecdotal tale about the tenth muse that no modern author has recounted.

In this tale, La Roche-Guilhen (?) also responds to the version by Scudéry by offering her own, innovative take on Sapho's story, telling us that she will narrate an

---

[98] For example, her *Astérie ou Tamerlan* was included in the *Œuvres de Madame de Villedieu*, 12 vols (Paris: Compagnie des Libraires, 1721), xi, pp. 1–150.

[99] See Isabelle Trivisani-Moreau, 'Anne de La Roche-Guilhen et la galanterie des anciens', in *La Galanterie des anciens*, ed. by Nédélec and Grande, pp. 177–91 (p. 179). They are *Arioviste, histoire romaine* (Paris: Barbin, 1674–75); *Intrigues amoureuses de quelques anciens Grecs* (The Hague: van Bulderen, 1690); *Amours de Neron* (The Hague: Troyel, 1695); *Histoire des favorites* (Amsterdam: Marret, 1697); *Sapho, ou l'heureuse inconstance* (The Hague: Troyel, 1695); *Histoires curieuses et galantes ou dernières œuvres de Mlle de La Roche-Guilhen* (Amsterdam: Marret, 1709), containing 'Agripine, histoire romaine' and 'Hieron, roi de Syracuse'; and *La Nouvelle Talestris, histoire galante* (Amsterdam: Marret, 1721). See also Helena Taylor, *The Lives of Ovid in Seventeenth-Century French Culture* (Oxford: Oxford University Press, 2017), pp. 97–106.

[100] It is mentioned in the catalogue of her works added to the 1703 edition of the *Histoire des Favorites* by Paul Marret. See Calame, *Anne de La Roche-Guilhen: romancière huguenote, 1644–1707*, pp. 63–64, and Trivisani-Moreau, 'Anne de La Roche-Guilhen et la galanterie des anciens', p. 180.

[101] La Roche-Guilhen (?), *Sapho ou l'heureuse inconstance*, np.

'anecdote' that has been overlooked.[102] Like Scudéry's Sapho, La Roche-Guilhen's leaves Lesbos and does not commit suicide, but instead of finding peace with the Lacedemonions and a platonic committed relationship with Phaon, she marries a man called Cercille.[103] While the differences in plot are themselves worthy of note and further study, it is particularly the fact of these differences, her reference to the 'anecdote', which is significant in that it draws attention to the act of reception itself, to the creative spaces of *galant* fiction, and thus to the very generic ethos of the *histoire galante*.

Unlike Villedieu or Scudéry, La Roche-Guilhen makes her economic motivations clear, which I argue suggests that Villedieu enabled a shift in practice, whereby it became acceptable to lay claim to such motivations. In the preface to her *Hieron, roi de Syracuse*, published in 1709, La Roche-Guilhen writes:

> Quoy que les romans ne soient plus à la mode, on est quelquefois obligé d'en faire: et il se trouve toujours des gens qui les lisent. [...] Ceux qui travaillent pour la seule gloire ne doivent produire que des chef-d'œuvres, mais quand on fait des livres par de certains motifs, on mérite tres certainement des indulgences pleinières.[104]

> Although novels are no longer in fashion, sometimes one is still sometimes obliged to write them and there are always people who read them. Those who work for glory alone should only produce masterpieces; but when one writes for other motives, one surely deserves plenary indulgence.

In a reversal of some of the usual tropes of modesty as the antitheses of financial gain, La Roche-Guilhen turns her need to write for profit into a gesture of humility (underscored by the religious language of 'indulgences pleinières'). She seems to draw a link between this humility and her decision to turn to ancient history: 'La vie d'Hiéron n'est point ignorée. Les auteurs célèbres nous l'ont apprise [...]. Cela suffit pour fournir des faits, des temps et des lieux qui sont les seules règles nècessaires pour ces sortes de bagatelles (The life of Hieron is not unknown. Famous authors have recounted it to us. And their versions provide the facts, times, and locations which are the only rules necessary for these sorts of frivolities).[105] She implies that she has not had to come up with a plot from scratch which has accelerated her process and thus made her writing more profitable for being more prolific. Her circumstances prevented her from ever soliciting a *privilège d'auteur*,

---

[102] On rhetoric of the genre of the secret history, see Rebecca Bullard, *The Politics of Disclosure, 1674–1725: Secret History Narratives* (London: Routledge, 2009).

[103] Joan DeJean mentions this text briefly, attributing it to La Roche-Guihen to underscore how the term 'galant' had taken on a more licentious meaning by the end of the century. DeJean, *Tender Geographies*, p. 256.

[104] Anne de La Roche Guilhen, 'Hieron, roi de Syracuse', in *Histoires curieuses ou dernières ouvrages de Mlle de La Roche-Guilhen*, pp. 248–50.

[105] Ibid., p. 248.

but La Roche-Guilhen's career and the value of historical fiction within attests to the influence of Villedieu's success.[106]

We see a variant example of this with Catherine Bernard, playwright, novelist, and *conteuse*, who followed her two historical novels, *Éléonor d'Yvrée* (1687) and *Le comte d'Amboise* (1689), with two extremely successful tragedies for the *Comédie-Française* (as the first woman to have her plays performed at this theatre), both of which were set in antiquity: her *Laodamia, Reine d'Épire* (1689), performed twenty-two times; and *Brutus* (1690), performed twenty-five times. They thus represent some of the most successful plays of the closing decades of the century.[107] The choice of classical subjects and the genre of tragedy allow for comparisons with the major figures of Corneille and Racine; and their success suggests a continued appetite for such theatre. There were some differences, however, in the authorial strategies surrounding each play: *Laodamia* was never published in Bernard's lifetime, and although it is set in ancient Epirus and the characters could be said to derive from a passing reference in Justin, the plot is an invention and not a new version of a classical source.[108] *Brutus*, on the other hand, was published in 1691, with a *privilège d'auteur* afforded to 'M. B', feminised in the second mention as 'ladite M. B', a dedication to Louis XIV's daughter, Madame La Duchesse de Bourbon-Condé, as well as a Preface.[109] It retells the famous story of Brutus from Livy and Plutarch, albeit not focusing on the best-known events of the rape of Lucretia, Brutus's expulsion of the Tarquins, and the founding of the Republic, but rather the later events leading up to his decision to have his sons, Titus and Tiberinus, executed for treason.[110]

While both plays could be seen to follow the model of Villedieu and Scudéry in privileging the sentimental lives of rulers and, in the case of *Laodamia*, a concern with female-centric narratives (*Laodamia* has been appraised for its representation of a powerful female ruler in a period of Salic law and its nuanced discussion of female friendship), it is particularly *Brutus* that merits attention here because of its overt rewriting of ancient history.[111] In the preface in which Bernard self-consciously notes that she is responding to critics, she defends herself against the

---

[106] La Roche-Guilhen, once exiled, used the extensive and partially clandestine networks of French publishers in Amsterdam. See Keller-Rahbé, 'Pratiques et usages des privilèges d'auteur', p. 82.

[107] Aurore Evain and others, eds, *Théâtre de femmes de l'Ancien Régime, Tome III, XVIIe–XVIIIe siècles* (Paris: Garnier, 2022), p. 31.

[108] Ibid., p. 37.

[109] Catherine Bernard, *Brutus, tragédie* (Paris: Gontier, 1691). The edition used here is Catherine Bernard, *Brutus*, in *Théâtre de femmes de l'Ancien Régime, Tome III, XVIIe–XVIIIe siècles*, ed. by Evain and others, pp. 101–74.

[110] Bernard's *Brutus* had a complex reception history: it was attributed to Fontenelle around the time of the controversy surrounding Voltaire's *Brutus* in 1730. See Nina Ekstein, 'Appropriation and Gender: The Case of Catherine Bernard and Bernard de Fontenelle', *Eighteenth-Century Studies*, 30.1 (1996), 59–80.

[111] See Derval Conroy, 'The Displacement of Disorder: Gynæcocracy and Friendship in Catherine Bernard's *Laodamia* (1689)', *Papers on French Seventeenth-Century Literature*, 67 (2007), 443–64.

132   WOMEN WRITING ANTIQUITY

accusations that she has painted Brutus too sympathetically.[112] As we saw in the discussion of Scudéry's representation of Brutus in her novel, *Clélie*, the Roman was famously depicted by Plutarch as being stony-faced at the deaths of his sons (*Lives I, Publicola*, VI), picking up on his response to Lucretia's rape where he 'castigated' Lucretius and Collatinus 'for their tears' (Livy, 1.59.4). Scudéry, following Livy's more sensitive account of his witnessing the death of his sons, softened her representation of Brutus in this scene.[113] Bernard also tempers his response to their death in her play (he wavers in his monologue in 5.6, and expresses his 'peine' in 5.7).[114] In the preface, she suggests that it is Livy's portrait of Brutus's 'sentiments' at his sons' execution that emboldened her, that gave her the 'témérité' to portray him as more sensitive.[115] She also argues that such a portrayal better suits the focus of her play on the intimate spaces and private life of this public figure—'je ne l'ai pas représenté dans le Sénat [...] mais dans un lieu, et dans le temps où il pouvait laisser agir les mouvements les plus secrets de son cœur' (I did not represent him in the Senate but in a place and at a time when he might allow the most secret movements of his heart to act)—and, relatedly, that it is better suited to contemporary mores:

> Quand même j'aurais un peu changé le caractère de Brutus, je n'aurais fait que rapprocher de nos mœurs une action qui en est fort éloignée, qui est extraordinaire même dans les mœurs romaines; et c'est, ce me semble, la pratique commune du théâtre que, pourvu que l'on conserve l'essentiel des actions, on est assez maître des motifs et des autres circonstances.[116]

> Even if I may have slightly changed Brutus's character, I would have only brought closer to our customs a story that is at a distance from them and that was extraordinary even for the Romans; such, it seems to me, are the common practices of theatre, that as long as one conserves the core events, one can be master of motivations and other details.

I suggest that Bernard is following Villedieu in her broad approach in changing historical details in theatre and following Scudéry in the precise version of Brutus.

---

[112] See also Nina Ekstein, 'A Woman's Tragedy: Catherine Bernard's *Brutus*', *Rivista di letterature moderne e comparate*, 48.2 (1995), 127–39.

[113] Livy: 'cum inter omne tempus pater voltusque et os eius spectaculo esset eminente animo patrio inter publicae poenae ministerium' ('while through it all men gazed at the expression on the father's face, where they might clearly read a father's anguish, as he administered the nation's retribution'). Livy, *History of Rome, Volume I: Books 1–2*, trans. by B. O. Foster, Loeb Classical Library 114 (Cambridge, MA: Harvard University Press, 1919), 2.5.

[114] Bernard, *Brutus*, p. 170. He also states to Titus, one of his sons: 'Je t'ai dû condamner; je ne m'en repens pas. / Mais je sens que ma mort va suivre ton trépas' (I ought to have condemned you, I do not regret this. But I feel that my own death will follow yours) (p. 170, lines 1469–70).

[115] Ibid., p. 106.

[116] Ibid.

Like Villedieu, Bernard modifies ancient history by removing some of the violence of the ancient story; she also explicates the stakes of her 'bold' actions in the preface in relation to both theatre and to antiquity. While she does not cite Scudéry, it is hard to imagine that she would not have been familiar with *Clélie* and the story of Brutus it contains: she seeks a classical source to justify a change which a reader will also recognise as having been effected and amplified already by Scudéry. Here, then, we have the familiar story of de-militarisation of heroes, of a focus on sentiment away from violence; but I think we also have the story of a lineage and a legacy of such approaches to antiquity filtered through a very precise example of the reworking of a single story (Brutus) and theme (father-son execution, as in Manlius sparing his son). Even if this is not a conscious nod to those authors and approaches, it still bears the trace of their influence, and Bernard's own temerity was perhaps far less risky given the guarantee of the commercial success of such an approach exemplified by Villedieu.

**

We do not know exactly how much writers were paid for their works but Henri-Jean Martin suggests a novel would have sold for 300 livres in 1690; and we might expect more for someone as successful as Scudéry or Villedieu.[117] As Turnovsky reminds us, it is hard to grasp the capital these actual figures relate to, not only in terms of conversion rates and income but also because, as he points out, the actual money itself only reveals so much about success in the literary market.[118] I have suggested in this chapter that Villedieu found a formula that united commercial success with the more abstract, symbolic prestige of the literary market—forces often considered to be at odds with each other—since her very version of ancient history was predicated on its wide appeal, on its being extricated from the exclusionary circles of the 'savants'. Her projection of her authorial identity embraced the entrepreneurship of the book trade, something which Scudéry avoided making explicit. Indeed, we might see more similarities between Villedieu and Gournay in the way that both authors invested their work with their names. She pushed against the paradigm of aristocratic detachment, but in doing so she was also in step with other key figures of her time. Villedieu's case therefore troubles the Bourdieusian dichotomy between commercial and intellectual prestige even if that dichotomy has occasionally come into play in relation to the reception of her works.

With her approach that values commercial success and a version of antiquity fit for a wider readership and speedy consumption, Villedieu shifts once more what we might understand 'literary value' to entail, moving it on from the more restrained relationship to the market represented by Scudéry. This is a question

---

[117] Henri-Jean Martin, 'L'Édition Parisienne au XVII siècle: quelques aspects économiques', *Annales*, 7.3 (1952), 303–18.

[118] Turnovsky, *The Literary Market*, p. 27.

that we will see again in Chapter 6 when we look at the work of the *conteuses* who defined a new genre in which they opposed the learned culture represented by antiquity while re-interpreting its literature. In the next chapter we will think about another, very different, approach to classical sources in the poetic work of Antoinette Deshoulières, who practised a detachment more in keeping with the paradigm of this period. However, as one of the few women to publish a full collection of poetry, under her own name—for which she too had solicited a *privilège d'auteur*—the question of authorial identity remains present.

5

Salon Verse and the Philosopher-Poet

In 1688 when Antoinette Deshoulières (1638?–1694) published her first collection of eighty-eight poems, the *Poésies de Mme Des Houlières*, she took an unusual step for an aristocratic female poet. If women of seventeenth-century Paris published their poetry at all, it was usually in multi-authored *recueils*, hybrid single-authored collections of verse and prose, or journals such as the *Mercure Galant*, and not in a single-authored poetry collection.[1] It took Deshoulières some time to make this move. She had in fact received the *privilège du roi* for her first collection in 1678, ten years before its publication: her hesitation is suggestive of the discomfort towards publication and professional writing we might expect of a woman of her class. After all, Deshoulières did publish her poetry in these more typical channels—her first poems appeared in the *Recueil des portraits et éloges en vers et en prose* (1659) and many of the poems which established her reputation, such as her pastoral 'idylls', first appeared in the *Mercure Galant* in the 1670s and 1680s.[2] However, by 1688 she was ready to publish the full collection, in which she gathered most of these poems.[3] This was reprinted in 1693 and she prepared a further collection that was published posthumously in 1695, and introduced by her daughter, Antoinette Thérèse. Many of her other poems were published in editions that came out after her death.[4] She wrote three plays, of which one, *Genséric*,

---

[1] There were occasional exceptions to this practice, notably Marie-Catherine Desjardins's *Recueil de poésies* (Paris: Barbin, 1662) and *Poésies de Madame la Comtesse de La Suze* (Paris: Sercy, 1666), a slim collection of eighteen poems, which was augmented by other people's works (such as Bussy-Rabutin). Less well-known are the collections by Mlle Certain, *Nouvelles Poésies* (Paris: Loyson, 1665); Madame de Lauvergne, *Recueil de poésies* (Paris: Barbin, 1680), and Madame de Sainctonge, *Diverses poésies* (Dijon: Fay, 1714). See Linda Timmermans, *L'Accès des femmes à la culture (1598–1715)*, 2nd edn (Paris: Champion, 2005), p. 189. Henriette Coligny de La Suze also published in multi-authored *recueils*, such as the *Recueil de pièces galantes en prose et en vers de Madame la Comtesse de la Suze, d'une autre dame et de Monsieur Pellisson* (Paris: Quinet, 1668). On Deshoulières as published poet, see Volker Schröder, 'Verse and Versatility: The Poetry of Antoinette Deshoulières', in *Teaching Seventeenth- and Eighteenth-Century French Women Writers*, ed. by Faith E. Beasley (New York: Modern Language Association of America, 2011), pp. 242–49.

[2] Her first two poems were published in the *Recueil des portraits et éloges en vers et en prose, dédié à son Altesse Royale Mademoiselle* (Paris: Sercy and Barbin, 1659), pp. 310–13, 502–08. She published a number of poems in the *Mercure Galant*, which publicised her idylls by referring back to her previous successes: 'Vous avez admiré Les Moutons, admirez Les Fleurs' (You enjoyed 'Sheep'; now you can enjoy 'Flowers') (*Le Nouveau Mercure Galant*, November 1677, p. 151), and for 'Les Oiseaux': 'C'est le dernier Idylle de Madame Deshoulières' (Here is Madame Deshoulières's latest idyll') (*Mercure Galant*, May 1679, p. 237).

[3] *Poésies de Madame Des Houlières* (Paris: Vve de Mabre-Cramoisy, 1688).

[4] *Poésies de Madame Deshoulières* (Paris: Villette, 1693); *Poésies de Madame Deshoulières* (Paris: Villette, 1695); *Poësies de Mme Deshoulières. Nouvelle édition, augmentée de toutes ses oeuvres posthumes [et des poësies de Mlle Deshoulières]* (Paris: Villette, 1705). There were twelve further editions in the eighteenth century. There have been two recent ones: Deshoulières, *L'Enchantement des*

Women Writing Antiquity. Helena Taylor, Oxford University Press. © Helena Taylor (2024).
DOI: 10.1093/oso/9780192870445.003.0005

136 WOMEN WRITING ANTIQUITY

was published and performed in 1680, but poetry was her primary creative practice.[5]

The aristocratic hesitation regarding the commerce of publishing was symbolic in the sense that she suffered some financial difficulty—although perhaps it was because of this difficulty that she was all the more reluctant to publish. Her family background was one of prestige: she was daughter of Melchior de Ligier de la Garde, *chevalier de l'ordre du roi* and *maître d'hôtel* to Anne of Austria; and wife, from age thirteen, of Guillaume de la Fon de Boisguérin, seigneur des Houlières, a lieutenant colonel in Condé's service. After the Fronde ended, and her husband had extracted himself from Condé's service, and once she and her husband had accepted the amnesty offered by Louis XIV, he was appointed as Governor of Sète, and she stayed in Paris.[6] She secured legal separation of goods and persons in 1658 to protect her assets from his creditors as his military assignments had depleted his resources; he was bankrupt, and she was alone in Paris, where she began to turn her hand to poetry and hosted a salon at the rue de l'Homme Armé. Their separation was a financial formality as they did seem to maintain occasional relations since they went on to have two more children.[7] She benefitted from the support of Madame de la Calprenède and Madame de Vilaines, and received a pension from the King in 1693, a year before she died. Her poetry afforded her renown: she won the inaugural poetry prize of the *Académie française* in 1671; was elected to the *Accademia dei Ricovrati* in 1684 and to the *Académie d'Arles* in 1689; and was dubbed the 'tenth muse' by Marie-Jeanne L'Héritier in a text written to commemorate her death.[8] She is also the only woman to figure under the definition of 'poète' in the sixth edition of the *Dictionnaire de l'Académie française* (1835).[9]

---

chagrins. Poésies Complètes, ed. by Catherine Hémon-Fabre and Pierre-Eugène Leroy (Paris: Bartillat, 2005); and *Madame Deshoulières: Poésies*, ed. by Sophie Tonolo (Paris: Garnier, 2010). Many of her poems were transcribed into mansuscripts circulating in the seventeenth century, notably the MS Tallemant des Réaux 672 and 673, Bibliothèque de La Rochelle (see the critical edition: *Le Manuscrit 673 de Tallemant des Réaux*, ed. by Vincenette Maigne (Paris: Klincksieck, 1994)). On the editorial history of her poetry, see Tonolo's edition, pp. 523–24. All references will be made in the text to Tonolo's edition.

[5] *Genséric* (Paris: Barbin 1680). See also *Fragments de l'Opéra de Zoroastre et Sémiramis* (written in 1679? and never published); *Fragments de la tragédie de Jules Antoine* (1681?), first published in *Œuvres de Mme et de Mlle Deshoulières, Nouvelle édition*, 2 vols (Paris: Libraires associés, 1754).

[6] There had apparently been some drama: when Condé learnt of their plan to accept the amnesty, he had them imprisoned in the fortress of Vilvoorde; they escaped in August 1657 and got back to Paris where they were received at court. See E. Angot, 'Mme Deshoulières et l'intrigue de Rocroy', *Revue d'Histoire littéraire de la France*, 27.3 (1920), 371–93 and Perry Gethner, 'Antoinette du Ligier de la Garde', <http://siefar.org/dictionnaire/en/Antoinette_du_Ligier_de_la_Garde>.

[7] See the biography in Perry Gethner, ed. and trans., *Challenges to Traditional Authority: Plays by French Women Authors, 1650–1700*, The Other Voice in Early Modern Europe: The Toronto Series 36 (Toronto: Iter Press, 2015), p. 166.

[8] She is Dioclée of Antoine Baudeau Somaize's *Le Grand Dictionnaire des prétieuses* (Paris: Ribou, 1661), p. 105. Marie-Jeanne L'Héritier, *Le Triomphe de Madame Des-Houlières, receue dixième muse au Parnasse* (Paris: Mazuel, 1694).

[9] 'Il se dit quelquefois en parlant d'une femme. Cette femme est poète. Madame Deshoulières était un poëte aimable' (It is sometimes used for a woman: this woman is a poet. Madame Deshoulières was a pleasant poet). *Dictionnaire de l'Académie française*, 6th edn (Paris: Didot frères, 1835), p. 444. In the 5th edition of 1798 under 'poétesse', it reads: 'Femme Poëte. Il est peu usité. On dit de Sapho,

SALON VERSE AND THE PHILOSOPHER-POET   137

Her wide-ranging poetic œuvre, which includes playful burlesque poems, salon games, pastoral idylls and eclogues, La Rochefoucauldian, melancholic 'Réflexions diverses', and a nonsense version of Lucretius, reveals her classical influences; and she also reworks Anacreon and Horace, engages extensively with Virgilian pastoral, and marshals Ovid. Her œuvre also bears the trace of her philosophical formation: she was tutored by the Gassendist, Jean Dehénault, who imparted learning of ancient atomism through Epicurus and the latter's main advocate, Lucretius. Because of this background and its expression in her work she was one of few women to be considered a 'libertine' by critics from Pierre Bayle to Frédéric Lachèvre.[10]

In this chapter, I explore the range of her poetic works, from poems categorised as more playful to those considered more serious. Building on recent criticism of philosophical poetry, and on Sophie Tonolo's work both on Deshoulières and on poetic forms which bridge the literary and the social (which I am calling 'salon verse'), I show how Latin poetry, namely Lucretius and Virgilian pastoral, proves productive for Deshoulières in the exploration of her own philosophical reflections, particularly regarding the limitation of man's reason and an Epicurean conception of the unity of man and the natural world.[11] Key to her philosophy is a position of scepticism: this is borne out most obviously in her scathing treatment of reason, but is also evident in her hermeneutics. Her elusive, equivocal slipperiness, manifest especially in her marshalling of burlesque—that is, comic inversion—and irony, means she delights in challenges of and to interpretation as she reflects on poetry's capacity to have or make meaning. Reworking classical models in particular allows her to reflect explicitly on questions of interpretation. Her scepticism is also evident in her relationship to the Quarrel of the Ancients and Moderns. On the one hand, she was a prominent and recognised Modern: a version of this quarrel had provided her with some (useful?) notoriety early in her career as she was presumed to be the author of a satirical sonnet criticising Racine's *Phèdre*, part of the wider 'querelle des sonnets' of 1677 over the

---

de Deshoulières, qu'elles étoient Poëtes; mais on ne dit pas La Poëte Sapho: ce seroit le cas de dire, La poétesse ... On l'évite' (Female poet: this term is little used. Of Sappho, and of Deshoulières, one says that they were poets; but one does not say 'the poet, Sappho': in that case, one would say 'the poetess', but this term is avoided). *Dictionnaire de l'Académie française*, 5th edn (Paris: Smits, 1798), p. 312.

[10] Frédéric Lachèvre, *Les Derniers Libertins* (Paris: Champion, 1924), pp. 25–63; Pierre Bayle, *Dictionnaire historique et critique par Mr. Pierre Bayle, cinquième edition*, 4 vols (Amsterdam: Brunel, 1740), II, p. 721. See also John J. Conley, *The Suspicion of Virtue: Women Philosophers in Neoclassical France* (Ithaca: Cornell University Press, 2002), pp. 45–74.

[11] Philippe Chométy, *'Philosopher en langage des dieux': La poésie d'idées en France au siècle de Louis XIV* (Paris: Champion, 2006); and Sophie Tonolo, *Divertissement et profondeur: l'épître en vers et la société mondaine en France de Tristan à Boileau* (Paris: Champion, 2005). There is a large corpus of texts arguing for the philosophical 'seriousness' of literary works: see, for instance, Natania Meeker, *Voluptuous Philosophy: Literary Materialism in the French Enlightenment* (New York: Fordham University Press, 2006).

138   WOMEN WRITING ANTIQUITY

Ancient Racine's *Phèdre* and the Modern Pradon's *Phèdre et Hippolyte*.[12] On the other hand, throughout her work she not only deviates from the Modern position in her rejection of progress and her preference for nature over man, but also seems to undermine and question the very Quarrel itself. Unlike the authors studied so far in this book, Deshoulières goes in for less self-representation, offering instead a slippery and fictive 'palette de "moi"', as Tonolo puts it: she does not include autobiography, as Gournay did, or construct an ideal intellectual like Scudéry, or figure herself as an author of *galant* fiction as Villedieu did.[13] Instead, concomitant to her reflection on the capacity of poetry is a subtle reflection on the status of the poet. In this chapter, I will start with analysis of her version of Lucretius, then look at her pastoral, before turning to her reflections on the role of the poet, which I show are mediated through her response to Anacreon and Horace. Deshoulières does not pursue a clear ideology of learning, or modesty, or *galanterie*, as we have seen thus far, but instead, with irony, scepticism and self-parody, interrogates authoritative dogmatism and 'thinks with' a range of ancient texts and their status to explore 'authority' as both authorial and epistemological.

'Imitation de Lucrèce en galimatias fait exprès'

Antoinette Deshoulières's 'Imitation de Lucrèce en galimatias fait exprès' (pp. 443–45) was first published posthumously in the collection of her complete works of 1705, but is thought to have been written and circulated relatively early in her career, probably in 1679.[14] The 'Imitation' reveals her philosophical formation and the influence of her Gassendist and Epicurean tutelage under Jean Dehénault.[15] It will form a starting point to my analysis of her work because it illustrates so brilliantly her playfulness, her self-conscious reflection on the act of reception, and

---

[12] Because of Deshoulières's known support of Pradon's play, her connections with the Modern *mores* of the Hôtel de Bouillon salon, which Pradon also frequented, and her friendship with the Duc de Nevers, to whom some attributed the sonnet, the *Sonnet burlesque* was credited to her in the later interventions in this *querelle*, shaping subsequent attribution. We do not know who wrote this sonnet, which was most likely a collective composition; however, Deshoulières did not deny the rumours of authorship. Georges Forestier, *Jean Racine* (Paris: Gallimard, 2006), pp. 549–72. On attribution and the corpus of this quarrel see *Poésies*, ed. by Tonolo, p. 17, pp. 479–82. For a detailed analysis of her stance as a quarreller, see Helena Taylor, 'Antoinette Deshoulières's Cat: Polemical Equivocation in Salon Verse', in *Women and Querelles in Early Modern France*, ed. by Helena Taylor and Kate E. Tunstall (= *Romanic Review*, 112.3 (2021)), pp. 452–69.

[13] Tonolo, *Divertissement et profondeur*, p. 409.

[14] *Poësies de Mme Deshoulières, nouvelle édition, augmentée de toutes ses œuvres posthumes*, p. 244. On the date, see *Poésies*, ed. by Tonolo, p. 532. On the influence of Lucretius on her work more widely, see Lacey Giles, 'The Reception of *De Rerum Natura* in the Poetry of Madame Deshoulières', *Studia z Historii Filozofii*, 3 (2021), 61–95.

[15] See also her 'Ode à Monsieur de la Rochefoucauld' (pp. 241–47), written, it is assumed, in 1678, but first published in 1688, which anticipates a line used in the 'Imitation' and singles out Epicurus as 'Le plus fort de ces grands maitres' (p. 246, l. 141).

the way she mobilises parody and burlesque to underscore the hermeneutical challenge posed by philosophical poetry. Deshoulières's 58-line poem opens and closes with the invocation of Venus and so echoes the 'Hymn to Venus' that introduces Lucretius's *De Rerum Natura* (*DRN*), but in the intervening stanzas—complex to the point of incomprehensible—some of the key ideas from other parts of his poem, particularly Book 1 (on atoms and void) and Book 4 (sex), are relayed. In so far as it is a version of Lucretius, it might be situated alongside two other recent versions which Deshoulières would have known: that of Jean Dehénault (his Hymn to Venus was circulated as a manuscript as early as 1649, but not published until 1694) and of Michel de Marolles, whose prose translation was published in 1650, and re-edited in 1659, and his verse version in 1677.[16]

Her decision not to publish this translation could be seen as a dissimulative strategy given the association of Lucretian ideas with atheism, even though Pierre Gassendi, whose writing was translated into French in 1674, revived the ancient atomism of Lucretius and Epicurus by making it theologically respectable.[17] It may also have been because Lucretius was not perceived as suitable for women. Although a woman is significant in the early modern reception of Lucretius (Lucy Hutchinson was the first woman to translate Lucretius in full into English, in an unpublished version, dated to the 1650s), aspects of Lucretius' *DRN* were not considered suitable for women readers: namely the atheistic vision and the descriptions of desire and sex.[18] Marolles inserts a warning into his verse translation of Book 4 (in which Lucretius gives his most explicit account of sex), a translation intended in part for a *mondain*, and perhaps feminine, audience: 'je ne crois pas que tout le monde soit propre à lire cette section. C'est pourquoi je conseille de bonne foi à plusieurs de s'abstenir' (I do not think that everyone should read this section; I therefore counsel in good faith many not to do so).[19]

---

[16] Jean Dehénault, 'Traduction du commencement du poème de Lucrèce', in *Recueil de pièces curieuses et nouvelles, tant en prose qu'en vers*, 2 vols (The Hague: Moetjens, 1694), II, 330–33. Michel de Marolles, *Le Poète Lucrèce latin et français de la traduction de M. D. M* (Paris: Quinet, 1650), revised as Marolles, *Les six livres de Lucrèce de la nature des choses* (Paris: Luyne, 1659); Marolles, *Les Six livres de Lucrèce de la nature des choses* (Paris: Langlois, 1677).

[17] Pierre Gassendi, *Syntagma philosophiae Epicuri cum refutationibus dogmatum quae contra fidem christianam ab eo asserta sunt* (Lyon: Guillaume Barbier, 1647). François Bernier, *Abregé de la Philosophie de Gassendi* (Paris: Langlois & Langlois, 1674). On Bernier's translation, his writing on India, and their relationship to literary-philosophical writing in the form of La Fontaine's *Fables*, see Faith E. Beasley, *Versailles meets the Taj Mahal: François Bernier, Marguerite de la Sablière and Enlightening Conversations in Seventeenth-Century France* (Toronto: University of Toronto Press, 2018), pp. 170–221.

[18] Indeed, Hutchinson was criticised for translating this poem in a verse by Sir Aston Cokain which closes 'The task is masculine, and he that can / Translate *Lucretius*, is an able man'. Sir Aston Cokain, 'To my ingenuous Friend Mr. *Alexander Brome* on his Essay to translate *Lucretius*', in *Small Poems of Divers Sorts* (London: Godbid, 1658), p. 204. See *The Works of Lucy Hutchinson, Vol. 1: The Translation of Lucretius: Part 1 Introduction and Text*, ed. by Ashley Reid Barbour, David Norbrook, and Maria Cristina Zerbino (Oxford: Oxford University Press, 2011), p. xxiii.

[19] Marolles, *Les six livres de Lucrèce* (1659), p. 256. On Marolles, see Florence de Caigny, 'Les commentaires de Marolles sur ses traductions de Lucrèce en prose: vers une réception moderne orientée', in *Traduire Lucrèce: pour une histoire de la réception française du De rerum natura (XVIe–XVIIIe*

140   WOMEN WRITING ANTIQUITY

Lucretius's influence was pervasive in this period as is manifest by his translations and commentaries; scholars have also stressed that Lucretian and/or Epicurean ideas resonated in literature and poetry in the seventeenth century.[20] Jessie Hock has recently explored how early modern readers of Lucretius found in his poem far-reaching reflections on poetics and the imagination.[21] Philippe Chométy has studied Deshoulières's version, recovering it as an important and valid object of study, countering its dismissal as nonsensical.[22] I draw in particular on these two perspectives here to argue that Deshoulières's apparently nonsensical version of Lucretius brings together two diverse voices that she deploys in her early poetry—the burlesque and the philosophical—and as such it constitutes an intervention in poetic hermeneutics: how far can poetry convey meaning and ideas? How does a reader create this meaning? How to negotiate the exclusive intended group of readers the poem was written to entertain and the place of the critic? By drawing on a tradition of burlesque versions of ancient poetry which undermine and subvert its authority, Deshoulières's version performs reception in a way that is provocatively destabilising: as Claudine Nédélec argues, burlesque versions of ancient texts are intended to subvert the classical canon (and doing so might be seen as Modern gestures).[23] With her 'Lucretius en galimatias', Deshoulières draws on masculine poetic modes ('galimatias' and the burlesque) and imitates a poet famed for being unsuitable for women, to reflect more broadly on translation and the gendered voice.

Her poem opens thus:

> Déesse en volupté féconde
> Toi dont le nom est révéré,
> Toi dont l'abîme est désiré,

---

siècle), ed. by Philippe Chométy and Michèle Rosellini (Paris: Champion, 2017), pp. 215–32; and Line Cottegnies, 'Michel de Marolles's 1650 French Translation of Lucretius and Its Reception in England' in *Lucretius and the Early Modern*, ed. by David Norbrook, Stephen Harrison, and Philip Hardie (Oxford: Oxford University Press, 2015), pp. 161–89. See also Montaigne's 'Sur des vers de Virgile' (III.5), *Essais III*, ed. by Alexandre Micha (Paris: Flammarion, 1969), pp. 56–112, and on Montaigne, see Wes Williams, 'Well Said/Well Thought: How Montaigne Read his Lucretius', in *Lucretius in the Early Modern*, ed. by Norbrook, Harrison, and Hardie, pp. 135–60.

[20] Philip Hardie, *Lucretian Receptions: History, the Sublime, Knowledge* (Cambridge: Cambridge University Press, 2009); Chométy and Rosellini, eds, *Traduire Lucrèce*; Pierre Vesperini, *Lucrèce: Archéologie d'un classique européen* (Paris: Fayard, 2017), and Bruno Roche, *Lumières Épicuriennes au XVIIᵉ Siècle: La Mothe Le Vayer, Molière, et La Fontaine, Lecteurs et Continuateurs de Lucrèce* (Paris: Champion, 2020). See also Alan Charles Kors, *Epicureans and Atheists in France, 1650–1729* (Cambridge: Cambridge University Press, 2016), Ada Palmer, *Reading Lucretius in the Renaissance* (Cambridge, MA: Harvard University Press, 2014), and Stephen Greenblatt, *The Swerve: How the World Became Modern* (New York: Norton, 2011).

[21] Jessie Hock, *The Erotics of Materialism: Lucretius and Early Modern Poetics* (Philadelphia: University of Pennsylvania Press, 2021).

[22] Philippe Chométy, 'Du *clinamen* au galimatias: l'Imitation de Lucrèce d'Antoinette Deshoulières', in *Traduire Lucrèce*, ed. by Chométy and Rosellini, pp. 257–84.

[23] Claudine Nédélec, *Les États et Empires du Burlesque* (Paris: Champion, 2004), p. 267. On Deshoulières's *épîtres en vers* as polemical, see Tonolo, *Divertissement et profondeur*, pp. 214–15 and pp. 283–84.

SALON VERSE AND THE PHILOSOPHER-POET   141

> De tous les habitants de l'un et l'autre monde
>> Je t'invoque fille de l'onde,
>> Vénus! Sers de port assuré
>> A ce qu'une étude profonde
> M'a, sur d'immenses faits, pour toi seule inspiré. (p. 443)

>> Goddess, fecund in sensousness
>> You, whose name is revered
>> You, whose abyss is desired,
> Of all inhabitants of this world and the other
>> I invoke you, daughter of the waves,
>> Venus! Serve as a safe harbour
>> To that [the poem] which a deep study
> Has, about immense feats, for you alone inspired me [to write].

Philippe Chométy has argued persuasively that Deshoulières's version contains both meaning and its deliberate undermining, both a 'système d'Epicure' and a 'polisonnerie', both 'une imitation de Lucrèce' and 'un jargon', such that Deshoulières is a philosopher-poet in both her investigations of Epicureanism and in her hermeneutical scepticism.[24] Deshoulières presents readers with a coherent Epicurean system which privileges the place of love/desire at the centre of the universe (which she does elsewhere, as I explore below): as Chométy shows, with the praise of Volupté, as well as in the frequency of liquid words later in the poem ('suc', 'fluidité', 'immersion'), Deshoulières is bringing in elements from Lucretius Book 4. John J. Conley also argues that this poem 'closely follows the theses of Lucretius: that matter is the fundamental principle of existence; that all beings represent variations of the material principle; that material objects cohere through an atomic structure.'[25]

However, this poem is also a performative exercise in disrupting meaning. This is immediately evident from the burlesque condensation of the opening lines: the 20 lines of praise for Venus of Lucretius's 61-line address to the goddess are compressed to three brief lines.[26] In part this recourse to a burlesque mode might be dissimulative because of the potentially 'libertine' or unorthodox nature of Epicureanism. Deshoulières's technique of equivocation is common to a number of her poems which engage with what Chométy calls 'la poésie d'idées'.[27] But this very disruption of meaning is also the purpose of the poem.[28] That this is playfully and provocatively one of the author's intentions is evident from the irony of, for

---

[24] Chométy, 'Du *clinamen* au galimatias', p. 266.
[25] Conley, *The Suspicion of Virtue*, p. 51.
[26] Lucretius, *On the Nature of Things*, trans. by W. H. D. Rouse, rev. by Martin F. Smith, Loeb Classical Library 181 (Cambridge, MA: Harvard University Press, 1924).
[27] Chométy, 'Du *clinamen* au galimatias', p. 259. See also Chométy, '*Philosopher en langage des dieux*'.
[28] Chométy, 'Du *clinamen* au galimatias', pp. 282–83.

142   WOMEN WRITING ANTIQUITY

instance, 'Conduis ma voix, belle Déesse / Pour chanter sur ma lyre en termes simples, et clairs' (Guide my voice, beautiful Goddess, to sing on my lyre in simple and clear terms) (p. 443, l. 10), whereby she plays with the reader's own desire for meaning.

The intention to disrupt meaning is also evident from the title: 'galimatias fait exprès.'[29] Galimatias—which means, according to the 1694 *Dictionnaire de l'Académie française*, 'discours embrouillé et confus qui semble dire quelque chose et ne dit rien' (disordered and confused discourse which seems to say something but says nothing), and, according to Godefroy, 'mélange confus et inintelligible'—may be a way for her to engage with a philosophically challenging and controversial work: 'galimatias' is thus another kind of shield.[30] The title might also be a playful allusion to Capitaine Galimatias of Furetière's *Nouvelle allégorique ou Histoire des derniers troubles arrivés au Royaume d'Éloquence* (1658) who declares war on La Reine Rhétorique, and prepares to attack her seat of power, the 'académie', from which he is excluded.[31] On the side of Galimatias, Prince of the country of 'Pedanterie', are a number of figures of speech—including *équivoques* and *ironie*, favourites of Deshoulières—considered also therefore to be on the wrong side of good taste and excluded from the purity and order represented by the *Académie française*. The battle ends with Galimatias's defeat and then a truce but Galimatias remains excluded from the *Académie*. The first part of her title is thus provocative, even iconoclastic. Deshoulières is likewise provocative on the question of gendered poetics. 'Galimatias' is a masculine poetic mode, as is made explicit in Furetière's allegory. Not only does he combat 'Queen Rhetoric' and genres that can be seen as polite and feminised (such as *galant* verse), but the only female writer to be mentioned in this convocation of troops is Madeleine de Scudéry and she is explicitly on the opposite side, aligned with Rhetoric as ruler of the 'Pays de Tendre'.

The second part of the title, the 'fait exprès', could be another anticipatory defence and pre-emptive move to protect potentially libertine elements of the poem from being taken seriously—namely, do not worry, you are really not meant to understand this as there is nothing to understand—or it might be intended to make Deshoulières immune to accusations of pedantry or being hard to follow,

---

[29] It is possible that this title might have been added by the later editor and is not Deshoulières's own.

[30] *Dictionnaire de l'Académie française* (Paris: Coignard, 1694), p. 509; Frédéric Godefroy, *Dictionnaire de l'ancienne langue française et de tous ses dialectes du 9e au 15e siècle*, 10 vols (Paris: Vieweg and Bouillon, 1881–1902), IX: *Complément. Carrel–Inaccostable* (Paris: Bouillon, 1898), p. 681. Edition used: <https://www.classiques-garnier.com/numerique-bases/godefroy>.

[31] Antoine Furetière, *Nouvelle allégorique ou Histoire des derniers troubles arrivés au Royaume d'Éloquence* (Paris: Luyne, 1658). On the etymology of 'galimatias', see Hugh Roberts, '"Capitaine Galimatias, homme obscur, et né de la lie du peuple" (Furetière). Le galimatias, vice de style et genre littéraire (fin XVIe–première moitié du XVIIe siècle)', in *Vices de style et défauts esthétiques XVIe–XVIIIe siècle*, ed. by Carine Barbafieri and Jean-Yves Vialleton (Paris: Classiques Garnier, 2017), pp. 361–75.

in that the poem is intentionally obfuscatory. And yet, the title seems performatively to protest too much, and thus draws attention to that very shield, as 'fait exprès' appears to suggest that there still could be meaning behind the unintelligible confusion or the apparent pedantry, and that this meaning has been deliberately disguised *precisely because of* its potentially provocative elements. 'Fait exprès' as an indication of intention and therefore of the poem's interpretability could equally, as Chométy astutely suggests, be a false illusion, an ironic nod to the contradiction that confronts the reader between the sense-making drive of interpretation and its deliberate resistance in galimatias.[32]

'Galimatias' also indicates a parody of *savant* discourse: the term 'galimatias' has semantic links with pedantry.[33] In this poem, Deshoulières parodies the terms specific to various scientific disciplines (astronomy, alchemy, geometry) to burlesque effect. For instance:

> L'ordre d'une cause excentrique,
> Fait par d'invisibles ressorts,
> Entrer en forme dans les corps,
> Tout le Pathos Académique. (p. 444, ll. 19–23)

> The order of an eccentric cause
> Makes by invisible movements
> Enter into the form of bodies
> All academic pathos.

With this parodic pedantry, then, Deshoulières seems to mock learned discourse. The capacity of 'galimatias' to invert norms affords Deshoulières the opportunity to parade her literary distinction: by showing she knows the rules of the game (in the Bourdieusian sense) *and* can break them, she demonstrates her superiority.[34] And yet, Deshoulières also shows herself to be part of this very discourse—to be a 'savante'—by virtue of the fact that she is writing a Lucretius poem 'en galimatias'. Some of this mockery is therefore directed against herself and her coterie of friends and the community of readers whose understanding of this poem relies on their knowledge of the original. The 'Imitation de Lucrèce' epitomises the way Deshoulières's writing peels away layers of authority in ever destabilising gestures which are often, ultimately, directed towards the poet herself. This element of self-parody is potentially another dissimulative shield, a way of distancing herself from the ideas expressed by her poetry with a self-reflexive twist that questions the authority of her poetic persona.

---

[32] Chométy, 'Du *clinamen* au galimatias', p. 269.

[33] Roberts, '"Capitaine Galimatias, homme obscur, et né de la lie du peuple"', p. 365.

[34] See ibid., p. 375.

144 WOMEN WRITING ANTIQUITY

As is evident in the following quotation, the burlesque is used on the level of the text—the jargon, such as 'limoneux' and 'transpirables', has a burlesque effect in context—but she makes her use of burlesque in her 'Imitation de Lucrèce' most evident in her allusion to another classical intertext: her evocation of Ovid's description of chaos at the beginning of the *Metamorphoses*, which itself inverts or burlesques elements of Lucretius' poem.[35] The third stanza is particularly Ovidian:

> Aussitôt des esprits fixes et végétables,
>> Les mouvements fuligineux
>> Rendent les désirs transpirables,
>> Et ces sources intarissables,
> Où la nature puise et sa force et ses feux,
>> En d'autres sources transmuables,
>> Rendent à jamais inflammables,
>> Tous les principes limoneux. (p. 444, ll. 26–34)

> Straightaway the sooty movements
>> of fixed and vegetable spirits
>> Render desires transpirable
>> And these abundant sources
> From which nature draws both her strength and her fire
>> Into other transmutable sources
>> Render forever inflammable,
>> all the silty principles.

Deshoulières signals her reference to Ovid's account of creation through her use of the term 'chaos' in the penultimate stanza: 'Plus on regarde, plus on fouille / Dans le chaos du vrai' (the more one looks, the more one rummages / In the chaos of truth) (p. 444, ll. 43–44), echoing the vocabulary used by Ovid: 'quem dixere chaos' ('which they call chaos').[36] Crucially, chaos is not a term used by Lucretius. With this additional classical reference, Deshoulières strengthens her claims to distinction, not least because by bringing in Ovid she also evokes the French burlesque versions of the opening of the *Metamorphoses* from the middle of the century, those by Charles Dassoucy and Louis Richer.[37] Such company

---

[35] See Stephen M. Wheeler, 'Ovid's Use of Lucretius in *Metamorphoses* 1.67–8', *The Classical Quarterly*, 45.1 (1995), 200–03. More widely, see Charles P. Segal, 'Intertextuality and Immortality: Ovid, Pythagoras and Lucretius in Metamorphoses 15', *Materiali e discussioni per l'analisi dei testi classici*, 46 (2001), 63–101; and Hardie, *Lucretian Receptions*, pp. 136–52.

[36] Ovid, *Metamorphoses, Volume I: Books 1–8*, trans. by Frank Justus Miller, rev. by G. P. Goold, Loeb Classical Library 42 (Cambridge, MA: Harvard University Press, 1916), 1.7.

[37] Charles Dassoucy, *L'Ovide en belle humeur de Mr Dassoucy, enrichi de toutes ses figures burlesques* (Paris: Sercy, 1650); Louis Richer, *L'Ovide Bouffon, ou les Métamorphoses travesties en vers burlesques* (Paris: Quinet, 1649). See Helena Taylor, *The Lives of Ovid in Seventeenth-Century French Culture* (Oxford: Oxford University Press, 2017), pp. 55–69.

places Deshoulières in the coteries of *savant* male poets, showing that it is both her classical knowledge and her ability to subvert these models which affords her distinction. Deshoulières's use of the burlesque mode is self-consciously disruptive. Deshoulières adds a further layer of discordance as a female poet writing in a mode usually associated with men, marking her gender with this discordance and this discordance with her gender.

There is also evident emphasis on pleasure in her 'Imitation', demonstrating what Jessie Hock calls the 'voluptuous style' of Lucretius, that is, 'a poetic and rhetorical mode grounded in the production of [poetic] pleasure' or 'voluptas'.[38] Deshoulières resists the tradition which feminises Lucretian 'voluptas' because of the association with Venus and thus (women's) bodies by instead writing a poem in which the production of intellectual pleasure prompted by the enjoyment of the parody is paramount. Her 'Imitation de Lucrèce' is a ludic and provocative poem intended for a close community of readers: so much of its force, of its pleasure, would have been derived from the fact that its audience knew the original poem, the identity of the author, and were the anticipated readers. To some degree, then, this already meta-poem is also an exploration of the social production and readership of verse written by and for a community: the 'galimatias' is exclusionary because the poem may well have made more sense to the original and intended readers. Because of Lucretius's complex status and Epicureanism's denial of divine power and the immortal soul, the reception of *DRN* has often been, as Hock argues in relation to Montaigne's 'Sur des vers de Virgile', a tense (and erotic) act of veiling and exposure.[39] Deshoulières's 'Imitation' can be placed in this tradition. She draws attention to this tension—both within the poem with her deliberate obfuscation of meaning, and extra-textually in her decision not to include this poem in her 1688 edition or any of the publications she prepared before she died, such that the exclusion is marked. In Deshoulières's case, I would argue that her emphasis on the tension between veiling and exposure is enhanced by her use of 'galimatias', and her (undisclosed, but known to friends) identity as a female poet and as a female reader of Lucretius, a prohibited category. Deshoulières's 'Imitation' relishes intellectual pleasure, figuring both classical reception and social modes of reading as pleasurable. Captain Galimatias—and galimatias—also problematise man's need to make sense of discourse or argument: Galimatias was also considered the enemy of reason.[40] In the next section, we will see how Deshoulières reflects more explicitly on the limitations of reason through her response to ancient pastoral poetry.

---

[38] Jessie Hock, 'Voluptous Style: Lucretius, Rhetoric and Reception in Montaigne's "Sur des vers de Virgile"', *Modern Philology*, 18.4 (2021), 492–514 (p. 493).

[39] Ibid., pp. 511–13.

[40] 'Galimatias' was an enemy of 'raison' according to Furetière commenting later in his *Dictionnaire universel*: see Roberts, '"Capitaine Galimatias, homme obscur, et né de la lie du peuple"', pp. 364–65.

146 WOMEN WRITING ANTIQUITY

Idylls and the Limits of Reason

Pierre Bayle, a fine reader of Deshoulières, does not include an article on her in his *Dictionnaire*, but he does mention her in his articles on Dehénault and on Ovid. In the latter, Bayle quotes her idylls to show how she engaged with questions of the conflict within man between reason and passion: this follows a discussion of Ovid's representation of chaos in the opening of his *Metamorphoses*, as mentioned above. Bayle focuses attention on Deshoulières's idylls, particularly 'Les Moutons', in which animals and the natural world act as a foil for man's shortcomings.[41] He quotes this idyll, introducing it thus:

> Quelle guerre n'y a t-il pas entre son ame et son corps, entre sa raison et ses sens, entre son ame sensitive et son ame raisonnable? La raison devroit calmer ce desordre et pacifier ces différends intestins; mais elle est juge et partie, et ses arrêts ne sont point exécutez et ne font qu'augmenter le mal. C'est ce qui a obligé l'un des plus solides, et des plus brillans esprits du XVII siècle de preferer à la condition de l'homme celle des moutons.

> What war is not waged between soul and body, between reason and the senses, between the sensitive and the reasonable soul? Reason should calm this disorder and pacify this inner strife; but it is judge and party, and its edicts are not executed and only serve to increase the harm. This is why one of the most sound and brilliant minds of the seventeenth century has preferred the condition of sheep to that of man.[42]

In this section, I examine Deshoulières's idylls in the light of Bayle's reading of their reflections on reason, and argue for their direct engagement with ancient pastoral. Deshoulières penned six pastoral poems with the title 'idyll', from her early 'Les Moutons' of 1674 to 'La Solitude' of 1690.[43] These idylls manifest a diverse range

---

[41] Bayle, Remarque H, 'Ovide', *Dictionnaire*, III, p. 560. Deshoulières's depiction of the combat between reason and passion is also presented in her 'Rondeau contre l'amour' where she evokes Ovid as a poet of love (p. 113).

[42] Frédéric Lachèvre also explicitly locates this poem in the debates about reason when he entitles it 'Contre la raison (les moutons)' in his short biography of Deshoulières, arguing for its connection to the sonnet against reason by Jacques Vallée Des Barreaux (1599–1673). Lachèvre, 'Antoinnette Deshoulières', in *Les Derniers libertins*, pp. 25–63 (p. 52). As Tonolo argues, 'tout comme la fable, l'idylle est née de la dénonciation du caractère artificiel du raisonnement logique' (like the fable, the idyll origininates in the condemnation of the artificial character of logical reasoning): 'De la querelle à l'idylle: quelques enjeux de la poésie de Mme Deshoulières', in *Concordia Discors: 41e congrès annuel de la North American Society for Seventeenth-Century French Literature*, ed. by Benoît Bolduc and Henriette Goldwyn, 2 vols (Tübingen: Narr, 2011), II, pp. 33–42 (p. 41).

[43] 'Les Moutons', her first idyll, published in *Le Nouveau Mercure Galant*, July 1677, pp. 133–41, was followed quickly by two further idylls, 'Les Fleurs', in *Nouveau Mercure Galant*, November 1677, pp. 151–58, and 'Les Oiseaux', in the *Mercure Galant*, May 1679, pp. 237–43. This cluster was followed by a later idyll, 'Le Ruisseau', printed in 1685 in the *Mercure Galant*, March, pp. 177–86. These were

of influences, and echo tropes in poems of her contemporaries or near contemporaries, particularly Théophile de Viau, François le Métel de Boisrobert and Antoine Girard de Saint-Amant.[44] Her idylls engage with some aspects of ancient pastoral, particularly Virgil's *Eclogues* (after all, the term 'idyll' could be intended to recall the work of Theocritus, creator of the pastoral genre and Virgil's model). In the next section, we will look in more detail at her engagement with Virgil's (and Renaissance) eclogues in her own eclogue poems, but some elements of Virgilian pastoral are relevant here in relation to her idylls and their philosophy. Ancient pastoral was predicated on the tension between the innocent world of the pastoral and the more complex shortcomings of human nature, a tension which Deshoulières develops; it is also a self-concious genre that paradoxically pairs the simplicity of the shepherds with the sophistication of the poet voicing them: as Philip Hardie suggests in relation to Virgil's *Eclogues*, 'much of the energy and interest of the *Eclogues* derives from the constant tension between the limiting case of a pastoral "idyll" and the forces that threaten to destabilize the idyll'.[45] Far from being naïve or idealistic, the pastoral genre poses moral, political, and philosophical questions, even if, as I will examine further, the ability of the genre to do so was contested in the late seventeenth century.[46] Pastoral or rustic poets of the Renaissance, such as Joachim Du Bellay, used the opposition between country and city inherent to the genre to criticise court life.[47] Deshoulières responds to this with her focus on human vice, particularly the vanities of the court and society: her pastoral idylls take on a 'moralist' character, and thus intersect with the work of her contemporaries, particularly La Rochefoucauld. By using nature as a foil to man's weakness, she draws on and develops the traditions of natural philosophy we saw her engage with above and participates in a key contemporary debate about the nature of the animal soul, as we will now explore.

Deshoulières infuses her pastoral with Epicureanism; in so doing, she responds to another feature of the ancient tradition. Ancient pastoral is sometimes associated with Epicurus because the *otium* of pastoral life can be paralleled with the

---

all included in her 1688 collection. She penned two further pastoral idylls, 'La Solitude', first published posthumously in the 1695 edition (p. 6), but thought to have been written in 1688 (see *Poésies*, ed. by Tonolo, p. 260). There is a further pastoral idyll, 'L'Hiver' (pp. 250–52), first published in the 1688 volume, which I will not analyse here. There were also two panegyric idylls, 'Pour la naissance Monsieur, duc de Bourgogne, Idylle (*Mercure Galant*, September 1682), pp. 71–78 (*Poésies*, ed. by Tonolo, pp. 116–17); and 'Idylle sur le retour de la santé du Roi' (*Mercure Galant*, September 1686), pp. 40–46 (*Poésies*, ed. by Tonolo, pp. 197–99).

[44] See *Poésies*, ed. by Tonolo, p. 215, p. 250, p. 260.

[45] Philip Hardie, *Virgil* (Cambridge: Cambridge University Press, 1998), pp. 5–6.

[46] See Philippe Chométy and Claudine Poulouin, 'Pour un siècle pastoral', in *Le Siècle Pastoral*, ed. by Philippe Chométy and Claudine Poulouin (= *Revue Fontenelle*, 10 (2012)), pp. 9–15 (p. 15); see also Louisa Mackenzie, *The Poetry of Place: Lyric, Language and Ideology in Renaissance France* (Toronto: Toronto University Press, 2011), p. 19.

[47] Joachim Du Bellay, *Divers jeux rustiques and et autres œuvres poétiques* (Paris: Morel, 1558). See also Isabelle Fernbach, 'From Copy to Copia: Imitation and Authorship in Joachim Du Bellay's *Divers Jeux Rustiques* (1558)', in *Virgilian Identities in the French Renaissance*, ed. by Isabelle Fernbach and Phillip John Usher (Rochester, NY: Boydell & Brewer, 2012), pp. 93–114.

148 WOMEN WRITING ANTIQUITY

Epicurean abstention from political life and retirement to the 'garden', and the attainment of pleasure through a state of tranquillity (*ataraxia*). Furthermore, in Virgil's sixth *Eclogue*, the 'Song of Silenus', the shepherd sings of the world's origin according to an Epicurean world system. Deshoulières makes the Epicureanism of the pastoral explicit with the recurring (Lucretian) images of nature being animated by love: 'Ce n'est point l'intérêt, l'ambition, la haine / Qui les anime: c'est l'amour' (They are not animated by self-interest, ambition or hatred, but love) ('La Solitude', p. 263, ll. 103–04), connecting this also to an Ovidian perception of nature's mutability and capacity for renewal. Deshoulières also makes the connection between Epicureanism and the pastoral explicit in her *Élégie* addressed to 'Généreux Licidas', a shepherd (p. 100). Licidas (Lycidas) is a pastoral name used by Theocritus and Virgil; here it is thought that she is addressing her (Epicurean) tutor, Dehénault, the 'berger' and her 'ami sage et fidèle' (p. 100, l. 1), as she reflects on the tension between 'sens' (the senses) and 'raison' and the ruinations of 'l'amour' compared to the tranquillity of 'sagesse'. 'Sage' and 'sagesse' are key recurring terms in her poetry; as I show, 'sagesse' epitomises a different sort of (self) knowledge to that represented by 'raison'.[48]

One of the ways Deshoulières demonstrates the limitations of man's reason is by praising the capacities of animals, as Bayle indicated. With this gesture, she is in the company of a number of other salon writers who, while perhaps favourable to much of Descartes's thought, particularly his valorisation of female intellectuals and the gender neutrality of his thinking subject, refuted his mechanistic representation of animals.[49] As Dennis Des Chene and Peter Sahlins show, the *bête-machine* was a complex and contested notion in Descartes's work and in its immediate reception; but the key elements of Descartes's (well-known) argument are as follows.[50] His 'new philosophy', particularly in the *Discours de la méthode* (1637), disputed the Aristotelian notion of a divided human soul and the notion of a hierarchy of souls (human, animal, vegetal). Instead, he unified the human soul and accounted for conflict between reason and passion by locating passions in the

---

[48] Plato called Anacreon 'sage' and we will see the importance of Anacreon in Deshoulières's writing. See Sophie Tonolo, 'Les métamorphoses d'Anacréon chez Mme Deshoulières: effets d'une tradition philologique et philosophique sur son lyrisme pastoral', *Le Siècle Pastoral*, ed. by Chométy and Poulouin, pp. 181–97 (pp. 184–87).

[49] René Descartes, *Discours de la méthode*, ed. by Laurent Renault (Paris: Garnier, 2000), pp. 91–95. See also Leonora C. Rosenfield, *From Beast-Machine to Man-Machine: Animal Soul in French Letters from Descartes to La Mettrie* (New York: Oxford University Press, 1941), pp. 154–79; Peter Sahlins, *1668: The Year of the Animal in France* (New York: Zone Books, 2017), pp. 277–310. On Descartes and feminism, see Marie-Frédérique Pellegrin, 'Cartesianism and Feminism', in *The Oxford Handbook of Descartes and Cartesianism*, ed. by Steven Nadler, Tad M. Schmaltz, and Delphine Antoine-Mahut (Oxford: Oxford University Press, 2019), pp. 565–78. For a full discussion of some of the contradictions in women's reception of Descartes, see Erica Harth, *Cartesian Women: Versions and Subversions of Rational Discourse* (Ithaca: Cornell University Press, 1992); and Rebecca Wilkin, *Women, Imagination and the Search for Truth in Early Modern France* (Aldershot: Ashgate, 2008), pp. 183–221.

[50] Dennis Des Chene, *Spirits and Clocks: Machine and Organism in Descartes* (Ithaca: Cornell University Press, 2001), pp. 1–12; Sahlins, *1668: The Year of the Animal in France*, pp. 28–31, pp. 277–310.

body and emphasising the separation between body and mind. Even though, as Susan James and others have argued, Descartes's argumentation takes these divisions in more complex directions, he nevertheless does describe the conflict as one of mind and body.[51] His conception of the soul or mind is distinguished further from that of Aristotle because not only is it unified, but it is also a site of thought. Where, for Aristotle, any animate thing that was capable of nutrition and reproduction (a plant or animal) could have a soul, Descartes argues that only creatures who can think have souls, and shows that only humans can think.[52] He elaborates a now-famous theory of a 'beast-machine' to explain that animals' actions are not governed by thought but are in fact mechanical functions of the body: animals cannot think and so do not have souls.[53]

Deshoulières combines her reflections on the limitations of human reason with her questioning of their superiority over—and differences from—animals in a sceptical gesture that is in dialogue with La Fontaine's 1678 *Discours à Madame de la Sablière* and recalls Montaigne's *Apologie de Raymond Sebond*, in which he argues for the limitations in humans' ability to comprehend the complexities of animals (for instance, the fact that we cannot understand them does not mean they cannot communicate) and stresses the complacency of a human-centred approach, as epitomised in his famous question: 'Quand je me joue à ma chatte, qui sait si elle passe son temps de moi plus que je ne fais d'elle?' (when I play with my cat, how do I know whether she is playing with me or I with her?) (II.12, 452c).[54]

As Bayle demonstrated, Deshoulières articulates her scepticism regarding the superiority of human reason in 'Les Moutons' (pp. 123–25): she suggests that man's reason cannot protect him from his desires and that such desires are the cause of unhappiness. She interrogates the limitations of human reason by comparing man to animal:

> Innocents animaux, n'en soyez point jaloux,
> Ce n'est pas un grand avantage
> Cette fière raison, dont on fait tant de bruit,
> Contre les passions n'est pas un sûr remède
> Un peu de vin la trouble, un enfant la séduit

---

[51] Susan James, *Passion and Action: The Emotions in Seventeenth-Century Philosophy* (Oxford: Clarendon Press, 1997), p. 259.

[52] James, *Passion and Action*, pp. 87–94.

[53] As Nathalie Grande and Nicole Aronson show, Madeleine de Scudéry also took a stance against the animal-machine in her novel *Clélie*, in her *Histoire de deux caméléons*, composed in 1673 and published in 1688, and in her letters to Catherine Descartes, poet and niece of the philosopher. Nathalie Grande, 'Une vedette des salons: le caméléon', in *L'Animal au XVII siècle*, ed. by Charles Mazouer (Tübingen: Gunter Narr Verlag, 2003), pp. 89–102; and Nicole Aronson, '"Que diable allait-il faire dans cette galère?": Mlle de Scudéry et les animaux', in *Les Trois Scudéry*, ed. by Alain Niderst (Paris: Klincksieck, 1993), pp. 523–32.

[54] Michel de Montaigne, 'Apologie de Raimond Sebond', *Essais II*, ed. by Alexandre Micha (Paris: Flammarion, 1969), pp. 105–268 (p. 119).

> Et déchirer un cœur qui l'appelle à son aide
> > est tout l'effet qu'elle produit.
> > > Toujours impuissante et sévère
> Elle s'oppose à tout, et ne surmonte rien. (p. 124, ll. 13–21)

> Innocent animals, don't be jealous of it,
> > This proud reason that so many clamour over,
> Is no great advantage,
> Is not a sure remedy against passions
> A bit of wine confuses it, a child seduces it
> And tearing apart a heart who calls on its aid
> > Is the only effect reason produces.
> > Powerless and severe always,
> It opposes everything and overcomes nothing.

This contrast between reason and passion was standard fare in this period—it might not, of course, be directly related to Descartes's writings of his *Discours* or his influential *Les Passions de l'âme* (1649). However, given Deshoulières's interest in contemporary philosophy and the differences between the Gassendist thought which so influenced her and some of Descartes's main ideas, we are justified in reading these comments as a form of engagement with philosophy as much as a recycling of literary tropes. 'Raison', which distinguishes man from animal in a Cartesian framework, is shown to be inadequate against 'passions' and so, implicitly, not a cause for superiority. Deshoulières laments man's vanity comparing it to the 'sagesse' of the sheep:

> Vous devez beaucoup moins redouter la colère
> > Des loups cruels et ravissants
> Que sous l'autorité d'une telle chimère,
> > Nous ne devons craindre nos sens.
> Ne vaudrait-il pas mieux vivre comme vous faites
> > Dans une douce oisiveté?
> Ne vaudrait-il pas mieux être comme vous êtes
> > Dans une heureuse obscurité,
> > Que d'avoir sans tranquillité
> > Des Richesses, de la Naissance
> > De l'Esprit et de la Beauté?
> Ces pretendus trésors dont on fait vanité
> > Valent moins que votre indolence. (p. 124, ll. 23–35)
> [...]

> Paissez, moutons, paissez sans règle, sans science
> > Malgré la trompeuse apparence,
> Vous êtes plus heureux et plus sages que nous. (p. 125, ll. 46–48)

You should have much less fear of the anger of
    cruel and ravishing wolves
Than under the authority of such a chimera
    We should fear our senses.
Wouldn't it be better to live as you do
    in sweet leisure?
Wouldn't it be better to be as you are
    In happy ignorance?
    Than to have without tranquillity
    Wealth, lineage, wit and beauty?
These apparent treasures which we vaunt
    are worth less than your idleness

[...]
Graze, sheep, graze without rule, without learning
    Despite deceptive appearances
You are happier and wiser than we are.

In a further move which contests the superiority of man, she compares human activities with those of plants in 'Les Fleurs' (pp. 170–72). Deshoulières recycles the Renaissance poetic trope of the short but sweet life of flowers to emphasise that they do not suffer in love, stressing that it is human self-consciousness which, so praised by Descartes, is the source of suffering:

Vous ne ressentez point la mortelle tristesse
    Qui dévore les tendres cœurs,
Lors que plein d'une ardeur extrême
    On voit l'ingrat objet qu'on aime
Manquer d'empressement, ou s'engager ailleurs. (pp. 171–2, ll. 15–19)

You do not feel the mortal sadness
    Which devours tender hearts
When, full of extreme ardour,
    One sees the ungrateful object of one's love
Lack enthusiasm or engage themselves to another.

This Lucretian idea that non-human life enjoys a harmonious relationship within the universe (they peacefully obey nature's laws in their cycle of rebirth) is also present in 'Les Oiseaux' (pp. 187–89). She contrasts the freedom of birds to man's enslavement to his passions but emphasises that this enslavement comes from man's inability to live by and accept his place in the natural universe and its 'premières lois'.

Nous aimons mieux par un bizarre choix,
Ingrats Escalves que nous sommes,

152 WOMEN WRITING ANTIQUITY

> Suivre ce qu'inventa le caprice des Hommes
>> Que d'obéir à nos premières Lois
>> Que votre sort est different du nôtre,
>> Petits Oiseaux qui me charmez!
>> Voulez vous aimer? vous aimez. (p. 188, ll. 29–33)

> We prefer through a bizarre choice
> Ungrateful slaves that we are,
> To follow whatever man's caprice has invented
>> Than to obey our first laws;
>> How different your fate is to ours
>> Little birds who delight me!
>> If you want to love? You love.

Conley reads this emphasis on birds' love as representative of Deshoulières's Epicurean 'refusal to limit love to the intentional activities of rational beings;' and this chimes with other reflections in salon writing on animals.[55] Deshoulières also suggests that birds possess a straightforwardness not embraced by man and laments the vanity and attention to appearances and artifice of 'perfides Humains':

> Et jamais dans les Bois on n'a vu les Corbeaux
>> Des Rossignols emprunter le ramage
>> Il n'est de sincère langage
> Il n'est de liberté que chez les Animaux. (p. 189, ll. 38–39)

> And never in the woods has one seen the ravens
>> Borrowing the song of nightingales
>> There is only sincere language
> There is only freedom among animals.

Animals are free; their ability to communicate in 'langage' that is 'sincère' and thus has moral properties is also an explicit refutation of Descartes's argument that animal communication is purely mechanical or repetitive and not demonstrative of thought, reason or empathy. Deshoulières's emphasis on sincerity here and the pitfalls of appearances, which recur in many of her poems, also makes this description a portrait *a contrario* of society as a place for insincerity.

Deshoulières's contrasting description of man and nature is then transformed into a more direct opposition as she details man's abuse of nature in the form of aggressive farming and cultivation of land. Here she writes against Virgil's *Georgics*,

---

[55] Conley, *The Suspicion of Virtue*, p. 58. Other writings include Scudéry's *Histoire de deux caméléons* where she describes an affective relationship between herself and one of them. I'm grateful to Lisa Nicholson for making this connection.

which praised such cultivation, and echoes, for instance, Pierre de Ronsard's *Elégie contre les bûcherons de la fôret de Gatine*, or his *Hymne de la Justice*, which laments the torments the plough inflicts upon the earth.[56] She writes:

> Contre nos trahisons la Nature en courroux
> Ne nous donne plus rien sans peine;
> Nous cultivons les Vergers et la Plaine,
> Tandis, petits Oiseaux, qu'elle fait tout pour vous. (p. 189, ll. 46–49)

> Against our betrayals nature enraged
> Gives us nothing anymore without pain;
> We have to cultivate orchards and plains
> While, little birds, she makes everything for you.

Man's violence over nature is explored most explicitly in the idyll she published in 1685, seven years after her initial three: 'Le Ruisseau' (pp. 215–19). Man is shown as being tyrannical towards nature, his 'Empire' (p. 217, l. 78). She gives a particular example of this mastery, relevant to the river she is addressing, when she evokes the fountain as a form of 'torture':

> Pourquoi vous mettre à la torture?
> Pourquoi vous renfermer dans cent Canaux divers,
> Et pourquoi renverser l'ordre de la Nature
> En vous forçant à jaillir dans les airs? (p. 217, ll. 65–67)

> Why do we submit you to torture?
> Why do we trap you in one hundred different canals
> And why do we reverse nature's order
> By forcing you to shoot into the air?

Her portrait of man in this poem is also negative, contrasting the 'franchise' of the river with the deceivers and flatterers who people 'le monde' (p. 218, ll. 89–90). The close of the poem, which courted some controversy in its possible suggestion of the soul as mortal, pursues this melancholy pessimism:

> Enfin dans cet horrible gouffre
> De misère et de vanité

---

[56] Pierre de Ronsard, Élégie XXIV, 'Élégie contre les bûcherons de la fôret de Gatine', in *Œuvres complètes*, ed. by Paul Laumonier, 7 vols (Paris: Société des Textes Français Modernes, 2009), v, 19–68; 'Hymne de la justice', ibid., ii, 47. Deshoulières allude à l'Élégie in 'La Solitude' when she states: 'parlez fôret', p. 263, l. 98. See also Mackenzie, *The Poetry of Place*, pp. 135–43, and Jennifer Oliver, 'When Is a Meadow Not a Meadow?': Dark Ecology and Fields of Conflict in French Renaissance Poetry', *Early Modern Écologies: Beyond English Ecocriticism*, ed. by Pauline Goul and John Philip Usher (Amsterdam: Amsterdam University Press, 2020), pp. 73–97.

Je me perds; et plus j'envisage
La faiblesse de l'Homme et sa malignité,
Et moins de la Divinité
En lui je reconnais l'Image.
Courez Ruisseau, courez, fuyez-nous, reportez
Vos ondes dans le sein des Mers dont vous sortez,
Tandis que pour remplir la dure destinée
Où nous sommes assujettis,
Nous irons reporter la vie infortunée
Que le hasard nous a donnée
Dans le sein du néant d'où nous sommes sortis. (pp. 218–19, ll. 103–15)

In this horrible chasm
Of misery and vanity
I lose myself; and the more I envisage
The feebleness of man and his malignity
The less I recognise the
Image of the divine in him.
Flow, river, flow, flee us, return
Your waves to the heart of the seas you come from;
While to fulfil the harsh destiny
To which we are subject
We will return the unfortunate life
Which chance has afforded us
To the heart of the nothingness from which we came.

These final three lines were quoted in Bayle's *Dictionnaire* entry on her tutor, Jean Dehénault, as an example of his possible influence on her work. Bayle remarks:

> Il est sûr qu'une personne, qui parleroit de la sorte dogmatiquement, nieroit l'immortalité de l'âme. Mais pour l'honneur de Madame Des Houlieres, disons qu'elle n'a suivi que des Idées Poétiques qui ne tirent point à conséquence. [...] Ne jugeons point d'elle par des Phrases Poëtiques. Ce n'est pas qu'on ne puisse cacher beaucoup de libertinage sous les privilèges de la versification.[57]

It is certain that no one, speaking dogmatically, would deny the immortality of the soul. To protect the honour of Madame Deshoulières, let us say that she was only pursuing poetic ideas which have no consequence. Let us not judge her by

---

[57] Bayle, Remarque D, 'Henault', *Dictionnaire*, II, p. 721.

her poetic phrases. It is not the case that one might hide much libertinage behind the privileges of versification.

Chométy's excellent reading of this passage emphasises Bayle's own logic of 'prétérition, paradoxe et ironie', and he stresses the parallels between Bayle's own suggestiveness here and Deshoulières's work, with the final sentence seeming particularly equivocal.[58] We are told both that there are no consequences to her poem and, as Bayle identifies in the opening sentence, that there might be one very serious and very controversial one: that she is denying the immortality of the soul. Bayle recognises in Deshoulières not only the philosophical engagement of her poetry, but also her capacity for equivocation, one of 'les privilèges de la versification'.

Her response to Virgil's *Georgics* can further be traced in her last idyll, 'La Solitude' (pp. 260–63), first published posthumously in 1695, but thought to have been written in 1688, which is a reflection on the pleasures of the rustic life of retreat. While it appears to echo elements of Virgil's *Georgics* (for instance *Georgics* 2, about the city dwellers who dream of living in the countryside, and *Georgics* 4 with references to the bees), it in fact draws more on what Sahlins calls the 'theriophilic' tradition of Montaigne and La Fontaine, to contest the idealisation of the taming of land in the *Georgics* where farming is lauded and to present such farming as a war waged against the earth. Men are criticised for this war and animals shown as more tranquil:

> Ici le Cerf, l'Agneau, le Paon, la Tourterelle,
> Pour la possession d'un champ ou d'un verger
>> N'ont point ensemble de querelle
>> Nul bien ne leur est étranger.
> Nul n'exerce sur l'autre un pouvoir tyrannique,
> Ils ne se doivent point de respects ni de soins,
> Ce n'est que par les nœuds de l'amour qu'ils sont joints. (p. 260–61, ll. 10–16)

> Here the deer, the lamb, the peacock, the dove
> To possess a field or an orchard
>> Do not quarrel with each other
>> No good is a stranger to them.
> They never exercise tyrannical power against each other,
> Respect or care are not obligations,
> It is only through bonds of love that they are joined.

---

[58] Chométy, 'Du *clinamen* au galimatias', p. 262.

156 WOMEN WRITING ANTIQUITY

Her vision is of nature as fair and egalitarian: she goes on to suggest that in nature 'tous les biens sont communs, tous les rangs sont égaux' (all their goods are in common, all their ranks are equal) (p. 261, l. 23). Echoing Montaigne who suggests that animals are more high-minded in that they do not subjugate each other, she suggests that the fiercest animals (bears, wolves) 'sont moins barbares que nous' (p. 262, l. 76), citing examples of human violence:

> Non, des meurtres sanglants, des noires trahisons
>   L'amour ne fournit plus aux hommes
> Les violents conseils ni les tendres raisons. (p. 263, ll. 111–13)

> No, bloody murders, black betrayals,
>   Love no longer gives men
> Either violent counsel or tender reason.

Like Montaigne, she also valorises what she calls 'instinct' among animals, and laments that humans are too proud to access this form of 'sagesse':

> En vain notre orgueil nous engage
> À ravaler l'instinct qui dans chaque saison
>   À la honte de la raison,
> Pour tous les Animaux est un guide si sage.
> Ah! n'avons-nous pas dû nous dire mille fois,
>   En les voyant être heureux sans richesse,
> Habiles sans étude, équitables sans lois
>   Qu'ils possèdent seuls la sagesse? (p. 262, ll. 54–61)

> In vain our pride engages us
> To suppress our instinct which, in each season,
>   To the shame of reason,
> For all animals is a wise guide.
> Ah! Have we not had to say to ourselves a thousand times,
>   Seeing animals happy without wealth
> Capable without study, fair without laws
>   That they alone are wise?

To elucidate this 'sagesse', she draws on particular examples: reptiles who are able to find remedies, ants for their industry, and bees for their social organisation. With this, she echoes similar lists from Montaigne's *Apologie* and La Fontaine's *Discours à Madame de la Sablière*.

With these idylls Deshoulières both contests Cartesian mechanism and rationalism, and signals her departure from elements of classical pastoral. Not only does she oppose parts of the *Georgics*, but by reorientating the threat to rustic tranquillity posed by the urban that underpins Virgil's *Eclogues* towards a more explicit vision of man's threat to nature, she also self-consciously modernises the tradition by drawing on more recent, French influences. As such, these poems also manifest Deshoulières's complex approach towards the authority of antiquity, here mobilised to question the twin authorities of reason and the human. Given the self-consciousness and artifice of the pastoral genre and the anxiety it provoked about the relationship between philosophy and poetry, her use of this tradition was also a way for Deshoulières to think through ideas of the poetic voice and the tradition of poetic philosophy. As we will now examine, she does so most prominently through her four eclogue poems which engage with the *querelle* about the eclogue of the 1680s.

Eclogues and Moderns

At the height of the Quarrel of the Ancients and Moderns of the late 1680s was a discrete quarrel about the pastoral genre. In 1688 Bernard Le Bovier de Fontenelle published a series of his own 'poésies pastorales' with an essay entitled 'Discours sur la nature de l'églogue' in which he was critical of the ancient genre, finding Theocritus's shepherds too realistic ('les bergers de Théocrite et leurs pareils sont trop bergers') and Virgil's too idealistic (indeed too philosophical), arguing instead that the pastoral needed to be modernised to correspond to the contemporary age.[59] This essay was combined with his *Digression sur les anciens et les modernes*, reinforcing the place of the debates about the eclogue within that wider Quarrel. With this text, he was responding in part to Hilaire-Bernard de Longepierre's (anonymous) 1686 translation of ancient Greek bucolic poets, Moschus and Bion, which Longepierre followed with another anonymous translation of Theocritus in 1688.[60] Fontenelle suggests that the eclogue genre is stronger when it allows for some deeper reflection on man's nature; but at the same time, he lambasts the lack of *vraisemblance* of shepherds who are too refined and sentimental: 'entre la grossiereté ordinaire des bergers de Théocrite, et le trop d'esprit de la plus part de nos bergers modernes, il y a un milieu à tenir' (there is a balance to be found between Theocritus' rustic shepherds and the over-refinement of the modern ones).[61] Longepierre, in contrast, holds up Theocritus as exemplary. This debate intersects in obvious ways with the Ancients and Moderns quarrel, particularly in relation to the 'primitive' nature of ancient Greek models, and was

---

[59] Bernard de Fontenelle, *Poésies pastorales de M.D.F. Avec un traité sur la nature de l'églogue, et une digression sur les anciens et les modernes* (Paris: Guerout, 1688), p. 177.

[60] Hilaire-Bernard de Longepierre, *Les idylles de Bion et de Moschus* (Paris: Aubouin, Emery, and Clousier, 1686); Longepierre, *Les idylles de Théocrite* (Paris: Aubouin, Emery, and Clousier, 1688).

[61] Fontenelle, *Poésies pastorales*, pp. 198–99.

158 WOMEN WRITING ANTIQUITY

continued by Charles Perrault and carried on well into the eighteenth century.[62] Fontenelle's criticism of the pastoral had considerable influence on the English Battle of the Books, as is evident from the attack on Fontenelle by Kneightly Chetwood added as a preface to Dryden's translation of Virgil in 1697.[63] This debate was also about poetic genres and the capacity of the eclogue to be philosophical. Fontenelle suggests that this is a category error as he implies in his criticism of Virgil's sixth 'Epicurean' Eclogue: 'je ne sçay du tout ce que c'est que cette pièce-là, je ne conçois point quel est le dessein, ni quelle liaison les parties ont entre elles' (I do not understand this one; I cannot grasp its purpose or how the parts fit together).[64] Marolles had made a similar comment in his 1649 prose translation of Virgil which he echoes in his 1673 verse version: 'comme ces sujets sont un peu trop élevez pour le poême pastoral, le poëte s'en excuse d'abord' (since these subjects are too lofty for the pastoral poem, the poet starts by apologising).[65]

In the four poems Deshoulières wrote entitled 'Églogue', she participates in this debate: her view of pastoral simplicity, her rejection of the 'civilisation' of modernity, which we also encountered in her idylls, prove a counterpoint to Fontenelle's argument and instead chime with her idealisation of the simplicity of nature. As Linda Timmermans reminds us, the eclogue in the late seventeenth century was not only or necessarily conceived of as an ancient poetic genre, given the importance of the pastoral to French novels, notably d'Urfé's *L'Astrée* (and Deshoulières includes a number of references to this work in her poetry);[66] however, I suggest that her eclogues engage with both the French pastoral tradition and the

---

[62] Charles Perrault affirms Fontenelle's gesture in the first volume of his *Parallèle des anciens et des modernes* which includes a poem called 'Le Génie: Épître à Monsieur de Fontenelle', *Parallèle des Anciens et des Modernes en ce qui regarde les arts et les sciences. Dialogues. Avec le Poème du Siècle de Louis le Grand, et une Épître en vers sur le Génie* (Paris: Coignard, 1688), p. 27. On Perrault's interventions in the quarrel about pastoral poetry, see Larry F. Norman, *The Shock of the Ancient: Literature and History in Early Modern France* (Chicago: University of Chicago Press, 2011), pp. 85–88. The quarrel continued into the eighteenth century: for instance, with Houdar de La Motte's 1754 'Discours sur l'églogue', ed. by Nathalie Dauvois, in *Textes critiques. Les raisons du sentiment*, ed. by Françoise Gevrey and Béatrice Guion (Paris: Champion, 2002), pp. 767–802. See Claudine Nédélec, 'Lyriques anciens et lyriques modernes à l'aune de la galanterie', *Littératures Classiques*, 77.1 (2012), 319–31. On Deshoulières's reception in this eighteenth-century quarrel, see Kim Gladu, 'Le débat sur le style pastoral au xviiie siècle: Madame Deshoulières, modèle de l'élégiaque galant', *Tangence*, 109 (2015), 89–109.

[63] Kneightly Chetwood, 'Preface to the Pastorals', in *The Works of Virgil*, trans. by John Dryden (London: Tonson, 1697), np. Fontenelle's essay was translated into English two years earlier in 1695: 'Of Pastorals', in René le Bossu, *Epick Poetry*, trans. by Pierre Motteux (London: Bennet, 1695), pp. 294–95. On Chetwood and the influence of this quarrel on Alexander Pope, see Joseph M. Levine, *The Battle of the Books: Literature and History in the Augustan Age* (Ithaca: Cornell University Press, 1994), pp. 181–90.

[64] Fontenelle, *Poésies pastorales*, p. 185. See also Philippe Chométy, 'Du poète-berger au berger-philosophe: Fontenelle, la pastorale et la poésie d'idées', *Le Siècle Pastoral*, ed. by Chométy and Poulouin, pp. 63–104.

[65] Michel de Marolles, *Les Œuvres de Virgile traduites en prose* (Paris: Quinet, 1649), p. 23; Marolles, *Toutes les œuvres de Virgile, traduites en vers françois* (Paris: Langlois, 1673), p. 29.

[66] For example, 'Lettre en vers de Madame Deshoulières à un des ses amis', in *Poésies*, ed. by Tonolo, pp. 167–69, is set 'proche des bords de Lignon', figuring the late Celadon. On the influence of *Astrée* on Deshoulières's ecologues, see M. E. Storer, 'Madame Deshoulières, jugée par ses contemporains', *Romanic Review*, 25 (1934), 367–74. See also Timmermans, *L'Accès des femmes à la culture*, p. 184.

ancient one and characterise her complex position in the Quarrel of the Ancients and Moderns.[67] This was not her first (oblique) engagement in the Quarrel of the Ancients and Moderns: the Pradon–Racine quarrel discussed in the introduction followed her 'Ballade à M. Charpentier sur son livre intitulé *Défense de la langue française pour l'inscription de l'arc de triomphe*', a satirical defence of François Charpentier, circulated in 1676, with which she contributed to the *querelle des inscriptions*, about whether to write monument inscriptions in French or Latin, another version of the Quarrel of the Ancients and Moderns in which she also took a Modern side.

Three of her eclogue poems are included in her 1688 collection: 'Célimène, Églogue'; 'Iris, Églogue'; 'Louis, Églogue'.[68] Her fourth eclogue, 'Daphnis, Églogue à Monsieur d'Audiffret', was first published posthumously in the 1695 collection she had prepared before she died. Tonolo suggests that Iris and Célimène were probably both composed in 1680, and Alain Niderst argues that Fontenelle composed his eclogue work in 1683–84.[69] In this respect, Deshoulières anticipates some of the questions Fontenelle and Longepierre debate, but it is difficult to say with any certainty who might have influenced whom. We do know that Deshoulières and Fontenelle were acquaintances and so it is very likely that their works were in dialogue with each other.

In what follows, I will show that Deshoulières's eclogues, witty and oblique though they are, differ from Fontenelle's not only in her celebration of simplicity but also in her presentation of these poems as philosophical. As in her idylls, in her eclogues she argues against the supremacy of reason and progress and valorises what Chométy describes as the 'figure mythique du berger premier savant' (the mythic figure of the first learned shepherd).[70] She capitalises on the self-consciousness and artifice that characterises the eclogue genre by reversing or modifying typical tropes, as we saw she does in her idylls, to reflect on the gendering of this 'premier savant' and the fabrication of the image of the philosopher-poet. In so doing, she engages in particular with a predecessor's identification with Virgil, namely Clément Marot's self-presentation as the French Virgil. Marot translated Virgil's first Eclogue as the opening of his *L'Adolescence clémentine* of 1513,[71] and playfully paralleled his identity with that of the Roman

---

[67] The genre is conceived as having an ancient lineage in Guillaume Colletet's 1657 *Discours du poëme bucolique où il est traité de l'églogue, de l'idylle, et de la bergerie* (Paris: Chamhoudry, 1657). He cites Octavian de Saint-Gélais as writing the first French eclogues because of his translation of Virgil in 1495; this tradition was then continued by Marot (Colletet, *Discours du poëme bucolique*, p. 20).

[68] Célimène, Églogue' was first published in this edition; 'Iris, Églogue' was first published in the *Mercure Galant* in 1684; and 'Louis, Églogue' was first published in the *Mercure Galant* in 1687.

[69] *Poésies*, ed. by Tonolo, p. 114. Alain Niderst, *Fontenelle à la recherche de lui-même, 1657–1702* (Paris: Nizet, 1972), p. 242.

[70] Philippe Chométy, 'Du poète-berger au berger-philosophe', pp. 11–12.

[71] *Œuvres complètes*, ed. by François Rigolot, 2 vols (Paris: Flammarion, 2007–08), i (2007), pp. 38–43.

160 WOMEN WRITING ANTIQUITY

poet through what Florian Preisig calls his 'jeu Marot/Maro', in which he forms
a pun out of his own name and its homophony with Virgil's: Publius Virgilius
Maro.[72]

The eclogues 'Célimène' (pp. 113–16) and 'Iris' (pp. 159–61) function as companion pieces: both are written in the third person but include long monologues
from the female characters; Célimène laments her lover's absence, Iris his unfaith-
fulness. The privileging of the female perspective and the inclusion of female
speech is perhaps the most significant of Deshoulières's innovations: as we saw
in relation to Gournay's eclogue poems in Chapter 2, and as we saw Ellen Osiensis argue, 'in the world of Virgilian pastoral, girls are not singers; they do not
perform; and while they are sometimes quoted, we never hear them speak'.[73]
It is possible that Deshoulières was aware of Gournay's eclogues, although the
latter's *Advis* was not re-published after 1641; it is more likely that she was continuing a tradition of French pastoral writing and more precisely the successful
eclogue poems by Madame de Villedieu included in her 1662 collection in which
female shepherdesses also have a voice.[74] Deshoulières's revision of the male-
orientated world of Virgil's *Eclogues* is underscored by the way her shepherdesses
otherwise share many of the traits of Virgil's love-lorn shepherds: like Virgil's
shepherds, Célimène is consumed by the threat of lost love, so much so that
she lets her sheep into the field without thinking of whether a wolf might get
them (Virgil's shepherds were also famously not very good at shepherding). And
yet, in both these poems, Deshoulières subverts the norms of the pastoral genre.
Célimène is denied the ability to enjoy the usual tropes of the pastoral lover
because her love is absent (for instance, she complains that they cannot frolic on
the grass); for Iris the pleasant grassland is defiled because Tirsis enjoys it with
another.

Deshoulières valorises the genre by self-consciously mixing poetic modes and
introducing philosophical themes. The Iris eclogue is written in Alexandrines,
underscoring the tragic proportions of her feelings and the depths of emotion that

---

[72] Florian Preisig, *Clément Marot et les métamorphoses de l'auteur à l'aube de la Renaissance* (Geneva:
Droz, 2004), pp. 109–26, p. 159. See also Bernard Renner, 'Virgil and Marot: Imitation, Satire and Per-
sonal Identity', in *Virgilian Identities*, ed. by Usher and Fernbach, pp. 19–37. Marot writes 'Vergille [...]
/ Maro s'appelle et Marot je me nomme, / Marot je suis et Maro ne suis pas' in 'L'Enfer', from 'Œuvres
de 1543', in *Œuvres complètes*, ed. by Rigolot, II, pp. 221–34 (p. 231). On Marot and Deshoulières, see
Poésies, ed. by Tonolo, pp. 43–46.

[73] Ellen Oliensis, 'Sons and Lovers: Sexuality and Gender in Virgil's Poetry', in *The Cambridge
Companion to Virgil*, ed. by Charles Martindale (Cambridge: Cambridge University Press, 2006),
pp. 294–331 (p. 297).

[74] See the five Eclogues in Desjardins, *Poésies*, pp. 1–33. Marie-Jeanne L'Héritier, whom we study in
the next chapter, included an Eclogue, 'Célimène', in her 1696 *Œuvres mêlées* which deliberately echoes
Deshoulières's poem: the second half of this eclogue is also a pastiche of 'Les Moutons', 'hélas, que vôtre
sort est doux auprès du nôtre, petits moutons, innocents animaux' (alas, your fate is sweet compared to
ours, little sheep, innocent animals) (pp. 345–48 (p. 348)). A number of French eclogues, including by
Desjardins, circulated in manuscript form, see, for instance, MS Conrart 5418 and MS Conrart 5422,
Bibliothèque de l'Arsenal, Paris.

can be conveyed by the pastoral poem. The ellipsis in lines 59–60 is particularly evocative: 'Mais ma raison s'égare … Ah! Quels soins, quels secours / Dois-je attendre de vous, qui servez leurs amours!' (But my reason wanders … Ah! What aid, what relief can I expect from you, you who serve their loves!) (p. 160). Iris explicitly laments losing control to her passions and her inability to reason, picking up themes we have seen elsewhere in Deshoulières's poetry—'L'absence, la raison, l'orgueil, rien ne me sert' (absence, reason, pride: nothing serves me) (p. 160, l. 28). Deshoulières also alludes to the debates about the philosopher-berger in one of Iris's complaints:

> Il voulut m'enseigner quelle herbe va paissant
> Pour reprendre sa force un Troupeau languissant;
> Ce que fait le Soleil des brouillards qu'il attire
> N'avait-il rien, hélas! de plus doux à me dire? (p. 159, ll. 23–26).

> He wanted to teach me which grass a languishing herd
> Would eat to regain their strength
> And what the sun does with the fogs it attracts;
> Alas, did he have nothing sweeter to tell me?

As Chométy argues, Deshoulières refers here to the phenomenon whereby a meteor is sublimated by the heat of the sun (comet sublimation).[75] Deshoulières's witty and knowing intervention in the debate about the eclogue presents Tirsis's philosophising as the antithesis of what would make him an adequate lover-berger in the eyes of Iris. With characteristic elusiveness, Deshoulières seems to be mocking the notion that shepherds should be 'philosophical' at the same time as she has Iris's lament engage in the philosophical questions of reason.

Deshoulières's eclogues thus draw more from Virgil than Theocritus in their philosophical bent: that preference is further evident in her use of the eclogue as a commemorative poem in 'Louis, Églogue' (pp. 219–24). Conferring immortality is part of the ancient tradition as is clear from Virgil's *Eclogue* 5 in which the speakers propose to exalt their dead fellow shepherd, Daphnis, 'to the stars'. It was also part of the Renaissance tradition: Marot had penned a ceremonial 'Églogue sur le trespas de tres haulte et tres illustre princesse ma dame Loyse de Savoye',[76] in which he very explicitly codifies the eclogue as Gallic by referring to French topography, flora and fauna.[77] Deshoulières takes this further: the location in 'Louis, Églogue' is not the usual *locus amoenus* of the rural shepherds but the cultivated gardens of Versailles; her poem has two speakers (like Virgil's polyphonic model), Iris and

---

[75] Chométy, 'Du poète-berger au berger-philosophe', p. 80.
[76] Marot, *Œuvres complètes*, ed. by Rigolot, I, pp. 204–12.
[77] On this see Robert J. Hudson, 'Bucolic Influence: Marot's Gallic Pastoral and Maurice Scève's Arion', *Romanic Review*, 105.3–4 (2014), 253–72.

162   WOMEN WRITING ANTIQUITY

Célimène, which refers us back to the other two eclogues of the 1688 collection. Where in 'Le Ruisseau' (which is also—pointedly—the poem that directly precedes 'Louis, Eclogue' in this collection), Deshoulières likens fountains to 'torture' (p. 217), here Célimène is full of praise for the artifice of the fountain: 'Admirez cet amas superbe / D'Eaux, de Marbres et d'Or qui brillent à nos yeux' (Admire this superb structure of water, marble, and gold which shines before our eyes) (p. 219, ll. 7–8), and for the gardens as evidence for Louis as 'Vainqueur de la Nature' (p. 220, l. 20). Deshoulières deliberately uses tropes of the pastoral throughout: Célimène's desire to praise her King is couched in terms that echo the shepherd's neglect of his sheep for his love—she does not care about herself or her health: 'Ce plaisir où je m'abandonne / Me tient lieu de tous les plaisirs' (this pleasure to which I abandon myself / takes the place of all other pleasures) (p. 222, ll. 78–80) and 'Je négligeai les autres soins / Mes infortunes domestiques / En sont de fidèles témoins' (I neglected other cares / my poor servants / are faithful witnesses of this) (p. 221, ll. 41–43). Recurring throughout this eclogue is also the (typical) eclogue self-referential theme of poetry composition. Célimène seems to stand for Deshoulières as she evokes the muse to guide her:

> A sa gloire en secret je consacrai mes jours,
> Et pour faire en tous lieux voler sa renommée,
> Des neufs savantes Sœurs j'implorai le secours. (p. 220, ll. 37–39)

> I consecrated my days in secret to his glory
> And to make his renown known everywhere
> I implored the aid of nine learned sisters.

With this poem Deshoulières draws out the artifice at the heart of the pastoral genre to make it match, stylistically, the artifice of Versailles. Using two female speakers again, and this time as celebrants of the King, Deshoulières also casts herself as panegyric poet.

Her ability to work closely with the ancient tradition, especially Virgil—an ability which strengthens my reading of her deliberate deviations from it—is most evident in her final eclogue, 'Daphnis, Églogue à Monsieur d'Audiffret' (pp. 360–65). It is a polyphonic poem between three male shepherds; Daphnis is lamenting the rejection of his lover, Iris, and Lysidor is consoling him, when Timandre enters to say that Iris is also heartbroken and all ends happily.[78] Daphnis is the bucolic hero of Theocritus' *Idyll* 1 and of Virgil's *Eclogue* 5, and often seen as inventor of the pastoral genre. Where Daphnis is the subject of the shepherds' song in both Theocritus's and Virgil's versions, here Deshoulières makes him narrate his own grief. By making Daphnis speak, she is perhaps echoing Ronsard's

---

[78] The composition date is unknown and this poem has some verse missing, see *Poésies*, ed. by Tonolo, p. 360.

eclogue which stages an amoebaean song contest between Daphnis and Thyrsis,[79] but the focus on heartache keeps its Virgilian antecedent in view. Across all of these eclogues, Deshoulières is characteristically equivocal in her 'defence' of this poetic genre, taking an oblique approach to this *querelle*, at once using some of her poems to demonstrate the genre's more philosophical capacities by exploring questions about reason, and also gently subverting some of its typical characteristics: in so doing she draws attention to the gender of the eclogue's speaking subject and thus of the 'premier savant' figure, and indeed of the poet.

Figuring the Poet: Versions of Anacreon and Horace

Underpinning Deshoulières's scrutiny of the epistemological properties of poetic genre is an implicit reflection on the role and status of the poet. In this final section, I want to examine that reflection further by looking at how she uses two other ancient poets: Anacreon and Horace. I close this chapter with an analysis of how she employs these—very different—poets to explore her status and authority as a poet, a gesture which is complemented by my reading of two further poems which contain a more direct reflection on what it meant to be a published woman of letters and a 'savante': the 'Épître chagrine' to Charlotte-Rose de Caumont de La Force published in her 1688 collection, written as advice to younger female friend, and her 'Épître à Madame de Maintenon', which forms a compelling companion to her Horatian Ode to Colbert.

One of her earliest published poems, after the two 'Portraits' that appeared in the *Recueil des portraits et éloges en vers et en prose* in 1659,[80] was her 'Sonnet sur l'or. Bouts rimés', written in the tradition of the ancient Greek lyric poet, Anacreon (what we would now call pseudo-Anacreon or the Anacreontea), and first published in a 1671 *Recueil* and included again in her 1688 collection.[81] In the 1688 edition of her poetry, this poem is followed by another Anacreontic verse, a 'Ballade' about drinking, and is preceded by her 'Imitation de la première ode d'Horace', thus making a trio of classical poems. The 'Sonnet sur l'or. Bouts rimés' (p. 106) playfully reworks the *topos* of the pleasures and moral ills of gold that has its poetic origins in Anacreontea 58, Ode to Gold.[82] It is possible that she was aware of the—interpretative—French version of this poem published by Claude-Denis Du Four de la Crespelière in 1670, and that she was aware of some contemporary

---

[79] 'Églogue: Daphnis et Thyrsis', in *Œuvres complètes*, ed. by Laumonier, IV, pp. 146–63.

[80] 'Portrait de Mlle de Vilenne fait par Mme Deshoulières', in *Recueil des portraits*, pp. 310–13; and 'Portrait de M. de Lignières fait par Mme Deshoulières', ibid., pp. 502–08; *Poésies*, ed. by Tonolo, pp. 87–94.

[81] *Recueil de poésies diverses dédié à Mgr le Prince de Conti par M. de la Fontaine*, 2 vols (Paris: Le Petit, 1671), II, p. 173. It may have been composed in 1667 or in 1670, see *Poésies*, ed. by Tonolo, p. 106.

[82] *Greek Lyric II: Anacreon, Anacreontea, Choral Lyric from Olympus to Alcman*, ed. and trans. by David Campbell, Loeb Classical Library 143 (Cambridge, MA: Harvard University Press, 1993).

164   WOMEN WRITING ANTIQUITY

uses of this *topos* by Pierre Le Moyne, Jean François Sarasin, and Laurent Drelin-
court, as suggested by Tonolo, but the more comprehensive French versions of
Anacreon by Anne Le Fèvre (Dacier) and Hilaire-Bernard de Longepierre did not
come out until some ten years later (though Deshoulières would have known Anne
Dacier from the salon of the artist Élisabeth Chéron).[83] According to a note in the
Recueil de pièces curieuses published by Adriaan Moetjens in 1694, which included
many of Deshoulières's poems, it is assumed that this poem was the result of a salon
game or poetic 'défi' and that Deshoulières had filled in the last words of a poem set
by Condé and circulated among acquaintances.[84] Its presentation in the 1688 edition both makes this insertion evident by having each final word follow an ellipsis,
and provides no context to explain the poem's origin or multiple authorship; it is
therefore recontextualised as her own. This poem emphasises the appealing and
even magical properties of gold before closing with the Anacreontic condemnation of its unsubstantial trappings. Deshoulières's reception of Anacreon informed
what Tonolo calls an 'atmosphère anacréontic' of the 1670s and 1680s: for instance,
La Fontaine also imitated the Greek lyric poet and we examined Scudéry's earlier
response to the Anacreontic tradition in Chapter 3.[85] Anacreon, like Ovid—and
indeed the two poets were sometimes paired—was conceptualised as a lyric poet;
and his focus on sentiment and sociability made him popular in salon culture.[86]
He had also been an important figure for the *Pléiade* poets, and Pierre de Ronsard, whose influence on Deshoulières was considerable, as we have seen, made

[83] *Poésies*, ed. by Tonolo, p. 106. Claude-Denis Du Four de la Crespelière, *Odes amoureuses, charmantes et bachiques des poètes grecs Anacreon, Sappho et Theocrite* (Paris: Loyson, 1670), p. 29. Earlier
translations include Rémi Belleau, *Les odes d'Anacreon ... traduites de grec en françois* (Paris: Wechel,
1556). As Tonolo shows, there was also the Italian tradition which she might have known (translations by Michelangelo Torcigliani, 1642; Francesco Antonio Cappone, 1670; and Bartolomeo Corsini,
1672): see Tonolo, 'Les métamorphoses d'Anacréon', p. 190. See also Anne LeFèvre [Dacier], *Les poésies
d'Anacréon et de Sapho* (Paris: Thierry, 1681); Hilaire-Bernard de Longepierre, *Les Poésies de Anacréon
et de Sapho* (Paris: Émery, 1684). The problem of who influenced whom is 'délicate' (Tonolo, 'Les
métamorphoses d'Anacréon', p. 191).

[84] *Recueil de pièces curieuses et nouvelles*, I, p. 578. This was a popular genre of salon verse: see, for
instance, the series of 'Sonnets en bouts rimés' included in Marie-Jeanne L'Héritier, *Œuvres mêlées de
Mlle L'H**** (Paris: Guignard, 1696), pp. 345–99. On the 'bouts-rimés' in the salon, see Emma Gilby,
'Présence d'esprit and Action in Seventeenth-Century France', in *The Places of Early Modern Criticism*,
ed. by Alexander Gavin, Emma Gilby, and Alexander Marr (Oxford: Oxford University Press, 2021),
pp. 176–90 (pp. 178–84).

[85] Tonolo, 'Les métamorphoses d'Anacréon', p. 191. Jean de La Fontaine, 'Contes et nouvelles', in
Œuvres complètes, ed. by Pierre Clarac (Paris: Seuil, 1965), pp. 242–43. See also Patricia Rosenmeyer,
The Poetics of Imitation: Anacreon and the Anacreontic Tradition (Cambridge: Cambridge University
Press, 1992).

[86] See Stéphanie Loubère, 'Figures et figuration d'Anacréon galant', in *La Galanterie des anciens*, ed.
by Nathalie Grande and Claudine Nédélec (Paris: Armand Colin, 2012), pp. 83–98. Deshoulières's
conception of Anacreon also made it into the eighteenth-century imaginary of this ancient poet.
Deshoulières features in Julien-Jacques Moutonnet-Clairfons, *Anacréon, Sapho, Bion et Moschus: traduction nouvelle en prose, suivie de la 'Veillée des fêtes de Vénus' et d'un choix de pièces de différents
auteurs* (Paris: Le Boucher, 1773). Anacreon (along with Ovid) is one of the lyric poets to celebrate Deshoulières in Marie-Jeanne L'Héritier's commemorative text, *Le Triomphe de Madame
Des-Houlières*, p. 414.

use of the newly available Anacreontic material in his collections published in the mid-sixteenth century.[87]

As one of her first published poems, this sonnet represents an intriguing choice: like her 'Imitation de Lucrèce', it anchors Deshoulières's poetics in knowing and witty salon games, which depend on one's inclusion. These sorts of poetic games feature elsewhere in the 1688 collection—for instance: the four rhyming poems she writes at the request of the Maréchal de Vivonne, 'Rimes': 'en ailles', 'en eilles', 'en illes', and 'en ouilles' (pp. 231–37). However, for all that Anacreon was important to salon culture, he was not necessarily an obvious choice for a woman entering the literary scene: as we saw in Chapter 3, his persona was frequently a lecherous old man who wrote primarily about drinking, women, and parties.

Deshoulières exploits the discordance between expectations of female modesty and the Anacreontic voice in the poem that directly follows this 'Sonnet' in the 1688 collection: the 'Ballade' (p. 107), which echoes the bacchic drinking poems associated with Anacreon and draws on Horace's Epode 13 celebrating the consolations of wine and song. In this Ballade, Deshoulières plays with notions of gender, propriety, and licentiousness. It opens:

> Il est saison de causer près du feu
> Le blond Phébus, chère Iris, se retire:
> L'Aquilon souffle; et d'un commun aveu,
> Point n'est ma chambre exposée à son ire
> Viens-y souper, j'ai du muscat charmant.
> Quand je te vois ma tendresse s'éveille,
> Désirerais être homme en ce moment,
> Ou quand ta voix se mêle follement
> Au doux glou glou que fait une bouteille. (pp. 107–08, ll. 1–9)

> It is the season for chatting by the fire
> Blond Phebus, dear Iris, retires;
> The Aquillon blows; and by mutual consent
> My room is not exposed to his ire;
> Come and dine here: I have a delicious muscat.
> When I see you, my tender feelings are awoken,
> I would desire to be a man at that moment,
> or when your voice mixes gaily
> with the sweet glugging sound of a bottle.

---

[87] See John O' Brien, *Anacreon Redivivus: A Study of Anacreontic Translation in Mid-Sixteenth-Century France* (Ann Arbor: Michigan University Press, 1995), pp. 155–200; and John O'Brien, 'Ronsard, Belleau and Renvoisy', *Early Music History*, 13 (1994), 199–215. On the publishing history of the Anacreontea, see Chapter 3.

166 WOMEN WRITING ANTIQUITY

Lines 1–4, as Tonolo shows, echo Horace's Epode 13.[88] The final line, repeated at
the end of each stanza, also situates the poem in the tradition of Anacreontic drinking poems. The Anacreontic persona is also echoed in the overt sexual virility of
the poet's address and the explicit gender-crossing ('je [...] désirerais être homme')
self-consciously draws attention to her own ventriloquism of a male poet; it also
troubles heteronormative assumptions. Beyond the licentiousness, a case could
also be made for reading this as an echo of Sappho's Fragment 31, 'He seems to me
equal to Gods', with its evocation of desire for another woman at a dinner party, so
that Deshoulières is, as in the editorial tradition and as we saw in Chapter 3 with
Scudéry, linking together these two lyric poets.

Such experiments with masculine poetic modes also come in the form of formal and public (rather than bacchic) verse, which allow Deshoulières to reflect
on the power of poetry as panegyric. The poem that introduces this classically
influenced trio in the 1688 collection, 'Imitation de la première Ode d'Horace,
Moecenas atavis. A Monsieur Colbert' (p. 103), is a version of Horace's first ode
dedicated to his patron Maecenas, adviser to Augustus (1.1). In this 'Imitation',
we encounter an injection of Deshoulières's own authorial persona: the poem is
marked by her own reflections on the vanity of glory. After an initial stanza praising Colbert, Deshoulières's 'Imitation' follows the logic and examples of Horace's
original which catalogues other occupations before culminating in a description
of the poet's own desire to sing the praises of their patron. Deshoulières uses
all the same examples as Horace: those who enjoy the tournament, the politician, the farmer, the merchant at sea, the drinker, the warrior, and the hunter.
The list in Horace's version contains some restrained criticisms (the politician
relies on a 'mob of fickle citizens', 7; merchants cannot rest for greed, 18; warriors engage in wars that mothers detest, 24; and the hunter 'neglects his soft wife
at home', 26), which allows him to emphasise the superiority of the poet's activities.
Deshoulières, by contrast, inflects every example with a negative comment about
the ambition of those pursuing these different occupations, turning the catalogue
into a more universal condemnation of man's vanity and foolishness. The 'jeune
audacieux' at the tournament thinks too highly of himself (17–20); the politician,
'l'ambitieux', is obsessed with glory (23–25); the farmer is 'avare'; the merchant is
foolhardy (37–40); the drinker is foolish (46–47). While she elaborates here her
pessimistic and sceptical view of man, decrying the vanity of glory, she does so in
a version of a poem well known for the explicit glory it will confer on the poet: the
final two lines of Horace's version read: 'quodsi me lyricis vatibus inseres / sublimi
feriam sidera vertice' ('But if you will include me among lyric bards / Then, my
head through the clouds, I shall collide with stars').[89] This sort of contradiction is

---

[88] *Poésies*, ed. by Tonolo, p. 107.
[89] Horace, *Odes and Epodes*, ed. and trans. by Niall Rudd, Loeb Classical Library 33 (Cambridge,
MA: Harvard University Press, 2004), 1.35–36.

common in her work: is she reinterpreting Horace's poem about glory to demonstrate its limits or are her criticisms of glory instances of *recusatio*? Deshoulières ostensibly makes a more 'modest' claim than Horace in the final lines:

> Pour moi de qui le cœur ne s'est trouvé sensible
> Qu'à l'innocent plaisir de bien faire des vers
> Seule au bord des ruisseaux je chante sur ma lyre
> Ou le Dieu des Guerriers, ou le Dieu des Amants
> Et ne changerais pas pour le plus vaste empire
>   Ces doux amusements.
>
> [...]
>
>   COLBERT, si vous daignez m'entendre,
> Si pour quelques momens mes chants peuvent suspendre
>   Les chagrins que traîne après soi
>   Cette profane politique
> Où le bien de l'État sans cesse vous applique
>   Quel sort plus glorieux pour moi? (pp. 105–6, ll. 67–83)

> As for me, whose heart is only sensitive
> To the innocent pleasure of writing verse well,
> Alone on the riverbank I sing on my lyre
> About either the god of warriors or the god of lovers
> And I would not change for the most vast empire
>   these sweet amusements ...
>
>   Colbert, if you deign to hear me,
> If for some moments my song might suspend
>   The difficulties that these profane politics
>   drag along with them
> and which the good of the state endlessly assails you with
>   What better glory might I expect?

She suggests that her glory will reside in offering Colbert some light relief and solace, rather than her name being placed among the stars, and her closing question rephrases as doubt the confidence of Horace's future tense. The close of this poem could be seen as a gesture of poetic modesty; and in the doubt it casts over man's recourse to glory, it could also be read as part of Deshoulières's sceptical philosophy. However, this modesty and scepticism are complicated in this poem because, in evoking Horace's famous poem about the poet's glory, she also asserts her place in the encomium tradition. She re-genders (and re-genres) Horace's closing gesture with the first-person description, 'seule au bord des ruisseaux je chante sur ma lyre', which stresses lyric and implicitly refers to another poet of the

168 WOMEN WRITING ANTIQUITY

lyre—Sappho.[90] The poem is thus in part about Deshoulières as poet, even though she denies her own quest for literary glory.

Her version of Horace has a continuation in her 'Épître à Madame de Maintenon' (pp. 208–10) from her 1688 collection, in which she compares Maintenon's position as respected confidante of the King to that of Maecenus to Augustus, thereby echoing her own imitation of Horace's Ode 1; with this poem, she implicitly casts herself as Horace (and Virgil), to whom Maecenas was patron. Although it is a common Modern gesture to compare Louis XIV with Augustus, Deshoulières's intertext identifies the male canon and alludes to her (contested) place within it. She echoes this later in a short poem published in 1747 (but dated 1687) addressed to the critic, grammarian, and essayist, Dominic Bouhours, known for his essay on 'le je-ne-sais-quoi' in his *Entretiens d'Ariste et d'Eugène* (1671) and his work of literary criticism, *La Manière de bien penser sur les ouvrages de l'esprit* (1687). In 'Au R. P. Bouhours sur son livre de l'art de bien penser sur les Ouvrages de l'esprit' (p. 464), she writes:

> Dans une liste triomphante
> De célèbres Auteurs que votre Livre chante
> Je ne vois point mon nom placé.
> À moi (n'est-il pas vrai?) vous n'avez point pensé;
> Mais aussi dans le même rôle
> Vous avez oublié Pascal,
> Qui pourtant ne pensait pas mal:
> Un tel compagnon me console.

> In a triumphant list
> Of famous authors which your book praises
> I do not see my own name.
> You must not have thought of me (surely?)
> But in the same vein
> You also forgot Pascal
> Who, however, was not a bad thinker:
> I'm consoled by such a companion.

---

[90] Sappho is not generally a figure of identification for Deshoulières. Deshoulières is identified with Sappho by others, such as Pierre Bayle (*Dictionnaire*, II, p. 720), and in the 'Lettre en prose et en vers à Sapho' attributed to her tutor, Jean Dehénault, and thought to be addressed to Deshoulières, see Frèdèric Lachèvre, 'Pièces libertines et philosophiques', *Les Œuvres de Jean Dehénault* (Paris: Champion, 1922), pp. 15–19, and *Les Derniers Libertins*, p. 28. See also Charles-Augustin Sainte-Beuve, *Portraits de femmes*, ed. by Gérald Antoine (Paris: Gallimard, 1998), p. 365. The 1694 Amsterdam edition of her poetry also makes the connection in a prefatory poem by Janus Broukhusius, *Les Poésies de Madame Deshoulières, édition nouvelle augmentée d'un tiers* (Amsterdam: Wetstein, 1694), np. She is also compared to Corinna in the caption for the engraving based on a portrait by Elisabeth Chéron included in the 1740 *Poésies de Madame et Mlle Deshoulières* (Brussels: Vve Foppens, 1740), np. See Anne Debrosse, *La Souvenance et le désir: la reception des poétesses grecques* (Paris: Classiques Garnier, 2018), pp. 371–73.

Her reference to Pascal in part refers to the quarrel between Bouhours and Ménage about Pascal and Vaugelas and, as such, is provocative: but this poem also draws attention to the male gendering of the canon.

This subtle, but provocative, allusion to quarrels, and this reflection on the status of the female poet, is most explicitly present in the final poem I will analyse here, in which she interrogates what it means specifically to be 'savante': her 'Épître Chagrine de Madame Deshoulières à Mademoiselle ***' (pp. 128–32) of her 1688 collection, assumed to be addressed to the *conteuse* and poet, Charlotte-Rose de Caumont de La Force, whom we will encounter in the next chapter.[91] Written in a version of the lament or complaint mode, her 'Épître chagrine' narrates the pitfalls of being a *savante*. It does so initially by emphasising the intrinsic and moral problems of this identity, in a manner that stresses its vanity and so seems to echo Scudéry's admonishments. The poem opens by linking the pursuit of being 'savante' with the pursuit of 'la gloire', thus condemning the demonstrative learning of this figure:

> Quel espoir vous séduit? Quelle gloire vous tente?
> > Quel caprice! à quoi pensez-vous?
> > Vous voulez devenir savante?
> Hélas! du bel Esprit savez-vous les dégoûts?
> Ce nom jadis si beau, si révéré de tous,
> > N'a plus rien, aimable Amarante,
> > Ni d'honorable ni de doux. (p. 128, ll. 1–7)

> What hope seduces you? What glory tempts you?
> > What caprice! What are you thinking of?
> > You want to become a learned woman?
> Alas! Do you know how distasteful the *bel esprit* has become?
> This name, once so beautiful, so revered by all
> > Is now nothing, dear Amarante,
> > Is no longer honourable or sweet.

She associates 'savante' here with the 'dégoût' of the 'bel esprit', in a usage that likens this category to pedants.[92] In the final stanza, Deshoulières draws on her own experience, claiming (in another instance of false modesty?) that she would

---

[91] It was first published in the *Mercure Galant* in November 1684 (p. 23). Significantly, it was entitled 'Epitre chagrine de Madame Deshoulières à Mademoiselle sur les savants et les sciences' in a manuscript version, MS Tralage 6542, Bibliothèque de l'Arsenal, Paris, II, fol. 220, as quoted in *Poésies*, ed. by Tonolo, p. 128. She also wrote two other 'Épîtres chagrines' addressed to Père La Chaise (p. 312) on the subject of *faux dévots*; and to Mlle de la Charce about false wooers and coquettes (p. 180). See also Tonolo, *Divertissement et profondeur*, for instance, pp. 30–31, pp. 222, p. 264.

[92] See also the Introduction.

never have drunk from the Hippocrene (source of the Muses) had she known what the reactions would be:

> J'ai su faire des Vers, avant de connaître
> Les chagrins attachés à ce maudit talent.
> > Vous que le ciel n'a point fait naître
> > Avec ce talent que je hais
> Croyez-en mes conseils, ne l'acquérez jamais. (p. 132, ll. 131–35)

> I became accomplished in writing verse before I realised
> The grief attached to this cursed talent.
> > You to whom the heaven did not provide at birth
> > The talent I hate
> Listen to my advice, and never acquire it.

It quickly becomes clear, however, that far from a generalised reflection on the perils of literary glory, the poem is an attack on a specific culture of *beaux esprits*, who create a difficult environment for a woman of letters to flourish—not because they disparage such women, but because they fawn on them and stifle them. Deshoulières does not mock the 'savante', but mocks the way in which this figure is revered by the group which is the real target of her attack: pedants. To some degree these enemies are generalised and abstracted (and enemies on which everyone can agree, in that pedants were such a standard target); but she is at pains to show that this is what she is not.[93] Deshoulières warns La Force of the fools she would have to suffer, as being a writer means subjecting oneself to the scrutiny and criticism of idiots:

> Pourrez-vous supporter qu'un Fat de qualité
> Qui sait à peine lire, et qu'un caprice guide
> > De tous vos ouvrages décide? (p. 129, ll. 25–28)
> [...]
> > Personne ne lit pour apprendre
> > On ne lit que pour critiquer (ll. 32–33)

> Will you be able to endure having a pompous fellow
> Who hardly knows how to read, guided by caprice
> > Judge your works?
> [...]
> > Nobody reads to learn
> > They only read to criticise.

---

[93] She targets pedants again, for instance in her 'Réflexions diverses' in her 1688 collection; see *Poésies*, ed. by Tonolo, pp. 190–97 (p. 196); and on this poem as against pedants and as an exploration of the status of the poet, see Tonolo, *Divertissement et profondeur*, pp. 30–31, p. 222.

The irony of her criticising critics is not only a way for her to pre-empt criticism, but also draws attention to the fact that this poem is an attack. The pedants (whom we might also call false savants) are more akin to Scudéry's Damophile: they too aspire to knowledge of antiquity:

> Dans la débauche et dans le jeu nourris
>   On les voit avec même audace
>   Parler et d'Homère, et d'Horace
>   Comparer leurs divins Écrits
> Confondre leurs beautés, leur tour, leurs caractères,
>   Si connus et si différents,
>   Traiter des Ouvrages si grands
>   De badinages, de chimères,
> Et cruels ennemis des Langues Etrangères
>   Être orgueilleux d'être ignorants. (p. 131, ll. 96–105)

> Nourished in debauchery and gambling
>   They can be seen with the same audacity
>   Talking about Homer and Horace
>   Comparing their divine writings,
> Confusing their beauties, their ruses, their characteristics,
>   So well-known and so different from each other,
>   Treating such great works as
>   Playful ephemera,
> And cruel enemies of foreign languages
>   They are proud of their ignorance.

However, these enemies are more specific: first, they are constructed in clear antithesis to *galants* and Moderns. And secondly, she refers in particular to theatre, singling out not the critics here, but the author's reaction to being judged:

> Irez-vous voir jouer une Pièce nouvelle,
> Il faudra pour l'Auteur être pleine d'égards:
> Il expliquera tout, mines, gestes, regards;
>   Et si sa pièce n'est pas belle,
> Il vous imputera tout ce qu'on dira d'elle,
>   Et de sa colère immortelle
> Il vous faudra courir tous les hasards (p. 130, ll. 54–60).

> If you go and see a new play
> You will need to be full of admiration for the author
> He will explain everything: expressions, gestures, looks
>   And if the play is no good

172 WOMEN WRITING ANTIQUITY

> He will attribute to you all that is said about it
> And you will run the risk of
> rousing his immortal anger.

This could be read as a nod to the *querelle des sonnets* of 1677, in which she probably played a role.[94] This is reinforced by a mock tragic stanza surely intended to echo Racine's *Phèdre*, where the poet fears the worst for the few who supporters who remain:

> Mais pour combien de temps aurez-vous leur secours?
> Hélas! J'en pâlis, j'en frisonne.
> Les trois fatales Sœurs qui n'épargnent personne,
> Sont prêtes à couper la trame de leurs jours. (pp. 132, ll. 109–13)

> But for how long will you have their help?
> Alas! I grew pale, I tremble as I think about this.
> The three fatal sisters who spare no one
> Are ready to cut the thread of their lives.

While this poem opens and closes with gestures that make it appear to be an exercise in modesty, it could equally be seen as provocative, a reflection on and continuation of the Racine–Pradon theatre quarrels of earlier in her career. In this respect, the frame of modesty and the claims to criticise criticism are also a way of deflecting the agonistic gesture present in the poem. This simultaneous engagement with and distancing from a quarrel could be another modest strategy of denial, but it is also particular to Deshoulières's ironic, equivocal, and playful poetic voice, her challenge to hermeneutics.[95]

**

Although Deshoulières does not yet quite have the revived status of some of the other women studied in this book, she was held in much esteem in her own time and was a key reference throughout the eighteenth century in France with her poems reprinted twenty-two times between 1705 and 1798.[96] She seems to have fallen out of literary favour in the nineteenth century. There are three aspects of

---

[94] Her 1680 play *Genséric* had also been attacked in an anonymous unpublished sonnet: see the MS Tallemant des Réaux 673, fol. 200 and see *Le Manuscrit 673 de Tallemant des Réaux*, ed. by Maigne, pp. 531–32.

[95] See Taylor, 'Antoinette Deshoulières's Cat'.

[96] For instance, when Fontenelle was received into the *Académie française*, her poetry was read aloud at the inauguration. She is highly praised in Claude Guyonnet de Vertron's *La Nouvelle Pandore ou les femmes illustres du siècle de Louis le Grand*, 2 vols (Paris, Vve Mazuel, 1698), for example, II, pp. 468–69. Vertron helped secure her membership of the *Académie d'Arles* and corresponded with Deshoulières who agreed to judge a sonnet competition in honour of the Duc de Saint-Aignan. See Miriam Speyer, 'Entre gazette mondaine et art poétique galant: les lettres dans La Nouvelle Pandore (1698)', *Arts et Savoirs*, 17 (2022) URL: http://journals.openedition.org/aes/4688.

SALON VERSE AND THE PHILOSOPHER-POET   173

her work which are made prominent in her eighteenth- and nineteenth-century reception: her success as a female poet, her involvement in the Racine–Pradon quarrel, and her position as a philosopher. She features in Olympe de Gouges's *Mirabeau aux Champs Élysées* (1791) with two other women, Madame de Sevigné and Ninon de l'Enclos, who are there to crown Mirabeau in an act that affirms female judgement.[97] Although Deshoulières has the smallest part of the three, she is represented as an advocate for women's equality and equal recognition to men: 'On ne veut pas que nous soyons sur la terre les égales des hommes: ce n'est qu'aux Champs-Élysées que nous avons ce droit' (On earth they do not want us to be equal to men; this is reserved for the Elysian Fields).[98] Her poetry was also a major reference in Henri Gaillard's *Rhétorique à l'usage des jeunes demoiselles* (1748), and in the preface she is cast, with Dacier, as an example of excellence and inspiration.[99] And yet, her involvement in the *querelle des sonnets* subjected her to the scorn often reserved for women polemicists: she is presumed to be one of the targets of Boileau's *Satire X*: 'au mauvais goût public la belle y fait la guerre' (the beauty waged war against the public's bad taste),[100] and Voltaire, who praised her poetry, wrote 'C'est dommage qu'elle soit l'auteur du mauvais sonnet contre l'admirable Phèdre de Racine [...] Une femme satirique ressemble à Méduse et à Scylla, deux beautés changées en monstres' (it is a shame that she wrote that poor sonnet against Racine's admirable *Phèdre*; a satirical woman resembles Medusa and Scylla, two beauties turned into monsters).[101] Finally, her position as philosopher is the particular focus of Sainte-Beuve's discussion of her work in his *Portraits de femmes*, in which he tried to reinstate her, although he too is critical of her inclination to satire.[102] All three of these aspects of her work are noted in the text written to commemorate her death, *L'Apothéose de Madame Des Houlières* (1694), dedicated to Madeleine de Scudéry, by Marie-Jeanne L'Héritier: she stresses Deshoulières's contributions as a woman poet, notes the diversity of Deshoulières's work, and defends her satire as proper and in keeping with *bienséance*.[103] For L'Héritier,

---

[97] See Jessica Goodman, 'Introduction', *Commemorating Mirabeau*: Mirabeau aux Champs-Elysées *and other texts*, ed. by Jessica Goodman (Cambridge: MHRA, 2017), pp. 1–51 (p. 31).

[98] 'Mirabeau aux Champs Elysées', in *Commemorating Mirabeau*, ed. by Goodman, p. 94.

[99] Henri Gaillard, *Rhétorique à l'usage des jeunes demoiselles* (Paris: Leclerc, 1748), np.

[100] Nicolas Boileau, *Œuvres complètes*, ed. by Françoise Escal, with an introduction by Antoine Adam (Paris: Gallimard, 1966), p. 74.

[101] 'Le Siècle de Louis XIV', in *Œuvres historiques*, ed. by René Pomeau (Paris: Gallimard, 1957), pp. 605–1274 (p. 1156). Her interventions in the Racine–Pradon quarrel were referred to by Augustin Simon Irailh, *Querelles litteraires ou mémoires pour servir à l'histoire des révolutions de la république des lettres, depuis Homère jusqu'à nos jours*, 2 vols (Paris: Durand, 1761), II, pp. 344–45. See also Volker Schröder, 'Madame Deshoulières, ou la satire au féminin', *Dix-septième siècle*, 258.1 (2013), 95–106.

[102] 'Elle semble plus moraliste qu'il ne convient à une bergère; il y a des pensées sous ses rubans et ses fleurs. Elle est un digne contemporain de M. de la Rochefoucauld [...] les allusions vengeresses du satirique peu galant' (She seems more of a moralist than suits a shepherdess; there is substance under her ribbons and flowers. She is a worthy contemporary of La Rochefoucauld [despite] the vengeful allusions of her hardly *galant* satire). Sainte-Beuve, *Portraits*, pp. 364–65. For a contemporary account of her philosophy, see Conley, *The Suspicion of Virtue*, pp. 45–74.

[103] L'Héritier, *Le Triomphe de Madame Des-Houlières*, p. 407.

174   WOMEN WRITING ANTIQUITY

Deshoulières epitomises the 'savante moderne': a category we will explore further in the next chapter.

For all that she was categorised thus, Antoinette Deshoulières nevertheless represents a complex Modern.[104] True, in her interventions in the Quarrel, she—albeit often obliquely—took a Modern side. The 1688 collection as a whole could be seen as a deliberate intervention in the Quarrel, coming out as it did at the Quarrel's height, especially since she had received a *privilège* a full ten years earlier and had delayed publication. Her Modern inclination is evident in other poems in this collection, which have not been the objects of study here: for instance, in the Gallic medievalism she promotes in her 1684 exchange of *Ballades* with the Duc de Saint-Aignan, longing for the mores of the 'siècle d'Amadis', published in the *Mercure Galant*, responding to the recent success of Lully's opera of the same title and drawing on the influence of 'Amadis de Gaule' on d'Urfé's *Astrée*.[105] Her medievalism can also be seen in her use of poetic genres that privileged medieval orality (chanson, rondeau) and her vaunting of the simplicity and innocence of nature.[106] Recourse to a French tradition rather than an ancient one, to a medieval period rather than a classical one, is a typical gesture of the Moderns, as we will explore further in the next chapter. As Marine Roussillon argues, Deshoulières's use of the medieval past in the Amadis cycle of *Ballades* exchanged with Saint-Aignan makes her an important figure in the *galant* and Modern deployment of that past.[107] This exchange of verse epistles was printed in full in the 1688 collection, both promoting from Deshoulières's side a Modern medievalism and staging a quarrel as a Modern through the moderate use of two sides and dialogue. The use of the 'ballade' form is not insignificant either to the Modern cause as it was an archaic verse form that harked back to the pre-Pleiad poet Clément Marot, whom she explicitly praises in a further poem, 'Rondeau sur le bel esprit' (p. 172). The 'ballade', like the 'rondeau', was not a classical form of verse, although Deshoulières does use plenty of these: odes, eclogues, and elegy, forms so vaunted by Du Bellay.[108]

This nostalgia, however, presents a more complex attitude than, for instance, Fontenelle's Modern optimism and vision of progress would allow: the premise of her position in the quarrel with Saint-Aignan, which he refutes, is that standards

---

[104] See also Tonolo, *Divertissement et profondeur*, p. 284.

[105] Sophie Tonolo, 'Aimer comme Amadis: une poétesse entre deux siècles', in *Origines: Actes du 39e congrès annuel de la North American Society for Seventeenth-Century French Literature*, ed. by Thomas M. Carr, Jr. and Russell Ganim (Tübingen: Narr, 2009), pp. 273–86. See also Alicia C. Montoya, *Medievalist Enlightenment: from Charles Perrault to Jean-Jacques Rousseau* (Cambridge: Boydell and Brewer, 2013), pp. 126–27.

[106] See Montoya, *Medievalist Enlightenment*, p. 118, pp. 125–27. On the importance of song as resistant to modern corruption, see Montoya, *Medievalist Enlightenment*, p. 141, and 'Introduction', in *Poésies*, ed. by Tonolo, pp. 69–70.

[107] Marine Roussillon, *Don Quichotte à Versailles: L'imaginaire médiéval du Grand Siècle* (Ceyzérieu: Champ Vallon, 2022), pp. 149–62.

[108] See Du Bellay, *La Deffence et l'illustration de la langue françoyse*, ed. Jean-Charles Monferran (Geneva: Droz, 2007), pp. 131–38. See Mackenzie, *The Poetry of Place*, pp. 17–19.

of courtship have slipped; likewise, as Tonolo argues, her uses of Marotic 'vieux langage' and Medieval atmosphere has a 'signification politique', looking back as it does to a pre-Frondian era of noble power.[109] In this respect, she might be seen to eschew, or at least not champion, the typical pro-Absolute values attributed to the Moderns.[110] Roussillon suggests that Deshoulières laments the fact that the court is no longer interested in arts, regretting the depoliticisation of pleasure.[111] It is also Deshoulières's philosophy, primarily her scepticism, her interest in ancient atomism, and her melancholy pessimism, which separates her from prominent Moderns and the related 'new science'.

Deshoulières's complexity as Modern underlines how far her interventions in the Quarrel and her sometime partisanship were a convenient 'stratégie d'auteur', as Tonolo argues.[112] Trying to fit her to a Modern mould might, therefore, be a red herring, but the difficulty in doing so is also revelatory for her attitude towards authority and categorisation. She is also slippery in her self-identification as 'savante' and both associates herself with and distances herself from that category. Her reflexive and ironic attitude at times seems to question both her own authority and that of her models; however, with this scepticism she also offers a strong intervention in the debates about reason and man's superiority over nature. Her appropriation of ancient texts and genres allows her to experiment with different poetic voices, to examine—with the cover of what Bayle calls 'les privilèges de la versification'—questions about human nature, and to mark her own innovations in relation to tradition. Deshoulières's poems evince a self-aware and ironic response to traditional forms of authority—classical, male, human—as well as to more contemporary forms of authority with which she might, as a woman, be aligned: modesty and the Moderns.

---

[109] Tonolo, 'Aimer comme Amadis', p. 283.
[110] Norman, *The Shock of the Ancient*, pp. 89–98.
[111] Roussillon, *Don Quichotte*, pp. 149–61.
[112] *Poésies*, ed. by Tonolo, p. 17.

6

Ancients and Moderns

Conteuses as Literary Critics

The fairy tale, which came to prominence in the 1690s, was a Modern genre par excellence: it privileged a French rather than ancient Greek or Roman genealogy and foregrounded medieval folkloric and feminine origins. The link between this genre and the Moderns was made evident by the major role Charles Perrault played in its development. With his 1694 collection of verse tales, 'Griselidis', 'Les Souhaits ridicules', and 'Peau d'âne', the latter of which is considered by Ruth Bottigheimer to be the first French fairy tale, and his *Histoires ou contes du temps passé* (1697), a collection of eight prose fairy tales, Perrault defined this genre as originating in the oral tales of lower-class women, featuring characters of lower status, and written in a concise and compact form.[1] The timing of his fairy tale publications was also significant for their Modern status: although he and the leader of the Ancients, Nicolas Boileau, his chief opponent in the Quarrel of the Ancients and Moderns, had officially 'reconciled' at the *Académie française* in 1694, the following year Perrault provocatively issued a re-edition of his three original fairy tales.[2] In addition to Perrault, the key architects of this genre, which, by its association with children and popular classes, as well as its diminutive form and apparent lack of ancient sources, had little prestige, were a group of women known as the 'conteuses'. For the most part, they self-consciously ascribed to this collective identity. In this chapter, I study some of them—Marie-Catherine d'Aulnoy, Charlotte-Rose de La Force (in brief), Marie-Jeanne L'Héritier, and Henriette-Julie de Murat—to show how they used their fairy tales and other writings to develop a conception of literature and of learning that made a bold Modern intervention in the Quarrel and which can be distinguished from that of Perrault by its emphasis on women and its complex interaction with Latin literature and the Greco-Roman past.

The 1690s were also the flashpoint of another quarrel, a discrete *querelle des femmes*: between Perrault and Boileau over the status and abilities of women, with Boileau's *Satire X contre les femmes* (1694) and Perrault's response, his *Apologie des*

---

[1] See Ruth B. Bottigheimer, *Fairy Tales: A New History* (New York: Excelsior Editions, 2009), p. 57. Charles Perrault, *Grisélidis, nouvelle. Avec le conte de Peau d'Âne et celui des Souhaits ridicules* (Paris: Coignard, 1694); Charles Perrault, *Histoires ou contes du temps passé avec des moralités* (Paris: Barbin, 1697).

[2] Charles Perrault, *Griselidis Nouvelle avec Le Conte de Peau d'Asne et celuy Des Souhaits ridicules. Quatrième édition* (Paris: Coignard, 1695). See Marine Roussillon, *Don Quichotte à Versailles: L'imaginaire médiéval du Grand Siècle* (Ceyzérieu: Champ Vallon, 2022), p. 165.

Women Writing Antiquity. Helena Taylor, Oxford University Press. © Helena Taylor (2024).
DOI: 10.1093/oso/9780192870445.003.0006

femmes of the same year.[3] Here, as he does elsewhere, Perrault advances his version of the Modern appropriation of 'female taste', that is, spontaneous, free from book learning, civilised and polite (the limitations of his championing of women have been examined by critics).[4] As explored throughout this study, women had long been a point of contention in the Quarrel of the Ancients and Moderns as they represented the broadening of literary publics and practices beyond erudite *savants*. In the 1690s these two quarrels—Ancients and Moderns and the *querelle des femmes*—were renewed and explicitly connected: for instance, Marie-Jeanne L'Héritier's 1694 response to Boileau's satire, her *Triomphe de Madame Deshoulières*, and her 1696 *Œuvres meslées*, which included this text, made a direct intervention in both debates, as I have argued elsewhere.[5]

The *conteuses* distinguished their tales from those of Perrault, investing the fairy tale genre with more sophistication than the apparent simplicity he vaunted: they favoured elite characters, their plots were more complex, their tone more ironic, and they valued more 'prestigious' sources, such as medieval troubadours, medieval romance, the fable, and even classical intertext.[6] Although recent critical work has shown the complex intertexts present in Perrault's *contes*, and his use of classical intertext, including Apuleius, in his prose tales in particular, in this chapter I focus primarily on his programmatic or theoretical statements of genre, using this as a counterpoint for those of the *conteuses*.[7] As Lewis C. Seifert and Domna Stanton suggest, with the stated dual classical and medieval heritage the *conteuses* 'bring into focus—and confront—two competing literary traditions' to equalise in prestige the foreign and the '(purportedly) indigenous', classical

---

[3] For a discussion of the other texts in this quarrel, see Anne E. Duggan, 'The *Querelle des femmes* and Nicolas Boileau's *Satire X*: Going beyond Perrault', *Early Modern French Studies*, 41.2 (2019), 144–57.

[4] Elizabeth Berg, 'Recognizing Differences: Perrault's Modernist Esthetic in *Parallèle des Anciens et des Modernes*', *Papers on French Seventeenth-Century Literature*, 18 (1983), 138–45 (pp. 144–45); Anne E. Duggan, *Salonnières, Furies, and Fairies: The Politics of Gender and Cultural Change in Absolutist France* (Newark: University of Delaware Press, 2005), pp. 121–64, and 'The *Querelle des femmes*'; and Lewis C. Seifert, *Manning the Margins: Masculinity and Writing in Seventeenth-Century France* (Ann Arbor: University of Michigan Press, 2009), pp. 86–91.

[5] Helena Taylor, 'Ancients, Moderns, Gender: Marie-Jeanne L'Héritier's "Le Parnasse reconnoissant ou le triomphe de Madame Des-Houlières"', *French Studies*, 70.1 (2017), 15–30; see also Roussillon, *Don Quichotte*, pp. 166–70. Marie-Jeanne L'Héritier de Villandon, 'Le Parnasse reconnaissant ou le Triomphe de Madame Deshoulières', in *Œuvres mêlées, contenant L'innocente tromperie; L'avare puni, Les enchantements de l'éloquence; Les aventures de finette, nouvelles, et autres ouvrages, en vers et en prose de Mlle L'H***, avec le Triomphe de Mme Des Houlières, tel qu'il a été composé par Mlle L'H**** (Paris: Guignard, 1696), pp. 404–24. The title page gives the publication date as 1696, but the 'achevé d'imprimer' is dated October 1695. All subsequent references to this edition are given in the text.

[6] See Lewis C. Seifert and Domna Stanton, 'Introduction', in *Enchanted Eloquence: Fairy Tales by Seventeenth-Century French Women Writers*, ed. and trans. by Lewis C. Seifert and Domna Stanton, The Other Voice in Early Modern Europe: The Toronto Series 9 (Toronto: Iter Press, 2010), pp. 1–46. See also Lewis C. Seifert, *Fairy Tales, Sexuality and Gender in France (1690–1715): Nostalgic Utopias* (Cambridge: Cambridge University Press, 1996), pp. 8–10.

[7] These arguments are made primarily by Ute Heidmann and Jean-Michel Adam, *Textualité et intertextualité des contes. Perrault, Apulée, La Fontaine, Lhéritier...* (Paris: Garnier, 2010).

178   WOMEN WRITING ANTIQUITY

mythology and folklore, ancient cultures and French.[8] Importantly, they also explicitly make a case for women and women as writers, moving beyond Perrault's appropriations of femininity.

The fairy tales of the *conteuses* are self-conscious and playful: they can be read, as Marc Fumaroli describes in a landmark essay on Marie-Jeanne L'Héritier, as a 'manifesto' or 'treatise' for the genre overall, as programmatic and metadiscursive.[9] In this self-reflection, they engage with the Quarrel, commenting on taste, authorship (and gender), and modernity. 'L'imaginaire médiéval', to use Marine Roussillon's phrase, in particular, was mobilised to define the values promoted by and attributed to *belles-lettres* or literature.[10] As such, fairy tales and the paratextual material in which the genre was theorised can also be read as a form of literary criticism.[11] Reading them in this way responds to recent work that has revealed the diverse forms and practices of criticism in this period, stressing that 'locations' of criticism were often marginal (paratext, correspondence) and signalling the importance of salon culture in making literary criticism a practice of women as well as men.[12]

In this chapter, I build on this scholarship, focusing not only on selected fairy tales by d'Aulnoy, La Force, L'Héritier, and Murat, but also including their other writing—Parnassus fictions, prefaces, dedications, periodicals, correspondence, and translations—which I likewise approach as examples of 'literary criticism'. Framing the diverse writings of the *conteuses* thus, I attend to their definitions of 'modernity', examining their rhetorical use of classical intertext and their emphasis on women. I show how across all their diverse works, these writers troubled hierarchisations of genre, reflected on the values and parameters of literature, and made their work a key site for the exploration and elaboration of both a theory and a practice of a Modern and feminine 'savoir'. Drawing on work that has shown this

---

[8] Seifert and Stanton, 'Introduction', p. 20. See also Nadine Jasmin, *Naissance du conte féminin. Mots et Merveilles: Les Contes de Fées de Madame d'Aulnoy (1690–1698)*, 2nd edn (Paris: Champion, 2021), pp. 33–194.

[9] Marc Fumaroli, 'Les enchantements de l'éloquence: *Les Fées* de Charles Perrault ou de la Littérature', in *Le Statut de la Littérature*, ed. by Marc Fumaroli (Geneva: Droz, 1982), pp. 153–86 (p. 164). See also Alicia C. Montoya, 'Continuities: The Medieval as Performance', in *Medievalist Enlightenment: from Charles Perrault to Jean-Jacques Rousseau* (Cambridge: Boydell and Brewer, 2013), pp. 107–44 (p. 129).

[10] Roussillon, *Don Quichotte*, pp. 163–87; see also Montoya, *Medievalist Enlightenment*, p. 4.

[11] On the relationship between the Quarrel and the development of criticism, see Larry F. Norman, 'La Querelle des anciens et des modernes, ou la métamorphose de la critique', in *Naissance de la critique littéraire*, ed. by Patrick Dandrey (= *Littératures classiques*, 86 (2015)), pp. 95–114; Alexis Tadié, 'Ancients, Moderns and the Language of Criticism', in *Ancients and Moderns in Europe: Comparative Perspectives*, ed. by Paddy Bullard and Alexis Tadié (Oxford: Voltaire Foundation, 2016), pp. 37–55.

[12] See Gavin Alexander, Emma Gilby, and Alexander Marr, 'Introduction', in *The Places of Early Modern Criticism*, ed. by Alexander Gavin, Emma Gilby, and Alexander Marr (Oxford: Oxford University Press, 2021), pp. 1–21 (p. 14). On salons, see also Joan DeJean, 'Rooms of their Own: Literary Salons in Seventeenth-Century France', in *The Cambridge History of Literary Criticism*, III: *The Renaissance*, ed. by Glyn P. Norton (Cambridge: Cambridge University Press, 2008), pp. 378–83.

'savoir' to be crucial for understanding the changing ideologies attributed to literature, I consider it in relation to their figuration of the female intellectual and their uses of Greco-Roman culture.[13] I show that for all that the *conteuses* gendered this learning as feminine, and so placed it in a tradition of difference *à la Scudéry*, they laid claim more comfortably (and sometimes more playfully) to erudition than Scudéry had done; and I explore how one *conteuse* in particular, Marie-Jeanne L'Héritier, articulated this 'savoir' through the vaunted figure of the 'savante moderne'.

Responding to Perrault: *Psyché et Cupidon* Renewed

As noted, critics have long registered differences in approach towards the fairy tale between Perrault and the *conteuses*: their preference for elite characters; ideological differences in terms of the representations of women; and their more complex plots and different genealogies, which include ancient models and, as we will analyse, the fable.[14] That their complex relationships to Perrault were a sort of power struggle has also been noted.[15] In this section, I will examine these tensions by considering what two authors, d'Aulnoy and La Force, did with a fable that Perrault had lambasted as 'ancien' and immoral. They mobilise Latin intertext not only to make their own mark but also to make the fairy tale a meta-discursive space for the very definition of the genre.

Marie-Catherine d'Aulnoy and Charlotte Rose de La Force both opened their first collections of fairy tales, in 1697 and 1698, with similar stories: *Gracieuse et Percinet* and *Plus belle que fée* are versions of what Paul Delarue and Marie-Louis Tenèze describe as 'conte-type 425', 'the search for a lost/disappeared husband', the model for which was Apuleius's 'Cupid and Psyche' from his second-century novel *The Golden Ass*.[16] The most recent and best-known version of this tale was La Fontaine's *Les Amours de Psyché et de Cupidon* (1669). Allusion to this intertext by d'Aulnoy and La Force is particularly noteworthy given that in the preface to the fourth edition of *Griselidis*, published in 1695, Perrault had criticised this fable (along with Petronius's 'Matron of Ephesus') as being too 'ancien' and lacking in morality.[17] In this preface, Perrault underscores the 'morale utile' of his collection,

---

[13] Roussillon, *Don Quichotte*, pp. 163–87; Fumaroli, 'Les enchantements de l'éloquence'.

[14] See Seifert and Stanton, 'Introduction'; see also Marianne Legault, *Female Intimacies in Seventeenth-Century French Literature* (Abingdon: Routledge, 2012), pp. 181–82. For a different perspective, see Heidmann and Adam, *Textualité et intertextualité des contes*.

[15] Anne Defrance, *Les Contes de fées et les nouvelles de Madame d'Aulnoy, 1690–1698* (Geneva: Droz, 1998), pp. 53–58; Duggan, *Salonnières*, pp. 201–09.

[16] Paul Delarue and Marie-Louise Tenèze, *Le Conte Populaire français. Catalogue raisonné des versions de France* (Paris: Maisonneuve and Larose, 2002).

[17] For more information on the publication history of 'Griselidis', see Elizabeth Storer, *La mode des contes de fées* (Paris: Champion, 1928), pp. 85–86.

180 WOMEN WRITING ANTIQUITY

attacking the tales by Petronius and Apuleius.[18] He suggests that he cannot fathom the moral lesson of the story of 'Cupid and Psyche': he finds the allegory present in this story (that Psyche stands for the soul) and her distress on discovering the identity of her lover to be 'une énigme impénétrable' (an impenetrable enigma).[19] He suggests that this tale, like most from antiquity, was written to please rather than instruct, and celebrates instead the Gallic tradition of tales of his 'aieux' (ancestors), for their 'morale louable et instructive' (praiseworthy and instructive moral lesson).[20] He does not mention La Fontaine here explicitly (perhaps out of polite restraint or polemical prowess), but he would surely have been thinking also of his celebrated recent version of the Psyche and Cupid story. La Fontaine, a professed Ancient in the Quarrel, had also claimed in his preface to *Les Amours de Psyché et de Cupidon* that his 'principal but est toujours de plaire' (main aim is always to please), seemingly to differ from the morality so central to Perrault's professed aesthetic.[21]

D'Aulnoy's 'Gracieuse et Percinet' is not only the first fairy tale d'Aulnoy published but it also initiates her *Contes des fées* (1697), the first collection to use this title and thus to name the genre.[22] 'Gracieuse et Percinet' has been read as programmatic for the collection as a whole, introducing readers to d'Aulnoy's ironic tone and ideological concern with the ethics of arranged and premature marriages.[23] La Force's 'Plus belle que fée' opens her 1698 *Les Contes des contes*, and in its very title seems to invite comparison with other works in the genre, especially Perrault's 'Les Fées' (1697), setting up her tale and her collection as superlative.[24] Both d'Aulnoy and La Force thus use these opening stories to announce their own aesthetics, making what can be read as a pointed response to Perrault all the more

---

[18] Charles Perrault, 'Préface', in *Contes* (Paris: Librairie Générale Française, 2006), p. 77–82 (p. 77).

[19] Ibid., p. 80.

[20] Ibid.

[21] Jean de La Fontaine, *Les Amours de Psyché et de Cupidon*, ed. by Françoise Charpentier (Paris: Flammarion, 1990), p. 38.

[22] She had already published one novel, *L'Histoire d'Hypolite, comte de Duglas* in 1690, which contained a fairy tale (not defined as such, but it describes a fairy tale world and is often seen as the first fairy tale), 'L'île de la Félicité'. 'Gracieuse et Percinet' is the first fairy tale to be named as such included as it is in d'Aulnoy's *Contes des fées* (Paris: Barbin, 1697–98). (This four-volume edition is rare; better known are the collections from 1698, and the posthumous ones of 1710 and 1725). D'Aulnoy is the first therefore to use the title 'conte *des* fées'; the genre is best known as 'conte *de* fées', a title used by Murat for her collection of 1698. See Jean Mainil, *Madame d'Aulnoy et le rire des fées: essai sur la subversion féérique et le merveilleux comique sous l'Ancien régime* (Paris: Kimé, 2001), pp. 228–39.

[23] See Madame d'Aulnoy, *Contes de fées*, ed. by Constance Cagnat-Debœuf (Paris: Gallimard, 2008), p. 38; Helena Taylor, '"Gracieuse et Percinet" de Madame d'Aulnoy: un conte programmatique', *Op. cit., revue des littératures et des arts*, 23 (2021), <https://revues.univ-pau.fr:443/opcit/index.php?id=704>. On her irony more generally, see Constance Cagnat-Debœuf, 'Préface', in Madame d'Aulnoy, *Contes de fées*, ed. by Cagnat-Debœuf, pp. 15–16.

[24] Charlotte-Rose Caumont de La Force, 'Plus belle que fée', in *Les Contes des contes* (Paris: Benard, 1698), pp. 1–96. Seifert shows that the title has its source in *Amadis de Gaule*. He also suggests that the title identifies the heroine with salon women and 'literalises and exaggerates the physical powers and pleasures designated by the metaphoric title "fée"' (*Fairy Tales*, p. 41).

significant: while they in part modify the model tale in light of Perrault's criticisms, they also inject more complex and differing interpretations which not only testify to the differences already noted between the 'compact' tales of Perrault and the 'complex' approaches of the *conteuses*, but reveal the role played by classical sources, including the fable, in that distinction.

'Cupid and Psyche' is signalled as an obvious intertext in both 'Plus belle que fée' and 'Gracieuse et Percinet' (the latter of which I will analyse in more detail): both stories feature a young princess, a sumptuous palace, a punitive older woman, tasks, which are similar across the three texts, that the princess has to accomplish, with the aid of her suitor, and their eventual marriage. In 'Plus belle que fée', we have two heroines and two suitors, one bad fairy, Nabote, persecuting the princesses, and one good fairy queen: the plot is therefore made more intricate with this consistent doubling. Emphasis is placed in particular on female friendship and solidarity as a counterpoint to the jealousy and venom that characterises Venus's attitude to Psyché in the versions by Apuleius and La Fontaine.[25]

Where Nadine Jasmin has analysed how d'Aulnoy took Modern liberties in her retelling of Apuleius's original, I focus here on her relationship with Apuleius's story as mediated through La Fontaine's text and Perrault's criticisms.[26] D'Aulnoy makes the allusions to the La Fontaine/Apulieus text explicit in 'Gracieuse et Percinet': Percinet, the fairy-man and suitor to Gracieuse, not only corresponds to Cupid in terms of the plot dynamic, but the comparison is signalled overtly. According to Constance Cagnat-Debœuf, his name derives from 'percer' (to pierce) and so echoes the action of Venus's son; and he is described thus: 'elle vit le prince Percinet aussi beau que l'on dépeint l'Amour' (she thought the Prince as beautiful as portrayals of Cupid).[27] D'Aulnoy further identifies *Psyché et Cupidon* as a key source: the opera performed at Percinet's Palace is 'les Amours de Psyché et de Cupidon, mêlés de danses et de petites chansons' (*The Loves of Psyche and Cupid* mixed with dances and short songs) (p. 62). This is a reference to the myth at the origin of her tale, and to its most recent adaptation as a *tragédie-ballet* by Molière, Corneille, Quinault, and Lully of 1671 (which was then turned into an opera by Lully and Thomas Corneille in 1678). Such an interjection is indicative of d'Aulnoy's ironic style and a gesture of Modern allegiance given that the genre of opera was considered a modern one.[28]

---

[25] See Legault on the unique representation of female friendship in 'Plus belle que fée', focusing on its pleasures, risks, and homoerotic tendencies (*Female Intimacies*, pp. 178–207); see Seifert on the body and its 'metonymic relations to' different sorts of pleasure in this text (*Fairy Tales*, p. 38).

[26] Jasmin, *Naissance du conte féminin*, pp. 70–71. On Ovid's influence, see ibid., pp. 61–69.

[27] 'Gracieuse et Percinet', in *Contes de fées*, ed. by Cagnat-Debœuf, pp. 49–74 (p. 60). All subsequent references to this edition will be given in the text. For Cagnat-Debœuf's discussion of Percinet's name, see p. 358, n. 2. His name also evokes 'Percival', the Gallic hero of Chrétien de Troyes.

[28] 'Les Opéra, les Poësies Galantes et le Burlesque. Il faut convenir que ces genres de Poësie sont nouveaux et n'ont point esté connus de toute l'Antiquité' (Opera, *galant* poetry, and the burlesque: these are new poetics genres which were not known in antiquity). Charles Perrault, *Parallèle des anciens et des modernes, en ce qui regarde la poësie* (Paris: Coignard, 1692), iii, pp. 280–81.

Has d'Aulnoy made the necessary moral corrections to this version, in line with Perrault's criticism? To a certain extent, yes: she has removed the problem of the allegory by replacing Psyché with Gracieuse (which was Perrault's first objection) and Percinet's identity is not hidden such that there is no discovery to displease her (his second). More significantly, in the style of Perrault's *contes*, d'Aulnoy inserts two moral lessons in the poem at the end: jealousy, in the form of Grognon, Gracieuse's wicked stepmother, is punished, which stands out from the versions by La Fontaine and Apuleius in which Venus is not punished for her cruelty. And Percinet's constant love is praised: 'Lorsque l'on aime avec constance, / Tôt ou tard, on se voit dans un parfait bonheur' (when one loves constantly, sooner or later, one will find perfect happiness) (p. 74). Gracieuse's virtue is rewarded and vice is punished, in line with Perrault's ideology.

However, the first moral lesson, the punishment of jealousy, is hardly demonstrated by the text: Grognon's punishment is less moral reprobation and more the result of a spat between Grognon and 'la mauvaise fée' whose help she had solicited in punishing Gracieuse, and who now wants to repair her fault. Grognon had wanted to strangle this fairy as Gracieuse continued to outsmart her. Grognon 'l'aurait étranglée si une fée était étranglable' (would have strangled her if a fairy were stranglable) (p. 72), with the neologism drawing attention to this description; at the end, la mauvaise fée 'chercha Grognon, et lui tordit le cou' (found Grognon and broke her neck) (p. 74). The ironic symmetry of the violence underscores how far her death is the result of an act of vengeance and not actually a punishment for her jealousy.

The second moral, Percinet's constancy, is also complicated by the narrative irony and the naivety, even foolishness, of Gracieuse. The very constancy of Percinet's love is risible given the excessive proof he needs to make of it: Gracieuse (and the reader) have no reason to doubt his love and he time and again proves himself, but she needs more proof. Each time he offers her happiness, she prefers to suffer. She, unwittingly and unnecessarily, keeps returning to dangerous situations: first she leaves the safety of the fairy palace to return home to ask her father—who had abandoned her for his new wife, Grognon—for permission to marry Percinet; then she willingly risks submitting once again to Grognon's punishing tasks, this time in the name of testing Percinet: 'elle lui répliqua que si Grognon lui faisait encore un mauvais tour, elle y consentirait' (she replied that if Grognon did one more bad thing to her, she would consent to marriage) (p. 72). When Grognon's furies strip her to whip her, the heroine possesses an exaggerated modesty, which also makes it impossible for Percinet to aid her: 'en toute autre détresse, Gracieuse aurait souhaité le beau Percinet; mais se voyant presque nue, elle était trop modeste pour vouloir que ce prince en fût témoin; et elle se préparait à tout souffrir comme un pauvre mouton' (in any other situation of distress, Gracieuse would have wished for the handsome Percinet; but given that she was almost naked, she was too modest to wish for her Prince to see her and she was prepared to suffer everything like a poor sheep) (pp. 56–57). This exaggeration, the avoidable mishaps in which Gracieuse finds herself, her foolish innocence, and d'Aulnoy's ironic interjections all serve to undermine this second moral. As Anne E. Duggan argues, d'Aulnoy questions the universality of moral maxims by closing her tale with morals that are often not fully upheld by what we have just read.[29]

The portrayal of Gracieuse also interrogates ideas of female heroism. Readers are cued to anticipate this questioning from the opening pages when the nurse warns Gracieuse: 'il faut que votre esprit vous élève autant que votre naissance: les princesses comme vous doivent de plus grands exemples que les autres' (your manner must raise your standing as much as your birth; princesses like you ought to be greater examples than others) (p. 52). In this injunction to be a 'good heroine', we also hear d'Aulnoy's voice asking what exactly a good heroine is. Gracieuse's 'vertu'—her modest *bienséance*, her obedience, her hesitation regarding love—is excessive (an excess highlighted by the fact this virtue characterises her name, meaning 'agréable' or 'douce').

The ideal of female heroism brings us to a second intertext for d'Aulnoy and another of Perrault's tales, 'Griselidis', the *conte* for which his preface condemning 'Cupid and Psyche' was written and which he held up as morally exemplary. Griselidis, the long-suffering wife, is submitted to trial after trial by her husband to test her fidelity and goodness; in the preface, Perrault explains that 'la morale de Griselidis [...] tend à porter les femmes à souffrir de leurs maris et à faire voir qu'il n'y en a point de si brutal ni de si bizarre, dont la patience d'une honnête femme ne puisse venir à bout' (the moral of Griselidis encourages women to suffer their husbands and reveals that there is nothing so brutal or strange that the patience of an *honnête* woman cannot overcome).[30] Although that moral is somewhat complicated by the playful dedication to Mademoiselle (Élisabeth-Charlotte d'Orléans) in which he admits that the tale might be a 'matière de risée' because of 'ses trop antiques leçons' (subject to mockery because of its old-fashioned lessons), her 'patience' is still praised.[31] D'Aulnoy offers a different conception of female heroism, not because Gracieuse is not also, in her way, patient and virtuous, but because the text offers a meta-commentary on heroism with the *non*-exemplarity of Gracieuse. D'Aulnoy shows a preference for equivocation and irony, for exaggeration and entertainment rather than instruction, questioning the necessity of this latter: this is typified when Gracieuse wants to tell her nurse that she has met Percinet, but 'à force de conter elle s'endormit; la nourrice s'en alla' (because she was telling the story, she fell asleep and the nurse left) (p. 57).[32] Not only does d'Aulnoy invert the norms when she has the young princess tell the nurse a tale, but she then has her princess fall asleep before being able to receive her advice.

[29] Duggan, *Salonnières*, p. 201.
[30] Perrault, *Contes*, p. 79.
[31] Ibid., pp. 89–90.
[32] See also Cagnat-Debœuf, 'Préface', *Contes de fées*, ed. by Cagnat-Debœuf, p. 16.

184 WOMEN WRITING ANTIQUITY

Are morals thus boring or soporific? D'Aulnoy takes a position here in relation to Perrault's attack on antiquity, not by directly praising ancient texts or morals, but rather by questioning his insistence on the Modern need for morals. In so doing, and in highlighting the innocence and naivety of Gracieuse, d'Aulnoy also draws attention to the negative consequences of women's lack of education, even denouncing the practice of premature and youthful marriage.[33]

As a programmatic *conte* that opens the first ever collection of *Contes des fées*, 'Gracieuse et Percinet' has a paradoxical status in so far as d'Aulnoy uses it to question some of the principles of the genre of the *conte* as established by Perrault. There is a gesture of self-definition here: d'Aulnoy's modernity is subversive, playful, heralding the parodic *contes* of the eighteenth century, but also invested in reforming aristocratic women's lives.[34] Her reworking of Apuleius's story (via La Fontaine) also suggests a complex and ambiguous relationship to the 'fable': she at once uses it as a prestigious model and adapts it to suit her ideology.[35] She explicitly thus uses a more diverse set of source texts than those declared by Perrault, offering a multi-layered genealogy, an approach we will now see to be prominent in the work of Marie-Jeanne L'Héritier.

Marie-Jeanne L'Héritier's 'Savantes Modernes'

The *conteuse* with perhaps the most complex (and the most analysed) relationship with Charles Perrault was Marie-Jeanne L'Héritier, his 'niece' (more precisely, daughter of his cousin) and protégée. She published her first miscellany, *Œuvres meslées*, in 1696; it contains four fairy tales described as 'nouvelles', other works in verse and prose, her 'Lettre à Madame D. G**', in which she theorises the fairy tale genre, and a Parnassus text, the *Triomphe de Madame Deshoulières*. After this, she published *L'Apothéose de Mademoiselle de Scudéry* in 1702; a periodical, *L'Érudition enjouée*, made up of three letters, in 1703;[36] another series of *contes*, *La Tour ténébreuse et les jours lumineux, contes anglais*, in 1705;[37] another Parnassus text, *La Pompe Dauphine ou Nouvelle Relation du Temple de Mémoire et des Champs Elysées*, in 1711; and a translation of Ovid's *Heroides* in 1732.[38] This translation, aimed, as she states in the preface, at women, can be seen as the culmination of her *galant* and Modern aesthetic: it is hybrid, as she uses a variety

[33] See Ibid., p. 38.
[34] See Mainil, *Madame d'Aulnoy et le rire des fées*, p. 248.
[35] On this tension between 'rivalité' (p. 44) and prestige, see Jasmin, *Naissance du conte féminin*, pp. 39–44, pp. 77–79.
[36] Marie-Jeanne L'Héritier, *L'Erudition Enjouée ou Nouvelles sçavantes, satyriques et galantes, écrites à une dame Françoise qui est à Madrid* (Paris: Ribou, 1703).
[37] *La Tour ténébreuse et les jours lumineux, contes anglais* (Paris: Veuve de Barbin, 1705).
[38] *La Pompe Dauphine ou Nouvelle Relation du Temple de Mémoire* (Paris: Veuve Saugrain, 1711) (all references will be in the text to this edition); and Marie-Jeanne L'Héritier, *Les Epîtres héroïques d'Ovide* (Paris: Brunet fils, 1732).

of verse forms and prose to translate the different heroines' laments; and there is a notable 'galantisation' of lexicon and of mores.[39] Although the latter provides her most direct engagement with antiquity, I will not study it in detail here, having analysed this text elsewhere;[40] nor do I explore in detail L'Héritier's *contes*, beyond brief analysis of two of them, given the attention they have received. Instead, I shall primarily focus on her more marginal, discursive texts: her *Lettres*, her Parnassus texts, and her periodical.

For L'Héritier, the genealogy of the fairy tale genre, in particular its link with a Gallic and female-orientated troubadour culture, is a recurrent topic of interest, and this emphasis, as well as her investment in promoting women as writers, distinguishes her from Perrault. L'Héritier also makes the allegorical or self-conscious properties of her *contes*—their capacity to reflect on their genre—more evident than Perrault, as is particularly clear in her 'Les Enchantments de l'éloquence', especially if compared to Perrault's parallel *conte*, 'Les Fées', as Jean Mainil has shown. Mainil argues that the differences between these two texts reveal L'Héritier's modernity to be more orientated towards a defence of learned women.[41] In this tale, L'Heritier demonstrates her articulation of a 'savoir mondain', drawing on a learned and ancient tradition of writing about eloquence, and, as Seifert shows, inscribes female discourse into a male tradition of oratory, reframing this to promote female success.[42] She makes it clear that her heroine, Blanche, is educated through reading novels, to the disapproval of her stepmother:

> La marquise auroit dû être touchée de voir le divertissement innocent où Blanche s'étoit réduite; mais quoyqu'elle sût à peine lire, elle se jetta sur le livre, et le luy arracha des mains, et après en avoir lû le titre avec beaucoup de difficulté, parce que c'étoit un nom Grec fort rébarbatif et qu'elle prononça très-mal, elle comprit enfin que ce livre étoit un roman. (pp. 179–80)

---

[39] 'J'espere du moins que les Dames me tiendront quelque compte de leur donner en vers des traductions qui n'avoient point paru depuis une si longue suite d'années' (I hope, at least, that women will acknowledge me for giving them a translation in verse of a text which has not been translated for a good number of years) (x). See Océane Puche, 'Les Epîtres héroïques de Marie-Jeanne L'Héritier: traduction et réception d'Ovide au XVIIe siècle' (unpublished doctoral thesis, Université de Lille, 2020) and Océane Puche, 'Defending Phaedra's Glory: The Corrective Translation of *Heroides* 4 by Marie-Jeanne L'Héritier in *Les Epîtres Héroïques* (1732)', in *Ovid in French: Reception by Women from the Renaissance to the Present*, ed. by Fiona Cox and Helena Taylor (Oxford: Oxford University Press, 2023), pp. 88–103.

[40] See also Helena Taylor, 'L'Adorateur du beau sexe': Madeleine de Scudéry et Marie-Jeanne L'Héritier, lectrices d'Ovide', in *Ovide en France du Moyen Âge à nos jours*, ed. by Stefania Cerrito and Marie Possamaï-Pérez (Paris: Classiques Garnier, 2021), pp. 243–63; and Helena Taylor, '*Belle* and *fidèle*?: Women Translating Ovid in Early Modern France', in *Ovid in French*, ed. by Cox and Taylor, pp. 67–87.

[41] Jean Mainil, '"Mes Amies les Fées": Apologie de la femme savante et de la lectrice dans les *Les Bigarrures ingénieuses* de Marie-Jeanne L'Héritier (1696)', *Féeries*, 1 (2003), 49–72 (pp. 60–72).

[42] Seifert, *Fairy Tales*, pp. 94–96.

> The Marquise should have been moved to witness the innocent entertainment Blanche had found for herself; but even though she could hardly read, she leapt on this book and ripped it from her hands and, having read the title with great difficulty, because it was in a very forbidding Greek which she pronounced badly, she understood that it was a novel.

With reference to this Greek title, L'Héritier identifies the classical heritage of her tales; but she also valorises the French Gallic tradition: 'Contes pour contes, il me paroît que ceux de l'antiquité Gauloise valent bien à peu près ceux de l'antiquité Grecque: et les fées ne sont pas moins en droit de faire des prodiges que les dieux de la Fable' (Stories for stories, it seems to me that those from Gallic antiquity are worth almost as much as those from Greek antiquity; and the fairies are just as permitted to perform miracles as the gods of myth) (p. 227). L'Heritier not only offers both ancient and modern origins for Blanche's knowledge but explicates this extradiegetically in relation to the origin of the *conte* itself; the narrator explains: 'Une dame très instruite des antiquités Grecques et Romaines, et encore plus savante dans les antiquités Gauloises, m'a fait ce conte quand j'étois enfant' (A woman very learned in ancient Roman and Greek culture, and even more learned in the world of ancient Gaul, told me this story when I was a child) (pp. 164–65). As with Perrault, the *conte* has a female storytelling origin; but unlike Perrault's case this woman is 'instruite' and 'savante' in both ancient culture and that of medieval Gaul. The adjectives of learning, 'instruite' and 'savante', are deliberately mobilised here to call upon, and equalise, different forms of learning in a gesture that upholds the dual heritage claimed by the *conteuses*, all the while indicating the superiority of the Gallic sources ('encore plus savante ...'). As Alicia C. Montoya shows, this comment also links the folkloric and French medieval tradition to a female one.[43]

L'Héritier's tales are female-centric and explicitly concerned with women's education and the articulation of their learning. The heroine of 'L'Adroite princesse ou les aventures de Finette', dedicated to Henriette-Julie de Murat, is so cultivated that she is called 'Finette'; like other heroines, she also challenges female-gendered norms of acquiescence, as is evident from the ironic description of her fending off a rapist by waving a hammer as if it were a fan: 'Riche-Cautèle, qui n'étoit pas un fort courageux personnage, et qui voyait toujours Finette armée du gros marteau dont elle badinait comme on fait d'un éventail, Riche-Cautèle, dis-je, consentit à ce que souhaitait la princesse, et se retira pour la laisser quelque temps méditer' (Riche-Cautéle, who was not brave, and who saw Finette armed with a large hammer which she toyed with carelessly as if it were a fan, agreed to what she wanted and withdrew so that she could have some time alone to think) (p. 265). L'Héritier's

---

[43] Montoya, *Medievalist Enlightenment*, p. 138.

contes and particularly 'Les Enchantements de l'éloquence' can be read as reflection on debates about taste and education, as 'une méditation, au fond très sérieuse, sur l'esprit de la culture mondaine, et sur la function de la littérature' (a serious reflection on *mondain* culture and the function of literature).[44] Lise Forment has shown how the motif of genealogy in L'Héritier's *contes* contributes to the Modern position, but does so in a way that is distinct, for its feminine emphasis, from the modernity of Perrault.[45] I want now to shift the attention away from the *contes* themselves, towards her other forms of literary practice and criticism. I will focus in particular on the genealogies she develops and her definition of the Modern aesthetic, looking at the place of 'savantes modernes', including herself, within this.

In her *Lettre à Madame D. G∗∗*, included in her *Œuvres meslées*, L'Héritier claims the prestigious heritage of the poems of the twelfth-century troubadours as the origins for the *conte* or fairy tale, also linking these tales to the novel which she shows to be derived from chivalric romances. This *Lettre* makes L'Héritier the foremost theorist of the fairy tale genre.[46] Montoya stresses how L'Héritier's genealogy, linking the troubadours to the novel, was a significant contribution to the burgeoning attempts to write a French national literary history, and would become commonplace in the eighteenth century;[47] and Roussillon stresses how L'Héritier's figuration of troubadours as 'galants' in this text makes them a vehicle for her Modern ethical, political, and aesthetic values.[48]

This text is also significant because L'Héritier articulates a further origin narrative for her genre: while she does valorise the intermediary roles of 'grandmères' and 'gouvernantes' in affirming the morality of these tales (p. 305), she condemns the interference of the 'simple' 'petit peuple' who 'ne savent pas ce que c'est la bienséance' (do not know what *bienséance* is) (p. 313)—those very simple and humble storytellers that Perrault had praised—as responsible for introducing 'adventures scandaleuses' (p. 312). Instead, L'Héritier praises the refined morals of those in contemporary Parisian society who have sought to return to the polite and morally correct origins ('remonter à leur source', p. 306) by producing *contes* in the style of the troubadours. In this respect, her *Lettre* offers an important companion to Huet's *Discours sur l'origine des romans* (1670), which is cited and

---

[44] Fumaroli, 'Les enchantements de l'éloquence', p. 185.

[45] Lise Forment, 'Marie-Jeanne L'Héritier dans la querelle des Anciens et des Modernes, ou comment être soi et nièce', in *Women and* Querelles *in Early Modern France*, ed. by Helena Taylor and Kate E. Tunstall (= *Romanic Review*, 112.3 (2021)), pp. 470–85. For the argument that L'Héritier defends Perrault's ideas, see Jean-Paul Sermain, *Le Conte de fées du classicisme aux Lumières* (Paris: Desjonquères, 2005), pp. 34–35.

[46] Montoya, *Medievalist Enlightenment*, p. 4.

[47] Ibid., p. 135.

[48] Marine Roussillon, 'Les "Galants Troubadours": Usages des Troubadours à l'âge classique', in *La Réception des troubadours en Languedoc et en France, XVI–XVIII siècle*, ed. by Jean-François Courouau and Isabelle Luciani (Paris: Classiques Garnier, 2015), pp. 109–24 (p. 110). See also Roussillon, *Don Quichotte*, pp. 174–79.

188   WOMEN WRITING ANTIQUITY

in which Huet sees Homer as a Greek troubadour.[49] L'Héritier also reflects on the
status and contributions of fictional genres, and particularly her own 'conte', gen-
erating a prestigious and exclusive genealogy that bypasses humble origins in a
gesture of aristocratic solidarity.[50]

She frames this ideology as it is explored in her *Contes* and elsewhere as an act
of taking a position, as agonistic, describing her actions metaphorically as 'entrer
en lice'. She closes the *Lettre*: 'Vous me tiendrez compte du moins d'avoir été si
vive à entrer en lice pour faire des Historiettes au sujet des Proverbes' (You will
take account of the fact at least that I was lively enough to enter the fray with my
little stories on the subject of proverbs) (p. 318). 'Entrer en lice'—appropriately—
refers literally to a medieval chevalier entering a tournament, but it can also have a
figurative meaning, that is, to commence a dispute or combat. The opponents she
anticipates are described negatively as 'critiques', a term she uses, like Deshoulières,
to imply pedantry and those steeped in school-book learning:[51]

> si je voulois me donner la liberté de nommer, je vous ferois une belle liste de ces
> critiques, et je vous ferois voir en meme temps que toute leur finesse consiste à
> examiner un ouvrage sur des principes d'ecoliers et sur les idées qu'ils croyent
> avoir puisées dans Horace ou dans Juvenal. (pp. 315–16)

> If I wanted to name names, I could give you a long list of these critics and I would
> show you at the same time that their entire skill lies in examining a work accord-
> ing to schoolboy principles and to ideas they think they have taken from Horace
> or Juvenal.

Rather than see her need for a tradition as an echo of the imitation so vaunted
by the Ancients of the Quarrel, as some have suggested, I argue that L'Héritier is
articulating her Modern offensive on the very territory of the Ancients, that is, by
using tradition and genealogy to support her defence of the Modern and French
fairy tale.[52] L'Héritier figures both her solidarity with the other women and the
publication of her *contes* as being agonistic, and presents her stance as Modern
and as confrontational, combining a defence of women with a defence of Modern
aesthetics.

---

[49] Pierre-Daniel Huet, 'Traité de l'origine des romans', in *Poétiques du roman. Scudéry, Huet, Du
Plaisir et autres textes théoriques et critiques du XVIIe siècle sur le genre romanesque*, ed. by Camille
Esmein (Paris: Champion, 2004), pp. 441–535 (p. 510–11).
[50] On the troubadours in Huet and L'Héritier, see Roussillon, 'Les "Galants Troubadours"', and
Roussillon, *Don Quichotte*, pp. 174–76.
[51] On the fluctuations of the term 'critique' and its relation to critical practice, see Gavin Alexander,
Emma Gilby, and Alexander Marr, 'Introduction', pp. 1–21.
[52] See Forment who also makes this argument ('Marie-Jeanne L'Héritier dans la querelle des Anciens
et des Moderns', p. 473). For the suggestion that her recourse to origins is at odds with a Modern
approach, see Marc Escola, *Contes de Charles Perrault, essai et dossier* (Paris: Gallimard, 2005), p. 68.

The sense of her distinction and her modernity is conveyed in the repeated claims to innovation made throughout this *Lettre*. It is innovation, in part, that drives her alignment with the troubadours as she underscores the meaning of the term—'ce nom est Provençal et il signifie trouveurs ou inventeurs' (the term name is Provencal and it means 'discoverers' or 'inventors') (p. 303)—and makes her own innovation and novelty clear. That novelty is combined with combat and she sees off her (Ancient) critics and detractors, accusing them of pedantry and an inability to speak French, forming a nicely symmetrical contrast with Gournay's attacks against those who could not read Latin: 'On les entend dire d'un ton grave: "ne voyez-vous pas qu'il n'y a point là de nominatif?" [...] la plupart ne sait pas parler François' (One hears them say, in a serious tone, 'do you not see that there is no nominative in that sentence?' ... most of them do not know how to speak French) (p. 316). Through her own criticisms then, and her claims to innovation, L'Héritier makes the *conte*, and the *conteuse*, exemplars of literary invention.

In the apotheosis text written to honour Antoinette Deshoulières, dedicated to Scudéry, and included in her *Œuvres meslées*, we witness her entering the 'lice'— this time directly targeting Nicolas Boileau, as I have examined elsewhere: the 'nouveau Juvenal', Boileau, is condemned by Minos to oblivion in a gesture that mimics his own attacks against Scudéry in his *Dialogue des héros du roman*.[53] It is also in this text that L'Héritier vaunts the term 'savantes modernes', using the substantive noun, which Scudéry had dubbed as 'terrible', positively as a term of value.[54] As part of the celebrations on Parnassus, L'Héritier describes two *Arcs de Triomphe*; on the relief on one side are the 'savantes de l'antiquité', 'illustres femmes' including Sappho, Erinna, Aspasia, Corinna. On another can be found the 'savantes modernes', including Christine de Pizan, Madeleine and Catherine Des Roches, Anna Maria van Schurman, Princesse Palatine, Marie de Rohan, 'Artenice' (Madame de Rambouillet), Comtesse de La Suze, Madame de Villedieu, Elena Cornaro Piscopia, and 'beaucoup d'autres' (p. 419). As Mainil has argued, there is a comparative and Modern perspective here, albeit muted: the 'savantes modernes' are shown to have surpassed their ancient counterparts.[55] Of the ancient Sappho, L'Héritier writes: 'quoiqu'elle ait été autant surpassée par une nouvelle Sapho, qu'elle a surpassé elle-même les plus fameux Poëtes de l'antiquité' (although she was surpassed by a new Sappho, she herself surpassed the most famous poets of antiquity) (p. 416). These 'savantes modernes' are not only 'modernes' because of their distinction from the ancients, but apart from Pizan and the Des Roches, they are contemporary to L'Héritier. In this respect, the modernity claimed is not only chronological but based on a periodisation of taste, of common

---

[53] See Helena Taylor, 'Ancients, Moderns, Gender'; and Sophie Raynard, 'Ancients vs. Moderns: The Women's Riposte', *Marvels and Tales*, 33.1 (2019), 116–39.

[54] Madeleine and Georges de Scudéry, 'Histoire de Sapho', *Artamène ou le Grand Cyrus* (Paris: Courbé, 1656), x, pp. 329–608 (p. 401). See also the Introduction and Chapter 3.

[55] Mainil, '"Mes amis les fées"', p. 55, p. 58.

190   WOMEN WRITING ANTIQUITY

culture: it is notable, for example, that Marie de Gournay is not in this list. This is reinforced in her 1702 *L'Apothéose de Madamoiselle de Scudéry* in which the highest praise is reserved for L'Héritier's (near) contemporaries: 'l'illustre' Madame Deshoulières, 'la célèbre' Madame de Villedieu, 'la sçavante' Mademoiselle de La Vigne, and 'la tendre et gracieuse' Comtesse de La Suze.[56] Gournay is present here but categorised with the medieval women, Christine de Pizan, the Comtesse de Die, and Marie de France. The progressive teleology we associate with the Moderns is demonstrated by this triumph; and 'modern' is an ideological, rather than temporal, marker.

As Parnassus fictions, these apotheoses can be seen as exercises in literary criticism—even though L'Héritier does not adopt the term 'critique', reserving it instead for her opponents. They celebrate an alternative female canon and attribute values across various genres in the descriptions and taxonomies of the different groups depicted in the celebratory parades which feature in both. While in the Deshoulières apotheosis these parades are organised more simply according to genre; in the Scudéry apotheosis authors and genres are organised according to muses, which allows for genres to be combined, and so lineages to be created, and traditional hierarchies of genre disputed.[57] Most significant are those genres and authors described as the 'favoris d'Erato', muse of lyric poetry (p. 27), because it is here that L'Héritier includes troubadours and contemporary novelists. Those 'favoris' include Tibullus, Propertius (Ovid would be in this group were he not busy as Scudéry's guide), troubadour poets and also novelists, Heliodorus, d'Urfé, La Calprenède, and others, though these novelists also possess the 'dons de Melpomene' (p. 29) (muse of tragedy). Scudéry is celebrated as diverse, her novels appealing to Erato, Melpomene, and Calliope (muse of eloquence and epic poetry, whom Scudéry herself uses as guide in her 'Songe d'Hésiode' from *Clélie*) (pp. 30–31). Thus L'Héritier combines and equalises the genres of lyric, epic, and tragedy and presents them all as ancestors of the novel. By linking the contemporary novel to ancient lyric poetry she also recalls what I argue Scudéry is doing in her early novels. Indeed, the echoes between L'Héritier's text and Scudéry's Parnassus-style dream, the 'Songe d'Hésiode' from *Clélie*, are evident and L'Héritier draws attention to this section of Scudéry's novel when she states that both Hésiode and Anacréon are pleased with how Scudéry represented them in *Clélie* (p. 22 and p. 52). In the 'Tableaux d'Histoire' in the Temple de Mémoire, we see the most illustrious figures from Scudéry's novel (p. 63). Their opinion is significant because it provides another occasion to champion the novel form: these characters 'étoient persuadez qu'ils étoient beaucoup plus fameux par les merveilleux romans où la scavante Scudéry a mis leur nom et leur principales avantures dans un si beau jour

---

[56] L'Héritier, *L'Apothéose de Mademoiselle de Scudéry* (Paris: Moreau, 1702), pp. 43–44. All subsequent references to this edition will be given in the text.

[57] Roussillon has argued that L'Héritier also challenges genre hierarchies in her *Œuvres meslées* (*Don Quichotte*, pp. 174–75).

qu'ils ne l'étoient par les éloges de quelques froids historiens' (they were convinced that they were much more famous because of the wonderful novels in which the learned Scudéry gave life to their names and principal deeds and not because of the praise of a few cold historians) (pp. 63–64)—and 'savante' as a prenominal adjective remains a term of praise.

In the following year, 1703, L'Héritier continued to experiment with genre and criticism. She set up a new literary periodical, *L'Érudition enjouée ou les nouvelles scavantes, satyriques et galantes*, presented as three letters to 'une dame française à Madrid', and dated June, August, and September/October.[58] In framing her periodical for a female reader outside Paris, L'Héritier was deliberately echoing the *Mercure Galant*, addressed to a provincial woman.[59] And like the *Mercure Galant*, *L'Érudition* is made up of fiction, poems, anecdotes and observations from salons and social gatherings, discussions of forthcoming publications, and recommendations. Christophe Schuwey describes the *Mercure Galant* as 'un salon de papier', while Roussillon shows how it intended 'construire et mettre en scène une communauté de valeurs' (to construct and represent a community of values): similarly, *L'Érudition*, although single-authored, performs and replicates the social space of the salon, and what has been seen as its interactive, dialogic, and pioneering practice of literary criticism.[60]

L'Héritier's *L'Érudition enjouée* can be read in the light of work that has seen periodicals as key to the shifting practices of literary criticism in the late seventeenth and early eighteenth centuries, especially as they also heralded 'changes in the sociology of literature', by targeting an enlarged reading public, and offering new reading methods and formats.[61] This periodical also exemplifies L'Héritier's ambitions as a transnational woman of letters, as Whitney Mannies has argued.[62] I suggest it also further reveals her conception of 'savoir'. The journal's title is a case in point: 'érudition' is qualified by 'enjouée' and its 'nouvelles' by 'sçavantes'. The title also adds to 'savantes' two further adjectives, 'satyriques et galantes', the first recalling a male-gendered literary tradition and the second a female one,

---

[58] It was then reprinted as Marie-Jeanne L'Héritier, 'L'Érudition enjouée ou nouvelles sçavantes, satyriques, et galantes, Écrite à une Dame Françoise, qui est à Madrid', in *Mélanges serieux, comiques et d'érudition* (Paris: Ribou, 1704). Subsequent references to this edition will be given in the text.

[59] See Whitney Mannies, 'The Periodical as Transnational Salon: Marie-Jeanne L'Héritier's *L'Érudition Enjouée* (1703)', *Eighteenth-Century Studies*, 53.4 (2020), 667–83.

[60] Christophe Schuwey, *Un entrepreneur des lettres au XVIIe siècle: Donneau de Visé, de Molière au 'Mercure Galant'* (Paris: Classiques Garnier, 2020), pp. 419–47 (p. 419). Roussillon, *Don Quichotte*, p. 154. *L'Érudition* performs the sharing of the 'nouvelles scavantes' it conveys. For instance, L'Héritier asks for feedback on a poem and states that she was pleased with how the story in the first letter had been received (2nd letter, p. 24; 3rd letter, p. 28).

[61] James Basker, 'Criticism and the Rise of Periodical Literature', in *The Cambridge History of Literary Criticism*, ed. by H. B. Nisbet and Clause Rawson, IV: *The Eighteenth Century* (Cambridge: Cambridge University Press, 2005), pp. 316–32 (p. 318). On how periodicals changed reading habits, also see Schuwey, *Un entrepreneur des lettres au XVIIe siècle*, pp. 177–200.

[62] Mannies, 'The Periodical as Transnational Salon', pp. 673–79.

192 WOMEN WRITING ANTIQUITY

the first (more typically) ancient and the second modern.[63] *L'Érudition enjouée* is thus a hybrid periodical, echoing both the *Mercure Galant* and the *Journal des Sçavans*, but also distinguishing itself from each of them. As we will see, with *L'Érudition enjouée* L'Héritier develops her conception of *savoir* as popularising learned sources and as valuing social learning.

She develops her multi-faceted notion of 'savoir' in the three *Lettres* of her periodical. In the opening pages, and at moments throughout, L'Héritier explicitly defines the 'nouvelles sçavantes' she seeks to relay (with 'savante' in this context positively connoted). She promises to send 'à quoy l'on s'occupe icy dans les belles lettres' (details of the fashions in *belles lettres*) (p. 4) because 'je suis ravie de l'inclination que vous me marqués que les dames de Madrid ont pour le sçavoir' (I am delighted to hear that the women of Madrid are inclined towards learning) (p. 4). This is a 'sçavoir' distinguished from, but also punctuated by and communicated alongside, pleasure; it is also aimed at women:

> je vais vous informer de tout ce que je sçay de nouvelles sçavantes: mais aussi ne pouvant me persuader qu'elles seront entierement du goût de toutes vos aimables amies, ainsi qu'elles seront du vôtre, en faveur des Dames que les nouveautés de l'empire des Lettres touchent peu, je vous écriray aussi des nouvelles badines et galantes; cependant comme je sçay bien que les nouvelles scavantes vous interesseront le plus, je vais commencer par celles de ce caractere. (p. 4)

> I will inform you of everything I know of learned news: but also—not convinced that this news will be entirely to the liking of all your amiable friends, as it will be to your own—in consideration of those women for whom news from the empire of letters is of little interest, I will also send you playful and *galant* news. However, since I know that you are most interested in learned news, I will start with that.

The first 'nouvelle sçavante' she imparts is the information that M. Moreau de Mantour's 'histoire des Amazones' is almost complete, information that she thinks will be particularly interesting to her women readers. Another, relayed in the 'Seconde Lettre' of July–August 1703, is the information that a new translation of Anacreon is about to come out (probably that of Antoine La Fosse which was published in 1704), which allows her to praise the one by Anne Dacier (1681) in aiding those without Greek, particularly women (p. 4). Her definition of 'nouvelles sçavantes' is also modulated by its antithesis, namely pedantry, as she is critical of 'scavans de College' and some academicians who 's'amusent à creuser des matieres

---

[63] 'Satire' was generally a mode avoided by 'moderns', especially women, as is evident from the fact that L'Héritier classes Deshoulières's poems as 'les satryriques agréables' (L'Héritier, *Le Parnasse Reconnoissant*, p. 407). See also Volker Schröder, 'Madame Deshoulières ou la satire au féminin', *Dix-septième siècle*, 258 (2013), 95–106; and Annalisa Nicholson, 'The Satire of the Salonnière: Women and Humour in Seventeenth-Century France, *Australian Journal of French Studies*, 59.4 (2022), 361–75.

insipides et frivoles qui ne font que desseicher l'esprit et l'obscurcir' (enjoy investigating insipid and unimportant matters which dull and darken the mind) ('Lettre' I, p. 7), giving as examples of such obscure knowledge the question of whether the Spartan women put collars on dogs or the name of the slave who warmed up Livia's bathwater. Some of that mockery is directed towards women in an anecdote about a woman who is known in certain circles as the 'Marquise de Rectangle' (p. 40) because of her passion for Descartes's philosophy and system of mathematics—is this little joke at the expense of 'la dame cartesienne', along the lines of Scudéry's mockery of Damophile and those who 'font la scavante'?

These definitions and examples of what constitutes 'érudition enjouée' and 'nouvelles sçavantes' set the context for her long discussion of the troubadours in the 'Troisième Lettre', where she figures them as origins for contemporary *galant* values and finds in their *cour d'amour* the model for the contemporary salon and its emphasis on women's authority and sociability.[64] She describes the *cour d'amour* thus: 'cette galante et docte compagnie qu'on nommoit *cour d'amour*, qui semble avoir été la sœur aînée de toutes les Academies de France' (this gallant and learned company called the 'cour d'amour' which could be seen as the older sister of all the French academies) (p. 10). Distinct to this court is its mixed-gendered company: 'elle fut toûjours composée de personnes les plus illustres de l'un et de l'autre sexe; et comme dans les siecles où elle brilla, un usage galant avoit établi une parfaite déférence pour les Dames, elles eurent toûjours la prérogative de présider dans l'assemblée de la Cour d'Amour' (it was always composed of the most illustrious people of both sexes; and, as in the centuries when it excelled, *galanterie* had established a perfect deference towards women: it was always women's prerogative to preside over the assembly of the *cour d'amour*) (p. 11). She lists some of the illustrious female members, including the Comtesse de Die and makes explicit the genealogy between her transnational salon and this *cour d'amour*, between *galanterie* and the social practices of this court, when she explains how the Duchesse de Maine has set up a similar assembly, *L'Ordre de l'Abeille*, in which guests were known as chevaliers and chevalières (pp. 17–18).[65]

---

[64] Her depiction of the troubadours is in dialogue with Jean de Nostredame, who wrote a key work on troubadours at the end of the sixteenth century, *Les vies des plus célèbres et anciens Poètes provensaux, qui ont floury du temps des comtes de Provence* (Lyon: Marsilii, 1575), and Pierre de Galaup de Chasteuil's *Discours sur les Arcs triomphaux dressez en la ville d'Aix, à l'heureuse arrivée de Monseigneur le Duc de Bourgogne, et de Monseigneur le duc de Berry* (Aix: Adibert, 1701). In response to an attack for its mixing of history and myth by Pierre-Joseph de Haitze, *Dissertations sur divers points de l'histoire de Provence* (Anvers: de l'imprimerie plantinienne, 1704), Galaup de Chasteuil also wrote an *Apologie des anciens historiens, et des troubadours, ou poetes provencaux* (Avignon: Perier, 1704). L'Héritier sides with Pierre de Galaup, provoking Pierre-Joseph de Haitze. On this quarrel, see Marine Roussillon, 'Les Troubadours dans les entrées royales d'Aix-en-Provence (1622 and 1701)', in *La Réception des troubadours en Provence, XVI–XVIII siècle*, ed. by Jean-François Courouau and Isabelle Luciani (Paris: Classiques Garnier, 2018), pp. 115–36.

[65] On the Duchesse de Maine's imitation 'cour d'amour', see Alicia C. Montoya, 'Jouer aux troubadours à l'aube des Lumières', in *La Réception des troubadours en Languedoc et en France, XVI–XVIII siècle*, ed. by Courouau and Luciani, pp. 95–108 (p. 100).

194   WOMEN WRITING ANTIQUITY

L'Héritier's 'savoir' mixes the erudition of classical and medieval learning with the new form of the fairy tale and the sociability of the periodical. She uses her catalogues of 'savantes modernes' as exemplary and implicitly includes among them her host of illustrious, literary female dedicatees: Marie de Launay de Razilly, Madame le Camus, Henriette-Julie de Murat, and the Duchesse d'Épernon. She also includes herself. This is evident from the letter to Madame de Mortaing which follows her third Parnassus fiction written to commemorate the death of the Dauphin in 1711, *La Pompe Dauphine ou Nouvelle Relation du Temple de Mémoire*, dedicated to the Duchess of Trimouille.[66] The *Pompe* itself echoes the celebration of women we traced in her other two Parnassus texts, with the connection made manifest when she has Deshoulières and Scudéry join the nine muses in a song of praise for the Dauphin (p. 65). In the 'Lettre à Madame de Mortaing', she offers philological and etymological reflection on this text (for instance exploring the cultural and linguistic history of 'apothéose', pp. 94–95) and offers her versions of two further ancient stories: the story of Arion, from Ovid's *Fasti* and Herodotus, both of whom she cites; and the story of Alectryon. Of this fable, she writes:

> elle n'est racontée que par des anciens auteurs pleins d'une si haute érudition que je n'ay guère de commerce avec eux. Cependant par je ne sçay quelle occasion, j'ay lû quelque part qu'Eustathe, Libanius et plusieurs autres Auteurs, doctissimes, en font mention. S'il m'en souvient bien voicy ce qu'ils en rapportent. (pp. 88–89)

> It is only told by ancient authors of such erudition that I rarely have anything to do with them. However, I don't know when it was, but I read somewhere that Eustatius, Libanius, and other, very learned authors mention it. If I remember correctly, this is what they said.

Unlike Scudéry, L'Héritier does cite her sources, and although she seems to be distinguishing the ones she has read from those of 'haute érudition', and tempers her statement with a modest vagueness, her reference to Eustatius (surely an erudite figure) and her superlative, 'doctissimes', places her own reading in this category. She suggests that the Alectryon fable has a moral truth, like her fairy tales, thereby implicitly offering this ancient source as another precursor for her fairy tale and, like d'Aulnoy, valorising the fable as source for the fairy tale.

In L'Héritier's work we witness a diverse practice of literary criticism, and a dynamic conception of French literary history that does not excise its connections to antiquity but which minimises these to emphasise a strong Gallic troubadour tradition, one that celebrates the contemporary arts of invention and evokes a female-centric world of social learning. The figure of the ideal 'savante

---

[66] On the dedicatees, see Roussillon, *Don Quichotte*, p. 166.

moderne' who emerges from across L'Héritier's work has shaken off the connotations of pedantry and pretension; 'savante' is appropriated, redefined according to L'Héritier's Modern learning. The ideal female intellectual is not only the expert conversationalist vaunted by Scudéry, but one who can also conduct philological and etymological analysis, who can quote their ancient and medieval sources, and whose irony enables a more forceful stance in relation to quarrels about modernity than that adopted by Scudéry. More than this, in using the term 'savante moderne', this ideal intellectual is given a referent, a name, of value—something we saw to be lacking in Scudéry's work and complex in Gournay's. At the same time, L'Héritier's new definition also reveals some of the limitations of what constitutes Modern as promoted by Perrault. In this chapter's final section, I now turn to the responses to Perrault's modernity by one of L'Héritier's dedicatees and another *conteuse*, Henriette-Julie de Murat, and explore further the dynamic practices of literary criticism by this generation of *conteuses*.

Henriette-Julie de Murat's *Fées Modernes*

Henriette-Julie de Murat (1668–1716), *conteuse*, author of a pseudo-*mémoire*, friend of L'Héritier and d'Aulnoy, and also known for the scandals involving her supposed adultery and lesbianism, distinguished herself from Perrault with rhetorical and performative uses of the terms 'ancien' and 'moderne'. In the preface which she addresses to 'fées modernes' from her third collection of fairy tales, the *Histoires sublimes et allégoriques* (1699), she makes a distinction, which echoes that of L'Héritier, between the sophisticated 'modern' Parisian fairies and their crude 'ancient' ancestors, who are shown to have left their mark on Perrault's 'Mother Goose Tales' (his *Histoires ou contes du temps passé*):

> Les anciennes Fées vos devancieres ne passent plus que pour des badines auprés de vous. Leurs occupations étoient basses et pueriles, ne s'amusant qu'aux servantes et aux nourrices. Tout leur soin consistoit à bien ballayer la maison, mettre le pot au feu, faire la lessive, remuer et endormir les enfans, traire les vaches, battre le beurre, et milles autres pauvretez de cette nature; et les effets les plus considerables de leur art se terminoient à faire pleurer des perles et des diamans, moucher des émeraudes et cracher des rubis. Leur divertissement étoit de dancer au clair de la lune, de se transformer en vieilles, en chats, en singes et en moynes-bourus, pour faire peur aux enfans, et aux esprits foibles. C'est pourquoy tout ce qui nous reste aujourd'huy de leurs faits et gestes ne sont que des contes de ma Mere l'Oye. Elles étoient presque toûjours vieilles, laides, mal-vétuës, et mal logées; et hors Melusine, et quelques demy douzaines de ses semblables, tout le reste n'étoient que des gueuses. Mais pour vous Mes Dames, vous avez bien pris une autre route: vous ne vous occupez que de grandes choses, dont les moindres sont de donner

de l'esprit à ceux et celles qui n'en ont point, de la beauté aux laides, de l'éloquence aux ignorans, des richesses aux pauvres, et de l'éclat aux choses les plus obscures. Vous estes toutes belles, jeunes, bien-faites, galament et richement vétuës et logées et vous n'habitez que dans la cour des Rois, ou dans des palais enchantez.[67]

The ancient fairies, your predecessors, pass for little more than fools next to you. Their activities were base and childish, amusing only to servants and nurses. They cared only to sweep the house well, put the pot on the fire, do the wash, rock and put the children to bed, milk cows, churn butter, and a thousand other low things of this nature; and the most considerable results of their art were limited to crying pearls and diamonds, blowing out emeralds from their noses, and spitting rubies. Their entertainment was to dance by the light of the moon; to transform into crones, cats, monkeys, and phantoms in order to scare children and weak spirits. That is why all that remains today of their deeds are only the *Tales of Mother Goose*. They were almost always old, ugly, poorly dressed, and poorly housed; and, except for Melusine and a few half-dozen like her, the rest were nothing but beggars. But as for you, Mesdames, you have taken a different road: You only concern yourselves with great things, the least of which consist of giving spirit to those who have none, beauty to the ugly, eloquence to the ignorant, riches to the poor, and clarity to the most obscure things. You are all beautiful, young, well formed, gallantly and richly dressed and housed, and you live in only the courts of Kings or in magic palaces.[68]

Like L'Héritier, Murat's distinction is class-based (as well as ageist) with the 'anciennes' fairies those of the lower classes and the 'modernes' from elite Parisian society. Just as significant is her pointed alignment of Perrault's 'contes de ma mère l'oye' with these unsophisticated tales which, she implies, do little more than scare children, and do not offer the moral clarities of the modern fairies who possess a civilising influence: 'Vous remplissez tous ces lieux de tant de graces par les douces influances que vous y répandez, que nous esperons que vous remettrez dans nos saisons déreglées, l'ordre naturel où elles ont été autrefois' ('You fill these places with so many charms, by the kind powers you sow there, that we hope you will restore in our unruly seasons the natural order they would have had otherwise').[69] Like L'Héritier, Murat signals the female-orientated nature of her tales, likening this to her contemporary culture of women writers, thus consolidating her community.

---

[67] Madame de Murat, 'Aux fées modernes', *Histoires sublimes et allégoriques, par Madame le Comtesse D***, dédiées aux fées modernes* (Paris: Delaulne, 1699), np.

[68] Translation from Holly Tucker and Melanie R. Siemens, 'Perrault's Preface to "Griselda" and Murat's "To Modern Fairies"', *Marvels and Tales*, 19.1 (2005), 125–30 (p. 129).

[69] Murat, 'Aux fées modernes', np; Tucker and Siemens, 'Perrault's Preface to "Griselda" and Murat's "To Modern Fairies"', p. 129.

The intertextual references used throughout her fairy tales attest to her use of varied and prestigious sources. For example, in her 'Isle de la Magnificence' of her *Histoires sublimes et allegoriques*, there is an interpolated story that echoes different tales from Ovid's *Metamorphoses*. In the 'Histoire de Grandimont, Roy des Arsades et de la Princesse Philomele', which is told within the 'Histoire de la Princesse Blanchette et du Prince Verdelet', Philomele, Grandimont's betrothed, is kidnapped by a sorcerer, Cameleor, disguised as an eagle. Cameleor comes to Grandimont to say he will never see Philomele again for she has been turned into a nightingale (we later discover: by a fairy, to protect her from Cameleor), and he then turns Grandimont into a lion (he will only return to a Prince once he has defeated a dragon). With the predator as eagle, L'Héritier echoes the story of Jupiter and Ganymede (Jupiter disguises himself as an eagle to kidnap him), as told in Ovid's *Metamorphoses* 10. The metamorphosis into a bird and the name Philomele—although the term metamorphosis is not used (and the process is transposed to a fairy tale context with it being the result of magic)—also echo Ovid's tale of the sisters Philomela and Procne (where Philomela becomes a swallow and Procne a nightingale). However, where silence characterises Philomela in Ovid's version, in Murat's the nightingale has the chance to tell her story to Grandimont once he has transformed back to a Prince and she into a Princess.[70]

Murat also mobilises ancient stories as literary criticism in her 1708 *Journal pour Mademoiselle de Menou*, a series of letters with literary interludes. This *Journal* is included in a much longer manuscript held at the Arsenal Library (MS 3471); it is attributed to her, and entitled 'Ouvrages de Mme la comtesse de Murat'. As Geneviève Clermidy-Patard shows in her critical edition of the *Journal*, Murat probably intended to publish this manuscript.[71] The *Journal*, which constitutes over half of the manuscript, comprises a series of letters she sent from Loches to her cousin, Mademoiselle de Menou, who lived in Boussay, between April 1708 and March 1709. Murat was writing from the Château de Loches, where she had been imprisoned in 1702 for her apparent lesbianism; this sentence had been mitigated to exile in 1707, with the freedom to leave the Château and explore the town and surrounding countryside. Her exile lasted until 1709 when she was ordered to live with her aunt in Limousin.[72] The letters, interspersed with stories and literary interludes, document daily life in the provincial town and draughty house: they mix intimate accounts of her illnesses and routines with short stories, poetry, literary interludes, and social digressions and observations. Clermidy-Patard aptly describes it as 'une gazette galante' and 'un journal personnel et même intime' as

[70] Murat, 'Histoire de la Princesse Blanchette et du Prince Verdelet', in *Histoires sublimes*, pp. 106–232.

[71] 'Introduction', in *Journal pour Mademoiselle de Menou*, ed. by Geneviève Clermidy-Patard (Paris: Classiques Garnier, 2014), pp. 11–51 (pp. 12–16). All subsequent references to the *Journal* will be given from this edition in the text.

[72] Ibid., p. 18.

198   WOMEN WRITING ANTIQUITY

it embraces a multiplicity of forms.[73] For the purposes of this chapter, I am not going to analyse this *Journal* in detail; however, I will pick out some key moments where Murat uses references to antiquity to develop what I suggest is a form of literary criticism.[74] I therefore approach this multi-genre *Journal* (addressed, like the *Mercure Galant*, to a woman in the provinces) in a similar vein to L'Héritier's literary criticism in her correspondence and her periodical.[75]

The Philomela story evoked in her fairy tale occurs again in the *Journal* when she consoles Menou for the death of her sparrow (letter dated 18th April, p. 64): 'Philomèle oublia ses malheurs pour ne chanter que des louanges de votre oiseau' (Philomela forgot her troubles to sing the praises of your bird). This playful letter is written in the style of a Parnassus text, like the three we analysed above by L'Héritier. It opens with a parody of the Parnassus genre:

À peine le brillant Phébus sortait du sein de l'onde qu'une fée de mes amies qui s'était mise dans le char de l'aurore pour arriver ici plus matin, est venue m'apprendre la mort de votre joli moineau, si aimable et si regretté, et les honneurs qu'il a reçus aux champs Élysées. (p. 64)

Hardly had bright Phebus risen from the ocean when one of my fairy friends, who took Aurora's chariot to get here earlier, came to inform me of the death of your lovely sparrow, so pleasant and much missed, and the honours it received in Parnassus.

Famous literary dead birds (including Philomèle) are there to welcome Menou's sparrow to the Champs Elysées, including the parrot belonging to Ovid's Corinna (*Amores* 2.6) who conducts the funeral oration and 'le galant moineau de Lesbie' (Lesbia's *galant* sparrow), from Catullus, who leads the celebration and declaims Catullus's verse. There is even an *arc de triomphe* decorated with birds. This letter is a light-hearted joke which relies on her reader's recognition of the Parnassus genre she is parodying: it also plays with the fact that avian laments in the Latin tradition were already parodic and draws on the more recent French tradition of burlesque uses of animals to mock human endeavour. That playfulness also reflects on Murat, as she both aligns herself with authors of these texts—and 'Parnasse' is a term Murat uses frequently in the *Journal*, at times in relation to her own practice (for example to introduce a poem she has composed, p. 231)—and parodies this authorship.

---

[73] Ibid., p. 26.
[74] For a detailed discussion of the *Journal*, see Clermidy-Patard, 'Introduction', in *Journal*, and Clermidy-Patard, *Madame de Murat et la 'défense des dames'. Un discours au féminin à la fin du règne de Louis XIV* (Paris: Classiques Garnier, 2012), pp. 357–406.
[75] Murat evokes the *Mercure Galant* ironically, offering her news as a more favourable source (*Journal*, p. 244); see Clermidy-Patard, 'Introduction', p. 29.

In this same letter she then includes a short story about the life of the ancient courtesan Rhodopis, which, she tells us, had initially been part of a longer envisaged project on famous courtesans of antiquity (p. 66). Rhodopis is also evoked by L'Héritier in her *Apothéose de Mlle de Scudéry*, where she is expelled from the Temple de Mémoire for causing disturbance.[76] The tale of Rhodopis intersects with that of Sappho because Sappho's brother, Charaxus, fell in love with Rhodopis and Sappho's disapproval of this liaison recurs in the accounts of her life. Significantly, Murat finds in the story of Rhodopis a possible origin for the story of Cinderella, evoking a tale told in Strabo's *Geography*. Rhodopis loses a shoe, which an eagle brings back to her: 'elle trouva cet augure glorieux pour elle: le bruit s'en répandit partout; et c'est sans doute sur cette aventure historique et singulière que l'on a formé tous les contes de Fées où une mule perdue fait bien souvent la fortune de l'héroïne' (she found this augury glorious: rumours about it spread and it is likely that it was this particular and historic adventure that formed the source of all the fairy tales in which a lost shoe can make the heroine's fortune) (pp. 74–75). She thus claims an ancient story as origin for the fairy tale. Murat's version of the Rhodope story is significant because of its insertion in her *Journal*: it becomes a hybrid piece of fiction, but placed as it is alongside personal anecdotes, it also becomes entwined with the story of her own life, giving it an intimacy and connection to the present.[77]

Such interweaving of literary criticism and fiction is most evident from her 'Dialogue des morts' in the 'Pot-pourri' section of her *Journal*, which also contains a series of poems. It has been well established in criticism that the *dialogue des morts* is a key Ancients and Moderns comparative genre, and as such is also a site for literary criticism. Murat's use of the genre here confirms this.[78] She asks Mlle de Menou if she knows Fontenelle's *Dialogues des morts*, in the style of which she has composed the following dialogue between Madame de Villedieu and 'Junie', whom readers will surely recognise as the protagonist from Villedieu's successful novel, *Les Exilés de la cour d'Auguste* (1672–78) (p. 250). The subject of this dialogue is 'si l'on pouvait prendre de l'amour pour une personne que l'on ne connaissait point, mais dont on aurait lu les ouvrages tendres, délicats et dignes d'admiration' (whether one can fall in love with someone one does not know but whose tender, delicate, and admirable works one has read) (p. 250), a subject which picks up on

---

[76] L'Héritier, *L'Apothéose de Mlle de Scudéry*, p. 61. See also Catherine Durand, *Les Belles Grecques, ou l'Histoire des plus fameuses courtisanes de la Grèce et Dialogues nouveaux des galantes modernes* (Paris: Veuve Saugrain and Prault, 1712), pp. 1–60.

[77] Her story is also told by Catherine Durand who likewise turns the Rhodopis story into a Sappho story and makes the reference to Rhodopis's shoe a model for subsequent stories (*Les Belles Grecques*, p. 33). Clermidy-Patard suggests that Murat's story was a way of competing with Durand as, although the latter's work was published in 1712, the 'approbation' dates to 1704, suggesting a version was available that year ('Introduction', *Journal*, p. 44; *Journal*, p. 66).

[78] See, for example, Lise Andries, 'Querelles et dialogues des morts au XVIIIe siècle', *Littératures classiques*, 81.2 (2013), 131–46.

200 WOMEN WRITING ANTIQUITY

Junie's declaration at the opening of Villedieu's novel.[79] Throughout the *Journal* up to this point, Murat has recommended Villedieu's fictions to Menou, noting their success (as discussed in Chapter 4), 'je ne sais si cela est du goût du siècle, mais ces sortes d'ouvrage ont fort réussi' (I do not know if this is the taste of the time, but these sorts of works have had great success) (p. 218), and praising the 'sensibles et tendres' qualities of her heroines (p. 218). She lends her copies and particularly singles out *Les Exilés*, which her friend will deliver to Menou along with Murat's 'pot-pourri' (p. 244). She thus establishes that her *dialogue des morts* is intended to be read alongside Villedieu's *Les Exilés*, and is better understood as a companion piece.

The dialogue is an exercise in literary criticism and in particular, as we saw in L'Héritier's work, a discussion of the state of the novel. The fictional 'Mme de Villedieu' explains her accommodation to prevailing taste by distinguishing her work from d'Urfé's *L'Astrée* and the Scudérys' *Artamène ou le Grand Cyrus*. Junie praises the success of Villedieu's work and her depiction of 'véritables portraits' rather than 'modèles' (p. 251):

> *Junie*
> 'Cela ne pouvait manquer de réussir; aussi l'on vit vos ouvrages courus, recherchés de tout le monde et jamais on ne fit tant d'éditions d'aucun livre de morale.'

> *Mme de Villedieu*
> 'Cela n'est point étonnant, c'était de l'amour et des bagatelles. La morale est à l'usage de peu de gens [...] mais les bagatelles et l'amour n'ont jamais ennuyé personne.'
>
> (p. 252)

> *Junie*
> 'That can't but succeed: we see your works as being popular, desired by everyone; one has never made as many editions of a moral work.'

> *Mme de Villedieu*
> 'It is not that surprising given that it is about trifles and love; morals interest very few people; but love and trifles have never bored anyone.'

---

[79] Junie says: 'Quand je lis les endroits passionnez de ses [d'Ovide] Elegies, où les divers caractères de l'Amour sont si naïvement dépeints, je sens une émotion de plaisir qui me fait désirer ardemment de voir l'homme admirable à qui je la dois' (When I read the passionate parts of his elegies, where the different characteristics of love are so simply portrayed, I feel an emotion of pleasure which makes me ardently desire to see the admirable man to whom I owe such a feeling). *Œuvres de Madame de Villedieu, Tome VIII contenant Les Exilez*, 12 vols (Paris: M. Clouzier, 1711), VIII, p. 5. See Helena Taylor, 'Ovid, *Galanterie* and Politics in Madame de Villedieu's *Les Exilés de la cour d'Auguste*', *Early Modern French Studies*, 37 (2015), 49–63.

What Junie then describes as 'Villedieu's' 'style badin' serves to dismantle much of the theory of the novel that vaunted its moral quality in favour of embracing its lightness and emotional sensibility.

Junie and 'Villedieu' then move on to discussing another key element of the seventeenth-century theory of the novel: *vraisemblance* and historical accuracy (a topic central to Villedieu's career, as we saw in Chapter 4). Junie, in a manner akin to the ancient characters in Gabriel Guéret's *Le Parnasse Réformé*, challenges 'Villedieu' for having cast her to a fictional island on the Aegean Sea, Thalassie, and for having made her, a woman of high rank, fall for a man of lower station: Ovid (p. 252). 'Villedieu' defends herself with the emotional veracity of her tale and its historical approximation (Junie recalls Julie, the daughter or granddaughter of Augustus, thought to have had an affair with the poet). 'Villedieu' then defends the persuasive power of what she describes as 'agréable' and 'charmant' works (p. 253). Murat uses this dialogue to engage in literary criticism, particularly criticism of the novel, but takes a new angle on the typical questions—and their responses—at the heart of the debates about this genre. With 'Madame de Villedieu', she stresses the importance of entertainment and uses commercial success as a form of defence; and gives short shrift to the usual points about morality and *vraisembalance* to instead champion the aesthetic qualities of the work—a response that confirms my earlier analysis of Villedieu's commerce-orientated approach to authorship. This 'dialogue des morts', labelled as such and introduced with a comparison to Fontenelle, is unusual not only for its setting in the wider *Journal* but also for its female-lead characters. Both Murat's and L'Héritier's works thus combine the textual transmission of translation, rewriting, and adaptation with a rhetorical use of antiquity: they maintain their valorisation of French culture, literary history, and new genres, but do so through an erudition and ideological engagement with the Greco-Roman past that explicitly questions the Modern appropriation of female taste and judgement that relies on women's exclusion from erudite culture.

**

If, as Schuwey and Roussillon argue, the periodical can be seen as a social space, creating and reflecting a community of readers and values, then many of the works analysed here, including but not limited to L'Héritier's periodical, *L'Érudition enjouée*, can also be seen as such. The dynamic works explored in this chapter reveal a community of reading that goes beyond the material and the temporal, constructing links with authors recently deceased (Deshoulières, Scudéry, Villedieu) and a genealogy that stretches back to both classical and medieval sources. The various different acts of literary criticism analysed in this chapter not only define an aesthetic practice and cultural mode (*galanterie*), but they also valorise 'new' genres (the fairy tale and, by extension for L'Héritier, the novel) and authors (women). Just as the fairy tale has been seen to construct authorship through the meta-discursive tropes common to this genre, so too do the other works by *conteuses*: L'Héritier figures herself, for instance, as both an author of fiction and a historian of literature.[80]

The Modern as it is defined by these authors has in common a strong sense of genealogy, be this in the line drawn from the troubadours to the novel, from the *cour d'amour* to the salon, from ancient genre to modern. Differences from Perrault's conception of 'modernity' emerge as we encounter a different conception of the history of French literature and of the sorts of learning and sources needed to be a legitimised female author. This chapter also saw a shift away from Scudéry's modest intellectual and a greater freedom to use irony, humour, even satire. With the complex layering of intertexts, the deployment of classical stories and genres, the *conteuses* studied here are no less Modern than Perrault; however, they also test the parameters of the definition of modernity that relies on a reductive stereotype of women's intellectual practice. In the next and final chapter we turn to a figure who embraced erudition, further challenging such stereotypes.

---

[80] See also Montoya, *Medievalist Enlightenment*, pp. 107–44.

7

The Career Classicist

Gender and Translation

Anne Dacier (1647–1720) cuts an exceptional figure: as a lauded 'savante', as an Ancient in the Homer Quarrel, and as an accepted and prominent participant in that Quarrel. She was the daughter of the leading Hellenist scholar, Tanneguy Le Fèvre, Professor at the Protestant Academy at Saumur, from whom she received an exceptional education in Latin and ancient Greek alongside her brother; after separating from her first husband, Jean Lesnier, she later married the scholar and pupil of her father, André Dacier.[1] Anne Dacier is distinct among the women analysed in this book not only for her knowledge of ancient Greek, but also for the scholarly genres of her writing: she produced editions in Latin for the *Ad usum Delphini* series as well as translations with commentary of Sappho and Anacreon (1681), and of authors who had received less attention in French: Plautus (1683), Aristophanes (1684), Terence (1688), and Homer's *Iliad* (1711) and *Odyssey* (1716).[2] She was also an untiring and unflinching participant in the Homer Quarrel of 1711–16, deploying rhetoric usually reserved for men. Dacier's willingness to engage directly in the Quarrel made for a divided reception, as is attested to by the polarised criticism she received after her death. Some cast her as erudite, but also modest and good at conversation, effacing her polemic and stressing her social abilities to modify the unseemliness of her conflict—while others lambasted her for being 'hommasse' and described her as 'vomiting torrents of insults'.[3] Focusing on her translations and her interventions in the Homer Quarrel, in this chapter I will explore the strategies Dacier deployed to make her career as a Classicist, examining in particular how she negotiated the usually irreconcilable identities of scholar, woman, and quarreller.

---

[1] I will refer to her by her married name of Dacier throughout.

[2] *Les Poésies d'Anacréon et de Sapho* (Paris: Thierry and Barbin, 1681); *Les Comédies de Plaute*, 3 vols (Paris: Thierry and Barbin, 1683); *Le Plutus et les Nuées d'Aristophane* (Paris: Thierry and Barbin, 1684); *Les Comédies de Térence*, 3 vols (Paris: Thierry and Barbin, 1688); *L'Iliade d'Homère*, 3 vols (Paris: Rigaud, 1711); *L'Odyssée d'Homère*, 3 vols (Paris: Rigaud, 1716). All references to these editions will hereafter be given in the text. On the fact that she turned to less-known authors, see Emmanuel Bury, 'Madame Dacier', in *Femmes savantes, savoir des femmes: Du crépuscule de la Renaissance à l'aube des Lumières*, ed. by C. Nativel (Geneva: Droz, 1999), pp. 209–22 (p. 219).

[3] 'Hommasse': François Cartaud de La Vilate, *Essai historique et philosophique sur le goût* (Paris: Maudouyt, 1736), p. 157; 'elle vomit [...] un torrent d'injures', Jean-Zorobabel Aublet de Maubuy, *Histoire des troubles et des démêlés littéraires: depuis leur origine jusqu'à nos jours*, 2 vols (Amsterdam, 1779), I, p. 12.

Women Writing Antiquity. Helena Taylor, Oxford University Press. © Helena Taylor (2024).
DOI: 10.1093/oso/9780192870445.003.0007

204   WOMEN WRITING ANTIQUITY

Dacier cuts an exceptional figure because she did not generally align herself with the Modern, feminised, and often modest literary culture and posture normally associated with women. For this reason, she has sometimes been compared to Marie de Gournay—Latinist, translator, polemicist, and also writing in favour of the ancients—whose work we analysed in Chapter 2.[4] Like Gournay, Dacier was bold in the demonstration of her erudition and strident in her stance as a quarreller. She was also a champion of women's education—not, like Gournay, through theoretical arguments and treatises, but in the way she directed her translations at female readers who might want to learn about ancient Greek and Roman literature. However, she also framed her gender differently to Gournay and to many of the women studied here. Although she made her female identity clear, publishing her works under her name and referring to it but on very few occasions,[5] she did not make her female sex or women's stories central to her authorial persona and work, beyond offering her translations to those without Latin and Greek.[6] Unlike other women writers engaged in classical reception, who tended to choose female-centred stories or amplify stories of female historical or mythological figures of antiquity, Dacier made no such changes or selections.[7] Although she is critical of Eustatius' commentary of Homer for his denigration of Homer's women (L'Iliade, I, p. 62), she resists using gender to shape her interpretation. This approach has in turn shaped her reception: Dacier was often singled out by contemporaries for her exceptional learning, was not subjected to the same levels of criticism and ridicule as the 'précieuses', and has since been catalogued in histories of Classical scholars and thinkers.[8] She tends not to be incorporated into the canon

[4] Myriam Dufour-Maître, 'Les "Belles" et les Belles-Lettres: femmes, instances du féminin et nouvelles configurations du savoir', in Le Savoir au XVIIe siècle, ed. by John D. Lyons and Cara Welch (Tübingen: Gunter Narr, 2003), pp. 35–64.

[5] She refers to it in a very early publication, a Latin edition of Callimachus in 1675, as I discuss below: Dacier [Le Fèvre], Preface, Callimachi Cyrenaei Hymni (Paris: Mabre-Cramoisy, 1675), np. Another rare example of her personal voice occurs in the preface to the Iliad translation of 1711 when she explains that she will have to delay working on her translation of the Odyssey to mourn the death of her daughter, Henriette-Susanne (L'Iliade, I, p. 71). This is likely a sincere expression of grief, despite the strategic and careful nature of her self-presentation; and yet, in expressing her grief in this preface, does she align herself with grieving women of epic? Can it be seen as a textual éloge, offering a monument to her daughter? (her father similarly had evoked her brother in his Méthode pour commencer les humanités grecques et latines (Saumur: Péan, 1672), p. 3).

[6] This is also noted by Fern Farnham, Madam Dacier: Scholar and Humanist (Monterey: Angel Press, 1976), p. 168; Eliane Itti, Madame Dacier, femme et savante du Grand Siècle (1645–1720) (Paris: L'Harmattan, 2012); p. 11; Rosie Wyles, 'Ménage's Learned Ladies: Anne Dacier (1647–1720) and Anna Maria van Schurman (1607–1678)', in Women Classical Scholars, ed. by Rosie Wyles and Edith Hall (Oxford: Oxford University Press, 2016), pp. 61–77 (p. 74); Suzanna van Dijk, Traces de femmes dans le journalisme français du XVIIIe siècle (Amsterdam: APA Holland University Press, 1988), p. 198; and Carol Pal, Republic of Women: Rethinking the Republic of Letters in the Seventeenth Century (Cambridge: Cambridge University Press, 2012), p. 271.

[7] See, for instance, Madeleine de Scudéry's versions of the stories of Clélie and Lucrèce in her Clélie: histoire romaine, 10 vols (Paris: Courbé, 1654–60), as studied in Chapter 3.

[8] See, for instance, Gilles Ménage, Historia Mulierum Philosopharum [The History of Women Philosophers] (Lyon: Rigaud, 1690) and Wyles, 'Ménage's Learned Ladies', pp. 61–77. For recent reception, see Wyles and Hall, eds, Women Classical Scholars; Pal, Republic of Women, pp. 266–86; and Karen

of French seventeenth- and early eighteenth-century 'women writers' which normally includes women writing in feminised genres or those who were vocal about the female cause.[9]

Dacier is also unique among seventeenth- and early eighteenth-century women writers for the prominent position she played in a quarrel which was not about the female sex—the *Querelle d'Homère*—for her Ancient stance, and for the way she was received as a legitimate opponent. On this final point she also differs significantly from Gournay who, although a prolific (Ancient) quarreller who engaged deeply in debates that went far beyond questions of male-female equality, was very often received with ridicule.[10] Some of the respect that Dacier commanded where Gournay did not was thanks to her more careful courting of politeness and social expectations in her social, if not printed, persona: to her perceived ability to distinguish between social and authorial identities. Some of the respect was due to the scholarly repute of her family. She benefited from what Neil Kenny, referring to a more general context, describes as the 'sociocultural legacy' conferred by her family, an inheritance that was both 'tangible and symbolic'.[11] It was not tangible in the sense of direct financial inheritance: when her father died in 1672, he was in financial difficulty having resigned from his professorship due to a quarrel with the consistory, and Dacier moved to Paris in order to make her living.[12] However, this familial inheritance *was* tangible in so far as her education and family networks meant that she was able to make money as a scholar and translator: in Paris, she was supported by Pierre-Daniel Huet, her father's friend, who enabled her to publish works for the series for the Dauphin; she was also aided by André Dacier, whom she married in 1683.[13] Together they would complete joint translations of

---

Green, 'Early Eighteenth-Century Debates: From Anne Dacier to Catharine Trotter Cockburn', in *A History of Women's Political Thought in Europe, 1700–1800* (Cambridge: Cambridge University Press, 2014), pp. 14–42. For a collection of resources pertaining to Dacier, see <https://madamedacier.humanum.fr/> run by SIEFAR and Université Lumière Lyon 2.

[9] Anne Dacier does not feature in either of the eighteenth-century chapters of Sonya Stephens, ed., *A History of Women's Writing in France* (Cambridge: Cambridge University Press, 2000) and is only mentioned in passing in the chapter on the seventeenth century (p. 66). She is not mentioned at all in either of the chapters dedicated to seventeenth- and eighteenth-century women writers, and is only referenced in passing in the chapter on seventeenth-century comedy in William Burgwinkle, Nicholas Hammond, and Emma Wilson, eds, *The Cambridge History of French Literature* (Cambridge: Cambridge University Press, 2011), p. 278.

[10] See Helena Taylor, 'Marie de Gournay et le Parnasse des femmes', in *Littéraire: pour Alain Viala*, ed. by M. M. Fragonard and others, 2 vols (Arras: Artois Presses Université, 2018), II, pp. 227–37.

[11] Neil Kenny, *Born to Write: Literary Families and Social Hierarchy in Early Modern France* (Oxford: Oxford University Press, 2020), p. 25. His study ends in 1650 and so does not go as late as Le Fèvre-Daciers but many of its arguments apply here.

[12] On Le Fèvre's difficulties, see Itti, *Madame Dacier*, pp. 61–76. It is thought that Dacier had returned to the family home in Saumur in 1669 following the death of her son and permanent separation from her first husband, her father's printer, Jean Lesnier.

[13] On making money from the series, see the letters she sent to Huet between May 1680 and September 1681, gathered in *La Collection Ad usum Delphini. L'Antiquité au miroir du Grand Siècle*, ed. by Caroline Volpilhac-Auger (Grenoble: Ellug, 2000), pp. 358–68. See also Eliane Itti, 'Tanneguy Le Fèvre et les époux Dacier entre mécénat privé et mécénat royal', *Littératures Classiques*, 72 (2010), 21–27.

Marc Anthony and Plutarch, examples of what Kenny calls collaborative 'family literature'.[14] The inheritance was also symbolic: her maiden and married names carried a weight of scholarly authority which protected her from the worst of ridicule while she was alive. Dacier did not share the aristocratic anxieties about publication we have encountered elsewhere in this study; however, for all that she was a professional scholar, nevertheless, as we will see, she did sometimes cultivate a more 'modest' approach, seeming to frame her contributions as activities of leisure, rather than the work of 'les véritables sçavants'.[15] And despite her exceptionality and the respect she commanded as a scholar, Dacier also had to negotiate perceptions of her gender. In this chapter, I analyse the different stages of Dacier's career as a translator to show that, for her, classical scholarship was professional, public, educational—and also personal, in that she invested her own reputation and authority in her interpretations as she self-consciously shaped a unique scholarly identity. This identity and her professional endeavours made their mark on the literary debates of the period as her translations were a prominent vehicle for championing the presence and alterity of 'foreign' cultures in French, and for advocating the literature of ancient Greece and Rome as a valuable heritage for French literary writing.

Formation: Sappho and Anacreon

By the time Anne Dacier came to publish her first translation, the poetry of Sappho and Anacreon in prose, in 1681, she was well established as a professional classical scholar. For the *Ad Usum Delphini* series, she had produced editions of Publius Annius Florus (1674), Dictys Cretensis (1680), Sextus Aurelius Victor (1681), and was working on one of Eutropius (1683); she had also published an edition of Callimachus in 1675, three years after her father's death. In this early publication, she includes an oft-cited comment. In the preface, she corrects foolish old men who think her father should not have educated her as he did.[16] While this is an important programmatic statement, in which she makes explicit reference to her gender, her access to learning, and her authority, it should also be seen for what it is: an isolated instance. As we will see, Dacier more typically preferred to assert her authority through her learning without explicitly making her case as a woman scholar representative—in which she differed significantly from Gournay.

---

[14] Kenny, *Born to Write*, p. 33. On their work see Christine Dousset-Seiden and Jean-Philippe Grosperrin, eds, *Les Époux Dacier* (= *Littératures Classiques*, 72.2 (2010)). She published, with André Dacier, *Réflexions morales de l'empereur Marc Antonin avec des remarques*, 2 vols (Paris: Barbin, 1691) and *Vies des hommes illustres de Plutarque, traduites en français, avec des remarques* (Paris: Barbin, 1694).

[15] Anne Dacier, *Des Causes de la corruption du goust* (Paris: Rigaud, 1714), p. 324. See also Linda Timmermans, *L'Accès des femmes à la culture sous l'ancien régime* (Paris: Champion, 1993), pp. 131–32.

[16] Dacier [Le Fèvre], 'Préface', *Callimachi Cyrenaei Hymni*, np.

Why did she choose to establish herself as a translator with a version of Sappho and Anacreon? This decision could be seen as a way of engaging directly with the legacy of her father who had produced a Latin version of Sappho and Anacreon in 1660, which had been reprinted in 1680, a year before her own translations were published.[17] (Such an intergenerational relationship was another form of 'family literature'.) His Lives of Anacreon and of Sappho included in his 1665 *Vies des poètes* also influenced the *Vies* of the two poets that Dacier inserted into her edition.[18] Dacier follows her father's selection of poetry attributed to the two poets, but she makes clear her distinction from him in correcting elements of his scholarship in the *remarques* included after each poem. Her choice must also surely be seen as a way of responding to, and—perhaps curiously, given her later Ancient stance— contributing to, the popularity of Anacreon and Sappho in *galant* salon culture, thanks, for instance, to versions by Claude Nicole (1666), Claude-Denis Du Four de la Crespelière (1670), and the wider reception of Greek lyric poets which we explored in Chapters 3 and 5 in relation to Scudéry and Deshoulières.[19] Her translation was published by Claude Barbin and Denys Thierry, *galant* publishers par excellence, as we examined in Chapter 4.

That Dacier was directly engaging with this culture is evident from the way she establishes her translation as *galant* by stating in her dedicatory preface to the Duc de Montausier that Anacreon represents 'ce que la Grece a eu de plus poly et de plus galant' (the most polite and *galant* aspects of Greece) (np).[20] She likewise makes this clear in the *Vie d'Anacréon* when, like her father, she defends Anacreon against criticism, stressing that his seeking of pleasure, especially drinking and the company of 'belles personnes', was within the bounds of a 'homme du monde' and a 'bel esprit'.[21] She also specifies that her target audience is women and those who want to learn the original language, which Du Four had done before her in his translation.[22] She opens her preface: 'En traduisant Anacreon en notre langue, j'ay voulu donner aux Dames le plaisir de lire le plus poly et le plus galand poëte Grec que nous ayons [...] dans cette pensee, je n'ai pas laissé un passage difficile sans l'éclaircir le mieux qu'il m'a esté possible' (by translating Anacreon into our language, I wanted to give women the pleasure of reading the most polite and *galant*

---

[17] Tanneguy Le Fèvre, *Anacreontis et Sapphonis Carmina* (Saumur: Lesnier, 1660).

[18] Tanneguy Le Fèvre, *Les vies des poètes grecs, en abrégé* (Paris: Sercy, 1665).

[19] Claude-Denis Du Four de la Crespelière, *Les Odes amoureuses, charmantes et bachiques des poètes grecs Anacréon, Sappho et Théocrite* (Paris: Loyson, 1670); Claude Nicole, *Recueil de diverses pièces choisies d'Horace, d'Ovide, Catulle, Martial, et Anacreon. Par M. Nicole* (Paris: Sercy, 1666).

[20] As we saw in Chapters 3 and 5, works attributed to Anacreon in this period have since been attributed rather to a tradition of his imitators, the Aanacreontea, with his own works only surviving in quotation.

[21] In the *remarques*, she frequently describes Anacreon's verse in the terms of mondain culture— 'galant', 'politesse', 'délicatesse'—see, for instance, p. 236, p. 240.

[22] '[...] cela me fait croire qu'il sera bien reçu des Dames dont il épargne la pudeur' (this makes me think he will be well received by women whose modesty he spares). Du Four, 'Au Lecteur', *Les Odes amoureuses*, np.

Greek poet that there is; with this in mind, I have tried to elucidate as well as possible any difficult passage) (np). Like Scudéry, she converts the bodily pleasure embraced by Anacreon into readers' intellectual pleasure. She explicitly states that she has in mind 'gens du monde'—whom she contrasts with 'savants', although this term is not used pejoratively—when she decided to keep her commentary light. This endeavour of providing access to knowledge chimes with her practice of translating into French works that were less well-known in the language.

However, we get a sense of the hybridity of this edition because she makes it clear that she is also targeting readers who may be familiar with Greek (namely, those 'savants') as she includes a parallel text to demonstrate that 'j'ai suivi mon Auteur avec la dernière exactitude' (I have followed my author with the utmost precision) (np). This dual audience is confirmed by the scholarly remarks which accompany each poem: although they are not relegated to the end of the book and so are readily accessible for the reader as they go along, the scholarly content of these remarks, concerned almost exclusively with philological matters, makes them relevant only to those literate in ancient Greek or at an advanced stage in their learning of this language. Like Jean Racine—also an Ancient in the Quarrel, who likewise attempted to placate both sides—she did not want to alienate a more *galant* audience at this point in her career at least, but she also sought to affirm her authority by nevertheless appealing to more erudite readers. In thus engaging with a 'stratégie de multiple alliance' at the outset of her translation career,[23] she was also taking the mainstream, fashionable approach towards ancient lyric: as Claudine Nédélec has discussed, no translator of lyric in the 1680s and at the height of the Quarrel attempted a real rupture with the idealisation of *galant* mores.[24]

In the prefatory material Dacier also institutes her authority as a translator. In her dedication, she deploys some of the usual tropes of modesty in an example of her subtle gendering of her professional persona: she credits the Duc de Montausier with the customary guidance in bringing this edition to publication, casting her own work as the product of leisure by comparing her 'petites occupations' to his 'grandes' (np)—although we might read this as a programmatic reference to the lyric genre, as Anacreon himself writes, in Dacier's translation: 'aportez moi la lyre d'Homère, mais que la corde qui chante les combats en soit ostée' (give me Homer's lyre; but remove from it the string that sings of military feats) (p. 249).[25] However, she also explicates her labour as a scholar as she makes it clear in the Anacreon preface that she does not agree with all her father's comments:

---

[23] On Racine see Tristan Alonge, *Racine et Euripide: la révolution trahie* (Geneva: Droz, 2017). On the 'stratégie de multiple alliance', see Alain Viala, *Naissance de l'écrivain: sociologie de la littérature à l'âge classique* (Paris: Minuit, 1985), pp. 167–68. See also the Introduction.

[24] Claudine Nédélec, 'Lyriques anciens et lyriques modernes à l'aune de la galanterie', *Littératures Classiques*, 77.1 (2012), 319–31 (p. 31).

[25] Ode 48: this is Ode 2 in Anacreontea, *Greek Lyric II: Anacreon, Anacreontea, Choral Lyric from Olympus to Alcman*, ed. and trans. by David Campbell, Loeb Classical Library 143 (Cambridge, MA: Harvard University Press, 1993).

'Mon pere a fait autrefois quelques Remarques sur cet Auteur, qui ont esté si bien receuës qu'il n'est pas necessaire que j'en parle ici. Cependant, quelque veneration que j'aye pour sa memoire, j'oseray dire que je ne suis pas toujours de son sentiment' (My father has already produced a commentary of this author, which was so well received that I do not need to discuss it here. However, with all due respect to his memory, I dare add that I am not always in agreement with him) (np).[26] The *remarques* are also peppered with reflections on the merits and shortcomings of previous editions (usually those of Henri Estienne and of her father). In her preface, she dismisses previous translations, of which she only mentions Rémi Belleau's: 'Il y a long-temps qu'il a esté traduit en François par Remi Belleau, mais outre que sa traduction est en vers et par consequent peu fidele, elle est en si vieux langage qu'il est impossible d'y trouver aucun agrément' (Anacreon was translated into French some time ago in French by Rémi Belleau, but not only is this translation in verse, and thus not very faithful, but it is in such an old style of language that it is impossible to find it charming) (np). She makes no mention of the two other, *galant* translations by Claude Nicole and Du Four: it is possible that she was not aware of the former, as it was included in a larger collection, but her exclusion of Du Four's is surely more condemnatory.

Her translation choices in relation to some of the more ribald aspects of Anacreon's verse suit her privileging of female readers and align with her commitment to (moral) instruction that we will see develop over her career: they may also reveal an awareness of her own gender as a translator and the resulting need for more decorum and pudeur. These choices primarily entail removing references to male genitalia and homoeroticism (without telling us that she has done so) which were retained in the Latin edition of her father and also kept—in some form—in the versions by Belleau and Du Four.[27] For example, in Ode 29 (17 in modern editions), the homoerotic 'Portrait of Bathyllis', she removes the description of Bathyllis as 'beloved' in the first line where it is retained by Le Fèvre as 'meos Bathyllum amores'; by Belleau as 'mon mignon'; and by Du Four as 'l'objet de mes plus chers delices' (the object of my dear pleasures).[28] She excises the description of the thighs and penis, which is kept by Le Fèvre, Belleau, and Du Four,[29] removing

---

[26] In her *Vie d'Anacréon* she makes some changes to her father's version, namely in her interest in the scholarly debate about the name of Anacreon's father, with which she opens her *Vie* (her father starts with the place of Anacreon's birth). Unlike her father, she then also pursues this question of lineage in her discussion of Plato's reference to Anacreon as being a relative of Solon (and so high-born, related to King Codrus). It is tempting to read her interest in lineage (and fathers) as an example of her own self-conscious awareness of her continuation and/or correction of her father's work.

[27] Rémi Belleau, *Les odes d'Anacréon ... traduites de grec en françois* (Paris: Wechel, 1556). It was typical of her not to point out omissions. See Itti, *Madame Dacier*, p. 131.

[28] Dacier, *Les Poésies d'Anacréon et de Sapho*, p. 147; Tanneguy Le Fèvre, *Anacreontis et Sapphonis Carmina*, p. 40; Belleau, *Les odes d'Anacréon*, p. 35; Du Four de la Crespelière, *Les Odes amoureuses*, p. 37.

[29] They all keep this section: Tanneguy Le Fèvre, 'femurque molle supra, / femur quod excit ignes / volo simplicem esse pubem/ iam cogitantem amores' (above his soft thigh, the thigh from which fire

210   WOMEN WRITING ANTIQUITY

the Greek text and signalling this replacement with asterisks (though she makes no reference to this in the *remarques*). Although some of this prudence is to be expected in a translation aimed at a *galant* and female readership, it is notable that she sometimes goes further than Du Four, who was writing for a similar audience, underscoring the importance of instruction to her approach and perhaps indicating a social awareness of the reception of her work as a female translator.

At the end of her collection of Anacreon odes, she includes a *Vie de Sappho* and then the two well-known Sappho odes (the 'Ode to Aphrodite', fragment 1, and the 'Ode to her friend', fragment 31) plus two epigrams, one about a fisherman, Pelagin, and the other about Timas, with *remarques* following each poem.[30] Although there is no preface accompanying this final section on Sappho, the *Vie* could be seen as a sort of hybrid *vie*-preface of the sort typically used to introduce *galant* translations, in which life, work, and translation are discussed together.[31] In keeping with this feature of the 'vie galante', Dacier weaves into the account of Sappho's life quotations in French from two further fragments, which we discussed in Chapter 3, and which do not feature in her father's version but are mentioned by Lilio Giraldi in his *Historiae poetarum tam Graecorum quam Latinorum dialogi decem* (1545).[32] The first is a fragment in which the speaker rejects marriage with a younger man (now fr. 121) and in the other the speaker is critical of another woman who will be forgotten (fr. 55), the second of which, as Dacier demonstrates, was reprised by Horace when he depicts Sappho in the Underworld (Odes 2.13). Dacier notes from this fragment the tensions and complexities in Sappho's social group and remarks: 'presque tous ses ouvrages estoient faits à la loüange de ses amies; mais une chose me surprend, c'est que ses amies ayent esté presque toutes étrangeres et qu'elle n'ait pû se faire aimer des Dames de son pays' (almost all her works were written in praise of her female friends; but one thing surprises me which is that her friends are almost all foreigners and she had very few friends among the women of her country) (p. 405). We might see here a continuation of the emphasis on the

---

comes out, I want there to be a simple member, that already knows love), *Anacreontis et Sapphonis Carmina*, p. 42; Belleau, 'fait luy son aine qui rougisse / son aine tendrette où soit vue/ entre les deux un petit feu' (make his groin enflamed, his tender groin where might be seen, between the two, a little fire), *Les odes d'Anacréon*, p. 36; and Du Four, 'que son aine soit molette et delicate, d'où sortent de petits feux charmants; je veux que la partie voisine soit simple et qu'elle commence déjà à ressentir les plus doux chatouillements de l'amour' (that his groin is soft and delicate from which come littte charming fires; I want the adjacent part to be simple and to already know the sweet tingles of love), *Les Odes amoureuses*, p. 38.

[30] These epigrams are from the Palatine Anthology: 159D and 158D in *Greek Lyric I: Sappho and Alcaeus*, ed. and trans. by David A. Campbell, Loeb Classical Library 142 (Cambridge, MA: Harvard University Press, 1982)). Dacier's selection is more limited than the Henri Estienne edition of some forty fragments. In making what are fragments look like complete poems, she follows the Henri Estienne version and that of her father but not that of Dionysus of Halicarnassus.

[31] For a discussion of the *vie galante*, see Helena Taylor, *The Lives of Ovid in Seventeenth-Century French Culture* (Oxford: Oxford University Press, 2017), pp. 35–42.

[32] Lilio Gregorio Giraldi, *Historiae poetarum tam Graecorum quam Latinorum dialogi decem* (Basel, 1545), pp. 972–80.

tensions and restrictions of sociable literary culture which Scudéry included in her portrayal of Sapho.

Unlike Scudéry's 'Histoire de Sapho', however, in the *Vie de Sappho* Dacier follows the traditional (and Ovidian) account which has Sappho love Phaon and kill herself when he rejects her.[33] Like Scudéry, however, Dacier is restrained, even censoring, in the representation of Sappho's bisexuality. In his 1665 *Vie de Sappho*, Tanneguy Le Fèvre had described fragment 31 as an 'ode de seize vers addressée à une fille dont elle estoit amoureuse' (an ode in sixteen lines, addressed to a girl whom she was in love with) which he then qualifies thus:

> Expliquons plustost le mot qui m'est échappé en parlant de *l'Ode de Seize Vers*; c'est, Monsieur, que Sappho fut d'une complexion fort amoureuse et que n'étant pas satisfaite de ce que les autres femmes rencontrent dans la compagnie des hommes qui ne leur sont pas desagreables, elle voulut avoir des maistresses aussi bien que des serviteurs.[34]

> Let me explain what I mean in relation to her *Ode in 16 lines*: it is, Sir, that Sappho was of a very passionate nature and not satisfied by what other women found in the company of the men who please them, she wanted to have mistresses as well as suitors.

Dacier would have been aware of this tradition, but is more circumspect, referring only obliquely to this as a rumour: 'si l'on en croit la plûpart des anciens qui ont écrit sa vie, elle ne vécut pas d'une manière fort reguliere après la mort de son mari' (if one believes the majority of ancient sources on her life, she did not live a conventional life after her husband's death) (p. 390). She also implies that these 'calomnies' are the result of jealousy:

> Ce qui me fait croire qu'il ne faut pas ajouter foy à tout ce que l'on trouve écrit contre elle. [...] Il ne faut pas douter que son merite ne lui eût fait bien des ennemis; car elle surpassoit en scavoir, non seulement toutes les femmes, quoi que de son temps il y en eût en Grece d'extrémement sçavantes; mais elle estoit même fort au dessus des plus excellens Poëtes. Je crois donc que ceux dont les vers auroient esté trouvez incomparables, si Sapho n'en eût jamais fait, ne furent pas de ses amis et que l'envie a fait écrire les calomnies dont on a tâché de la noircir. (pp. 393–94)[35]

---

[33] Joan DeJean has criticised Dacier for 'promoting a fiction of Sappho that could be assimilated to the contemporary tradition of sexually pitiable females who strengthen rather than threaten orders of male bonding'. Joan DeJean, *Fictions of Sappho: 1546–1937* (Chicago: University of Chicago Press, 1989), p. 96.

[34] Le Fèvre, *Abrégé des vies*, pp. 25–26.

[35] Longepierre, three years later, is less restrained than Dacier in his discussion of Sappho's sexuality and criticised her for her unlicenced behaviour. Hilaire-Bernard de Longepierre, *Les Poésies de Anacréon et de Sapho* (Paris: Émery, 1684), pp. 351–52.

212 WOMEN WRITING ANTIQUITY

All this makes me think that we should not pay any heed to what we find written against her. [...] It is likely that her success made her many enemies, for her learning not only far exceeded that of all women, even though there were at that time some very learned women in Greece, but it also surpassed male poets. I think therefore that those whose verse would be unparalleled had Sappho not also written her poetry were not friends to her and that jealousy inspired the slander that attempted to tarnish her reputation.

Jacqueline Fabre-Serris and Joan DeJean suggest that we can read some identification here between Dacier and Sappho, as both a female intellectual and the subject of jealous gossip (rumours had circulated about the legitimacy of her and André's eldest daughter, Marie).[36] However, Dacier also distances herself from Sappho: her praise is not unequivocal. She states: 'au reste, quoy que je sois persuadée qu'il y a eu beaucoup de médisance dans tout ce que l'on a dit contre Sapho, je ne crois pas pourtant qu'elle ait esté d'une sagesse exemplaire. Elle ne fut pas exempte de passion; tout le monde sçait qu'elle aima Phaon, et qu'elle l'aima d'une maniere fort violente' (although I am persuaded that there was a great deal of scandal-mongering in everything said against Sappho, I do not think however that she was of an exemplary wisdom. She was not exempt from passion: everyone knows that she loved Phaon, and that she did so violently) (pp. 395–96). The way she plays down Sappho's bisexuality and criticises her passionate love affairs demonstrates Dacier's morally instructive approach, and, as in her Anacreon translations, perhaps reveals a sensitivity regarding her own position as a woman writing in public with fewer liberties than her father.

And yet, in her translations, Dacier allows for more ambiguity in terms of Sappho's sexuality than she does in this *Vie*. She follows the norm in making the object of desire in fragment 1 unequivocally masculine: instead of the now-accepted female participle of line 24 (κωὐκ ἐθέλοισα—'even if she is not willing', which retrospectively gives a gender to the previous third-person verbs of lines 21–23, 'if she runs away', etc.), Dacier uses the practices of the time with a second-person verb that translates as 'whenever you order it'. Without the marked gender of the female participle, the grammatical gender of the third-person subject is male, allowing for a heterosexual reading. Dacier makes this reading explicit in her translation by using the male pronoun, as expected, 's'il te fuit' (p. 411), but also by adding a reference to the lover as a 'jeune homme' (ibid.).[37] In the remarks, Dacier makes

---

[36] Jacqueline Fabre-Serris, 'Anne Dacier (1681), Renée Vivien (1903): Or What Does It Mean for a Woman to Translate Sappho?', in *Women Classical Scholars*, ed. by Wyles and Hall, pp. 78–102 (pp. 79–81); DeJean, *Fictions of Sappho*, p. 95. The couple converted to Catholicism in 1685, a month before the Revocation of the Edict of Nantes. See Eliane Itti, 'L'Abjuration des époux Dacier, le 20 septembre 1685', in *Bulletin de la Société de l'Histoire du Protestantisme Français*, 157 (2011), 159–85.

[37] This was also the approach taken by Du Four who also uses a male pronoun 'si maintenant il te fuit' (*Les Odes amoureuses*, p. 83); Longepierre does the same: 'il te fuit' (*Les Poésies de Anacréon et de Sapho*, p. 379).

it clear that she interprets the male pronoun of this poem as Phaon: 'S'il te fuit: Cecy me paroist purement historique, car Phaon quitta Lesbos pour fuïr Sapho' (*If he flees you*: this seems purely historical as Phaon left Lesbos to flee Sappho) (pp. 415–16).[38] However, with her fragment 31—the poem which for Tanneguy Le Fèvre proved Sappho's bisexuality—Dacier introduces more ambiguity. She makes the gender of the addressee explicitly feminine by giving the poem a title in French (which it does not have in Longinus, or in Estienne's or Belleau's versions), but neutralises the passion in her French by using 'À son amie' ('to her friend'), which Du Four had done before her, and following her father's Latin title 'ad amicam suam'.[39] It seems, therefore, that Dacier 'side-steps' the homosexuality by using 'amie' (friend) rather than 'aimée' (beloved) and in the preface she describes this as 'une ode qu'elle fit pour une de ses amies' (p. 403).[40] And yet her Greek title, 'ΕΙΣ ΤΗΝ ΕΡΟΜΕΝΗΝ', transliterated as *eis tēn erōmenēn* (p. 418), allows for a more explicitly erotic reading. This means 'to the female who is loved in an *erōs* sense', that is, sexually, rather than 'friendly' love, for which the term would be *philia*. More importantly, in Greek culture there was a common formulation of the (homosexual) relationship between an older male and a younger man; the younger man was known as the *erōmenos*, 'the male who is loved in an *erōs* sense', with the masculine version of the participle used by Dacier. So not only is the title clearly about sexual love, it is also a strong parallel for Greek terminology for homosexual love, but transferred to the female realm.[41] In the remarks which directly follow this poem (and so are easily accessible to the reader), Dacier also clearly describes the emotion expressed in this poem for Sappho's 'amie' as a violent and passionate 'amour', which, although it could denote friendship, seems ambiguous in this context: 'Sapho, pour marquer la violence de son amour [...]' (Sappho, to mark the violence of her love [...]) (p. 422). Lesbian love, then, *is* present in Dacier's version of Sappho, 'hidden' perhaps from many readers in this Greek title, but also readily available in her notes on the poem. Her translation speaks of the tension between the need for decorum and her scholarly drive for accuracy.

Dacier's unfussy and direct translations also have the effect of strongly conveying the erotic charge of Sappho's verse. This can be seen particularly with regard to fragment 31 when compared to the translations by Belleau and Du Four, as well as the one included by Nicolas Boileau in his translation of Longinus (the original source for this poem).[42] For example, Belleau embellishes the original: Sappho's 'At once a subtle fire has stolen beneath my flesh', which Dacier translates closely

---

[38] She then quotes in full her father's Latin translation of fragment 1 as if to bolster the authority of her version, although his Latin translation removes the need for a gendered pronoun: 'si fugit nunc te' (*Anacreontis et Sapphonis Carmina*, p. 98).

[39] Le Fèvre, *Anacreontis et Sapphonis Carmina*, p. 98.

[40] Fabre-Serris, 'Anne Dacier', p. 90.

[41] My thanks to Emily Hauser for her advice on this point.

[42] With this reading, I nuance Fabre-Serris's emphasis on her embellishments (p. 93): they are less remarkable than those of her contemporaries and predecessors who are not analysed by Fabre-Serris.

as 'un feu subtil se glise dans mes veines' (a subtle fire slips into my veins) (p. 419), becomes in Belleau 'un petit feu qui furette / Dessous ma peau tendrelette / Tant de beauté me dement!' (a little fire which slipped / under my tender little skin / so much beauty drives me mad!).[43] Du Four's 1670 version is also interpretative: 'je brusle d'amour / Ce Dieu pour ton sujet à toute heure m'oppresse (I burn with love / This God for you oppresses me constantly).[44] Boileau's 1674 version, attacked for being bland and flat, is in Alexandrines which gives an element of control to the disordered sentiments and makes the poem more French. He also changes some of the most powerful imagery: sweat, which is not 'pleasing', is replaced with 'je tombe en de douces langueurs' (I fall into pleasurable languor).[45] He turns the series of physical effects, each described with a different verb in the original, into a list of adjectives (line 3 here):

> Un nuage confus se répand sur ma veuë
> Je n'entends plus, je tombe en de douces langueurs,
> Et pasle, sans haleine, interdite, éperduë,
> Un frisson me saisit, je tremble, je me meurs.[46]

> An opaque cloud covers my vision
> I no longer hear and I fall into pleasurable languish
> Pale, breathless, speechless, lost
> A shiver runs through me: I tremble and I die.

Instead, Dacier, closer to the force of the original, writes:

> mes yeux se couvrent d'épais nuages, je n'entens qu'un bruit confus, une sueur froide coule de tout mon corps, je tremble, je deviens pâle, je suis sans poulx et sans mouvement, enfin il me semble que je n'ay plus qu'un moment à vivre. (pp. 419–21)

> my eyes are covered with thick cloud; I only hear a confused noise; cold sweat runs over my body, I tremble, I become pale, I am without pulse and without movement; it seems I only have one moment left to live.

Her translation of Anacreon and Sapho was well received initially: Hilaire-Bernard de Longepierre praised it in the preface to his verse versions of Anacreon and

---

Nicolas Boileau-Despréaux, *Œuvres diverses du sieur D***, avec le Traité du sublime* (Paris: Thierry, 1674). On the publication history of Sappho's fragments, see Chapter 3.

[43] *Greek Lyric I*, ed. and trans. by Campbell; Belleau, *Les odes d'Anacréon*, p. 61.

[44] Du Four, *Les Odes amoureuses*, p. 86.

[45] Boileau, *Œuvres diverses du sieur D****, p. 26. On its criticisms, see DeJean, *Fictions of Sappho*, p. 85—though Longepierre calls it 'une excellente traduction' (*Les Poésies de Anacréon et de Sapho*, p. 382).

[46] Boileau, *Œuvres diverses du sieur D****, p. 26.

Sappho published three years later in 1684. It was also singled out for praise in the funeral *Éloge* for Dacier in the *Journal des Sçavans*, and her later rival, Antoine Houdar de La Motte, addressed to her an Ode praising this translation in 1707.[47] Early in her career as a translator, Dacier chose authors who would appeal to readers with Greek and those without, balancing scholarly directness and accuracy with her attempts to accommodate female readers and a more *galant* style, following her father's influence without compromising her own scholarly pride, and navigating assertions of scholarly authority and an instructive moral restraint. Crucially, for all that Dacier's Anacreon and Sappho translation does reveal—and shape—literary tastes, she does not explicitly mobilise this text or her approach as ideological, as a direct intervention in the wider questions about how to interpret and adapt ancient literature. Some two years later this would change: like Gournay, Dacier turned translation into an instrument of polemic.

Plautus, Aristophanes, and Terence: Translation as Polemic

After this first foray into translation, Dacier turned her hand to translating ancient comedy with three plays by Plautus (*Amphytiron*, *The Rope*, and *Epidicus*, 1683), two by Aristophanes (*Plutus* and *The Clouds*, 1684), and Terence's complete works of six plays (1688)—once again Barbin and Thierry published the first editions of these translations. The choice of Plautus and particularly of Aristophanes is striking given their unfavourable reception in France: indeed her Aristophanes translation was received with mixed success.[48] She may have chosen these authors because Tanneguy's syllabus at Saumur had also included these two plays by

---

[47] Antoine Houdar de La Motte, 'Ode I. À Madame Dacier. Sur son Anacréon', in *Odes de M. D**** (Paris: Dupuis, 1707), pp. 87–89. This positive reception was fairly short-lived: when François Gacon came to publish his verse versions of 1712, he was dismissive of all previous ones, particularly the prose version by Dacier or 'Eufrosine' who wrote in 'la prose grossière'. François Gacon, *Les Odes d'Anacréon et de Sapho en vers français* (Rotterdam: Fritsch and Böhm, 1712), np. There were two late eighteenth-century translations: the first makes no reference to previous editions and the second mostly cites Gacon, though uses Tanneguy Le Fèvre's *Vie* as a template, but damningly quotes the 1772 *Nouveau Dictionnaire Historique*, which states 'on ne parle plus des versions de Mme Dacier en prose, de Belleau en vers et de quelques autres postérieures' (we no longer talk about Madame Dacier's prose version or that of Belleau in verse or any other earlier ones), L. Poinsinet de Sivry, *Anacréon, Sapho, Moschus, Bion, Tyrtée, etc. traduits en vers français* (Nancy: Antoine, 1758), p. 4. See also J. Moutonnet de Clairfons, *Anacréon, Sapho, Bion et Moschus. Traduction nouvelle en prose* (Paris: Bastien, 1780). For a discussion, see Stéphanie Loubère, 'Figures et figuration d'Anacréon galant', in *La Galanterie des anciens*, ed. by Nathalie Grande and Claudine Nédélec (= *Littératures Classiques*, 77 (2012)), pp. 83–98.

[48] This was the case even though Racine had created a version of Aristophanes' *The Wasps* with his *Plaideurs* (1668) and Molière had adapted Plautus' *Amphytiron* in the same year. On the mixed success of Dacier's Aristophanes translations, see Malika Bastin-Hammou, 'Anne Dacier et les premières traductions françaises d'Aristophane: l'invention du métier de femme philologue', *Littératures classiques*, 72.2 (2010), 85–99 (p. 85). There were only four re-editions of Aristophanes compared around twenty of Terence: see Jean-Philippe Grosperrin, 'Les époux Dacier: une bibliographie', *Littératures classiques*, 72.2 (2010), 259–86.

216　WOMEN WRITING ANTIQUITY

Aristophanes; and he had himself penned a translation of the more controversial *Ecclesiazusae* (*Assemblywomen*): Dacier was once again prudent in opting for the two Aristophanes plays that could be more readily accommodated to a polite readership.[49]

With these translations, we encounter a similar concern with *bienséance* and moral instruction that was evident in her first translation, especially in relation to the male homosexuality present in some of these plays. However there is also a clear desire to champion and redeem these playwrights, as scholars have noted, as well as a surer conception of her translation practice.[50] This practice is marked by a drive to educate and an emphasis on 'utility', traces of which we have encountered already, as well as a sensitivity and attention to the different capacities of Greek, Latin, and French as she formulates versions of her position on language and translation that would later be central to the Homer Quarrel.[51] In these comedy translations of the 1680s, she also aligns translation as a practice with polemic, by rendering prominent instances within these texts where rhetoric and argument are key—such as the debate between Right and Wrong Argument in Aristophanes' *The Clouds* and the authorial positioning in Terence's prologues. Translation is subtly yoked to polemic at this point in her career: she maintains a (personal) distance from the fray of the Quarrel of the Ancients and Moderns, a distance we will see measured very differently when it comes to the Homer Quarrel.

Education and utility are two tenets of Dacier's translation practice: they are the guiding principles for her Plautus translation. In the preface, she writes:

J'ay consulté long-temps de quelle maniere je devois m'y prendre et j'ay vû que pour faire un ouvrage utile, il ne suffisoit pas de donner une simple traduction, qu'il faloit ajouter des remarques et mettre à la teste de chaque Comedie un examen selon les regles du Theatre, pour en faire remarquer les defauts et les beautez. (np)

I spent a long time considering how I ought to go about it and I saw that to write a useful book, one must do more than offer a simple translation, and that one must add comments and add at the beginning of each play an observation according to the rules of theatre to note its faults and beauties.

---

[49] Le Fèvre, *Méthode*; and Tanneguy Le Fèvre, 'Ecclesiazusae', *Tanaquili Fabri Epistolae* (Saumur: Lesnier, 1659). See Rosie Wyles, 'Aristophanes and the French Translations of Anne Dacier', in *Brill's Companion to the Reception of Aristophanes*, ed. by Philip Walsh (Leiden: Brill, 2016), pp. 195–216 (pp. 197–98).

[50] See Bastin-Hammou, 'Anne Dacier et les premières traductions françaises d'Aristophane', and Wyles, 'Aristophanes'.

[51] On Dacier's theories of language and translation, and her sensitivity to the 'world-disclosing' capacities of foreign languages, see Julie Candler Hayes, 'Meaning and Modernity: Anne Dacier and the Homer Debate', in *Translation, Subjectivity, and Culture in France and England, 1600–1800* (Stanford: Stanford University Press, 2009), pp. 121–40 (p. 125).

Her educational approach is fitting for the readers for whom she intends these works. She makes it clear that she is aiming for a dual audience: 'la traduction est pour ceux qui ne peuvent lire les originaux ou qui prennent plaisir à juger de chaque langue. [...] Les remarques peuvent estre utiles à ceux qui veulent estudier et l'examen peut estre d'un grand usage pour tous ceux qui veulent apprendre à bien juger des pieces de Theatre ou qui voudroient travailler eux-mesmes avec succez' (the translation is for those who cannot read the originals or who will take pleasure in judging both languages. The commentary should be useful to those who want to study and the preface for those who want to better learn to judge these plays or who themselves want to work with success) (np). With this subtle emphasis away from the diverting *galant* 'plaisir' she evoked in her Anacreon and Sappho translation to the scholarly pleasure of comparing Latin and French and of education, Dacier establishes a context for her first strong attack on contemporary taste:

> Ce n'estoit pas à Plaute à deviner le goust que nous avons aujourd'huy, c'est à nous à prendre celuy de son siecle. [...] Si on n'a la force de remonter jusques à ces temps-là et d'y fixer son esprit on ne goûtera que fort difficilement les plus belles choses de l'Antiquité et l'on fera la mesme faute que si pour juger des anciens tableaux on les examinoit par rapport à l'air et aux manieres de son temps. Les plus grandes beautez d'Homere ne pourroient se soûtenir contre cette maxime et ces divins endroits qui luy ont attiré l'admiration de tous les siecles, luy attireroient aujourd'huy nos railleries ou nostre mépris. (np)

> It was not for Plautus to guess at today's taste; it is for us to take on that of his time. [...] If one does not have the strength to go so far back in time and to place one's imagination there, one will have considerable difficulty in appreciating the beautiful things of antiquity and one will commit the same mistake as if one judged old paintings by the style of our time. What is most beautiful in Homer would not withstand such an approach and the most divine elements of his writing which have been admired for centuries would today attract scorn and disdain.

Her reference to the attacks sustained by Homer is an allusion to those of Jean Desmarets de Saint Sorlin and lays the groundwork for her later interventions in the Homer Quarrel.[52] Her comments here also suggest her willingness to take a strident position in the Quarrel of the Ancients and Moderns, simmering in 1683 but not at its height, and to frame her approach to translation through its prism.

Her forthright engagement with the issues at the heart of the Quarrel of the Ancients and Moderns gathers strength in her preface to the 1684 Aristophanes

---

[52] Jean Desmarets de Saint-Sorlin, *La Comparaison de la langue et de la poésie française avec la grecque et la latine* (Paris: Billaine, 1670); *Défense du poème héroïque* (Paris: Le Gras, 1675); *Défense de la poésie et de la langue française* (Paris: Le Gras, 1675).

218 WOMEN WRITING ANTIQUITY

edition. She states that there are three types of readers: the good, the mediocre, and the closed-minded. Her description of the third type is a caricature of the Moderns: 'ils ne jugent jamais que par rapport à eux-mesmes, ils veulent se reconnoistre en tout et ils condamnent absolument tout ce qui ne leur ressemble point' (they only judge in relation to themselves: they want to see themselves in everything and condemn everything that does not resemble them) (np). She goes on to argue:

> Ce qui empesche aujourd'hui la pluspart des hommes de goûter les ouvrages des anciens, c'est qu'on ne veut jamais perdre de vûë son siècle et qu'on veut le reconnoistre en tout. Il n'est rien de plus injuste, les siecles se suivent sans se ressembler, et si les hommes sont toûjours dans ce préjugé qu'il n'y a rien de bon que ce qui porte les marques de leur siècle, il se trouvera que les meilleurs ouvrages n'auront qu'une vie fort limitée et que les plus grands écrivains découragez par une imagination si mortifiante, n'auront plus la force de travailler pour une immortalité qu'ils ne devront pas se promettre. (np)

> The main factor preventing most people from enjoying the works of the ancients is their inability to look beyond their own century and their desire to recognise it in everything. There is nothing more unfair: after all, centuries follow rather than resemble each other and if people always take this limited view that it is only the character of their century that is of any interest, then the best works will only have a short life and the greatest writers, discouraged by such mortifying lack of imagination, will not have the motivation to work since their immortality seems unlikely.

The strident agonistic tone marks a shift from the modern, *galant*-orientated preface of her Sappho and Anacreon edition. It underscores how far Dacier envisages her translations as interventions in these debates and so the rhetoric of the preface is important in its own right, even if some of the claims are not necessarily borne out by her translation and she sometimes 'manipulates her position' as point of access by not always making it clear what she has changed and how, especially since her Aristophanes translation does not contain a parallel text.[53]

However, some of the claims *are* borne out by her translation: she makes some key changes which are important within the wider context of the simmering Quarrel. In the set piece of the debate between 'Right Discourse' and 'Wrong Discourse' from *The Clouds*, Dacier enacts a meta-discursive intervention on the questions of rhetoric, gender, education (key elements of the Quarrel), linking her acts of translation with argument. Placed as a centrepiece in *The Clouds*, this debate is

---

[53] On her manipulations, see Wyles, 'Aristophanes', p. 196. Bastin-Hammou is critical of the discrepancies between rhetoric and practice ('Anne Dacier et les premières traductions françaises d'Aristophane', p. 94).

between tradition and progress in relation to education, or as James White would have it in his 1759 translation, 'Genius of Ancient Education' and 'Genius of Modern Education', usefully underscoring how closely this debate maps on to some of the questions at the heart of the Quarrel.[54] In Dacier's version the figures are female-gendered as 'La Justice' and 'L'Injustice', whom she refers to in the preface as 'deux femmes' (np). Dacier offers linguistic reasons for this transposition as, she claims, no other terms would work in French. Rosie Wyles, justifiably, is not persuaded by this reasoning and thinks that the re-gendering allows Dacier to avoid the homosexual accusation made against 'Wrong Discourse' by 'Right Discourse': after all, Pierre Brumoy in his 1730 translation uses the masculine nouns 'L'injuste' and 'Le juste'.[55] The transposition to female nouns also allows Dacier subtly to reflect on gender. The re-gendering is not itself wholly a positive given that it actually allows for effective use of misogynistic tropes, as Justice is framed as an old hag—'une vieille radoteuse et une sotte' (an old, foolish woman who rambles on) (p. 230)—even though a case can be made for Dacier's own alignment with the views of Justice. It is tempting to suggest that her decision to transpose this debate to female-gendered subjects was a way of indicating that women might be able to engage effectively in quarrels about education and antiquity, all the while with sufficient distance that she herself is kept out of the fray—for the time being at least.

This centrality of rhetoric and argument to Dacier's translation practice is further evident in the way she moves the *parabasis*—the address to the audience on behalf of the author—that occurs at the end of Act 1 of *The Clouds* to the position of prologue. As critics have noted, this is one of the main changes she makes to this play, and her principal motivation is thought to be adherence to contemporary dramatic rules of time: she says 'cela est plus à nos manières car aujourd'huy on ne veut rien qui interrompe le cours de l'action Theatrale' (this is more in line with our practice, as today we avoid anything which interrupts the course of the theatrical action) (p. 271).[56] It is also more in keeping with the tradition of including prefaces or *discours* as introductory arguments in printed versions of texts: in her additional remarks discussing Aristophanes' *parabasis*, she emphasises the importance of an author's self-defence.

---

[54] James White, *The Clouds. Comedy translated from Aristophanes* (London: Payne, 1759), pp. 113–37. On this, see Wyles, 'Aristophanes', p. 211.

[55] Wyles, 'Aristophanes', p. 207. For all that Dacier plays down the homosexuality, she does manage to allude to contemporary accusations of effeminacy that Ancients made against Moderns in the complaints of La Justice about modern education (pp. 233–34). Furthermore, she implicitly retains some of the hints at sodomy with her repeated use of the term 'infâme' (eg. p. 230, p. 240) for 'wide-arsed' ('εὐρυπρώκτων'), translated on both occasions without a corresponding remark. For the connection between 'infâme' and sodomy, see Jonathan Patterson, 'Obscenity and Censorship in the Reign of Henri III', *Renaissance Quarterly*, 70.4 (2017), 1321–65.

[56] Bastin-Hammou, 'Anne Dacier et les premières traductions françaises d'Aristophane', p. 97.

220   WOMEN WRITING ANTIQUITY

She develops further her theory of translation in the preface to her Terence translation of 1688. Despite the three volumes of these translations coming out during the flashpoint of the Quarrel, here she makes no attacks on readers' taste: perhaps she did not want to be seen to be directly engaging in this phase of the Quarrel proper; perhaps she was not willing to bend to its terms (after all, in the Homer Quarrel, she sets the frame of debate).[57] She emphasises the importance of remaining close to the original, but also suggests that the style and beauty of the French need not be compromised:

> Je m'éloigne le moins que je puis du texte, persuadée que quand on peut dire ce que Terence a dit et comme il l'a dit, il est impossible de faire mieux et que c'est la perfection. Mais comme le genie et le tour des langues sont differents, la nostre ne peut pas toûjours suivre Terence. J'ay donc esté obligée de chercher les beautez de nostre langue, comme il a cherché les beautez de la sienne. (np)

> I try to stay as close as possible to the text and I think that there is nothing better than saying what Terence said in the way he said it. But since the genius and characteristics of languages are different, ours cannot always follow that of Terence. I am therefore obliged to seek the beauties of our language, just as he sought the beauties of his own.

She demonstrates her prowess as a multilinguist (a skill some of her Modern interlocutors did not share), drawing on her deep knowledge of linguistic difference to support her approach to translation.[58] Dacier also accommodates Terence to modern sensibilities, but does so to champion this playwright, rather than discredit him: she stresses how he excels in 'la peinture des mœurs' and 'politesse', defending him against the charges of immorality that she shows were laid more generally against comedy by Quintilian. To some degree, as it was in the cases of Plautus and Aristophanes, this accommodation is borne out by her translation choices: for instance, for the fact that Pamphilius in *The Mother-in-Law* did not have sex with his wife on their wedding night, 'virginem non attigit' (1.136), Dacier changes this to him not *speaking* to his wife (III, p. 267). She also consistently translates 'leno' ('pimp') with the less sexual 'marchand des esclaves', although she is frank in her relaying of the repeated acts of buying and selling women, and she is also diligent in her translation of insults.[59] And as we saw in her translation of Aristophanes,

---

[57] On the phenomenon of female quarrellers, see Helena Taylor and Kate E. Tunstall, eds, *Women and Querelles in Early Modern France* (= *Romantic Review*, 112.3 (2021)).

[58] See Candler Hayes, 'Meaning and Modernity', p. 129.

[59] For instance, in Terence's *The Self-Tormenter*, she does a good job of translating the insults: for example, in *Phormio*, 'sterculinum' ('you shit!') becomes 'âme de boue!' (soul of mud) (III, p. 103). Terence, *Phormio. The Mother-in-Law. The Brothers*, ed. and trans. by John Barsby, Loeb Classical Library 23 (Cambridge, MA: Harvard University Press, 2001).

she consistently plays down the homoeroticism, particularly in her version of *The Eunuch*.[60]

In this preface, we get another rare instance of her presentation as a female scholar when she describes consulting three Terence manuscripts in the Royal Library, which she tells us she did after her translations were in press, but before she wrote the preface. This research is presented modestly: she only went on the advice of the librarian Melchisédech Thévenot and had to overcome her discomfort at making such a visit: 'J'avois beaucoup de repugnance à en venir là; il me sembloit que les manuscrits estoient si fort au dessus d'une personne de mon sexe, que c'estoit usurper les droits des savants que d'avoir seulement la pensée de les consulter' (I felt much aversion to going there: it seemed to me that consulting manuscripts was far above someone of my sex and that even to consider consulting them was to usurp the rights of learned gentleman) (np). Despite this claim to a sense of being an imposter, she then proceeds to enumerate, for twelve pages, with evident excitement, all the ways in which these beautifully illustrated manuscripts confirm ('prouvent', np) her readings in relation to the changes she has made to previous editions and commentaries, particularly her proposed act divisions, and understanding of the actors' gestures, props, and movement. This is an example of one of the rare occasions when Dacier draws attention to her gender, but the modesty is quickly undermined by her scholarly precision and zeal.

Dacier embeds her reflections on authority in her representation of Terence's prologues, using the prologues to explore her own philosophy of reception and transmission; and it is here that we glimpse some of the attention to polemic we saw in her other theatre translations.[61] The prologues are an important feature of

---

[60] For instance, the homoerotic innuendos and suggestiveness of the predator/prey in the hare joke (l. 425) are removed with the excision of this line entirely, though it is replaced on this occasion with an asterisk to signal its removal (I, p. 321). The sexual innuendo of Act 3 Scene 2 is kept but only discreetly: regarding the Eunuch, Thraso says 'ego illum eunuchum, si opus sit, vel sobrius' ('I know what I'd do to that eunuch, even when sober') (l. 479): Dacier's version is 'en verité, à un besoin il passeroit pour une fille, et sans avoir bu on s'y meprendroit' (in truth, if need he would pass for a girl, and without having had a drink one would be mistaken) (I, p. 332). Terence, *The Woman of Andros. The Self-Tormentor. The Eunuch*, ed. and trans. by John Barsby, Loeb Classical Library 22 (Cambridge, MA: Harvard University Press, 2001).

[61] Terence's *Heauton Timorumenos* or *The Self-Tormentor*, also sometimes known as his 'third play', had been the subject of a particular quarrel which had started in the 1640s between the Abbé d'Aubignac and Gilles Ménage, and related to the question of the duration of the play, and broader questions of theatrical time. The matter seemed to be resolved by the time of Dacier's translation and she makes no direct mention of it in her preface, although in the commentary she emphasises that she considers the night to be short constituting only a brief interval in the action. Ménage, however, took the opportunity offered by Dacier's 1688 translation of Terence to publish his views for a third time in 1690, although d'Aubignac was now dead. In this 1690 text Ménage recounts a story of a visit to see Madame Dacier in October 1687 when he found out she was working on a Terence translation. She informed him that she did not agree with his assessment; Ménage remains persuaded of his original view but explains that he has decided to dedicate this Discours to her 'afin de l'attirer de mon parti par mes nouvelles raisons' (to try to persuade her by new justifications). Ménage, *Discours de Ménage sur l'Heautontimorumenos de Térence* (Utrecht: Schouten, 1690), np. Ménage also dedicates his *Historia Mulierum Philosopharum* (1690) to Dacier.

222   WOMEN WRITING ANTIQUITY

Terence's work, introducing every play, and functioning as a chance for the play-wright to defend and frame his work.[62] She includes separate 'remarques' for the prologues which constitute a sort of meta-prologue for her own translations. A key term for Terence, and a recurring theme of his own defence, is the word 'contaminare', which is how he describes his own approach to Menander's plays, his Greek model and source. Dacier is particularly attentive to this theme, using it as a way into discussing questions of adaptation and reception. In the *remarques* accompanying the prologue to *L'Andrienne*, Dacier explores the different meanings of 'contaminare' as both 'mesler' (mix) and 'gâter' or 'corrompre' (spoil) and argues that the correct translation is the former. She defends Terence against the critics who charge him with this second meaning, adding 'J'ai un peu étendu cette remarque parce que j'ai vû des gens d'ailleurs tres-habiles et d'un goût excellent qui ont eu beaucoup de peine à revenir de leurs prejugez' (I have expanded on this comment because I have seen many very capable people with excellent taste who struggle to revise their initial opinions) (I, p. 209). In the prologue to the *The Eunuch*, Terence states that the 'maxime' that one cannot reuse material would mean that (in Dacier's translation) 'on ne pourra plus parler ni écrire, car on ne peut rien dire aujourd'huy qui n'ait esté dit autrefois' (one can no longer speak or write because one cannot say anything today that has not been said before) (I, p. 251). In the *remarques* on this point, Dacier writes:

> j'ai un peu étendu ce vers dans ma traduction, pour faire mieux sentir la force du raisonnement de Terence [...] Terence ne témoigne ici aucun chagrin contre ceux qui avoient traité avant lui les mesmes caracteres qu'il traite, au contraire, il veut faire voir qu'on a la liberté de faire ce qu'ils ont fait, comme on a celle de se servir des mesmes lettres, des mesmes mots, des mesmes noms, des mesmes nombres et que si l'on veut se faire un scrupule de suivre les idées communes et generales, il faudra aussi s'empescher de parler parce qu'il n'est pas plus difficile de dire des choses nouvelles qu'il est d'inventer des caracteres nouveaux. Ce passage est plein de force. (I, p. 461)

> I have expanded a little on this verse in my translation to strengthen the force of Terence's reasoning. [...] Terence does not show any ill will towards those who have treated before him the same figures that he treats; on the contrary, he wants to show that one has the liberty to do what they have done, just as one has the liberty to use the same letters, the same words, the same names, the same numbers and that if one is going to have scruples about following general and common ideas, one must also stop oneself from speaking because it is not more

---

[62] See Ọbáfẹ́mi Kujọrẹ, 'A Note on Contaminatio in Terence', *Classical Philology*, 69.1 (1974), 39–42; and R. K. Ehrman, 'Terentian Prologues and the Parabases of Old Comedy', *Latomus*, 44.2 (1985), 370–76.

difficult to say new things than it is to invent new figures. This passage is full of force.

Referring twice to the 'force' of Terence's argument and emphasising her own attention to it, Dacier defends here the principle of deference towards earlier models, confirming a stance that directly engages with some of the questions of the contemporary Quarrel of the Ancients and Moderns, but doing so in such a way that maintains Dacier's personal distance from it: a change we will see in the next stage of her career as she translates and defends Homer.

Gender in the *Querelle d'Homère*

The Homer Quarrel not only represents the pinnacle of Dacier's career but is constructed as such by Dacier herself. Scholars have devoted detailed attention to the importance of Dacier's arguments in this Quarrel for our wider understanding of the reception of antiquity and for ideas about language and translation in this period; but less attention has been paid to the relation of this Quarrel to her authorial persona and to her career.[63] Recent scholarship on quarrels has shown how the self-conscious conceptualisation of a quarrel as either irenic or agonistic was fundamental to the ethics and ethos of the quarreler, and critical attention has also been brought to the strategic use of a quarrel in an author's career.[64] Scholars have also demonstrated how the rhetoric used for quarrelling mapped onto the different positions, with the Moderns favouring a more 'moderate', polite evenhanded *disputatio*, and the Ancients a more one-sided argument.[65] Drawing on these approaches, in this section I argue that Dacier's conception of quarrelling, as it is revealed in her interventions in the 1711–16 *Querelle d'Homère* in particular, is agonistic and that this approach is disguised under a posture of instruction. Her interventions in the Quarrel were strategic, and not simply motivated by vocation or feeling: she stakes her reputation on victory; her authorial identity and the Quarrel are thus connected.[66]

---

[63] On Dacier's role in the Quarrel, see in particular Larry F. Norman, *The Shock of the Ancient: Literature and History in Early Modern France* (Chicago: University of Chicago Press, 2011); see also Itti, *Madame Dacier*, pp. 259–78.

[64] Kate E. Tunstall, '"Ne nous engageons point dans des querelles": un projet de guerre perpétuelle?', *Revue de Synthèse*, 137 (2016), 345–72; see also Georges Forestier and Claude Bourqui, 'Comment Molière inventa la querelle de *L'école des femmes* ...', in *Le Temps des querelles*, ed. by Jeanne-Marie Hostiou and Alain Viala (= *Littératures classiques*, 81 (2013)), pp. 185–97.

[65] Béatrice Guion, '"Une dispute honnête": la polémique selon les Modernes', *Littératures Classiques*, 59 (2006), 157–72.

[66] See also Helena Taylor, 'Polemical Translation, Translating Polemic: Anne Dacier's Rhetoric in the Homer Quarrel', *Modern Language Review*, 116.1 (2021), 21–41. Some of this section of the chapter reprises one section of that article.

224 WOMEN WRITING ANTIQUITY

Dacier's 1711 three-volume translation of the *Iliad* with commentary was pitched to be provocative, even possibly to rekindle the Ancient–Modern debate. As critics have argued, both preface and translation were deliberately and self-consciously engaging with some of the issues that had underpinned the Quarrel of the Ancients and Moderns, apparently resolved with the reconciliation between Nicolas Boileau and Charles Perrault in 1694, but as we saw in Chapter 6, reignited with Perrault's 1695 edition of his fairy tales.[67] In relation to Homer, the Quarrel had been continued by Antoine Houdar de La Motte, academician and playwright, who published a verse translation of the first book of the *Iliad* in 1701: a translation he describes as a test case to ascertain whether to publish a full version, which he did in 1714, as I discuss below. In the preface he claims not to take a part in the 'dispute' but defends the liberties he has taken and modifications made to suit contemporary taste and *bienséance*.[68] The praise for Homer contained in Dacier's 1711 preface knowingly combats many of the arguments used against him by Charles Perrault and Jean Desmarets, in particular in her defence against charges of rusticity, crude manners and morals, and paganism; it also argues for a close translation method and the need for prose to best capture the original. Dacier makes it clear in her Homer preface that her translation is not for 'les sçavants qui lisent Homère en sa langue' (those learned gentlemen who read Homer in his language), but that it is intended to be educational and accessible, for 'le plus grand nombre' (the majority) and for those who are learning ancient Greek (pp. 35–36). She provokes the Moderns by being disparaging about the capabilities of French to animate the text in the same way as the original, offering the much-cited analogy of her prose translation to a mummified Helen, lacking in the life and vitality of the living woman but making evident the structural details of her beauty (p. 37).[69] She then goes on to suggest—equally provocatively—that French *verse* translations, generally preferred by the Moderns, are completely unable to render this structural beauty and that 'les poëtes traduits en vers cessent d'estre poëtes' (poets translated into verse are no longer poets) (p. 39).

Three years after the publication of her 1711 prose translation of the *Iliad*, Houdar de La Motte proceeded to publish a truncated translation of his *Iliad* in verse in which he cut Homer's twenty-four books down to twelve, with a preface in

---

[67] Charles Perrault, *Griselidis Nouvelle avec Le Conte de Peau d'Asne et celuy Des Souhaits ridicules. Quatrième édition* (Paris: Coignard, 1695). On Dacier, see also Norman, *The Shock of the Ancient*, pp. 1–2. Candler Hayes also argues for the importance of paying heed to this *Iliad* preface as an intervention in this quarrel, 'Meaning and Modernity', p. 130. On Homer in the seventeenth century, see Noémie Hepp, *Homère en France au XVIIe siècle* (Paris: Klincksieck, 1998).

[68] Antoine Houdar de La Motte, *Le Premier livre de l'Iliade d'Homère en vers français* (Paris: Emery, 1701), np.

[69] She then goes on to explain that an elegant translation 'devient non seulement la fidelle copie de son original mais un second original mesme' (becomes not only the faithful copy of its original but even a second original) (*L'Iliade*, p. 43); she then echoes this exact phrasing in her *Causes*, p. 329.

which he was openly critical of Homer.[70] La Motte's text sparked controversy and a flurry of arguments back and forth between 1714 and 1716: Dacier responded with *Des Causes de la corruption du goust* (1714), a forensically detailed account reiterating her arguments of the *Iliad* preface and tearing apart La Motte's preface and his translation;[71] to which La Motte replied with his *Réflexions sur la Critique*, in three parts, printed in 1715.[72] The Quarrel also prompted satirical responses and press coverage, as I will discuss.[73] After a number of other interventions, including by Jean Boivin and the Abbé Terrasson,[74] peace was apparently restored between Dacier and La Motte in April 1716, thanks to the interventions of the Marquise de Lambert.[75] However, the Ancient, Jean Hardouin, then offered an interpretation of Homer in his *Apologie d'Homère* (1716) that Dacier could not condone, leading her to pen a further refutation, which she anticipates in the preface to her *Odyssée* of 1716,[76] and which was explicitly intended, at that point, to be her last word in the Quarrel, the *Homère defendu contre l'Apologie du R. P. Hardouin ou Suite des causes de la corruption du goust* (1716).[77] Dacier's actual final word in the quarrel was her seventeen-page attack on Pope's Preface to his *Iliad* translation in her *Réflexions sur la première partie de la préface de Mr Pope*, the last work she wrote, published as an appendix to the second edition of her *Iliad* in 1719, a year before she died.[78]

As with many early modern *querelles*, Dacier and La Motte also self-reflexively explored the ethics of *how* to quarrel in the very works in which they mounted their positions. This is evident in their different translations of the *Iliad*, which constitute the first round of texts in the *Querelle d'Homère*. The controversial question

---

[70] Antoine Houdar de La Motte, *L'Iliade, poëme avec un discours sur Homère* (Paris: Dupuis, 1714). References to this work will be given in the text.

[71] Anne Dacier, *Des Causes de la Corruption du Goust* (Paris: Rigaud, 1714). References to this work will be given in the text.

[72] Houdar de La Motte, *Réflexions sur la Critique* (Paris: Dupuis, 1715), in three parts: all these parts were then published together in one volume as *Réflexions sur la Critique, second édition corrigée et augmentée* (Paris: Dupuis, 1716). References to this work will be given in the text.

[73] For satirical theatre, see Louis Fuzelier's *Arlequin defenseur d'Homère*, first performed at the Foire Saint Laurent in Paris in 1715, and printed in *Le Théâtre de la Foire ou l'Opéra Comique*, 8 vols (Paris: Ganeau, 1721), II, pp. 3–43; Ignace Limojon de Saint-Didier, 'L'Iliade, tragi-comédie', in *Le Voyage du Parnasse*, 2 vols (Rotterdam: Fritsch and Bohm, 1717), II, pp. 267–317; Abbé Faure, *Homère danseur de corde* (Paris: Prault, 1716); Pierre de Marivaux, *L'Homère travesti ou l'Iliade en vers burlesques* (Paris: Prault, 1716).

[74] François Gacon, *Homère vengé ou Réponse à M. de La Motte sur l'Iliade* (Paris: Ganeau, 1715); Jean Boivin, *Apologie d'Homère et Bouclier d'Achille* (Paris: Jouenne, 1715); Jean Terrasson, *Dissertation critique sur L'Iliade d'Homère*, 2 vols (Paris: Fournier, 1715); Etienne Fourmont, *Examen pacifique de la querelle de Madame Dacier et Monsieur de la Motte*, 2 vols (Paris: Rollin, 1716).

[75] See Farnham, *Madam Dacier*, pp. 178–79.

[76] Jean Hardouin, *Apologie d'Homère* (Paris: Rigaud, 1716); Anne Dacier, *L'Odyssée d'Homère traduite en françois avec des remarques*, 3 vols (Paris: Rigaud, 1716). References to this work will be given in the text.

[77] Anne Dacier, *Homère defendu contre l'Apologie du R. P. Hardouin ou Suite des Causes de la Corruption du Goust* (Paris: Coignard, 1716).

[78] *L'Iliade d'Homère, traduite en françois [...] Seconde édition [...] avec quelques réflexions sur la préface angloise de M. Pope*, 3 vols (Paris: Rigaud, 1719), III, np.

of Achilles' anger after the death of Patroclus in Book 22 allows for self-reflexive positioning on the question of combat. Dacier is sensitive to Achilles' suffering at Patroclus's death by Hector: she argues that Achilles' anger is poetically justified; she also defends his desecration of Hector's corpse. In contrast, the scene between Achilles and Hector is one of the main episodes that La Motte changes. He signals this change in the Preface when he describes Achilles' behaviour as 'défectueuse', citing its incompatibility with contemporary mores (*L'Iliade*, pp. 167–68). His translation of Achilles' actions also injects more moral judgement than is present in the original or Dacier's rendering: 'À quel excès alors la vengeance l'égare! / Ce n'est plus un Héros, c'est un tigre barbare' (To what excesses does his vengeance stray? / He is no longer a hero, but a barbaric tiger) (p. 184). Dacier, in contrast, does not censure the anger, but argues that Homer does not glorify Achilles and that for reasons of poetics, his depiction should be respected: 'Homere, comme je l'ay desja dit souvent, ne donne pas ce caractere d'Achille comme un caractere moralement bon, mais comme un caractere vicieux et qui n'est bon que poëtiquement' (Homer, as I have said often before, does not offer Achilles as a morally good character but as a character full of vice who is only good in terms of poetics) (*L'Iliade*, III, 545).[79] That aesthetics should trump ethics is no surprise given the Ancient defence of antiquity's differences, but Dacier is quick to point out that her aesthetic preference for Homer is not, as it is with La Motte, a personal reaction, but one that is based on learning. Being able to interpret Achilles' anger correctly is, for Dacier, a sign of being a 'lecteur instruit': 'il a revestu ce caractere d'Achille d'une valeur estonnante mais c'est pour le rendre plus éclatant et non pas plus loüable [...]. Il n'y a donc point d'illusion dans le Poëte et jamais cette illusion prétenduë ne passa jusqu'au Lecteur bien instruit' (He has afforded this character with considerable distinction but this was to make him more striking not more worthy of praise. There is no illusion in this poet's work, and this so-called illusion would never convince an educated reader) (*Causes*, p. 271). La Motte aligns morality with personal readings; Dacier pairs it with learning.

The frontispiece which introduces the 1711 edition of Dacier's translation (Figure 1), an engraving of Antoine Coypel's 'La colère d'Achille', with title in Greek, is aptly chosen given the centrality of Achilles' anger in the moral debates about Homer and Dacier's insistence on her duty to depict it faithfully. It can be read as programmatic for her approach and as a polemical statement in keeping with her response to some of the debates about Homer in her preface. The agonistic quality of this frontispiece is confirmed by the riposte of La Motte's own frontispiece (Figure 2), which is itself overtly provocative. It depicts Mercury guiding Homer to pass his lyre to La Motte as he rises from his writing desk and has the caption: 'choisis, tout n'est pas prétieux'. This echoes a line from the Ode 'L'Ombre

---

[79] See also Norman, *The Shock of the Ancient*, p. 87, pp. 206–08.

Figure 1 Frontispiece, Anne Dacier, *L'Iliade d'Homère*, 3 vols (Paris: Rigaud, 1711), I, np.
Image reproduced with the permission of The Provost and Fellows of Worcester College, Oxford.

228 WOMEN WRITING ANTIQUITY

Figure 2 Frontispiece, Antoine Houdar de La Motte, *L'Iliade, poëme avec un discours sur Homère* (Paris: Dupuis, 1714).

Image reproduced with the permission of The Provost and Fellows of Worcester College, Oxford.

de Homère' (pp. 175–80), included after La Motte's own preface, his *Discours sur Homère*, in which the ancient bard addresses La Motte:

> Choisis, tout n'est pas précieux.
> Prend mes hardiesses sensées,
> Et du fonds vif de mes pensées,
> Songe toujours à t'appuyer;
> Du reste je te rends le maître
> A quelque prix que ce puisse être,
> Sauve-moi l'affront d'ennuyer.
> Mon siècle eût des Dieux trop bizares,
> Des héros d'orgeuil infectez,
> Des Rois indignement avares,
> Défauts autrefois respectez.
> Adoucis tout avec prudence
> Que de l'exacte bienséance
> Ton ouvrage soit revêtu
> Respecte le goût de ton âge [...] (pp. 177–78)

> Choose: not everything is precious.
> Take my reasonable audacity
> And in the lively depths of my thoughts
> Dream always of finding inspiration
> I make you master of the rest;
> At whatever price is necessary,
> Save me from the affront of being tedious.
> My century had strange gods,
> Heroes infected with pride,
> Kings who were undignified in their greed
> Faults that were once respected.
> Sweeten everything with prudence
> So that your work is clothed
> In precise bienséance
> Respect the taste of your time [...]

La Motte's frontispiece is in dialogue with that of Dacier, emphasising La Motte's personal (and moral) responsibility in changing Homer's text, where Dacier's showed her exactitude and learning.

In the next round of texts, Dacier's *Causes de la corruption du goust* and La Motte's *Réflexions sur la critique*, this distinction between a premise of learning and of (personal) morality becomes intimately connected to their authorial postures. In the *Causes*, Dacier twins military metaphors with a posture of reluctance. She figures her position and her language as that of combat, but does so using *recusatio*: 'la douleur de voir ce Poëte si indignement traité, m'a fait résoudre à le deffendre, quoyque cette sorte d'ouvrage soit tres opposé à mon humeur, car je suis tres paresseuse et tres pacifique, et le seul nom de guerre me fait peur' (the pain of seeing this poet treated so unfairly has made me resolve to defend him, although this sort of work goes against my temperament, since I am very lazy and very peaceful in nature and the very word 'war' scares me) (*Causes*, pp. 3–4). This *recusatio* is repeated a few pages later as she identifies with 'les guerriers les moins braves' of Homer's poem: 'je suis à peu près comme ces guerriers' (I am a little like those [least brave] warriors) (p. 12). Even within this *recusatio*, the reference points are male warriors: she steers clear of the Amazons or other female military figures, such as Bellona, used by other women writers, as we have seen. Her self-representation as 'pacifique' must in part, nevertheless, be accounted for by the hostility she anticipated as a female quarreller.[80] However, Dacier does not give her gender as a reason for her posture of reluctance, but rather stresses learning: she disapproves of polemic that is vehement and personal, and instead posits her own method of quarrelling as instructive. In the *Causes* she explains:

> Mais pour ne pas faire de cet ouvrage un de ces ouvrages purement polemiques, et que je hais parce qu'ils me paroissent plus propres à divertir les lecteurs qu'à instruire, je tascheray de me tirer de cette voye commune de dispute et de faire une espece de Traité qui fera une recherche des *Causes de la Corruption du Goust*. (p. 14)

> To ensure that this does not become one of those purely polemical works, which I hate because they seem to me more intended to entertain readers than to instruct them, I will try to keep myself away from this common route of dispute and to write a treatise enquiring into the *Causes of the Decline in Taste*.

The *praeteritio* that opens the passage here reveals a reluctance to be associated with the ordinary mode, 'cette voye commune'. Dacier's insistence on instruction is of course itself a claim to morality, based as it is on the classical adage that promotes the usefulness of literature, *plaire et instruire*. But unlike La Motte's, her morality is grounded in a tradition of learning, rather than a personal response: she claims her restraint derives from her reputation as a distinguished scholar (indeed, she offers Tacitus's *Dialogue on oratory or the causes of corrupt eloquence [Dialogus de oratoribus]* as her model (p. 15)). In so doing, she both stresses that learning underpins her approach and uses her accepted authority as a *savante* to justify a text which is actually polemical, to disguise her rhetoric—despite these claims, the argumentative techniques used in the *Causes* recall the conventions of

---

[80] This posturing is evident throughout her work: for instance, in the 1711 edition of the *Iliad* she writes: 'Il ne m'appartient point de parler de guerre, cela est trop au-dessus de moi' (It is not fitting for me to talk of war, it is far above me) (p. li).

sixteenth-century polemic.[81] A mere fourteen pages are devoted to a treatise on the decline of taste and the remaining 614 (!) are an attentive line-by-line refutation of her target text, La Motte's Preface and translation. Dacier is far from 'pacifique', 'moins brave', or indeed 'paresseuse', in this text.

We see evidence of her combative approach in her co-opting of the sort of misogynist rhetoric typically used by male Ancients against women. Dacier echoes many of Boileau's gendered attacks against Scudéry, especially his attacks against the effeminacy of her novel heroes, in *her* attacks against *La Motte*: in her *Causes* she criticises opera and novels for their championing of effeminacy and suggests this has influenced La Motte (p. 27), later repeating that he was too influenced by novels in his approach to Homer (p. 97), having already herself criticised novels for their corruption in her *Iliad* Preface (*L'Iliade*, I, p. 69). She also discredits La Motte's authority by sarcastically imagining a 'fiction' in which his poem would be respected by the learned and only criticised by ignorant 'cavaliers' and 'femmes peu instruites des beautés de la Poësie' (women with little instruction in the beauties of poetry) (*Causes*, p. 51). Such an approach also extends to the representation of Homer's female figures: on the controversial question of how to approach Jupiter's violence against Juno, attacked by La Motte as indecent (*Réflexions*, p. 50), Dacier remains true to Homer's text, citing authenticity (*Causes*, p. 352).[82] She also criticises La Motte's portrayal of Minerva, to whom La Motte gives more agency by amplifying her speeches, by employing the gendered terms typically used to satirise women: 'Voila un plaisant langage pour Minerve. Une précieuse ridicule ne sçauroit mieux s'exprimer' (Here Minerva uses some pleasant terms. A ridiculous pretentious young woman would not know how to express herself better) (*Causes*, p. 477). She thus pre-empts any such attack being used against her.

She also presents herself as being akin but also superior to male 'savants' and to members of the *Académie française*. The *Académie* should have known better than to admit and encourage La Motte; she asserts that her husband and Boileau are the only ones who 'se sont élevez contre ces égarements de la raison' (who have risen up against these affronts to reason) (p. 32), and she is shocked that no one else from the *Académie* has come to Homer's defence. She nominates herself to do so instead, in a gesture that both aligns her with this body and sets her apart as superior:

> Je sçay bien qu'il y en a qui gemissent de cet attentat et je suis témoin de l'indignation que quelques-uns en ont conceûë, mais cette indignation d'une partie ne suffit pas pour justifier tout le corps et le public attendoit quelque chose de plus de cette Compagnie [...] Il vaut mieux que je deffende Homere toute seule. (pp. 32–33)

---

[81] See Emily Butterworth, *Poisoned Words: Slander and Satire in Early Modern France* (Cambridge: Legenda, 2006), p. 4.
[82] These translators used Latinised names for the divinities.

232 WOMEN WRITING ANTIQUITY

> I know that there are those who wince at this attack and I am witness to the indignation of certain parties, but the indignation of one does not exculpate the whole body and the public expect better of this company [...] I had better defend Homer on my own.

She condemns the 'indignation' of some of the *académiciens* as weak and insufficient and thus valorises her own heroism in coming to Homer's defence.

After Dacier's *Causes* and the first three parts of La Motte's *Réflexions* were published, the two apparently reconciled in April 1716. La Motte reflects on this reconciliation in the second edition of the *Réflexions sur la critique*, which he had re-published after peace was restored: at the end, he tells us that instead of adding his promised fourth part in which he would have extended his quarrel, he inserts a short, italicised passage declaring:

> Voilà la dispute finie entre Madame Dacier, Monsieur Boivin et moi; et le fruit de nôtre dispute est une amitié sincère et reciproque, dont ils me permettront de me faire honneur devant le Public. [...] Il faut que les disputes des gens de lettres ressemblent à ces conversations animées où après des avis différens et soûtenus de part et d'autre avec toute la vivacité qui en fait le charme, on se sépare en s'embrassant et souvent plus amis que si l'on avoit été froidement d'accord. (pp. 295–96)

> The dispute between Madame Dacier, Monsieur Boivin and me is hereby finished and the fruit of our dispute is a sincere and reciprocal friendship, and they will allow me to be proud of this in public [...] Disputes among intellectuals should resemble the sorts of animated conversations, in which, after having argued for different opinions, with a charming vivacity, the parties part with an embrace and often more friendliness than if they had been coldly in agreement.

La Motte mixes public and private here, suggesting that private friendships have resolved a public dispute. He presents the resolution of the Quarrel as being consensus ('to agree to disagree'); 'warm', 'lively', 'charming': harmony reigns. La Motte's ethics are based on identification, both between reader and text—as his main issue with Homer was, as we saw, the difference between ancient and contemporary morals—and, as is evident in this passage, between peers.

Dacier's own representation of the resolution of her conflict with La Motte, a few months after his declaration of peace, makes for a stark contrast and confirms her resistance to the social niceties that would see the Quarrel dismissed; she will not reduce its stakes. The text she published immediately after their 'reconciliation' was her *Odyssée* translation. Fern Farnham sees this last text as offering 'an end to the argument' with La Motte; I would suggest instead that her *Odyssée* Preface and the 'last word' it anticipates, her *Homère defendu* against Jean Hardouin, demonstrate her agonistic approach.[83] In the *Odyssée* Preface she does not declare the Quarrel over, but instead she meets La Motte's overtures with silence, not mentioning him once throughout its ninety-four pages. While she refrains from mentioning the Quarrel itself until the final eight pages, the main subject of her Preface—epic poetry—allows her to revisit many of her arguments from a different angle. At the end, far from offering a gesture of consensus, she reflects on the effect of the Quarrel on Homer's reception, suggesting 'ce Poëte de mesme est sorti avec un nouvel esclat de toutes ces querelles, et de ces guerres qu'on luy a faites' (this poet has actually come out of these quarrels and the attacks against him with new renown) (I, p. 86).[84] If Homer emerges as newly brilliant then so, implicitly, does his champion defender: Dacier. She then launches an attack on Perrault and finishes the one which she started in her *Causes* against Terrasson. The 'reconciliation' with La Motte simply means she no longer names him.

At the end of the *Odyssée* Preface she targets her (intended) final opponent, Jean Hardouin, and anticipates her next move in the Quarrel, her *Homère defendu*. She figures her refutation of Hardouin's text as her last battle:

> Un autre combat m'appelle, il faut refuter l'Apologie que le R.P Hardouin, un des plus sçavants hommes du siecle, vient de faire de ce Poëte. [...] Ma Réponse ne se fera pas longtemps attendre et j'ose esperer que les amateurs d'Homere ou plustost les amateurs de la raison, la verront avec quelque plaisir. Je finis-là ma carriere. (I, pp. 91–2)

> Another battle calls me: I must refute the recent Apology by the R.P Hardouin, one of the most learned men of this time. My response will be ready soon and I hope that those who admire Homer, or rather, those who admire reason, will read it with pleasure. I will finish my career with this.

She then amplifies the announcement of her retirement contained in 'je finis-là ma carriere' with an (unreferenced) quotation from Virgil's *Aeneid* 5.485: 'hic caestus artemque repono' ('here I lay down my boxing gloves and my art').[85] These lines in Virgil's *Aeneid* are spoken by Entellus, the aging champion boxer goaded back to the ring for a final fight against the young Dares. Entellus is prevented from beating the young man to death and, on receiving the award for the fight, a bull, he announces his retirement, 'hic *victor* caestus artemque repono' ('here, as *victor*,

---

[83] Farnham, 'That Madame Dacier fully subscribed to these sentiments [those quoted above from the end of La Motte's *Réflexions*] may be doubted, but she was willing to put an end to their argument'. Farnham, *Madam Dacier*, p. 179.

[84] Dacier, 'Préface', in *L'Odyssée*, I, 4–92.

[85] 'Carrière' potentially contains a metaphor of violence as it also refers to a run conducted on horseback or a joust. Virgil, *Eclogues. Georgics. Aeneid: Books 1–6*, trans. by H. Rushton Fairclough, rev. by G. P. Goold, Loeb Classical Library 63 (Cambridge, MA: Harvard University Press, 1916).

234 WOMEN WRITING ANTIQUITY

I lay down my boxing gloves and my art').[86] Dacier's removal of the term 'victor' might be an example of her reluctance to appear too polemical. However, it is also a rhetorical trick because the learned reader will fill in the missing word and crown her as victor. This self-conscious closing of her engagement in the Homer Quarrel with an image of competition, in which the line between sport and violence is crossed, picks up on the 'guerrier' with which she opened it in the *Causes*, confirming the consistency of her approach. It also confirms the crucial connection between the Quarrel and her career by showing that both should be ended together. Dacier was less conciliatory in her Homer Quarrel texts than critics have suggested, because winning mattered to her reputation. She adopted an agonistic approach, wearing the armour of her learning.

We have seen how Dacier negotiated the complex identity of female quarreller with denial and preterition; to some degree, the gendered criticism she received during her lifetime from her opponents was similarly coded and indirect, and not as prevalent as we might expect.[87] This is especially evident from La Motte's criticisms where he rarely attacks her gender head on. The emphasis he places on reciprocity in the 'conciliatory' gestures discussed above from the 1716 edition of his *Réflexions* are also present in his 1715 edition. He articulates clearly his ethics of moderation and respect, his Modern irenism:

> Quelques auteurs au contraire n'ont d'autre vûë dans la dispute, que d'entendre et de faire entendre la raison [...] Ce caractère me paroît si estimable que je me le proposerai toûjours pour modelle dans la dispute où je suis obligé d'entrer. J'examinerai les objections de Me Dacier comme si je me les étois faites à moi-même. (p. 4)

> Some authors, in contrast, seek in dispute only mutual understanding and reason [...] This approach seems to be so worthy of esteem that I will use it as a model for any dispute that I am obliged to enter. I will examine Mme Dacier's objections as if I had made them against myself.

While not overtly declaring her rhetoric unsuitable for a woman, he does so in coded language when he describes her violence. He complains of her ruthlessness:

---

[86] See also the *Ad Usum Delphini* Latin edition, *P. Virgilii Maronis Opera, interpretatione et notis illustravit Carolus Ruaeus,...ad usum serenissimi Delphini* (Paris: Bernard, 1675), p. 478.

[87] For instance, the Abbé Terrasson, a Modern, takes a polite approach in his *Dissertation critique sur L'Iliade*: he positions Dacier as an authority in that he is reliant on her translations but also offers corrections of her readings and interpretations, especially regarding the morals of Achilles. Although occasionally sarcastic, his criticisms are not gendered. She was highly praised and well received by fellow Ancients, who make of her gender a positive attribute. Etienne Fourmont's *Examen pacifique de la querelle*, despite its apparently neutral title, is very strongly on Dacier's side. He writes: 'Madame Dacier paroit ici comme un de ces genereuses Amazones qui ne souffrent pas que l'on entre sur leurs terres; M. de la M. est comme un des enfants d'Apollon' (Madame Dacier seems here like one of those magnanimous Amazons who will not allow others onto their territory; M. de La Motte is like a child of Apollo) (i, p. 5).

'elle me traite sans scrupule comme mort et Homere comme vivant' (she treats me without scruple as if I were dead and Homer were alive) (p. 23), and uses military language to describe her discourse: 'Me D. combat encore [...]' (p. 116); her strategies are 'petites ruses de guerre' (little war-like ruses) (p. 131). He explicitly contrasts his 'modération' with her approach: 'Mme D. s'amuse à prouver sçavamment ma propre pensée en me faisant un crime de ma modération' (It pleases Mme D. to demonstrate, in a learned, knowing way, my own thoughts by making a crime of my moderation) (p. 93); and 'Mme D. a pris apparemment cet usage pour un privilege de l'érudition; elle ne m'épargne pas ces sortes d'injures' (Mme D. apparently assumes that this approach is a privilege of erudition; she does not spare me these sorts of insults) (p. 24). La Motte's (passive-aggressive) restraint towards Dacier, as Suzanna van Dijk shows, cultivates a flattering image of himself as *galant* and tactful.[88] That 'privilège d'érudition' also comes in for attack as he—implicitly—accuses Dacier of *savant* pedantry. This is explicitly gendered on one occasion. He picks up on one of the rare instances in which *Dacier* alludes to her gender when, buried in her commentary on the *Iliad* Book 6.490, she mentions that she has been bold in doing more than restricting herself to the distaff to which Homer relegated women (*L'Iliade*, I, pp. 518–19). La Motte responds sarcastically, enumerating the 'merits' of her temerity:

> Laissez la quenoüille aux femmes, vous êtes née pour des occupations plus grandes. Donnez-nous encore l'Odissée et beaucoup d'autres ouvrages, s'il est possible; joignez-y des notes savantes pour éclaircir les faits et les usages [...]; nous vous ferons honneur des fruits qu'on tirera de vos traductions et s'il arrive que l'Iliade et l'Odissée tombent, parce que vous les aurez bien fait connoître, la postérité vous sera obligée de leur chute même. (*Réflexions*, pp. 282–83)

> Leave the distaff for other women; you were born for loftier occupations. Give us the *Odyssey* and other works still, if possible: and add learned commentaries to clarify facts and customs [...]; we will honour you with the fruits we take from these translations and if it happens that the *Iliad* and the *Odyssey* should go out of fashion because you have made them so well known, then posterity will be obliged to you for their very decline.

Her pedantry, her 'notes savantes', have revealed the true flaws of the original text, so that her very defence has undermined Homer: her scholarship is excellent, but to save Homer, she should have remained at the distaff.

As van Dijk argues, Dacier's confrontational approach sometimes posed a challenge for the reading and literary public, evident from the comments in the press. More than her direct opponents, commentators and reviewers were critical of

---

[88] Van Dijk, *Traces de femmes*, p. 210.

236 WOMEN WRITING ANTIQUITY

her forthright and ruthless tone, implying it was inappropriate for a woman.[89] Instances of attack can particularly be found in the strongly partisan Modern *Nouveau Mercure Galant*, directed by Hardouin Le Fèvre de Fontenay. For example, Jean-François Le Pons, author of the *Lettre à M*** sur l'Iliade de M. de la Motte*, which, written in 1714 before her *Causes* was published, had been polite towards Dacier,[90] suggests in May 1715 that the *Causes* 'scandalizât tout ensemble les gens sensez' (scandalised all reasonable people), although he does not mention Dacier by name.[91] In a supplement to the December issue, Fontenay describes 'le procedé injurieux de cette Sçavante envers son adversaire' (the offensive conduct of this learned lady towards her opponent), and summarises the pro-Dacier intervention by Etienne Fourmont as justifying 'les excés injurieux de Madame Dacier' (the offensive excesses of Madame Dacier).[92] However, it was not all negative. The February 1715 edition of the more even-handed *Journal des Sçavans* contained a positive review of Dacier's *Causes*, and claims that she has so excelled in this sort of writing, which is described as 'le didactique et le polémique', that she should have undertaken more of it.[93] In the next month's instalment, the reviewer defends her quarrelling method, saving Dacier from the accusation of making a personal attack: 'on voit par là, comme par tout le reste du Livre, que Madame Dacier n'en veut qu'aux sentiments de M. de la Motte, qu'elle n'attaque nullement son mérite personnel' (it is evident from this, as it is from the whole book, that she is only attacking the ideas of M. de la Motte and not attacking him personally).[94]

---

[89] See van Dijk, *Traces de femmes*, pp. 208–9. For instance, 'j'aurois voulu qu'une Dame eût paru une Dame dans ses Ouvrages, qu'elle eût par tout répandu les fleurs et les grâces, et par conséquent qu'elle ne fût pas entrée dans les sentiments d'un Savant offensé' (I would have wanted a woman to seem like a woman in these works, to see her scatter flowers and grace everywhere, then she would not have seemed like an offended savant). *Journal Littéraire*, vi (1715), p. 466. Quoted in van Dijk, *Traces de femmes*, p. 211.

[90] Le Pons, *Lettre à M*** sur l'Iliade de M. de la Motte* (Paris: Seneuze, 1714). He refrains from naming her when he discusses the Ancients, 'laissons crier les adorateurs d'Homère', which he also describes as a 'culte' (p. 7). Although he is vehemently critical of the *Iliade*, describing it as 'ce tout monstrueux' (p. 17), he is respectful and polite about her translation—'elle a entendu Homère autant qu'on le peut entendre aujourd'hui, elle sçait beaucoup mieux encore la langue française' (she understood Homer as well as one can today and she knows a lot more about the French language) (p. 22).

[91] Abbé de Pons, 'Dénonciation faite à Monseigneur le Chancelier d'un Libelle injurieux, qui, revêtu de l'autorité du sceau, paroît dans le monde sous le titre d'Homère vengé', in *Nouveau Mercure Galant*, May 1715, pp. 58–100 (p. 70).

[92] [Fontenay], 'Critique sur l'Examen pacifique de M. l'Abbé de Fourmont', in a supplement to the *Nouveau Mercure Galant*, December 1715, pp. 35–36. On the adjective 'injurieux' and for further discussion of these journals, see David D. Reitsam, *La Querelle d'Homère dans la presse des Lumières: l'exemple du Nouveau Mercure Galant* (Tübingen: Narr, 2021), pp. 125–28. On the uncertain attribution of this essay, see also Reitsam, *La Querelle d'Homère*, p. 127.

[93] *Journal des Sçavans*, 25 February 1715, p. 113.

[94] *Journal des Sçavans*, 4 March 1715, p. 141. A few months later, in the June edition, La Motte's *Réflexions* were reviewed: his *Réflexions*, not polemic or didactic, are 'si sages et si judicieuses' (3 June 1715, p. 338) and, as he perhaps intended, he is praised for treating a woman with 'le respect dû au sexe et la plus scrupuleuse politesse' (p. 347). A similar approach is taken in the *Nouveau Mercure Galant*— for instance, La Motte had 'tous les égards qu'un galant homme doit à son beau sexe' (all the regard that a *galant* gentleman should have towards the fair sex) (March 1715, p. 327). On this, see Reitsam, *La Querelle d'Homère*, pp. 125–26.

It was only really after her death that the attacks become vitriolic, personal, and notably gendered. This distinction is important as it shows how her status and the respect she commanded kept the wolves at bay during her lifetime. Although Dacier was praised as a source of influence and inspiration for women throughout the eighteenth century, particularly, for instance by the Marquise de Lambert who suggests that she is 'une autorité qui prouve que les femmes [...] sont capables [de savoir]' (an authority who proves women are capable of learning), she was also subjected to misogynist attack.[95] Cartaud de La Vilate's 1736 *Essai historique et philosophique sur le goût* which was quoted in Simon-Augustin Irailh's *Querelles Littéraires* (1761) is a particularly forceful example. Cartaud makes the usual attacks against a 'savante', namely describing her in physical terms as 'grotesque' and suggesting that time spent on study led to neglect of her personal attributes.[96] For Cartaud, her knowledge was masculine and unseemly: 'il sied aussi mal à une femme de s'herisser d'une certaine érudition, que de porter des moustaches. Une femme sçavante a quelque chose de trop hommasse' (it is as unseemly for a woman to clothe herself in such erudition as it is for her to sport a moustache. A learned lady has a rather too mannish quality).[97] He explicitly contrasts her rhetoric with that of La Motte, noting the inversion of the expectations of their gender: 'On dit à cette occasion que M. de la Mothe écrivoit comme une femme galante qui auroit de l'esprit et que Madame Dacier écrivoit comme un pédant' (One could say that on this occasion M. de La Motte wrote like a lively, *galant* lady and that Madame Dacier wrote like a male pedant).[98] Irailh is a little more measured in that he only quotes *some* of Cartaud's attack, with the warning that Cartaud is one of the 'ennemis de cette illustre savante'; however, he also uses negatively inflected gendered language to criticise her. Although he is dismissive of both her translation—all the while noting that her learning is extraordinary—and that of La Motte, he takes Dacier to task for her quarrelling rhetoric and her lack of moderation, while praising La Motte for his restraint.[99] Jean Aublet de Maubuy, who likewise defends La Motte in his *Histoire des troubles et des démêlés littéraires* (1779), is also forceful in his gendered attack on Dacier; with regard to her text against Harduoin, he writes: 'Madame Dacier cria *haro* contre lui: hérissée de Grec et de Latin, elle se présenta hardiment pour le combattre, ce qu'elle fit avec une espèce de fureur' (Dacier railed

---

[95] 'J'estime infiniment Mad. D. Notre sexe lui doit beaucoup: elle a protesté contre l'erreur commune qui nous condamne à l'ignorance' (I have great esteem for Madame D. Our sex owes her much: she protested against the common error which condemns us to ignorance). Undated letter to Claude Buffier, in *Œuvres de Madame la Marquise de Lambert, avec un abrégé de sa vie* (Lausanne: Bousquet, 1748), p. 383.

[96] Cartaud de La Vilate, *Essai historique*, pp. 156–58 (p. 156).

[97] Ibid., p. 157.

[98] Ibid., p. 158.

[99] *Querelles Littéraires ou mémoires pour servir à l'histoire des révolutions de la république des lettres*, 4 vols (Paris: Durand, 1761), II, p. 315. Earlier, he writes: 'L'autheur, dans son livre, est une femme des Halles en furie' (the author of this book is a screeching market woman), contrasting this with the 'dissertation modérée, fine et délicate' of La Motte (p. 311).

238   WOMEN WRITING ANTIQUITY

against him: adorned with Greek and Latin, she boldly presented herself for battle, which she undertook with a certain fury).[100] La Motte is on the side of moderation and *politesse*, Dacier a wild combatant.[101]

Of the satires written in response to the quarrel, Ignace Limojon de Saint-Didier's *Iliade, tragi-comédie* (1717) is most indicative of the other current in her reception: that which played down her forthright participation in the quarrel in favour of a more feminine, modest, and gentle representation. This text is included within his *Voyage du Parnasse* and is in part a satire attacking La Motte, and is favourable towards Dacier. In showing this favour, however, Limojon turns her into a softer maternal figure and has Apollon come to the rescue, as she is not able to resolve the dispute herself. In this short three-act play in verse, which is also a reworking of Racine's *Iphigénie*, signalled by references to specific acts and scenes of Racine's play in the margins, 'L'Iliade' is a young girl (Iphigenia) to be sacrificed by La Motte and La Pucelle, his lover, to Du Puis (La Motte's publisher); le Bon Goust, Iliade's lover, and Dacier, her mother, are trying to save her. This play stages an inversion of the rhetoric of La Motte and Dacier by making La Motte the aggressor and turning Dacier into a maternal figure keen to save her child.

In this representation, Limojon anticipates some of the ways that those favourable to Dacier dealt with her caustic rhetoric, particularly after her death. The quarrelling or polemical aspect of her interventions was played down: a feminine *ethos* of modesty was emphasised in the memorials and accounts of her life.[102] For instance, in the fourteen-page funeral *éloge* in the *Journal des Sçavans*, all her interventions in the quarrel are presented as being driven by her desire to teach and correct (no mention is made of her caustic rhetoric): hers was 'une vie si précieuse aux gens de lettres' (a life so precious to people of letters).[103] It is particularly in the *éloge* of the *Journal de Trévoux* that her modesty is stressed. Here, her interventions in the *Querelle d'Homère* are described as judicious and well received, diverting attention away from their polemical tone, and her social reconciliation with La Motte is emphasised: 'la gayeté de la table et la politesse de cet ennemi

---

[100] Maubuy, *Histoire des troubles et des démêlés littéraires*, I, p. 14.

[101] See Myriam Dufour-Maître, 'Femmes, querelles galantes du XVIIᵉ siècle et histoire littéraire', in *Women and Querelles in Early Modern France*, ed. by Taylor and Tunstall, pp. 372–88.

[102] See Itti, *Madame Dacier*, p. 313; and van Dijk, *Traces de femmes*, pp. 219–20. She is briefly mentioned in the *Nouveau Mercure*, December 1720, explaining that La Motte praised her at a gathering (p. 188). See 'Ode à la louange de Madame Dacier. Prononcée à l'Académie dans une Séance publique', in *Œuvres de Monsieur Houdar de La Motte*, 2 vols (Paris: Prault, 1754), I, pp. 259–64.

[103] *Journal des Sçavans*, December 1720, pp. 593–607 (p. 607). The Marquise de Lambert takes a similar view: 'elle a associé l'érudition aux bienséances' (she combined *bienséance* with erudition), p. 383. Saint-Simon also takes this view: 'elle n'étoit savante que dans son cabinet ou avec des savants, partout ailleurs simple, unie, avec de l'esprit, agréable dans la conversation, où on ne se seroit pas douté qu'elle sût rien de plus que les femmes les plus ordinaires' (She was only learned in her rooms or in other learned company; elsewhere she was straightforward, without airs, witty, pleasant in conversation, and one would never have suspected that she knew anything more than the most ordinary of women). Saint-Simon, *Mémoires*, 7 vols (Paris: Gallimard, Bibliothèque de la Pléiade, 1963), VI, pp. 633–34.

d'Homere la désarmerent' (the good cheer and the politeness of the dinner table of this enemy of Homer disarmed her).[104] Her modesty is foregrounded:

> Sa modestie étoit si grande, que jamais elle ne parloit de science ni de ce qu'elle avoit fait et qu'elle ne faisoit jamais paroître dans ses conversations l'avantage qu'elle pouvait avoir de ce côté-là sur la plûpart de ceux avec qui elle s'entretenoit [...] Ceux qui ne la connoissoient point ne pouvoient découvrir en elle qu'une femme ordinaire qui ne sçavoit que garder les bienséance de son sexe.[105]

> Her modesty was so great that she never spoke of learning or of what she had achieved and she never let show in her conversations the intellectual advantage she could have over most of her interlocutors [...] Those who did not know her would only encounter an ordinary woman who knew how to behave according to the *bienséance* of her sex.

This description with its emphasis on Dacier's conversational skills, her ability to blend in and not 'faire la savante' (though this construction is not used), echoes, at points almost verbatim, Scudéry's portrait of Sapho which we analysed in Chapter 3. That echo is most likely not deliberate but such was the influence of Scudéry's conception of the modest female intellectual that its key contours filtered through. The *éloge* then quotes an anecdote whereby a German 'savant' asked Dacier to add her name and a sentence to his book of 'sçavants hommes de l'Europe', which she declined to do, embarrassed, and after his insistence she added her name and a line in Greek from Sophocles—'le silence est l'ornement des femmes' (silence is a woman's ornament).[106] This gesture speaks of that tension between modesty and learning we traced in her early works and which characterises so many of the gestures of the women studied in this book: note that she adds this comment in ancient Greek, an act which reinforces the *praeteritio* already contained in the statement by undercutting the gesture of modesty as well as the silence. The intention of this story is, however, to underscore her modesty; this, combined with the defanged descriptions of her *Querelle* texts, strips Dacier of her rhetorical bite. What comes across clearly in these portraits is that she is 'saved' from pedantry by social skills (where Gournay seems to have failed): although her books might be uncompromisingly erudite, *in person* she was modest so all is right with the world. The reference to the dinner party in the *Trévoux éloge*, which echoes La Motte's own presentation of their reconciliation, reinforces this sociability. But Dacier's own representation and articulation of her knowledge across

---

[104] *Journal de Trévoux*, January 1721, pp. 88–115 (p. 106). Of the *Causes*: 'cet ouvrage fut reçu avec un grand applaudissement et un des meilleurs juges sur ces matieres lui donna cet éloge, que c'étoit un excellent traité de Rhetorique et de Poëtique' (this work was received with acclaim and one of the best judges of such subjects said it was an excellent treatise of both rhetoric and poetics) (p. 105).

[105] Ibid., pp. 107–08.

[106] Ibid., p. 109.

240 WOMEN WRITING ANTIQUITY

her *œuvre* is not social, sociable, or acquiescent: Dacier's authorial persona and authority rest instead on her erudition.

**

Dacier proves a fascinating and complicated case in a study on gender and classical reception. To some extent, her mastery of Latin and Greek, her boy's education at the hands of one of the most prominent Hellenists (and educators) in France, the 'sociocultural' inheritance of her family, and her learned editions, translations, and commentaries all meant that she did not face the normal obstacles and prejudices confronting women in this period. We should not therefore overstate the barriers she overcame 'as a woman', and this is all the clearer when she is compared to other women writing across this period. She is distinct from all the other women studied in this book, even Marie de Gournay, whom Dacier otherwise resembles in her erudition and quarrelling. To this end, then, her exclusion from the canons of seventeenth- and eighteenth-century 'women writers' might be because of an understanding of women as defined by marginalisation or as defined as writing in feminised genres or for feminised causes—or the exclusion might be because of a conception of 'writing' that does not include translation.

And yet, for all her exceptionality, she still engaged in her own way with the modesty expected of her, navigating gender expectations, and so her exclusion from the category of 'woman writer' dismisses the complexities of her situation. These expectations are evident both from the *éloges* which emphasise her modesty, and from the accusations that she was manly, vomiting her unbridled anger. In relation to her final work, her *Réflexions* on Pope's *Iliad* Preface, often dismissed as the erroneous ravings of an old woman, and assumed, incorrectly, to be based on a faulty translation, critics risk rehearsing some of the language and tropes inherited from this misogyny, as I have argued elsewhere.[107] Dacier was also aware of the potential for overstepping the boundaries expected of her sex in relation to her quarrelling gestures: it is this, as we have seen, more than her learning, which prompted strategic claims to being 'pacifique' in works where she is so clearly a 'guerrièr(e)'. She reminds us of the importance of nuance in all our approaches to writing by women—not all women faced the same obstacles, not all women wrote for a putatively collective identity, not all were interested in the same causes or writing in feminised genres. And yet ideas of female gender entailed expectations to be negotiated, worked around, confronted. This study has used gender as a unifying category, but it also questions and disrupts notions of unity and unification among women writing in this period.

---

[107] On this quarrel with Pope, see Taylor, 'Anne Dacier's Rhetoric', and Howard D. Weinbrot, '"What Must the World Think of Me?": Pope, Madame Dacier, and Homer: The Anatomy of a Quarrel', in *Eighteenth-Century Contexts: Historical Inquiries in Honor of Philip Harth*, ed. by Howard D. Weinbrot, Peter J. Schakel, and Stephen E. Karian (Madison: University of Wisconsin Press, 2001), pp. 183–206.

Coming at the end of this book, Dacier completes an arc that is appropriate to the study of the reception of Greco-Roman literature in this period: from the beginnings of the French, Modern aesthetic so resisted by Marie de Gournay to the re-articulation and re-orientation of some of those questions in the Homer Quarrel. With Gournay and Dacier, the study is thus flanked by two 'savante', Ancient women, in a century which is also known for the 'salonnière' and the attendant modesty, feminised genres and sociability that this role entailed. Throughout this study we have seen the limitations of those labels when imposed extradiegetically. I have stressed the importance of attending instead to the complexities of authorial persona and posture as it meets creative and critical practice; and the importance of examining how and *why* divisions in knowledge were constructed by women at the time, and what this reveals about authorial posture and the literary field more widely.

As we have seen, all the writers in this corpus were writing in and shaping a time of change in terms of what was meant by 'savoir' and ideologies underpinning literature. In the March 1715 issue of the *Nouveau Mercure Galant*—which, as we examined above, was mostly critical of Dacier—there is a general discussion of the Dacier–La Motte dispute. This is used as a way into a reflection on the meaning of 'savant':

> Définissons un peu le vray sçavant et nous jugerons ensuite de nos dettes reciproques. Le vray sçavant est celuy qui a acquis un grand nombre de connoissance et qui a cultivé et formé son jugement de manière qu'il sçait faire usage des connoissances acquises au gré de la droite raison. Nos Sçavants Grecs ont grand interêt à rejetter ma définition. D'accord: mais quelle est la leur? Le Sçavant, c'est celuy qui sçait du Grec? Cela n'est pas possible. Les langues ne sont pas des sciences, elles ne portent par elles-mêmes aucunes lumieres à l'esprit. Un homme pourroit sçavoir vingt langues differentes et être une grosse bête, un ignorant, un stupide personnage. [...] c'est un homme, diroit on, qui a passé sa vie à apprendre des mots. Il auroit fourny dans le monde une carrière honorable si du travail ingrat dont il a servi sa memoire, il en avoit servi son esprit et son jugement.[108]

> Let us define a little the true learned man and then we will judge our reciprocal debt. A true learned man is one who has acquired a great deal of knowledge and who has cultivated and formed his judgement in such a way that he knows how to make use of this knowledge according to reason. Our learned Greeks have real reason to reject my definition. Fine: what is their definition? Is a learned man someone who knows Greek? This is not possible. Languages are not sciences, they do not bear in themselves any enlightenment of the mind. A man could know twenty different languages and be an idiot, an ignorant and stupid person. He is a man (people would say) who has spent his life learning words. He would have

---

[108] *Nouveau Mercure Galant*, March 1715, pp. 10–12.

provided the world with a reasonable career if instead of this ungrateful work of memorising he had instead attended to his mind and his judgement.

It's typically Modern stuff—the difference between being educated and genuine knowledge, between book learning and the imagination, which draws on a longer history of associating pedantry with rote learning of languages—but what interests me is that it is the dispute propelled by Dacier which is driving this redefinition of the 'savant' and that her position in this Quarrel, her quarrel *tout court*, is implicitly understood as being about the nature of learning. In contrast to Gournay's struggle with the category error of the female intellectual and Scudéry's inability to offer a positive substantive for her ideal intellectual, here the reviewer suggests the opposite: that it is the traditional conception of the 'learned man', literate in ancient languages, who is an impossibility, an aporia, because this is not true 'savoir'. Lurking within the struggle to define the 'savante', therefore, is also a question that goes beyond gender to attend to practices of learning and the figure of the intellectual more widely. Throughout this study we have encountered definitions of 'savante' as aspirational, as oppositional, as identifying, as distancing, and we have traced its different inflections in meaning from pedantry to *mondainité*; many of these definitions have been self-serving, strategic and/or exclusionary. We have also considered how the definitions of 'savante'—and more widely the figure of the female intellectual—mapped onto evolving ideas about literature, and particularly French literature. This comment usefully takes us back to the point from which we started, that the definition of a practitioner is related to defining a practice; that ideologies require, are shaped by, and in turn shape, adherents to those ideologies. And for all that a community, or even a 'field', might be made up of opposing positions (after all, community can be built on dissensus rather than consensus), this comment also reminds us, as Gournay had explored, of how definitions can be normative and of how failing to fit into accepted moulds can be existentially threatening to the necessarily social identity of the (female) intellectual.[109]

---

[109] On communities of dissensus, see Alexis Tadié and Anne-Lise Rey, 'Introduction', in *Disputes et territoires épistémiques*, ed. by Tadié and Rey (= *Revue de Synthèse*, 137 (2016)), pp. 223–26 (p. 223).

8
Conclusion

This study has examined the ways in which the struggle to define the female intellectual in seventeenth-century France mapped onto the broader struggle for a definition of literature and literary knowledge in a context of significant cultural change. Scholarship has attended to the 'feminisation' of taste in this period, and the expanding of literary practitioners and publics to include women; it has also considered the figure or type of the 'savante', particularly from the perspective of satire, and its relationship to changing gender norms.[1] This study has altered the focus by placing responses by women to the figure of the female intellectual at the centre, examining them alongside women's receptions of the most learned form of literary culture—from ancient Greece and Rome—to reveal the correspondence of posture and practice to ideologies of literature. This approach has offered a way into analysing the relationship between terminology, legitimacy, and authorial identity; the shifting values attributed to literature and to authorship; changing modes of receiving the classical past; and contested ideas of what French literature should be in this period. The methodology adopted here has also allowed me to reframe early modern classical reception through the prisms of ideology and authorial strategy.[2]

I have thus shifted some of the trends in classical reception studies, traditionally often formalist and source-text orientated in method, with my focus on the ideological significance of Greco-Roman culture in this period and on the place of classical reception in authorial self-fashioning and career strategy. I have shown how for many of the authors studied here classical reception, broadly conceived, was important to their biographical professional identities because of the lucrative nature of such reception, either as philologists (Gournay, Dacier), or writers of fiction (particularly Scudéry, Villedieu, La Roche-Guilhen, Bernard), even as we have also traced their diverse approaches towards the literary market and the business of the book trade. Indeed, I have demonstrated how this reception was also central to the rhetorical framing of those professional identities, from Scudéry's posture of

---

[1] Key works in this area include Linda Timmermans, *L'Accès des femmes à la culture (1598–1715)*, 2nd edn (Paris: Champion, 2005); Myriam Dufour-Maître, *Les Précieuses: naissance des femmes de lettres en France au XVIIe siècle*, 2nd edn (Paris: Champion, 2008); and Domna Stanton, *The Dynamics of Gender in Early Modern France: Women Writ, Women Writing* (New York: Routledge, 2014).

[2] This builds on a methodology I developed in my first book, *The Lives of Ovid in Seventeenth-Century French Culture* (Oxford: Oxford University Press, 2017).

Women Writing Antiquity. Helena Taylor, Oxford University Press. © Helena Taylor (2024).
DOI: 10.1093/oso/9780192870445.003.0008

244   WOMEN WRITING ANTIQUITY

aristocratic detachment that entailed the downplaying of her labours as a (Classical) scholar, to Villedieu's commercially orientated ancient history that implicitly questioned the opposition between cultural and economic value by legitimising commercial success.

I have also, I hope, brought attention to writers not usually considered to be Classicists who are not often included in detail in reception studies—Scudéry, the *conteuses*, Deshoulières, Villedieu—alongside the two figures who do more commonly feature in such studies, namely, Gournay and Dacier. Alongside traditional forms of reception in familiar genres—rewriting, intertextual reference, translation, fictionalisation—I have included Parnassus fictions, non-fictional essays, periodicals, journals, and autobiographical writing. I show how they all fit under the broad category of adaptation: sometimes the ancient Greek and Roman past is a rhetorical construction, a foil against which to pitch Modern, innovative ideas or a way of investing one's ethos with erudition; sometimes this adaptation has been directly textual in the form of translation or fictional rewritings of ancient history. The nature of this corpus has meant that the translations studied have primarily been examples of erudite philology (by Gournay and Dacier), and in both cases by women who vaunted ancient culture and its authority; that is far from the full picture of translation in this period, in which it was very frequently a modernising and domesticating activity. Embedded in this diversity of reception and genre is also analysis of the seventeenth-century reflections on the relationship between classical heritage and the constitution of genre (evident especially in relation to the novel and the *conte de fées*, but also, to less well-known genres or modes, such as the eclogue), where we see sometimes a tension, sometimes a lineage and more often a combination, between ancient heritage and a French tradition. That complex tension is also writ large in the broader ideological stakes entailed by how ancient culture was adapted, rewritten, and received: not only as it pertains to the question of whether to assimilate it to French taste and literature, but also to the elaboration of what constitutes such taste and such literature.

We witness across this corpus some clear examples of solidarity between women intellectuals and writers, especially in the genealogies analysed in the *conteuses* chapter, whereby French literature is linked to a feminine troubadour history, the *cours d'amour*, and to a line of significant women from Pizan to Scudéry; that solidarity is also extended back to ancient women intellectuals in works by the *conteuses*, and by Marie Gournay, Madeleine Scudéry, and Anne Dacier. However, this book has also alighted on the limitations of such solidarity, evident in the reception of Gournay, and the ambivalent 'gate-keeping' of Scudéry whose alter-ego 'Damophile' is a figure of ridicule. Running through the work analysed here are anxieties about the social space of the salon (we see this in Gournay's reprimands of contemporary readers, in Scudéry's Sapho, hounded by persistent hangers-on, in Antoinette Deshoulières's representations of flatterers who are a nuisance) even as we also encounter a celebration of these spaces, whether fictional or historical, physical or, in the case of Marie-Jeanne L'Héritier's periodical, virtual. Such emphasis on tensions chimes with this study's intentions to interrogate ideas of women's collectivity both in the period and in its reception, by focusing on individuals and drawing attention to the different ideologies underpinning the categories of 'woman writer' and 'Classicist', 'salonnière' and 'savante', provoking reflection on the historiography of those groupings and taking an approach to the women studied here that is led by an understanding of gender as a category of analysis and not an essential characteristic.

A common stylistic tool used by the women studied here is humour.[3] For all that women were subject to mockery, and the pursuit of recognition and a name was a serious one, humour, irony, satire, and even mockery itself were modes of many of the writers in my corpus. Scudéry's gentle satire of Damophile is one case in point, but, as shown, Villedieu, Deshoulières, L'Héritier, Marie-Catherine d'Aulnoy, and Henriette-Julie de Murat in particular all deploy irony, and a self-aware and sometimes self-directed humour that merits note as a means of communicating an idea, of shaping meaning, targeting a specific and exclusionary audience, and as a strategy of entertainment and success. But we also encounter the limitations of the qualities of humour that are socially acquiescent: Gournay in particular, and also Dacier, in her reluctance to invest her authorial persona with the grace she is credited with possessing socially, could be seen as versions of Sara Ahmed's celebratory 'feminist killjoy': they are not willing to laugh at their own expense or smooth over an intellectual confrontation—in print at least—with social niceties.[4] Humour surfaces in this book as expressing the need for recognition, even approval, and so a willingness to please and entertain, as well as more confident in-jokes and irony: it pertains to the social dynamics that are shown to have shaped the figure of the female intellectual.

Finally, in this book I have attempted to hold in tension an author's ethos, her immediate reception, and her legacy in order to explore and confront how these women have been categorised and what that means for the historiography of gender and learning. In the remainder of this Conclusion I turn to the legacy of the term and type of the '(femme) savante' and its relationship with the various ambivalent avatars that emerge across the eighteenth, nineteenth, and early twentieth centuries in France and England: Bluestocking, le Bas-Bleu, and the Girton Girl.

For the immediate inheritor of the figure of the 'femme savante' we need to look to mid-eighteenth-century England at the 'Bluestocking Circle' of Elizabeth Montagu and Elizabeth Vesey's salons. When first used in 1756 in the correspondence of Elizabeth Montagu, the term 'Bluestocking' was a descriptor in gentle jest for

---

[3] See Annalisa Nicholson, 'The Satire of the Salonnière: Women and Humour in Seventeenth-Century France', *Australian Journal of French Studies*, 59.4 (2022), 361–75.

[4] See Sara Ahmed, <https://feministkilljoys.com/>, and Sara Ahmed, *The Feminist Killjoy Handbook* (London: Allen Lane, 2023).

246 WOMEN WRITING ANTIQUITY

the dress of one of the male attendees of her salon, Benjamin Stillingfleet.[5] In the 1760s and early 1770s, it was a term used by its referents to describe men and women of this circle without negative connotations. However, as Sylvia Harcstark Myers shows, by the late 1770s it came almost exclusively to connote women's learning and to be used increasingly in a pejorative way, especially from the 1790s in the strongly reactionary political climate when women's learning was seen to be dangerous.[6] Like 'savante', then, 'Bluestocking' only came to have a pejorative meaning when it was associated primarily with women; naming thus enabled the articulation of a fear or anxiety. As Myers argues, 'Bluestocking' was sometimes connected to the French terms, 'femme savante' or 'précieuses ridicules', with pejorative intent.[7] This was still the case in the twentieth century: as Myers shows, Richard Wilbur's 1977 translation of Molière's *Les Femmes savantes* often uses 'Bluestocking' as a substitute for 'femme savante'; and Howard C. Barnard uses 'Bluestocking' for 'précieuse' in his 1966 translation of Fénélon's *On Education*.[8]

The Bluestocking Circle was a group of intellectuals interested in arts, literature, and education: classical literature played a key role in their pursuits. There were overt connections with the French salons; indeed, Montagu styled her salon on those hosted by women in eighteenth-century Paris. Just as that of Madeleine de Scudéry, Bluestocking feminism has been seen as somewhat ambivalent with its focus on women's education alongside promotion of female respectability and conduct: members of this circle did not resist gender roles in ways that some of their contemporaries did.[9] Many women also laid claim to the term 'Bluestocking', even while it had negative associations, so that, like 'savante' again, the term was also (re)appropriated to have a positive meaning.[10]

The term 'Bluestocking' also fed back into French culture in the late eighteenth century and into the nineteenth by way of its calque, 'Les Bas-Bleus', as is recognised in the definition of the current *Dictionnaire de l'Académie française*, which is preceded by the following information:

---

[5] Sylvia Harcstark Myers, *The Bluestocking Circle: Women, Friendship and the Life of the Mind in Eighteenth-Century England* (Oxford: Oxford University Press, 1990), p. 6.

[6] Myers, *The Bluestocking Circle*, pp. 9–10. See also Nicole Pohl and Betty A. Schellenberg, 'A Bluestocking Historiography', in *Reconsidering the Bluestockings*, ed. by Nicole Pohl and Betty A. Schellenberg (= *Huntingdon Library Quarterly*, 65.1–2 (2002)), pp. 1–19 (p. 5).

[7] For instance, William Pitt Scargill links the Bluestockings with 'précieuses ridicules' in his novel *Bluestocking Hall* (1827). As Myers explains, quoting Scargill, the protagonist 'doesn't wish to be with pedantic people and have to "talk science all day to a set of *précieuses ridicules*"'. Quoted in Myers, *The Bluestocking Circle*, pp. 294–95. He also 'refers disparagingly to his aunt and her "Aspasias"' (ibid., p. 295), thus linking this movement with classical learning.

[8] See Myers, *The Bluestocking Circle*, pp. 300–1.

[9] Harriet Guest, 'Bluestocking Feminism', in *Reconsidering the Bluestockings*, ed. by Pohl and Schellenberg, pp. 59–80.

[10] For example, Myers shows that when 'Lucy Martin Donnelly (1870–1948) wrote "The Heart of a Bluestocking" in the *Atlantic Monthly* (October 1908) she celebrates the joys of an academic life [...] and sees herself in a tradition of "Blue Stockings"'. Myers, *The Bluestocking Circle*, p. 299.

Bas-Bleu: Calque de l'anglais *blue-stocking*, issu par ellipse de *The Blue-Stocking Society*, nom donné à un salon littéraire, d'après la couleur des bas portés par un de ses familiers, brillant causeur.

Femme à prétentions littéraires, pédante.[11]

Bas-Bleu: calque from the English term 'bluestocking', a term derived from The Bluestocking Society, the name given to a literary salon, so called because of the colour of the stockings worn by one of its attendees, a brilliant conversationalist.

A woman with literary pretensions, a pedant.[12]

The term 'Le Bas-Bleu' connotes all that was pejorative about the seventeenth-century 'femme savante', particularly unwomanliness, and in this respect it is more absolutely a negative term than 'Bluestocking' (or 'savante'): indeed, the self-declared Bluestocking Hannah More sought to distance herself and the Bluestockings from their French equivalents.[13] That connotation of manliness is evident from the well-known series of forty plates 'Les Bas-Bleus' by Honoré Daumier printed in August 1844 in *Le Charivari* magazine, in which women are ridiculed for neglecting their wifely or motherly duties while studying or are presented as haggard and unattractive in their pursuit of knowledge. Frédéric Soulié's satire, *Physiologie du Bas-Bleu* (1841–42), both makes the link to the 'femme savante' clear from its opening pages—'Molière les appelait des femmes savantes: nous les avons nommées Bas-Bleus' (Molière called them 'femmes savantes'; we call them Bas-Bleus)[14]—and stresses the unwomanliness of the 'bas-bleu' by emphasising the masculine gender of the noun:

Mais j'aime ce nom, qui ne signifie absolument rien, par cela seul qu'il dénonce cette espèce féminine par un mot du genre masculin. Tant que la femme reste blanchisseuse, actrice, couturière, danseuse, cantatrice, reine, on peut écrire grammaticalement parlant: elle est jolie, elle est fine, elle est adroite, elle est bien tournée, elle a une grâce ravissante, elle est d'une beauté parfaite. Mais, du

---

[11] *Dictionnaire de l'Académie française*, <https://www.dictionnaire-academie.fr/>.

[12] It also features with a similar definition in the 8th edition (1935) under 'bas', but not in the 7th edition of 1870, not perhaps having sufficient cultural currency by that point. 'Fig., Bas-bleu, se dit d'une Femme à prétentions littéraires, en souvenir d'un lord anglais à bas bleus qui fréquentait assidûment le salon de lady Montagu' (A woman with literary pretensions, recollecting an English Lord who regularly frequented Lady Montagu's salon). *Dictionnaire de l'Académie française* (Paris: Hachette, 1935), p. 127.

[13] Hannah More, 'The "Bas-Bleu" or Conversation' [1783], published in Hannah More, *Florio: a tale: for fine gentlemen and fine ladies: and, the bas bleu; or, conversation: two poems* (London: Cadell, 1786), pp. 67–89. See Pohl and Schellenberg, 'A Bluestocking Historiography', p. 4; and Moyra Haslett, 'Becoming Bluestockings: Contextualising Hannah More's "The Bas Bleu"', *Journal for Eighteenth-Century Studies*, 33.1 (2010), 89–114.

[14] Frédéric Soulié, *Physiologie du Bas-Bleu* (Paris: La Vigne, 1841–42), p. 5.

moment qu'une femme est *Bas-Bleu*, il faut absolument dire d'elle: il est malpropre, il est prétentieux, il est malfaisant, il est une peste. Cependant le bas-bleu est femme.[15]

But I like this name, which means nothing, for the simple reason that it denounces this feminine figure with a masculine noun. As long as women are laundry-women, actresses, seamstresses, [female] dancers, [female] singers, queens, one can describe them with grammatical correctness: she is pretty, she is delicate, she is graceful, she is well presented, she has ravishing grace, she is a perfect beauty. But from the minute that a woman is a Bas-Bleu [a masculine noun], one must absolutely say of her: he is clumsy, he is pretentious, he is wicked, he is a nuisance. And yet, the Bas-Bleu is a woman.

The masculine noun of 'Bas-bleu' being applied to women suitably reveals the disruption of gender norms that a learned woman represents. Soulié also makes an explicit link back to the salons of the seventeenth century, suggesting that Scudéry, Madame de Sévigné, and Emilie Du Châtelet were 'les premières graines de ces fleurs si rares' (the first seeds of these rare flowers) of the 'bas-bleu aristocrate'.[16]

For Jules Barbey d'Aurevilly (1808–1889), who wrote 'Les Bas-bleus' (1878) as part of his series *Les Œuvres et les hommes*, Scudéry, Sévigné, and d'Aulnoy were not 'bas-bleus' but were 'précieuses', 'd'une insupportable manière d'être' (in an unsufferable manner).[17] For Barbey d'Aurevilly, the 'Bas-Bleu' was a product of the French Revolution and the nineteenth century, and significantly, the term refers to a professional writer (he opposes commercial interest to ability, in a move we have encountered in this book): 'c'est la femme littéraire. C'est la femme qui fait métier et marchandise de littérature. C'est la femme qui se croit cerveau d'homme et demande sa part dans la publicité et dans la gloire' (A Bas-Bleu is a literary woman. A woman who makes a living and business from literature. A woman who thinks she has a man's brain and who demands her share of public attention and glory).[18] His descriptions do however share a link with the pejorative uses of the meaning of 'savante' as denoting false learning or failed aspiration (as in 'faire la sçavante': to play the learned lady): to be a 'Bas-Bleu' 'il ne faut qu'une plume, une écritoire, et un faux orgeuil' (you only need a pen, a writing desk and an inflated sense of arrogance).[19] Barbey also, like Soulié, registers discomfort with the gendering of learning implicit in the phenomenon, not by focusing on the male gender of this term but on the female gender of a new term, 'professoress', as—once

[15] Ibid., p. 6.
[16] Ibid., p. 15.
[17] Jules Barbey d'Aurevilly, 'Les Bas Bleus', in *Les Œuvres et les hommes*, 26 vols (Paris: Amyot, 1860–1909), v (1878), p. xii.
[18] Ibid., p. xii.
[19] Ibid.

again—a way into attacking the phenomenon: 'd'étranges *professoresses* (car le bas-bleuisme bouleverse la langue comme il bouleverse le bon sens) se sont mises à faire solennellement des conférences et ont pu trouver des publics' (strange *professoresses* [for bluestockingism upturns language as it upturns good sense] have solemnly started giving lectures and have found audiences).[20]

The question of whether to 'feminise' professional titles—a question we explored in the Introduction in relation to the quarrel about the term 'autrice' between Marie de Gournay and Guez de Balzac and the wider masculinisation of French heralded by the seventeenth-century grammarians—remains a divisive issue, with the *Académie française* only 'permitting' the use of feminised terms for certain *métiers* and *fonctions* in 2019 (but it has not gone so far as to permit 'l'écriture inclusive').[21] The Anglo-American tradition, possibly because English is rarely an inflected language, prefers 'neutral' terms that are also inclusive of nonbinary or genderqueer identities (either the historically male-gendered but not genderless, such as actor; or a gender-neutral circumlocution: postal worker, firefighter, headteacher, etc).

Next in this line of negative or contested figures for the female intellectual might be the late nineteenth-century/early twentieth-century phenomenon of the 'Girton Girl'. This refers, literally, to women who studied at Girton College in Cambridge, the first college for women founded by Emily Davies in 1869, but the term came to stand more broadly for a certain type of female intellectual. Like 'Bluestocking' and 'savante', the term could have a positive or negative force depending on the context, but its charged meaning derived essentially from a distrust of learned women. Girton College was founded to provide women with an education equal to men's and thus with a specific focus on Classics among other subjects (which contrasts with Newnham College, the other women-only Cambridge college, founded in 1871, which established a curriculum specific to its women students and was involved in wider university curriculum reform).[22] Andrew Lang's late nineteenth-century 'Ballad of the Girton Girl' opens 'She has just "put her gown on" in Girton / She is learned in Latin and Greek' and later says 'She has lectured on Scopas and Myrton'.[23] As Isobel Hurst points out, this poem highlights two features of the 'Girton Girl': that she makes her knowledge public and that Latin and Greek mark her out for distinction because Classics is a 'marker of seriousness'.[24] Or rather, what for men would be a mark of distinction

---

[20] Ibid., p. xvii.

[21] <https://www.academie-francaise.fr/sites/academie-francaise.fr/files/rapport_feminisation_noms_de_metier_et_de_fonction.pdf>. On 'l'écriture inclusive', see <https://www.academie-francaise.fr/actualites/lettre-ouverte-sur-lecriture-inclusive>.

[22] See Isobel Hurst, *Victorian Women Writers and the Classics: The Feminine of Homer* (Oxford: Oxford University Press, 2006), pp. 85–88.

[23] *The Poetical Works of Andrew Lang*, ed. by Mrs. Lang, 4 vols (London: Longmans, Green & Co., 1923), I, 189–90.

[24] Hurst, *Victorian Women*, p. 86.

(this learning, as represented by the gown) becomes for women an image of ridiculous aping. A satirical image in *Punch* by George du Maurier, entitled 'St Valentine's Day at Girton', underscores the prominence of Classics, particularly Greek, with a Girton Girl smoking (a gesture which recalls satirical images of the 'New Woman', that is, a woman seeking radical change), reading a Valentine card from her boyfriend and enjoying its Greek inscription from *Antigone* (the incongruity of this source presumably was intended).[25] The Girton Girl was also queer coded, 'masculine' in her learning: a 1913 biography of Queen Christina of Sweden, reputed in the seventeenth century for lesbianism and cross-dressing, described her as a 'Girton Girl on the throne'.[26]

But 'Girton Girl' was also a term and a type that was defended, particularly in Oscar Wilde's periodical *Woman's World* which sought to give a positive image of women's higher education (Greek played a key role here with Sappho as a role model);[27] and other periodicals tried to 'normalise' the image of the Girton Girl to advocate for higher education.[28] That the image of the Girton Girl should find itself at the heart of topical debates about education reform chimes with a finding of this present study: that 'savante', and, more broadly, the contested identity of the female intellectual, became ideologically charged at a time when ideas of what constituted 'savoir' and how it should be expressed were in flux, subject to significant debate, and indicative of wider cultural currents.

We have not yet shaken off the complex associations entailed by women and learning. In 2019 the then UK Prime Minister Boris Johnson called former UK PM, David Cameron, a 'girly swot': this could be seen as one of the more recent instances of a long line of gendered terms that use the clever woman as a figure of ridicule. Like many of the terms analysed above, it has also been appropriated positively.[29] Evidence for this discomfort and for the enduring negative image of the 'savante' can be found in the most recent definition of the substantive 'savant/e' in the *Dictionnaire de l'Académie française*:

---

[25] *Punch*, 26 February 1876. See also Susanna Cerasuolo, 'We Must Do This Well If We Do It At All': Reports On The First Women's College, Girton, Cambridge', <https://open.conted.ox.ac.uk/resources/documents/%E2%80%98we-must-do-well-if-we-do-it-all%E2%80%99-reports-first-women%E2%80%99s-college-girton-cambridge.>

[26] See Sarah Waters, '"A Girton Girl on a Throne": Queen Christina and Versions of Lesbianism, 1906–1933', *Feminist Review*, 46 (1994), 41–60.

[27] See also, on the performing of Greek in women's colleges, Yopie Prins, *Ladies' Greek: Victorian Translations of Tragedy* (Princeton: Princeton University Press, 2017), pp. 152–201.

[28] See Petra Clark, 'The Girton Girl's "Academical Home": Girton College in the Late-Victorian Periodical Press', *Victorian Periodicals Review*, 52.4 (2019), 659–78 (p. 660); and Isobel Hurst, 'Ancient and Modern Women in the *Woman's World*', *Victorian Studies*, 52.1 (2009), 42–51.

[29] Journalist Steph McGovern wore the 'Girly Swot' t-shirt on BBC1's 'Have I Got News For You?'. It is now merchandise: <https://www.girlyswotshop.co.uk/>.

Personne d'un grand savoir, d'une grande érudition; spécialement, celui, celle qui se distingue dans le domaine de la recherche scientifique (en ce sens, s'emploie surtout au masculin) [...] Marie Curie fut un grand savant ou une grande savante.

Someone with considerable learning and great erudition; specifically, he or she who distinguishes themselves in the domain of academic/scientific research (in this sense, it is mostly used in the masculine) [...] Marie Curie was a great savant or a great savante.[30]

Given the *Académie française*'s inclusion of gendered *métiers* and *fonctions*—see the terms 'autrice' and 'auteure' under 'auteur',—and, in the above entry, the explicit acknowledgement of a possible but not-favoured use of the feminine, the entry's preference for 'savant' to designate a scientist or, more widely, an academic (there is an ambiguity in meaning here) is surely more than a case of a 'neutral' use of a male grammatical term.[31] Instead, it speaks of the long, complex history of the term 'savante' and, behind this, the related gendering of learning, with 'science' being masculinised in this instance. Madeleine de Scudéry might not have made it into the *Académie française* in her lifetime, but some three hundred years later she has made her mark on its dictionary.

---

[30] *Dictionnaire de l'Académie française*: <https://www.dictionnaire-academie.fr/>.

[31] Under 'auteur' in the current online edition is a note: 'La féminisation des noms de métiers et de fonctions se développant dans l'usage, comme l'a constaté le rapport de l'Académie française rendu public le 1er mars 2019, il est à noter que les formes féminines autrice, auteur ou, moins bien, auteure se rencontrent également' (the feminisation of the names of professions or titles has developed according to usage, as stated in the report of this Académie: the feminine forms 'autrice', 'auteur', or the less appropriate, 'auteure', are all used). <https://www.dictionnaire-academie.fr/>.

Bibliography

Primary sources

Paris, Bibliothèque de l'Arsenal, MS Conrart 5418
Paris, Bibliothèque de l'Arsenal, MS Conrart 5422
Paris, Bibliothèque de l'Arsenal, MS Tralage 6542
La Rochelle, Bibliothèque de La Rochelle, MS Tallemant des Réaux 672 and 673
Anacreon, Odae (Paris: Estienne, 1554)
Anacréon, Sapho, Bion et Moschus. Traduction nouvelle en prose, trans. by Julien-Jacques Moutonnet de Clairfons (Paris: Bastien, 1780)
L'Anti-Gournai, ou l'Anti-Gontier, servant de response à l'adieu de l'ame, fait par le pere Gontier sous le nom de la Damoiselle de Gournai ([n.p.]: [n. pub], [n.d.])
Ablancourt, Nicolas Perrot d', trans., *La Retraite des Dix-Mille, de Xénophon, ou l'Expédition de Cyrus contre Artaxerxès* (Paris: Vve Camusat and Le Petit, 1648)
Aubignac, François Hédélin d', *Deux dissertations concernant le poème dramatique, en forme de Remarques sur deux tragédies de M. Corneille intitulées Sophonisbe et Sertorius* (Paris: Brueil, 1663)
Aubignac, Abbé d', *Dissertations contre Corneille*, ed. by Nicholas Hammond and Michael Hawcroft (Exeter: University of Exeter Press, 1995)
Aulnoy, Marie-Catherine Le Jumel de Barneville baronne d', *Contes des fées* (Paris: Barbin, 1697–98)
Aulnoy, Marie-Catherine Le Jumel de Barneville baronne d', *Contes de fées*, ed. by Constance Cagnat-Debœuf (Paris: Gallimard, 2008)
Aurevilly, Jules Barbey d', 'Les Bas Bleus', in *Les Œuvres et les hommes*, 26 vols (Paris: Amyot, 1860–1909), v (1878)
Balzac, Jean Louis Geuz de, 'Lettre à Monsieur Girard', *Œuvres de Monsieur de Balzac*, 2 vols (Paris: Billaine, 1665), i, p. 257
Bayle, Pierre, *Dictionnaire historique et critique par Mr. Pierre Bayle, revue, corrigée et augmentée, cinquième édition*, 4 vols (Amsterdam: Brunel; Leiden: Luchtmans; The Hague: Gosse; Utrecht: Neaulme, 1740).
Belleau, Rémi, *Les odes d'Anacréon ... traduites de grec en françois* (Paris: Wechel, 1556)
Bernard, Catherine, *Brutus, tragédie* (Paris: Gontier, 1691)
Bernier, François, *Abregé de la Philosophie de Gassendi* (Paris: Langlois & Langlois, 1674)
Bertaut, Jean de, *Traduction un peu paraphrasée du deuxiesme livre de l'Aeneide de Virgile* ([n.p]: [n. pub.], 1603)
Boccaccio, Giovanni, *On Famous Women*, trans. by Guido Guarino (London: Allen and Unwin, 1964)
Boileau-Despréaux, Nicolas, *Œuvres diverses du sieur D***, avec le Traité du sublime* (Paris: Thierry, 1674)
Boileau-Despréaux, Nicolas, *Œuvres complètes*, ed. by Françoise Escal, introduction by Antoine Adam (Paris: Gallimard, 1966)
Boivin, Jean, *Apologie d'Homère et Bouclier d'Achille* (Paris: Jouenne, 1715)

BIBLIOGRAPHY   253

Buffet, Marguerite, *Nouvelles Observations sur la langue Françoise [...] avec Les Eloges des Illustres Sçavantes, tant anciennes que modernes* (Paris: Cusson, 1668)

Catullus, *Catullus, et in eum commentarius M. Antonij Mureti* (Venice: Muret, 1554)

Catullus, *Catullus*, trans. by Francis Cornish, 2nd edn by G. P. Goold, Loeb Classical Library 6 (Cambridge, MA: Harvard University Press, 1988)

Certain, Mademoiselle de, *Nouvelles Poésies ou Diverses pièces choisies, tant en vers qu'en prose, de mademoiselle Certain* (Paris: Loyson, 1665)

Chastillon, François Joulet de, *Six oraisons de Ciceron* (Paris: Estienne, 1609)

Chetwood, Kneightly, 'Preface to the Pastorals', in *The Works of Virgil*, trans. by John Dryden (London: Tonson, 1697)

Chevreau, Urbain, *La Belle Lucresse romaine, tragédie* (Paris: Quinet, 1637)

Cicero, *On Ends*, ed. and trans. by H. Rackham, Loeb Classical Library 40 (Cambridge, MA: Harvard University Press, 1914)

Cicero, *M Tulli Ciceronis Philippicae Orationes XIIII* (Bale: Froben, 1551)

Cicero, *Philippic II*, ed. and trans. by D. R. Shackleton Bailey, rev. by John T. Ramsey and Gesine Manuwald, Loeb Classical Library 189 (Cambridge, MA: Harvard University Press, 2010)

Cokain, Aston, *Small Poems of Divers Sorts* (London: Godbid, 1658)

Colletet, Guillaume, *Discours du poëme bucolique où il est traitté de l'églogue, del'idylle, et de la bergerie* (Paris: Chamhoudry, 1657)

Cousin, Victor, *La Jeunesse de Mme de Longueville: études sur les femmes illustres et la société du XVIIe siècle* (Paris: Dider, 1853)

Cousin, Victor, *La Société française au XVIIe siècle d'après Le Grand Cyrus de Mlle de Scudéry* (Paris: Didier, 1858)

Dacier, Anne [Le Fèvre], *Callimachi Cyrenaei Hymni* (Paris: Mabre-Cramoisy, 1675)

Dacier, Anne [Le Fèvre], *Les poésies d'Anacréon et de Sapho* (Paris: Thierry, 1681)

Dacier, Anne [Le Fèvre], *Les Comédies de Plaute*, 3 vols (Paris: Thierry and Barbin, 1683)

Dacier, Anne, *Le Plutus et les Nuées d'Aristophane* (Paris: Thierry and Barbin, 1684)

Dacier, Anne, *Les Comédies de Térence*, 3 vols (Paris: Thierry and Barbin, 1688)

Dacier, Anne, *L'Iliade d'Homère*, 3 vols (Paris: Rigaud, 1711)

Dacier, Anne, *Des Causes de la Corruption du Goust* (Paris: Rigaud, 1714)

Dacier, Anne, *Homère defendu contre l'Apologie du R. P. Hardouin ou Suite des Causes de la Corruption du Goust* (Paris: Coignard, 1716)

Dacier, Anne, *L'Odyssée d'Homere traduite en francois avec des remarques par Madam Dacier*, 3 vols (Paris: Rigaud, 1716)

Dacier, Anne, *L'Iliade d'Homère, traduite en françois [...] Seconde édition [...] avec quelques réflexions sur la préface angloise de M. Pope*, 3 vols (Paris: Rigaud, 1719)

Dacier, Anne and André Dacier, *Réflexions morales de l'empereur Marc Antonin avec des remarques*, 2 vols (Paris: Barbin, 1691)

Dacier, Anne and André Dacier, *Vies des hommes illustres de Plutarque, traduites en français, avec des remarques* (Paris: Barbin, 1694)

Dassoucy, Charles, *L'Ovide en belle humeur de Mr Dassoucy, enrichi de toutes ses figures burlesques* (Paris: Sercy, 1650)

Dehénault, Jean, 'Traduction du commencement du poème de Lucrèce', in *Recueil de pièces curieuses et nouvelles tant en prose qu'en vers*, 2 vols (The Hague: Moetjens, 1694), II, pp. 330–33

Dehénault, Jean, *Les Œuvres de Jean Dehénault*, ed. by Frédéric Lachèvre (Paris: Champion, 1922)

254 BIBLIOGRAPHY

Descartes, René, *Discours de la méthode*, ed. by Laurent Renault (Paris: Garnier, 2000)

Deshoulières, Antoinette, *Genséric* (Paris: Barbin, 1680)

Deshoulières, Antoinette, *Poésies de Madame Des Houlières* (Paris: Vve de Mabre-Cramoisy, 1688)

Deshoulières, Antoinette, *Poésies de Madame Deshoulières* (Paris: Villette, 1693)

Deshoulières, Antoinette, *Poésies de Madame Deshoulières, édition nouvelle augmentée d'un tiers* (Amsterdam: Wetstein, 1694)

Deshoulières, Antoinette, *Poésies de Madame Deshoulières* (Paris: Villette, 1695)

Deshoulières, Antoinette, *Poësies de Mme Deshoulières. Nouvelle édition, augmentée de toutes ses oeuvres posthumes [et des poësies de Mlle Deshoulières]* (Paris: Villette, 1705)

Deshoulières, Antoinette, *Poésies de Madame et Mlle Deshoulieres* (Brussels: Vve Foppens, 1740)

Deshoulières, Antoinette, *Œuvres de Mme et de Mlle Deshoulières, Nouvelle édition*, 2 vols (Paris: Libraires associés, 1754)

Deshoulières, Antoinette, *L'Enchantement des chagrins. Poésies Complètes*, ed. by Catherine Hémon-Fabre and Pierre-Eugène Leroy (Paris: Bartillat, 2005)

Deshoulières, Antoinette, *Madame Deshoulières: Poésies*, ed. by Sophie Tonolo (Paris: Garnier, 2010)

Desmarets de Saint-Sorlin, Jean, *La Comparaison de la langue et de la poésie française avec la grecque et la latine* (Paris: Billaine, 1670)

Desmarets de Saint-Sorlin, Jean, *Défense de la poésie et de la langue française* (Paris: Le Gras, 1675)

Dictionnaire de l'Académie française, 2 vols (Paris: Coignard, 1694)

Dictionnaire de l'Académie française, 6th edn (Paris: Didot frères, 1835)

Dictionnaire de l'Académie française, 8th edn (Paris: Hachette, 1935)

Dictionnaire de l'académie française, 9th edn, https://www.dictionnaire-academie.fr

Dictionnaire universel françois et latin [Dictionnaire de Trévoux], 4th edn, 6 vols (Paris: Vve Delaulne, 1743)

Dionysus of Halicarnassus, *Anquitatum Romanarum* (Paris: R. Estienne, 1546)

Dionysus of Halicarnassus, *De compositione* (Paris: R. Estienne, 1547)

Dionysus of Halicarnassus, *Roman Antiquities*, trans. by Earnest Cary, Loeb Classical Library 319 (Cambridge, MA: Harvard University Press, 1937)

Du Bellay, Joachim, *La Deffence et illustration de la langue française* (Paris: Angelier, 1549)

Du Bellay, Joachim, *Divers jeux rustiques and et autres œuvres poétiques* (Paris: Morel, 1558)

Du Bellay, Joachim, *La Deffence et l'illustration de la langue françoyse*, ed. by Jean-Charles Monferran (Geneva: Droz, 2007)

Du Bosc, Jacques, *L'Honnête femme* (Paris: Billaine, 1632)

Du Four de la Crespelière, Claude-Denis, *Les Odes amoureuses, charmantes et bachiques des poètes grecs Anacréon, Sappho et Théocrite* (Paris: Loyson, 1670)

Du Perron, Jacques Davy, *Partie du premier livre de l'Ænéide de Virgile* (Paris: Estienne, 1610)

Durand, Catherine, *Les Belles Grecques, ou l'Histoire des plus fameuses courtisanes de la Grèce et Dialogues nouveaux des galantes modernes* (Paris: Veuve Saugrain and Prault, 1712)

Du Ryer, Pierre, *Lucrèce, tragédie* (Paris: Sommaville, 1638)

Du Ryer, Pierre, *Les Histoires de Hérodote* (Paris: Sommaville, 1645)

Du Ryer, Pierre, *Les Décades de Tite-Live*, 2 vols (Paris: Sommaville, 1653)

Estienne, Robert, *Dictionnaire françois-latin* (Paris: Estienne, 1539)

BIBLIOGRAPHY 255

Faure, Abbé, *Homère danseur de corde* (Paris: Prault, 1716)

Fontenelle, Bernard de, *Poésies pastorales de M.D.F. Avec un traité sur la nature de l'eglogue, et une digression sur les anciens et les modernes* (Paris: Guerout, 1688)

Fontenelle, Bernard de, 'Of Pastorals', in René le Bossu, *Epick Poetry*, trans. by Pierre Motteux (London: Bennet, 1695), pp. 294–95

Fougerolles, François, *Le Diogène français tiré du grec ou Diogène Laërtien touchant les vies traduites et paraphrasées sur le grec par M. François de Fougerolles* (Lyon: Huguetan, 1601)

Fourmont, Etienne, *Examen pacifique de la querelle de Madame Dacier et Monsieur de la Motte*, 2 vols (Paris: Rollin, 1716)

Furetière, Antoine, *Nouvelle allégorique ou Histoire des derniers troubles arrivés au Royaume d'Éloquence* (Paris: Luyne, 1658)

Furetière, Antoine, *Dictionnaire universel* (Amsterdam: Leers, 1690)

Fuzelier, Louis, *Arlequin defenseur d'Homère*, in *Le Théâtre de la Foire ou l'Opéra Comique*, 8 vols (Paris: Ganeau, 1721)

Gacon, François, *Les Odes d'Anacréon et de Sapho en vers français* (Rotterdam: Fritsch and Böhm, 1712)

Gacon, François, *Homère vengé ou Réponse à M. de La Motte sur l'Iliade* (Paris: Ganeau, 1715)

Gaillard, Antoine, *La furieuse monomachie de Gaillard et de Braquemart*, in *Œuvres du Sieur Gaillard* (Paris: Dugast, 1634), pp. 1–26

Gaillard, Henri, *Rhétorique à l'usage des jeunes demoiselles* (Paris: Leclerc, 1748)

Galaup de Chasteuil, Pierre de, *Discours sur les Arcs triomphaux dressez en la ville d'Aix, à l'heureuse arrivée de Monseigneur le Duc de Bourgogne, et de Monseigneur le duc de Berry* (Aix: Adibert, 1701)

Galaup de Chasteuil, Pierre de, *Apologie des anciens historiens, et des troubadours, ou poetes provencaux* (Avignon: Perier, 1704)

Gassendi, Pierre, *Syntagma philosophiae Epicuri cum refutationibus dogmatum quae contra fidem christianam ab eo asserta sunt* (Lyon: Guillaume Barbier, 1647)

Giraldi, Giglio Gregorio, *Historiae poetarum tam Graecorum quam Latinorum dialogi decem* (Basel, 1545)

Gournay, Marie de, *Le Promenoir de Monsieur de Montaigne, par sa fille d'alliance* (Paris: Angelier, 1594)

Gournay, Marie de, *Versions de quelques pieces de Virgile, Tacite et Salluste avec L'Institution de Monsieur, frère unique du roi* (Paris: Fleury, 1619)

Gournay, Marie de, *L'Ombre de la Damoiselle de Gournay* (Paris: Libert, 1626)

Gournay, Marie de, *Les Advis ou les presens de la Damoiselle de Gournay* (Paris: Tousssaint de Bray, 1634)

Gournay, Marie de, *Les Advis ou les presens de la Damoiselle de Gournay, troisième edition* (Paris: Du Bray, 1641)

Gournay, Marie de, *Apology for the Woman Writing and Other Works*, trans. by Richard Hillman and Colette Quesnel, The Other Voice in Early Modern Europe (Chicago: Chicago University Press, 2002)

Gournay, Marie de, *Œuvres complètes*, ed. by Jean-Claude Arnould, Évelyne Berriot, Claude Blum, Anna Lia Franchetti, Marie-Claire Thomine, and Valerie Worth-Stylianou, 2 vols (Paris: Champion 2002)

Granet, François, *Recueil de dissertations sur plusieurs tragédies de Corneille et de Racine*, 2 vols (Paris: Gissey, 1739)

Greek Lyric I: Sappho and Alcaeus, ed. and trans. by David A. Campbell, Loeb Classical Library 142 (Cambridge, MA: Harvard University Press, 1982)

256   BIBLIOGRAPHY

Greek Lyric II: Anacreon, Anacreontea, Choral Lyric from Olympus to Alcman, ed. and trans. by David Campbell, Loeb Classical Library 143 (Cambridge, MA: Harvard University Press, 1993)

Guéret, Gabriel, *Le Parnasse Réformé* (Paris: Jolly, 1668)

Guillaume, Jacquette, *Les Dames Illustres* (Paris: Jolly, 1665)

Haitze, Pierre-Joseph de, *Dissertations sur divers points de l'histoire de Provence* (Anvers: de l'imprimerie plantinienne, 1704)

Hardouin, Jean, *Apologie d'Homère* (Paris: Rigaud, 1716)

Hay, Mary, 'Mary of Jars, Lady of Gournay', in *Female Biography; or Memoirs of Illustrious and Celebrated Women of All Ages and Countries*, 6 vols (London: Phillips, 1803), II, pp. 445–51

Heinsius, Daniel, *Pub. Terentii Comoediae sex* (Amsterdam: Janson, 1618)

Horace, *Odes and Epodes*, ed. and trans. by Niall Rudd, Loeb Classical Library 33 (Cambridge, MA: Harvard University Press, 2004)

Huet, Pierre-Daniel, 'Traité de l'origine des romans', in *Poétiques du roman. Scudéry, Huet, Du Plaisir et autres textes théoriques et critiques du XVIIe siècle sur le genre romanesque*, ed. by Camille Esmein (Paris: Champion, 2004), pp. 441–535

Hutchinson, Lucy, *The Works of Lucy Hutchinson, Vol. 1: The Translation of Lucretius: Part 1 Introduction and Text*, ed. by Ashley Reid Barbour, David Norbrook, and Maria Cristina Zerbino (Oxford: Oxford University Press, 2011)

Irailh, Augustin Simon, *Querelles litteraires ou mémoires pour servir à l'histoire des révolutions de la république des lettres, depuis Homère jusqu'à nos jours*, 4 vols (Paris: Durand, 1761)

Journal des Sçavans (Paris, 1665–1792)

Journal de Trévoux (Trévoux, 1701–67)

Journal Littéraire (The Hague, 1713–37)

La Fontaine, Jean de, *Recueil de poésies diverses dédié à Mgr le Prince de Conti par M. de la Fontaine*, 2 vols (Paris: Le Petit, 1671)

La Fontaine, Jean de, *Œuvres complètes*, ed. by Pierre Clarac (Paris: Seuil, 1965)

La Fontaine, Jean de, *Les Amours de Psyché et de Cupidon*, ed. by Françoise Charpentier (Paris: Garnier-Flammarion, 1990)

La Force, Charlotte-Rose Caumont de, *Les Contes des contes* (Paris: Benard, 1698)

La Forge, Jean de, *Le Cercle des femmes sçavantes* (Paris: Loyson, 1663)

Lambert, Marie-Thérèse de Marguenat de Courcelles marquise de, *Œuvres de Madame la Marquise de Lambert, avec un abrégé de sa vie* (Lausanne: Bousquet, 1748)

La Motte, Antoine Houdar de, *Le Premier livre de l'Iliade d'Homère en vers français* (Paris: Emery, 1701)

La Motte, Antoine Houdar de, 'Ode I. À Madame Dacier. Sur son Anacréon', in *Odes de M. D**** (Paris: Dupuis, 1707), pp. 87–89

La Motte, Antoine Houdar de, *L'Iliade, poëme avec un discours sur Homère* (Paris: Dupuis, 1714)

La Motte, Antoine Houdar de, *Réflexions sur la Critique*, 3 vols (Paris: Dupuis, 1715)

La Motte, Antoine Houdar de, *Réflexions sur la Critique, second édition corrigée et augmentée* (Paris: Dupuis, 1716)

La Motte, Antoine Houdar de, *Œuvres de Monsieur Houdar de La Motte*, 2 vols (Paris: Prault, 1754)

La Motte, Antoine Houdar de, 'Discours sur l'églogue', ed. by Nathalie Dauvois, in *Textes critiques. Les raisons du sentiment*, ed. by Françoise Gevrey and Béatrice Guion (Paris: Champion, 2002), pp. 767–802

BIBLIOGRAPHY   257

Lang, Andrew, *The Poetical Works of Andrew Lang*, ed. by Mrs. Lang, 4 vols (London: Longmans, Green & Co., 1923)

La Roche-Guilhen, Anne de, *Arioviste, histoire romaine* (Paris: Babrin, 1674–75)

La Roche-Guilhen, Anne de, *Intrigues amoureuses de quelques anciens Grecs* (The Hague: van Bulderen, 1690)

La Roche-Guilhen, Anne de, *Amours de Neron* (The Hague: Troyel, 1695)

La Roche-Guilhen, Anne de, *Sapho ou l'heureuse inconstance* (The Hague: Troyel, 1695)

La Roche-Guilhen, Anne de, *Histoire des favorites* (Amsterdam: Marret, 1697)

La Roche-Guilhen, Anne de, *Histoires curieuses ou dernières ouvrages de Mlle de La Roche-Guilhen* (Amsterdam: Marret, 1709)

La Roche-Guilhen, Anne de, 'Astérie ou Tamerlan', in *Œuvres de Madame de Villedieu*, 12 vols (Paris: Compagnie des Libraires, 1721), xii, pp. 1–150

La Roche-Guilhen, Anne de, *La Nouvelle Talestris, histoire galante* (Amsterdam: Marret, 1721)

La Suze, Henriette Coligny de, *Poésies de Madame la Comtesse de la Suze* (Paris: Sercy, 1666)

Lauvergne, Madame de, *Recueil de poésies* (Paris: Barbin, 1680)

Laval, Antoine de, *Desseins de professions nobles et publiques* (Paris: Langelier, 1605)

La Vilate, François Cartaud de, *Essai historique et philosophique sur le goût* (Paris: Maudouyt, 1736)

Le Fèvre, Tanneguy, *Tanaquili Fabri Epistolae* (Saumur: Lesnier, 1659)

Le Fèvre, Tanneguy, *Anacreontis et Sapphonis Carmina* (Saumur: Lesnier, 1660)

Le Fèvre, Tanneguy, *Les vies des poètes grecs, en abrégé* (Paris: Sercy, 1665)

Le Fèvre, Tanneguy, *Méthode pour commencer les humanités grecques et latines* (Saumur: Péan, 1672)

Le Moyne, Pierre, *Gallerie des femmes fortes* (Paris: Sommaville, 1647)

Le Pons, Jean-François, *Lettre à M*** sur l'Iliade de M. de la Motte* (Paris: Seneuze, 1714)

L'Héritier de Villandon, Marie-Jeanne, *Le Triomphe de Madame Des-Houlières, receue dixième muse au Parnasse* (Paris: Mazuel, 1694)

L'Héritier de Villandon, Marie-Jeanne, *Œuvres mêlées, contenant L'innocente tromperie; L'avare puni, Les enchantements de l'éloquence; Les aventures de finette, nouvelles, et autres ouvrages, en vers et en prose de Mlle L'H***, avec le Triomphe de Mme Des Houlières, tel qu'il a été composé par Mlle L'H**** (Paris: Guignard, 1696)

L'Héritier de Villandon, Marie-Jeanne, *L'Apothéose de Mademoiselle de Scudéry* (Paris: Moreau, 1702)

L'Héritier de Villandon, Marie-Jeanne, *L'Erudition Enjouée ou Nouvelles sçavantes, satyriques et galantes, écrites à une dame Françoise qui est à Madrid* (Paris: Ribou, 1703)

L'Héritier de Villandon, Marie-Jeanne, 'L'Érudition enjouée ou nouvelles sçavantes, satyriques, et galantes, Écrite à une Dame Françoise, qui est à Madrid', in *Mélanges serieux, comiques et d'érudition* (Paris: Ribou, 1704)

L'Héritier de Villandon, Marie-Jeanne, *La Tour ténébreuse et les jours lumineux, contes anglais* (Paris: Veuve de Barbin, 1705)

L'Héritier de Villandon, Marie-Jeanne, *La Pompe Dauphine ou Nouvelle Relation du Temple de Mémoire et des Champs Elysées* (Paris: Veuve Saugrain, 1711)

L'Héritier de Villandon, Marie-Jeanne, *Les Epîtres héroïques d'Ovide* (Paris: Brunet fils, 1732)

Limojon de Saint-didier, Ignace François, 'L'Iliade, tragi-comédie', in *Le Voyage du Parnasse*, 2 vols (Rotterdam: Fritsch and Bohm, 1717), ii, pp. 267–317

258   BIBLIOGRAPHY

Livy, *History of Rome, Volume 1, Books 1–2*, trans. by O. B. Foster, Loeb Classical Library 114 (Cambridge, MA: Harvard University Press, 1919)

Longepierre, Hilaire-Bernard de, *Les Poésies de Anacréon et de Sapho* (Paris: Émery, 1684)

Longepierre, Hilaire-Bernard de, *Les idylles de Bion et de Moschus* (Paris: Aubouin, Emery, and Clousier, 1686)

Longepierre, Hilaire-Bernard de, *Les idylles de Théocrite* (Paris: Aubouin, Emery, and Clousier, 1688)

Longinus, *Dionysii Longini rhetoris praestantissimi liber de grandi, siue sublimi orationis genere* (Basel: Robortello, 1554)

Lucretius, *On the Nature of Things*, trans. by W. H. D. Rouse, rev. by Martin F. Smith, Loeb Classical Library 181 (Cambridge, MA: Harvard University Press, 1924)

Le Manuscrit 673 de Tallemant des Réaux, ed. by Vincenette Maigne (Paris: Klincksieck, 1994)

Marivaux, Pierre de, *L'Homère travesty ou l'Iliade en vers burlesques* (Paris: Prault, 1716)

Marolles, Michel de, *Les œuvres de Virgile traduites en prose* (Paris: Quinet, 1649)

Marolles, Michel de, *Le Poète Lucrèce latin et français de la traduction de M. D. M* (Paris: Quinet, 1650)

Marolles, Michel de, *Mémoires de Michel de Marolles*, 2 vols (Paris: Sommaville, 1656–57)

Marolles, Michel de, *Les Six comédies de Térence* (Paris: Lamy, 1659)

Marolles, Michel de, *Les Six livres de Lucrèce de la nature des choses* (Paris: Luyne, 1659)

Marolles, Michel de, *Les Épistres Héroïdes d'Ovide* (Paris: Lamy, 1661)

Marolles, Michel de, *Les Six livres de Lucrèce de la nature des choses* (Paris: Langlois, 1677)

Marolles, Michel de, *Toutes les œuvres de Virgile, traduites en vers françois* (Paris: Langlois, 1673)

Marot, Clément, *Œuvres complètes*, ed. by François Rigolot, 2 vols (Paris: Garnier-Flammarion, 2007–08)

Maubuy, Jean-Zorobabel Aublet de, *Histoire des troubles et des démêlés littéraires: depuis leur origine jusqu'à nos jours*, 2 vols (Amsterdam, 1779)

Le Mercure Galant (Paris: 1672–74)

Le Mercure Galant (Paris: 1678–1714)

Ménage, Gilles, *Observations sur la langue française*, 2 vols (Paris: Barbin, 1676)

Ménage, Gilles, *Discours de Ménage sur l'Heautontimorumenos de Térence* (Utrecht: Schouten, 1690)

Ménage, Gilles, *Historia Mulierum Philosopharum* [The History of Women Philosophers] (Lyon: Rigaud, 1690)

Montaigne, Michel de, *Les Essais de Michel Seigneur de Montaigne, Édition nouvelle* (Paris: Angelier, 1595)

Montaigne, Michel de, *Les Essais*, ed. by Alexandre Micha, 3 vols (Paris: Garnier-Flammarion, 1969)

Montaigne, Michel de, *Les Essais*, ed. by Michel Magnien, Catherine Magnien-Simonin, and Alain Legros (Paris: Gallimard, 2007)

More, Hannah, *Florio: a tale: for fine gentlemen and fine ladies: and, the bas bleu; or, conversation: two poems* (London: Cadell, 1786)

Moutonnet-Clairfons, Julien-Jacques, *Anacréon, Sapho, Bion et Moschus: traduction nouvelle en prose, suivie de la 'Veillée des fêtes de Vénus' et d'un choix de pièces de différents auteurs* (Paris: Le Boucher, 1773)

Murat, Henriette-Julie de Castelnau Comtesse de, *Histoires sublimes et allégoriques, par Madame le Comtesse D***, dédiées aux fées modernes* (Paris: Delaulne, 1699)

Murat, Madame de [Henriette-Julie de Castelnau, Comtesse de], *Journal pour Mademoiselle de Menou*, ed. by Geneviève Clermidy-Patard (Paris: Classiques Garnier, 2014)

BIBLIOGRAPHY   259

Nicole, Claude, *Recueil de diverses pieces choisies d'Horace, d'Ovide, Catulle, Martial, et Anacreon. Par Monsieur le President Nicole* (Paris: Sercy, 1666)

Nicot, Jean, *Dictionnaire françois-latin* (Paris: Du Puys, 1573)

Nostredame, Jean de, *Les vies des plus célèbres et anciens Poètes provensaux, qui ont floury du temps des comtes de Provence* (Lyon: Marsilii, 1575)

Nouveau dictionnaire de l'académie française, 2 vols (Paris: Coignard, 1718)

Le Nouveau Mercure Galant (Paris, 1677)

Le Nouveau Mercure Galant (Paris, 1714–16)

Le Nouveau Mercure (Paris, 1717–21)

Ovid, *Metamorphoses, Volume I: Books 1–8*, trans. by Frank Justus Miller, rev. by G. P. Goold, Loeb Classical Library 42 (Cambridge, MA: Harvard University Press, 1916)

Ovid, *Fasti*, trans. by James G. Frazer, rev. by G. P. Goold, Loeb Classical Library 253 (Cambridge, MA: Harvard University Press, 1931)

Oxford English Dictionary Online: https://www.oed.com/

Perrault, Charles, *Parallèle des Anciens et des Modernes en ce qui regarde les arts et les sciences. Dialogues. Avec le Poème du Siècle de Louis le Grand, et une Épître en vers sur le Génie* (Paris: Coignard, 1688)

Perrault, Charles, *Grisélidis, nouvelle. Avec le conte de Peau d'Âne et celui des Souhaits ridicules* (Paris: Coignard, 1694)

Perrault, Charles, *Griselidis, Nouvelle avec Le Conte de Peau d'Ane et celuy des Souhaits ridicules. Quatrième édition* (Paris: Coignard, 1695)

Perrault, Charles, *Histoires ou contes du temps passé avec des moralités* (Paris: Barbin, 1697)

Perrault, Charles, *Contes* (Paris: Librairie Générale Française, 2006)

Le Petit Robert online: <https://petitrobert-lerobert-com>

Philostratus, *Apollonius of Tyana, Volume I: Life of Apollonius of Tyana, Books 1–4*, ed. and trans. by Christopher P. Jones, Loeb Classical Library 16 (Cambridge, MA: Harvard University Press, 2005)

Pindari Olympia, Pythia, Nemea, Isthmia. Caeterorum octo lyricorum carmina, Alcaei, Sapphus, Stesichori, Ibyci, Anacreontis, Bacchylidis, Simonidis, Alcmanis, nonnulla etiam aliorum (Paris: H. Estienne, 1560)

Plutarch, *Lives I*, trans. by Bernadotte Perrin, Loeb Classical Library 46 (Cambridge, MA: Harvard University Press, 1914)

Poinsinet de Sivry, Louis, *Anacréon, Sapho, Moschus, Bion, Tyrtée, etc. traduits en vers français* (Nancy: Antoine, 1758)

Poullain de la Barre, François, *De l'égalité des sexes; De l'éducation des dames; De l'excellence des hommes*, ed. by Marie-Frédérique Pellegrin (Paris: Vrin, 2011)

Recueil de pièces curieuses et nouvelles, tant en prose qu'en vers, 2 vols (The Hague: Moetjens, 1694)

Recueil de pièces galantes en prose et en vers de Madame la Comtesse de la Suze, d'une autre dame et de Monsieur Pellisson (Paris: Quinet, 1668)

Recueil des portraits et éloges en vers et en prose, dédié à son Altesse Royale Mademoiselle (Paris: Sercy and Barbin, 1659)

*Remarques sur la tragédie de Sophonisbe de Mr Corneille envoyées à Madame la Duchesse de R** par Monsieur L. D.* (Paris: Sercy, 1663)

Remerciment des Beurrières (Niort, 1610)

Richelet, Pierre, *Dictionnaire de la langue française* (Geneva: Wider, 1680)

Richer, Louis, *L'Ovide Bouffon, ou les Métamorphoses travesties en vers burlesques* (Paris: Quinet, 1649)

Roederer, Pierre-Louis, *Fragments de divers mémoires pour servir à l'histoire de la société polie en France* (Paris: Didot Frères, 1834)

260   BIBLIOGRAPHY

Ronsard, Pierre de, *Œuvres complètes*, ed. by Paul Laumonier, 7 vols (Paris: Société des Textes Français Modernes, 2009)

Sainctonge, Louise-Geneviève de, *Diverses poésies* (Dijon: Fay, 1714)

Saint-Évremond, Charles de, *La Comédie des Académistes* ([n.p.]: [n.pub.], [n.d.])

Saint-Simon, Louis de Rouvroy, duc de, *Mémoires*, 7 vols (Paris: Gallimard, Bibliothèque de la Pléiade, 1963)

Sainte-Beuve, Charles-Augustin, *Portraits de femmes*, ed. by Gérald Antoine (Paris: Gallimard, 1998)

Sallust, *The War with Catiline. The War with Jugurtha*, ed. by John T. Ramsey, trans. by J. C. Rolfe, Loeb Classical Library 116 (Cambridge, MA: Harvard University Press, 2013)

Scudéry, Georges de, *Ibrahim ou le Grand Bassa*, 4 vols (Paris: Sommaville, 1641–4)

Scudéry, Georges de, *Ibrahim ou le grand Bassa*, ed. by Rosa Pellegrini and Antonella Arrigoni (Paris: Presses de l'Université de Paris-Sorbonne, 2003)

Scudéry, Georges and Madeleine de, *Les Femmes illustres ou les harangues héroïques* (Paris: Sommaville, 1642)

Scudéry, Georges and Madeleine de, *Artamène ou le grand Cyrus*, 10 vols (Paris: Courbé, 1649–53)

[Scudéry, Madeleine de?], *Lettres amoureuses de divers auteurs de son temps* (Paris: Courbé, 1641)

Scudéry, Madeleine de, *Clélie, histoire romaine*, 10 vols (Paris: Courbé, 1654–60)

Scudéry, Madeleine de, *Conversations sur divers sujets*, 2 vols (Paris: Barbin, 1680)

Scudéry, Madeleine de, *'De l'air galant' et autres Conversations*, ed. by Delphine Denis (Paris: Champion, 1998)

Scudéry, Madeleine de, *Clélie, Histoire romaine*, ed. by Chantal Morlet-Chantalat, 5 vols (Paris: Champion, 2001–05)

Scudéry, Madeleine de, *The Story of Sapho*, trans. by Karen Newman, The Other Voice in Early Modern Europe (Chicago: Chicago University Press, 2003)

Scudéry, Madeleine de, *Selected Letters, Orations, and Rhetorical Dialogues*, trans. by Jane Donawerth and Jane Strongson, The Other Voice in Early Modern Europe (Chicago: Chicago University Press, 2004)

Scudéry, Madeleine de, *Clélie, histoire romaine*, ed. by Delphine Denis (Paris: Gallimard, 2006)

Scudéry, Madeleine de, *Lucrèce and Brutus: Glory in the Land of Tender*, ed. and trans. by Sharon Nell, The Other Voice in Early Modern Europe: The Toronto Series 84 (Toronto: Iter Press, 2021)

Scudéry, Madeleine de, Paul Pellisson et leurs amis, *Chroniques du Samedi. Suivis de pièces diverses*, ed. by Alain Niderst, Delphine Denis and Myriam Dufour-Maître (Paris: Champion, 2002)

Sévigné, Marie de Rabutin-Chantal de, *Lettres de Madame de Sévigné de sa famille et de ses amis* (Paris: Hachette, 1862)

Sévigné, René-Renaud, *Correspondance du chevalier de Sévigné et de Christine de France, duchesse de Savoi*, ed. by Jean Lemoine and Frédéric Saulnier (Paris: Renouard, 1911)

Somaize, Antoine Baudeau, *Le Grand dictionnaire des prétieuses* (Paris: Ribou, 1661)

Sorel, Charles, *La Bibliothèque française* (Paris: Compagnie des Libraires, 1667)

Soulié, Frédéric, *Physiologie du Bas-Bleu* (Paris: La Vigne, 1841–42)

Tacitus, *Histories: Books 1–3*, trans. by Clifford H. Moore, Loeb Classical Library 111 (Cambridge, MA: Harvard University Press, 1925)

Tallemant des Réaux, Gédéon, *Historiettes*, ed. by Antoine Adam, 2 vols (Paris: Gallimard, 1961)

Tallemant des Réaux, Gédéon, *Historiettes*, ed. by Michel Jeanneret and Antoine Adam (Paris: Gallimard, 2013)

Terence, *The Woman of Andros. The Self-Tormentor. The Eunuch*, ed. and trans. by John Barsby, Loeb Classical Library 22 (Cambridge, MA: Harvard University Press, 2001)

Terence, *Phormio. The Mother-in-Law. The Brothers*, ed. and trans. by John Barsby, Loeb Classical Library 23 (Cambridge, MA: Harvard University Press, 2001)

Terrasson, Jean, *Dissertation critique sur L'Iliade d'Homère*, 2 vols (Paris: Fournier, 1715)

Valerius Maximus, *Memorable Doings and Sayings, Volume II: Books 6–9*, ed. and trans. by D. R Shackleton Bailey, Loeb Classical Library 493 (Cambridge, MA: Harvard University Press, 2000)

Vertron, Claude Guyonnet de, *La Nouvelle Pandore ou les femmes illustres du siècle de Louis le Grand*, 2 vols (Paris: Vve Mazuel, 1698)

Villedieu, Marie-Catherine de [Desjardins], *Alcidamie* (Paris: Barbin, 1661)

Villedieu, Marie-Catherine de [Desjardins], *Manlius* (Paris: Barbin, 1662)

Villedieu, Marie-Catherine de [Desjardins], *Recueil de poésies* (Paris: Barbin, 1662)

Villedieu, Marie-Catherine de [Desjardins], *Nitétis* (Paris: Quinet and Barbin, 1664)

Villedieu, Marie-Catherine de [Desjardins], *Carmente, histoire Grecque par Mademoiselle Desjardins* (Paris: Barbin, 1668)

Villedieu, Madame de, *Cléonice, ou le roman galant* (Paris: Barbin, 1669)

Villedieu, Madame de, *Les Amours des Grands Hommes, par M. de Villedieu* (Paris: Barbin, 1671)

Villedieu, Madame de, *Les Annales galantes de Grèce* (Paris: Barbin, 1687)

Virgil, P. *Virgilii Maronis Opera, interpretatione et notis illustravit Carolus Ruaeus,... ad usum serenissimi Delphini* (Paris: Bernard, 1675)

Virgil, *Eclogues. Georgics. Aeneid: Books 1–6*, trans. by H. Rushton Fairclough, rev. by G. P. Goold, Loeb Classical Library 63 (Cambridge, MA: Harvard University Press, 1916)

Visé, Jean Donneau de, *Deffense de la Sophonisbe de Monsieur de Corneille* (Paris: Barbin, 1663)

Visé, Jean Donneau de, *Deffence du Sertorius de Monsieur de Corneille* (Paris: Barbin, 1663)

Visé, Jean Donneau de, *Jean Donneau de Visé et la querelle de Sophonisbe: écrits contre l'abbé d'Aubignac*, ed. by Bernard J. Bourque (Tübingen: Narr, 2014)

Voltaire, 'Le Siècle de Louis XIV', in *Œuvres historiques*, ed. by René Pomeau (Paris: Gallimard, 1957), pp. 605–127

White, James, *The Clouds. Comedy translated from Aristophanes* (London: Payne, 1759)

Secondary sources (since 1900)

Ahmed, Sara, *The Feminist Killjoy Handbook* (London: Allen Lane, 2023)

Alcover, Madeleine, 'The Indecency of Knowledge', *Rice University Studies*, 64 (1978), 25–39

Alexander, Gavin, Emma Gilby, and Alexander Marr, 'Introduction', in *The Places of Early Modern Criticism*, ed. by Alexander Gavin, Emma Gilby, and Alexander Marr (Oxford: Oxford University Press, 2021), pp. 1–21

Alonge, Tristan, *Racine et Euripide: la révolution trahie* (Geneva: Droz, 2017)

Amossy, Ruth, *La Présentation du soi: ethos et identité verbale* (Paris: Presses Universitaires de la France, 2010)

Andries, Lise, 'Querelles et dialogues des morts au XVIIIe siècle', *Littératures classiques*, 81.2 (2013), 131–46

262 BIBLIOGRAPHY

Angot, E., 'Mme Deshoulières et l'intrigue de Rocroy', *Revue d'Histoire littéraire de la France*, 27.3 (1920), 371–93

Arnould, Jean-Claude, 'Marie de Gournay polémique', *Littératures Classiques*, 59.1 (2006), 237–50

Aronson, Nicole, 'Mademoiselle de Scudéry et l'Histoire Romaine dans "Clélie"', *Romanische Forschungen*, 88 (1976), 183–94

Aronson, Nicole, '"Que diable allait-il faire dans cette galère?": Mlle de Scudéry et les animaux', in *Les Trois Scudéry*, ed. by Alain Niderst (Paris: Klincksieck, 1993), pp. 523–32

Aulotte, Robert, 'Sur quelques traductions d'une ode de Sappho au XVIe siècle', *Bulletin de l'Association Guillaume Budé: Lettres d'humanité*, 17 (1958), 107–22

Ayres-Bennett, Wendy, *Sociolinguistic Variation in Seventeenth-Century France: Methodology and Case Studies* (Cambridge: Cambridge University Press, 2004)

Ayres-Bennett, Wendy, 'Women as Authors, Audience, and Authorities in the French Tradition', in *Women in the History of Linguistics*, ed. by Wendy Ayres-Bennett and Helena Sanson (Oxford: Oxford University Press, 2020), pp. 91–120

Basker, James, 'Criticism and the Rise of Periodical Literature', in *The Cambridge History of Literary Criticism*, ed. by H. B. Nisbet and Clause Rawson, IV: *The Eighteenth Century* (Cambridge: Cambridge University Press, 2005), pp. 316–32

Bastin-Hammou, Malika, 'Anne Dacier et les premières traductions françaises d'aristophane: l'invention du métier de femme philologue', *Littératures classiques*, 72.2 (2010), 85–99

Bauschatz, Cathleen, 'Marie de Gournay and the Crisis of Humanism', in *Humanism in Crisis: The Decline of the French Renaissance*, ed. by Philippe Desan (Ann Arbor, MI: University of Michigan Press, 1991), pp. 279–94

Bauschatz, Cathleen, 'Marie de Gournay's Gendered Images for Language and Poetry', in *Montaigne et Marie de Gournay*, ed. by Marcel Tétel (Paris: Champion, 1997), pp. 251–67

Bauschatz, Cathleen, 'To Choose Ink and Pen: French Renaissance Women's Writing', in *A History of Women's Writing in France*, ed. by Sonya Stephens (Cambridge: Cambridge University Press, 2000), pp. 41–63

Beasley, Faith E., 'Marguerite Buffet et la sagesse mondaine', in *Le Savoir au XVII siècle*, ed. by John D. Lyons and Cara Welch (Tübingen: Narr, 2002), pp. 227–38

Beasley, Faith E., *Salons, History and the Creation of Seventeenth-Century France* (Aldershot: Ashgate, 2006)

Beasley, Faith E., *Versailles meets the Taj Mahal: François Bernier, Marguerite de la Sablière and Enlightening Conversations in Seventeenth-Century France* (Toronto: University of Toronto Press, 2018)

Beasley, Faith E., 'Seventeenth-Century Women Writers and the Novel: a Challenge to Literary History', in *The History of the Novel in French*, ed. by Adam Watt (Cambridge: Cambridge University Press, 2021), pp. 95–112

Beaulieu, Jean-Philippe, 'Marie de Gournay ou l'occultation d'une figure auctoriale', *Renaissance and Reformation*, 24.2 (2000), 23–34

Beaulieu, Jean-Philippe, ed., *D'une écriture à l'autre. Les Femmes et la traduction sous l'Ancien Régime* (Ottawa: Ottawa University Press, 2004)

Beaulieu, Jean-Philippe, '"Moy Traductrice": le façonnement de la figure auctoriale dans le paratexte des traductions de Marie de Gournay', *Renaissance and Reformation*, 35.4 (2012), 119–34

Beaulieu, Jean-Philippe and Hannah Fournier, '"Les interests du sexe": dédicataires féminins et réseaux de sociabilité chez Marie de Gournay', *Renaissance and Reformation*, 28.1 (2004), 47–59

Belle, Marie-Alice, 'Locating Early Modern Women's Translations: Critical and Historiographical Issues', in *Women's Translations in Early Modern England and France*, ed. by Marie-Alice Belle (= *Renaissance and Reformation*, 35.4 (2012)), pp. 5–23

Belle, Marie-Alice and Brenda Hosington, eds, *Thresholds of Translation: Paratexts, Print, and Cultural Exchange in Early Modern Britain (1473–1660)* (Palgrave Macmillan, 2018)

Berg, Elizabeth, 'Recognizing Differences: Perrault's Modernist Esthetic in *Parallèle des Anciens et des Modernes*', *Papers on French Seventeenth-Century Literature*, 18 (1983), 138–45

Bichard-Thomine, Marie-Claire, 'Des métaphores chez Marie de Gournay: réflexion linguistiques et practique littéraire', in *Marie de Gournay et l'édition de 1595*, ed. by Jean-Claude Arnould (Paris: Champion, 1996), pp. 175–92

Bichard-Thomine, Marie-Claire, 'Les Traités linguistiques', in Marie de Gournay, *Œuvres complètes*, ed. by Jean-Claude Arnould, Évelyne Berriot, Claude Blum, Anna Lia Franchetti, Marie-Claire Thomine, and Valerie Worth-Stylianou, 2 vols (Paris: Champion 2002), I, pp. 44–55

Bichard-Thomine, Marie-Claire, 'Les traités sur l'éducation du prince', in Gournay, *Œuvres complètes*, ed. by Jean-Claude Arnould, Évelyne Berriot, Claude Blum, Anna Lia Franchetti, Marie-Claire Thomine, and Valerie Worth-Stylianou, 2 vols (Paris: Champion 2002), I, pp. 98–108

Bombart, Mathilde, *Guez de Balzac et la querelle des Lettres: écriture, polémique et critique dans la France du premier XVIIe siècle* (Paris: Champion, 2007)

Bonnel, Roland and Catherine Rubinger, eds, *Femmes savantes et femmes d'esprit: Women Intellectuals of the French Eighteenth Century* (New York: Peter Lang, 1994)

Bottigheimer, Ruth B., *Fairy Tales: A New History* (New York: Excelsior Editions, 2009)

Bourque, Bernard J., *All the Abbé's Women: Power and Misogyny in Seventeenth-Century France, through the Writings of Abbé d'Aubignac* (Tübingen: Narr, 2015)

Bowden, Caroline, 'Women in Educational Spaces', in *The Cambridge Companion to Early Modern Women's Writing*, ed. by Laura Lunger Knoppers (Cambridge: Cambridge University Press, 2009), pp. 85–96

Brammall, Sheldon, 'The Politics of the Partial Translations of the *Aeneid* by Dudley Digges and Marie de Gournay', *Translation and Literature*, 22.2 (2013), 182–94

Broad, Jacqueline and Karen Green, 'From the Reformation to Marie le Jars de Gournay', in *A History of Women's Political Thought in Europe 1400–1700* (Cambridge: Cambridge University Press, 2009), pp. 110–39

Broad, Jacqueline and Karen Green, 'The Fronde and Madeleine de Scudéry', in *A History of Women's Political Thought in Europe 1400–1700* (Cambridge: Cambridge University Press, 2009), pp. 180–98

Bromilow, Pollie E., 'Power through Print: The Works of Hélisenne de Crenne', in *Women and Power at the French Court, 1483–1563*, ed. by. Susan Broomhall (Amsterdam: Amsterdam University Press, 2018), pp. 287–305

Brown, Hilary, *Women and Early Modern Cultures of Translation: Beyond the Female Tradition* (Oxford: Oxford University Press, 2022)

Bullard, Rebecca, *The Politics of Disclosure, 1674–1725: Secret History Narratives* (London: Pickering and Chatto, 2009)

264 BIBLIOGRAPHY

Burch, Laura J., 'Madeleine de Scudéry: peut-on parler de la femme philosophe?', *Revue philosophique de la France et de l'étranger*, 138.3 (2013), 361–75

Burgwinkle, William, Nicholas Hammond, and Emma Wilson, eds, *The Cambridge History of French Literature* (Cambridge: Cambridge University Press, 2011)

Burke, Peter, *A Social History of Knowledge: From Gutenberg to Diderot* (Cambridge: Polity Press, 2000)

Bury, Emmanuel, 'Madame Dacier', in *Femmes savantes, savoir des femmes: Du crépuscule de la Renaissance à l'aube des Lumières*, ed. by Colette Nativel (Geneva: Droz, 1999), pp. 209–22

Butterworth, Emily, *Poisoned Words: Slander and Satire in Early Modern France* (Cambridge: Legenda, 2006)

Butterworth, Emily, 'Women's Writing in the Sixteenth-Century', in *The Cambridge History of French Literature*, ed. by William Burgwinkle, Nicholas Hammond, and Emma Wilson (Cambridge: Cambridge University Press, 2011), pp. 211–19

Butterworth, Emily, and Rowan Tomlinson, 'Scandal', in *Renaissance Keywords*, ed. by Ita Mac Carthy (Leeds: Legenda, 2013), pp. 80–100

Caigny, Florence de, 'Les commentaires de Marolles sur ses traductions de Lucrèce en prose: vers une réception moderne orientée', in *Traduire Lucrèce. Pour une histoire de la réception française du* De rerum natura *(XVIe–XVIIIe siècle)*, ed. by Philippe Chométy and Michèle Rossellini (Paris: Champion, 2017), pp. 215–32

Calame, Alexandre, *Anne de La Roche-Guilhen: romancière huguenote, 1644–1707* (Geneva: Droz, 1972)

Caldicott, C. E. J., *La carrière de Molière: entre protecteurs et éditeurs* (Amsterdam: Rodopi, 1998)

Calvert, Ian, *Virgil's English Translators: Civil Wars to Restoration* (Edinburgh: Edinburgh University Press, 2021)

Candler Hayes, Julie, *Translation, Subjectivity, and Culture in France and England, 1600–1800* (Stanford: Stanford University Press, 2009)

Caron, Philippe, *Des belles-lettres à la littérature: une archéologie des signes du savoir profane en langue française (1680–1760)* (Louvain: Peeters, 1992)

Cave, Terence, *Pré-histoires: textes troublés au seuil de la modernité* (Geneva: Droz, 1999)

Cerasuolo, Susanna, 'We Must Do This Well if We Do It at all': Reports on the First Women's College, Girton, Cambridge', <https://open.conted.ox.ac.uk/resources/documents/%E2%80%98we-must-do-well-if-we-do-it-all%E2%80%99-reports-first-women%E2%80%99s-college-girton-cambridge>

Chométy, Philippe, 'Du poète-berger au berger-philosophe: Fontenelle, la pastorale et la poésie d'idées', *Revue Fontenelle*, 10 (2012), 63–104

Chométy, Philippe, 'Du *clinamen* au galimatias: l'Imitation de Lucrèce d'Antoinette Deshoulières', in *Traduire Lucrèce. Pour une histoire de la réception française du* De rerum natura *(XVIe–XVIIIe siècle)*, ed. by Philippe Chométy and Michèle Rosellini (Paris: Champion, 2017), pp. 257–84

Chométy, Philippe and Claudine Poulouin, 'Pour un siècle pastoral', *Revue Fontenelle*, 10 (2012), 9–15

Chométy, Philippe and Michèle Rosellini, eds, *Traduire Lucrèce: pour une histoire de la réception française du De rerum natura (XVIe–XVIIIe siècle)* (Paris: Champion, 2017)

Churchill, Laurie J., Phyllis R. Brown and Jane E. Jeffrey, eds, *Women Writing Latin: from Roman Antiquity to Early Modern Europe*, 3 vols, III: *Early Modern Women Writing Latin* (London: Routledge, 2002)

Clark, Petra, 'The Girton Girl's "Academical Home": Girton College in the Late-Victorian Periodical Press', *Victorian Periodicals Review*, 52.4 (2019), 659–78

Clarke, Danielle, 'The Politics of Translation and Gender in the Countess of Pembroke's *Antonie*', *Translation and Literature*, 6.2 (1997), 149–66

Clarke, Danielle, *The Politics of Early Modern Women's Writing* (Harlow: Pearson, 2001)

Clarke, Danielle, 'Translation', in *The Cambridge Companion to Early Modern Women's Writing*, ed. by Laura Lunger Knoppers (Cambridge: Cambridge University Press, 2010), pp. 167–80

Clarke, Danielle and Elizabeth Clarke, eds, *'This Double Voice': Gendered Writing in Early Modern England* (Basingstoke: Palgrave Macmillan, 2000)

Clément, Michèle and Edwige Keller-Rahbé, eds, *Privilèges d'auteurs et d'autrices en France (XVI–XVII siècles). Anthologie critique* (Paris: Garnier Classiques, 2017)

Clermidy-Patard, Geneviève, *Madame de Murat et la 'défense des dames'. Un discours au féminin à la fin du règne de Louis XIV* (Paris: Classiques Garnier, 2012)

Code, Lorraine, *What Can She Know? Feminist Theory and the Construction of Knowledge* (Ithaca: Cornell University Press, 1991)

Conley, John J., *The Suspicion of Virtue: Women Philosophers in Neoclassical France* (Ithaca: Cornell University Press, 2002)

Conley, John J., 'Tutor, Salon, Convent: The Formation of Women Philosophers in Early Modern France', *British Journal for the History of Philosophy*, 27.4 (2019), 786–805

Conley, John J., 'Against Uniformity: Gournay's Philosophy of Language and Literature', *Women Philosophers in Early Modern France*, ed. by Derval Conroy (= *Early Modern French Studies*, 43.1 (2021)), pp. 21–38

Conroy, Derval, 'The Displacement of Disorder: Gynæcocracy and Friendship in Catherine Bernard's *Laodamia* (1689)', *Papers on French Seventeenth-Century Literature*, 67 (2007), 443–64

Conroy, Derval, 'Engendering Equality: Gynæcocracy in Gournay, Poullain de la Barre and Suchon', in *Ruling Women: Government, Virtue and the Female Prince in Seventeenth-Century France*, 2 vols (Basingstoke: Palgrave Macmillan, 2016), I, pp. 83–91

Conroy, Derval, 'A Defence and Illustration of Marie de Gournay: Bayle's Reception of "Cette Savante Demoiselle"', *French Studies Bulletin*, 40.152 (2019), 51–54

Conroy, Derval, 'Casting Models: Female Exempla of the Ancient Near East in Seventeenth-Century French Drama and Gallery Books (1642–62)', in *Beyond Greece and Rome: Reading the Ancient Near East in Early Modern Europe*, ed. by Jane Grogan (Oxford: Oxford University Press, 2020), pp. 212–34

Conroy, Derval, ed., *Towards an Equality of the Sexes in Early Modern France* (London: Routledge, 2021)

Cottegnies, Line, 'Michel de Marolles's 1650 French Translation of Lucretius and its Reception in England', in *Lucretius and the Early Modern*, ed. by David Norbrook, Stephen Harrison, and Philip Hardie (Oxford: Oxford University Press, 2015), pp. 161–89

Cottegnies, Line, John Thompson and Sandrine Parageau, eds, *Women and Curiosity in Early Modern England and France* (Leiden: Brill, 2016)

Couton, Georges, *La Vieillesse de Corneille* (Paris: Maloine 1949)

Cox, Fiona, *Sibylline Sisters: Virgil's Presence in Contemporary Women's Writing* (Oxford: Oxford University Press, 2011)

Cox, Fiona, *Ovid's Presence in Contemporary Women's Writing: Strange Monsters* (Oxford: Oxford University Press, 2017)

Cox, Fiona, 'An Amazon in the Renaissance: Marie de Gournay's Translation of *Aeneid* 2', in *Virgil and his Translators*, ed. by Susanna Braund and Martirosova Torlone (Oxford: Oxford University Press, 2018), pp. 97–106

266   BIBLIOGRAPHY

Cox, Fiona and Elena Theodorakopoulos, eds, *Homer's Daughters: Homer's Presence in Women's Writing in Twentieth-Century and Beyond* (Oxford: Oxford University Press, 2019)

Crawford, Julie, *Mediatrix: Women, Politics, and Literary Production in Early Modern England* (Oxford: Oxford University Press, 2014)

Cuénin, Micheline, *Roman et société sous Louis XIV: Madame de Villedieu (Marie-Catherine Desjardins, 1640–1683)*, 2 vols (Paris: Champion, 1979)

Dawson, Hannah, *The Penguin Book of Feminist Writing* (London: Penguin, 2023)

Debaisieux, Martine, 'Marie de Gournay cont(r)e la tradition: du *Proumenoir de Monsieur de Montaigne* aux versions de l'*Énéide*', *Renaissance and Reformation*, 21.2 (1997), 45–58

Debrosse, Anne, 'Promenades désenchantées en "mer Dangereuse": Madeleine de Scudéry, Sapho et Erinne aux prises avec le monde', *Études Épistémè*, 27 (2015), <http://journals.openedition.org/episteme/464>

Debrosse, Anne, *La Souvenance et le désir: la reception des poétesses grecques* (Paris: Classiques Garnier, 2018)

Defrance, Anne, *Les Contes de fées et les nouvelles de Madame d'Aulnoy, 1690–1698* (Geneva: Droz, 1998)

DeJean, Joan, *Fictions of Sappho: 1546–1937* (Chicago: University of Chicago Press, 1989)

DeJean, Joan, *Tender Geographies: Women and the Origins of the Novel in Early Modern France* (New York: Columbia University Press, 1991)

DeJean, Joan, *Ancients against Moderns: Cultures Wars and the Making of a fin de siècle* (Chicago: Chicago University Press, 1997)

DeJean, Joan, 'Rooms of their Own: Literary Salons in Seventeenth-Century France', in *The Cambridge History of Literary Criticism*, III, *The Renaissance*, ed. by Glyn P. Norton (Cambridge: Cambridge University Press, 2008), pp. 378–83

Delarue, Paul and Marie-Louise Tenèze, *Le Conte Populaire français. Catalogue raisonné des versions de France* (Paris: Maisonneuve and Larose, 2002)

Démoris, René, 'Écriture féminine en *je* et subversion des savoirs chez Mme de Villedieu (*Les Mémoires d'Henriette-Sylvie de Molière*)', in *Femmes savantes, savoir des femmes: du crépuscule de la Renaissance à l'aube des Lumières*, ed. by Colette Nativel (Geneva: Droz, 1999), pp. 197–208

Des Chene, Dennis, *Spirits and Clocks: Machine and Organism in Descartes* (Ithaca: Cornell University Press, 2001)

Deslauriers, Marguerite, 'Marie de Gournay and Aristotle on the Unity of the Sexes', in *Feminist History of Philosophy: The Recovery and Evaluation of Women's Philosophical Thought*, ed. by Eileen O'Neill and Marcy P. Lascano (New York: Springer, 2019), pp. 281–99

Devincenzo, Giovanna, *Marie de Gournay: un cas littéraire* (Paris: Presses de l'Université de Paris-Sorbonne, 2002)

Devincenzo, Giovanna, 'Les "après-diners" de la Rue Saint-Honoré ou Marie de Gournay, amoureuse de la langue française', *Bulletin de la société internationale des amis de Montaigne*, 68 (2018), 105–16

Devincenzo, Giovanna, *Des mots et des femmes à l'origine de la langue française. XVI*e *–XVII*e *siècles* (Paris: Hermann, 2018)

Devincenzo, Giovanna, 'The Rhetoric of Equality: Marie de Gournay, Linguist and Philosopher', in *Towards an Equality of the Sexes in Early Modern France*, ed. by Derval Conroy (New York: Routledge, 2021), pp. 60–73

Devincenzo, Giovanna, '"On ne parle plus ainsi": Marie de Gournay et le destin de la langue française', *Cahiers de recherches médiévales et humanistes*, 43 (2022), 497–510

Dijk, Suzanna van, *Traces de femmes dans le journalisme français du XVIIIe siècle* (Amsterdam: APA Holland University Press, 1988)

Dodds, Lara, and Michelle M. Dowd, 'Happy Accidents: Critical Belatedness, Feminist Formalism, and Early Modern Women's Writing', *Criticism*, 62.2 (2020), 169–93

Donaldson, Ian, *The Rapes of Lucretia: A Myth and its Transformations* (Oxford: Clarendon Press, 1982)

Dousset-Seiden, Christine and Jean-Philippe Grosperrin, eds, *Les Époux Dacier* (= *Littératures Classiques* 72.2 (2010))

Dubois, Claude-Gilbert, 'Autour de l'*Adieu de l'ame du roy Henry de France* (1610) de Marie de Gournay', *Journal of Medieval and Renaissance Studies*, 25.3 (1995), 477–87

Dufour-Maître, Myriam, 'Les "Belles" et les Belles-Lettres: femmes, instances du féminin et nouvelles configurations du savoir', in *Le Savoir au XVIIe siècle*, ed. by John D. Lyons and Cara Welch (Tübingen: Narr, 2003), pp. 35–64

Dufour-Maître, Myriam, 'Les "antipathies": académies des dames savantes et ruelles des précieuses, un discours polémique dans l'espace des Belles-Lettres', *Bonnes lettres / Belles lettres*, ed. by Claudine Poulouin et Jean-Claude Arnould (Paris: Champion, 2006), pp. 271–92

Dufour-Maître, Myriam, *Les Précieuses: naissance des femmes de lettres en France au XVIIe siècle*, 2nd edn (Paris: Champion, 2008)

Dufour-Maître, Myriam, 'Trouble dans la galanterie? Préciosité et questions de genre', *Littératures classiques*, 90.2 (2016), 107–18

Dufour-Maître, Myriam, 'Femmes, querelles galantes du dix-septième siècle et histoire littéraire', in *Women and* Querelles *in Early Modern France*, ed. by Helena Taylor and Kate E. Tunstall (= *Romanic Review*, 112.3 (2021)), pp. 372–88

Duggan, Anne E., 'Clélie, Histoire Romaine, or Writing the Nation', in *Le Savoir au XVIIe siècle*, ed. by John Lyons and Cara Welch (Tübingen: Narr, 2003), pp. 71–79

Duggan, Anne E., *Salonnières, Furies and Fairies: The Politics of Gender and Cultural Change in Absolutist France* (Newark: University of Delaware Press, 2005)

Duggan, Anne E., 'The *Querelle des femmes* and Nicolas Boileau's *Satire X*: Going beyond Perrault', *Early Modern French Studies*, 41.2 (2019), 144–57

Earley, Benjamin, 'Herodotus in Renaissance France', in *Brill's Companion to the Reception of Herodotus in Antiquity and Beyond*, ed. by Jessica Priestley and Vasilika Zali (Leiden: Brill, 2016), pp. 120–42

Ehrman, R. K., 'Terentian Prologues and the Parabases of Old Comedy', *Latomus*, 44.2 (1985), 370–76

Ekstein, Nina, 'A Woman's Tragedy: Catherine Bernard's *Brutus*', *Rivista di letterature moderne e comparate*, 48.2 (1995), 127–39

Ekstein, Nina, 'Appropriation and Gender: The Case of Catherine Bernard and Bernard de Fontenelle', *Eighteenth-Century Studies*, 30.1 (1996), 59–80

Ekstein, Nina, 'Sophonisbe's Seduction: Corneille Writing against Mairet', in *Studies in Early Modern France*, VIII: *Strategic Rewriting*, ed. by D. L. Rubin (Charlottesville: Rookwood Press, 2002), pp. 104–18

Escola, Marc, *Contes de Charles Perrault, essai et dossier* (Paris: Gallimard, 2005)

Evain, Aurore, 'Histoire d'autrice, de l'époque latine à nos jours', *SÊMÉION, Travaux de sémiologie*, 6 (2008), 53–62

Evain, Aurore, Perry Gethner, and Henriette Goldwyn, eds, *Théâtre de femmes de l'Ancien Régime. XVIIe siècle, Tome II, XVIIe siècle* (Paris: Garnier, 2016)

268   BIBLIOGRAPHY

Evain, Aurore, Perry Gethner, Henriette Goldwyn, eds, with the collaboration of Derval Conroy, Séverine Genieys-Kirk, and Alicia C. Montoya, *Théâtre de femmes de l'Ancien Régime, Tome III, XVIIe–XVIIIe siècles* (Paris: Garnier, 2022)

Ezell, Margaret J. M., *Writing Women's Literary History* (Baltimore and London: Johns Hopkins University Press, 1993)

Fabre-Serris, Jacqueline, 'Anne Dacier (1681), Renée Vivien (1903): Or What Does It Mean for a Woman to Translate Sappho?', in *Women Classical Scholars: Unsealing the Fountain from the Renaissance to Jacqueline de Romilly*, ed. by Rosie Wyles and Edith Hall (Oxford: Oxford University Press, 2016), pp. 78–102

Farnham, Fern, *Madam Dacier: Scholar and Humanist* (Monterey, CA: Angel Press, 1976)

Ferguson, Margaret W., *Dido's Daughters: Literacy, Gender, and Empire in Early Modern England and France* (Chicago: Chicago University Press, 2003)

Fernbach, Isabelle, 'From Copy to Copia: Imitation and Authorship in Joachim Du Bellay's *Divers Jeux Rustiques* (1558)', in *Virgilian Identities in the French Renaissance*, ed. by Isabelle Fernbach and Phillip John Usher (Rochester, NY: Boydell & Brewer 2012), pp. 93–114

Ferreyrolles, Gérard, ed., *La Polémique au xviie siècle* (= *Littératures classiques*, 59 (2006))

Finglass, P. J., 'Editions of Sappho since the Renaissance', in *The Cambridge Companion to Sappho*, ed. by P. J. Finglass and Adrian Kelly (Cambridge: Cambridge University Press, 2021), pp. 247–60

Flandrois, Isabelle, *L'Institution du Prince au début du XVIIe siècle* (Paris: Presses Universitaires de France, 1992)

Fogel, Michèle, *Marie de Gournay: itinéraires d'une femme savante* (Paris: Fayard, 2004)

Fogel, Michèle, 'La Damoiselle de Gournay, qui a tousjours bien servi au public', in *Les Femmes et l'écriture de l'histoire, 1400–1800*, ed. by Sylvie Steinberg and Jean-Claude Arnould (Mont Saint-Aignan: Publications des Universités de Rouen et du Havre, 2008), pp. 205–17

Font Paz, Carme and Nina Geerdink, eds, *Economic Imperatives for Women's Writing in Early Modern Europe* (Leiden: Brill, 2018)

Forestier, Georges, *Jean Racine* (Paris: Gallimard, 2006)

Forestier, Georges and Claude Bourqui, 'Comment Molière inventa la querelle de *L'école des femmes* ...', in *Le Temps des querelles*, ed. by Jeanne-Marie Hostiou and Alain Viala (= *Littératures classiques*, 81 (2013)), pp. 185–97

Forment, Lise, 'Marie-Jeanne l'Héritier dans la querelle des Anciens et des Moderns, ou comment être soi et nièce', *Women and Querelles in Early Modern France*, ed. by Helena Taylor and Kate E. Tunstall (= *Romanic Review*, 112.3 (2021)), pp. 470–85

Foucault, Michel, 'Qu'est-ce qu'un auteur?', *Bulletin de la société française de philosophie*, 63 (1969), 73–104

Fournier, Hannah, 'Women Translators in France', in *The Encyclopedia of Women in the Renaissance: Italy, France and England*, ed. by Diana M. Robin, Anne Larsen, and Carole Levin (Santa Barbara: University of California Press, 2007), pp. 373–74

Franchetti, Anna Lia, *L'Ombre discourante de Marie de Gournay* (Paris: Classiques Garnier, 2006)

Fumaroli, Marc, 'Les enchantements de l'éloquence: *Les Fées* de Charles Perrault ou De La Littérature', in *Le Statut de la Littérature*, ed. by Marc Fumaroli (Geneva: Droz, 1982), pp. 153–86

Fumaroli, Marc, 'Les Abeilles et les araignées', in *La Querelle des anciens et des modernes*, ed. by Anne-Marie Lecoq (Paris: Gallimard, 2001), pp. 7–218

Gaines, James F., *Pierre Du Ryer and His Tragedies: From Envy to Liberation* (Geneva: Droz, 1987)

Gaines, James F., 'Lucrèce, Junie and Clélie: Burdens of Female Exemplarity', *Journal of the Western Society for French History*, 17 (1990), 515–21

Gargam, Adeline, *Les femmes savantes, lettrées et cultivées dans la littérature française des Lumières ou La conquête d'une légitimité: 1690–1804*, 2 vols (Paris: Champion, 2013)

Gethner, Perry, 'Antoinette du Ligier de la Garde', <http://siefar.org/dictionnaire/en/Antoinette_du_Ligier_de_la_Garde>

Gethner, Perry, ed. and trans., *Challenges to Traditional Authority: Plays by French Women Authors, 1650–1700*, The Other Voice in Early Modern Europe: The Toronto Series 36 (Toronto: Iter Press, 2015)

Gilby, Emma, *Descartes's Fictions: Reading Philosophy with Poetics* (Oxford: Oxford University Press, 2019)

Gilby, Emma, '*Présence d'esprit* and Action in Seventeenth-Century France', in *The Places of Early Modern Criticism*, ed. by Alexander Gavin, Emma Gilby, and Alexander Marr (Oxford: Oxford University Press, 2021), pp. 176–90

Giles, Lacey, 'The Reception of *De Rerum Natura* in the Poetry of Madame Deshoulières', *Studia z Historii Filozofii*, 3 (2021), 61–95

Gladu, Kim, 'Le débat sur le style pastoral au xviiie siècle: Madame Deshoulières, modèle de l'élégiaque galant', *Tangence*, 109 (2015), 89–109

Godefroy, Frédéric, *Dictionnaire de l'ancienne langue française et de tous ses dialectes du 9e au 15e siècle*, 10 vols (Paris: Vieweg and Bouillon, 1881–1902)

Goldsmith, Elizabeth C. and Dena Goodman, eds, *Going Public: Women and Publishing in Early Modern France* (Ithaca: Cornell University Press, 1995)

Goldwyn, Henriette, '*Manlius*—l'héroïsme inversé', in *Actes de Wake Forest*, ed. by M. R. Margitic and B. R. Wells (Tübingen: Narr, 1987), pp. 421–37

Goodman, Dena, *The Republic of Letters: A Cultural History of the Enlightenment* (Ithaca: Cornell University Press, 1994)

Goodman, Jessica, ed., *Commemorating Mirabeau: Mirabeau aux Champs-Elysées and other texts* (Cambridge: MHRA, 2017)

Gordon, Daniel, *Citizens without Sovereignty: Equality and Sociability in French Thought, 1670–1789* (Princeton: Princeton University Press, 1994)

Grande, Nathalie, *Stratégies de romancières: de 'Clélie' à 'La Princesse de Clèves': 1654–1678* (Paris: Champion, 1999)

Grande, Nathalie, 'Une vedette des salons: le caméléon', in *L'animal au XVII siècle*, ed. by Charles Mazouer (Tübingen: Gunter Narr Verlag, 2003), pp. 89–102

Grande, Nathalie, 'Discours paratextuel et stratégie d'écriture chez Madame de Villedieu', in *Madame de Villedieu romancière: nouvelles perspectives de recherche*, ed. by Edwige Keller-Rahbé (Lyon: Presses Universitaires de Lyon, 2004), pp. 163–74

Grande, Nathalie, 'Claude Barbin, un libraire pour les dames', *Revue de la BNF*, 3 (2011), 22–27

Grande, Nathalie, 'La métamorphose galante de l'histoire antique: modalités et enjeux d'une poétique', in *La Galanterie des anciens*, ed. by Nathalie Grande and Claudine Nédélec (= *Littératures classiques*, 77 (2012)), pp. 229–44

Grande, Nathalie, 'Qui furent les femmes savantes? Réflexions sur l'accès des femmes à la science au temps de Louis XIV', in *Femmes de sciences de l'Antiquité au XIXe siècle. Réalités et représentations*, ed. by Adeline Gargam (Dijon: Editions universitaires de Dijon, 2014), pp. 57–67

270 BIBLIOGRAPHY

Grande, Nathalie, 'La métamorphose galante de l'histoire antique: modalités et enjeux d'une poétique', *Littératures classiques*, 77.1 (2012), 229–44

Grande, Nathalie, 'Introduction générale', in Madame de Villedieu, *Les Amours des grands hommes*, ed. by Nathalie Grande (Paris: Garnier, 2015), pp. 7–49

Grande, Nathalie and Edwige Keller-Rahbé, 'Villedieu, ou les avatars d'un nom d'écrivain(e)', *Littératures Classiques*, 3.61 (2006), 5–32

Grande, Nathalie and Claudine Nédélec, 'Avant-propos', in *La Galanterie des anciens*, ed. by Nathalie Grande and Claudine Nédélec (= *Littératures classiques*, 77 (2012)), pp. 5–13

Green, Karen, 'Women's Writing and the Early Modern Genres Wars', *Hypatia*, 28.3 (2013), 499–515

Green, Karen, 'Eighteenth-Century Debates: From Anne Dacier to Catharine Trotter Cockburn', in *Women's Political Thought in Europe 1700–1800* (Cambridge: Cambridge University Press, 2014), pp. 14–42

Greenblatt, Stephen, *The Swerve: How the World Became Modern* (New York: Norton, 2011)

Grosperrin, Jean-Philippe, 'Les époux Dacier: une bibliographie', *Littératures classiques*, 72.2 (2010), 259–86

Guest, Harriet, 'Bluestocking Feminism', in *Reconsidering the Bluestockings*, ed. by Nicole Pohl and Betty A. Schellenberg (= *Huntingdon Library Quarterly*, 65.1–2 (2002)), pp. 59–80

Guion, Béatrice, '"Une dispute honnête": la polémique selon les Modernes', *Littératures Classiques*, 59 (2006), 157–72

Haase-Dubosc, Danielle, 'Intellectuelles, femmes d'esprit et femmes savantes au XVIIe siècle', *Clio. Histoire, femmes et sociétés*, 13, 2001, <https://doi.org/10.4000/clio.133>

Hagengruber, Ruth, 'Cutting through the Veil of Ignorance: Rewriting the History of Philosophy', in *The History of Women's Ideas*, ed. by Karen Green and Ruth Hagenhruber (= *The Monist*, 98.1 (2015)), pp. 34–42

Hamerton, Katherine J., 'A Feminist Voice in the Enlightenment Salon: Madame de Lambert on Taste, Sensibility and the Feminine Mind', *Modern Intellectual History*, 7.2 (2010), 209–38

Hammond, Nicholas, 'Authorship and Authority in Molière's *Le Misanthrope*', in *Essays on French Comic Drama from the 1640s to the 1780s*, ed. by D. Connon and G. Evans (Bern: Peter Lang, 2000), pp. 55–70

Hardie, Philip, *Virgil* (Cambridge: Cambridge University Press, 1998)

Hardie, Philip, *Lucretian Receptions: History, the Sublime, Knowledge* (Cambridge: Cambridge University Press, 2009)

Hardwick, Lorna and Stephen Harrison, eds, *Classics in the Modern World: A Democratic Turn?* (Oxford: Oxford University Press, 2013)

Harneit, Rudolf, 'Diffusion Européenne des Œuvres de Madame de Villedieu au siècle de Louis XIV', in *Madame de Villedieu romancière: nouvelles perspectives de recherche*, ed. by Edwige Keller-Rahbé (Lyon: Presses Universitaires de Lyon, 2004), pp. 29–70

Harth, Erica, *Cartesian Women: Versions and Subversions of Rational Discourse in the Old Regime* (Ithaca: Cornell University Press, 1992)

Haslett, Moyra, 'Becoming Bluestockings: Contextualising Hannah More's "The Bas Bleu"', *Journal for Eighteenth-Century Studies*, 33.1 (2010), 89–114

Heidmann, Ute and Jean-Michel Adam, *Textualité et intertextualité des contes. Perrault, Apulée, La Fontaine, Lhéritier...* (Paris: Garnier, 2010)

Hepp, Noémie, 'L'utilisation d'Hérodote et de Xénophon dans *Le Grand Cyrus* ou les tabous de Sapho', *Les Trois Scudéry: actes du colloque du Havre*, ed. by Alain Niderst (Paris: Klincksieck, 1993), pp. 359–66

Hepp, Noémie, *Homère en France au XVIIe siècle* (Paris: Klincksieck, 1998)

Herdman, Emma, 'Folie and Salmacis: Labé's Rewriting of Ovid', *The Modern Language Review*, 108.3 (2013), 782–801

Hock, Jessie, *The Erotics of Materialism: Lucretius and Early Modern Poetics* (Philadelphia: University of Pennsylvania Press, 2021)

Hock, Jessie, 'Voluptuous Style: Lucretius, Rhetoric and Reception in Montaigne's "Sur des vers de Virgile"', *Modern Philology*, 18.4 (2021), 492–514

Hogg, Chloé, 'On Not Cutting Off Manlius's Head: Villedieu's (Non) Querelle and the Politics of Literary Reconciliation' (unpublished paper, Modern Languages Association Conference, Chicago, January 2019)

Hosington, Brenda M., 'Women Translators and the Early Printed Book', in *A Companion to the Early Printed Book in Britain 1476–1558*, ed. by Vincent Gillespie and Susan Powell (Cambridge: Brewer, 2014), pp. 248–71

Houdard, Sophie, 'Les fictions du non-mariage: Mme de Villedieu et le personnage de la femme naturelle et publique', *Littératures classiques*, 55.3 (2004), 225–42

Hudson, Robert J., 'Bucolic Influence: Marot's Gallic pastoral and Maurice Scève's Arion', *Romanic Review*, 105.3–4 (2014), 253–72

Huguet, Edmond, *Dictionnaire de la langue française du seizième siècle*, 7 vols (Paris: Champion and Didier, 1925–67)

Humble, Noreen, 'The Well-Thumbed Attic Muse: Cicero and the Reception of Xenophon's Persia in the Early Modern Period', in *Beyond Greece and Rome: Reading the Ancient Near East in Early Modern Europe*, ed. by Jane Grogan (Oxford: Oxford University Press, 2020), pp. 29–52

Hurst, Isobel, *Victorian Women Writers and the Classics: The Feminine of Homer* (Oxford: Oxford University Press, 2006)

Hurst, Isobel, 'Ancient and Modern Women in the *Woman's World*', *Victorian Studies*, 52.1 (2009), 42–51

Hutton, Sarah, '"Blue-eyed Philosophers Born on Wednesdays": An Essay on Women and History of Philosophy', in *The History of Women's Ideas*, ed. by Karen Green and Ruth Hagenhruber (= *The Monist*, 98.1 (2015)), pp. 7–20

Hutton, Sarah, '"Context" and "Fortuna" in the History of Women Philosophers: A Diachronic Perspective', in *Methodological Reflections on Women's Contributions and Influence in the History of Philosophy*, ed. by Sigridur Thorgeirsdottir and Ruth Edith Hagengruber (Cham: Springer, 2020), pp. 29–42

Hutton, Sarah, 'Science and Natural Philosophy', in *The Routledge History of Women in Early Modern Europe*, ed. by Amanda L. Capern (London: Routledge, 2021), pp. 386–403

Ibbett, Katherine, *Liquid Empire* (forthcoming)

Ilsley, Marjorie Henry, *A Daughter of the Renaissance: Marie le Jars de Gournay, her Life and Works* (The Hague: Mouton, 1963)

Itti, Eliane, 'Tanneguy Le Fèvre et les époux Dacier entre mécénat privé et mécénat royal', *Littératures Classiques*, 72 (2010), 21–27

Itti, Eliane, 'L'Abjuration des époux Dacier, le 20 septembre 1685', in *Bulletin de la Société de l'Histoire du Protestantisme Français*, 157 (2011), 159–85

Itti, Eliane, *Madame Dacier, femme et savante du Grand Siècle (1645–1720)* (Paris: L'Harmattan, 2012)

272 BIBLIOGRAPHY

James, Susan, *Passion and Action: The Emotions in Seventeenth-Century Philosophy* (Oxford: Clarendon Press, 1997)

Jameson, Fredric, *A Singular Modernity: Essay on the Ontology of the Present* (London: Verso, 2013)

Jasmin, Nadine, *Naissance du conte féminin. Mots et Merveilles: Les Contes de Fées de Madame d'Aulnoy (1690–1698)*, 2nd edn (Paris: Champion, 2021)

Jed, Stephanie, *Chaste Thinking: The Rape and Lucretia and the Birth of Humanism* (Bloomington: Indiana University Press, 1989)

Keller-Rahbé, Edwige, 'Madame de Villedieu, "La Poule aux œufs d'or" de Claude Barbin?', in *Les Arrières-Boutiques de la Littérature: auteurs et imprimeurs-libraires au XVIe et XVIIe siècles*, ed. by Edwige Keller- Rahbé (Toulouse: Presses Universitaires de Toulouse-Le Mirail, 2010), pp. 87–111

Keller-Rahbé, Edwige, 'Pratiques et usages du privilège d'auteur chez Mme de Villedieu et quelques autres femmes de lettres du XVIIe siècle', *Œuvres & Critiques*, 35.1 (2010), 69–94

Keller-Rahbé, Edwige, 'L'île de Théras dans *Les Annales galantes de Grèce* (1687) de Madame de Villedieu. Une réécriture libertine d'Hérodote?', in *L'Île au XVIIe siècle: jeux et enjeux*, ed. by Christian Zonza (Tübingen: Narr, 2010), pp. 205–23

Keller-Rahbé, Edwige, '"Je crois déjà les entendre dire que je viole le respect dû à la sacrée Antiquité": Mme de Villedieu et la galanterie des anciens, ou le savoir-faire d'une mondaine', in *La Galanterie des anciens*, ed. by Nathalie Grande and Claudine Nédélec (= *Littératures Classiques*, 77 (2012)), pp. 161–75

Kenny, Neil, *The Uses of Curiosity in Early Modern France and Germany* (Oxford: Oxford University Press, 2004)

Kenny, Neil, *Born to Write: Literary Families and Social Hierarchy in Early Modern France* (Oxford: Oxford University Press, 2020)

Knoppers, Laura Lunger, 'Introduction: Critical Framework and Issues', in *The Cambridge Companion to Early Modern Women's Writing*, ed. by Laura Lunger Knoppers (Cambridge: Cambridge University Press, 2009), pp. 1–18

Kors, Alan Charles, *Epicureans and Atheists in France, 1650–1729* (Cambridge: Cambridge University Press, 2016)

Kraus, Chris, *I Love Dick* (London: Serpent's Tail, 2016)

Krier, Isabelle, 'Marie de Gournay, une philosophie des égalités, à l'aube du XVIIe siècle', *Cités*, 89.1 (2022), 103–18

Kruer, Megan, 'The End of Marriage: Sexual Violence after *Clélie*', *Papers on French Seventeenth Century Literature*, 83 (2015), 313–25

Kuizenga, Donna, 'Madame de Villedieu englished: les traductions en anglais des ouvrages de Villedieu au XVIIe siècle', in *Madame de Villedieu romancière: nouvelles perspectives de recherche*, ed. by Edwige Keller-Rahbé (Lyons: Presses Universitaires de Lyon, 2004), pp. 145–60

Kujọrẹ, Ọbafẹmi, 'A Note on Contaminatio in Terence', *Classical Philology*, 69.1 (1974), 39–42

Lachèvre, Frédéric, *Les Derniers libertins* (Paris: Champion, 1924)

Lallemand, Marie-Gabrielle, 'Galanterie des conquérants: l'Alexandre de la Calprenède et le Cyrus des Scudéry', in *La Galanterie des anciens*, ed. by Nathalie Grande and Claudine Nédélec (= *Littératures Classiques*, 77 (2012)), pp. 99–112

Langlands, Rebecca, *Sexual Morality in Ancient Rome* (Cambridge: Cambridge University Press, 2006)

Larsen, Anne R., 'A Women's Republic of Letters: Anna Maria van Schurman, Marie de Gournay, and Female Self-Representation in Relation to the Public Sphere', *Early Modern Women*, 3 (2008), 105–26

Larsen, Anne R. and Anna Maria van Schurman, '*The Star of Utrecht*': *The Educational Vision and Reception of a Savante* (London: Routledge, 2006), pp. 121–22

Le Doeuff, Michèle, *Le Sexe du savoir* (Paris: Aubier, 1998)

Legault, Marianne, *Female Intimacies in Seventeenth-Century French Literature* (Abingdon: Routledge, 2012)

Lennox, Charlotte, *The Female Quixote*, ed. by Margaret Dalziel (Oxford: Oxford University Press, 2008)

Letexier, Gérard, 'Des nouvelles historiques exemplaires: *Les Annales galantes*', in *Madame de Villedieu romancière: nouvelles perspectives de recherche*, ed. by Edwige Keller-Rahbé (Lyon: Presses universitaires de Lyon, 2004), pp. 201–18

Levine, Joseph M., *The Battle of the Books: Literature and History in the Augustan Age* (Ithaca: Cornell University Press, 1994)

Lévy-Lelouche, Claire, 'Quand le privilege de librairie publie le roi', in *De la publication: entre Renaissance et Lumières*, ed. by Christian Jouhaud and Alain Viala (Paris: Fayard, 2002), pp. 139–59

Lilti, Antoine, 'Les salons d'autrefois: XVIIe ou XVIIIe siècle ?', *Les Cahiers du Centre de Recherches Historiques*, 28–29, 2002, <http://journals.openedition.org/ccrh/1032>

Lilti, Antoine, *Le Monde des salons: sociabilité et mondainité à Paris au XVIIIe siècle* (Paris: Fayard, 2005)

Lodge, Anthony, *French: from Dialect to Standard* (London: Routledge, 1993)

Loubère, Stéphanie, 'Figures et figuration d'Anacréon galant', in *La Galanterie des anciens*, ed. by Nathalie Grande and Claudine Nédélec (= *Littératures Classiques*, 77 (2012)), pp. 83–98

Lyons, John D. and Cara Welch, eds, *Le Savoir au XVII siècle* (Tübingen: Narr, 2002)

Mac Carthy, Ita, ed., *Renaissance Keywords* (Leeds: Legenda, 2013)

Mackenzie, Louisa, *The Poetry of Place: Lyric, Language and Ideology in Renaissance France* (Toronto: Toronto University Press, 2011)

McQuade, Paula and Jaime Goodrich, eds, *Beyond Canonicity: the Future(s) of Early Modern Women Writers* (= *Criticism*, 63 (2021))

Mainil, Jean, *Madame d'Aulnoy et le rire des fées: essai sur la subversion féérique et le merveilleux comique sous l'Ancien régime* (Paris: Kimé, 2001)

Mainil, Jean, '"Mes Amies les Fées": Apologie de la femme savante et de la lectrice dans les *Les Bigarrures ingénieuses* de Marie-Jeanne L'Héritier (1696)', *Féeries*, 1 (2003), 49–72

Mannies, Whitney, 'The Periodical as Transnational Salon: Marie-Jeanne l'Héritier's *L'Érudition Enjouée* (1703)', *Eighteenth-Century Studies*, 53.4 (2020), 667–83

Marshall, Sharon, 'The Aeneid and the Illusory Authoress: Truth, Fiction and Feminism in Hélisenne de Crenne's Eneyde' (unpublished doctoral thesis, University of Exeter, 2011)

Martin, Henri-Jean, 'L'Édition Parisienne au XVII siècle: quelques aspects économiques', *Annales*, 7.3 (1952), 303–18

Martin, Henri-Jean, *Livre, pouvoirs et société à Paris au XVIIe siècle, 1598–1701*, 3rd edn (Geneva: Droz, 1999)

Matthes, Melissa, *The Rape of Lucretia and the Founding of Republics: Readings in Livy, Machiavelli and Rousseau* (University Park: Penn State University Press, 2000)

Meeker, Natania, *Voluptuous Philosophy: Literary Materialism in the French Enlightenment* (New York: Fordham University Press, 2006)

BIBLIOGRAPHY

Meli, Cinthia, 'L'Audace pour mot d'ordre: l'invention de l'intrigue et des caractères dans le Manlius de Marie-Catherine Desjardins', in *Madame de Villedieu et le théâtre*, ed. by Nathalie Grande and Edwige Keller-Rahbé (Tubingen: Gunter Narr, 2009), pp. 107–17

Meli, Cynthia, 'La Critique dramatique à l'épreuve de la polémique: l'abbé d'Aubignac et la querelle de *Sophonisbe*, *Littératures classiques*, 89, (2016), 43–54

Montoya, Alicia C., *Medievalist Enlightenment: From Charles Perrault to Jean-Jacques Rousseau* (Cambridge: Boydell and Brewer, 2013)

Montoya, Alicia C., 'Jouer aux troubadours à l'aube des Lumières', in *La Réception des troubadours en Languedoc et en France, XVI–XVIII siècle*, ed. by Jean-François Courouau and Isabelle Luciani (Paris: Classiques Garnier, 2015), pp. 95–108

Moriarty, Michael, 'French Criticism in the Seventeenth Century', in *The Cambridge History of Literary Criticism*, III: *The Renaissance*, ed. by Glyn P. Norton (Cambridge: Cambridge University Press, 2008), pp. 555–65

Morlet-Chantalat, Chantal, *La Clélie de Mademoiselle de Scudéry: de l'épopée à la gazette: un discours féminin de la gloire* (Paris: Champion, 1994)

Morlet-Chantalat, Chantal, 'Pythagore et Sapho: réincarnation galante d'un philosophe mythique', in *Madeleine de Scudéry: une femme de lettres au XVIIe siècle*, ed. by Delphine Denis and Anne-Élisabeth Spica (Arras: Artois Presses Université, 2002), pp. 123–31

Morrison, Mary, 'Henri Estienne et Sappho', *Bibliothèque d'Humanisme et Renaissance*, 24.2 (1962), 388–91

Mueller, Marlies, *Les Idées politiques dans le roman héroïque de 1630 à 1670* (Lexington, KT: French Forum, 1984)

Myers, Sylvia Harcstark, *The Bluestocking Circle: Women, Friendship and the Life of the Mind in Eighteenth-Century England* (Oxford: Oxford University Press, 1990)

Nativel, Colette, ed., *Femmes savantes, savoirs des femmes: du crepuscule de la Renaissance à l'aube des Lumières* (Geneva: Droz, 1999)

Nédélec, Claudine, 'Équivoques de l'auctorialité au XVIIe siècle', *Les Cahiers du Centre de Recherches Historiques*, 33 (2004), <http://journals.openedition.org/ccrh/235>

Nédélec, Claudine, *Les États et Empires du Burlesque* (Paris: Champion, 2004)

Nédélec, Claudine, 'Lyriques anciens et lyriques modernes à l'aune de la galanterie', *Littératures Classiques*, 77.1 (2012), 319–31

Newman, Karen, 'The French Disease', *Comparative Literature*, 64.1 (2012), 33–48

Nicholson, Annalisa, 'The Satire of the Salonnière: Women and Humour in Seventeenth-Century France', *Australian Journal of French Studies*, 59.4 (2022), 361–75

Niderst, Alain, *Fontenelle à la recherche de lui-même, 1657–1702* (Paris: Nizet, 1972)

Niderst, Alain, 'L'histoire romaine dans les romans de Madeleine de Scudéry', in *Le Roman Historique*, ed. by Pierre Ronzeaud (Tübingen: Narr, 1983), pp. 11–22

Niderst, Alain, 'Le Brutus de Madeleine de Scudéry', in *Bruto il maggiore nella letteratura francese e dintorni*, ed. by Franco Piva (Fasano: Schena, 2002), pp. 75–87

Norman, Larry F., *Modernités de Perrault*, ed. by Jean-Pierre Van Eslande and Larry F. Norman (= *Cahiers parisiens / Parisian Notebooks*, 4, (2008)), pp. 190–288

Norman, Larry F., *The Shock of the Ancient: Literature and History in Early Modern France* (Chicago: University of Chicago Press, 2011)

Norman, Larry F., 'La Querelle des anciens et des modernes, ou la métamorphose de la critique', in *Naissance de la critique littéraire*, ed. by Patrick Dandrey (= *Littératures classiques*, 86 (2015)), pp. 95–114

Nunn, Robert, 'The Rape of Lucretia in Madeleine de Scudéry's *Clélie*', in *Violence et fiction jusqu'à la Révolution*, ed. by Martine Debaisieux and Gabrielle Verdier (Tübingen: Narr, 1998), pp. 245–49

O'Brien, John, 'Ronsard, Belleau and Renvoisy', *Early Music History*, 13 (1994), 199–215

O'Brien, John, *Anacreon Redivivus: a Study of Anacreontic Translation in Mid-Sixteenth-Century France* (Ann Arbor: Michigan University Press, 1995)

Oliensis, Ellen, 'Sons and Lovers: Sexuality and Gender in Virgil's Poetry', in *The Cambridge Companion to Virgil*, ed. by Charles Martindale (Cambridge: Cambridge University Press, 2006), pp. 294–331

Oliver, Jennifer, 'When Is a Meadow Not a Meadow?': Dark Ecology and Fields of Conflict in French Renaissance Poetry', in *Early Modern Écologies: Beyond English Ecocriticism*, ed. by Pauline Goul and John Philip Usher (Amsterdam: Amsterdam University Press, 2020), pp. 73–97

Pal, Carol, *Republic of Women: Rethinking the Republic of Letters in the Seventeenth Century* (Cambridge: Cambridge University Press, 2012)

Palmer, Ada, *Reading Lucretius in the Renaissance* (Cambridge, MA: Harvard University Press, 2014)

Patterson, Jonathan, 'Marie de Gournay, Poetry and Gender: In Search of "La vraye douceur"', *Seventeenth-Century French Studies*, 32.2 (2010), 206–20

Patterson, Jonathan, 'Obscenity and Censorship in the Reign of Henri III', *Renaissance Quarterly*, 70.4 (2017), 1321–65

Pellegrin, Marie-Frédérique, 'La science parfait: savants et savantes chez Poulain de la Barre', in *Penser au féminin au XVIIième siècle*, ed. by Vicent Guillin and Marie-Frédérique Pellegrin (= *Revue Philosophique de La France et de l'Étranger*, 138.3 (2013)), pp. 377–92

Pellegrin, Marie-Frédérique, 'Cartesianism and Feminism', in *The Oxford Handbook of Descartes and Cartesianism*, ed. by Steven Nadler, Tad M. Schmaltz, and Delphine Antoine-Mahut (Oxford: Oxford University Press, 2019), pp. 565–79

Pellegrin, Marie-Frédérique, *Pensées du corps et différences des sexes à l'époque moderne* (Lyon: ENS-Editions, 2020)

Pellegrin, Marie-Frédérique, 'Equality, Neutrality, Differentialism: Descartes, Malebranche, and Poulain de la Barre', in *Towards an Equality of the Sexes in Early Modern France*, ed. by Derval Conroy (London: Routledge, 2021), pp. 22–38

Pender, Patricia, *Early Modern Women's Writing and the Rhetoric of Modesty* (Basingstoke: Palgrave, 2012)

Pfister, Laurent, 'L'Auteur, propriétaire de son oeuvre ? La formation du droit d'auteur du xvie siècle' (unpublished doctoral thesis, Université Robert Schuman, Strasbourg, 1999)

Philo, Jean-Mark, *An Ocean Untouched and Untried: The Tudor Translations of Livy* (Oxford: Oxford University Press, 2020)

Plazenet, Laurence, *L'ébahissement et la délectation: réception comparée et poétiques du roman grec en France et en Angleterre aux XVIe et XVIIe siècles* (Paris: Champion, 1997)

Plazenet, Laurence, 'What Did Heliodorus's Name Stand for in the Works of Mlle de Scudéry?', in *Re-Wiring the Ancient Novel. Volume 1: Greek Novels*, ed. by Edmund Cueva, Stephen Harrison, Huge Mason, William Owens, and Saundra Schwartz (Groningen: Barkhuis, 2018), pp. 289–312

Pohl, Nicole and Betty A. Schellenberg, 'A Bluestocking Historiography', in *Reconsidering the Bluestockings*, ed. by Nicole Pohl and Betty A. Schellenberg (= *Huntingdon Library Quarterly*, 65.1–2 (2002)), pp. 1–19

Power, Henry, *Epic into Novel: Henry Fielding, Scriblerian Satire and the Consumption of Classical Literature* (Oxford: Oxford University Press, 2015)

276 BIBLIOGRAPHY

Preisig, Florian, *Clément Marot et les métamorphoses de l'auteur à l'aube de la Renaissance* (Geneva: Droz, 2004)

Prins, Yopie, *Ladies' Greek: Victorian Translations of Tragedy* (Princeton: Princeton University Press, 2017)

Prochasson, Christophe and Anne Rasmussen, *Comment on se dispute: les formes de la controverse* (= *Mil neuf cent. Revue d'histoire intellectuelle*, 25.1 (2007))

Puche, Océane, 'Les Epîtres héroïques de Marie-Jeanne L'Héritier: traduction et réception d'Ovide au XVIIe siècle' (unpublished doctoral thesis, Université de Lille, 2020)

Puche, Océane, 'Defending Phaedra's Glory: The Corrective Translation of *Heroides* 4 by Marie-Jeanne L'Héritier in *Les Epîtres Héroïques* (1732)', in *Ovid in French: Reception by Women from the Renaissance to the Present*, ed. by Fiona Cox and Helena Taylor (Oxford: Oxford University Press, 2023), pp. 88–103

Rathery, Edmé-Jacques-Benoît and Boutron, eds, *Mademoiselle de Scudéry: sa vie et sa correspondence* (Paris: Techener, 1873)

Raynard, Sophie, 'Ancients vs. Moderns: The Women's Riposte, *Marvels and Tales*, 33.1 (2019), 116–39

Reed, Gervais, *Claude Barbin: libraire de Paris sous le règne de Louis XIV* (Geneva: Droz, 1974)

Reitsam, David D., *La Querelle d'Homère dans la presse des Lumières: l'exemple du Nouveau Mercure galant* (Tübingen: Narr, 2021)

Renner, Bernard, 'Virgil and Marot: Imitation, Satire and Personal Identity', in *Virgilian Identities in the French Renaissance*, ed. by John P. Usher and Isabelle Fernbach (Cambridge: Boydell and Brewer, 2012), pp. 19–37

Roberts, Hugh, '"Capitaine Galimatias, homme obscur, et né de la lie du peuple" (Furetière). Le galimatias, vice de style et genre littéraire (fin XVIe-première moitié du XVIIe siècle)', in *Vices de style et défauts esthétiques XVIe–XVIIIe siècle*, ed. by Carine Barbafieri and Jean-Yves Vialleton (Paris: Classiques Garnier, 2017), pp. 361–75

Roberts, Hugh, Guillaume Peureux, and Lise Wajeman, eds, *Obscénités Renaissantes* (Geneva: Droz, 2011)

Roche, Bruno, *Lumières Épicuriennes au XVIIe Siècle: La Mothe Le Vayer, Molière, et La Fontaine, Lecteurs et Continuateurs de Lucrèce* (Paris: Champion, 2020)

Roller, Matthew, 'Exemplarity in Roman Culture: the Cases of Horatius Cocles and Cloelia', *Classical Philology*, 99.1 (2004), 1–56

Rosenfield, Leonora C., *From Beast-Machine to Man-Machine: Animal Soul in French Letters from Descartes to La Mettrie* (New York: Oxford University Press, 1941)

Rosenmeyer, Patricia, *The Poetics of Imitation: Anacreon and the Anacreontic Tradition* (Cambridge: Cambridge University Press, 1992)

Ross, Sarah C. E., *Women, Poetry and Politics in Seventeenth-Century Britain* (Oxford: Oxford University Press, 2015)

Roussillon, Marine, 'Les "Galants Troubadours": Usages des Troubadours à l'âge classique', in *La Réception des troubadours en Languedoc et en France, XVI–XVIII siècle*, ed. by Jean-François Courouau and Isabelle Luciani (Paris: Classiques Garnier, 2015), pp. 109–24

Roussillon, Marine, 'Les Troubadours dans les entrées royales d'Aix-en-Provence (1622 and 1701)', in *La Réception des troubadours en Provence, XVI–XVIII siècle*, ed. by Jean-François Courouau and Isabelle Luciani (Paris: Classiques Garnier, 2018), pp. 115–36

Roussillon, Marine, *Don Quichotte à Versailles: L'imaginaire médiéval du Grand Siècle* (Ceyzérieu: Champ Vallon, 2022)

Russo, Elena, *La Cour et la ville: de la littérature classique aux lumières* (Paris: Presses Universitaires de France, 2002)

BIBLIOGRAPHY 277

Russo, Elena, review [of Antoine Lilti], *The World of the Salons: Sociability and Wordliness in Eighteenth-Century Paris* (Oxford: Oxford University Press, 2015), *Reviews in History*, <https://reviews.history.ac.uk/review/2041>

Sahlins, Peter, *1668: The Year of the Animal in France* (New York: Zone Books, 2017)

Schapira, Nicolas, 'Quand le privilège de librairie publie l'auteur', in *De la publication: entre Renaissance et Lumières*, ed. by Christian Jouhaud and Alain Viala (Paris: Fayard, 2002), pp. 121–37

Schapira, Nicolas, 'Écrivains et élites urbaines au XVIIe siècle: peut-on se passer du modèle du salon?', in *La ville et l'esprit de société*, ed. by Katia Béguin and Olivier Dautresme (Tours: Presses universitaires François-Rabelais, 2004), pp. 17–32

Schiebinger, Londa, *The Mind Has No Sex? Women in the Origins of Modern Science* (Cambridge, MA: Harvard University Press, 1989)

Schneider, Robert A., *Dignified Retreat: Writers and Intellectuals in the Age of Richelieu* (Oxford: Oxford University Press, 2019

Schröder, Volker, 'Verse and Versatility: The Poetry of Antoinette Deshoulières', in *Teaching Seventeenth- and Eighteenth-Century French Women Writers*, ed. by Faith E. Beasley (New York: Modern Language Association of America, 2011), pp. 242–49

Schröder, Volker, 'Madame Deshoulières, ou la satire au féminin', *Dix-septième siècle*, 258.1 (2013), 95–106

Schuwey, Christophe, *Un entrepreneur des lettres au XVIIe siècle: Donneau de Visé, de Molière au 'Mercure Galant'* (Paris: Classiques Garnier, 2020)

Scott, Joan W., 'Gender: A Useful Category of Historical Analysis', *The American Historical Review*, 91.5 (1986), 1053–75

Segal, Charles P., 'Intertextuality and Immortality: Ovid, Pythagoras and Lucretius in Metamorphoses 15', *Materiali e discussioni per l'analisi dei testi classici*, 46 (2001), 63–101

Seifert, Lewis C., *Fairy Tales, Sexuality and Gender in France (1690–1715): Nostalgic Utopias* (Cambridge: Cambridge University Press, 1996)

Seifert, Lewis C., *Manning the Margins: Masculinity and Writing in Seventeenth-Century France* (Ann Arbor: University of Michigan Press, 2009)

Seifert, Lewis C. and Domna Stanton, 'Introduction', in *Enchanted Eloquence: Fairy Tales by Seventeenth-Century French Women Writers*, ed. and trans. by Lewis C. Seifert and Domna Stanton, The Other Voice in Early Modern Europe: The Toronto Series 9 (Toronto: Iter Press, 2010), pp. 1–46

Sermain, J.-P., *Le Conte de fées du classicisme aux Lumières* (Paris: Desjonquères, 2005)

Simonin, Charlotte, 'Des seuils féminins? Le péritexte chez Mme de Villedieu', *Littératures Classiques*, 61 (2006), 151–72

Speyer, Miriam, 'Entre gazette mondaine et art poétique galant: les lettres dans *La Nouvelle Pandore* (1698)', *Arts et Savoirs*, 17 (2022) http://journals.openedition.org/aes/4688

Stanton, Domna C., 'Woman as Object and Subject of Exchange: Marie de Gournay's 'Le Proumenoir' (1594)', *L'Esprit Créateur*, 23.2 (1983), 9–25

Stanton, Domna C., 'Auto-gynography: The Case of Marie de Gournay's *Apologie pour celle qui escrit*', in *Autobiography in French Literature* (Columbia, SC: University of South Carolina, 1985), pp. 18–31

Stanton, Domna C., 'The Demystification of History and Fiction in "Les Annales Galantes"', in *L'Image du souverain dans le théâtre de 1600 à 1650. Actes de Wake Forest*, ed. by Milorad R. Margitić and Byron R. Wells (Tübingen: Narr, 1987), pp. 339–60

Stanton, Domna C., *The Dynamics of Gender in Early Modern France: Women Writ, Women Writing* (New York: Routledge, 2014)

BIBLIOGRAPHY

Stephens, Sonya, ed., *A History of Women's Writing in France* (Cambridge: Cambridge University Press, 2000)

Stevenson, Jane, *Women Latin Poets* (Oxford: Oxford University Press, 2005)

Stevenson, Jane, 'Women Writers and the Classics', in *The Oxford History of Classical Reception in English Literature*, ed.by Patrick Cheney and Phillip Hardie, 5 vols (Oxford: Oxford University Press, 2015), II, pp. 129–43

Storer, Elizabeth, *La mode des contes de fées* (Paris: Champion, 1928)

Storer, Elizabeth, 'Madame Deshoulières, jugée par ses contemporains', *Romanic Review*, 25 (1934), 367–74

Tadié, Alexis, 'Peut-on traduire les querelles?', *Le Temps des querelles*, ed. by Jeanne-Marie Hostiou and Alain Viala (= *Littératures classiques*, 81 (2013)), pp. 211–26

Tadié, Alexis, 'Ancients, Moderns and the Language of Criticism', in *Ancients and Moderns in Europe: Comparative Perspectives*, ed. by Paddy Bullard and Alexis Tadié (Oxford: Voltaire Foundation, 2016), pp. 37–54

Tadié, Alexis, 'The Language of Quarrels', in *Theories of Quarrels*, ed. by Alexis Tadié (= *Paragraph*, 40.1, 2017)), pp. 81–96

Tadié, Alexis and Anne-Lise Rey, 'Introduction', in *Disputes et territoires épistémiques*, ed. by Tadié and Rey (= *Revue de Synthèse*, 137 (2016)), pp. 223–26

Tamas, Jennifer, *Au non des femmes: libérer nos classiques du regard masculin* (Paris: Seuil, 2023)

Taylor, Helena, 'Ovid, *Galanterie* and Politics in Madame de Villedieu's *Les Exilés de la cour d'Auguste*', *Early Modern French Studies*, 37 (2015), 49–63

Taylor, Helena, 'Ancients, Moderns, Gender: Marie-Jeanne L'Héritier's "Le Parnasse reconnoissant ou le triomphe de Madame Des-Houlières"', *French Studies*, 70.1 (2017), 15–30

Taylor, Helena, *The Lives of Ovid in Seventeenth-Century French Culture* (Oxford: Oxford University Press, 2017)

Taylor, Helena, 'Marie de Gournay et le Parnasse des femmes', in *Littéraire: pour Alain Viala*, ed. by M. M. Fragonard, D. Glynn, S. Guyot, and M. Roussillon, 2 vols (Arras: Artois Presses Université, 2018), II, pp. 227–37

Taylor, Helena, 'État présent: The Quarrel of the Ancients and Moderns', *French Studies*, 74.4 (2020), 605–20

Taylor, Helena, 'L'Adorateur du beau sexe': Madeleine de Scudéry et Marie-Jeanne L'Héritier, lectrices d'Ovide', in *Ovide en France du Moyen Âge à nos jours*, ed. by Stefania Cerrito and Marie Possamaï-Pérez (Paris: Classiques Garnier, 2021), pp. 243–63

Taylor, Helena, 'Antoinette Deshoulières's Cat: Polemical Equivocation in Salon Verse', in *Women and Querelles in Early Modern France*, ed. by Helena Taylor and Kate E. Tunstall (= *Romanic Review*, 112.3 (2021)), pp. 452–69

Taylor, Helena, '"Gracieuse et Percinet" de Madame d'Aulnoy: un conte programmatique', *Op. cit., revue des littératures et des arts*, 'Agrégation 2022', 23 (2021), <https://revues.univ-pau.fr:443/opcit/index.php?id=704>

Taylor, Helena, 'Introduction: "C'est une femme qui parle"', in *Women and* Querelles *in Early Modern France*, ed. by Helena Taylor and Kate E. Tunstall (= *Romanic Review*, 112. 3 (2021)), pp. 363–71

Taylor, Helena, 'Polemical Translation, Translating Polemic: Anne Dacier's Rhetoric in the Homer Quarrel', *Modern Language Review*, 116.1 (2021), 21–41

Taylor, Helena, 'Belle and fidèle? Women Translating Ovid in Early Modern France', in *Ovid in French: Reception by Women from the Renaissance to the Present*, ed. by Fiona Cox and Helena Taylor (Oxford: Oxford University Press, 2023), pp. 67–87

Taylor, Helena and Kate E. Tunstall, eds, *Women and* Querelles *in Early Modern France* (= *Romanic Review*, 112.3 (2021))

Tidman, Gemma, *The Emergence of Literature in Eighteenth-Century France: The Battle of the School Books*, Oxford University Studies in the Enlightenment (Liverpool: Liverpool University Press, 2023)

Timmermans, Linda, *L'Accès des femmes à la culture (1598–1715)*, 2nd edn (Paris: Champion, 2005)

Tonolo, Sophie, *Divertissement et profondeur: l'épître en vers et la société mondaine en France de Tristan à Boileau* (Paris: Champion, 2005)

Tonolo, Sophie, 'Aimer comme Amadis: une poétesse entre deux siècles', in *Origines: Actes du 39e congrès annuel de la North American Society for Seventeenth-Century French Literature*, ed. by Thomas M. Carr, Jr. and Russell Ganim (Tübingen: Narr, 2009), pp. 273–86

Tonolo, Sophie, 'De la querelle à l'idylle: quelques enjeux de la poésie de Mme Deshoulières', in *Concordia Discors: 41e congrès annuel de la North American Society for Seventeenth-Century French Literature*, ed. by Benoît Bolduc and Henriette Goldwyn, 2 vols (Tübingen: Narr, 2011), II, pp. 33–42

Tonolo, Sophie, 'Les métamorphoses d'Anacréon chez Mme Deshoulières: effets d'une tradition philologique et philosophique sur son lyrisme pastoral', *Revue Fontenelle*, 10 (2012), 181–97

Trivisani-Moreau, Isabelle, 'Anne de La Roche-Guilhen et la galanterie des anciens', in *La Galanterie des anciens*, ed. by Claudine Nédélec and Nathalie Grande (= *Littératures Classiques*, 77, (2012)), pp. 177–91

Tucker, Holly and Melanie R. Siemens, 'Perrault's Preface to "Griselda" and Murat's "To Modern Fairies"', *Marvels and Tales*, 19.1 (2005), 125–30

Tunstall, Kate E., '"Ne nous engageons point dans des querelles": un projet de guerre perpétuelle?', in *Disputes et territoires épistémiques*, ed. by Alexis Tadié and Anne-Lise Rey (= *Revue de Synthèse*, 137 (2016)), pp. 345–72

Tunstall, Kate E. and Wilda Anderson, eds, *Naming, Un-Naming, and Re-Naming in Early Modern and Enlightenment Europe* (= *Romance Studies*, 31.3–4 (2013))

Turnovsky, Geoffrey, *The Literary Market: Authorship and Modernity in the Old Regime* (Philadelphia: University of Pennsylvania Press, 2010)

Turnovsky, Geoffrey, 'Chroniques des *Chroniques du Samedi*: l'invention d'un manuscrit', *Les Dossiers du Grihl* [Online], 11-2 2017, https://doi.org/10.4000/dossiersgrihl.6795

Vanacker, Beatrijs and Lieke van Deinsen, eds, *Portraits and Poses: Female Intellectual Authority, Agency and Authorship in Early Modern Europe*, (Leuven: Leuven University Press, 2022)

Venesoen, Constant, *Marie de Gournay: Textes relatifs à la calomnie* (Tübingen: Narr, 1998)

Verhaart, Floris, *Classical Learning in Britain, France and the Dutch Republic, 1690–1750: Beyond the Ancients and Moderns* (Oxford: Oxford University Press, 2020)

Vesperini, Pierre, *Lucrèce: Archéologie d'un classique européen* (Paris: Fayard, 2017)

Viala, Alain, *Naissance de l'écrivain: sociologie de la littérature à l'âge classique* (Paris: Minuit, 1985)

Viala, Alain, 'D'une politique des formes: la galanterie', *Dix-septième siècle*, 183 (1994), 143–51

Viala, Alain, 'The Theory of the Literary Field and the Situation of the First Modernity', in *Theory and the Early Modern* (= *Paragraph*, 29.1 (2006)), pp. 80–93

280   BIBLIOGRAPHY

Viala, Alain, *La France galante: essai historique sur une catégorie culturelle, de ses origines jusqu'à la Révolution* (Paris: Presses Universitaires de France, 2008)

Viala, Alain, 'Des stratégies dans les lettres', in *On ne peut pas tous réduire à des stratégies: pratiques d'écriture et trajectoires sociales*, ed. by Nicolas Schapira and Dinah Ribard (Paris: Presses Universitaires de France, 2013), pp. 183–200

Viala, Alain, 'Un temps de querelles', in *Le Temps des querelles*, ed. by Jeanne-Marie Hostiou and Alain Viala (= *Littératures classiques*, 81 (2013)), pp. 5–22

Viala, Alain, *L'Adhésion littéraire* (Montreuil: Le Temps des Cerises, 2022)

Viennot, Éliane, 'La Querelle de la langue', in *La France, les femmes et le pouvoir, 2. Les résistances de la société (17ᵉ–18e siècles)* (Paris: Perrin, 2008), pp. 78–84

Viennot, Éliane, *Non, le masculin ne l'emporte pas sur le féminin! Petite Histoire des résistances de la langue française* (Paris: Éditions iXe, 2014)

Volpilhac-Auger, Caroline, ed., *La Collection Ad usum Delphini. L'Antiquité au miroir du Grand Siècle* (Grenoble: Ellug, 2000)

Walters, Tracey L., *African American Literature and the Classicist Tradition: Black Women Writers from Wheatley to Morrison* (Basingstoke: Palgrave Macmillan, 2007)

Waters, Sarah, '"A Girton Girl on a Throne": Queen Christina and Versions of Lesbianism, 1906–1933', *Feminist Review*, 46 (1994), 41–60

Weinbrot, Howard D., '"What Must the World Think of Me?": Pope, Madame Dacier, and Homer: The Anatomy of a Quarrel', in *Eighteenth-Century Contexts: Historical Inquiries in Honor of Philip Harth*, ed. by Howard D. Weinbrot, Peter J. Schakel, and Stephen E. Karian (Madison: University of Wisconsin Press, 2001), pp. 183–206

Wheeler, Stephen M., 'Ovid's Use of Lucretius in *Metamorphoses* 1.67–8', *The Classical Quarterly*, 45.1 (1995), 200–03

Wiesner-Hanks, Merry, *Women and Gender in Early Modern Europe*, 4th edn (Cambridge: Cambridge University Press, 2019)

Wilkin, Rebecca, *Women, Imagination and the Search for Truth in Early Modern France* (Aldershot: Ashgate, 2008)

Williams, Wes, 'Well Said/Well Thought: How Montaigne Read his Lucretius', in *Lucretius and the Early Modern*, ed. by David Norbrook, Stephen Harrison, and Philip Hardie (Oxford: Oxford University Press, 2015), pp. 135–60

Wilson, Emily, *Mocked with Death: Tragic Over-living from Sophocles to Milton* (Baltimore: Johns Hopkins University Press, 2005)

Wilson, Emily, 'Epilogue: Translating Homer as a Woman', in *Homer's Daughters: Women's Responses to Homer in the Twentieth Century and Beyond*, ed. by Fiona Cox and Elena Theodorakopoulos (Oxford: Oxford University Press, 2019), pp. 279–98

Wiseman, Susan, 'Exemplarity, Women and Political Rhetoric', in *Rhetoric, Women, and Politics in Early Modern England*, ed. by Jennifer Richards and Alison Thorne (London: Routledge, 2007), pp. 129–48

Worth-Stylianou, Valerie, 'Marie de Gournay et la traduction: défense et illustration d'un style', in *Marie de Gournay et l'édition de 1595 des Essais de Montaigne*, ed. by Jean-Claude Arnould (Paris: Champion, 1996), pp. 193–206

Worth-Stylianou, Valerie, 'Marie de Gournay, traductrice', in *Œuvres complètes*, ed. by Jean-Claude Arnould, Évelyne Berriot, Claude Blum, Anna Lia Franchetti, Marie-Claire Thomine, and Valerie Worth-Stylianou, 2 vols (Paris: Champion, 2002), I, pp. 56–79

Worth-Stylianou, Valerie, '"C'est, pourtant, l'œuvre d'une Fille": Mlle Desjardins à l'Hôtel de Bourgogne', *Littératures Classiques*, 51 (2004), 105–20

Worth-Stylianou, Valerie, 'Virgilian Space in Renaissance French Translations of the *Aeneid*', in *Virgilian Identities in the French Renaissance*, ed. by John P. Usher and Isabelle Fernbach (Cambridge: Boydell & Brewer, 2012), pp. 117–40

Worth-Stylianou, Valerie, '"Bugge-Beares" or "Bouquets"?: Translations of the Latin Quotations in Florio's and Gournay's Versions of the Essais', in *Montaigne in Transit: Essays in Honour of Ian Maclean*, ed. by Neil Kenny, Richard Scholar, and Wes Williams (Cambridge: Legenda, 2016), pp. 155–70

Wyles, Rosie, 'Aristophanes and the French Translations of Anne Dacier', in *Brill's Companion to the Reception of Aristophanes*, ed. by Philip Walsh (Leiden: Brill, 2016), pp. 195–216

Wyles, Rosie, 'Ménage's Learned Ladies: Anne Dacier (1647–1720) and Anna Maria van Schurman (1607–1678)', in *Women Classical Scholars*, ed. by Rosie Wyles and Edith Hall (Oxford: Oxford University Press, 2016), pp. 61–77

Wyles, Rosie and Edith Hall, eds, *Women Classics Scholars: Unsealing the Fountain from the Renaissance to Jacqueline de Romilly* (Oxford: Oxford University Press, 2016)

Zonza, Christian, 'La houlette et le sceptre: une écriture entre fiction et histoire', *Littératures classiques*, 61.3 (2006), 219–34

Index

For the benefit of digital users, indexed terms that span two pages (e.g., 52–53) may, on occasion, appear on only one of those pages.

Ablancourt, Nicolas Perrot d', 74–75
Académie d'Arles, 136
Académie française, 8–9, 16–17, 25, 34–35, 65–66, 136, 176, 231, 249, 251, see also *Dictionnaire de l'Académie française*
Accademia dei Ricovrati, 64–65, 136
Achilles, 225–229
ad usum delphini, 203, 205–206
Aeneas, 55–60
agon, 16–17, 25, 174, 188–189, 218, 223
Amadis de Gaule, 174
amateurism, 3–4, 12–13, 15–16, 21, 70–71, 104, 135–136, 243–244
Amazons, 54–56, 82–83, 99–100, 192–193, 229–230
Amyot, Jacques, 87–88
Anacreon, 21, 23–24, 87–89, 137–138, 163–166, 192–193, 203, 206, 217, 218, *see also* Anne Dacier, Antoinette Deshoulières, Madeleine de Scudéry
ancient Near East, 3 n. 7, 67–68, 74–75
animal-machine, 22, 148–149, 156–157, *see also* Descartes
animal soul, 16–17, 22, 148–149
Apuleius, 177–179
Arete, 37–38
Aristophanes, 23–24, 203, 215, *see also* Anne Dacier
Aristotle, 19–20, 87–88, 148–149
Arsenal library, 2–3 n. 3, 160 n. 74, 197–198
Aspasia, 37–38, 189–190, 245–246 n. 7
Aubignac, Abbé d', 113–119
auctrix, 8–9
Augustus, 104–106, 168
Aulnoy, Marie-Catherine d', 3, 22–23, 103, 107–108, 176, 178–179, 194, 245, see also *conteuses*
Gracieuse et Percinet, 22–23, 179
Aurevilly, Jules Barbey d', 248–249
authorship, 2–3, 10–11, 22–23, 25, 73, 75, 110–111, 120–121, 123, 125–126, 135–138, 178, 184, 198, 201–202, 243–245

autobiography, 20–21
autrice, 8–10, 249

Balzac, Guez de, 8–9, 249
Barbin, Claude, 15–16, 21–22, 102, 103–111, 118–119, 128, 207
Bas-Bleu, le, 24, 245–249
Battle of the Books, the, 157–158
Bayle, Pierre, 65, 137, 146–149, 154–155, 175
Beasley, Faith E., 7 n. 32, 12–13, 19, 86 n. 70, 101–102, 139 n. 17
Beaulieu, Jean-Philippe, 26 n. 5, n. 7, 41, 49–50 n. 90, 53, 55–56, 118
beaux esprits, 170
Belleau, René, 80–81 n. 49, 163–165 n. 83, 208–210, 212–214, 214–215 n. 47
belles-lettres, 7, 17–18, 74, 178, 192
Bernard, Catherine, 3, 21–22, 103, 104, 128, 243–244
Bertaut, Jean, 52–57
bienséance, 48–49, 58, 64–65, 113–114, 172–174, 183, 187–188, 216, 224, 226–229, 238–239
birds, 151–152, 197–198
Bluestocking, 24, 245–249
Boccaccio, 73–74, 95, 97–98
Boileau, Nicolas, 16–17, 52–53, 70–72, 90–91, 101–102, 172, 176–177, 213–214, 224, 231
Boisrobert, François le Métel de, 146–147
Boivin, Jean, 224–225
Bouhours, Dominic, 168–169
Bourdieu, Pierre, 70–71, 133, 143
Brown, Hilary, 10–11, 43–44 n. 75
Brumoy, Pierre, 218–219
Brutus, 21, 69–70, 86–87, 89, 131–133, *see also* Madeleine de Scudéry
Buffet, Marguerite, 1–2 n. 4, 4–5 n. 19
Butterworth, Emily, 1–2 n. 3, 25 n. 1, 28–29, 29 n. 16, 31–32 n. 21, 35–36 n. 38, 38, 39 n. 57, 63–64 n. 130, 230–231 n. 81

canon, 2–3, 63–66, 100–102, 168

categorisation of learning, 2–3, 7–8, 10–15, 19–20, 25, 29, 63–66, 73, 100–102, 172–175, 184, 201–205, 234–240, 242, 244–245, see also *savante*, woman writer
Catullus, 80–82, 198
Charaxus, 199
Chauveau, François, 86
Chéron, Elisabeth, 163–165
Chevreau, Urbain, 89–90
Chométy, Philippe, 140–143, 155, 159–161
Churchill, Laurie, 13–14, 19–20 n. 93
Cicero, 20–21, 26, 37–38, 47–50, 55–56
Classicist, 3, 13–15, 23–24, 72, 203–206, 243–245
Classics, 13–15, 23–24, 243–245, 249–250
Clermidy–Patard, Geneviève, 197–198, 199 n. 77
Cloelia, 67–68, 85, 87, 89–90, 97–98
Clusium, 85, 97–98, 166
Colbert, Jean-Baptiste, 166–168
community, 1–2, 12–13, 71, 79, 91, 143, 145, 191, 196, 201–202, 242, 244–245, see also salon
Condé, Prince de, 74–75, 136, 163–165
Conley, John J., 141, 152
Conroy, Derval, 3–4 n. 10, 34–35 n. 28, 45 n. 78, 65–66 n. 137, 74–75
conteuses, 22–23, 133–134, 176
conversation, 12–13, 48–49, 70–71, 73, 87–89, 93, 194–195, 203, 232, 238–240, 246
Corinne/Corinna, 37–38, 83–84, 167–168 n. 90, 189–190, 198
Corneille, Pierre, 63–64, 87, 113–119, 181
Corneille, Thomas, 181
cour d'amour, 193, 202, 244–245
Cousin, Victor, 12
Coypel, Antoine, 226–229
Cupid and Psyche, 22–23, 184
Curie, Marie, 250

Dacier, Anne, 3, 12–15, 17–18, 23–24, 39, 54, 63–65, 100–101, 107–108, 128–129, 163–165, 192–193, 203
  ad usum delphini, 203, 205–206, 243–245
  Des Causes de la corruption du goût, 224–225, 229–232
  family, 203, 205–206
  female cause, 204–208, 224, 231, 234–235
  Homer Quarrel, 16–17, 203–206, 223, see also *querelle d'Homère*
  as quarreller, 203, 217–219, 223
  reception of, 203–206, 234–240
  as *savante*, 203–206, 240–241

Tanneguy Le Fèvre, 100–101, 203, 206–213, 215–216
  translation of Aristophanes, 203, 215
  translation of Plautus, 203, 215
  translation of Sappho and Anacreon, 203, 206, 217–218
  translation of Terence, 203, 215
  views on education, 1–2, 207–208, 217, 221, 224, 226–230, 239–240
Dacier, André, 203, 205–206, 231
Damo, 37–38, 91, 92
Dassoucy, Charles, 144–145
Davies, Emily, 249–250
Debrosse, Anne, 2–3 n. 3, 69–70 n. 10, 73–74, 80–81 n. 49, 82–83, 84–85 n. 63, 167–168 n. 90
Dehénault, Jean, 22, 137, 138–139, 146
DeJean, Joan, 2–3 n. 6, 3–4, 4–5 n. 14, 7–8 n. 38, 10–11 n. 51, 17–18, 67–68 n.2, 71, 73–74, 78–79 n. 42, 80–81 n. 47, n. 55, 86 n. 69, 101–102 n. 132, 110–111, 125 n. 84, 125–126 n. 86, 129–130 n. 103, 178 n.12, 211 n.33, 212, 213–214 n. 45
Descartes, René, 7–8, 12–13, 22, 120–121, 148–152, 156–157, 192–193
Deshoulières, Antoinette, 3, 12–13, 22, 61–62, 64–65, 103, 107–108, 133–135, 188, 189–191, 194, 201–202, 244–245, see also *querelle des sonnets*
  Anacreon, 137–138, 163–166
  animal-machine, 22, 148–149, 156–157
  atomism, 22, 137, 138–139, 141, 174–175
  burlesque, 137–138, 140, 144–145
  eclogues, 137, 146–147, 157, 244
  family, 136
  Horace, 137–138, 163, 165–168
  idylls, 135–136, 146
  'Imitation de Lucrèce en galimatias fait exprès', 137–138, 151, 165
  literary market, 136
  as Modern, 137–138, 140, 157, 168, 171–175
  Ovid, 137, 144–146
  pastoral, 137–138, 146, 157
  pedantry, 142–143, 169–172
  philosophy of nature, 137–138, 146
  as poet, 135–136, 143, 163
  reception of, 172–175
  satire, 143
  savante, 163, 169–172
  Virgil, 137–138, 146–148, 152–153, 155, 156–157, 168
Desjardins, Marie-Catherine, *see* Madame de Villedieu
Desmarets de Saint Sorlin, Jean, 217, 224

284 INDEX

Des Roches, Madeleine and Catherine, 50–51, 189–190
dialogue des morts, 199–201
Dictionnaire de l'Académie française (1694), 5–6, 8–9 n. 49, 142, 144–145 n. 40
   Dictionnaire de l'Académie française (1835), 12, 136
   Dictionnaire de l'Académie française (1935), 246 n.12
   Dictionnaire de l'Académie française (current), 246, 250–251
Dido, 37–38, 55–60
Die, Comtesse de, 189–190
Dijk, Suzanna van, 234–235
Diogenes Laertius, 34, 36, 37–38 n. 46, 91
Dionysus of Halicarnassus, 85, 97–100
Donneau de Visé, Jean, 110–111, 113–119
Dryden, John, 157–158
Du Bellay, Joachim, 39–40, 51–52, 146–147, 174
Du Bosc, Jacques, 95–96
Du Châtelet, Emilie, 248
Du Four de la Crespelière, Claude-Denis, 163–165, 207, 208–210, 212–214
Dufour-Maître, Myriam, 3–4, 7–8 n. 38, 12 n.63, 17n. 79, 67–68 n. 2–3, 68 n. 5, 71 n. 16, 72, 73 n. 23–24, 74, 75 n. 34, 79 n. 45–46, 82–83 n. 60, 84–85, 86–87 n. 72, 204–205 n. 4, 237–238 n. 101, 243 n. 1
Duggan, Anne E., 3–4, 7–8 n. 38, 17 n. 80, 72 n. 19, 86 n. 69, 86–87 n. 72, n.74, 87–88 n. 76, 176–177 n. 3–4, 179 n. 15, 182–183
Du Perron, Jacques Davy, 52–53, 55–57, 65
Dutch, 27–28, 60–61, 64–65, 109, 128–129

eclogues, 22, 60–62, 137, 146–147, 244
   quarrel about, 22, 157
England, 245–247, 249–250
Epicurus, 22, 137–139, 145, 147–148, 158–159
Erinne/Erinna, 37–38, 73–74, 84–85 n. 63, 189–190
Estienne, Henri, 80–81, 208–209, 210–211 n. 30, 212–213
Estienne, Robert, 5–6 n. 20
Eustatius, 194, 204–205
Evain, Aurore, 8–9, 111–112 n. 35, 128–129 n. 97, 131 n. 107
exemplar tradition, 89–90, 97

fairy tales, 16, 22, 176–179, 184–189, 194–197, 201–202, 244 see also *conteuses*, Marie-Catherine d'Aulnoy, Charlotte de La Force, Marie-Jeanne L'Héritier, Henriette-Julie de Murat

feminised professions, 8–10, 24, 249–251
feminism, *see also* Anne Dacier, Marie-Jeanne L'Héritier, Madeleine de Scudéry, Marie de Gournay, woman writer
   of difference, 2–3, 21, 69–70, 246
   of equality, 2–3, 20–21, 69–70
   of the Moderns, 17, 176–179, 184, 202
   scholarship, 7–11, 19, 26, 33
femme savante, 1–3, 18, 20–21, 73, 243, see also *savante*
Fénelon, François, 7, 245–246
Fontenay, Hardouin Le Fèvre, 235–236
Fontenelle, Bernard de, 157–160, 174–175, 199–200
Foucault, Michel, 125–126
France, Marie de, 189–190
Franchetti, Anne Lia, 26 n.3, 29 n. 15, 32, 40–41 n. 58, n. 64, 41–42 n. 69, 56–57 n. 105, 59–60 n. 119
French language, 2–3, 39, 51, 220, 224
Fronde, 74–75, 86–87
Fumaroli, Marc, 16–17 n.77, 178, 178–179 n. 13, 186–187 n. 44
Furetière, Antoine, 5–6 n. 25–28, 8–9 n. 49, 76–77 n. 40, 90–91, 142, 145 n. 40

Gaillard, Henri, 172
galanterie, 13–14, 21–22, 68, 86–87, 92–93, 101–104, 107–108, 111, 124, 126, 128–129, 137–138, 171, 184–185, 201–202, 206
galimatias, 22, 49–50, 138
Gargam, Adeline, 7, 7–8 n.37, 11
Gassendi, Pierre, 22, 137, 138–139, 150
gender (approaches to), 3, 10–11, 19, 23–24, 240–241, 243–245
Gethner, Perry, 104–106 n. 7, 111–112 n. 35, 118–119, 119 n. 55, 121 n. 66, 122 n.69, 128–129 n. 97, 136 n. 5–6
Giraldi, Lilio Gregorio, 80–81, 83–85, 210–211
girly swot, 250
Girton College, 249–250
Girton Girl, 24, 249–250
Godefroy, Frédéric, 5–6, 90–91, 142
Gouges, Olympe de, 172
Gournay, Marie de, 1–2, 4–5, 8–9, 12–15, 17–21, 25, 67–68, 103, 133, 137–138, 189, 240–245
   Adieu de l'âme du roi, 34–35
   agonistic rhetoric, 39, 214–215
   alchemy, 28–29, 35–36
   Anna Maria van Schurman, 27–28
   'Apologie pour celle qui escrit', 28–37
   autobiography, 26, 29, 206

'Copie de la Vie de la Damoiselle de Gournay, envoyée à Hinhenctum Anglois', 29–31
'De la façon d'escrire de Messieurs L'Eminentissime Du Perron et Bertuat Illustrissime Evesque de Sées', 51–53, 55
'Discours à Sophrosine', 26, 37–38
Égalité des hommes et des femmes, 25, 29–30, 37–38, 57, 63
ethos, 29
family, 27–29, 50–51
feminism, 25, 29, 48–49, 65–66, 74
Greek language, 25, 29, 36n. 40
'Grief des Dames', 29–30, 36–37, 40–41
language reform, 25, 39, 51, 249
Latin language, 15–16, 25, 29–31, 43–44
learning, 25, 29
money, 28–29, 34–36, 63
Montaigne, 26–29, 34, 39, 43–44, 60–61, 65–66
'La Pincture des mœurs', 29–30
poetry (Bouquet de Pinde), 60, 160
reception of, 63–66, 189–190, 203, 205–206
Renaissance poetics, 25, 39–40, 51
salon, 25, 63, 65–66
slander, 25, 34–35, 64–65
translation theory, 39, 51, 62
translation of Cicero, 26, 47–50
translation of Ovid, 26, 39
translation of Sallust, 26, 41–44, 46–47
translation of Tacitus, 26, 41–46
translation of Virgil, 26, 51
Grande, Nathalie, 69, 71, 72 n. 19, 99–100 n. 118, 104–106 n. 6, n. 9, n. 11, 106–107 n. 14, 107–108 n. 21–23, 110–111 n. 30, 111–112 n. 35, 118 n. 25, 123, 124–125 n. 79, 125, 126 n. 86, 128–129, 149 n. 53
Greek language, 1–3, 23–25, 29, 36n. 40, 192–193, 203–206, 223, 224, 241–242
Greek lyric, 69–70, 88–89, 92–93, 100, 163–165, 167–168, 190–191, 208, *see also* Anacreon, Sappho
Guéret, Gabriel, 201
Guillaume, Jacquette, 1–2 n. 4, 4–5 n. 19

Hardouin, Jean, 225–226, 232–233
historical fiction, 21, 67, 131–132, *see also* Madeleine de Scudéry and Madame de Villedieu
Hector, 225–226
Helen, 224
Heliodorus, 87–88, 190–191
Herodotus, 3 n.7, 67–68, 70–71, 74–75, 104–106, 194
Hesiod, *see* 'Songe d'Hésiode'

Hock, Jessie, 140, 145
Homer, 16–17, 23–24, 83–84, 99–100, 187–188, 203–206, 208–209, 217, 223
homosexuality, 73–74, 80–81, 195, 211–213, 218–221, 249–250
Horace, 22, 63, 80–81, 137–138, 163, 165–168, 210–211
Huet, Pierre-Daniel, 68, 187–188, 205–206
Huguet, Edmond, 5–6
Humanism, 3–5
humour, 202, 245
Hurst, Isobel, 4–5 n. 70, 249–250
Hutchinson, Lucy, 139
Hypatia, 37–38

Irailh, Simon-Augustin, 172–174 n. 101, 237–238
irenism, 223, 234
irony, 22, 122, 124–125, 137–138, 141–142, 171, 180–181 n.23, 182–184, 194–195, 202, 245

Jed, Stephanie, 89–90 n. 84, 96
Journal des sçavans, 100–101, 191–192, 214–215, 235–236, 238–239
Journal de Trévoux, 238–240
Juno, 231
Jupiter, 231

Keller-Rahbé, Edwige, 103, 104 n. 5, 104–106 n. 11, 106–108, 110–111 n. 30, 111, 118–123, 124–125 n. 79, 125–126, 130–131 n. 106
Kenny, Neil, 50–51, 125–126 n. 87, 205–206
keywords, 1–2

La Calprenède, Gautier de, 70–71, 90–91 n. 87, 190–191
La Calprenède, Madame de, 136
Lachèvre, Frédéric, 137, 146 n. 42, 167–168 n. 90
Lafayette, Marie-Madeleine, 110–111
La Fontaine, Jean de, 149, 155, 179
La Force, Charlotte Rose Caumont de, 3, 22–23, 163, 169–170, 176, 178–179
Plus belle que fée, 22–23, 179
La Forge, Jean de, 1–2 n. 4, 4–5 n. 19
Lambert, Marquise de, 224–225, 232, 237–238, 238–239 n. 103
La Mothe Le Vayer, François de, 25
La Motte, Antoine Houdar de, 16–17, 214–215, 223, 228, 241
Lang, Andrew, 249–250
Langlands, Rebecca, 94 n. 97, 95–96, 97 n.109

286 INDEX

language reform, 2–3, 8–10, 16–17, 20–21, *see also* Marie de Gournay
La Roche-Guilhen, Anne de, 3, 21–22, 104, 128, 243–244
La Rochefoucauld, François de, 137, 138–139 n. 15, 146–147, 172–174 n. 102
La Suze, Henriette-Coligny de, 83–85, 135–136 n.1, 189–190
Latin language, 1–3, 7–9, 13–16, 19–21, 23–25, 29, 30–31, 43–44, 67–68, 72, 74–75, 80–81, 85, 91 n. 90, 158–159, 184–185, 189–190, 203–206
La Vilate, Cartaud de, 203 n.3, 237–238
Le Fèvre, Anne, *see* Anne Dacier
Le Fèvre, Tanneguy, 100–101, 203, 204–205 n. 5, 205–213, 214–215 n. 47, 215–216 n. 49
legitimacy, 2–3, 14–16, 22–23, 25, 28–29, 54, 69, 109–110, 119–121, 243, *see also* literary value
Le Moyne, Pierre, 95, 97–98, 163–165
Lennox, Charlotte, 101–102
Le Pons, Jean-François, 235–236
Lesbos, 80–83, 92, 129–130, 212–213
L'Héritier de Villandon, Marie-Jeanne, 3, 22–23, 63–64, 100–101, 103, 136, 172, 176–179, 184, 201, 244–245, see also *conteuses*
   L'Apothéose de Mademoiselle de Scudéry, 184–185, 189–190, 194–195, 199, 220
   contes, 146–188, 194–195
   L'Érudition enjouée, 22–23, 184–185, 191–195, 201–202
   feminism, 186–191
   'Lettre à Madame D. G.', 184–185, 187–190, 194–195
   La Pompe Dauphine, 184–185, 194–195
   savoir, 184
   translation of Ovid's *Heroides*, 184–185
   La Triomphe de Madame Deshoulières, 184–185, 189–191, 194–195
Limojon de Saint-Didier, Ignace François, 238–239
lineage, 27–28, 39, 81 n. 55, 82, 84–85, 87–88, 127–128, 158–159 n. 67, 184, 201–202, 208–209 n. 26, 244
literary criticism, 18, 22–23, 176
literary field, 2–3, 7–8 n. 38, 12–13, 16, 17–18, 67–71, 241, 242
literary market, 15–16, 21–22, 43–44, 70–71, 102, 110–111, 128, 133–134, 136, 243–244, *see also* money, Villedieu

literary value, 2–3, 7–8, 12–15, 21–22, 69–72, 109–111, 133–134, 178, 190–221, 243–244
literature, practices of, 2–3, 7–8, 110–111, 191–193, 243–244
Livy, 67–68, 85, 89–90, 93, 96, 98, 99–100
Loges, Madame des, 25, 28–29
Longepierre, Hilaire-Bernard de, 157–159, 163–165, 211 n. 35, 212–213 n. 37, 214–215
Longinus, 80–81 n. 51, 212–214
Louis XIII, 34–35, 54
Louis XIV, 74–75, 120–126, 136, 161–162, 168
Lucrèce/Lucretia, 21, 69–70, 85, 86–87, 89
Lucretius, 22, 137–138, 151, *see also* Antoinette Deshoulières
Lully, Jean-Baptiste, 169, 181
Luyne, Guillaume de, 106–107

Madrid, 192
Maintenon, Madame de, 168
Mairet, Jean, 113–114
Malherbe, François de, 25, 29–30, 40–41, 52–53, 55–56 n. 105, 64–65, 87 n. 75
Marolles, Michel de, 25, 34–35 n.30, 49–50, 65, 138–139, 157–158
Marot, Clément, 61–62, 159–162, 174–175
Matthes, Melissa, 89–90 n. 84, 100
Maubuy, Jean Aublet de, 203 n. 3, 237–238
medievalism, 174–178, 184, 201–202
Ménage, Gilles, 8–9 n.48, 65, 91–92, 169, 204–205 n. 8, 221–222 n. 61
Menander, 221–222
Menou, Mademoiselle de, 197–200
Mercure Galant, 107, 110–111 n. 29, 135–136, 146–147 n. 43, 159 n. 68, 169 n. 91, 174, 191–192, 197–198, see also *Nouveau Mercure Galant*, *Nouveau Mercure*
Mercury, 226–229
Minerva, 231
modesty, 54–56, 63, 64–65, 67, 127–128, 130–131, 137–138, 165–170, 172, 175, 182–183, 203, 207–208 n. 22, 208–209, 221, 238–241
Moetjens, Adriaan, 138–139 n.16, 163–165
Molière, 4–5, 104–106, 110–111, 181, 215–216 n. 48, 245–247
mondainité, 3–4, 11–13, 22–23, 139, 185–187, 207–208 n. 21, 242
money, 15–16, 21–22, 28–29, 34–36, 63, 71, 75, 109–111, 120–121, 130–131, 133–134, 205–206, 243–244, *see also* literary market and amateurism
Montagu, Elizabeth, 245–246

Montaigne, Michel de, 1, 20–21, 26, 27–30, 34, 39, 43–44, 48–49 n. 84, 60–61, 65–66, 139 n. 19, 145, 149, 155–156, *see also* Gournay

Montausier, Duc de, 207–209

Montoya, Alicia C., 174 n. 105–106, 178 n. 9–10, 186–187, 193 n. 65, 201–202 n. 80

Montpensier, Mademoiselle de, 111–112

More, Hannah, 247

Morlet-Chantalat, Chantal, 83–84 n. 62, 86, 87–88 n. 76, 91 n. 89

Murat, Henriette-Julie de, 3, 12–13, 22–23, 107–108, 176, 178–179, 195, 245
  Histoires sublimes et allégoriques, 22–23, 195–197
  Journal pour Mademoiselle de Menou, 197–201

muses, 170, 190–191

Nédélec, Claudine, 69, 87–88 n. 77, 140, 157–158 n. 62, 208

Nell, Sharon, 86–87, 90–91 n. 87, 95–96 n. 104, n.107, 98–99 n. 116

Newman, Karen, 4–5, 76 n.38, 80–81 n. 47

Newnham College, 249–250

Nicholson, Lisa, 78–79, 191–192 n. 63, 245 n.3

Nicole, Claude, 207–209

Niderst, Alain, 12 n. 63, 67–68 n. 3, 72 n. 19, 79–80 n. 46, 90–91 n. 87, 94 n. 94, 159

Ninon de l'Enclos, 172

Norman, Larry, 2–3 n. 6, 18, 72 n. 20, 157–158 n. 62, 174–175 n. 110, 178 n. 11, 223 n. 63, 224 n. 67, 225–226 n. 79

novel (genre), 13–14, 69–72, 84–85, 89, 97, 178–179, 184, 201–202, 244

Nouveau Mercure, 238–239 n. 102

Nouveau Mercure Galant, 235–236, 241, see also *Mercure Galant*

opera, 181

Orléans, Elisabeth-Charlotte de, 183–184, 189–190

Ovid, 22, 26, 39 n. 50, 62, 67–68, 73–74, 104–106, 124–125, 129, 137, 144–146, 163–165, 184–185, 190–191, 194, 197–198

Parnassus, 22–23, 184–185, 189–191, 194, 198

pastoral, 16–17, 22, 137–138, 146, 157

Patroclus, 225–226

pedantry, 5–7, 21, 142–143, 169–172, 189, 234–235, 239–240, 242

Pellegrin, Marie-Frédérique, 3–4 n. 10, 7–8 n. 39–n. 40, 148–149 n. 49

Pellisson, Paul, 68, 87–88

periodicals, 22–23, 178–179, 191–193, 201–202, 235–236, 250, see also *Journal des sçavans, Mercure Galant, Nouveau Mercure Galant, Journal de Trévoux*

Perrault, Charles, 16–17, 22–23, 52–53, 68, 157–158, 176–179, 184–188, 194–196, 202, 224, 232–233
  Preface to *Grisélidis*, 179, 183

Petronius, 179–180

Phaon, 73–74, 77, 79–83, 129–130, 211, 212–213

philology, 3–4, 13–14, 19–20, 243–244, *see also* Latin language, Greek language, Classicist

Philostratus, 80–81

Piscopia, Elena Cornaro, 189–190

Pizan, Christine de, 3–4, 57, 63–64, 73–74, 189–190

Plautus, 23–24, 203, 215–217

pleasure, 88–89, 145, 147–148, 155, 161–165, 174, 180–181 n. 24, n. 25, 192, 207–208, 217

Plutarch, 67–68, 85, 97–100, 104–106, 205–206

polemic, 16–17, 20–21, 23–24, 26, 39, 64–65, 73–74, 118–119, 172–174, 179–180, 203–205, 215, 226–231, 233–234, 235–236 n. 94, 238–239

politesse, 4–5, 28–29, 48–49, 95–96, 207–208 n. 21, 220–221, 235–236 n. 94, 237–238

Pope, Alexander, 224–225, 240

Porsenna, 85, 97–100

Poullain de la Barre, François, 7–8

Pradon, Jean, 137–138, 158–159, 172, see also *querelle des sonnets*

précieuse, 1–2, 7, 7–8 n. 38, 11–13, 65, 71, 104–107, 111–112, 125–126, 204–205, 231, 245–246, 248–249

Propertius, 55–56, 190–191

Publius Valerius Publicola, 85, 99–100, 131–132

Pythagoras, 37–38, 91–92

Quarrels, 2–3, 15, 241–243
  Quarrel of the Ancients and Moderns, 2–3, 15, 22–23, 52–53, 72, 87–88, 92–93, 111, 137–138, 157–159, 174, 176, 203
  querelle d'Homère, la, 3, 16–17, 23–24, 203–206, 217, 223
  querelle des femmes, la, 3–4, 16–17, 176–177
  querelle de Sophonisbe, la, 111, *see also* Villedieu, *Manlius*
  querelle des sonnets, la 137–138, 172
  querelle du Cid, la, 25, 113–114

288 INDEX

Quinault, Philippe, 181
Quintilian, 220–221

Racine, Jean, 12–13, 137–138, 158–159, 172,
    208, 238
Rambouillet, Marquise de, 28–29, 75, 189–190
reason, 146
recusatio, 166–167, 229–230
Rhodopis, 199
Richelet, Pierre, 5–6 n. 26
Richer, Louis, 144–145
Roederer, Pierre-Louis, 12
Rohan, Marie de, 189–190
Rome, 45–47, 49–50, 69–70, 84–85, 89,
    104–106, 111
Ronsard, Pierre de, 20–21, 51–52, 60–62, 80–81
    n. 49, 152–153, 162–165
Roussillon, Marine, 16 n. 76, 174–175, 176 n. 2,
    176–177 n. 5, 178, 178–179 n. 13, 187,
    187–188 n. 50, 190–191 n. 57, 191, 193 n.
    64, 194 n. 66, 201–202
Ryer, Pierre du, 74–75, 85 n. 65, 87, 89–90, 95,
    104–106, 111–112

Sablière, Marguerite de la, 12–13, 149, 156
Saint-Aignan, Duc de, 121, 174–175
Saint-Amant, Antoine Girard de, 146–147
Saint Augustine, 69
Saint-Simon, Duc de, 238–239 n. 103
Sainte-Beuve, Charles-Augustin, 101–102,
    167–168 n. 90, 172–174
Sallust, 20–21, 26, 41–44, 46–47
salonnière, 2–3, 241
salons, *see also* Marie de Gournay, Madeleine de
    Scudéry, community
  women's authority in, 3–4
  as contested, 11–13
  representation of, 78–80, 82–83, 169–171,
    191, 193–195, 201–202, 210–211,
    244–245
Sappho, 23–24, 67–70, 73, 80–81, 88–89, 91,
    92–93, 129, 168, 189–190, 199, 203, 206,
    217–218
Sarasin, Jean François, 163–165
satire, 78–79, 108, 137–138, 143, 202, 245
Saumur, 203, 215–216
savant, 5–6, 92–93, 103–104, 111, 116, 121–122,
    127–129, 143, 144–145, 159–160,
    162–163, 224, 234–236, 239–242
savante, 1–3, 23–24, 241–242
  Dacier as, 203–206, 240–241
  dictionary definitions 5–6, 8–10, 76
  used by Deshoulières, 163, 169–172
  used by Gournay, 30–32, 63, 73, 194–195

used by L'Héritier, 184
used by Scudéry, 4–5, 21, 73, 251
savante femme, 1–3, see also *femme savante*,
    savante
savoir, 2–5, 18, 21, 32, 65, 67–68, 73, 100–101,
    178–179, 184, 237–238, 241–242, 250, *see
    also* Marie-Jeanne L'Héritier
sexual difference, 3–4, 7, 25, *see also* feminism
Schapira, Nicolas, 119–121
Schurman, Anna Maria van, 27–28, 37–38 n.
    45, 54 n. 100, 64–65, 73 n. 24, 100–101,
    189–190
Schuwey, Christophe, 110–111, 191, 201–202
Scott, Joan W., 10–11 n. 54
Scudéry, Georges de, 4–5, 25–P2, 70–71, 74–75,
    83–84, 87–88, 120–121
Scudéry, Madeleine de, 3–5, 7–8, 12–15, 21,
    63–65, 67, 137–138, 142, 172, 178–179,
    189–191, 194, 201–202, 243–245
  Anacreon, 21, 23–24, 87–89
  ancient sources, 74–75, 85, 97–98, *see also*
    Plutarch, Livy, Herodotus, Xenophon,
    Valerius Maximus
  Artamène ou le Grand Cyrus, 4–5, 67–68,
    70–71, 73, 74–75, 99–100, 200
    'Histoire de Sapho', 4–5, 10–11, 21, 74–83,
    129–130, 210–211, 251
  Brutus, 21, 69–70, 86–87, 89, 131–133
  Carte de Tendre, 86
  Clélie, 21, 67–68, 70–73, 85, 89, 97
    'Songe d'Hésiode, 83–85, 190–191
  Clélie, 85, 97
  Damophile, 31–32, 75, 78–81, 171, 193,
    244–245
  family, 68, 71
  feminism, 69–70, 246
  Les Femmes Illustres, 21, 67–68, 73–74,
    82–83, 95–98
  Latin language, 67–68, 72, 74–75, 80–81, 85,
    91 n. 90
  literary market, 70–71, 102, 110–111,
    127–128, 133–134
  Lucrèce (Lucretia), 21, 69–70, 85, 86–87, 89,
    97
  reception of, 100–102, 231
  salon, 71, 73, 79–80 n.46
  Sapho, 67–68, 73, 88–89, 91, 92–93, 100–101,
    129–130, 244–245
  savante (representation of), 4–5, 21, 67–68,
    73, 194–195
Seifert, Lewis C., 17 n. 80, 69–70, 177–178, 179
    n. 14, 180–181 n. 24–25, 185
Sévigné, Madame de, 172, 248
Sextus Tarquin, 89–90, 94–99

Socrates, 36–37, 55–56, 104–106
Sophocles, 239–240
Stanton, Domna, 3–4, 7, 7–8 n. 40, 10–11 n. 51, 26 n. 5, 29 n.15, 59–60 n. 119, 78–79 n. 43, 104 n. 5, 177–178, 179 n.14, 243 n.1
Stevenson, Jane, 13–14, 19–20 n.93, 73–74 n. 27, 167–168 n. 128
Strabo, 199
Suchon, Gabrielle, 19–20
Sweden, Queen Christina of, 93 n. 93, 249–250

Tacitus, 20–21, 26, 41–46, 230–231
Tallemant des Réaux, Gédéon, 29–30, 64–65, 68 n. 5, 104–106 n. 10, 113–115
Tarquin the Proud, 85–87, 91, 93
taste, 2–3, 17–18, 20–21, 32, 47–49, 52–53, 63–64, 69, 70–71, 92, 100, 116, 142, 172–174, 176–178, 186–187, 189–190, 199–201, 214–215, 217, 220–222, 224, 229–231, 243–244, *see also* literary value, novel, literature (practices of), Dacier, *Des Causes de la corruption du goût*
Terence, 23–24, 203, 220–223
Terrasson, Abbé, 224–225, 232–233, 234 n. 87
Theocritus, 61–62, 146–147, 157–158, 161–162, 201–202
Théophile de Viau, 146–147
Thierry, Denys, 207
Tibullus, 190–191
Timmermans, Linda, 3–4, 7, 7–8 n. 37, 27–28 n. 9, 104–106 n. 9, 135–136 n. 1, 158–159, 205–206 n.15, 243 n.1
Tonolo, Sophie, 1 n.4, 137–138, 140 n. 23, 146 n. 42, 147–148 n. 48, 159, 159–160 n. 72, 163–166, 170 n. 93, 174 n. 105, 174–175
tragedy, 111, 131, 190–191
troubadours, 16–17, 177–178, 185, 187–191, 193, 194–195, 202, 244–245
Tullia the Elder, 93
Tullia the Younger, 93
Turnovsky, Geoffrey, 12 n. 63, 15–16, 21–22, 103–104, 109–111, 120–121, 123, 133

Urfé, Honoré d', 87–88, 104–106, 158–159, 174, 190–191, 200

Valerius Maximus, 89–90 n. 85, 97–100
Valois, Marguerite de, 25
Venus, 138–142, 145, 181–182
Versailles, 161–162
Vesey, Elizabeth, 208–210

Viala, Alain, 3–4, 4–5 n. 15, 13–16, 16 n.76, 17–18 n. 83, 70–71, 1 n. 1, 106–107 n.15, 207–208 n. 23
Villedieu, Madame de, 3, 14–16, 21–22, 64–65, 102, 103, 137–138, 201–202, 243–244
  Les Amours des grands hommes, 104–107, 109, 119–120, 124–126
  Les Annales galantes de Grèce, 104–107, 109, 126–127
  and Claude Barbin, 103–111, 118–119, 128
  career, 104–107, 109–111, 119, 127
  Carmente, 104–107, 119–120, 123–124
  commercial prowess, 109–111, 117, 119–121, 127–128, 133–134, 201
  Les Exilés de la cour d'Auguste, 104–107, 109, 119–120, 126, 199–201
  Le Favory, 104–107, 119–120, 122–123
  as fictional character, 22–23, 199–201
  galant historical fiction, 103–104, 111, 119, 124–128
  Les Galanteries Grenadines, 106–107, 119–120, 126
  Manlius, 21–22, 104–106, 111, 121–125, 132–133
  naming, 103–106, 121–123, 125–126
  Nitetis, 104–106, 118–119, 121–124
  paratext, 119
  prefaces, 119
  privilèges d'auteur, 21–22, 103, 106–107, 111, 119
  poetry, 103–106, 111–112, 119, 122, 125, 135–136 n. 1
  Portrait des faiblesses humaines, 104–107, 109
  and Antoine Boësset, le Sieur de Villedieu, 104–107, 125
Virgil, 8–9, 26, 51, 61–62, 137–138, 146–148, 152–153, 155, 156–157, 168, 234–235
Voltaire, 172
vraisemblance, 111, 113–119

Wilde, Oscar, 250
Wilkin, Rebecca, 1–2 n. 5, 7–8 n. 38–39, 148–149 n. 49
Wilson, Emily, 72, 94–95
woman writer, 3, 10–11, 23–24, 124–126, 240–241, 243–245
Woman's World, The, 250
Worth-Stylianou, Valerie, 41–42 n. 70, 43 n. 74, 51–52 n. 95–96, 57, 58 n. 111
Wyles, Rosie, 13–14 n. 69, 204–205 n. 6, 215–216 n. 49–50, 218 n. 53, 218–219

Xenophon, 3 n.7, 67–68, 74–75